T0190494

More information about this series at https://link.springer.com/bookseries/558

Lecture Notes in Computer Science 1

Christian Wallraven · Qingshan Liu ·
Hajime Nagahara (Eds.)

Pattern Recognition

6th Asian Conference, ACPR 2021
Jeju Island, South Korea, November 9–12, 2021
Revised Selected Papers, Part I

 Springer

Editors
Christian Wallraven ⓘD
Korea University
Seoul, Korea (Republic of)

Qingshan Liu ⓘD
Nanjing University
Nanjing, China

Hajime Nagahara ⓘD
Osaka University
Osaka, Japan

ISSN 0302-9743   ISSN 1611-3349 (electronic)
Lecture Notes in Computer Science
ISBN 978-3-031-02374-3   ISBN 978-3-031-02375-0 (eBook)
https://doi.org/10.1007/978-3-031-02375-0

This Springer imprint is published by the registered company Springer Nature Switzerland AG
The registered company address is: Gewerbestrasse 11, 6330 Cham, Switzerland

Preface

Pattern recognition stands at the core of artificial intelligence and has evolved significantly in recent years. This proceedings comprises the high-quality original research papers presented at the 6th Asian Conference on Pattern Recognition (ACPR 2021), which was successfully held in Jeju Island, South Korea, during November 9–12, 2021. The conference was planned to welcome all participants from around the world to meet physically in the beautiful surroundings of Jeju Island to exchange ideas, as we did in past conferences of the ACPR series. Due to the COVID-19 pandemic constraints, many of us could only join the conference virtually. Nevertheless, we tried our best to overcome various challenges to prepare and actually hold the conference both in person and online. With all your participation and contributions, we believe ACPR 2021 was a special and memorable conference!

ACPR 2021 was the sixth conference in the series since it was launched in 2011 in Beijing. ACPR 2011 was followed by ACPR 2013 in Okinawa, Japan; ACPR 2015 in Kuala Lumpur, Malaysia; ACPR 2017 in Nanjing, China; and ACPR 2019 in Auckland, New Zealand. As we know, ACPR was initiated to promote pattern recognition theory, technologies, and applications in the Asia-Pacific region. Over the years, it has welcomed authors from all over the world. This year, we had participants from 13 countries.

ACPR 2021 focused on four important areas of pattern recognition: pattern recognition and machine learning, computer vision and robot vision, signal processing, and media processing and interaction, covering various technical aspects.

ACPR 2021 received 154 submissions from authors in 13 countries. The program chairs invited 110 Program Committee members and a pool of additional reviewers to assist with the paper selection process. Each paper was single blindly reviewed by at least three reviewers. This rigorous procedure ensured unbiased review. The review committee made the hard decision to accept 26 papers for oral presentation and 59 papers for poster presentation. This resulted in an acceptance rate of 16.9% for oral presentation and 38.3% for poster presentation, giving a total acceptance rate of 55.2%.

The technical program of ACPR 2021 was scheduled over four days including four tutorials, a workshop, three keynote speeches, nine oral sessions, two poster sessions, and a spotlight.

The keynote speeches were given by internationally renowned professors. Lei Zhang, from Hong Kong Polytechnic University, talked about "Gradient centralization and feature gradient decent for deep neural network optimization", Andreas Dengel, from DFKI and the University of Kaiserslautern, talked about "Combining Bird Eye View and Grass Root View for Earth Observation", and Jure Leskovic, from Stanford University, talked about "Graph Neural Networks and Beyond".

Organizing a large event during the COVID-19 pandemic is a challenging task, requiring teamwork, intensive coordination, and collaboration across rather different geolocations and time zones. We would like to thank the organizing committee for their hard work and the steering committee for their guidance. The publication chairs, workshop chairs, tutorial chairs, exhibition/demo chairs, sponsorship chair, finance chair, local organizing chairs, and webmaster all led their respective committees and worked together closely to make ACPR 2021 successful. Our special thanks go to the many reviewers for their constructive comments on the papers. We thank all the authors who submitted their papers to ACPR 2021, which is the most important part for a scientific conference. Finally, we would like to acknowledge all volunteers and students from our local organizing team.

Seong-Whan Lee
Cheng-Lin Liu
Yasushi Yagi
Christian Wallraven
Qingshan Liu
Hajime Nagahara

Organization

Steering Committee

Seong-Whan Lee	Korea University, South Korea
Cheng-Lin Liu	CASIA, China
Umapada Pal	ISI, India
Tieniu Tan	CAS, China
Yasushi Yagi	Osaka University, Japan

General Chairs

Seong-Whan Lee	Korea University, South Korea
Cheng-Lin Liu	CASIA, China
Yasushi Yagi	Osaka University, Japan

Program Chairs

Christian Wallraven	Korea University, South Korea
Qingshan Liu	Nanjing University of Information Science and Technology, China
Hajime Nagahara	Osaka University, Japan

Publication Chairs

Unsang Park	Sogang University, South Korea
Wei Xiong	Institute for Infocomm Research, Singapore

Publicity Chairs

Jean-Marc Ogier	University of La Rochelle, France
Umapada Pal	ISI, India
Richard Zannibi	RIT, USA

Workshop Chairs

Soo-Hyung Kim	Chonnam National University, South Korea
Byoungchul Ko	Keimyung University, South Korea

Tutorial Chairs

Chang D. Yoo   KAIST, South Korea
Jingdong Wang   Microsoft Research Asia, China

Exhibition/Demo Chairs

Sung Chan Jun   Gwangju Institute of Science and Technology,
                               South Korea
Dong Gyu Lee   Kyungpook National University, South Korea

Sponsorship Chair

Soo-Hyung Kim   Chonnam National University, South Korea

Finance Chair

Wonzoo Chung   Korea University, South Korea

Local Organizing Chairs

Tea-Eui Kam   Korea University, South Korea
Sungjoon Choi   Korea University, South Korea

Webmaster

Hyun-Seung Chung   Korea University, South Korea

Program Committee

Alireza Alaei   Southern Cross University, Australia
Sung-Ho Bae   Kyung Hee University, South Korea
Saumik Bhattacharya   IIT Kharagpur, India
Michael Blumenstein   University of Technology Sydney, Australia
Sukalpa Chanda   Østfold University College, Norway
Andrew Tzer-Yeu Chen   University of Auckland, New Zealand
Songcan Chen   Nanjing University, China
Gong Cheng   Nanjing University, China
Sungjoon Choi   Korea University, South Korea
Jaesik Choi   KAIST, South Korea
Michael Cree   Waikato University, New Zealand
Jinshi Cui   Peking University, China
Andreas Dengel   University of Kaiserslautern, Germany

Junyu Dong	Ocean University, China
Bo Du	University of Wollongong, Australia
Jianjiang Feng	Tsinghua University, China
Fei Gao	Zhejiang University, China
Guangwei Gao	Nanjing University, China
Hitoshi Habe	Kindai University, Japan
Renlong Hang	Nanjing University, China
Tsubasa Hirakawa	Chubu University, Japan
Maiya Hori	Kyushu University, Japan
Kazuhiro Hotta	Meijo University, Japan
Masaaki Iiyama	Kyoto University, Japan
Yoshihisa Ijiri	LINE Corporation, Japan
Kohei Inoue	Kyushu University, Japan
Koichi Ito	Chiba University, Japan
Yumi Iwashita	NASA, USA
Xiaoyi Jiang	University of Münster, Germany
Xin Jin	Peking University, China
Taeeui Kam	Korea University, South Korea
Kunio Kashino	NTT Communication Science Laboratories, Japan
Yasutomo Kawanishi	Nagoya University, Japan
Hiroaki Kawashima	Kyoto University, Japan
Sangpil Kim	Korea University, South Korea
Jinkyu Kim	Korea University, South Korea
Byoungchul Ko	Keimyung University, South Korea
Hui Kong	University of Macau, China
Shang-Hong Lai	National Tsing Hua University, Taiwan
Dong-Gyu Lee	Kyungpook National University, South Korea
Namhoon Lee	POSTECH, South Korea
Xuelong Li	Northwestern Polytechnical University, China
Zhu Li	University of Missouri, USA
Zechao Li	Nanjing University of Science and Technology, China
Junxia Li	Nanjing University of Information Science and Technology, China
Jia Li	Pennsylvania State University, USA
Weifeng Liu	China University of Petroleum-Beijing, China
Huimin Lu	National University of Defense Technology, China
Feng Lu	University of Virginia, USA
Jiayi Ma	Wuhan University, China
Yasushi Makihara	Osaka University, Japan
Brendan McCane	University of Otago, New Zealand

Haiyuan Wu	Wakayama University, Japan
Guiyu Xia	Macau University of Science and Technology, China
Guisong Xia	Wuhan University, China
Yong Xu	Nanjing University of Posts and Telecommunications, China
Yanwu Xu	Pittsburgh University, USA
Takayoshi Yamashita	Chubu University, Japan
Hirotake Yamazoe	Hyogo University, Japan
Junchi Yan	Shanghai Jiao Tong University, China
Weiqi Yan	Auckland University of Technology, New Zealand
Keiji Yanai	University of Electro-Communications, Japan
Wankou Yang	Southeast University, China
Xucheng Yin	University of Science and Technology Beijing, China
Xianghua Ying	Peking University, China
Kaihua Zhang	Nanjing University of Information Science and Technology, China
Shanshan Zhang	University of Bonn, Germany
Hao Zhang	eBay, USA
Cairong Zhao	Tongji University, China
Jiang-Yu Zheng	Indiana University-Purdue University Indianapolis, USA
Wangmeng Zuo	Harbin Institute of Technology, China

Contents – Part I

Object Detection and Anomaly

Segmentation, Grouping and Shape

Face and Body and Biometrics

Adversarial Learning and Networks

Contents – Part II

Applications, Medical and Robotics

Classification

One-Shot Image Learning Using Test-Time Augmentation

Keiichi Yamada$^{(\boxtimes)}$ and Susumu Matsumi

Department of Information Engineering, Meijo University, Nagoya, Aichi, Japan
`yamadak@meijo-u.ac.jp`

Abstract. Modern image recognition systems require a large amount of training data. In contrast, humans can learn the concept of new classes from only one or a few image examples. A machine learning problem with only a few training samples is called few-shot learning and is a key challenge in the image recognition field. In this paper, we address one-shot learning, which is a type of few-shot learning in which there is one training sample per class. We propose a one-shot learning method based on metric learning that is characterized by data augmentation of a test target along with the training samples. Experimental results demonstrate that expanding both training samples and test target is effective in terms of improving accuracy. On a benchmark dataset, the accuracy improvement by the proposed method is 2.55% points, while the improvement by usual data augmentation which expands the training samples is 1.31% points. Although the proposed method is very simple, it achieves accuracy that is comparable or superior to some of existing methods.

Keywords: Image classification · One-shot learning · Test-time augmentation

1 Introduction

Image recognition performance has significantly improved with the development of deep learning technology. Achieving high performance with modern image recognition systems requires a large amount of labeled data for training. However, collecting and annotating data generally incurs enormous effort and cost. In addition, it is sometimes practically difficult to provide large amounts of training data. In contrast, humans can learn the concept of new classes from one or a few image examples and recognize the images of those classes. The type of machine learning problem in which there are only a few training samples is called few-shot learning (FSL).

FSL exhibits low performance when using common supervised learning methods because the models overfit to a small number of training samples. Therefore, FSL generally uses prior knowledge from meta-training data.

© Springer Nature Switzerland AG 2022
C. Wallraven et al. (Eds.): ACPR 2021, LNCS 13188, pp. 3–16, 2022.
https://doi.org/10.1007/978-3-031-02375-0_1

This paper addresses image classification problem, particularly one-shot learning (OSL), which is a type of FSL in which the training data (referred to as the support data in FSL) include only one sample per class. This paper proposes an approach of OSL which is characterized by data augmentation of a test target along with one training sample per class. We reveal the properties of this method and demonstrate its performance through experiments on the miniImageNet and tieredImageNet datasets.

2   Related Work

Basic FSL approaches include metric learning [10, 15, 25, 28], meta-learning [5, 12, 18, 21], and data augmentation [2, 6, 16, 19, 22]. These approaches are occasionally combined.

In the metric-learning-based approach, an embedding space in which samples of the same class are close together is learned from meta-training data. There are various methods depending on how the test target is classified using the support data in the embedding space. Examples include Matching networks [28] and Prototypical networks [25]. Note that the proposed method is based on metric-learning.

Data augmentation is widely used in image recognition including deep learning [23]. The standard image data augmentation techniques include flipping, shifting, rotating, rescaling, and random cropping of the training images. Data augmentation is also used in FSL to address the shortage of training samples [2, 6, 16, 19, 22]. However, data augmentation in previous FSL studies expands the support data, whereas the proposed method expands both the support data and the test target simultaneously.

Test-time augmentation is a method that expands a test target and uses the averages of the output predictions as the final prediction results. This method is often used in general image recognition [7, 8, 26]. We apply a type of test-time augmentation to OSL. To the best of our knowledge, research focusing on the use of test-time augmentation for OSL has not been reported to date.

3   Problem Definition

Three datasets are used for training and testing, including meta-training, in FSL. They are the base set (D_b), which contains the meta-training data for obtaining prior knowledge; the support set (D_s), which contains the support data consisting of a small number of samples for learning novel classes; and the testing set (D_q), which contains the test targets for testing the FSL results. The classes in datasets D_s and D_q are mutual and are both C_{novel}. The class that D_b has is C_{base}, and there are no mutual classes between D_b and D_s. In other words,

$$D_b = \{(x_i, y_i)\}_{i=1}^{N_b}, \ y_i \in C_{\text{base}} \tag{1}$$

$$D_s = \{(x_i, y_i)\}_{i=1}^{N_s}, \ y_i \in C_{\text{novel}} \tag{2}$$

$$D_q = \{(x_i, y_i)\}_{i=1}^{N_q}, \ y_i \in C_{\text{novel}} \tag{3}$$

$$C_{\text{base}} \cap C_{\text{novel}} = \phi, \tag{4}$$

where the label of data x_i is expressed as y_i. Here, x_i is an image.

The FSL problem where the number of novel classes $|C_{\text{novel}}|$ is N and D_s has K labeled samples for each class is referred to as N-way K-shot learning. K is generally 1 to 5. This paper addresses OSL, a type of FSL in which $K = 1$. In the case of OSL, $Ns = N$. The objective of FSL is to obtain a model f that predicts the label y_q of a test target x_q in D_q when D_b and D_s are given, which is expressed as follows.

$$\hat{y}_q = f(x_q; D_b, D_s), \ (x_q, y_q) \in D_q. \tag{5}$$

4   Proposed Method

Figure 1 shows an overview of the proposed method for a 5-way OSL case, where x_1–x_5 are the support data, and x_q is the test target whose correct class is the class of x_1. An example in an actual image is shown in Fig. 3.

The learning and prediction of the proposed method are based on metric learning. Here, we employ a convolutional neural network (CNN) as an embedded function $g(x; \theta)$ with θ as parameter. Metric learning is performed by training the CNN with D_b as the supervised training data, and parameter θ of the embedded function is obtained. Then, the class y_q of x_q is predicted with classifier h using D_s as the supervised training data in this embedded space.

$$\hat{y}_q = h\Big(g(x_q; \theta(D_b)); \big\{(g(x_i; \theta(D_b)), y_i)\big\}_{i=1}^{N_s}\Big),$$
$$(x_q, y_q) \in D_q, \ (x_i, y_i) \in D_s. \tag{6}$$

We employ the nearest neighbor classifier with the cosine distance as h.

The proposed method expands both the support data $x_i, i = 1, ..., N_s$ in D_s and the test target x_q. The transformation function to expand an image x J times is given as $a_j(x), j = 1, ..., J$. Then, the average vector in the embedded space g of the data where x_i in D_s is expanded J times is expressed as $\text{mean}\{g(a_j(x_i))\}_{j=1}^{J}$. In addition, the average vector in the embedded space g of the data where the test target x_q is expanded J times is expressed as $\text{mean}\{g(a_j(x_q))\}_{j=1}^{J}$. In the proposed method, when a set of $\text{mean}\{g(a_j(x_i))\}_{j=1}^{J}$ with its teacher label y_i, $i = 1, ..., N_s$, is given, the class of x_q is predicted by determining the class of $\text{mean}\{g(a_j(x_q))\}_{j=1}^{J}$ using classifier h. In other words, we obtain the following:

$$\hat{y}_q = h\Big(\text{mean}\{g(a_j(x_q))\}_{j=1}^{J}; \big\{(\text{mean}\{g(a_j(x_i))\}_{j=1}^{J}, y_i)\big\}_{i=1}^{N_s}\Big),$$
$$(x_q, y_q) \in D_q, \ (x_i, y_i) \in D_s, \tag{7}$$

where $\theta(D_b)$ in g is omitted to keep the formula simple.

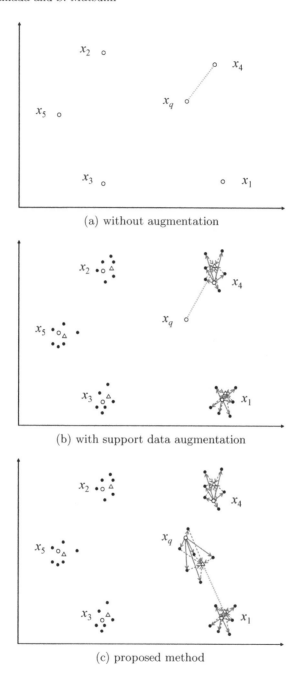

(a) without augmentation

(b) with support data augmentation

(c) proposed method

Fig. 1. Illustration of the proposed method, showing an example of 5-way OSL where x_1–x_5 are the support data and x_q is the test target whose correct class is the x_1 class. The circle represents the embedded vector of each original image. The black dots represent the embedded vectors of the expanded images, and the triangle mark represents the average vector. An example in an actual image is shown in Fig. 3.

5   Experimental Methods

5.1   Datasets

The miniImageNet [28] and tieredImageNet [19] datasets, which are commonly used as benchmarks for FSL, were used in our experiment.

The miniImageNet dataset, which is a subset of ImageNet [3], is a 100-class dataset of 600 labeled images per class. Here, the image resolution was 84×84 pixels. According to [18], 64 classes were used as the base class, 16 classes were used as the validation class, and 20 classes were used as the novel class.

The tieredImageNet dataset is also a subset of ImageNet; however, it is a larger dataset than miniImageNet. The classes in the tieredImageNet are grouped according to the hierarchical structure of WordNet. Each class includes an average of 1,282 images. According to [19], 20 superclasses (351 classes) were used as the base class, 6 superclasses (97 classes) were used as the validation class, and 8 superclasses (160 classes) were used as the novel class. The images were resized to 84×84 pixels.

5.2   Backbone

Conv-4 and ResNet-18 were used as the backbone of the embedded function.

Conv-4 is a CNN with four Conv blocks formed from a convolution layer with 3×3 filters, batch normalization, the ReLU activation function, and a 2×2 max pooling layer. In our experiment, the number of filters for the four Conv blocks was 64-64-64-64. Three fully connected layers were connected after the fourth Conv block. The first two fully connected layers had 512 units with the ReLU activation function. Dropout with a rate of 0.5 was applied between these fully connected layers. The export from the first fully connected layer (fc1) was used as a 512-dimension embedded vector. The results of our preliminary experiments indicated that the accuracy of OSL was higher when using the export from fc1 as the embedded vector than when using the export from the fourth Conv block (maxpool4), as shown in Table 1.

The structure of our ResNet-18 is essentially the same as the 18-layer residual network described in [7]. However, the first 7×7 convolution was changed to 3×3 convolution. In addition, by removing the 3×3 max pooling and changing the stride of the first residual block convolution to 1, the first two down-sampling processes were eliminated. In addition, after the global average pooling (GAP), we added one fully connected layer of 512 units with the ReLU activation function. The export from this fully connected layer was used as a 512-dimension embedded vector. The results of our preliminary experiments demonstrated that the accuracy of OSL was higher when using the export from the added fully connected layer (added fc1) as the embedded vector than when using the GAP export, as in Table 1.

5.3   Training Methods

Conv-4 and ResNet-18 were both trained from scratch on D_b using mini-batch stochastic gradient descent with weight decay and momentum using cross-entropy loss. Here, the batch size, weight decay, and momentum were $25, 5 \times 10^{-4}$, and 0.9, respectively. The learning rate of Conv-4 was 10^{-3} for the first 60 epochs, followed by 10^{-4} for 10 epochs and 10^{-5} for 10 epochs. The learning rate of ResNet-18 was 3×10^{-2} for 60 epochs, followed by 10^{-3} for 10 epochs and 10^{-4} for 10 epochs for miniImageNet. For tieredImageNet, it was 10^{-2} for 80 epochs, followed by 10^{-3} for 10 epochs and 10^{-4} for 10 epochs. During training of these CNNs, we added general jitter of random crop, rotation, and horizontal flip.

Table 1. 5-way and 10-way OSL accuracy and 95% confidence interval on miniImageNet for different embeddings. For Conv-4, using the export from the first fully connected layer (fc1) for the embedded vector has higher accuracy than export from the fourth Conv block (maxpool4). For ResNet-18, using the export from the first fully connected layer added afterward (added fc1) for the embedded vector has higher accuracy than export from the global average pooling (GAP).

Backbone	Embedding	Accuracy (%)	
		5-way	10-way
Conv-4	maxpool4	44.93 ± 0.51	30.69 ± 0.38
	fc1	$\mathbf{50.18 \pm 0.57}$	$\mathbf{34.77 \pm 0.44}$
ResNet-18	GAP	55.90 ± 0.59	39.96 ± 0.48
	added fc1	$\mathbf{57.52 \pm 0.60}$	$\mathbf{41.14 \pm 0.50}$

5.4   Experimental Conditions

The transformation function $a_j(x)$ shown in Table 2 was used to expand image data x. Here, the shift(x, d_h, d_v) function shifts x by d_h in the horizontal direction and d_v in the vertical direction, the flip(x) function flips x horizontally, and the rotate(x, d_r) function rotates x by d_r. In our experiment, a_1–a_5 were used when expanding the data 5 times (5×), a_1–a_{10} were used when expanding the data 10×, a_1–a_{18} were used when expanding the data 18×, and a_1–a_{22} were used when expanding the data 22×. Note that Δ and Δ_r were fixed to 5 pixels and 5°C, respectively.

   We compared the proposed method with the following five scenarios. When expanding the support data D_s but not averaging the embedded vectors, and not expanding the test target x_q,

$$\hat{y}_q = h\left(g(x_q); \left\{\{(g(a_j(x_i)), y_i)\}_{j=1}^{J}\right\}_{i=1}^{N_s}\right). \tag{8}$$

Table 2. Transformation function $a_j(x)$ to expand image data x; a_1-a_5 are used when expanding the data 5×, a_1-a_{10} are used when expanding the data 10×, a_1-a_{18} are used when expanding the data 18×, and a_1-a_{22} are used when expanding the data 22×. Δ is 5 pixels and Δ_r is 5°.

$a_1(x) = \text{shift}(x, 0, 0)$	$a_{12}(x) = \text{shift}(x, \Delta, -\Delta)$
$a_2(x) = \text{shift}(x, \Delta, 0)$	$a_{13}(x) = \text{shift}(x, -\Delta, \Delta)$
$a_3(x) = \text{shift}(x, -\Delta, 0)$	$a_{14}(x) = \text{shift}(x, -\Delta, -\Delta)$
$a_4(x) = \text{shift}(x, 0, \Delta)$	$a_{15}(x) = \text{flip}(\text{shift}(x, \Delta, \Delta))$
$a_5(x) = \text{shift}(x, 0, -\Delta)$	$a_{16}(x) = \text{flip}(\text{shift}(x, \Delta, -\Delta))$
$a_6(x) = \text{flip}(\text{shift}(x, 0, 0))$	$a_{17}(x) = \text{flip}(\text{shift}(x, -\Delta, \Delta))$
$a_7(x) = \text{flip}(\text{shift}(x, \Delta, 0))$	$a_{18}(x) = \text{flip}(\text{shift}(x, -\Delta, -\Delta))$
$a_8(x) = \text{flip}(\text{shift}(x, -\Delta, 0))$	$a_{19}(x) = \text{rotate}(x, \Delta_r)$
$a_9(x) = \text{flip}(\text{shift}(x, 0, \Delta))$	$a_{20}(x) = \text{rotate}(x, -\Delta_r)$
$a_{10}(x) = \text{flip}(\text{shift}(x, 0, -\Delta))$	$a_{21}(x) = \text{flip}(\text{rotate}(x, \Delta_r))$
$a_{11}(x) = \text{shift}(x, \Delta, \Delta)$	$a_{22}(x) = \text{flip}(\text{rotate}(x, -\Delta_r))$

When expanding D_s and averaging the embedded vectors, and not expanding x_q,

$$\hat{y}_q = h\left(g(x_q); \left\{(\text{mean}\{g(a_j(x_i))\}_{j=1}^{J}, y_i)\right\}_{i=1}^{N_s}\right). \tag{9}$$

When not expanding D_s, and expanding x_q but not averaging the embedded vectors,

$$\hat{y}_q = h\left(\{g(a_j(x_q))\}_{j=1}^{J}; \{(g(x_i), y_i)\}_{i=1}^{N_s}\right). \tag{10}$$

When not expanding D_s, and expanding x_q and averaging the embedded vectors,

$$\hat{y}_q = h\left(\text{mean}\{g(a_j(x_q))\}_{j=1}^{J}; \{(g(x_i), y_i)\}_{i=1}^{N_s}\right). \tag{11}$$

When expanding D_s but not averaging the embedded vectors, and expanding x_q but not averaging the embedded vectors,

$$\hat{y}_q = h\left(\{g(a_j(x_q))\}_{j=1}^{J}; \left\{\{(g(a_j(x_i)), y_i)\}_{j=1}^{J}\right\}_{i=1}^{N_s}\right). \tag{12}$$

When there were multiple test elements, as in (10) and (12), the classes were determined based on the total closest distance. The proposed method and these comparison methods were implemented using MatConvNet [27].

6   Experimental Results

Figure 2 shows main results. This figure presents the 5-way OSL accuracy on miniImageNet for the cases of not expanding the data (1×) and expanding the data by 22× when using Conv-4 as the backbone. For the latter case, the accuracy of the comparison methods (8)–(12) and the proposed method (7) are shown. As the figure shows, the accuracy when expanding both the support data and test target (12)(7) was higher than when expanding only the support data (8), (9) or only the test target (10)(11). The accuracy of the proposed method (7) was 2.55% points higher than when not expanding the data (1×), while the accuracy improvement by usual data augmentation which expands only the support data (9) was 1.31% points. When comparing using the averaged embedded vector and not using it ((9) vs (8), (11) vs (10), (7) vs (12)), the accuracy of the former was slightly higher. Furthermore, the use of the average vector has the advantage of reducing the search cost of the nearest neighbor classifier h.

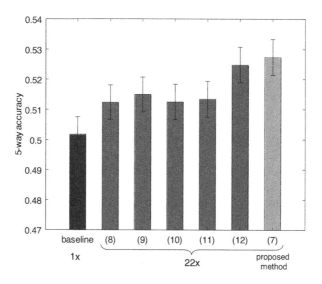

Fig. 2. 5-way OSL accuracy and 95% confidence interval for the cases of not expanding the data (1×) and expanding the data by 22× on miniImageNet for Conv-4. The accuracy of the proposed method (7) which expands both the support data and test target is significantly higher than the cases (8)–(11) which expand either the support data or the test target.

Table 3 presents the 5-way and 10-way OSL accuracy on miniImageNet for Conv-4 when the data were expanded 5×, 10×, 18×, and 22×. In this table, the accuracy of the comparison methods (8)–(12) and the proposed method (7) are shown in order from top to bottom. Here, *exp* and *ave* in the table signify using data expansion and average of the embedded vectors, respectively. As can be seen, for any case, including the comparison methods, the accuracy when expanding the data was higher than when not expanding the data (50.18% for 5-way and 34.77% for 10-way, as displayed in Table 1). Out of these methods, the proposed method (the bottom row of the table) had the highest accuracy. When examining the relationship between expansion rate and accuracy, the larger the expansion rate was, the higher the accuracy was. The rightmost column in the table displays the costs of the nearest neighbor search for each respective case. Here, N and J are the number of the way (i.e., the number of novel classes) and expansion rates, respectively. Since the search cost when no data expansion was applied is N, the proposed method can improve the accuracy without increasing the search cost.

Table 4 presents the accuracy of 5-way OSL on miniImageNet and tieredImageNet for Conv-4 and ResNet-18 when not expanding the data ($1\times$) and when using the proposed method of expanding the data by $22\times$. For any combination of dataset and backbone, the accuracy improved by 1.3–3.3% points with the proposed method of expanding the data by $22\times$ compared to the case of not expanding the data.

Table 3. 5-way and 10-way OSL accuracy (%) on miniImageNet for each expansion rate when using Conv-4 as the backbone. The bottom row is the proposed method. The terms exp and ave signify using data expansion and the embedded vector averaging for the support data D_s and the test target x_q, respectively. The rightmost column presents the calculation costs of the nearest neighbor search.

D_s		x_q		$5\times$		$10\times$		$18\times$		$22\times$		cost
Exp	Ave	Exp	Ave	5-way	10-way	5-way	10-way	5-way	10-way	5-way	10-way	
✓	–	–	–	50.83	35.40	51.17	35.65	51.25	35.75	51.23	35.75	NJ
✓	✓	–	–	50.87	35.40	51.24	35.73	51.40	35.87	51.49	35.97	N
–	–	✓	–	50.63	35.18	50.96	35.46	51.10	35.59	51.25	35.69	NJ
–	–	✓	✓	50.78	35.32	51.04	35.54	51.18	35.67	51.34	35.79	N
✓	–	✓	–	51.32	35.85	52.01	36.41	52.29	36.70	52.48	36.89	NJ^2
✓	✓	✓	✓	**51.47**	**35.96**	**52.09**	**36.49**	**52.42**	**36.79**	**52.73**	**37.08**	N

Table 4. 5-way OSL accuracy and 95% confidence interval for no data expansion ($1\times$), and the proposed method when expanding the data $22\times$.

Dataset	Backbone	5-way accuracy (%)	
		$1\times$	$22\times$
miniImageNet	Conv-4	50.18 ± 0.57	$\mathbf{52.73 \pm 0.60}$
	ResNet-18	57.52 ± 0.60	$\mathbf{58.84 \pm 0.61}$
tieredImageNet	Conv-4	56.15 ± 0.46	$\mathbf{59.45 \pm 0.47}$
	ResNet-18	65.13 ± 0.50	$\mathbf{67.42 \pm 0.50}$

In Table 5, the proposed method is compared with several existing methods in terms of accuracy. Here, regular FSL which does not use unlabeled data were the comparative target, and semi-supervised FSL [11,13,19,29] that uses external unlabeled data and transductive FSL [4,13,17,20,29] that uses information from

Table 5. Proposed method (Ours) compared with several existing methods in terms of accuracy.

Dataset	Backbone	Model	5-way accuracy (%)
miniImageNet	Conv-4	MatchingNet [28]	43.56 ± 0.84
		MAML [5]	48.70 ± 1.84
		ProtoNet [25]	49.42 ± 0.78
		Baseline++ [1]	48.24 ± 0.75
		TapNet [30]	50.68 ± 0.11
		DSN [24]	51.78 ± 0.96
		Support-based init [4]	50.69 ± 0.63
		Ours (22×)	**52.73** ± 0.60
miniImageNet	ResNet-18	MatchingNet [1,28]	52.91 ± 0.88
	ResNet-18	MAML [1,5]	49.61 ± 0.92
	ResNet-18	ProtoNet [1,25]	54.16 ± 0.82
	ResNet-18	Baseline++ [1]	51.87 ± 0.77
	ResNet-12	TapNet [30]	61.65 ± 0.15
	ResNet-12	DSN [24]	**62.64** ± 0.66
	WRN-28-10	Support-based init [4]	56.17 ± 0.64
	ResNet-18	Ours (22×)	58.84 ± 0.61
tieredImageNet	Conv-4	MAML [5,13]	51.67 ± 1.81
		ProtoNet [13,25]	53.31 ± 0.89
		MetaOptNet-SVM [9]	54.71 ± 0.67
		TapNet [30]	57.11 ± 0.12
		Support-based init [4]	58.42 ± 0.69
		Ours (22×)	**59.45** ± 0.47
tieredImageNet	ResNet-12	ProtoNet [24,25]	61.74 ± 0.77
	ResNet-12	MetaOptNet-SVM [9]	65.99 ± 0.72
	ResNet-12	DSN [24]	66.22 ± 0.75
	WRN-28-10	Support-based init [4]	**67.45** ± 0.70
	ResNet-18	**Ours** (22×)	**67.42** ± 0.50

test data other than the test target were excluded. As can be seen, the simple proposed method (Ours) achieved accuracy that is comparable or superior to the methods listed in the table. Although the accuracy of the proposed method was lower than DSN in the miniImageNet+ResNet case, it was higher than that in the miniImageNet+Conv-4, tieredImageNet+Conv-4, and tieredImageNet+ResNet cases.

Figure 3 shows the results of visualizing the distribution of the embedded vector using t-SNE [14]. The figure shows an example of 5-way OSL when expanding the image data by 22×. Here, x_1–x_5 are the support data, and x_q is the test target. The plot points indicate the embedded vectors of the original image and the expanded images of each class. ◯ represents the original image vector, while △ represents the average of the expanded image vectors. The figure also shows the original image. In this example, x_q was incorrectly identified as the x_4 class when no data expansion was applied; however, x_q was correctly identified as the x_1 class when using the proposed method. When examining the original image vector ◯ and expanded average vector △ of x_1, x_4, and x_q, the figure demonstrates that while x_q was close to x_4 in the original image vector, x_q was closer to x_1 in the expanded average vector.

Fig. 3. Example of visualizing the embedded vector distribution using t-SNE when expanding image data by 22×. x_1–x_5 are the support data; x_q is the test target. The plot points indicate the embedded vectors of the original image and the expanded images of each class. ◯ represents the original image vector while △ represents the average of the expanded image vectors.

Table 6 shows the results of expanding the data by 18× when transforming image x with a random shift amount rather than expanding the image using transformation functions a_1–a_{18} with a fixed shift amount Δ of 5. This table displays the accuracy of 5-way and 10-way OSL on miniImageNet for Conv-4. For transformation with a random shift amount, two random values Δ_1 and Δ_2 that were sampled per transformation from a uniform distribution of [-10, 10] were used and transformed with shift(x, Δ_1, Δ_2). Here, the probability of horizontal flip was 0.5 (9 out of 18). Table 6 also shows the results of expanding with a_1–a_{18} with the shift amount Δ fixed at a value of 5, which was also shown in Table 3,

Table 6. OSL accuracy (%) when transforming with a random shift amount instead of fixing the shift amount when expanding the data 18× on miniImageNet for Conv-4.

D_s		x_q		random Δ		fixed Δ	
Exp	Ave	Exp	Ave	5-way	10-way	5-way	10-way
✓	−	−	−	49.42	33.92	51.25	35.75
✓	✓	−	−	49.79	34.22	51.40	35.87
−	−	✓	−	48.92	33.55	51.10	35.59
−	−	✓	✓	49.07	33.71	51.18	35.67
✓	−	✓	−	51.61	36.07	52.29	36.70
✓	✓	✓	✓	52.10	36.45	**52.42**	**36.79**

for the purpose of comparison. Table 6 shows that using a fixed shift amount, as the proposed method, resulted in higher accuracy than using a random shift amount. We believe the reason for this result is that when the shift amount is determined randomly per image, there are differences in the expansion method between images.

7 Conclusion

In this paper, we have proposed an OSL method for image classification that is characterized by the data expansion of a test target along with support data. The experimental results demonstrate that expanding both the support data and test target is effective in terms of improving accuracy. Accuracy can be improved without increasing the cost of nearest neighbor search using the average of the embedded vectors of the expanded images. The proposed method achieved performance that is comparable or superior to some existing methods on the miniImageNet and tieredImageNet datasets despite being a rather simple method. Tasks for future research include learning the transformation function and the parameters from meta-training data, and combining this method with other methods.

References

1. Chen, W.Y., Liu, Y.C., Kira, Z., Wang, Y.C.F., Huang, J.B.: A closer look at few-shot classification. In: International Conference on Learning Representations (2019)
2. Chen, Z., Fu, Y., Wang, Y.X., Ma, L., Liu, W., Hebert, M.: Image deformation meta-networks for one-shot learning. In: 2019 IEEE/CVF Conference on Computer Vision and Pattern Recognition (CVPR), pp. 8672–8681 (2019)
3. Deng, J., Dong, W., Socher, R., Li, L.J., Li, K., Fei-Fei, L.: Imagenet: a large-scale hierarchical image database. In: 2009 IEEE Conference on Computer Vision and Pattern Recognition, pp. 248–255 (2009)

4. Dhillon, G.S., Chaudhari, P., Ravichandran, A., Soatto, S.: A baseline for few-shot image classification. In: International Conference on Learning Representations (2020)
5. Finn, C., Abbeel, P., Levine, S.: Model-agnostic meta-learning for fast adaptation of deep networks. In: Proceedings of the 34th International Conference on Machine Learning. Proceedings of Machine Learning Research, vol. 70, pp. 1126–1135 (2017)
6. Hariharan, B., Girshick, R.: Low-shot visual recognition by shrinking and hallu-cinating features. In: 2017 IEEE International Conference on Computer Vision (ICCV), pp. 3037–3046 (2017)
7. He, K., Zhang, X., Ren, S., Sun, J.: Deep residual learning for image recognition. In: 2016 IEEE Conference on Computer Vision and Pattern Recognition (CVPR), pp. 770–778 (2016)
8. Krizhevsky, A., Sutskever, I., Hinton, G.E.: Imagenet classification with deep con-volutional neural networks. In: Proceedings of the 25th International Conference on Neural Information Processing Systems, vol. 1, pp. 1097–1105 (2012)
9. Lee, K., Maji, S., Ravichandran, A., Soatto, S.: Meta-learning with differentiable convex optimization. In: 2019 IEEE/CVF Conference on Computer Vision and Pattern Recognition (CVPR), pp. 10649–10657 (2019)
10. Li, W., Wang, L., Xu, J., Huo, J., Gao, Y., Luo, J.: Revisiting local descriptor based image-to-class measure for few-shot learning. In: 2019 IEEE/CVF Conference on Computer Vision and Pattern Recognition (CVPR), pp. 7253–7260 (2019)
11. Li, X., et al.: Learning to self-train for semi-supervised few-shot classification. In: Advances in Neural Information Processing Systems, vol. 32 (2019)
12. Li, Z., Zhou, F., Chen, F., Li, H.: Meta-SGD: learning to learn quickly for few-shot learning. arXiv preprint arXiv:1707.09835 (2017)
13. Liu, Y., et al.: Learning to propagate labels: transductive propagation network for few-shot learning. In: International Conference on Learning Representations (2019)
14. van der Maaten, L., Hinton, G.: Visualizing data using t-SNE. J. Mach. Learn. Res. 9(86), 2579–2605 (2008)
15. Oreshkin, B., Rodríguez López, P., Lacoste, A.: Tadam: Task dependent adap-tive metric for improved few-shot learning. In: Advances in Neural Information Processing Systems, vol. 31, pp. 721–731 (2018)
16. Qi, H., Brown, M., Lowe, D.G.: Low-shot learning with imprinted weights. In: 2018 IEEE/CVF Conference on Computer Vision and Pattern Recognition, pp. 5822–5830 (2018)
17. Qiao, L., Shi, Y., Li, J., Tian, Y., Huang, T., Wang, Y.: Transductive episodic-wise adaptive metric for few-shot learning. In: 2019 IEEE/CVF International Confer-ence on Computer Vision (ICCV), pp. 3602–3611 (2019)
18. Ravi, S., Larochelle, H.: Optimization as a model for few-shot learning. In: Inter-national Conference on Learning Representations (2017)
19. Ren, M., et al.: Meta-learning for semi-supervised few-shot classification. In: Inter-national Conference on Learning Representations (2018)
20. Rodríguez, P., Laradji, I., Drouin, A., Lacoste, A.: Embedding propagation: smoother manifold for few-shot classification. In: Vedaldi, A., Bischof, H., Brox, T., Frahm, J.-M. (eds.) ECCV 2020. LNCS, vol. 12371, pp. 121–138. Springer, Cham (2020). https://doi.org/10.1007/978-3-030-58574-7_8
21. Rusu, A.A., et al.: Meta-learning with latent embedding optimization. In: Interna-tional Conference on Learning Representations (2019)
22. Schwartz, E., et al.: Delta-encoder: an effective sample synthesis method for few-shot object recognition. In: Advances in Neural Information Processing Systems, vol. 31 (2018)

23. Shorten, C., Khoshgoftaar, T.M.: A survey on image data augmentation for deep learning. J. Big Data **6**, 60 (2019). https://doi.org/10.1186/s40537-019-0197-0
24. Simon, C., Koniusz, P., Nock, R., Harandi, M.: Adaptive subspaces for few-shot learning. In: 2020 IEEE/CVF Conference on Computer Vision and Pattern Recognition (CVPR), pp. 4135–4144 (2020)
25. Snell, J., Swersky, K., Zemel, R.: Prototypical networks for few-shot learning. In: Advances in Neural Information Processing Systems, vol. 30, pp. 4077–4087 (2017)
26. Szegedy, C., et al.: Going deeper with convolutions. In: 2015 IEEE Conference on Computer Vision and Pattern Recognition (CVPR), pp. 1–9 (2015)
27. Vedaldi, A., Lenc, K.: MatConvNet: convolutional neural networks for MATLAB. In: Proceedings of the 23rd ACM International Conference on Multimedia, pp. 689–692 (2015)
28. Vinyals, O., Blundell, C., Lillicrap, T., kavukcuoglu, K., Wierstra, D.: Matching networks for one shot learning. In: Advances in Neural Information Processing Systems, vol. 29, pp. 3630–3638 (2016)
29. Wang, Y., Yao, Q., Kwok, J.T., Ni, L.M.: Generalizing from a few examples: a survey on few-shot learning. ACM Comput. Surv. **53**(3), 1–34 (2020)
30. Yoon, S.W., Seo, J., Moon, J.: TapNet: neural network augmented with task-adaptive projection for few-shot learning. In: Proceedings of the 36th International Conference on Machine Learning. Proceedings of Machine Learning Research, vol. 97, pp. 7115–7123 (2019)

Offline Handwritten Mathematical Expression Recognition via Graph Reasoning Network

Jia-Man Tang[1]($\boxtimes$), Jin-Wen Wu[2,3], Fei Yin[2], and Lin-Lin Huang[1]

[1] Beijing Jiaotong University, Beijing, China
{jiamantang,huangll}@bjtu.edu.cn
[2] National Laboratory of Pattern Recognition, Institute of Automation of Chinese Academy of Sciences, Beijing, China
{jinwen.wu,fyin}@nlpr.ia.ac.cn
[3] School of Artificial Intelligence, University of Chinese Academy of Sciences, Beijing, China

Abstract. Handwritten mathematical expression recognition (HMER) remains a challenge due to the complex 2-D structure layout and variable writing styles. Recently, large progress has been made by using deep encoder-decoder networks, which treat HMER as an Image-to-Sequence task and parse the math expression into a sequence (i.e. LaTeX). However, (1) mathematical expression is a 2-D structure pattern and sequence representation can not explicitly explore the structural relationship between symbols. (2) Image-to-Sequence as recurrent models can not infer in parallel during test stage. In this paper, we formulate mathematical expression recognition as an **Image-to-Graph** task and propose a Graph Reasoning Network (GRN) for offline HMER task. Compared with sequence representation, graph representation is more interpretable and more consistent with human visual cognition. Our method builds graph on math symbols detected from image, aggregates node and edge features via a Graph Neural Network (GNN) and parses the graph to give Symbol Layout Tree (SLT) format recognition result via node and edge classification. Experiments on public datasets show that our model achieve competitive results against other methods and can interpret the located symbols and inter-relationship explicitly.

Keywords: Handwritten Mathematical Expression Recognition · Symbol detection · Parallel reasoning

1 Introduction

Handwritten Mathematical Expression Recognition (HMER) is an important module of Optical Character Recognition (OCR) system. HMER has a wide range of applications such as educational scoring, office automation and information retrieval. With the prevalence of handwritten input devices, HMER attracts

© Springer Nature Switzerland AG 2022
C. Wallraven et al. (Eds.): ACPR 2021, LNCS 13188, pp. 17–31, 2022.
https://doi.org/10.1007/978-3-031-02375-0_2

a lot of attention in the community. Researches on mathematical expression recognition could be traced back to 1960s [7]. HMER needs to recognize math symbols as well as parse the 2-D structure among them. Mathematical expression can be represented according to specific rules. Markup language (i.e. LaTeX) and Symbol Layout Tree (SLT) [32] are two of the common representations.

Due to the variable style of handwritten mathematical symbols and complicated 2-D structure, HMER still remains a very challenging task. Unlike typeset expressions, the scale and style of handwritten symbols of different people usually vary a lot, which increases the difficulty in recognizing mathematical symbols. In addition to different writing styles, visual ambiguity of some mathematical symbols also downgrades the recognition result. For example, the uppercase letter 'X' and lowercase letter 'x' and operator '\times' are very similar in handwritten expressions, which needs more context information to distinguish them correctly. Apart from the handwritten symbolic diversity, parsing the complex 2-D spatial layout of mathematical expressions is even more challenging.

In order to recognize HME, grammar-based methods like [16] were introduced to tackle this problem. Though these methods can explicitly segment the primitives and learn an alignment between input primitives and target tokens, they require much grammar knowledge and manual features, therefore are less efficient and robust compared with data driven methods.

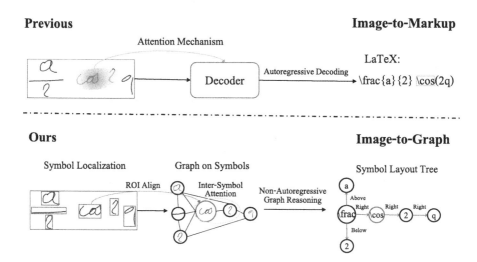

Fig. 1. A brief illustration of Image-to-Markup methods and our Image-to-Graph method. For Image-to-Markup systems, the decoder focus on relevant regions of symbols with an implicit attention mechanism which can not learn a precise alignment between input symbols and output targets. However, our Image-to-Graph method explicitly parses detected symbols to SLT format targets, and thus is more interpretable.

Recently, attention-based encoder-decoder models have achieved significant progress in sequence-to-sequence learning tasks such as speech recognition [5], machine translation [4] and image captioning [18]. Inspired by this, many works like [10, 27] formulate mathematical expression recognition as Image-to-Sequence task, i.e. Image-to-Markup [10]. Given the input formula $\mathbf{x}$ and its markup language representation $\mathbf{y}$, these methods are typically designed to transform the input $\mathbf{x}$ to high-level feature representation by an encoder and generate output prediction $\hat{\mathbf{y}}$ with an decoder. However, such approaches commonly have three defects: (i) Sequential methods can not explicitly exploit the 2-D structure information which is critical for parsing the formula. (ii) The encoder-decoder framework can not explicitly detect or segment the primitives and learn a precise alignment between input $\mathbf{x}$ and its output prediction $\hat{\mathbf{y}}$. (iii) Besides, the encoder-decoder method can not test in parallel and is computation-expensive.

To solve the problems mentioned above, some works like [22, 29] treats HMER as graph learning task. Inspired by these methods, we formulate offline HMER as Image-to-Graph learning problem $I_x \rightarrow G_y$ [31] and parse symbols and their relationships in parallel. A brief comparision between Image-to-Markup methods and our method can be seen in Fig. 1.

With the rapid development of graph learning, Graph Neural Network (GNN) has achieved impressive progress in graph data classification. To better exploit the 2-D structure information in the formula, we propose a Graph Reasoning Network (GRN) module to parse the input math image I_x to a graph and classify math symbols and their spatial relations simultaneously.

The main contribution of our work are as follows: (1) We formulate offline HMER as **Image-to-Graph** task which can explicitly leverage the spatial information of mathematical expression and is interpretable. (2) Our method is able to recognize math symbols and their relationships in parallel, which is concise and efficient.

The rest of this paper is organized as follows: Sect. 2 briefly reviews some representative work on HMER task. Section 3 describes the proposed model in detail. Section 4 presents our preliminary experiment results on public HMER datasets and discuss future plans. Section 5 concludes our current work.

2   Related Work

A typical framework of mathematical expression recognition mainly consists of three sub-tasks: symbol detection, symbol recognition and 2-D structure analysis. Existing HMER methods can be roughly classified into three categories: grammar based methods, Image-to-Markup methods and the newly emerging graph parsing methods.

2.1   Grammar Based Methods

Grammar based methods were prevalent in early stage of mathematical expression recognition research because they can recognize math symbols and parse the structure at the same time. Alvaro et al. [2,3] recognize math formulas based on context-free string grammars. Yamam et al. [30] presented a method using probabilistic context-free grammars. Macle et al. [21] proposed a method using relational grammars and fuzzy sets. However, these methods usually require much grammar knowledge and largely relies on the accuracy of symbol detection and segmentation. Meanwhile, the features for symbol segmentation and classification are designed artificially. So, they are less efficient and less robust compared with data driven ones.

2.2 Image-to-Markup Methods

With the success of encoder-decoder framework in sequence learning, encoder-decoder methods have been proposed to parse math expressions.

Deng et al. [9] proposed a method named WYGIWYS which employs a convolutional neural network (CNN) for feature extraction and an attention module for parsing like machine translation. A similar idea was also adopted by Le et al. [17]. These methods employ a CNN or RNN to encode the input formula and then a recurrent decoder to generate the target markup sequentially. Zhang et al. [33] proposed an improved model with coverage based attention mechanism, which can alleviate the over-segmentation and under-segmentation problems in basic parsing methods. To improve the performance later, Zhang et al. presented a DenseNet [14] based model with multi-scale attention to tackle the problem caused by pooling. Wu et al. [27] introduced an Image-to-Markup approach with paired adversarial learning (PAL) to learn better features against the variation of writing styles. Its improved version PAL-v2 [28] utilizes a pre-aware unit to enhance the accuracy of attention. Le et al. [17] use bidirectional RNNs to directly encode online formula inputs. Zhang et al. [35] proposed a tree-structure decoder to explicitly utilize the tree structure information in markup language.

2.3 Graph Parsing Methods

Recently, graph learning has attracted much attention. Graph neural networks have been successfully applied to visual understanding tasks like image captioning [8], scene graph generation [31] and text page segmentation [19]. Yang et al. proposed a graph model named Graph R-CNN [31] to understand scene contents. Li et al. [19] presented a page segmentation approach based on graph attention network (GAT) [25], with nodes representing primitive regions and edges representing geometric relationship. Node features and edge features are extracted using a CNN, which is trained jointly with the GAT.

Compared with sequence representation, graph representation is more natural and flexible for representing math expressions. Mahdavi and Zanibbi [22] proposed a graph based parsing model named QD-GGA to parse online handwritten formula into a SLT. It generates a Line-of-Sight (LOS) graph [13] over strokes, and extracts a SLT on the graph based on nodes and edges classification. Wu et al. [29] encoded the source graph on online handwritten strokes and decoded the graph with a graph decoder sequentially.

Motivated by the graph based methods [22, 29], we treat HMER as a graph learning and relational parsing task. Our method is designed for offline HMER. Instead of building graph on online strokes, we need to detect symbols from image as nodes of graph, and take advantage of the feature aggregation of GNN to improve the node and edge classification performance.

3   Method

3.1   Overview

Our method consists of two modules: Symbol Localization and Graph Reasoning Network. First, mathematical symbols in the image are detected using a math symbol detector. Second, a Line-of-Sight [13] graph $G(V, E)$ is generated based on the detected symbols, of which each node $v_i \in V$ represents a detected math symbol and each edge $e_{i,j} \in E$ represents the relationship between source node v_i and destination node v_j. Finally, GRN based on GAT [25] is employed to parse the symbol graph and extract the final SLT. The architecture of our method is illustrated in Fig. 2.

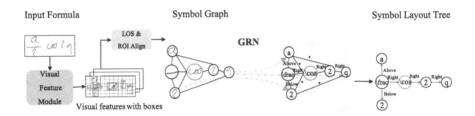

Fig. 2. An overview of our method. Firstly, visual features of math formula image with bounding boxes are generated through a visual feature module. Secondly, a symbol graph is constructed based on detected symbols according to the Line-of-Sight rule and graph features are obtained by ROI Align. Finally, the symbol graph is parsed by GRN and the SLT of the formula is obtained. In the figure, '*' stands for 'No-Relation' between two nodes.

3.2   Symbol Localization

To explicitly focus on math symbols in the image, we adopt a single stage general object detector named YOLOv5 [15] to detect symbols. In order to keep the simplicity of the detection module and improve the recall of symbol detection, we only detect symbols in the image ignoring their classes.

For symbol features generation, we implement a visual feature module. We adopt a modified ResNet50 [12] module to learn visual symbol features. To extract node features F_v of the graph, we perform RoIAlign [11] on the last three stages of ResNet50 given the detected bounding boxes to extract symbol features and project the features of each symbol F_{v_i} to a certain dimension using fully connected layer.

Following [19], for each edge $e_{i,j}$, we first compute the smallest enclosing bounding box that surrounds node v_i and v_j exactly. Then we perform RoIAlign based on the enclosing bounding box and use FC layer to project the edge feature $F_{e_{i,j}}$ to a certain dimension. See Fig. 3 for more details.

3.3   Graph Reasoning Network

Graph Representation. Mathematical expressions can be represented by SLT, which represents symbols and their relationships along the writing lines. In order to generate a symbol graph given the detection results, we follow [13] to generate a Line-of-Sight symbol graph with K-Nearest Neighbors (e.g. K=3). For each symbols, an edge is firstly added to its K nearest symbols to improve the edge recall, then follow the Line-of-Sight rule to generate symbol graph. We add a 'Background' class to the node class set, which means a false positive detection box. Similarly, a 'No-Relation' class is added to the edge class set, which indicates there is no relationship between the source node v_i and destination node v_j. To extract SLT from the generated Line-of-Sight graph $G(V,E)$, we need to classify the nodes and edges and filter out the 'Background' nodes and 'No-Relation' edges.

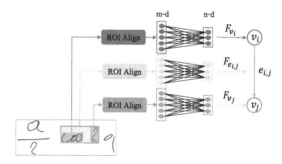

Fig. 3. Node features and edge features extraction. We perform ROIAlign based on symbol boxes and their smallest enclosing box to extract node features and edge features respectively.

Architecture. In order to extract the SLT of a formula, we parse the symbol graph with GRN. By adding edge classification task to vanilla GAT, our GRN is able to preform node classification and edge classification simultaneously. The input of our GRN are node features $F_V \in \mathbb{R}^{|V| \times N}$ and edge features $F_E \in \mathbb{R}^{|E| \times N}$, where $|V|$ and $|E|$ are node number and edge number, N is node and edge feature dimension. The general architecture of GRN is illustrated in Fig. 4

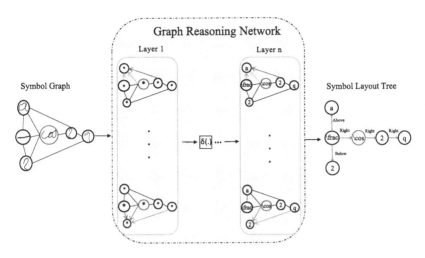

Fig. 4. The architecture of Graph Reasoning Network. Symbol graph is parsed by our Graph Reasoning Network and the SLT is finally obtained by filtering 'Background' nodes and 'No-Relation' edges out. The different edge colors in each layer stand for different inter-symbol attention, $\delta(\cdot)$ denotes non-linear transformation.

In the k-th GRN layer, we update the edge features $F_{e_{i,j}}^k$ by concatenating edge features in the $k-1$-th layer with its source node features $F_{v_i}^{k-1}$ and destination node features $F_{v_j}^{k-1}$ and performing a non-linear transformation:

$$F_{e_{i,j}}^k = \delta(W^k[F_{v_i}^{k-1}||F_{e_{i,j}}^{k-1}||F_{v_j}^{k-1}]), \tag{1}$$

where $W^k \in \mathbb{R}^{N' \times (2N+N)}$ is the weight matrix, δ is the LeakyReLU activation function, $||$ stands for the concatenation. By updating edge features, the model can better integrate the contextual information in the neighbors.

Then the *self-attention mechanism* is used to compute self-attention coefficient $r_{i,j}$ of every neighboring node pair(v_i, v_j):

$$r_{i,j} = a(W_V F_{v_i}||W_V F_{v_j}||W_E F_{e_{i,j}}), \tag{2}$$

where a denotes the self-attention mechanism,e.g. linear transformation, W_V and W_E are the learnable parameters for nodes and edges. Then we normalize $r_{i,j}$ among all the neighbors of node i using softmax function:

$$\alpha_{i,j} = softmax(r_{i,j}) = \frac{exp(\beta r_{i,j})}{\sum_{k \in \mathcal{N}_i} exp(\beta r_{i,k})}, \tag{3}$$

where $\mathcal{N}_i$ is the neighbors of v_i, β is the temperature usually set to 1. Once obtain the normalized attention coefficient $\alpha_{i,j}$, we can update the node features in k-th layer by:

$$F_{v_i}^k = \delta(\sum_{j \in \mathcal{N}_i} \alpha_{i,j} W_V F_{v_j}^{k-1}). \tag{4}$$

During the inference stage, a symbol graph is constructed over the detected regions, and then the nodes and edges of the symbol graph are classified into corresponding symbols and spatial relationships. Nodes predicted as 'Background' and edges predicted as 'No-Relation' are removed from the symbol graph to generate the final SLT.

3.4 Training Details

We first pretrain the detector on the math dataset, then jointly fine-tuning with the GRN. Three layers of GRN are employed, since more layers would result in over-smoothing and drops the performance. Our model is optimized via the SGD optimizer with a momentum of 0.9 and weight decay of 0.0005. The initial learning rate is set to 0.01 and is adjusted according to the sinusoidal learning rate adjustment strategy. The detector adopts the GIoU loss as regression loss and Binary Cross Entropy loss as objectness loss.

$$\mathcal{L}_{reg} = 1 - GIoU = 1 - IoU + \frac{A^c - \mu}{A^c}, \tag{5}$$

$$\mathcal{L}_{obj} = BCE(pred, y), \tag{6}$$

where c is the smallest enclosing box of predicted box p and ground truth box g, A^c is the area of c, μ is the union of p and g and $pred$ is the output objectness distribution. In the GRN, the loss of node prediction $\mathcal{L}_n$ and edge prediction $\mathcal{L}_e$ are computed using Cross Entropy loss respectively.

$$\mathcal{L}_n = - \sum_{v_i \in V} \log \hat{p}_{v_i}, \tag{7}$$

$$\mathcal{L}_e = - \sum_{e_{i,j} \in E} \log \hat{p}_{e_{i,j}}, \tag{8}$$

where $\hat{p}_{v_i}$ represents output probability of node v_i and $\hat{p}_{e_{i,j}}$ represents output probability of edge $e_{i,j}$. And the overall loss function is described in Eq. 9. The coefficients of the overall loss are determined experimentally. Specifically, $\lambda_1 = 0.05$, $\lambda_2 = 1$ and $\lambda_3 = \lambda_4 = 2$.

$$\mathcal{L} = \lambda_1 \times \mathcal{L}_{reg} + \lambda_2 \times \mathcal{L}_{obj} + \lambda_3 \times \mathcal{L}_n + \lambda_4 \times \mathcal{L}_e. \tag{9}$$

Our model is implemented on the PyTorch platform and DGL library and optimized on 4 Nvidia TITAN XP GPUs with 12GB memory.

4 Experiment

4.1 Datasets

We train our model on CROHME datasets from the Competition on Recognition of Online Handwritten Mathematical Expressions [23] and OffRaSHME dataset from the Competition on Offline Recognition and Spotting on Handwritten Mathematical Expressions [26].

The hanwritten mathematical expressions of CROHME are collected with online devices. The stroke data is described by lists of (x,y) coordinates and stored in the InkML files. There are 101 symbol classes and 6 structural relation classes ('Right', 'Above', 'Below', 'Superscript', 'Subscript' and 'Inside') in CROHME datasets. In our setting, a 'Background' class and 'No-Relation' class are added to symbol class set and relation class set respectively. The CROHME training set contains 8,836 formulas and the test sets for CROHME 2014/2016/2019 contain 986/1,147/1,199 formulas respectively. Since the CROHME formulas are online handwritten formulas, we render them into offline images and pad the images to specific size (e.g. 256×1,024).

The OffRaSHME contains the same handwritten math symbol classes and relations classes as CROHME. The OffRaSHME training set contains 19,749 offline handwritten formulas images with 10,000 formulas annotated at symbol level and the test set contains 2,000 formulas with symbol level annotations. Unlike the formula images rendered from online strokes in CROHME, the offline formula images in OffRaSHME are more natural and closer to the real handwritten images which contain more handwritten information. We train our model on the 10,000 training images and evaluate our model on 2,000 images.

4.2 Results

The main metric for HMER is expression recognition rate (ExpRate) which means the ratio of correctly recognized formulas over the test set. And structure rate (StruRate) denotes the correct structure recognition rate ignoring symbol classification.

OffRaSHME. In order to prove the effectiveness of our GRN in parsing graph data, we repalce GRN module with a Multi-Layer Perceptron (MLP). Experiments were conducted on OffRaSHME dataset to compare our GRN against MLP. To be consistent with GRN, two MLPs with three layers are employed to classify nodes and edges of the symbol graph. Classification results are list in Table 1.

Table 1. Classification results on OffRaSHME. All metrics presented below are in %.

Module	Node Acc	Edge Acc	ExpRate	StruRate
MLP	91.25	96.10	40.10	59.35
GRN	94.61	98.34	56.95	74.70

As is shown in Table 1, since our proposed GRN can aggregate context information between nodes, thus outperforms MLP by a large margin.

For reference, Table 2 presents our preliminary results and the participants of the OffRaSHME. Note that it's unfair to directly compare our method against the participants of OffRaSHME, since our method is only trained on 10,000 formula images and we do not apply tricks like model ensemble and data augmentation. The winner USTC-iFLYTEK combines a string decoder [36] and a Tree Decoder [35] to parse the formula. We compared our method with Tree Decoder on CROHME without using data augmentation and model ensemble in Table 4. Our current results show the promise of the proposed method for offline HMER.

Table 2. Results on OffRaSHME. "≤ 1 error" and "≤ 2 error" indicate expression recognition rate when 0 to 2 structural or symbol errors can be tolerated.

Methods	ExpRate	≤ 1 error	≤ 2 error	StruRate
USTC-iFLYTEK [35]	79.85	89.85	92.00	92.55
SCUT-DLVCLab [20]	72.90	86.05	88.80	89.45
TUAT [24]	71.75	82.70	85.80	86.60
HCMUS-I86 [26]	66.95	79.65	83.60	84.00
SYSU [6]	61.35	77.30	81.55	82.90
MLE [26]	46.85	61.15	65.80	67.45
Ours	56.95	72.75	77.55	74.70

CROHME. To evaluate the performance of our explicit localization, detection results are listed in Table 3. 'UPV' [1] and 'Tokyo' [23] are the winner of CROHME 2014 and 2016 using official training data respectively. Experiment results show the advantages of our model in symbol level detection.

Table 3. Symbol level evaluation on CROHME. "Det" denotes the detection /segmentation precision and "Det+Class" denotes the symbol accuracy based on detection.

Methods	CROHME 2014		CROHME 2016	
	Det	Det+Class	Det	Det+Class
UPV [1]	90.71	84.18	–	–
Tokyo [23]	–	–	93.35	87.58
Ours	95.60	88.23	96.40	90.03

We benchmark our model against SOTAs on CROHME 2014/2016/2019 test sets. Our preliminary results on CROHME 2014/2016/2019 are listed in Table 4. For fair comparison, ensemble models are not included.

As is shown in the Table 4, our model achieves comparable results against current SOTA models. On CROHME 2014/2016/2019 test sets, our model achieves a recognition rate of 47.67%, 49.87% and 50.71% respectively. Although our performance is far from being satisfactory compared with up-to-date SOTA systems, our model can learn an alignment between input formula and output SLT explicitly. Our model can learn the correspondence between predicted symbols and the regions in the input image. Therefore, our model is structural interpretable. Moreover, different from sequential decoders, our model can run in parallel which is computation friendly. Our model is faster than most of the models mentioned in the table. The test time on CROHME 2014 for TAP is 377 sec, the WAP and the ensemble of TAP + WAP take 196 sec and 564 sec respectively and the PAL-v2 takes more than 300 sec. The test time of our model is around 140 sec. Although QD-GGA takes only 59 sec on CROHME 2014 test set, our performance outperforms QD-GGA by a large margin. Our current model is concise and straightforward. The preliminary results demonstrate that our model is a promising method.

4.3 Visualization

To better explore the limitation of our current model and discuss the future improvement, we visualize some typical errors on OffRaSHME and CROHME.

The first sort of typical errors is detection error. Due to the variable writing styles, some symbols may be merged into one symbol while some symbols may be separated into multiple parts. As is shown in Fig. 5, symbol ')' and '=' in formula I are detected as one symbol and later classified as 'F'. Symbol 'p' in formula II are detected as two parts and classified as '1' and ')'. Similarily, symbol '$\pm$' in formula III is separated into two parts and classified as '+' and '-', and symbol '$\backslash ldots$' in formula IV is detected and classified as three consecutive '$\backslash dot$'s.

The second sort of errors is classification errors. In this situation, each symbol in the formula is detected correctly. However, some handwritten symbols are similar in visual shapes and hard to recognize correctly. As is shown in Fig. 5, symbol '3' in formula V is wrongly classified as '5', symbol '$\backslash prime$' in formula VI is wrongly classified as 'i', symbol 'q' in formula VII is wrongly classified as '9' and symbol 'z' in formula VIII is classified as '2'. Some of these misclassifications are challenging even for humans.

We speculate that these errors are caused by the lack of semantic information. Since we currently only utilize visual features of formulas, it's likely to encounter these errors. In the future work, we will improve our model by considering semantic information to improve detection and graph parsing performance.

Table 4. Comparison against State-of-the-art HMER models on CROHME 2014/2016/2019.

Datasets	Methods	ExpRate	≤ 1 error	≤ 2 error	StruRate
CROHME 2014	WYGIWYS	28.70	–	–	–
	UPV	37.22	44.22	47.26	–
	TAP	46.90	–	–	–
	QD-GGA	32.40	45.06	55.23	–
	PAL-v2	48.88	64.50	69.78	–
	Tree Decoder [35]	49.10	64.20	67.80	68.60
	WS WAP [24]	53.65	–	–	–
	Ours	47.67	62.47	67.95	64.91
CROHME 2016	Tokyo	43.94	50.91	53.70	61.60
	QD-GGA	32.84	46.88	59.12	–
	PAL-v2	49.61	64.08	70.27	–
	DenseWAP [34]	40.10	54.30	57.80	59.20
	Tree Decoder	48.50	62.30	65.30	65.90
	WS WAP	51.96	64.34	70.10	–
	Ours	49.87	64.25	69.65	65.91
CROHME 2019	QD-GGA	40.65	60.01	64.96	60.22
	DenseWAP	41.70	55.50	59.30	60.70
	Tree Decoder	51.40	66.10	69.10	69.80
	Ours	50.71	66.47	70.56	67.89

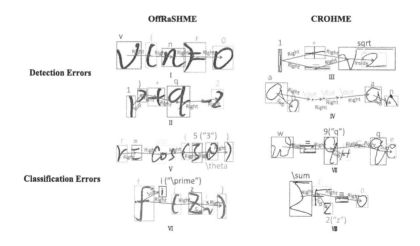

Fig. 5. Error visualization. For classification errors, ground truth is in the brackets.

5 Conclusion

In this paper, we formulate offline HMER as an Image-to-Graph task and proposed a simple but competitive Graph Reasoning Network to model the input formula image I_x to symbol graph $G(V, E)$. The graph representation of handwritten mathematical expression is more consistent with human visual cognition, more natural and interpretable compared with sequence representation. Our model is able to explicitly utilize the spatial information and computation friendly. Experiment results on public datasets demonstrate that our method is competitive and promising.

Acknowledgments. This work has been supported by the National Key Research and Development Program Grant 2020AAA0109702, and the National Natural Science Foundation of China (NSFC) grants 61733007.

References

1. Alvaro, F., Sánchez, J.A., Benedí, J.M.: Offline features for classifying handwritten math symbols with recurrent neural networks. In: 2014 22nd International Conference on Pattern Recognition, pp. 2944–2949. IEEE (2014)
2. Alvaro, F., Sánchez, J.A., Benedí, J.M.: Recognition of on-line handwritten mathematical expressions using 2D stochastic context-free grammars and hidden Markov models. Pattern Recogn. Lett. **35**, 58–67 (2014)
3. Álvaro, F., Sánchez, J.A., Benedí, J.M.: An integrated grammar-based approach for mathematical expression recognition. Pattern Recogn. **51**, 135–147 (2016)
4. Bahdanau, D., Cho, K., Bengio, Y.: Neural machine translation by jointly learning to align and translate. arXiv preprint arXiv:1409.0473 (2014)
5. Bahdanau, D., Chorowski, J., Serdyuk, D., Brakel, P., Bengio, Y.: End-to-end attention-based large vocabulary speech recognition. In: 2016 IEEE International Conference on Acoustics, Speech and Signal Processing (ICASSP), pp. 4945–4949. IEEE (2016)
6. Chan, C.: Stroke extraction for offline handwritten mathematical expression recognition. IEEE Access **8**, 61565–61575 (2020)
7. Chan, K.F., Yeung, D.Y.: Mathematical expression recognition: a survey. Int. J. Doc. Anal. Recogn. **3**(1), 3–15 (2000). https://doi.org/10.1007/PL00013549
8. Dai, B., Zhang, Y., Lin, D.: Detecting visual relationships with deep relational networks. In: Proceedings of the IEEE Conference on Computer Vision and Pattern Recognition, pp. 3076–3086 (2017)
9. Deng, Y., Kanervisto, A., Rush, A.M.: What you get is what you see: a visual markup decompiler (2016)
10. Deng, Y., Kanervisto, A., Ling, J., Rush, A.M.: Image-to-markup generation with coarse-to-fine attention. In: International Conference on Machine Learning, pp. 980–989. PMLR (2017)
11. He, K., Gkioxari, G., Dollár, P., Girshick, R.: Mask R-CNN. In: Proceedings of the IEEE International Conference on Computer Vision, pp. 2961–2969 (2017)
12. He, K., Zhang, X., Ren, S., Sun, J.: Deep residual learning for image recognition. In: Proceedings of the IEEE Conference on Computer Vision and Pattern Recognition, pp. 770–778 (2016)

13. Hu, L., Zanibbi, R.: Line-of-sight stroke graphs and Parzen shape context features for handwritten math formula representation and symbol segmentation. In: 2016 15th International Conference on Frontiers in Handwriting Recognition (ICFHR), pp. 180–186. IEEE (2016)
14. Huang, G., Liu, Z., Van Der Maaten, L., Weinberger, K.Q.: Densely connected convolutional networks. In: Proceedings of the IEEE Conference on Computer Vision and Pattern Recognition, pp. 4700–4708 (2017)
15. Jocher, G., et al.: ultralytics/yolov5: v5.0 - YOLOv5-P6 1280 models, AWS, Supervise.ly and YouTube integrations, April 2021. https://doi.org/10.5281/zenodo.4679653
16. Julca-Aguilar, F., Mouchère, H., Viard-Gaudin, C., Hirata, N.S.: A general framework for the recognition of online handwritten graphics. Int. J. Doc. Anal. Recogn. (IJDAR) **23**(2), 143–160 (2020)
17. Le, A.D., Nakagawa, M.: Training an end-to-end system for handwritten mathematical expression recognition by generated patterns. In: 2017 14th IAPR International Conference on Document Analysis and Recognition (ICDAR), vol. 1, pp. 1056–1061. IEEE (2017)
18. Li, L., Tang, S., Deng, L., Zhang, Y., Tian, Q.: Image caption with global-local attention. In: Proceedings of the AAAI Conference on Artificial Intelligence, vol. 31 (2017)
19. Li, X.-H., Yin, F., Liu, C.-L.: Page segmentation using convolutional neural network and graphical model. In: Bai, X., Karatzas, D., Lopresti, D. (eds.) DAS 2020. LNCS, vol. 12116, pp. 231–245. Springer, Cham (2020). https://doi.org/10.1007/978-3-030-57058-3_17
20. Li, Z., Jin, L., Lai, S., Zhu, Y.: Improving attention-based handwritten mathematical expression recognition with scale augmentation and drop attention. In: 2020 17th International Conference on Frontiers in Handwriting Recognition (ICFHR), pp. 175–180. IEEE (2020)
21. MacLean, S., Labahn, G.: A new approach for recognizing handwritten mathematics using relational grammars and fuzzy sets. Int. J. Doc. Anal. Recogn. (IJDAR) **16**(2), 139–163 (2013). https://doi.org/10.1007/s10032-012-0184-x
22. Mahdavi, M., Zanibbi, R.: Visual parsing with query-driven global graph attention (QD-GGA): preliminary results for handwritten math formula recognition. In: Proceedings of the IEEE/CVF Conference on Computer Vision and Pattern Recognition Workshops, pp. 570–571 (2020)
23. Mouchère, H., Viard-Gaudin, C., Zanibbi, R., Garain, U.: ICFHR 2016 CROHME: competition on recognition of online handwritten mathematical expressions. In: 2016 15th International Conference on Frontiers in Handwriting Recognition (ICFHR), pp. 607–612. IEEE (2016)
24. Truong, T.N., Nguyen, C.T., Phan, K.M., Nakagawa, M.: Improvement of end-to-end offline handwritten mathematical expression recognition by weakly supervised learning. In: 2020 17th International Conference on Frontiers in Handwriting Recognition (ICFHR), pp. 181–186. IEEE (2020)
25. Veličković, P., Cucurull, G., Casanova, A., Romero, A., Lio, P., Bengio, Y.: Graph attention networks. arXiv preprint arXiv:1710.10903 (2017)
26. Wang, D.H., et al.: ICFHR 2020 competition on offline recognition and spotting of handwritten mathematical expressions-OFFRASHME. In: 2020 17th International Conference on Frontiers in Handwriting Recognition (ICFHR), pp. 211–215 (2020). https://doi.org/10.1109/ICFHR2020.2020.00047

27. Wu, J.-W., Yin, F., Zhang, Y.-M., Zhang, X.-Y., Liu, C.-L.: Image-to-markup generation via paired adversarial learning. In: Berlingerio, M., Bonchi, F., Gärtner, T., Hurley, N., Ifrim, G. (eds.) ECML PKDD 2018. LNCS (LNAI), vol. 11051, pp. 18–34. Springer, Cham (2019). https://doi.org/10.1007/978-3-030-10925-7_2

28. Wu, J.-W., Yin, F., Zhang, Y.-M., Zhang, X.-Y., Liu, C.-L.: Handwritten mathematical expression recognition via paired adversarial learning. Int. J. Comput. Vis. **128**(10), 2386–2401 (2020). https://doi.org/10.1007/s11263-020-01291-5

29. Wu, J.W., Yin, F., Zhang, Y.M., Zhang, X.Y., Liu, C.L.: Graph-to-graph: towards accurate and interpretable online handwritten mathematical expression recognition. In: Proceedings of the AAAI Conference on Artificial Intelligence, vol. 35, pp. 2925–2933 (2021)

30. Yamamoto, R., Sako, S., Nishimoto, T., Sagayama, S.: On-line recognition of handwritten mathematical expressions based on stroke-based stochastic context-free grammar. In: Tenth international workshop on frontiers in handwriting recognition. Suvisoft (2006)

31. Yang, J., Lu, J., Lee, S., Batra, D., Parikh, D.: Graph R-CNN for scene graph generation. In: Ferrari, V., Hebert, M., Sminchisescu, C., Weiss, Y. (eds.) Computer Vision – ECCV 2018: 15th European Conference, Munich, Germany, September 8-14, 2018, Proceedings, Part I, pp. 690–706. Springer International Publishing, Cham (2018). https://doi.org/10.1007/978-3-030-01246-5_41

32. Zanibbi, R., Blostein, D.: Recognition and retrieval of mathematical expressions. Int. J. Doc. Anal. Recogn. (IJDAR) **15**(4), 331–357 (2012). https://doi.org/10.1007/s10032-011-0174-4

33. Zhang, J., Du, J., Dai, L.: A GRU-based encoder-decoder approach with attention for online handwritten mathematical expression recognition. In: 2017 14th IAPR International Conference on Document Analysis and Recognition (ICDAR), vol. 1, pp. 902–907. IEEE (2017)

34. Zhang, J., Du, J., Dai, L.: Multi-scale attention with dense encoder for handwritten mathematical expression recognition. In: 2018 24th International Conference on Pattern Recognition (ICPR), pp. 2245–2250. IEEE (2018)

35. Zhang, J., Du, J., Yang, Y., Song, Y.Z., Wei, S., Dai, L.: A tree-structured decoder for image-to-markup generation. In: International Conference on Machine Learning, pp. 11076–11085. PMLR (2020)

36. Zhang, J., et al.: Watch, attend and parse: an end-to-end neural network based approach to handwritten mathematical expression recognition. Pattern Recogn. **71**, 196–206 (2017)

Circulant Tensor Graph Convolutional Network for Text Classification

Xuran Xu, Tong Zhang$^{(\boxtimes)}$, Chunyan Xu, and Zhen Cui

School of Computer Science and Engineering, Nanjing University of Science and Technology, Nanjing, China
tong.zhang@njust.edu.cn

Abstract. Graph convolutional network (GCN) has shown promising performance on the text classification tasks via modeling irregular correlations between word and document. There are multiple correlations within a text graph adjacency matrix, including word-word, word-document, and document-document, so we regard it as heterogeneous. While existing graph convolutional filters are constructed based on homogeneous information diffusion processes, which may not be appropriate to the heterogeneous graph. This paper proposes an expressive and efficient circulant tensor graph convolutional network (CTGCN). Specifically, we model a text graph into a multi-dimension tensor, which characterizes three types of homogeneous correlations separately. CTGCN constructs an expressive and efficient tensor filter based on the t-product operation, which designs a *t*-linear transformation in the tensor space with a block circulant matrix. Tensor operation t-product effectively extracts high-dimension correlation among heterogeneous feature spaces, which is customarily ignored by other GCN-based methods. Furthermore, we introduce a heterogeneity attention mechanism to obtain more discriminative features. Eventually, we evaluate our proposed CTGCN on five publicly used text classification datasets, extensive experiments demonstrate the effectiveness of the proposed model.

Keywords: Tensor · Graph convolutional network · Text classification

1 Introduction

Text classification aims to conclude the types/labels of documents based on textual content. For example, an e-mail can be identified as spam if it contains advertisements words. As a footstone of natural language processing tasks, text classification has been widely applied to information filtering [29], sentiment analysis [5], recommender systems [7], and document summarization [16]. Early works on text classification are derived from the development of statistical learning and the rise of traditional machine learning methods. Exactly, the document feature is modeled into a vector based on the statistics of words, e.g., term frequency-inverse document frequency (TF-IDF) [24], bag-of-words, and n-grams [27], then a classifier model is employed. General classifier models include

© Springer Nature Switzerland AG 2022
C. Wallraven et al. (Eds.): ACPR 2021, LNCS 13188, pp. 32–46, 2022.
https://doi.org/10.1007/978-3-031-02375-0_3

support vector machine (SVM) and Bayesian inference. Although promising performance has been achieved, however, hand-crafted features are under expressive and the generalization ability of traditional machine learning models is inadequate. Recently, deep learning methods are flourishing in the computer vision domain, which promotes the development of natural language processing simultaneously. For example, convolutional neural network (CNN) is used to extract word features for sentence-level classification tasks in [12]. Recurrent neural network (RNN) [17] concatenates the previous state and the current state together and achieves better performance on the text classification task with the advantage of modeling sequence. Moreover, long short-term memory (LSTM) as one variant of RNN has been shown its superiority in modeling long sequences by flowing the information with dynamically calculating weights in [32]. Despite the success of these deep neural networks in text classification, they only consider the sequence of words in the document. Therefore, they are incapable of constructing irregular correlations between words.

More recently, graph neural network obtains growing attention in the task of text classification. Yao et al. [30] firstly model document and word as nodes and introduce graph convolutional network to diffuse information between nodes. Experimental results demonstrate their proposed Text GCN outperforms state-of-the-art methods and is capable of learning more discriminative features. Afterwards, researchers have been trying to explore more effective GCN-based models for text classification tasks [31]. Although irregular correlations between word-word, word-document, and document-document can be modeled in the above researches, these correlations are constructed in the single adjacency matrix, which can not be well modeled by traditional homogeneous graph convolutional network. Hence, Hu et al. take the heterogeneity of text graph into consideration in [15]. Although the heterogeneity of text graph from the information diffusion process is modeled, they ignore the diversity of feature spaces. According to literature [1, 19], more contextual information contributes to text classification tasks. Liu et al. construct a text graph tensor that integrates semantic, syntactic, and sequential contextual information in [18] and propose to diffuse node information based on the multi-graph convolutional network. However, the multi-graph convolutional network is two-stage that separately conducts intra-graph to diffuse homogeneous information and inter-graph propagation to harmonize heterogeneous information instead of the natural extension of the GCN in tensor space.

Considering existing methods are exposed to the following challenges: i) Matrix feature space for text graph is under expressive; ii) How to construct heterogeneous correlation among text graph; iii) How to efficiently harmonize heterogeneous feature space. We aim to construct an expressive text graph feature space and explore an efficient heterogeneous information harmonization strategy in this paper. Specifically, we construct a text graph tensor that describes the topology structure between document and word, co-occurrence correlation among words in the whole corpus, co-occurrence correlation between word and document. Based on these three types of feature space and correlations, we design an expressive heterogeneous text graph tensor feature space. To further overcome the limitation that GCN-based methods are not suitable for the heterogeneous text graph tensor information diffusion process, we propose a circulant tensor graph convolutional network (CTGCN). CTGCN is based on the tensor operation t-product, which can be interpreted as the extension of a linear transformation in the tensor space. Based on the mimetic matrix properties of the t-product, CTGCN not only expressively encodes specific feature space but also harmonizes different types of features. Inspired by channel attention [28], we finally utilize a heterogeneity attention mechanism to obtain more discriminative features. Experimental results demonstrate that our proposed CTGCN efficiently encodes information between high-dimension feature tensors. In summary, our contributions are three folds:

- We construct an expressive heterogeneous text graph tensor that integrates topology structure, words co-occurrence, and word-document co-occurrence.
- We introduce a tensor operation t-product to deal with high-dimension correlations and naturally propose a circulant tensor graph convolutional network that efficiently conducts information diffusion in the tensor space. Moreover, for the specific text classification task, the circulant tensor graph convolutional network harmonizes different feature spaces.
- Experiments on the five open text classification datasets demonstrate that our proposed CTGCN compares favorably with state-of-the-art models.

2   Related Work

Graph convolutional network is proposed to generalize convolution operation from low-dimensional regular grid structures, e.g., image, video, and speech to high-dimensional irregular structures, e.g., social networks, protein structure, citation network. However, the early spectral graph convolutional network [3] is limited by the computation cost of Laplacian matrix eigendecomposition. To tackle this issue, a fast localized spectral graph convolutional network [4] parameterizes filters as Chebyshev polynomial. Then Kipf et al. [13] further propose a localized first-order approximation of spectral graph convolutions, which is widely used in various GCN-based models, formulated as $\mathbf{H}^{(l+1)} = \sigma(\tilde{\mathbf{D}}^{-\frac{1}{2}}\tilde{\mathbf{A}}\tilde{\mathbf{D}}^{-\frac{1}{2}}\mathbf{H}^{(l)}\mathbf{W}^{(l)})$. Moreover, there are a proportion of works start to research tensor graph convolutional neural networks. For example, Zhang et al. utilize the Kronecker sum operation to model dynamic graphs to learn an optimal conjunctive graph. Another tensor graph convolutional network introduces the M-product operation to conduct spatial and temporal message passing. However, these two models are constructed for the dynamic graph.

With the development of graph convolution theory, the GCN-based methods are widely applied to computer vision and natural language processing. Yao et al. [30] firstly propose to model document and word as a heterogeneous graph and introduce GCN model to diffuse information between nodes. Afterwards, Zhang et al. [31] integrate a dual attention mechanism with GCN to capture more discriminative features. Specifically, they combine connection-attention and hop-attention to capture more long dependencies. However, they both ignore that text graph is heterogeneous and the single feature space is under expressive. Hence, Hu et al. [15] present a flexible heterogeneous information network then employ node-level and type-level attentions for short text classification. Ragesh et al. model documents as a heterogeneous graph that encodes relationships among words, documents, and labels [23]. Closer to our work, Liu et al. [18] propose to construct a text graph tensor that consists of multi-type contextual information and introduce a multi-graph convolutional network. Although great improvements have been obtained, it unsolved the problem of extending the graph convolutional network to tensor space.

3   Preliminaries

In this section, we first briefly describe the standardized tensor conception based on the prior literature [9]. Then we introduce the t-product operation proposed in [11,21] and corresponding linear-algebraic properties. Finally, we present the construction of our proposed text graph tensor.

3.1   Tensor Notation

Tensor is used to denote multi-dimension data and can be referred to as $\mathcal{X} \in \mathbb{R}^{I_1 \times I_2 \times \cdots \times I_M}$, where M is the tensor order and I_n is the number of elements in the respective dimension n. In this paper, tensor, matrix, and vector are denoted by boldface Euler script, bold uppercase, and bold lowercase respectively, such as $\mathcal{X}, \mathbf{X}, \mathbf{x}$. We consider the case that M is equal to 3 and write as $\mathcal{X} \in \mathbb{R}^{l \times m \times n}$. For a third-order tensor, we can obtain its slice matrix by fixing one index, e.g., $\mathcal{X}_{i::}, \mathcal{X}_{:j:}$, and $\mathcal{X}_{::k}$ denote horizontal, lateral, and frontal slides of tensor $\mathcal{X}$. Moreover, the lateral slice $\mathcal{X}_{:j:}$ can be further interpreted as a vector of tubes by fixing the third index. We show the schematic of slices operation in Fig. 1 for a better understanding. Meanwhile, the kth frontal slice of $\mathcal{X}$ can be denoted more compactly as $\mathbf{X}^{(k)}$ and the pth lateral slice of $\mathcal{X}$ can be denoted as $\overrightarrow{\mathbf{X}}_p$.

Definition 1. (circ, MatVec, fold) Circ operation creates a block circulant matrix from the slice of a third-order tensor and MatVec operation unfolds tensor to the matrix. According to [11], for $\mathcal{X} \in \mathbb{R}^{l \times m \times n}$ with frontal slice $\mathbf{X}^{(1)}, \mathbf{X}^{(2)}, \cdots, \mathbf{X}^{(n)}$, circ and MatVec operation are defined as follows:

$$
circ(\mathcal{X}) = \begin{bmatrix} \mathbf{X}^{(1)} & \mathbf{X}^{(n)} & \cdots & \mathbf{X}^{(2)} \\ \mathbf{X}^{(2)} & \mathbf{X}^{(1)} & \cdots & \mathbf{X}^{(3)} \\ \vdots & \vdots & \ddots & \vdots \\ \mathbf{X}^{(n)} & \mathbf{X}^{(n-1)} & \cdots & \mathbf{X}^{(1)} \end{bmatrix}, \quad MatVec(\mathcal{X}) = \begin{bmatrix} \mathbf{X}^{(1)} \\ \mathbf{X}^{(2)} \\ \vdots \\ \mathbf{X}^{(n)} \end{bmatrix}, \quad (1)
$$

where $circ(\mathcal{X}) \in \mathbb{R}^{ln \times mn}$ and $MatVec(\mathcal{X}) \in \mathbb{R}^{ln \times m}$. Operation $fold(\cdot)$ can be regard as inverse operation of $MatVec(\cdot)$, which folds a matrix back to a tensor. Therefore, we have

$$
\mathcal{X} = fold(MatVec(\mathcal{X})). \quad (2)
$$

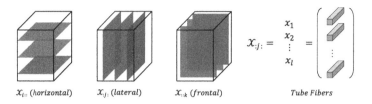

$\mathcal{X}_{i::}$ *(horizontal)* $\mathcal{X}_{:j:}$ *(lateral)* $\mathcal{X}_{::k}$ *(frontal)* $\quad$ *Tube Fibers*

Fig. 1. The schematic of lateral, horizontal and frontal slides of tensor.

Definition 2. (t-product) T-product denotes an algebraic formulation of tensors and its remarkable property is the preservation of tensor order. Here we utilize notation $*$ to denote t-product operation between tensors, then

$$\mathcal{X} * \mathcal{W} = fold(circ(\mathcal{X}) \cdot MatVec(\mathcal{W})), \qquad (3)$$

where $\mathcal{X} \in \mathbb{R}^{l \times m \times n}$, $\mathcal{W} \in \mathbb{R}^{m \times p \times n}$, and $(\mathcal{X} * \mathcal{W}) \in \mathbb{R}^{l \times p \times n}$. We can observe that the t-product does not change the order of tensor, which provides a basic condition for generalizing the concepts of linear algebra for tensors.

Proposition 1. *Tensors as t-linear operators can be analogous to matrices as linear operators.*

Proof. According to the above notation that we define, the pth lateral slice of tensor $\mathcal{W}$ is written as $\overrightarrow{\mathbf{W}}_p \in \mathbb{R}^{m \times n}$ and it can be reoriented as a third-order tensor $\overrightarrow{\mathcal{W}}_p \in \mathbb{R}^{m \times 1 \times n}$, a similar operation also can be defined on tensor $\mathcal{X}$. According to [2,10], the t-product of tensor $\mathcal{X}$ and $\overrightarrow{\mathcal{W}}_p$ can be formulated as

$$T(\overrightarrow{\mathcal{W}}_p) = \mathcal{X} * \overrightarrow{\mathcal{W}}_p = \sum_{i=1}^{m} \overrightarrow{\mathcal{X}}_i * \mathbf{w}_i , \quad \overrightarrow{\mathcal{W}}_p := \begin{bmatrix} \mathbf{w}_1 \\ \mathbf{w}_2 \\ \vdots \\ \mathbf{w}_m \end{bmatrix}. \qquad (4)$$

In general, $\overrightarrow{\mathcal{X}}_i * \mathbf{w}_i$ will not be defined unless $m = 1$. Here T defines a linear combination of the lateral slices of tensor $\mathcal{X}$ and $T(\overrightarrow{\mathcal{W}}_p) \in \mathbb{R}^{l \times 1 \times n}$. Therefore, t-product operation can be interpreted as t-linear operation. It is a natural expansion of linear transformation to tensor space. We display the schematic of t-product operation in Fig. 2 for a better understanding.

3.2   Graph Construction

There are word-word, word-document, and document-document correlations in the text graph. Significantly, documents are connected by words. Text GCN [30] directly constructs these three types of connections with an adjacency matrix,

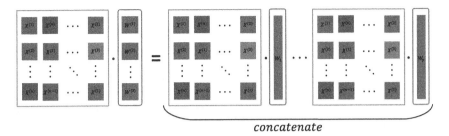

concatenate

Fig. 2. The schematic of t-linear operator.

while traditional graph convolution filters can not handle these heterogeneous correlations. In this paper, we construct a text graph tensor from three perspectives: i) The topology structure of the text graph indicates whether the word appears in the document. ii) The words co-occurrence graph that depicts correlations between words in the whole corpus. iii) The word-document co-occurrence graph that depicts correlations between word and document.

Topology Graph. Intricate similarity calculations between word and document are apt to blurring the topology connection between word and document. To tackle this problem, we construct a 0–1 adjacency matrix based on whether the word appears in the document, describing the hard connection between word and document.

Words Co-occurrence Graph. The second graph depicts correlations between words. We utilize point-wise mutual information (PMI) to denote the edge weights. PMI is calculated by

$$\text{PMI}(i,j) = log\frac{p(i,j)}{p(i)p(j)}, \tag{5}$$

where p is the probability function, $p(i,j)$ denotes the probability of word i, j appear in the sliding window simultaneously.

Word-Document Co-occurrence Graph. The third graph depicts correlations between word and document. We utilize TF-IDF to denotes the edge weights. TF-IDF is calculated by

$$\text{TF-IDF}_{ij} = \text{TF}_{ij} * \text{IDF}_i = \frac{n_{ij}}{\sum_k n_{k,j}} * log\frac{\mid D \mid}{\mid \{j : t_i \in d_j\} \mid}, \tag{6}$$

where term frequency (TF) denotes the frequency that word appear in the document. Therefore, n_{ij} is the number of times the word t_i appears in document d_j.

Considering the length of documents is different, $\sum_k n_{k,j}$ term is used to normalized. Inverse document frequency (IDF) describes the importance of word. $|D|$ is the total number of documents, and $\{j : t_i \in d_i\}$ calculates the number of documents that contain the word t_i.

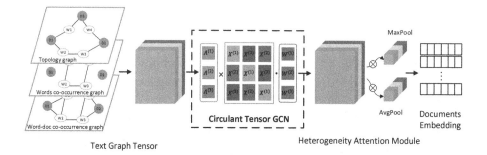

Fig. 3. The architecture of circulant tensor graph convolutional network.

4   The Proposed Method

4.1   Circulant Tensor Graph Convolutional Network

The overall architecture of our proposed model is shown in Fig. 3, including two main modules named the circulant tensor GCN and heterogeneity attention module. Considering heterogeneous correlations between word and document, a text graph tensor can be referred to as $\mathbf{G} = \{\mathcal{G}_1, \mathcal{G}_2, \cdots, \mathcal{G}_R\}$, here $\mathcal{G}_r$ represents the state of graph for specific rth relationship, and we have $|\mathcal{G}_1| = |\mathcal{G}_r| = N$, where N is the number of nodes. The feature tensor of nodes is formulated as $\mathcal{X} \in \mathbb{R}^{N \times D \times R}$ and the adjacency tensor of graph is $\mathcal{A} \in \mathbb{R}^{N \times N \times R}$. According to Proposition 3.1, the t-product has been proved to be a t-linear transformation in tensor space. We can model tensor graph convolutional network as:

$$\widetilde{\mathcal{H}} = \delta(\hat{\mathcal{A}} \; \widetilde{\times}_3 \; \mathcal{X} * \mathcal{W}), \tag{7}$$

here we define the propagation rule of graph convolutional network in the tensor space. On the above formulation, there are some notations defined as follows:

– Laplacian adjacency tensor $\hat{\mathcal{A}}$: We consider that the extension of Laplacian adjacency tensor to the tensor space should be along with the third dimension. Specifically, for any $r = 1, \cdots, R$, we define $\widetilde{\mathbf{A}}^r = \mathbf{I}_N + \mathbf{A}^{(r)}$ that adds self-connections and its diagonal degree matrix $(\widetilde{\mathbf{D}}^{(r)})_{ii} = \sum_j \widetilde{\mathbf{A}}_{ij}^{(r)}$, then laplacian adjacency matrix can be denoted as

$$\hat{\mathbf{A}}^{(r)} = (\widetilde{\mathbf{D}}^{(r)})^{-\frac{1}{2}} \widetilde{\mathbf{A}}^{(r)} (\widetilde{\mathbf{D}}^{(r)})^{-\frac{1}{2}}, \tag{8}$$

$[\hat{\mathbf{A}}^{(1)}, \hat{\mathbf{A}}^{(2)}, \cdots, \hat{\mathbf{A}}^{(R)}]$ can be reoriented as adjacency tensor $\hat{\mathcal{A}} \in \mathbb{R}^{N \times N \times R}$.

– Batch tensor product $\widetilde{\times}_3$: The operator performs batch processing along the third dimension. Given two tensors, $\mathcal{A} \in \mathbb{R}^{N \times N \times R}$ and $\mathcal{X} \in \mathbb{R}^{N \times D \times R}$, we define the calculation as follows:

$$[\mathcal{A} \ \widetilde{\times}_3 \ \mathcal{X}]^{(k)} = \mathbf{A}^{(k)} \times \mathbf{X}^{(k)}. \tag{9}$$

– Circulant Tensor Graph filters $\mathcal{W}$: $\mathcal{W} \in \mathbb{R}^{D \times D' \times R}$ denotes a filter.
– Activation function δ: $Relu(\cdot)$ or $Leaky \ Relu(\cdot)$.

For a specific correlation r, circulant tensor graph convolutional network follows the layer-wise propagation rule:

$$\begin{aligned}
\widetilde{\mathbf{H}}^{(r)} = \ & \delta \ (\hat{\mathbf{A}}^{(r)} \cdot \mathbf{X}^{(r)} \cdot \mathbf{W}^{(1)} \\
& + \sum_{i=1}^{r-1} \hat{\mathbf{A}}^{(i)} \cdot \mathbf{X}^{(i)} \cdot \mathbf{W}^{(r-i+1)} \\
& + \sum_{i=r+1}^{R} \hat{\mathbf{A}}^{(i)} \cdot \mathbf{X}^{(i)} \cdot \mathbf{W}^{(R-i+r+1)}), \ for \ r = 1, \ldots, R.
\end{aligned} \tag{10}$$

We can observe that the circulant tensor graph convolutional network forms a unified framework that combines spatial correlations diffusion process with heterogeneous information harmonization process.

In this paper, we consider a two-layer circulant tensor graph convolutional network for text classification. Our forward model is formulated as

$$\widetilde{\mathcal{H}} = \delta(\hat{\mathcal{A}} \ \widetilde{\times}_3 \ \delta(\hat{\mathcal{A}} \ \widetilde{\times}_3 \ \mathcal{X} * \mathcal{W}_1) * \mathcal{W}_2), \tag{11}$$

where $\mathcal{W}_1 \in \mathbb{R}^{D \times D' \times R}$ and $\mathcal{W}_2 \in \mathbb{R}^{D' \times D'' \times R}$. Finally, we can obtain document embedding $\widetilde{\mathcal{H}} \in \mathbb{R}^{N \times D'' \times R}$.

4.2 Heterogeneous Attention Module

We then introduce the heterogeneity attention module shown in Fig. 3, which aims to obtain more discriminative features. Specifically, heterogeneity attention is calculated by

$$\alpha_{heter} = \sigma(MLP(AvgPool(\widetilde{\mathcal{H}})) + MLP(MaxPool(\widetilde{\mathcal{H}}))), \tag{12}$$

where σ denotes the sigmoid function, $AvgPool(\mathcal{H})$ and $MaxPool(\mathcal{H})$ perform average-pooling and max-pooling operations along the feature axis. Hence, we have $AvgPool(\mathcal{H}) \in \mathbb{R}^{N \times 1 \times R}$ and $MaxPool(\mathcal{H}) \in \mathbb{R}^{N \times 1 \times R}$. Notably, we do not perform pooling along the node axis, so different nodes show different attention on the heterogeneous information, which is particularly important for the heterogeneous graph. Then we have

$$\mathcal{H}_{out} = \delta(\alpha_{heter} \ \otimes \ \widetilde{\mathcal{H}}), \tag{13}$$

where δ is activation function.

4.3   Loss Function

For the text classification task, the document is annotated with a single label. In the final layer, we first unflatten tensor $\mathcal{H}_{out} \in \mathbb{R}^{N \times D'' \times R}$ to matrix $\mathbf{H} \in \mathbb{R}^{N \times (D'' \times R)}$ and feed it into a multi-layer perceptron classifier. We formulate it as: $\mathbf{Z} = softmax(MLP(\mathbf{H}))$. Then we define the loss function with cross-entropy loss and it can be formulated as:

$$\mathcal{L} = - \sum_{d \in \mathcal{Y}_D} \sum_{c=1}^{C} \mathbf{Y}_{dc} \, ln\mathbf{Z}_{dc}, \qquad (14)$$

l where $\mathcal{Y}_D$ is the set of training documents and Y is the label indicator matrix.

5   Experiments

5.1   Dataset

We evaluate CTGCN on five benchmark datasets including 20-News groups (20NG)[1], Ohsumed[2], R52, R8[3], and Movie Review (MR)[4]. The 20-News groups dataset consists of news reviews with 20 different topics and each topic has the same proportion. The Ohsumed dataset comes from an online medical information database MEDLINE. Original Ohsumed dataset is multi-label, therefore, a document can be assigned to many categories. However, in this paper, the Ohsumed dataset chooses one most frequent categories as its single label. Datasets R52 and R8 are cut from the Reuters dataset. MR is a movie review dataset, each review only consists of a sentence and there are only two categories in the whole dataset. Table 1 depicts the fundamental information of datasets.

Table 1. Datasets statistics

Dataset	Train	Words	test	Nodes	Classes	Average length
20NG	11314	42757	7532	61603	20	221
MR	7108	18764	3554	29426	2	20
Ohsumed	3357	14157	4043	21557	23	136
R52	6532	8892	2568	17992	52	70
R8	5485	7688	2189	15362	8	66

---

[1] http://qwone.com/~jason/20Newsgroups/.

[2] http://disi.unitn.it/moschitti/corpora.htm.

[3] https://www.cs.umb.edu/~smimarog/textmining/datasets/.

[4] https://www.cs.cornell.edu/people/pabo/movie-review-data/.

5.2   Implementation Details

We construct a two-layers circulant tensor graph convolutional network with 256 and 128 filters respectively. We use pre-trained word embedding from Text GCN [30] as word-document co-occurrence graph input feature and use GloVe word embeddings as words co-occurrence graph input feature, moreover, topology structure feature is initialized with Gaussian random distribution. The dimension of input feature is 200. In the training process, the drop rate is set to 0.3 for the first layer and changes to 0.5 for the second layer. Our model is optimized by Adam optimizer with a learning rate of 0.01 and a decay weight of 1e-6. Finally, CTGCN is trained to minimize cross-entropy loss with 1200 epochs.

5.3   Comparison with State-of-the-art

We comprehensively compare our model with traditional machine learning models and deep learning models, including TF-IDF+LR [30], CNN [12], LSTM [17], Bi-LSTM, PV-DBOW [14], PV-DM [14], PTE [26], fastText [8], SVEM [25], LEAM [22], Graph-CNN-C [4], Graph-CNN-S [3], Graph-CNN-F [6] and Text GCN [30]. A more detailed introduction of these models is described in [30]. According to Table 2, we observe that the traditional machine learning method

Table 2. Performance on five datasets: 20NG, MR, Ohsumed, R52 and R8. "–" denotes the original paper didn't report the results.

Methods	20NG	MR	Ohsumed	R52	R8
TF-IDF+LR	83.19	74.59	54.66	86.95	93.74
CNN-rand	76.93	74.98	43.87	85.37	94.02
CNN-non-static	82.15	**77.75**	58.44	87.59	95.71
LSTM	65.71	75.06	41.13	85.54	93.68
LSTM(pre-trained)	75.43	77.33	51.10	90.48	96.09
PV-DBOW	74.36	61.09	46.65	78.29	85.87
PV-DM	51.14	59.47	29.50	44.92	52.07
PTE	76.74	70.23	53.58	90.71	96.69
fastText	79.38	75.14	57.70	92.81	96.13
fastText(bigrams)	79.67	76.24	55.69	90.99	94.74
SWEM	85.16	76.65	63.12	92.94	95.32
LEAM	81.91	76.95	58.58	91.84	93.31
Graph-CNN-C	81.42	77.22	63.86	92.75	96.99
Graph-CNN-S	–	76.99	62.82	92.74	96.80
Graph-CNN-F	–	76.74	63.04	93.20	96.89
Text GCN	86.34	76.74	68.36	93.56	97.07
CTGCN	**86.92**	77.69	**69.73**	**94.63**	**97.85**

TF-IDF+LR obtains great performance on five datasets, especially it outperforms most deep learning methods on 20NG datasets. It can be concluded that the TF-IDF term significantly makes for modeling document information. And representative deep learning models CNN-rand and LSTM fail to observably improve the performance. While CNN-non-static and LSTM (pre-trained) that further propose to utilize pre-trained word embedding as an input feature obtain a great improvement. Then PV-DM and PV-DBOW concentrate on how to construct document embedding from word embedding. Graph-based models obtain great improvements on the five datasets by constructing irregular correlations between word and document. The difference between these three Graph-CNN models (Graph-CNN-C, Graph-CNN-S, and Graph-CNN-F) is graph convolution filters, they use Chebyshev filter, Spline filter, and Fourier filter respectively. We also observe that the GCN-based models generally outperform traditional machine learning models and deep learning models, which strongly demonstrates the expression ability of graph structure and the efficiency of graph convolutional network. We can observe that Text GCN significantly improves the accuracy of text classification. Our proposed CTGCN further generalizes text graph convolution to tensor space. Compared to Text GCN, our proposed CTGCN obtains about 1% improvement on all datasets, especially for the Ohsumed dataset, CTGCN obtains about 1.5% improvement. Notably, our proposed CTGCN compares tolerably with the CNN-non-static model on the dataset MR. Further exploration of our proposed model is conducted in the following section.

5.4   Ablation Study

There are three types of correlations constructed on the proposed text graph tensor, to explore the effectiveness of every correlation, we design the ablation experiments. Specifically, we just choose two types of correlations to construct text graph tensor and conduct circulant tensor graph convolution. As shown in Table 3, we observe that word-document correlation plays an important role for the dataset 20NG and MR. Especially for the MR dataset, when we ignore word-document correlation, the accuracy of CTGCN decrease by 2.25%. For the dataset Ohsumed, it can be observed that words co-occurrence correlation is more important. When word-document correlation is ignored, the accuracy of CTGCN is decreased by 1.3%. Experimental results demonstrate that all three correlations contribute to modeling document information and different datasets may have different concerns on these correlations.

Table 3. Analysis of the effectiveness of topology structure, words co-occurrence, and word-document co-occurrence correlations.

Model	Topology	Words	Word-doc	20NG	MR	Ohsumed	R52	R8
CTGCN	✓	✓		85.61	75.44	69.11	94.20	97.49
		✓	✓	86.56	77.29	69.68	94.35	97.72
	✓		✓	86.47	77.12	68.44	94.04	97.62
	✓	✓	✓	**86.92**	**77.69**	**69.73**	**94.63**	**97.85**

5.5   Tensor Graph Convolutional Network

Liu et al. [18] also propose a tensor graph convolutional networks (TensorGCN) for text classification, however, i) TensorGCN constructs text graph tensor from three perspectives: semantic, syntactic, and sequential contextual information, which requires specialized prior knowledge of words and pre-trained language models, it is of great difficulty for researchers to reproduce. We construct a text graph tensor that describes word-document topology structure, word-word co-occurrence, and word-document co-occurrence correlation, instead of introducing prior knowledge. ii) TensorGCN model introduces multi-graph to conduct graph tensor information diffusion. They use intra-graph propagation to aggregate information from neighborhood nodes in a single graph and inter-graph to harmonize heterogeneous information between graphs, which is a two-stage graph convolution. Our proposed CTGCN utilizes tensor operation t-product to model an efficient and expressive framework that naturally extends graph convolutional network to the tensor space. We reproduce TensorGCN model and use our proposed text graph tensor as input, showing the comparison results in Table 4. We can observe that our proposed model outperforms TensorGCN, therefore, CTGCN is better at harmonizing heterogeneous correlations. We use t-SNE [20] to visualize document embeddings in Fig. 4, it can be observed that our proposed CTGCN is capable of learning a more discriminative feature embedding.

Table 4. Comparison of text GCN, TensorGCN and CTGCN.

Methods	20NG	MR	Ohsumed	R52	R8
Text GCN	86.34	76.74	68.36	93.56	97.07
TensorGCN	85.70	76.08	65.16	93.93	96.71
CTGCN	**86.92**	**77.69**	**69.73**	**94.63**	**97.85**

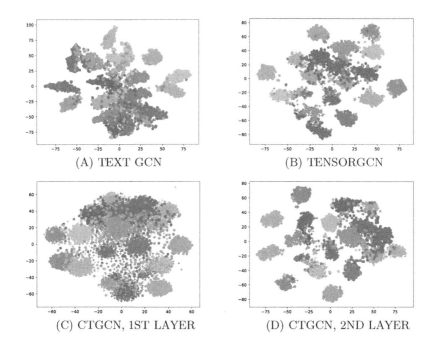

(A) TEXT GCN

(B) TENSORGCN

(C) CTGCN, 1ST LAYER

(D) CTGCN, 2ND LAYER

Fig. 4. The t-SNE visualization of test set document embedding in 20 NG.

6   Conclusion

In this paper, we have proposed a novel circulant tensor graph convolutional network for heterogeneous text classification tasks. We constructed a text graph tensor that integrates topology structure, words co-occurrence, and word-document co-occurrence information. Our proposed CTGCN introduces a tensor operation t-product to model high-dimension graph-structure data, it naturally extends graph convolutional network to the tensor space. Experimental results demonstrate that circulant tensor operation is capable of efficiently harmonizing heterogeneous features and capturing high-dimensional correlations. Moreover, considering that circulant tensor graph convolutional network has shown promising performance for heterogeneous graphs, we intend to employ it to model dynamic graphs that consist of high-dimension temporal correlation.

References

1. Bastings, J., Titov, I., Aziz, W., Marcheggiani, D., Sima'an, K.: Graph convolutional encoders for syntax-aware neural machine translation. arXiv preprint arXiv:1704.04675 (2017)
2. Braman, K.: Third-order tensors as linear operators on a space of matrices. Linear Algebra Appl. **433**(7), 1241–1253 (2010)
3. Bruna, J., Zaremba, W., Szlam, A., Lecun, Y.: Spectral networks and locally connected networks on graphs. Comput. Sci. (2014)

4. Defferrard, M., Bresson, X., Vandergheynst, P.: Convolutional neural networks on graphs with fast localized spectral filtering. In: Advances in Neural Information Processing Systems, pp. 3844–3852 (2016)
5. Feldman, R.: Techniques and applications for sentiment analysis. Commun. ACM **56**(4), 82–89 (2013)
6. Henaff, M., Bruna, J., LeCun, Y.: Deep convolutional networks on graph-structured data. arXiv preprint arXiv:1506.05163 (2015)
7. Huang, Z., Chung, W., Ong, T.H., Chen, H.: A graph-based recommender system for digital library. In: Proceedings of the 2nd ACM/IEEE-CS Joint Conference on Digital Libraries, pp. 65–73. ACM (2002)
8. Joulin, A., Grave, E., Bojanowski, P., Mikolov, T.: Bag of tricks for efficient text classification. arXiv preprint arXiv:1607.01759 (2016)
9. Kiers, H.A., Mechelen, I.V.: Three-way component analysis: principles and illustrative application. Psychol. Methods **6**(1), 84 (2001)
10. Kilmer, M.E., Braman, K., Hao, N., Hoover, R.C.: Third-order tensors as operators on matrices: a theoretical and computational framework with applications in imaging. SIAM J. Matrix Anal. Appl. **34**(1), 148–172 (2013)
11. Kilmer, M.E., Martin, C.D.: Factorization strategies for third-order tensors. Linear Algebra Appl. **435**(3), 641–658 (2011)
12. Kim, Y.: Convolutional neural networks for sentence classification. arXiv preprint arXiv:1408.5882 (2014)
13. Kipf, T.N., Welling, M.: Semi-supervised classification with graph convolutional networks. arXiv preprint arXiv:1609.02907 (2016)
14. Le, Q., Mikolov, T.: Distributed representations of sentences and documents. In: International Conference on Machine Learning, pp. 1188–1196 (2014)
15. Linmei, H., Yang, T., Shi, C., Ji, H., Li, X.: Heterogeneous graph attention networks for semi-supervised short text classification. In: Proceedings of the 2019 Conference on Empirical Methods in Natural Language Processing and the 9th International Joint Conference on Natural Language Processing (EMNLP-IJCNLP), pp. 4823–4832 (2019)
16. Litvak, M., Last, M.: Graph-based keyword extraction for single-document summarization. In: Proceedings of the workshop on Multi-source Multilingual Information Extraction and Summarization, pp. 17–24. Association for Computational Linguistics (2008)
17. Liu, P., Qiu, X., Huang, X.: Recurrent neural network for text classification with multi-task learning. arXiv preprint arXiv:1605.05101 (2016)
18. Liu, X., You, X., Zhang, X., Wu, J., Lv, P.: Tensor graph convolutional networks for text classification. In: Proceedings of the AAAI Conference on Artificial Intelligence, vol. 34, pp. 8409–8416 (2020)
19. Luo, Y., Uzuner, Ö., Szolovits, P.: Bridging semantics and syntax with graph algorithms-state-of-the-art of extracting biomedical relations. Brief. Bioinform. **18**(1), 160–178 (2017)
20. Van der Maaten, L., Hinton, G.: Visualizing data using t-SNE. J. Mach. Learn. Res. **9**(11) (2008)
21. Newman, E., Horesh, L., Avron, H., Kilmer, M.: Stable tensor neural networks for rapid deep learning. arXiv preprint arXiv:1811.06569 (2018)
22. Peng, H., et al.: Large-scale hierarchical text classification with recursively regularized deep graph-CNN. In: Proceedings of the 2018 World Wide Web Conference on World Wide Web, pp. 1063–1072. International World Wide Web Conferences Steering Committee (2018)

23. Ragesh, R., Sellamanickam, S., Iyer, A., Bairi, R., Lingam, V.: Hetegcn: heterogeneous graph convolutional networks for text classification. In: Proceedings of the 14th ACM International Conference on Web Search and Data Mining, pp. 860–868 (2021)
24. Ramos, J., et al.: Using TF-IDF to determine word relevance in document queries. In: Proceedings of the First Instructional Conference on Machine Learning, vol. 242, pp. 133–142. Piscataway, NJ (2003)
25. Shen, D., et al.: Baseline needs more love: On simple word-embedding-based models and associated pooling mechanisms. arXiv preprint arXiv:1805.09843 (2018)
26. Tang, J., Qu, M., Mei, Q.: PTE: predictive text embedding through large-scale heterogeneous text networks. In: Proceedings of the 21th ACM SIGKDD International Conference on Knowledge Discovery and Data Mining, pp. 1165–1174. ACM (2015)
27. Wang, S., Manning, C.D.: Baselines and bigrams: simple, good sentiment and topic classification. In: Proceedings of the 50th annual meeting of the association for computational linguistics: short papers-volume 2, pp. 90–94. Association for Computational Linguistics (2012)
28. Woo, S., Park, J., Lee, J.Y., Kweon, I.S.: CBAM: convolutional block attention module. In: Proceedings of the European Conference on Computer Vision (ECCV), pp. 3–19 (2018)
29. Wyle, M.: A wide area network information filter. In: Proceedings First International Conference on Artificial Intelligence Applications on Wall Street, pp. 10–15. IEEE (1991)
30. Yao, L., Mao, C., Luo, Y.: Graph convolutional networks for text classification. In: Proceedings of the AAAI Conference on Artificial Intelligence, vol. 33, pp. 7370–7377 (2019)
31. Zhang, X., Zhang, T., Zhao, W., Cui, Z., Yang, J.: Dual-attention graph convolutional network. In: Palaiahnakote, S., Sanniti di Baja, G., Wang, L., Yan, W.Q. (eds.) ACPR 2019. LNCS, vol. 12047, pp. 238–251. Springer, Cham (2020). https://doi.org/10.1007/978-3-030-41299-9_19
32. Zhou, P., Qi, Z., Zheng, S., Xu, J., Bao, H., Xu, B.: Text classification improved by integrating bidirectional LSTM with two-dimensional max pooling. arXiv preprint arXiv:1611.06639 (2016)

NASformer: Neural Architecture Search for Vision Transformer

Bolin Ni[1,2], Gaofeng Meng[1,2,3(✉)], Shiming Xiang[1,2], and Chunhong Pan[1]

[1] NLPR, Institute of Automation, Chinese Academy of Sciences, Beijing, China
`nibolin2019@ia.ac.cn`, {`gfmeng,smxiang,chpan`}`@nlpr.ia.ac.cn`
[2] School of Artificial Intelligence, University of Chinese Academy of Sciences, Beijing, China
[3] Center for Artificial Intelligence and Robotics, HK Institute of Science and Innovation, Chinese Academy of Sciences, Beijing, China

Abstract. Vision transformer has shown strong representation power by modeling the long-range dependencies. However, the self-attention mechanism in transformer has a quadratic complexity to the sequence length, limiting the generalization to dense prediction downstream tasks. Besides, it is challenging to design the architecture for vision transformer manually. To alleviate these two issues, we propose an efficient and parameter-free self-attention mechanism, named *dilated window*, which limits the self-attention to non-overlapping windows but still retains the ability to refer to global features. The *dilated window* scheme relies only on changes to data layout (reshapes and transpositions), which can be implemented with one line code. Furthermore, based on that, we proposed an efficient and effective hierarchical vision transformer architecture called *NASformer* by using one-shot neural architecture search. The searched architectures are superior to achieve better performances than recent state-of-the-arts, such as ViT, DeiT, and Swin on many vision tasks, including image classification, object detection, and semantic segmentation.

Keywords: Vision transformer · Neural architecture search · Computer vision

1 Introduction

Transformer based on self-attention [37] has been dominating the field of natural language processing, as its great power of learning the global features. In the light of this, many works [12,25,34,41,46,50] try to explore the potential of self-attention in vision tasks. Recently, ViT [12] attempted to replace the traditional convolutional layers with vanilla transformer blocks and achieved remarkable performance surprisingly. In particular, it splits the image into non-overlapped grid patches, and then these patches are projected and fed into a stacked transformer block as a sequence. Inspired by ViT, various improvement emerged, *e.g.*,

© Springer Nature Switzerland AG 2022
C. Wallraven et al. (Eds.): ACPR 2021, LNCS 13188, pp. 47–61, 2022.
https://doi.org/10.1007/978-3-031-02375-0_4

Table 1. Comparison to related works. Note that our proposed NASformer not only retains the global receptive field but also ensures the high efficiency.

Methods	Structure	Attention types	Handling windows	Parameter-free communication	Development friendly	Automate search
ViT [12]	Isotropic	Global	N/A	✓	✓	✗
PVT [41]	Pyramid	Global	N/A	✓	✓	✗
Swin [25]	Pyramid	Expanded local*	Shift windows	✓	✗	✗
Twins [6]	Pyramid	Local + Global	N/A	✗	✓	✗
NASformer	Pyramid	Local + Global	Dalite windows	✓	✓	✓

*: Like CNN, the local receptive field is expanded gradually.

better training strategies [34], better position embedding [7], going deeper [50]. All these works seem to emphasize the tremendous success of vision transformer.

However, there are two key issues standing in the way of the prosperity of vision transformer: 1) *High computation complexity and memory requirement of self-attention.* 2) *The ambiguous architecture design principle of vision architecture.* For the first issue, the self-attention has a quadratic complexity to the sequence length. It makes it awkward to work on fine-grained patch sizes and considerably undermines the generalization of vision transformer in dense prediction downstream tasks such as object detection and semantic segmentation, which benefit from or require fine feature information computed from high-resolution images. Some works [3,25] try to limit the self-attention in non-overlapped local windows, but their approaches are either inefficient or unfriendly to development. For the second issue, unlike the well-explored design principle for CNNs [29], how to design a great architecture is ambiguous so far. From a macroscopic point of view, though [18,41] introduce the hierarchical structure into vision transformer to compute multi-scale features, how to determine the block numbers and embedding dimension for each block is still unclear. In the micro aspect, how to strike a good combination of the critical factors in self-attention such as the heads number and Multi-Layer Perceptron (MLP) ratio is also problematic.

To address the two issues above, in this paper, we try to answer two key questions: 1) *How to globally represent long-range dependencies at an acceptable price.* 2) *How to determine the optimal architecture for vision transformer.*

For the first question, inspired by [45], we proposed a new scheme named *dilated window* that limits self-attention to non-overlapped windows while also allowing for cross-window connection. We dilate the window so that each window does not gaze on a connected local region but a dis-connected global region for a global view. Most importantly, we alternately utilized the regular window-based self-attention and proposed dilated window-based self-attention, which guarantees the effective information exchange between different local windows. Note that our proposed method is parameter-free and relies only on changes to the data layout, which is easy to implement (one line code) and development-friendly. Table 1 shows the comparison between our method and others.

For the second question, neural architecture search (NAS) as a potent approach for automating the design of networks has shown its superiority to manual design [42,52]. Though there is no consensus about the design principle of vision transformer, many works [3,6,38,46–48] have sought to modify the structure of vision transformer manually. Consequently, we use one-shot NAS method to search the macro- and micro structure. From a macroscopic point (stage-level), we search the 1) *blocks number in each stage.* 2) *the embedding in each stage.* In a micro aspect (block-level), the 3) *MLP ratio,* 4) *window size,* 5) $Q - K - V$ *dimension* and 6) *the number of heads* are searched.

In summary, we make the following contributions:

- We propose a new approach to compute self-attention, named *dilatedwindow* based self-attention, and produce hierarchical feature representation with linear computational complexity to input image size.
- Integrated with the dilated window scheme, we design a search space for vision transformer and employ the one-shot NAS method to search for an optimal architecture named NASformer.
- We achieve state-of-the-art results on sufficient experiments, including image classification, object detection, and semantic segmentation. The remarkable results prove the powerful modeling ability of NASformer, and it can serve as a general-purpose backbone for computer vision.

2   Related Work

2.1   Vision Transformer

Recently, ViT [12] firstly introduced a pure transformer architecture for vision tasks and achieved competitive performance to state-of-the-art CNN models. Motivated by it, a series of works [15, 34, 35, 46, 50] is proposed to explore the design of vision transformer. The improvements can be divided into two categories. Some approaches seek to modify the structure of vision transformer, and others attempt to reduce the complexity of the global self-attention mechanism to be applied to big input resolution.

For the first category, DeiT [34] suggested a great training strategy that most works adopt. CPVT [7] makes efforts on the positional embedding to utilize the vision transformer on multi-scale input. Similar to common CNN structure, PVT [41] down-samples the feature map gradually and extract multi-scale features by using spatial-reduction attention to reduce the dimension of *key* and *value.* However, there is no consensus about designing the structure of the transformer block, and some conclusions even contradict each other. This motivates us to utilize one-shot NAS method to help us to design the architecture of the vision transformer.

For the second category, many works [3, 25, 36] limit the self-attention within some non-overlapped windows. In order to avoid the lack of information communication between different windows, HaloNet [36] proposes to exchange information by overlapped *key* and *value* in self-attention but leave the *query* non-overlapped. Swin [25] proposed to use the regular window and shifted window alternatively. RegionViT [3] exploits extra regional token to communicate across windows. It is worth noting that either HaloNet [36] or Swin [25] expand the receptive field gradually, which brings a problem that they both can not capture the global dependence under big input resolution and the small number of layers of transformer. Different from that, our proposed dilated window-based self-attention could capture the global dependence regardless of the layer number of transformer and the resolution of the input image. What is more, our proposed method is parameter-free and development-friendly. As opposed to that, the roll operation in Swin [25] is not supported in ONNX [9] and RegionVit [3] needs extra computation and parameters.

2.2   Neural Architecture Search

Neural Architecture Search (NAS) is proposed to accelerate the principled and automated discovery of high-performance networks. The approaches could be divided into three categories: reinforcement learning [13,51,52], revolution algorithms [31,44] and differential methods [5,11,24,27]. To avoid training thousands of architecture candidates from scratch separately, the weight-sharing strategy is proposed in [28]. The key idea is to train an over-parameterized supernet where all subnets share weights. SPOS [14] introduces a simple and effective way to train the supernet. In each iteration, it only samples one random path and trains the path using one batch of data. Once the training process is finished, the subnets can be ranked by inheriting the shared weights. However, all the algorithms mentioned above are designed to search either CNNs or RNNs, rather than transformers.

For transformer, few works are employing NAS to improve architectures. Evolved Transformer [32] utilize evolution algorithms to search the inner architecture of transformer block. This study relies on mass computing resources, which is unrealistic for most researchers. HAT [39] proposes to design hardware-aware transformers with NAS to enable low-latency inference on resource-constrained hardware platforms. BossNAS [21] explores hybrid CNN-transformers with block-wisely self-supervised. Unlike the above studies, we focus on pure vision transformer architectures.

3   Preliminary

3.1   Window Based Self-Attention

In order to alleviate the high computation cost of origin multi-head self-attention, Window-based Multi-head Self-Attention (WMSA) is proposed to compute the attention map in local non-overlapped windows [19,25,30,40]. Usually, the windows have the same size and evenly partition the image. The parameters are shared across different windows. In a word, the WMSA share the same structure with MSA except for the receptive field. The WMSA reduces the computation complexity of the global self-attention mechanism significantly. Specifically, for a feature map $X \in R^{h \times w \times C}$, the computation complexity of global MSA and

WMSA are as follow:

$$\mathcal{O}(MSA) = 4hwC^2 + 2(hw)^2 C$$
$$\mathcal{O}(WMSA) = 4hwC^2 + 2M^2 hwC$$
(1)

where M represents the number of patches in a window. It could be seen that WMSA is significantly more efficient than MSA when $M \ll H$ and $M \ll W$. What is more, it grows linearly with HW when M is fixed.

3.2 One-shot NAS

One-shot NAS [1,2,14,22] was proposed to overcome the high computation cost of original NAS pipeline in which abundant networks are trained independently from scratch [27,51,52]. The search space $\mathcal{A}$ is encoded in a supernet, denoted as $\mathcal{N}(\mathcal{A}, W)$ where W is the weight of the supernet. Weight sharing is the core part of one-shot NAS. Specifically, the subnet $\alpha \in \mathcal{A}$ in $\mathcal{N}$ share the weight of all operations. The most common one-shot method formula the search of optimal subnet α^* as a two-stage optimization problem.

The first stage is optimizing the weight W as follow

$$W_{\mathcal{A}} = \arg \min_{W} \mathcal{L}_{\text{train}} \left(\mathcal{N}(\mathcal{A}, W) \right)$$
(2)

where $\mathcal{L}_{\text{train}}$ is the loss function on the training dataset. We adopt the single-path uniform sampling strategy to train the supernet [14].

The second stage is to search the optimal subnet α^* on the supernet with the weight $W_{\mathcal{A}}$, which is formulated as

$$\alpha^* = \arg \max_{\alpha \in \mathcal{A}} Acc_{val} \left(\mathcal{N}(\alpha, w_\alpha) \right)$$
(3)

where w_α denotes the weight of subnet α and Acc_{val} is the accuracy of subnet α on the validation dataset. Specifically, considering the stability and speed, we utilize evaluation search [31] to search the optimal α^*.

4   NASformer

In this section, we introduced our proposed dilated window-based self-attention in Sect. 4.1 and followed by an overall architecture of NASformer in Sect. 4.2. The search space are presented in Sect. 4.3. Lastly, we introduce the whole pipeline of vision transformer search, including supernet training and optimal subnet search, in detail in Sect. 4.4.

4.1 Dilated Window Based Self-Attention

The shortcut of window-based self-attention is obvious. It lacks the connection across different windows and results in that each token only could capture the feature from other tokens within the local window, limiting the representation power of the model, especially on high-resolution input images.

To alleviate this issue, inspired by the widely used dilation convolution in semantic segmentation [45], we proposed dilated window-based self-attention. The advantage of dilation convolution is the expansion of the receptive field without adding parameters. With the same motivation, the dilated window aims to cover tokens as far as possible, as illustrated in Fig. 1. Figure 1 (b) shows the regular window-based self-attention mechanism under which tokens only communicate with those of the same color in a local field. Different from that, Fig. 1 (c) shows the dilated window mechanism. Each window is dilated to cover tokens as far away as possible. Without increasing the window size and extra computation cost, tokens could exchange information with more distant tokens, rather than local tokens. Note that, unlike the dilated convolution, which has a specific dilation factor, the dilation factor of the dilated window is fixed and determined by the size of both feature map and window.

In practical, for a $2D$ feature map with size (H, W) and windows with size (M, M), we just need to reshape the feature map to $(M, \frac{H}{M}, M, \frac{W}{M})$ and transpose the second and third axis to $(M, M, \frac{H}{M}, \frac{W}{M})$. This change of data layout is pretty easy to implement on any deep learning framework.

Compared to the Swin [25] which shift the windows to exchange information from the neighboring windows, our proposed dilated window-based self-attention has two advantages: (1) The shift operation in Swin [25] only connect the neighboring windows and can not exchange information with distant windows. Though this phenomenon could be alleviated with the layers going deep, it still limits the modeling power, especially in a small model. (2) The shift operation is not friendly for deployment, as it is not supported in ONNX. Our proposed dilated window-based self-attention just relies on a basic change of data layout.

Last, as shown in Fig. 1, we stack the regular window based self-attention and dilated window based self-attention alternatively in the whole architecture. The blocks in NASformer are computed as

$$
\begin{aligned}
\hat{\mathbf{z}}^l &= \text{WMSA}\left(\text{LN}\left(z^{l-1}\right)\right) + z^{l-1}, \\
z^l &= \text{MLP}\left(\text{LN}\left(\hat{\mathbf{z}}^l\right)\right) + \hat{\mathbf{z}}^l, \\
\hat{\mathbf{z}}^{l+1} &= \text{DWMSA}\left(\text{LN}\left(\mathbf{z}^l\right)\right) + \mathbf{z}^l \\
\mathbf{z}^{l+1} &= \text{MLP}\left(\text{LN}\left(\hat{\mathbf{z}}^{l+1}\right)\right) + \hat{\mathbf{z}}^{l+1}
\end{aligned}
\tag{4}
$$

where $\hat{z}^l$ and z^l denote the output of regular window based self-attention and dilated window based self-attention in block l, respectively.

4.2   Overall Architecture of NASformer

First of all, we introduce the architecture of the vision transformer. The architecture we set up follows the settings in Swin [25], except the shift window-based self-attention. The shift window-based self-attention is replaced by dilated window-based self-attention.

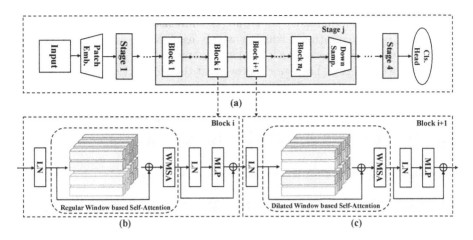

Fig. 1. Illustration of dilated window based self-attention. One color corresponds to one separate window. The self-attention is computed within the local window. The regular window based self-attention block and dilated window based self-attention block are utilized alternatively in the backbone. (Color figure online)

As shown in Fig. 1, the image with size $H \times W \times 3$ is first split into non-overlapped patches with size $p \times p$ and each patch is projected to a vector named patch embedding with C dimension by a linear projection. Like the most hierarchical CNN architectures, the architecture has 4 stages and the resolution of each stage is $\frac{H}{2^{i+1}} \times \frac{W}{2^{i+1}}$ where $i = 1, 2, 3, 4$. To produce a hierarchical representation, there is a 2×down-sampling module in the last of the first 3 stages to down-sample the feature map. The down-sampling module simply concatenates the features of each 2×2 neighboring tokens, and a linear projection is applied to it to reduce the dimension. Note that there are no convolution layers applied in our proposed NASformer. The proposed architecture could conveniently replace the backbone in most methods for many vision tasks. For image classification, the average embedding of all tokens is utilized, followed by a fully connected classifier.

4.3   Search Space for Heterogeneous Transformer

Based on the architecture mentioned above, we build a *heterogeneous* search space in which the embedding dim and block numbers are elastic. Specifically, for each stage, the *stage level* searchable variables are the (1) number of blocks and (2) the embedding dimension. For each block, the *block level* searchable variables are (3) the window size, (4) the number of heads, (5) the MLP ratio, and (6) the $Q - K - V$ dimension. $Q - K - V$ dimension means the dimension in *query*, *key* and *value* are identical.

We have to emphasize again that our proposed transformer is *heterogeneous*, which means that the *block level* searchable variables of different blocks in the same stage could be diverse. Our setting is not groundless. Voita et al. [38] show that many heads are redundant. [48] reduce the dimension of *key* and *value*. [47] set the MLP ratio to 3 rather 4 which is widely used. Many works [6,46,47] use the different configurations of block numbers and embedding dimensions. [3] uses the different window size. Their works prove that the architecture of vision transformer still has room for exploration and inspires us to search for the optimal architecture. As for the structure hyper-parameters that does not exclusive to vision transformer, such as the number of stages and the multiplier of downsampling, we fix them as most works do [6,25,41].

4.4   Search Pipeline

We follow the two-stage one-shot NAS methods: train the supernet, and search the optimal architecture.

Phase 1: Train the Supernet. We build a supernet with the maximum parameters. In particular, the supernet stacks the maximum number of blocks in each stage. Every block has the maximum embedding dimension, $Q - K - V$ dimension, the MLP ratio, and the number of heads. Note that the window size does not influence the supernet configuration. It is only related to the floating-point operations(FLOPs). Every possible architecture in the predefined space is a subnet of the supernet. To decouple the weights of the individual subnet, we perform uniform path sampling for the training [14]. In other words, in each iteration, only one subnet is sampled uniformly from the supernet to start the forward/backward propagation and update the weights. This is expressed as

$$W_{\mathcal{A}} = \underset{W}{\mathrm{argmin}} \mathbb{E}_{\alpha \sim \Gamma(\mathcal{A})} \left[\mathcal{L}_{\text{train}} \left(\mathcal{N}(\alpha, W(\alpha)) \right) \right] \tag{5}$$

where $\Gamma(\mathcal{A})$ is a prior distribution of $\alpha \in A$. $\mathcal{L}_{\text{train}}$ is the cross-entropy loss. This equation is an implementation of Eq. (2). We uniformly sample the α from the $\Gamma(\mathcal{A})$. Different from the [14], the uniform sampling in our proposed search space is two-steps.

step.1 For stage $i(i = 1, 2, 3, 4)$, uniformly sample the blocks number n_i and embedding dimension d_i.

step.2 For block $j(j = 1, \cdots, n_i)$ in stage i, uniformly sample the window size w_i^j, the MLP ratio m_i^j, the $Q - K - V$ dimension q_i^j, and the number of heads h_i^j. The architecture α is formulated as

$$\begin{aligned} \alpha &= \{n_i, d_i, block_i | i = 1, 2, 3, 4\} \\ block_i &= \{w_i^j, m_i^{\,j}, q_i^j, h_i^j | j = 1, 2, \cdots, n_i\} \end{aligned} \tag{6}$$

Phase 2: Searching with Evolutionary Algorithm. The last step in the one-shot NAS framework is to search the optimal architecture as Eq. (3) described. Considering the stability and speed, we choose the evolutionary algorithm [14]. A population of architectures is initialized randomly, with their performance on the validation dataset. The top-k architectures are picked from the population as parents to generate the child subnets by mutation and crossover. For mutation, we randomly sample some architectures in the population to be mutated. A candidate mutates its depth with probability P_d firstly. Then it mutates each block with a probability of P_m to produce a new architecture. For crossover, two randomly selected architectures are crossed to produce a new one. For every new architecture, we evaluate the performance of the validation dataset.

Table 2. Comparison of different backbones on ImageNet-1K classification. All the performance is obtained at resolution 224×224.

Models	Top-1 Acc	Top-5 Acc	#Params	FLOPs	Model type
ResNet50 [17]	76.2%	92.9%	26M	4.1G	CNN
RegNetY-4GF [29]	80.0%	–	21M	4.0G	CNN
T2T-ViT-14 [46]	80.7%	–	22M	6.1G	Transformer
DeiT-S [34]	79.9%	95.0%	22M	4.7G	Transformer
ViT-S/16 [12]	78.8%	–	22M	4.7G	Transformer
Twins-PCPVT-S [6]	81.2%	–	24M	3.8G	Transformer
Twins-SVT-S [6]	81.7%	–	24M	2.9G	Transformer
Swin-T [25]	81.3%	–	28M	4.5G	Transformer
NASformer-T (Ours)	**82.3%**	**95.8%**	**31M**	**4.6G**	Transformer
ResNet152 [17]	78.3%	94.1%	60M	11G	CNN
BoTNet-S1-110 [33]	82.8%	96.4%	55M	10.9G	CNN + Trans
T2T-ViT-24 [46]	82.2%	–	64M	15G	Transformer
Twins-PCPVT-B [6]	82.7%	–	44M	6.7G	Transformer
Twins-SVT-B [6]	83.2%	–	56M	8.6G	Transformer
Swin-S [25]	83.0%	–	50M	8.7G	Transformer
NASformer-S (Ours)	**83.7%**	**96.4%**	**50M**	**9.5G**	Transformer
RegNetY-16GF [29]	80.4%	–	83M	16G	CNN
ViT-B/16 [12]	79.7%	–	86M	18G	Transformer
DeiT-B [34]	81.8%	95.6%	86M	18G	Transformer
Twins-PCPVT-L [6]	83.1%	–	61M	9.8G	Transformer
Twins-SVT-L [6]	83.7%	–	99M	15.1G	Transformer
Swin-B [25]	83.3%	–	88M	15.4G	Transformer
NASformer-B (Ours)	**83.9%**	**96.6%**	**71M**	**13.6G**	Transformer

5   Experiments

5.1   Implementation Details

Supernet Training. Our setting is similar to DeiT [34]. Specifically, We employ an AdamW [26] optimizer for 300 epochs with a cosine decay learning rate scheduler, 0.05 weight decay and 20 epochs for linear warm-up. The initial learning rate is 1×10^{-3} and the minimal learning rate is 1×10^{-5}. The label smoothing is 0.1. For various model sizes, we adopt the different stochastic depth rate, 0.2 for *tiny*, 0.3 for *small* and 0.5 for *base*. The batch size is 1024.

Evolutionary Search. The implementation of evolutionary search follows the protocol in SPOS [14]. The population size is 50 and the generation step is 20. Each step, we choose the top-10 architecture to be parents. The mutation probability P_m and P_d are both set to 0.1.

Retrain. When the evolutionary search is finished, we need to retrain the weight of the searched architecture. We use the exactly same training setting as supernet training.

Table 3. Results on COCO object detection using cascaded mask R-CNN.

Backbone	Params.(M)	Cas. Mask R-CNN w/ FPN 1×						Cas. Mask R-CNN w/ FPN 3×					
		AP^b	AP^b_{50}	AP^b_{75}	AP^m	AP^m_{50}	AP^m_{75}	AP^b	AP^b_{50}	AP^b_{75}	AP^m	AP^m_{50}	AP^m_{75}
ResNet-50 [17]	82	41.2	59.4	45.0	35.9	56.6	38.4	46.3	64.3	50.5	40.1	61.7	43.4
Swin-T [25]	86	48.1	67.1	52.2	41.7	64.4	45.0	50.4	69.2	54.7	43.7	66.6	47.3
NASformer-T	89	**48.3**	**67.7**	**52.2**	**42.0**	**64.7**	**45.1**	**50.6**	**69.5**	**55.0**	**43.9**	**66.9**	**47.5**
X-101-32 [43]	101	44.3	62.7	48.4	38.3	59.7	41.2	48.1	66.5	52.4	41.6	63.9	45.2
X-101-64 [43]	140	45.3	63.9	49.6	39.2	61.1	42.2	48.3	66.4	52.3	41.7	64.0	45.1
Swin-S [25]	107	50.3	69.6	54.8	43.4	66.7	47.0	51.8	70.4	56.3	44.7	67.9	48.5
Swin-B [25]	145	50.5	69.5	55.0	43.5	66.9	46.9	51.9	70.7	56.3	45.0	68.2	48.8
NASformer-S	107	**50.9**	**70.2**	**55.1**	**43.9**	**67.4**	**47.2**	**52.8**	**71.7**	**56.8**	**45.4**	**68.7**	**49.5**

5.2   Image Classification

Settings. We retrain it with the setting in Sect. 5.1 on the training dataset of ImageNet [10]. Considering the various resource constraint, we provide three models with different size: NASformer-tiny(31M), NASformer-small(50M), NASformer-base(71M), respectively.

Results. As shown in Table 2, our proposed NASformer-T/S/B consistently has a better performance compared to the CNN models, transformer models, and hybrid models. Compared to the state-of-the-art CNN models, with similar parameters and FLOPs, NASformer-T is +2.3% higher accuracy than RegNetY-4GF. NASformer-B surpasses the RegNetY-16 by +3.5% with fewer parameters and FLOPs. Compared to the state-of-the-art transformer models, NASformer-T is +1.0% higher accuracy than Swin-T and +3.5% higher accuracy than ViT-S/16. NASformer-S is +0.7% higher accuracy than Swin-S. NASformer-B is +0.6% higher accuracy than Swin-B with 17M fewer parameters. All these results prove that NASformer is a very competitive backbone.

5.3   Object Detection

Settings. We conduct the object detection experiments on COCO2017 [23] dataset. We choose Cascade Mask R-CNN [16] as method. All the experiments are conducted on MMDetection [4], and we utilize the default hyperparameters provided by it.

Table 4. Results on ADE20K Semantic Segmentation using UperNet.

Method	Backbone	#param (M)	mIoU (%)	mIoU (ms+flip%)
UperNet	ResNet-50 [17]	67	42.05	42.78
	DeiT-S [34]	52	43.15	43.85
	Swin-T [25]	60	44.51	45.81
	NASformer-T	63	**44.79**	**46.16**
	ResNet-101 [17]	86	43.82	44.85
	DeiT-B [34]	121	44.09	45.68
	Swin-S [25]	81	47.64	49.47
	NASformer-S	81	**48.00**	**49.19**

Table 5. The effectiveness of dilated window. Local Transformer is obtained by removing the shifted window in Swin.

Backbone	Method	Top-1 Acc. (%)	ONNX support
Local transformer-T	N/A	80.3	✓
	shifted window	81.3	✗
	dilated window	81.4	✓
Local transformer-S	N/A	82.0	✓
	shifted window	83.0	✗
	dilated window	83.1	✓

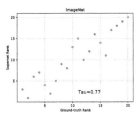

Fig. 2. The correlation between the supernet ranking and ground-truth ranking. We uniformly sample 20 models from the trained supernet and evaluate them on ImageNet validation dataset to obtain supernet rank. The ground-truth rank is obtained by training these models from scratch.

Results. We report the box AP and mask AP for $1\times, 3\times$ schedule on Table 3. Compared to CNN models, NASformer-T surpasses ResNet-50 by 4.3 box AP and 3.8 mask AP for $3\times$ schedule. NASformer-S is $+4.7$ higher box AP than ResNeXt-101-32 and $+4.5$ higher box AP than ResNeXt-101-64 for $3\times$ schedule. Compared to the other transformer models, NASformer-T is $+0.2$ higher box AP than Swin-T. Notably, our NASformer-S is $+1.0$ higher box AP than Swin-S and $+0.9$ higher box AP than Swin-B, with fewer parameters. Under the $1\times$ schedule, NASformer still outperforms other backbones.

5.4 Semantic Segmentation

Settings. We conduct semantic segmentation experiments on ADE20K [49] dataset. All the experimetns are conducted on MMSegmentation [8] and deafult hyperparameters are used.

Results. We list the mIoU on validation dataset of ADE20K in Table 4.Compared to CNN models, NASformer-T is +2.74 mIoU higher than ResNet-50, and NASformer-S is +4.18 mIoU higher than ResNet-101. Compared to other transformer models, NASformer-T is +1.64 mIoU higher than DeiT-S and +0.28 mIoU higher than Swin-T. NASformer-S is +3.91 mIoU higher than DeiT-B and +0.36 mIoU higher than Swin-S.

5.5 Ablation Study

The Effectiveness of Dilated Window-Based Self-Attention. To verify the effectiveness of our proposed dilated window-based self-attention, we replace the shifted window-based self-attention in Swin [25] with the dilated window-based self-attention. As shown in Table 5, the dilated window-based self-attention has better performance(+0.1) than shifted window method. Though the improvement is slight, our dilated window method is friendly to developers as it is supported by ONNX and could be deployed on various platforms. Therefore, dilated window-based self-attention is an effective method to capture the global feature in local self-attention. It not only gains high performance but also guarantees efficiency. This experiment also implies that the good performance of NASformer relies both on the dilated window and NAS approach.

The Effectiveness of Supernet Training. We conduct experiments to verify if the weight-sharing supernet training is effective. In detail, we uniformly select 20 subnets from the trained supernet and evaluate them on ImageNet [10] validation set. Then, these subnets are initialized and trained from scratch to obtain the ground-truth performance. At last, we rank the 20 models by the performance with the inherited weights and fully optimized weights and compute the Kendall rank correlation coefficient [20] between these two types of ranks as the ranking correlation. It can be seen from Fig. 2 that there is a strong positive correlation between the two types of ranks, which suggests that the search pipeline is effective in selecting the optimal architecture.

6   Conclusion

We proposed a new dilated window-based self-attention mechanism in this work, which could capture the global dependencies and has linear computational complexity to input image size. Moreover, we design a vast search space for vision transformer and leverage one-shot NAS method to search the optimal architecture. Extensive experiments well demonstrate that our proposed models outperform many concurrent ViT variants on three vision tasks, including image classification, object detection, and action recognition.

Acknowledgement. This work was supported in part by the National Natural Science Foundation of China under Grant No. 61976208.

References

1. Bender, G., Kindermans, P.J., Zoph, B., Vasudevan, V., Le, Q.: Understanding and simplifying one-shot architecture search. In: ICML (2018)
2. Brock, A., Lim, T., Ritchie, J.M., Weston, N.: Smash: one-shot model architecture search through hypernetworks. In: ICLR (2018)
3. Chen, C.F., Panda, R., Fan, Q.: Regionvit: regional-to-local attention for vision transformers. arXiv preprint arXiv:2106.02689 (2021)
4. Chen, K., et al.: MMDetection: open MMLab detection toolbox and benchmark. arXiv preprint arXiv:1906.07155 (2019)
5. Chen, X., Xie, L., Wu, J., Tian, Q.: Progressive differentiable architecture search: bridging the depth gap between search and evaluation. In: ICCV (2019)
6. Chu, X., et al.: Twins: revisiting the design of spatial attention in vision transformers. arXiv preprint arXiv:2104.13840 (2021)
7. Chu, X., et al.: Conditional positional encodings for vision transformers. arXiv preprint arXiv:2102.10882 (2021)
8. Contributors, M.: MMSegmentation: openmmlab semantic segmentation toolbox and benchmark. https://github.com/open-mmlab/mmsegmentation (2020)
9. Contributors, O.: Open neural network exchange (2020). https://github.com/onnx/onnx
10. Deng, J., Dong, W., Socher, R., Li, L.J., Li, K., Fei-Fei, L.: Imagenet: a large-scale hierarchical image database. In: CVPR (2009)
11. Dong, X., Yang, Y.: Searching for a robust neural architecture in four GPU hours. In: CVPR (2019)
12. Dosovitskiy, A., et al.: An image is worth 16×16 words: transformers for image recognition at scale. In: ICLR (2021)
13. Ghiasi, G., Lin, T.Y., Le, Q.V.: Nas-fpn: Learning scalable feature pyramid architecture for object detection. In: Proceedings of the IEEE/CVF Conference on Computer Vision and Pattern Recognition, pp. 7036–7045 (2019)
14. Guo, Z., et al.: Single path one-shot neural architecture search with uniform sampling. In: ECCV (2020)
15. Han, K., Xiao, A., Wu, E., Guo, J., Xu, C., Wang, Y.: Transformer in transformer. arXiv preprint arXiv:2103.00112 (2021)
16. He, K., Gkioxari, G., Dollár, P., Girshick, R.: Mask R-CNN. In: ICCV (2017)
17. He, K., Zhang, X., Ren, S., Sun, J.: Deep residual learning for image recognition. In: CVPR (2016)
18. Heo, B., Yun, S., Han, D., Chun, S., Choe, J., Oh, S.J.: Rethinking spatial dimensions of vision transformers. arXiv preprint arXiv:2103.16302 (2021)
19. Hu, H., Zhang, Z., Xie, Z., Lin, S.: Local relation networks for image recognition. In: Proceedings of the IEEE/CVF International Conference on Computer Vision, pp. 3464–3473 (2019)
20. Kendall, M.G.: A new measure of rank correlation. Biometrika **30**(1/2), 81–93 (1938)
21. Li, C., et al.: Bossnas: exploring hybrid CNN-transformers with block-wisely self-supervised neural architecture search. arXiv preprint arXiv:2103.12424 (2021)
22. Li, L., Talwalkar, A.: Random search and reproducibility for neural architecture search. In: UAI (2019)
23. Lin, T.-Y., et al.: Microsoft COCO: common objects in context. In: Fleet, D., Pajdla, T., Schiele, B., Tuytelaars, T. (eds.) ECCV 2014. LNCS, vol. 8693, pp. 740–755. Springer, Cham (2014). https://doi.org/10.1007/978-3-319-10602-1_48

24. Liu, H., Simonyan, K., Yang, Y.: DARTS: differentiable architecture search. In: ICLR (2019)
25. Liu, Z., et al.: Swin transformer: hierarchical vision transformer using shifted windows. arXiv preprint arXiv:2103.14030 (2021)
26. Loshchilov, I., Hutter, F.: Decoupled weight decay regularization. In: ICLR (2019)
27. Luo, R., Tian, F., Qin, T., Chen, E., Liu, T.Y.: Neural architecture optimization. In: NeurIPS (2018)
28. Pham, H., Guan, M., Zoph, B., Le, Q., Dean, J.: Efficient neural architecture search via parameters sharing. In: ICML (2018)
29. Radosavovic, I., Kosaraju, R.P., Girshick, R., He, K., Dollár, P.: Designing network design spaces. In: CVPR (2020)
30. Ramachandran, P., Parmar, N., Vaswani, A., Bello, I., Levskaya, A., Shlens, J.: Stand-alone self-attention in vision models. arXiv preprint arXiv:1906.05909 (2019)
31. Real, E., Aggarwal, A., Huang, Y., Le, Q.V.: Regularized evolution for image classifier architecture search. In: AAAI (2019)
32. So, D., Le, Q., Liang, C.: The evolved transformer. In: International Conference on Machine Learning. PMLR (2019)
33. Srinivas, A., Lin, T.Y., Parmar, N., Shlens, J., Abbeel, P., Vaswani, A.: Bottleneck transformers for visual recognition. arXiv preprint arXiv:2101.11605 (2021)
34. Touvron, H., Cord, M., Douze, M., Massa, F., Sablayrolles, A., J'egou, H.: Training data-efficient image transformers and distillation through attention. arXiv preprint arXiv:2012.12877 (2020)
35. Touvron, H., Cord, M., Sablayrolles, A., Synnaeve, G., Jégou, H.: Going deeper with image transformers. arXiv preprint arXiv:2103.17239 (2021)
36. Vaswani, A., Ramachandran, P., Srinivas, A., Parmar, N., Hechtman, B., Shlens, J.: Scaling local self-attention for parameter efficient visual backbones. In: Proceedings of the IEEE/CVF Conference on Computer Vision and Pattern Recognition, pp. 12894–12904 (2021)
37. Vaswani, A., et al.: Attention is all you need. In: NeurIPS (2017)
38. Voita, E., Talbot, D., Moiseev, F., Sennrich, R., Titov, I.: Analyzing multi-head self-attention: specialized heads do the heavy lifting, the rest can be pruned. In: ACL (2019)
39. Wang, H., Wu, Z., Liu, Z., Cai, H., Zhu, L., Gan, C., Han, S.: Hat: Hardware-aware transformers for efficient natural language processing. In: ACL (2020)
40. Wang, H., Zhu, Y., Green, B., Adam, H., Yuille, A., Chen, L.-C.: Axial-deepLab: stand-alone axial-attention for panoptic segmentation. In: Vedaldi, A., Bischof, H., Brox, T., Frahm, J.-M. (eds.) ECCV 2020. LNCS, vol. 12349, pp. 108–126. Springer, Cham (2020). https://doi.org/10.1007/978-3-030-58548-8_7
41. Wang, W., et al.: Pyramid vision transformer: a versatile backbone for dense prediction without convolutions. arXiv preprint arXiv:2102.12122 (2021)
42. Williams, R.J.: Simple statistical gradient-following algorithms for connectionist reinforcement learning. Mach. Learn. 8(3–4), 229–256 (1992). https://doi.org/10.1007/BF00992696
43. Xie, S., Girshick, R., Dollár, P., Tu, Z., He, K.: Aggregated residual transformations for deep neural networks. In: CVPR (2017)
44. Yang, Z., et al.: Cars: continuous evolution for efficient neural architecture search. In: Proceedings of the IEEE/CVF Conference on Computer Vision and Pattern Recognition, pp. 1829–1838 (2020)
45. Yu, F., Koltun, V.: Multi-scale context aggregation by dilated convolutions. arXiv preprint arXiv:1511.07122 (2015)

46. Yuan, L., et al.: Tokens-to-token VIT: training vision transformers from scratch on imagenet. arXiv preprint arXiv:2101.11986 (2021)
47. Yuan, L., Hou, Q., Jiang, Z., Feng, J., Yan, S.: Volo: vision outlooker for visual recognition (2021)
48. Zhang, Q., Yang, Y.: Rest: an efficient transformer for visual recognition. arXiv preprint arXiv:2105.13677 (2021)
49. Zhou, B., Zhao, H., Puig, X., Fidler, S., Barriuso, A., Torralba, A.: Scene parsing through ade20k dataset. In: CVPR (2017)
50. Zhou, D., et al.: Deepvit: towards deeper vision transformer. arXiv preprint arXiv:2103.11886 (2021)
51. Zoph, B., Le, Q.V.: Neural architecture search with reinforcement learning. In: ICLR (2016)
52. Zoph, B., Vasudevan, V., Shlens, J., Le, Q.V.: Learning transferable architectures for scalable image recognition. In: CVPR (2018)

Interference Distillation for Underwater Fish Recognition

Jian Pang[1], Weifeng Liu[1(✉)], Baodi Liu[1], Dapeng Tao[2], Kai Zhang[1], and Xiaoping Lu[3]

[1] China University of Petroleum (East China), Qingdao, China
pangjian@stu.kust.edu.cn, liuwf@upc.edu.cn
[2] Yunnan University, Kunming, China
[3] Haier Industrial Intelligence Institute Co., Ltd., Qingdao, China

Abstract. Underwater fish recognition has great value for marine ecological monitoring and management. However, the underwater environment poses great challenges due to absorption and scattering of light which leads to interference images obstructing fish species recognition. In this paper, we use the teacher-student model to distill the interference in underwater fish images, which intends to classify the fish species more efficiently. Specifically, the processed fish image and the raw fish image are used to generate the distance matrix separately, and the interference information is distilled at the feature level by reducing the discrepancy of the two distance matrix, which promotes the network to extract discriminative clues. The KL-Divergence is utilized to further lower the noise in the original data distribution. The results of experiments conducted on several datasets verify that the proposed method is effective and outperforms the competitors.

Keywords: Underwater fish recognition · Teacher-student model · Interference distillation · KL-Divergence

1 Introduction

Fish species recognition is one of the most prominent topics of research for the underwater environment. Marine biologists and researchers can analyze the habits and health of fish species according to their types and numbers, which is of great significance to the protection and improvement of the marine ecological environment. The majority of available studies focus on the identification of fish specimens outside of the water because underwater classification poses challenges such as background noises and poor image quality [2,21]. We argue that the underwater images produced by the effects of light scattering and absorption will have a serious impact on recognition(several samples are shown in Fig. 1). On the contrary, the image processed by the existing algorithm [9] has the features of higher contrast and clearer target, which may be helpful for recognition. Based on this assumption, we propose a novel method that employs the teacher-student model to distill the interference information in the raw image.

© Springer Nature Switzerland AG 2022
C. Wallraven et al. (Eds.): ACPR 2021, LNCS 13188, pp. 62–74, 2022.
https://doi.org/10.1007/978-3-031-02375-0_5

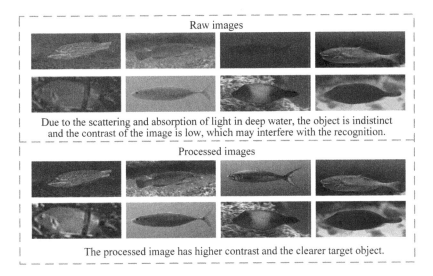

Fig. 1. Randomly sampled images from the raw underwater dataset and corresponding processed images.

Some currently available studies aim to capture detailed features for improving the identification ability by reforming the network structure [10,12]. Also, the traditional method exploits low-level features for fish recognition [1]. This type of method has unsatisfactory performance and did not consider the impact of low-quality images due to light scattering and absorption on recognition. Fish images collected underwater containing a lot of noise and interference will seriously affect the recognition performance. In this paper, we consider the interference caused by poor quality images due to light scattering and absorption in the deep water and proposed a novel algorithm with superior performance. Knowledge distillation [6] can be used to reduce the interference in the underwater image through the guidance of the teacher network to transfer the constructive knowledge of students'.

This paper aims at finding a solution to reduce the impact of interference on fish classification. The pipeline of the proposed method is shown in Fig. 2. The teacher-student model is used as the backbone for feature extraction. The images input to the student network and teacher network are the raw underwater images and the processed images separately. Two fully connected layers are respectively connected to the end of the teacher network and the student network as a classifier. We distill the knowledge of the student model in two ways. One way called Feature Similarity Alignment(FSA) is to push the internal relationship calculated by the batch images similarity according to the student output closer to the teachers'. To further constrain the student predictive distribution, KL-Divergence is introduced to minimize the discrepancy between two predicted outputs of teacher and student networks. Experiments prove the superiority and effectiveness of our approach. Our contributions are summarized as follows:

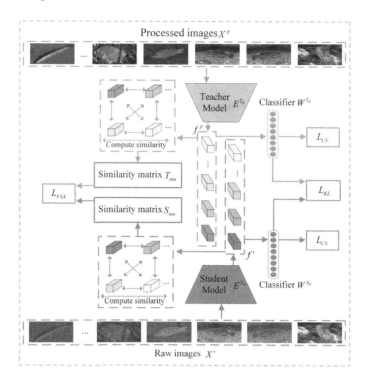

Fig. 2. An illustration of our approach. The raw images are sampled from underwater datasets. The processed images are obtained by processing raw images through the algorithm [9]. A teacher-student model is utilized to extract features with a classifier added at the end. The proposed method consists of two parts: Feature Similarity Alignment(FSA) and KL-Divergence.

- We consider the impact of light scattering and absorption in underwater images on fish identification and propose a novel method for distilling interference clues.
- The proposed feature similarity alignment and KL-Divergence constraint the student model to learn undisturbed feature representations at the feature level and the distribution level, respectively.
- Extensive experiments have proved the superiority of our approach. The ablation study demonstrates the effectiveness of each proposed loss function.

The rest of the paper is organized as follows: Sect. 2 gives a brief overview of related work. Section 3 demonstrates the proposed method. Section 4 discusses the experimental results. Finally, the conclusions and a discussion are presented in Sect. 5.

2   Related Work

2.1   Underwater Fish Recognition

Before the advent of Convolutional Neural Networks(CNN), traditional fish recognition algorithms mainly relied on manual features, such as color-based, geometric, and texture [1,13]. Saitoh et al. [13] effectively improve the accuracy by combining geometric features and semantic information. Besides, Ananthara-jah et al. [1]propose a region-based session variability modeling approach, which is beneficial to learning the invariant feature representation of fish under different environments. With the advancement of artificial intelligence, convolutional neural networks have been greatly improved and have shown great advantages in many visual tasks. Jager et al. [7] combine CNN features with SVM for more accurate performance. Qiu et al. [12] believe that fish recognition is a fine-grained image classification problem [11,16,19,20], which is more challenging than common image classification, especially with low-quality and small-scale data. To reduce the impact of interference in low-quality underwater images on performance, they exploit super-resolution reconstruction technology to increase the sample diversity and improves performance with the help of designed squeeze-and-excitation blocks [12]. However, these methods do not take into account the imaging characteristics of underwater images. Due to the scattering and absorption of light, the low-quality image will interfere with fish identification.

2.2   Knowledge Distillation

Hinton et al. [6] pioneered the concept of distilling knowledge that migrating potential knowledge from a complex teacher network to a student network. To reveal the mechanism of knowledge distillation, Wang et al. [18] gives a comprehensive overview of knowledge distillation and provide explanations on how it works. Mathematically, traditional cross-entropy is usually utilized to constrain the output of the student model to imitate the teachers' output. This encouragement mechanism helps the student model have better generalization performance [17]. In some cases, the performance of the student is even better than the teacher. These studies argued that the teacher distribution provided much richer information compared to just one-hot labels. Shen et al. [15] proposed a method of integrating multiple teacher networks for joint learning. Specifically, the KL-Divergence is calculated by averaging the predicted results of multiple teachers and the results of the student model. Furthermore, the discriminator is used for distillation to get more accurate results [14]. However, due to the special imaging properties of underwater images, this type of research cannot be directly used in underwater fish recognition tasks.

3   The Proposed Method

In Fig. 2, The developed method consists of two parts. Feature Similarity Alignment(FSA) reduces the matrix difference obtained by calculating image similarity to distill interference at the feature level, and the other part employs

KL-Divergence to align the predicted results of the teacher-student model. The ResNet-50 pre-trained on ImageNet [3] is used in both teacher and student models as the feature extraction network. The fully connected layer is added to the end of the network for classification.

3.1 Supervised Training

Given a raw fish dataset $\{\boldsymbol{X}^s, \boldsymbol{Y}^s\}$, where $\boldsymbol{X}_s = \{x_i^s\}_{i=1}^{N_s}$ has N_s images contain C classes. Each image x_i^s corresponds to a label $y_i \in \boldsymbol{Y}_i^s$. The processed fish dataset is denoted as $\boldsymbol{X}^p = \{x_i^p\}_{i=1}^{N_s}$. Note that the label y_i of the processed image x_i^p and the raw image x_i^s are consistent. Define E^{T_θ} and E^{S_θ} to represent the teacher network and the student network respectively. At the end of the network, a fully connected layer is added for classification denoted as W^{T_θ} and W^{S_θ} for the teacher and the student separately.

For the classification task, the popular loss function cross-entropy was employed to jointly optimize E^{T_θ} and E^{S_θ} in the form of,

$$L_{CE}(E^*, W^*) = \sum_{c=1}^{C} -I(c, \hat{y}_i^c) log \hat{y}_i^c, \tag{1}$$

where $\hat{y}_i^c$ is the predicated logits of class c. E^* denotes E^{T_θ} or E^{S_θ}. W^* represents the classifier corresponding to E^*. Following the [5], we introduce label smoothing to prevent over-fitting. It can be formulated as:

$$I(c, \hat{y}_i^c) = \begin{cases} 1 - \varepsilon, & \text{if } c = \hat{y}_i^c \\ \frac{\varepsilon}{C-1}, & \text{otherwise} \end{cases} \tag{2}$$

where ε is a smoothing parameter and set to 0.1 empirically. C is the number of species.

3.2 Distillation by Feature Similarity Alignment

Only adopting cross-entropy to optimize the network is far from meeting the requirements. Underwater images are affected by light scattering and absorption, this would mislead the feature representation towards learning interference information. To solve this problem, we use the discrepancy of features between the underwater image and the processed image to distill the interference clues. Define the raw underwater image as x_i^s and the corresponding processed image as x_i^p. $f_i^p = E^{T_\theta}(x_i^p)$ and $f_i^s = E^{S_\theta}(x_i^s)$ respectively represent the output features of the teacher network and student network. We argue that the divergence between $E^{T_\theta}(x_i^p)$ and $E^{S_\theta}(x_i^s)$ is caused by the inconsistent representation for two types of input images. In order to reduce the interference contained in the underwater image, the Feature Similarity Alignment(FSA) was designed for narrowing the differences between the raw image features and the processed image features.

The similarity matrix of the raw image features is obtained by calculating the following formula:

$$\boldsymbol{T}_{mn} = \|f_m^s - f_n^s\|_2, \qquad m, n = 1, 2, \ldots, B, \tag{3}$$

The same operation can be performed on the processed images to obtain the similarity matrix:

$$\boldsymbol{S}_{mn} = \|f_m^p - f_n^p\|_2, \qquad m, n = 1, 2, \ldots, B, \tag{4}$$

where B denotes the batch-size. $\boldsymbol{T}_{mn}$ represents intrinsic relevance of the batch processed images, and $\boldsymbol{S}_{mn}$ represents intrinsic relevance of the batch raw images. Our goal is to distill the interference information in the output result of the student model, which can be achieved by pushing the intrinsic similarity matrix of the raw images close to the processed images'. It can be described by:

$$\boldsymbol{L}_{FSA}(E^{\boldsymbol{S}_\theta}) = \frac{1}{B^2}\|\boldsymbol{T}_{mn} - \boldsymbol{S}_{mn}\|_1, \tag{5}$$

Because the input image of the teacher model is clearer, the feature details are more abundant. Through feature alignment, the interfering components in the output features of the student model can be reduced.

3.3   Distillation by KL-Divergence

KL-Divergence is a measure metric of how differences between two probability distributions. In the former section, the feature similarity alignment was employed to distill the interference, while ignoring the gap between the probability distributions. Therefore, KL-Divergence is utilized to further constrain the student network for interference distillation. In our method, we optimize the student model $E^{\boldsymbol{S}_\theta}$ by minimizing the KL-Divergence between its outputs P^{S_θ} and the teacher outputs P^{T_θ}. It can be expressed as:

$$\boldsymbol{L}_{KL}(E^{\boldsymbol{S}_\theta}, W^{\boldsymbol{S}_\theta}) = -\sigma^2 \frac{1}{N_s} \sum_{i=1}^{N_s} P^{T_\theta}(f_i^p) \log(\frac{P^{S_\theta}(f_i^s)}{P^{T_\theta}(f_i^p)}), \tag{6}$$

where N_s is the number of samples. $P^{T_\theta}(f_i^p) = softmax(W^{T_\theta}(f_i^p)/\sigma)$ and $P^{S_\theta}(f_i^s) = softmax(W^{S_\theta}(f_i^s)/\sigma)$ represent the teacher's and the student's softmax prediction respectively. σ is the hyper-parameter that balances the predicted logits and is set to 10 empirically.

It should be noted that only cross-entropy is involved to optimize the teacher network. The overall loss function for the student network consists of three parts: cross-entropy loss in Eq. (1), feature similarity alignment in Eq. (5), and KL-Divergence in Eq. (6). It can be formulated as:

$$\boldsymbol{L} = \boldsymbol{L}_{CE} + \alpha \boldsymbol{L}_{FSA} + \beta \boldsymbol{L}_{KL}, \tag{7}$$

where α and β are hyper-parameters that balance the importance of the two loss functions.

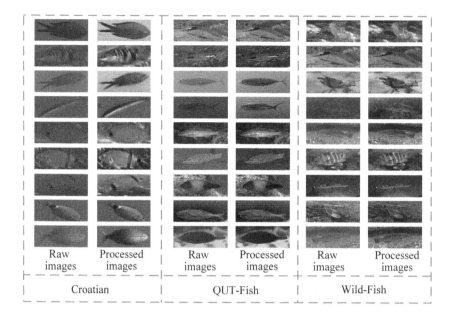

| Raw images | Processed images | Raw images | Processed images | Raw images | Processed images |
| Croatian | | QUT-Fish | | Wild-Fish | |

Fig. 3. Several fish images from Croatian [7], QUT-Fish [1], and Wild-Fish [23] with the corresponding processed images.

4   Experiments

4.1   Training Setting

Implementation Details. During training, the images processed by method [9] are feed to the teacher model. The raw images are as input to the student model. It should be noted that only the student model is used to test the raw underwater images. The ResNet-50 pre-trained on ImageNet [3] is used in both teacher and student models as a backbone network, each of them are followed by a global average pooling and batch normalization to process the features, and finally, a fully connected layer is added for classification. The model has trained 120 epochs in total. The batch-size is set to 16 in all experiments. We select Adam [8] with weight decay 0.0005 as the optimizer. During training, the warmup strategy [5] is introduced to adjust the learning rate. Specifically, the initial learning rate is set to 0.00035, then changed to 1/10 of its previous value when the current epoch reaches 40th and 90th respectively. We use the Pytorch platform to conduct related experiments on an NVIDIA GTX1080Ti. The smoothing parameter ε in Eq. (2) is set to 0.1. The σ in Eq. (6) is set to 10. For three datasets Croatian [7], QUT-Fish [1] and Wild-Fish [23], (α, β) are set to (1, 20), (0.5, 8) and (1, 20) separately.

Datasets and Evaluation Protocol. We adopt three underwater fish datasets (Croatian [7], QUT-Fish [1], Wild-Fish [23]) to evaluate the proposed method.

The method proposed by Li et al. [9] has excellent performance for processing underwater images, so it was employed to process the underwater images. Several samples of the raw image and the processed image are shown in Fig. 3. Croatian [7] contains a total of 794 images in 12 categories. All the training and test images in Croatian are resized to 30×60. We divide it 60% for training and the remaining for the test. QUT-Fish [1] contains a total of 3,960 images of 468 species, but only some of the images are from underwater (1209 images of 193 categories), the rest are taken on land. We take 60% of the underwater images for training, and the rest for testing. Since the image pixels in this dataset are relatively large, therefore both the training and test images are resized to 300×600. For the Wild-fish dataset [23], we following the split setting [23] to acquire training and test images and resize them to 100×150. The images in all the above datasets are processed by random cropping and horizontal flipping, without using data augmentation such as random erasing and data mixture. We summarize the details of the split setting for various datasets in Table 1. Note that all the following experimental results are presented by top-1.

Table 1. Details of training and test images for three datasets.

Datasets	Total		Train		Test	
	#Class	#Image	#Class	#Image	#Class	#Image
Croatian	12	794	12	472	12	322
QUT-Fish	193	1209	193	636	193	573
Wild-Fish	43	2957	43	1648	43	1309

4.2   Results and Comparison

There are two types of comparison methods. The One is designed for underwater fish recognition tasks, including Croatian [7], ISV [1], TLSE [12]. The other are popular networks that perform well on classification tasks, including ResNet-34, ResNet-50, ResNet-101 [4], OsNet-x0-5 and OsNet-x1-0 [22], where ResNet-50 and ResNet-101 are widely used in various fine-grained classification tasks. OsNet is the newly released classification network that employs a unified aggregation gate to dynamically integrate Multiple scale features. The difference between OsNet-x0-5 and OsNet-x1-0 lies in the number of channels inside the network, that represent the scope of vision. Due to the excellent performance and scalability of OsNet, it can be applied to many classification tasks.

From Table 2, we can observe that the proposed method is significantly better than TLSE [12], which has the best performance in fish recognition tasks. The top-1 reaches 99.22%/74.22% on the Croatian/QUT-Fish dataset, surpassing TLSE by 16.27%/17.22%. The reason possibly owning to ignoring the generated interference clues during super-resolution reconstruction. In addition, the squeeze-and-excitation module designed in TLSE didn't take into account the scattering and absorption of light. Our method is also better than ResNet-like networks with various depths, especially compared with ResNet-101 which has double parameters. Compared with the latest recognition network OsNet, the proposed method still has a leading position on the three datasets. The main reason for the superior performance of our algorithm is that these classification networks are ignoring the interference caused by the underwater environment. We considering the light scattering and absorption in the raw images, and promotes a model to extract discriminative features that are not affected by the environment.

Table 2. Experimental results of the proposed methods and state-of-the-art methods on three popular datasets. Here, "–" denotes not reported. The Bold indicates the optimal value. The accuracy is reported by top-1.

Methods	Croatian	QUT-Fish	Wild-Fish
Croatian	66.78	–	–
ISV	–	46.7	–
TLSE	82.95	57.00	–
ResNet-34	96.09	62.50	56.25
ResNet-50	96.09	64.85	58.59
ResNet-101	97.66	64.85	57.81
OsNet-x0-5	96.88	63.23	61.71
OsNet-x1-0	96.88	67.97	59.38
Ours	**99.22**	**74.22**	**62.50**

Table 3. Ablation study of the proposed method on three datasets. *Baseline* is obtained by the student network only using cross-entropy loss. L_{FSA} and L_{KL} correspond to Eq. (5) and Eq. (6) respectively. The Bold indicates the optimal value. The accuracy is reported by top-1.

Methods	Croatian	QUT-Fish	Wild-Fish
Baseline	96.09	64.84	58.59
Baseline+L_{FSA}	97.66	69.53	60.94
Baseline+L_{KL}	97.66	68.75	61.72
Baseline+L_{FSA}+L_{KL}	**99.22**	**74.22**	**62.50**

4.3   Ablation Study

Table 3 visualizes the results of the ablation experiment. The result of the *Baseline* is obtained by the student network only using cross-entropy loss. The proposed method consists of two parts, namely Feature Similarity Alignment(FSA) and KL-Divergence. From the comparison between *"Baseline"* and $Baseline+L_{FSA}$, the top-1 accuracy improved 1.57%, 4.69%, and 2.35% when tested on Croatian, QUT-Fish, and Wild-Fish respectively. It can be seen that when Baseline and $Baseline+L_{FSA}$ are combined, the performance of the three data sets is improved. These results demonstrate the proposed FSA is effective and valid on both datasets. When adding KL-Divergence to *Baseline*, it can also improve model performance. Finally, when the two sub-modules are combined, the model reached the best, especially on Croatian, the recognition reaches 99.22%. The results prove that integration is more effective than any submodule individually, which shows the complementarity of the two methods.

4.4   Parameter Selection and Analysis

α and β in Eq. (7) measure the impact of the corresponding loss function on the overall model respectively. In order to explore the effect of the proposed method on performance, we conduct a series of experiments for parameter analysis on QUT-Fish and Wild-Fish datasets. It is worth noting that β is set to 0 when analyzing the performance of α, and vice versa. By observing the top-1 accuracy under different parameters, we will select the value with better performance as the weight in the final loss.

Effect of the Parameter. α. α controls the strength of the FSA, and its performance is shown in Fig. 4. It can be seen that when $\alpha = 0$, the top-1 of QUT-Fish, and Wild-Fish reached 64.48% and 58.59%, respectively. The performance gradually rises with the increase of α. The accuracy on QUT-Fish is relatively good when α reached 0.5. When α takes 1 and 3, it performs best on the Wild-Fish with the accuracy of 60.94%. In acquire the ideal performance in the comparison experiment, α is set to 0.5 and 1 for the QUT-Fish and Wild-Fish respectively.

Effect of the Parameter. β. β is used to adjust KL-Divergence. Figure 5 visualizes the effects of β on our approach. When $\beta = 0$, the top-1 of QUT-Fish hover around 64.0%. It is elevated greatly when β from 0 to 8. The top-1 reached the best accuracy 68.75% with $\beta = 8$. Subsequently, the recognition rate began to slowly decline. For the Wild-Fish, the performance maintains a small fluctuation around 58.0% when β goes from 0 to 18. Until β reaches 20, the model is optimal with the top-1 is 61.72%. Through observation, the acceptable values of β for QUT-Fish and Wild-Fish are set to 8 and 20 individually.

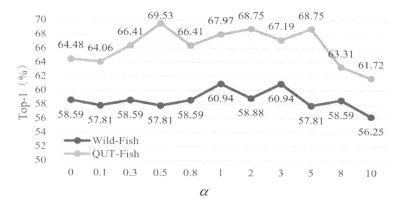

Fig. 4. Performance analysis under different values of α. The accuracy is reported by top-1.

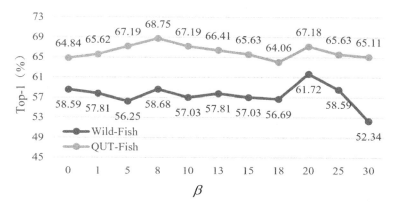

Fig. 5. Performance analysis under different values of β. The accuracy is reported by top-1.

5 Conclusions

To solve the interference of light absorption and scattering on fish recognition. We proposed a novel method, which employs a teacher-student model to distill the interference in underwater images. Specifically, the processed fish image and the raw fish image are used to generate the distance matrix separately, and the interference information is distilled at the feature level by reducing the discrepancy of the two distance matrix, which promotes the network to extract discriminative clues. The KL-Divergence is utilized to further lower the noise in the raw data distribution. We selected different depths of ResNet networks that performed well on classification tasks to compare the experimental performance. In addition, the newly released network OsNet with stronger generalization ability is also adopted for comparison. The result proves that the proposed method has superior performance, surpassing the compared methods by a large margin. The ablation study certified the effectiveness of each proposed loss function. Finally, through parameter analysis, we can catch sight of the influence of each function on the model to provide a guarantee for the selection of the optimal parameters. In the future, we will explore a framework that integrates image processing and recognition for the identification of underwater creatures.

Acknowledgements. This work was supported by the Major Scientific and Technological Projects of CNPC under Grant ZD2019-183-008 and the Open Project Program of the National Laboratory of Pattern Recognition (NLPR) (Grant No. 20200009).

References

1. Anantharajah, K., et al.: Local inter-session variability modelling for object classification. In: IEEE Winter Conference on Applications of Computer Vision, pp. 309–316. IEEE (2014)
2. Chuang, M.C., Hwang, J.N., Rose, C.S.: Aggregated segmentation of fish from conveyor belt videos. In: 2013 IEEE International Conference on Acoustics, Speech and Signal Processing, pp. 1807–1811. IEEE (2013)
3. Deng, J., Dong, W., Socher, R., Li, L.J., Li, K., Fei-Fei, L.: Imagenet: a large-scale hierarchical image database. In: 2009 IEEE Conference on Computer Vision and Pattern Recognition, pp. 248–255. Ieee (2009)
4. He, K., Zhang, X., Ren, S., Sun, J.: Deep residual learning for image recognition. In: Proceedings of the IEEE Conference on Computer Vision and Pattern Recognition, pp. 770–778 (2016)
5. He, L., Liao, X., Liu, W., Liu, X., Cheng, P., Mei, T.: Fastreid: a pytorch toolbox for general instance re-identification. arXiv preprint arXiv:2006.02631 (2020)
6. Hinton, G., Vinyals, O., Dean, J.: Distilling the knowledge in a neural network. arXiv preprint arXiv:1503.02531 (2015)
7. Jager, J., Simon, M., Denzler, J., Wolff, V., Fricke-Neuderth, K., Kruschel, C.: Croatian Fish Dataset: Fine-grained Classification of Fish Species in Their Natural Habitat. BMCV, Swansea (2015)
8. Kingma, D.P., Ba, J.: Adam: a method for stochastic optimization. In: ICLR 2015. arXiv preprint arXiv:1412.6980 9 (2015)
9. Li, C., et al.: An underwater image enhancement benchmark dataset and beyond. IEEE Trans. Image Process. **29**, 4376–4389 (2019)
10. Li, H., Pang, J., Tao, D., Yu, Z.: Cross adversarial consistency self-prediction learning for unsupervised domain adaptation person re-identification. Inf. Sci. **559**, 46–60 (2021)
11. Mo, X., Wei, T., Zhang, H., Huang, Q., Luo, W.: Label-smooth learning for fine-grained visual categorization. In: Palaiahnakote, S., Sanniti di Baja, G., Wang, L., Yan, W.Q. (eds.) ACPR 2019. LNCS, vol. 12046, pp. 17–31. Springer, Cham (2020). https://doi.org/10.1007/978-3-030-41404-7_2
12. Qiu, C., Zhang, S., Wang, C., Yu, Z., Zheng, H., Zheng, B.: Improving transfer learning and squeeze-and-excitation networks for small-scale fine-grained fish image classification. IEEE Access **6**, 78503–78512 (2018)
13. Saitoh, T., Shibata, T., Miyazono, T.: Feature points based fish image recognition. Int. J. Comput. Inf. Syst. Ind. Manage. Appl. **8**, 12–22 (2016)
14. Shen, Z., He, Z., Xue, X.: Meal: multi-model ensemble via adversarial learning. In: Proceedings of the AAAI Conference on Artificial Intelligence, vol. 33, pp. 4886–4893 (2019)

15. Shen, Z., Savvides, M.: Meal v2: Boosting vanilla resnet-50 to 80%+ top-1 accuracy on imagenet without tricks. arXiv preprint arXiv:2009.08453 (2020)
16. Sun, N., Mo, X., Wei, T., Zhang, D., Luo, W.: The effectiveness of noise in data augmentation for fine-grained image classification. In: Palaiahnakote, S., Sanniti di Baja, G., Wang, L., Yan, W.Q. (eds.) ACPR 2019. LNCS, vol. 12046, pp. 779–792. Springer, Cham (2020). https://doi.org/10.1007/978-3-030-41404-7_55
17. Walawalkar, D., Shen, Z., Savvides, M.: Online ensemble model compression using knowledge distillation. In: Vedaldi, A., Bischof, H., Brox, T., Frahm, J.-M. (eds.) ECCV 2020. LNCS, vol. 12364, pp. 18–35. Springer, Cham (2020). https://doi.org/10.1007/978-3-030-58529-7_2
18. Wang, L., Yoon, K.J.: Knowledge distillation and student-teacher learning for visual intelligence: a review and new outlooks. IEEE Trans. Pattern Anal. Mach. Intell. (2021)
19. Wang, Q., Huang, W., Xiong, Z., Li, X.: Looking closer at the scene: multiscale representation learning for remote sensing image scene classification. IEEE Trans. Neural Networks Learn. Syst. (2020)
20. Wen, Z., Ke, Z., Xie, W., Shen, L.: Clustering-based adaptive dropout for CNN-based classification. In: Palaiahnakote, S., Sanniti di Baja, G., Wang, L., Yan, W.Q. (eds.) ACPR 2019. LNCS, vol. 12046, pp. 46–58. Springer, Cham (2020). https://doi.org/10.1007/978-3-030-41404-7_4
21. White, D.J., Svellingen, C., Strachan, N.J.: Automated measurement of species and length of fish by computer vision. Fish. Res. **80**(2–3), 203–210 (2006)
22. Zhou, K., Yang, Y., Cavallaro, A., Xiang, T.: Learning generalisable omni-scale representations for person re-identification. IEEE Trans. Pattern Anal. Mach. Intell. (2021)
23. Zhuang, P., Wang, Y., Qiao, Y.: Wildfish: a large benchmark for fish recognition in the wild. In: Proceedings of the 26th ACM International Conference on Multimedia, pp. 1301–1309 (2018)

Action and Video and Motion

Contact-Less Heart Rate Detection
in Low Light Videos

Tamal Chowdhury[1]([✉]), Sukalpa Chanda[2]([✉]), Saumik Bhattacharya[3],
Soma Biswas[4], and Umapada Pal[1]([✉])

[1] Computer Vision and Pattern Recognition Unit, Indian Statistical Institute,
Kolkata, India
tgchowdhury101@gmail.com, umapada@isical.ac.in
[2] Department of Computer Science and Communication, Østfold University College,
Halden, Norway
sukalpa@ieee.org
[3] Department of Electronics and Electrical Communication Engineering. Indian
Institute of Technology, Kharagpur, India
saumik@ece.iitkgp.ac.in
[4] Department of Electrical Engineering, Indian Institute of Science, Bangalore, India
somabiswas@iisc.ac.in

Abstract. Heart Rate is considered as an important and widely
accepted biological indicator of a person's overall physiological state.
Remotely measuring the heart rate has several benefits in different medical and in computational applications. It helps monitoring the overall
health of a person and analyse the effect of various physical, environmental and emotional factors of an individual. Various methods have been
proposed in recent years to measure the heart rate remotely using RGB
videos. Most of the methods are based on skin color intensity variations
which are not visible to the naked eye but can be captured by a digital
camera. Signal processing and traditional machine learning techniques
have tried to solve this problem using mainly frequency domain analysis of this time varying signal. However these methods are primarily
based on face detection and ROI selection in a sufficiently illuminated
environment, and fail to produce any output in low lighting conditions
which is of utmost importance for the purpose of constant monitoring.
Here, we have proposed a 1-dimensional convolutional neural network
based framework that processes a magnified version of the time series
color variation data in the frequency domain to build an autonomous
heart rate monitoring system. With the help of artificial illumination
this method can even perform well in low light conditions. Also, we have
collected our own dataset that currently contains short frontal face video
clips of 50 subjects along with their ground truth heart rate values both
in normal and low lighting conditions. We have compared our method
with the heuristic signal processing approach to validate its efficacy. (A
demo video of the working of our system can be found here)

Keywords: Remote Heart Rate Detection · Lowlight · Artificial
illumination · Convolutional Neural Network

© Springer Nature Switzerland AG 2022
C. Wallraven et al. (Eds.): ACPR 2021, LNCS 13188, pp. 77–91, 2022.
https://doi.org/10.1007/978-3-031-02375-0_6

1   Introduction

Today's professional world is demanding in terms of time and energy. Hence it is not feasible for any person to monitor family members physically while they are at work, staying in other rooms or outdoors. Remote monitoring of vital physiological parameters in human is predominantly sensor based. Using a sensor-based device, information regarding a physiological condition such as heartbeat can be obtained remotely, but this is inconvenient since the sensor needs to be physically connected to the body of the person. Few contact-less methods do exists to procure vital statistics like body temperature, but unfortunately those methods demand special equipment like thermal imaging cameras to detect temperature [19] or are constrained with proper face detection as a prerequisite to detect body temperature [3].

The contributions of this research are as follows:

- With the help of artificial illumination our method can work in both low and normal lighting conditions
- Pretrained Single Shot Detector (SSD) with ResNet base is used for better face detection and tracking.
- Color magnification technique has been incorporated to better capture the subtle color variation signal.
- We have used 1D convolutional neural network on the frequency spectrum of the color variation data to predict the heart rate of a subject.

2   Related Works

Remote heart rate (HR) detection has been a topic of research for more than a decade. In 2007, Pavlidis et al. [13] first proposed facial region based measurements for heart rate detection. In the same year Garbey et al. [5] used facial thermal imaging with bioheat models for detecting heart rate. In 2008, Verkruysse et al. [17] used Photoplethysmography (PPG) to estimate HR from human facial videos. Since then, PPG has been a popular technique and used in many of the research works for remote heart rate monitoring. In principle it takes into account the blood volume changes due to cardiac activity. As the amount of light absorbed by the skin is a function of blood volume PPG technique measures the amount of light reflected or transmitted by illuminating the skin with the help of a light-emitting diode (LED). However, this method requires a proper environmental setting. In recent years, color based methods for heart rate detection for HR detection has gained a lot of attention that uses regular commercial cameras. In 2010, Poh et al. [15] developed a system for automatic heart rate measurement from webcam. Poh et al. (2011) [14], Pursche et al. (2012) [16], Kwon et al. (2012) [9] Isabel (2016) [2] adopted similar methods. These methods incorporate face detection followed by blind source separation (BSS) on the temporal changes of face color to detect the heart rate. Independent Component Analysis (ICA) was applied to separate the PPG signal from the three color channels (RGB). The signal was then transferred into the frequency domain to find the frequency with the max power and the heart rate was estimated. Previous research suggests [17] that the green channel contains the strongest plethysmographic signal comparative to other color channels. Li et al. [11] proposed a framework incorporating face tracking and Normalized Least Mean Square adaptive filtering methods to eliminate the effect of motion and inconsistent illuminationn from the color signal. Lee et al. [10] adopted a self-supervised approach using a transductive meta-learner. The work produces state-of-the-art results and also addresses the problem of distributional variance of the data during deployment. In 2011 Da et al. [4], captured head motion using accelerometers to monitor HR. Balakrishnan et al. [1] proposed a motion-based approach that tracks the subtle head oscillations due to cardiovascular activity which showed promising results on a self-collected dataset. However, both color and motion-based methods are prone to noise and can easily be influenced by inconsistent illumination and subject's movements. However, the potential of learning-based methods which have enjoyed a huge success in recent years in other application domain, is yet to be fully explored for contactless HR monitoring. In this paper, we propose a novel learning-based framework for remote heart rate detection which can work in both normal and low lighting conditions.

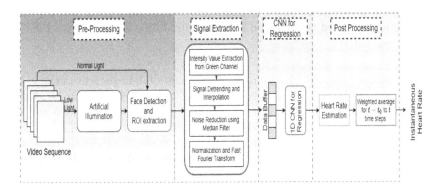

Fig. 1. Schematic diagram of the Proposed Heart Rate Detection method

3   Method

In this section, we provide a detailed discussion of the methodologies that we have used to get the heart rate from a frontal face RGB video. The proposed algorithm comprises of following elements: (a) artificial illumination to enable face detection and signal processing even in low light conditions (b) color magnification technique to better capture the subtle color variation of the skin (c)selecting a region of interest (ROI) from the face area to extract the color intensity values, (d)signal processing in frequency domain to extract the primary signal components and (e)1-D CNN for mapping the frequency spectrums to the corresponding heart rate. Figure 1 gives an overall block diagram of the proposed method.

3.1   Artificial Illumination

Most the methods for remote heart rate detection utilises face detection algorithm at some stage to extract the ROI and capture the color variation from it. But the performance of the state-of-the-art face detection algorithms is very poor in the low light conditions. To increase the robustness of the method to work also in poor lighting settings we utilized the Zero-Deep Curve Estimation [6] technique to artificially illuminate the videos so that the face detection algorithm can detect and extract the ROI easily. Given an input image $I(x)$ the method estimates the best fitting quadratic light enhancement curve $(LE(I(x); \alpha))$ parameterised by α. The equation of the curve is formalised as:

$$LE(I(x); \alpha) = I(x) + \alpha I(x)(1 - I(x)) \tag{1}$$

To cope up with challenging low light conditions the curve is applied iteratively on input image as:

$$LE_n(x) = LE_{n-1}(x) + A_n LE_{n-1}(x)(1 - LE_{n-1}(x)) \tag{2}$$

where A is a parameter map with the same dimension as the input image and n is the total number of iterations. The value of n is more for images captured in darker environment. Hence, it performs pixel-wise mapping of the input using the estimated curve to obtain the final illuminated image. For our low light videos, we have applied this method in a frame-by-frame manner to get the light enhanced version.

Measure of Luminance. To quantify the amount of light present in the videos we have used two measures namely luminance and perceived lightness. Luminance is a measure of the amount of light falling on a surface. It is a linear perception of lightness as is captured by a digital camera, whereas perceived lightness is a non-linear approximation of human vision. To calculate the luminance of a RGB pixel the R, G and B values are scaled between $0 - 1$. Then these values are linearized using gamma decoding as:

$$V_{lin} = \begin{cases} V/12.92, & \text{if } V \leq 0.04045 \\ (V + 0.055/1.055)^{2.4} & V > 0.04045, \end{cases}$$

Then the luminance (Y) is calculated as:

$$Y = 0.216 * R_{lin} + 0.7152 * G_{lin} + 0.0722 * B_{lin} \tag{3}$$

Perceived lightness (L) is calculated from Y as:

$$L = \begin{cases} 903.3 * Y, & \text{if } Y \leq 0.008856 \\ Y_{1/3} * 116 - 16 & Y > 0.008856, \end{cases}$$

The luminance and perceived lightness of an image is then calculated by averaging the luminance and perceived lightness of all the pixels and further averaging over all the frames for a video stream.

3.2   Color Magnification

Due to the cardiovascular activities, the color of our skin changes continuously. Different physical and mental states contribute to a change of the natural rhythm of the heart which in turn reflects on the skin color variation over time. However, this variation is so subtle that it is not visible to our eyes and directly processing these videos without any pre-processing cannot capture this variation well. To overcome this issue, we have used Eulerian Video Magnification technique [18] to amplify the change. Given an input frame $I(x,t)$, at a time step t, the method synthesizes a output signal $\tilde{I}(x,t)$ as:

$$I(x,t) = f(x + (1 + \alpha)\delta(t)) \tag{4}$$

where $f(x)$ is the local image $I(x,0)$, $\delta(t)$ is a displacement function and α is the magnification factor. The method suggests that the color amplification signal obtained matches with the photoplethysmogram and hence can safely be used for our purpose. A magnification factor of 15 is used for each of the video (Fig. 2).

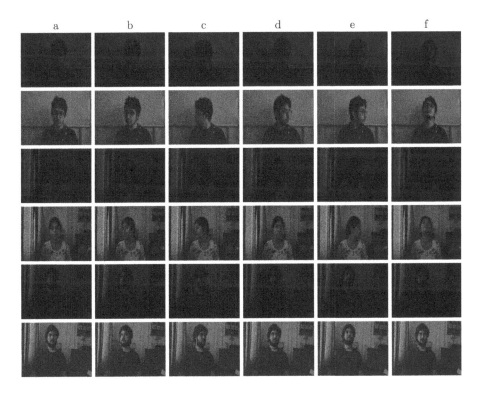

Fig. 2. Before ($1_{st}, 3_{rd}, 5_{th}$ rows) and after ($2_{nd}, 4_{th}, 6_{th}$ rows) artificial illumination of lowlight videos of 6 poses marked in a, b, c, d, e and f.

3.3   Face Detection and ROI Selection

In this method we have used a deep learning-based face detection algorithm which is more robust and accurate than the traditional face detection algorithms and works well on different adverse situations like side faces and also when eyes are closed.

The algorithm is based on the Single Shot Multibox Detector [12] framework with a ResNet-10 backbone. A pre-trained model has been used to detect the faces from the videos and dlib's [7] ensemble regression tree-based facial landmark detection model is used to estimate 68 important facial landmark coordinates from the detected face region. These coordinates are then used to select 2 rectangular ROI's just below the subject's eyes (on the cheeks). The face detection and the selection of good ROI's are extremely crucial for

Fig. 3. Face detection using and ROI selection result

extracting the color variation signal from the skin which is fundamental for the algorithm to work. Hence, selecting a better and robust face detection algorithm can help to improve the face tracking and ROI selection process which in turn produces better results (Fig. 3).

Table 1. Effect of artificial illumination on 10 randomy selected low light video samples. Here, AVL: Average Video Luminance, IL: Increaed Luminance, APL: Average Perceived Lightness, IPL: Increased Perceived Lightness

Subject no	Before illumination		Face	After illumination		Face detection
	AVL	IL	Detection	APL	IPL	
1	0.0068	0.105	False	6.14	38.72	True
2	0.0053	0.063	False	4.78	30.15	True
3	0.0064	0.076	False	5.78	33.13	True
4	0.0074	0.093	False	6.68	36.55	True
5	0.0121	0.166	False	10.63	47.75	True
6	0.0086	0.122	False	7.76	41.53	True
7	0.0076	0.096	False	6.86	37.14	True
8	0.0059	0.074	False	5.33	32.70	True
9	0.0106	0.140	False	9.48	44.23	True
10	0.0094	0.128	False	8.48	42.46	True

3.4   Extraction of Frequency Spectrums from Color Variation Data

After selecting the ROIs total green channel color intensity values are extracted at each time frame. A queue of length 100 is used as a data buffer to store the intensity values of last 100 time stamps. To remove the linear trend from the data, linear detrending technique is used. One dimensional piece-wise linear interpolation is used to increase the number of data points. Then to remove the effect of noise from the data a median filter is used. As previous studies suggest that there exists a strong correlation between the frequency response of the color variation signal and the HR, we have carried out our experiments in frequency domain that gives a more clear picture of the corresponding signal components in a particular frequency range and hence, better information encoding. After that Fast Fourier Transform (FFT) is used to obtain the frequency spectrum from the 1D signal. Given the one-dimensional color variation signal $s(t)$, it's FFT is calculated as (Table 1):

$$S(k) = \sum_{n=0}^{N-1} s(t)e^{-2\pi ikn/N} \tag{5}$$

Considering the frequency of human heart rate the algorithm chooses only frequencies in the range of 0.4 Hz to 3 Hz. The frequency output obtained is directly correlated with the cardiovascular activity of the subject, which in turn can provide the heart rate information.

3.5   1D Convolutional Neural Network

The frequency spectrums obtained from the color variation data buffer are then used to train our convolutional neural network. The network consists of one input layer, four hidden layers and an output layer. The problem is framed as a regression problem where the network outputs a continuous output value (Heart rate in Bpm) given a frequency spectrum. The first hidden layer consists of a 1-dimensional convolutional layer with a kernel size of 3 and stride 3 followed by a batch normalization layer. ReLU is used as the activation function. 128 such feature maps are generated at the output of the first hidden layer. Those are then passed into the second hidden layer which comprises of a convolutional layer with kernel size 1 and stride 3 followed by a batch normalization layer and ReLU activation. 1-dimensional max-pooling is used at the end of second hidden layer to reduce the dimension of the feature maps while preserving the most important information. The second hidden layer also generates 128 feature maps of length 3 which are then flattened and passed into a fully connected layer or dense layer. Finally, the output of this dense layer is passed into another dense layer which outputs the heart rate value in beats per minute (BPM). Figure 4 shows the architecture of the proposed model.

3.6   Post-processing

During inference, the network outputs a heart rate value in a continuous man-ner for each consecutive frequency spectrum obtained from the color variation data buffer. This color intensity-based heart rate calculation is often prone to noise due to several environmental factors like inconsistent illumination and light reflection that affect the instantaneous values of the RGB channels. To alleviate this effect and to get the heart rate at a particular time step t a weighted average is calculated on the heart rates obtained for the 10 previous time steps. The weights are taken as a linear function of the time stamp where the present time stamp (t) has maximum weightage and the $t - 9_{th}$ time stamp has minimum weightage. The dataset and codes used in this paper can be found at https:// github.com/TomChow01/Heart-Rate-Detection-RGB-Videos-

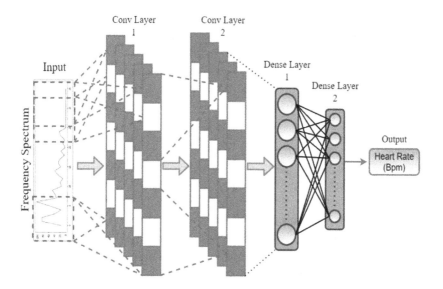

Fig. 4. Architecture of the proposed model

4   Experimental Details

4.1   Dataset Description

We have collected 50 short video clips of duration 25–35 s from 50 different subjects both in normal and low light condition. The subjects are in the age group of 7–55 years. The videos are collected using a mobile camera of 16 megapixel, with a resolution of 1280 × 720 and a tripod at a distance of 2 meters to ensure stabilization. The frame rate per second is 30. The videos are stored in .mp4 format. A pulse meter was put on the finger of the subjects during the data collection procedure and the reading (Heart rate in BPM) was taken at the end of video capturing process. First normal light videos were captured in an indoor environment with sufficient artificial lighting. Next, low light videos were captured after turning of all but one light to ensure at least some amount of light reaches the camera. Some of the videos captured (both in normal and low lighting conditions) during our data collection phase are presented in Fig. 5. To address the challenge of abrupt motion, different types of head movements were also incorporated by the subjects during the video capturing process.

4.2   Training

We trained and validated the model using the frequency data extracted from the low light video samples in a 5-fold cross validation manner where each fold contains 10 video samples. Then for each instance of the model we fit the model using 4 folds and the remaining 5th fold is used for testing purpose. This is done until each of the folds have been used as the test set once. Frequency spectrums are extracted from the color variation data extracted from the videos following the steps mentioned above. It is assumed that during the short video capturing process the heart rate does not change significantly. Hence, for all the frequency spectrums of a particular subject the heart rate is taken to be constant. A batch size of 32 is used during training. The problem is framed as a regression problem

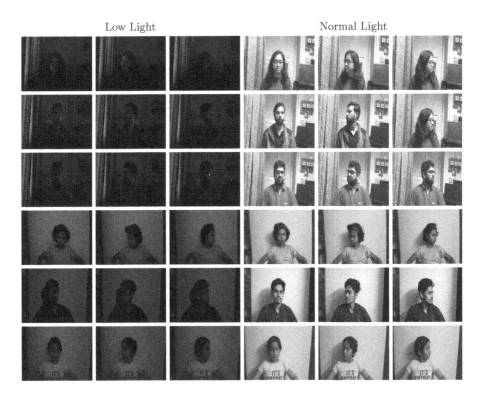

Fig. 5. Examples of some of the videos captured in Normal and Low Lighting Conditions

and the CNN is trained to minimize the mean square error (MSE) between the predicted and ground truth heart rate values. Adam [8] is used as an optimizer to update the network parameters with a fixed learning rate of 0.0001. For each fold of the training dataset, the model is trained for 500 epochs and the performance is measured on the test set.

5   Results and Discussion

In this section, we have discussed the performance of our model during training and inference period. For each fold of the training data, four segments have been used for training and the one is used for testing.

5.1   Evaluation Metrics

The performance of our method is validated based on two statistical measures. The first one is the root mean square error (RMSE), calculated as $RMSE = \frac{1}{N}\sum_{n=1}^{N}(HR_{pred}(n) - HR_{gt}(n))^2$ and the second one is the Pearson's correlation (ρ) that measures the extent of linear correlation between the HR_{pred} and HR_{gt} and the statistical significance of the model output. ρ varies between -1 and 1, where 1 indicates a perfect positive correlation and -1 stands for a perfect negative correlation.

5.2   Performance on Low Light Videos

The RMSE/bpm and pearson correlation (ρ) values of each fold on the test data during the five fold cross validation are depicted in Table 2.

Table 2. Performance of the proposed method on test set for low light videos in terms of RMSE (root mean squared error) and Pearson Correlation(ρ) for each fold

Subject	Fold 1		Fold 2		Fold 3		Fold 4		Fold 5	
	Actual	Predicted	Actual	Predicted	Actual	Predicted	Actual	Predicted	Actual	Predicted
1	70	75	87	85	100	94	85	90	78	82
2	85	82	68	76	91	90	53	62	117	100
3	90	84	80	80	57	63	78	80	93	87
4	72	66	73	78	90	89	75	78	90	92
5	98	94	110	97	90	94	95	92	93	90
6	83	83	90	87	72	73	90	86	113	108
7	85	86	115	102	85	81	93	98	70	74
8	73	76	80	81	95	96	98	95	82	83
9	65	66	80	88	88	90	100	106	100	102
10	80	87	77	76	65	60	84	81	92	90
RMSE	4.26		7.11		3.70		4.72		6.36	
ρ	0.89		0.95		0.96		0.94		0.93	

Table 3. Comparison of the Performance of heuristic and proposed method on test dataset (10 subjects) of the fold with lowest test error. The heart rates are measured in beats per minute

Sl. no.	Actual HR	Heuristic (normal light)	Proposed (normal light)	Proposed (low light)
1	100	84	102	94
2	91	78	94	90
3	57	68	66	63
4	90	81	94	89
5	90	83	90	94
6	72	58	70	73
7	85	76	85	81
8	95	90	92	96
9	88	74	87	90
10	65	82	62	60
RMSE (bpm)	–	12.09	3.64	3.70
ρ	–	0.60	0.96	0.96

The small variations of these metrics suggest the statistical stability of our method. Table 3 shows the actual heart rates, HR obtained by the heuristic method that assumes a linear relationship between the peak frequency and the HR, and the proposed method for the 10 test subjects from the fold with lowest rmse value. The results indicate that the model does a descent job for predicting the heart rates in the range 70–90 bpm. The performance declines when actual heart rate exceeds 100 bpm. This may be due to the lesser number of subjects with high HR value in the training dataset. We also grouped the HRs of test datasets for all 5 fold into three categories, low (<70 bpm), normal (70–85 bpm) and high (> 85 bpm) and measured the performance. The RMSE values for these 3 categories are 5.38, 3.16 and 14.92, respectively, whereas the ρ values are 0.81, 0.85 and 0.68, respectively. All the training and inference was carried out on a system with 1 single core hyper threaded Xeon Processors @2.3 GHz, 1 T K80 GPU and 16 GB of RAM. The system was meant to be a real time HR monitor. However, during the inference period of different models involved the processing speed is affected slightly. The FPS of the final output is recorded to be in between 12–15.

5.3 Performance on Normal Light Videos

As mentioned earlier in Subsect. 4.1, our dataset consists of videos from 50 subjects under regular light as well as under low light condition. We were curious to note the generalization capability of the proposed model by testing the system with videos taken under normal lighting condition. The five-fold framework as discussed in Subsect. 5.2 is maintained here. For every fold, 40 low light videos were used for training and 10 other "Normal" light videos were used for testing. The results are depicted in Table 4:

Table 4. Performance of the proposed method on test set for normal light videos in terms of RMSE (root mean squared error) and Pearson Correlation(ρ) for each fold

Subject	Fold 1		Fold 2		Fold 3		Fold 4		Fold 5	
	Actual	Predicted	Actual	Predicted	Actual	Predicted	Actual	Predicted	Actual	Predicted
1	70	72	87	82	100	102	85	95	78	80
2	85	87	68	70	91	94	53	58	117	108
3	90	80	80	82	57	66	78	82	93	80
4	72	78	73	76	90	94	75	76	90	95
5	98	90	110	106	90	90	95	90	93	90
6	83	84	90	88	72	70	90	88	113	102
7	85	86	115	108	85	85	93	96	70	76
8	73	70	80	75	95	92	98	92	82	80
9	65	66	80	84	88	87	100	98	100	96
10	80	82	77	71	65	62	84	82	92	88
RMSE	4.73		4.33		3.64		4.73		6.93	
ρ	0.87		0.96		0.96		0.93		0.91	

5.4 Effect of Color Magnification

Color magnification plays an important role in the overall framework. We have investigated the effect of color magnification on the performance of our model. Table 5 demonstrates the effect of color magnification factor on the performance of heart rate detection method. The RMSE/bpm, and ρ values (both in normal and low lighting conditions) indicate, initially with the increase of α, as mentioned in Eq. 4, the performance of the model improves. But after certain value of α the performance starts deteriorating as shown in Fig. 6 and Fig. 7

Table 5. Effect of color magnification factor (α) on the model performance. The RMSE and ρ values are presented for the test set of best performing fold for each magnification factor.

Magnification factor (α)	Normal light		Low light		Magnification factor (α)	Normal light		Low light	
	RMSE	ρ	RMSE	ρ		RMSE	ρ	RMSE	ρ
2	12.63	0.70	16.36	0.62	12	11.0	0.90	10.8	0.82
4	11.40	0.78	16.64	0.60	14	7.12	0.96	7.22	0.95
6	11.20	0.85	15.02	0.68	16	7.23	0.95	7.63	0.94
8	9.84	0.88	12.8	0.78	18	11.60	0.82	12.6	0.80
10	10.28	0.80	14.0	0.70	20	14.92	0.74	15.4	0.64

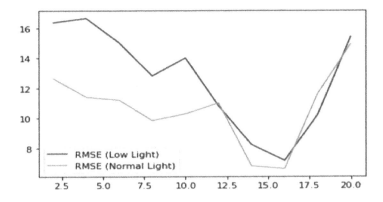

Fig. 6. Effect of color magnification on the RMSE value

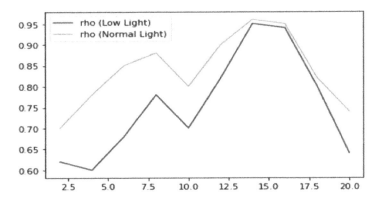

Fig. 7. Effect of color magnification on ρ vaue

6   Conclusion

Existing methods for remote heart rate detection have several limitations and their performance degrades in situations such as abrupt motion of subject, and inappropriate lighting conditions. Many ideas have been proposed to address the above-mentioned issues and the performance of these methods is getting better over the years. However, no attempt has been made to extract a person's HR in low light environment which can be beneficial for continuous monitoring in different environmental conditions. In our work we have integrated an artificial light enhancement technique with a learning-based method to build a robust framework for the same purpose. Further, we have collected our own dataset for all the training and testing purposes that contains videos in both low light and normal lighting conditions. Different signal processing strategies have been adapted to coagulate the information content of the color variation signals and the learning-based approach helps to disregard the effect of unwanted intensity change due to artificial illumination process. Improvement in face detection, ROI selection and noise reduction algorithms along with better learning algorithms can further improve the performance and reliability of such systems. Future works, will be more focused towards real time contactless HR monitoring for moving subjects and variable lighting conditions which will play a key role in remote monitoring to get the physiological status of a person.

Acknowledgement. This is a collaborative research work between Indian Statistical Institute, Kolkata, India and Østfold University College, Halden, Norway. Funding is provided by BabySensor AS, Norway.

References

1. Balakrishnan, G., Durand, F., Guttag, J.: Detecting pulse from head motions in video. In: Proceedings of the IEEE Conference on Computer Vision and Pattern Recognition, pp. 3430–3437 (2013)
2. Bush, I.: Measuring heart rate from video. In: Standford Computer Science, in press (2016)
3. Cheng, X., et al.: Non-invasive measuring method of skin temperature based on skin sensitivity index and deep learning. arXiv preprint arXiv:1812.06509 (2018)
4. Da He, D., Winokur, E.S., Sodini, C.G.: A continuous, wearable, and wireless heart monitor using head ballistocardiogram (BCG) and head electrocardiogram (ECG). In: 2011 Annual International Conference of the IEEE Engineering in Medicine and Biology Society, pp. 4729–4732. IEEE (2011)
5. Garbey, M., Sun, N., Merla, A., Pavlidis, I.: Contact-free measurement of cardiac pulse based on the analysis of thermal imagery. IEEE Trans. Biomed. Eng. **54**(8), 1418–1426 (2007)
6. Guo, C., et al.: Zero-reference deep curve estimation for low-light image enhancement. In: Proceedings of the IEEE/CVF Conference on Computer Vision and Pattern Recognition, pp. 1780–1789 (2020)
7. King, D.E.: Dlib-ml: a machine learning toolkit. J. Mach. Learn. Res. **10**, 1755–1758 (2009)
8. Kingma, D.P., Ba, J.: Adam: a method for stochastic optimization. arXiv preprint arXiv:1412.6980 (2014)
9. Kwon, S., Kim, H., Park, K.S.: Validation of heart rate extraction using video imaging on a built-in camera system of a smartphone. In: 2012 Annual International Conference of the IEEE Engineering in Medicine and Biology Society, pp. 2174–2177. IEEE (2012)
10. Lee, E., Chen, E., Lee, C.-Y.: Meta-rPPG: remote heart rate estimation using a transductive meta-learner. In: Vedaldi, A., Bischof, H., Brox, T., Frahm, J.-M. (eds.) ECCV 2020. LNCS, vol. 12372, pp. 392–409. Springer, Cham (2020). https://doi.org/10.1007/978-3-030-58583-9_24
11. Li, X., Chen, J., Zhao, G., Pietikainen, M.: Remote heart rate measurement from face videos under realistic situations. In: Proceedings of the IEEE Conference on Computer Vision and Pattern Recognition, pp. 4264–4271 (2014)
12. Liu, W., et al.: SSD: single shot MultiBox detector. In: Leibe, B., Matas, J., Sebe, N., Welling, M. (eds.) ECCV 2016. LNCS, vol. 9905, pp. 21–37. Springer, Cham (2016). https://doi.org/10.1007/978-3-319-46448-0_2
13. Pavlidis, I., Dowdall, J., Sun, N., Puri, C., Fei, J., Garbey, M.: Interacting with human physiology. Comput. Vis. Image Underst. **108**(1–2), 150–170 (2007)

14. Poh, M.Z., McDuff, D.J., Picard, R.W.: Advancements in noncontact, multiparameter physiological measurements using a webcam. IEEE Trans. Biomed. Eng. **58**(1), 7–11 (2010)
15. Poh, M.Z., McDuff, D.J., Picard, R.W.: Non-contact, automated cardiac pulse measurements using video imaging and blind source separation. Opt. Express **18**(10), 10762–10774 (2010)
16. Pursche, T., Krajewski, J., Moeller, R.: Video-based heart rate measurement from human faces. In: 2012 IEEE International Conference on Consumer Electronics (ICCE), pp. 544–545. IEEE (2012)
17. Verkruysse, W., Svaasand, L.O., Nelson, J.S.: Remote plethysmographic imaging using ambient light. Opt. Express **16**(26), 21434–21445 (2008)
18. Wu, H.Y., Rubinstein, M., Shih, E., Guttag, J., Durand, F., Freeman, W.: Eulerian video magnification for revealing subtle changes in the world. ACM Trans. Graph. (TOG) **31**(4), 1–8 (2012)
19. Zheng, Y., Wang, H., Hao, Y.: Mobile application for monitoring body temperature from facial images using convolutional neural network and support vector machine. In: Mobile Multimedia/Image Processing, Security, and Applications 2020, vol. 11399, p. 113990B. International Society for Optics and Photonics (2020)

Spatio-temporal Weight of Active Region for Human Activity Recognition

Dong-Gyu Lee[1]([✉]) and Dong-Ok Won[2]

[1] Department of Artificial Intelligence, Kyungpook National University,
Daegu 41566, Republic of Korea
dglee@knu.ac.kr

[2] Department of Artificial Intelligence Convergence, Hallym University,
Chuncheon 24252, Republic of Korea

Abstract. Although activity recognition in the video has been widely studied with recent significant advances in deep learning approaches, it is still a challenging task on real-world datasets. Skeleton-based action recognition has gained popularity because of its ability to exploit sophisticated information about human behavior, but the most cost-effective depth sensor still has the limitation that it only captures indoor scenes. In this paper, we propose a framework for human activity recognition based on spatio-temporal weight of active regions by utilizing human a pose estimation algorithm on RGB video. In the proposed framework, the human pose-based joint motion features with body parts are extracted by adopting a publicly available pose estimation algorithm. Semantically important body parts that interact with other objects gain higher weights based on spatio-temporal activation. The local patches from actively interacting joints with weights and full body part image features are also combined in a single framework. Finally, the temporal dynamics are modeled by LSTM features over time. We validate the proposed method on two public datasets: the BIT-Interaction and UT-Interaction datasets, which are widely used for human interaction recognition performance evaluation. Our method showed the effectiveness by outperforming competing methods in quantitative comparisons.

Keywords: Human activity recognition · Human-human interaction · Spatio-temporal weight

1 Introduction

Recognition of human activity is still developing in computer vision, a field with many applications such as video surveillance, human computer interface and automated driving. In previous studies, the bag-of-words approach or preset motion attributes were commonly used in human activity recognition [10,11,24,36]. Recent deep learning-based representation methods such as 3D convolutional neural networks(CNN) [8], two-stream CNN [27], and multi-stream

© Springer Nature Switzerland AG 2022
C. Wallraven et al. (Eds.): ACPR 2021, LNCS 13188, pp. 92–103, 2022.
https://doi.org/10.1007/978-3-031-02375-0_7

CNN [31] have shown promising results for the human activity recognition problem. However, recognizing human activity accurately remains a challenging task, compared to other aspects of computer vision and machine learning. The use of RGB information imposes limitations on extensibility and versatility because it is often influenced by recording conditions, such as illumination, size, resolution, and occlusion.

With the advent of depth sensors such as Microsoft Kinect, Asus Xtion, and Intel RealSense, instead of using RGB camera, action recognition using 3D skeleton sequences has attracted substantial research attention, and many advanced approaches have been proposed [4,9,18,20,32,35]. Human actions can be represented by a combination of movements of skeletal joints in 3D space. In addition, there has also been major advances in skeleton-based human activity recognition researches [2,3,25,29,34]. They models what happens between two or more people based on their joint information. Although the human skeleton can provide sophisticated information about human behavior, most depth sensors are currently limited to indoor applications with close distance; these conditions are necessary to estimate articulated poses accurately. However, Human activity recognition using articulated poses outdoors could have many more practical applications. Therefore, we address such settings: namely, activity recognition problems where articulated poses are estimated from RGB videos.

In recent studies, deep learning-based approaches have achieved excellent results in estimating the human body joints from RGB videos through pose evaluation [6,7,26]. It has become possible to extract accurate multiple human poses with joint information from RGB video in real time. Because pose estimation and action recognition are closely related problems, some studies simultaneously address these two tasks. A multi-task deep learning approach performed joint 2D and 3D pose estimation from still images and human action recognition from video in a single framework [19]. An AND-OR graph-based action recognition approach utilizes hierarchical part composition analysis [33]. Even though the end-to-end approach has advantages for optimization of the task, it has limited extensibility to videos in varying real-world environments. Furthermore, an approach to research involving interactions, rather than single human actions, methodologically distinct; another problem is that requires the large amount of training data.

In this paper, we propose a novel framework for human activity recognition from RGB video based on spatio-temporal weight of active joints. The proposed framework extracts individual human body joints using publicly available pose estimation method, and recognizes human interaction based on joint motion, local path image, and full-body images with spatio-temporal weight of active region. Therefore, the proposed framework selectively focuses on the informative joints in each frame in an unconditioned RGB video. Figure 1 shows that the interaction regions differ in human activity. In the case of a handshake, hand interaction occurs, but a punch can be understood as head and hand interaction, and a hug as interaction between torso and hand.

Fig. 1. An example of human body joints with spatio-temporal active region analysis: stretched right hand is interacting three different body part of other person in each activity.

We presents our contributions as follows: first, the proposed framework is based on the RGB video, so it has the benefit that activity recognition can be performed using in the wild without constraints. Second, the spatio-temporal weight of the active region is given to activity relevant motion or poses, that makes the model can focus on important cue of human activity. Third, the experimental result shows the effectiveness of proposed method for the human behavior understanding. This framework allows us to develop a highly extensible application. Furthermore, by not performing separate learning for estimation, detection, and tracking tasks, the proposed framework can be extended to varying datasets in an unconditioned environment.

2   Proposed Method

2.1   Preprocessing

In the most recent studies, video representation through a CNN-based approach has shown good results. We first normalize the RGB pixel data and extract feature vector from images to process input images through CNN. We perform human object detection using Faster-RCNN [22] with the Inception-resnet-v2 network [30]. The detection result provides (x, y) coordinates with height and width. We also perform joint estimation using Part Affinity Fields (PAF) [7] on the same images.

The composition of the estimated joints using PAF is shown in Fig. 2. The PAF provides 18 joints for each human object. In addition, the average of joints 8 coordinate and joint 11 coordinate is designated as point 18 for utilization of the torso information; this is referred to as the hip. For each human subject, we denote each joint as $j_i = \{j_0, ..., j_{18}\}$. The pose estimation in an RGB frame often causes a missing joint. Thus, if the previous n frames have failed to estimate a joint, the value in current frame is used for interpolation and restoration. We use the bounding box to filter out bad results using constraints. First, both the head and torso of each object must be included in the bounding box. If a failure occurs in estimating the head (index 0), the average coordinate of $j_{14}, ..., j_{17}$ is

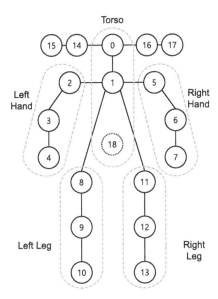

Fig. 2. An illustration of joint indexes from estimated human pose to corresponding five body parts (torso, left hand, right hand, left leg, and right leg).

used as the head position. In this way, noisy objects and poorly estimated joints for interaction can be removed.

In order to consider the local image associated with the body parts in active region, we extract the $(n \times n)$-size image feature from each joint location of index 0 (head position) and 3 (right elbow), 4 (right hand), 9 (right knee), 10 (right foot), 6 (left elbow), 7 (left hand), 12 (left knee), and 13 (left foot). The last fully connected layer of the Inception-resnet-v2 network is used to extract its feature vector, $\mathbf{pf}_j^t$. The input image patches are extracted where the $([x - n/2 : x + n/2], [y - n/2 : y + n/2])$, center is in position (x, y).

2.2 Body Joint Exploitation

We extract four type of joint-based body part features to express the behavior of an individual human. At each time step, for each subject, the 2D coordinates of the 19 body joints are obtained. To consider the characteristics of different behaviors, the motion features were extracted according to the status of the joints. First, we create five body parts using joints from 0 to 18 defined in each frame: right arm p_1 (2, 3, 4), left arm p_2 (5, 6, 7), right leg p_3 (8, 9, 10), left leg p_4 (11, 12, 13), and torso p_5(0, 1, 18). Each number denotes the joint index, and their 2D coordinates are defined as $j_{i^n, (x,y)}$. We then calculate the spatio-temporal weight of five body parts that are created by combining joints and extract the motion feature by using each body part. After defining the five body parts, we calculate the inner angle of each part, θ_{in} as follows:

$$\mathbf{a} = (j_{i^1,x} - j_{i^2,x}, j_{i^1,y} - j_{i^2,y}),$$
$$\mathbf{b} = (j_{i^1,x} - j_{i^3,x}, j_{i^1,y} - j_{i^3,y}),$$
$$\theta = arccos\left(\frac{\mathbf{a} \cdot \mathbf{b}}{|\mathbf{a}||\mathbf{b}|}\right) \tag{1}$$

We also calculate the angle between each part using (1). The outer angle θ_{out} denotes the value for connected part, which is calculated using following joint indexes as input in each frame: (1, 2, 3), (1, 5, 6), (1, 8, 9) and (1, 11, 12). The inner angle represents the relative position of the joint inside the body part, and the outer angle represents the shape of the body part. θ_{in} and θ_{out} can express scale-invariant human posture information for the five body parts. This is also an important cue to express the movement of the body parts by changing the position of each joint. For all points in the body parts, the average value of the difference between each previous point and each current point of the sequence, normalized by n length, is used to calculate the motion velocity, v_p^t and acceleration $\hat{v}_j^t$.

2.3   Full-Body Image Representation

We also conduct full-body image-based activity descriptor to capture overall appearance change. The method used here exploits the SCM descriptor used for human interaction recognition [15,16]. Extracting a feature vector from a full-body image has proved useful. Since joint estimation from RGB images includes a failure case, a full-body image can compensate for the missing parts.

From the bounding box of the human object region, we extract weights from the last fully connected layer of the inception-resnet-v2 network. Then we generate a sub-volume for each object $\mathbf{f}_{oi}^t = [p, \delta x, \delta y]$, where p denotes the average of feature vectors in a sub-volume. A series of frame-level image feature vectors of object oi at time t for l consecutive frames, are averaged into a single feature vector. Then, K-means clustering is performed on the training set to generate codewords $\{w_k\}_{k=1}^K$, where k denotes the number of clusters. Each of sub-volume feature $\mathbf{f}_{oi}^t$ is assigned to the corresponding cluster w_k following the BoW paradigm. The index of the corresponding cluster k_{oi}^t is codeword index, which is also the index of the row and column of the descriptor. Here, we should note that, we use the oj_l coordinates from joint estimation to obtain more precise information.

A descriptor using sub-volume features is constructed from each sub-volume of an object $v_{oi}^t = (\mathbf{f}, x, y, k)$. We measure the Euclidean distance between sub-volumes oi and oj. The overall spatial distance between sub-volume oi and the other oj in segment t for $\#pairs$, where $oj \neq oi$, is aggregated as follows:

$$r^t = \frac{1}{2} \sum_{oi} \sum_{oj \neq oi} dist_{oi,oj}^t. \tag{2}$$

The participation ratio of the pair in the segment t is represented using distance difference between sub-volume oi and oj to the global motion activation. The feature scoring function based on sub-volume clustering is calculated as follows:

$$f_p = log \left(\frac{||w_{oi}^t - \mathbf{f}_{oi}^t|| + ||w_{oj}^t - \mathbf{f}_{oj}^t||}{2} + \psi \right). \tag{3}$$

After computing all required values between all sub-volumes, we finally construct the SCM descriptor, as follows:

$$M^t(k_{oi}^t, k_{oj}^t) = \frac{1}{N} \sum_{oi,oi \neq oj} \sum_{1:t} \frac{s_{oi}^t}{\epsilon^t} \frac{r^t}{dist_{oi,oj}^t} f_p(\mathbf{f}_{oi}^t, \mathbf{f}_{oj}^t), \tag{4}$$

where N is the normalization term. The value between oi, oj is assigned to the SCM descriptor using the corresponding cluster index, k_{oi}^t and k_{oj}^t, of each sub-volume. Each of the descriptors is generated for every non-overlapped time step. Therefore, the descriptor is constructed in a cumulative way.

2.4 Spatio-temporal Weight for Classification

In this section, we present the joint based spatio-temporal weight of active region. The basic idea of spatio-temporal weight of active region is the assumption that, when human interaction occurs, the body parts that constitute each action will be of different importance. Spatio-temporal weights of each body part of the person who leads the action and other person have different depends on interactive motions. For example, when person 1 punches person 2, person 1 reaches out to person 2's head and person 2 would be pushed back without motion towards person 1. If person 1 performs a push action, person 2's response will look similar to a punch, but person 1 will reach out to person 2's torso, and two hands will reach out. We try to capture these subtle differences between similar activities, and reflect the difference in the weights. The weight of body parts between persons is calculated as follows:

$$A_{p,t} = S \times \frac{\sum_p^5 |d_{p,t} - d_{p,t-1}|}{|d_{p,t} - d_{p,t-1}|} \tag{5}$$

where d denotes the relative distance between each pair of body parts among the interacting persons. The calculated part weight, $A_{p,t}$ is multiplied by the velocity $wv_p^t = A_{p,t} \times v_p^t$ and acceleration $w\hat{v}_j^t = A_{p,t} \times \hat{v}_j^t$ to determine the weight. The motion feature m_p^t is created by concatenating θ_{in}, θ_{out}, a weighted wv_p^t, and $w\hat{v}_j^t$. The weight is also multiplied by the image patch feature vector from each joint. Since an interacting body part with a high weight plays an important role in the activity, this also gives a high weight to the joint-based image feature extracted from the position of the body part as $\mathbf{wf} = \mathbf{pf} \otimes A_p$.

The overall framework is illustrated in Fig. 3. From a given video, estimated joints are processed through three different streams: joint patch feature extraction, body part motion features with spatio-temporal weight extraction, and

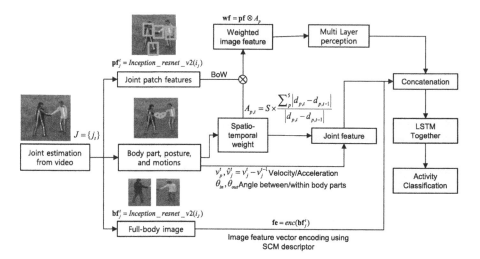

Fig. 3. Illustration of the overall framework combining spatio-temporal weight, joint feature and image feature. The first joint estimation from the video denotes human body joint extraction from RGB input.

full-body image feature extraction. At each step, The generated motion features m_p^t and joint-based weighted image patch features $\mathbf{wf}_p^t$, and SCM descriptor after multi layer perception are concatenated and used as LSTM inputs. The final vector is used as input to LSTM Together, and the activity classification task is the output of the LSTM after processing t segments.

3   Experiment

In this section, we validate the effectiveness of the proposed method on the BIT-Interaction dataset [11] and UT-Interaction dataset [23], which are common and widely used in human interaction recognition research. The performance of the proposed method is shown by comparing the performance with that of the competing methods. In this experiment, the joint estimation was done using PAF [7]. To extract joint patch features and full-body image features, we use the weight of the Inception-resnet-v2 network [30], implemented in Tensorflow [1].

The BIT-Interaction dataset used in the experimental evaluation consists of eight classes of human interactions: bow, boxing, handshake, high-five, hug, kick, pat, and push. Each class contains 50 clips. The videos were captured in a very realistic environment, including partial occlusion, movement, complex background, varying sizes, view point changes, and lighting changes. The sample images of this dataset is shown in Fig. 4(1)–4(b). Both images have the environmental difficulties that are occlusion and complex background. For this dataset, we used a training set with from 1 to 34 index for each class (a total of 272 clips) and the remaining from 35 to 50 index as the test set (128 clips) following official standard in the literature [5,10,13].

(a) BIT: Bow   (b) BIT: Boxing

(c) UT #1: Push   (d) UT #2: Kick

Fig. 4. Sample frames of the BIT-Interaction dataset (a-b), UT-Interaction dataset Set #1 (c) and Set #2 (d).

Table 1. Comparison of the recognition results on the BIT-Interaction dataset

Method	Accuracy (%)
Linear SVM (BoW)	64.06
Dynamic BoW [24]	53.13
MTSSVM [13]	76.56
MSSC [5]	67.97
MMAPM [10]	79.69
Kong et al. [12]	90.63
Liu et al. [17]	84.37
SCM [16]	88.70
Proposed Method	**92.67**

The experimental results for quantitative comparison on the BIT-Interaction dataset, compared with the competing methods, are shown in Table 1. The table lists the average classification accuracy for eight classes. The proposed method achieved better overall performance over than all the other comparison methods, with 92.67% recognition accuracy for human interaction activity recognition. This result is better than the competing methods. In addition, it shows better performance than SCM-based technique [15], that only considers full-body images. This means that it is better to use the joint-based high-level motion information than to utilize the low-level image features alone.

The UT-Interaction dataset used in the experimental evaluation consist of six classes of human interactions: push, kick, hug, point, punch, and handshake. Each class contains 10 clips for each set. The dataset is composed of two sets of video which were captured in different environments; set #1 and set #2. The set #1 videos were captured in a parking lot background. However, the backgrounds in set #2 of the UT-Interaction dataset consisted of grass and jittering twigs, which could be noise to local patches. We performed leave-one-out cross validation for the performance in the Table 2 and Table 3 as done in previous studies [5, 10, 16, 21, 24, 28].

Table 2. Comparison of the recognition results on the UT-Interaction dataset (set #1).

Method	Accuracy (%)
Bag-of-Words (BoW)	81.67
Integral BoW [24]	81.70
Dynamic BoW [24]	85.00
SC [5]	76.67
MSSC [5]	83.33
MMAPM [10]	**95.00**
SCM et al. [16]	90.22
Mahmood et al. [21]	83.50
Slimani et al. [28]	90.00
Proposed Method	91.70

Table 3. Comparison of the recognition results on the UT-Interaction dataset (set #2).

Method	Accuracy (%)
Bag-of-Words (BoW)	80.00
Dynamic BoW [24]	70.00
Lan et al. [14]	83.33
SC [5]	80.00
MSSC [5]	81.67
MMAPM [10]	86.67
SCM [16]	89.40
Mahmood et al. [21]	72.50
Slimani et al. [28]	83.90
Proposed Method	**89.70**

Table 2 compares the classification accuracy measured on the UT-Interaction #1. In set #1, the proposed method achieved 91.70 % recognition accuracy. The performance of MMAPM was very high and the proposed method has the second highest performance. On the other hand, our method achieved the highest performance in set #2 as shown in Table 3. This is because set #2 has a noisier background than the set #1, so the proposed method of using human structural characteristics through joint estimation works better than competing methods based on image features only. In real-world scenarios, considering the complexities of environmental change, the proposed method is highly effective.

4   Conclusion and Future Work

Despite numerous studies, it is still challenging and difficult to recognize the complex activity of people in video. However, the complex activity of two or more people interacting with each other requires a higher level of scene understanding than robust image representation. In this study, we showed that robust activity recognition results can be obtained by acquiring joint information of the human that is estimated from RGB videos are informative to understand the human activity. The spatio-temporal weight to actively interacting body parts improve the recognition accuracy than RGB-only methods. This indicates that the relationship between objects plays a key role in complex activity recognition. In addition, the proposed method has high practicality, in the sense that it can overcome the limitations of existing sensors that uses depth information to exploit the skeleton information and increase the possibility of using a common RGB camera. In future research, we intend to expand this work to show robust performance even in interactions involving more people or non-human objects.

Acknowledgment. This work was supported by the National Research Foundation of Korea (NRF) grant funded by the Korea government (MSIT) (No.2021R1C1C1012590).

References

1. Abadi, M., et al.: TensorFlow: large-scale machine learning on heterogeneous systems (2015). https://www.tensorflow.org/. software available from tensorflow.org
2. Baradel, F., Wolf, C., Mille, J.: Human action recognition: pose-based attention draws focus to hands. In: ICCV Workshop on Hands in Action (2017)
3. Baradel, F., Wolf, C., Mille, J.: Pose-conditioned spatio-temporal attention for human action recognition. arXiv preprint arXiv:1703.10106 (2017)
4. Butepage, J., Black, M.J., Kragic, D., Kjellstrom, H.: Deep representation learning for human motion prediction and classification. In: Proceedings of the IEEE Conference on Computer Vision and Pattern Recognition, pp. 6158–6166 (2017)
5. Cao, Y., et al.: Recognize human activities from partially observed videos. In: Proceedings of the IEEE Conference on Computer Vision and Pattern Recognition, pp. 2658–2665 (2013)
6. Cao, Z., Hidalgo, G., Simon, T., Wei, S.E., Sheikh, Y.: OpenPose: realtime multi-person 2D pose estimation using Part Affinity Fields. In: arXiv preprint arXiv:1812.08008 (2018)

7. Cao, Z., Simon, T., Wei, S.E., Sheikh, Y.: Realtime multi-person 2d pose estimation using part affinity fields. In: CVPR (2017)
8. Ji, S., Xu, W., Yang, M., Yu, K.: 3d convolutional neural networks for human action recognition. IEEE Trans. Pattern Anal. Mach. Intell. **35**(1), 221–231 (2013)
9. Ke, Q., Bennamoun, M., An, S., Sohel, F., Boussaid, F.: A new representation of skeleton sequences for 3d action recognition. In: 2017 IEEE Conference on Computer Vision and Pattern Recognition (CVPR), pp. 4570–4579. IEEE (2017)
10. Kong, Y., Fu, Y.: Max-margin action prediction machine. IEEE Trans. Pattern Anal. Mach. Intell. **38**(9), 1844–1858 (2016)
11. Kong, Y., Jia, Y., Fu, Y.: Learning human interaction by interactive phrases, pp. 300–313 (2012)
12. Kong, Y., Jia, Y., Fu, Y.: Interactive phrases: semantic descriptions for human interaction recognition. IEEE Trans. Pattern Anal. Mach. Intell. **36**(9), 1775–1788 (2014)
13. Kong, Y., Kit, D., Fu, Y.: A discriminative model with multiple temporal scales for action prediction. In: Proceeding of European Conference on Computer Vision, pp. 596–611 (2014)
14. Lan, T., Chen, T.-C., Savarese, S.: A hierarchical representation for future action prediction. In: Fleet, D., Pajdla, T., Schiele, B., Tuytelaars, T. (eds.) ECCV 2014. LNCS, vol. 8691, pp. 689–704. Springer, Cham (2014). https://doi.org/10.1007/978-3-319-10578-9_45
15. Lee, D.G., Lee, S.W.: Human activity prediction based on sub-volume relationship descriptor. In: Proceedings of the IEEE International Conference on Pattern Recognition, pp. 2060–2065 (2016)
16. Lee, D.G., Lee, S.W.: Prediction of partially observed human activity based on pre-trained deep representation. Pattern Recogn. **85**, 198–206 (2019)
17. Liu, J., Kuipers, B., Savarese, S.: Recognizing human actions by attributes. In: Proceedings of the IEEE Conference on Computer Vision and Pattern Recognition, pp. 3337–3344 (2011)
18. Liu, J., Wang, G., Duan, L.Y., Abdiyeva, K., Kot, A.C.: Skeleton-based human action recognition with global context-aware attention lstm networks. IEEE Trans. Image Process. **27**(4), 1586–1599 (2018)
19. Luvizon, D.C., Picard, D., Tabia, H.: 2d/3d pose estimation and action recognition using multitask deep learning. In: The IEEE Conference on Computer Vision and Pattern Recognition (CVPR), vol. 2 (2018)
20. Luvizon, D.C., Tabia, H., Picard, D.: Learning features combination for human action recognition from skeleton sequences. Pattern Recogn. Lett. **99**, 13–20 (2017)
21. Mahmood, M., Jalal, A., Sidduqi, M.: Robust spatio-temporal features for human interaction recognition via artificial neural network. In: International Conference on Frontiers of Information Technology, pp. 218–223. IEEE (2018)
22. Ren, S., He, K., Girshick, R., Sun, J.: Faster R-CNN: towards real-time object detection with region proposal networks. In: Advances in Neural Information Processing Systems, pp. 91–99 (2015)
23. Ryoo, M.S., Aggarwal, J.K.: UT-Interaction Dataset, ICPR contest on Semantic Description of Human Activities (SDHA) (2010). http://cvrc.ece.utexas.edu/SDHA2010/Human_Interaction.html
24. Ryoo, M.S.: Human activity prediction: early recognition of ongoing activities from streaming videos. In: Proceedings of the IEEE International Conference on Computer Vision, pp. 1036–1043 (2011)

25. Shahroudy, A., Liu, J., Ng, T.T., Wang, G.: Ntu rgb+ d: a large scale dataset for 3d human activity analysis. In: Proceedings of the IEEE Conference on Computer Vision and Pattern Recognition, pp. 1010–1019 (2016)
26. Simon, T., Joo, H., Matthews, I., Sheikh, Y.: Hand keypoint detection in single images using multiview bootstrapping. In: CVPR (2017)
27. Simonyan, K., Zisserman, A.: Two-stream convolutional networks for action recognition in videos. In: Advances in Neural Information Processing Systems, pp. 568–576 (2014)
28. el houda Slimani, K.N., Benezeth, Y., Souami, F.: Learning bag of spatio-temporal features for human interaction recognition. In: International Conference on Machine Vision, vol. 11433, p. 1143302 (2020)
29. Song, S., Lan, C., Xing, J., Zeng, W., Liu, J.: An end-to-end spatio-temporal attention model for human action recognition from skeleton data. In: AAAI, vol. 1, pp. 4263–4270 (2017)
30. Szegedy, C., Ioffe, S., Vanhoucke, V., Alemi, A.A.: Inception-v4, inception-resnet and the impact of residual connections on learning. In: AAAI, vol. 4, p. 12 (2017)
31. Tu, Z., et al.: Multi-stream CNN: learning representations based on human-related regions for action recognition. Pattern Recogn. **79**, 32–43 (2018)
32. Wang, H., Wang, L.: Modeling temporal dynamics and spatial configurations of actions using two-stream recurrent neural networks. In: e Conference on Computer Vision and Pa ern Recognition (CVPR) (2017)
33. Xiaohan Nie, B., Xiong, C., Zhu, S.C.: Joint action recognition and pose estimation from video. In: Proceedings of the IEEE Conference on Computer Vision and Pattern Recognition, pp. 1293–1301 (2015)
34. Yun, K., Honorio, J., Chattopadhyay, D., Berg, T.L., Samaras, D.: Two-person interaction detection using body-pose features and multiple instance learning. In: 2012 IEEE Computer Society Conference on Computer Vision and Pattern Recognition Workshops (CVPRW), pp. 28–35. IEEE (2012)
35. Zhu, W., et al.: Co-occurrence feature learning for skeleton based action recognition using regularized deep LSTM networks. In: AAAI, vol. 2, p. 6 (2016)
36. Zhu, Y., Nayak, N., Gaur, U., Song, B., Roy-Chowdhury, A.: Modeling multi-object interactions using "string of feature graphs." Comput. Vision Image Understanding **117**(10), 1313–1328 (2013)

Motor Imagery Classification Based on CNN-GRU Network with Spatio-Temporal Feature Representation

Ji-Seon Bang[1] and Seong-Whan Lee[2(✉)]

[1] Department of Brain and Cognitive Engineering, Korea University, Seoul, Republic of Korea
js_bang@korea.ac.kr
[2] Department of Artificial Intelligence, Korea University, Seoul, Republic of Korea
sw.lee@korea.ac.kr

Abstract. Recently, various deep neural networks have been applied to classify electroencephalogram (EEG) signal. EEG is a brain signal that can be acquired in a non-invasive way and has a high temporal resolution. It can be used to decode the intention of users. As the EEG signal has a high dimension of feature space, appropriate feature extraction methods are needed to improve classification performance. In this study, we obtained spatio-temporal feature representation and classified them with the combined convolutional neural networks (CNN)-gated recurrent unit (GRU) model. To this end, we obtained covariance matrices in each different temporal band and then concatenated them on the temporal axis to obtain a final spatio-temporal feature representation. In the classification model, CNN is responsible for spatial feature extraction and GRU is responsible for temporal feature extraction. Classification performance was improved by distinguishing spatial data processing and temporal data processing. The average accuracy of the proposed model was 77.70% (±15.39) for the BCI competition IV_2a data set. The proposed method outperformed all other methods compared as a baseline method.

Keywords: Brain-computer interface (BCI) · Electroencephalography (EEG) · Motor imagery (MI) · Convolutional neural network (CNN) · Gated recurrent unit (GRU)

This work was partly supported by Institute of Information & Communications Technology Planning & Evaluation (IITP) grant funded by the Korea government (MSIT) (No. 2015-0-00185, Development of Intelligent Pattern Recognition Softwares for Ambulatory Brain Computer Interface, No. 2017-0-00451, Development of BCI based Brain and Cognitive Computing Technology for Recognizing User's Intentions using Deep Learning, No. 2019-0-00079, Artificial Intelligence Graduate School Program (Korea University)).

ⓒ Springer Nature Switzerland AG 2022
C. Wallraven et al. (Eds.): ACPR 2021, LNCS 13188, pp. 104–115, 2022.
https://doi.org/10.1007/978-3-031-02375-0_8

1   Introduction

Brain-computer interfaces (BCI) allows users to control external devices with their intentions, which are decoded from users' brain signals [1–5]. Motor imagery (MI) tasks are widely used for BCI paradigms. Sensory motor rhythms [6–8] are induced when humans mentally simulate certain movements in their minds. Whenever a subject imagines the movement of the particular body part, the corresponding parts of the brain are activated. This brain activity can be recorded and used to control external devices.

There are many studies to achieve better classification performance of MI. Common spatial pattern (CSP) [9] and its variants are the most commonly used feature extraction methods. CSP finds the set of spatial filters that maximizes the distance of variance for multiple classes [10]. Common spatio-spectral pattern (CSSP) [11] is extended versions of CSP. It provides a temporal delay to obtain various features.

In the process of decoding the electroencephalography (EEG) signal for the BCI system, feature extraction is particularly important. As MI signals have high variability between and within subjects, decoding accuracy can be improved by extracting the subject-specific features of each subject [12–14]. However, performance can often be reduced because this part is usually not well considered [15].

Recently, the use of neural network methods has increased in the BCI field [16–22], for various BCI classification tasks. Cecotti *et al.* [16], Manor *et al.* [17], and Sturm *et al.* [18] focused on the EEG time series of each channel. Stober *et al.* [19] and Bashivan *et al.* [20], targeted frequency components using fast Fourier transform (FFT) and short-time Fourier transform (STFT). Sakhavi *et al.* [21] adopted spatial filter on the EEG time series data and Bang *et al.* [22] focused on spatio-spectral domain of the EEG signal.

Here, convolutional neural networks (CNN) is one of the artificial neural network models that has several convolutional layers and a fully connected layer. The neurons in the CNN jointly implement a complex nonlinear mapping by adapting the weights of each neuron. The CNN was first designed to recognize two-dimensional images [23], and the network functions by convolving the images with a two-dimensional kernel in the convolutional layer.

On the other hand, unlike CNN, which specializes in spatial information, there also exists recurrent neural network (RNN) that specializes in time information. Gated recurrent unit (GRU) is a type of RNN, known to show the highest performance in the RNN family to date. The network of RNN is connected in chronological order, and, like an inductive graph, a connection is formed between nodes to handle the time dynamics. Distinctive characteristic of GRU is that it is consisted of two gates: update gate and reset gate. Meanwhile, long short term memory (LSTM) is one of the RNN family network. It contains input and forgetting gates, which play similar role to update gate. However, when the amount of data is small, GRU is known to perform better because it contains less parameters. The use of GRUs is more appropriate as EEG signals have a relatively small number of data compared to other data such as image.

Here, we propose a method for classifying MI signals with combined CNN and GRU network. Especially, we classified brain signals when imagining right-hand and left-hand movement. We adopted CNN to handle spatial information and GRU to handle temporal information. To generate input features for the classification, we first adopted spatial feature representation with normalized sample covariance matrix (NSCM) [24] for each temporal band. Then we concatenated them to generate the final input feature map for the CNN-GRU network.

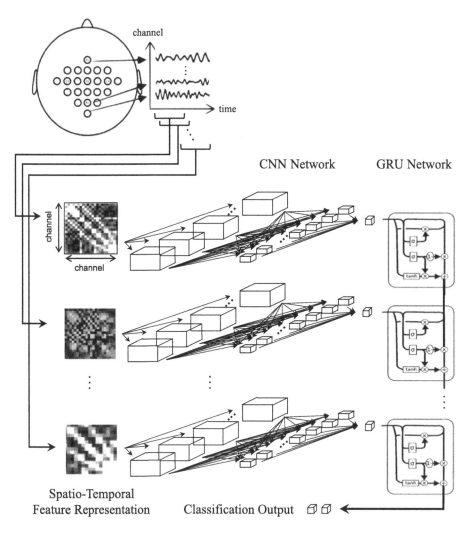

Fig. 1. The framework of the proposed CNN-GRU network with spatio-temporal feature representation.

The concept of the proposed method is similar to CSSP, which provides a temporal delay to obtain various features. However, unlike CSP, our method extracts spatial and temporal information separately. First, the CNN network extract features from NSCM feature maps within each time point. The reason for adopting CNN is that the NSCM feature maps contain spatial information. From this process, a key feature value is extracted at each point. After that, the GRU network extract features on the time domain. As the GRU network is specialized for classification on time-series, we adopted it for the second process. By dividing the steps of feature extraction, we were able to further refine classification to improve performance.

Meanwhile, [25] is a previous study which adopted CNN and RNN to classify EEG signal. Here, the model was proposed for detecting Parkinson's disease. Although it may be considered to share commonalities with proposed method as it used a CNN and RNN mixture model, the previous method differs from the proposed model in that it used *channel × time* EEG configuration for classification. The previous paper only applied basic pre-processing method such as band-passed filtering and segmentation to the raw EEG signal. On the other hand, in the proposed method, we devised a formation of feature representation in which the model can extract features well before designing the network model, namely spatio-temporal feature representation.

2   Method

In this section, we will introduce what we considered for the proposed method. Also, we will give a brief explanation of the EEG signal. Specifically, we will first focus on how to generate an input matrix that contains spatial and temporal information from each of the EEG trials. Then we will explain the design of the CNN-GRU network that can handle spatio-temporal feature representation. Figure 1 presents the overview of the proposed method. Further detailed information will be explained below.

2.1   Spatio-temporal Feature Generation

When analyzing EEG data, bandpass filtering is a common pre-processing method. It removes unnecessary artifacts and specifies the signal of interest. for the filtering band, we specified a common frequency range of 8–30 Hz, so that it can be applied equally to all subjects. 8–30 Hz includes alpha-band and beta-band, which are brain signals that are active when a person is awake and focused. It is also a commonly used frequency band when classifying MI signals.

The segmented signal is normalized by adopting a function named local average reference. The reference channel for the function was electrode Cz. Then, the normalized signal was compressed with NSCM. NSCM is a type of covariance matrix. In general, the covariance matrix is known to extract the informative features well in MI classification. CSP families, which were most widely used machine learning method for the MI classification, are all based on covariance-based feature extraction. For this reason, we generated input feature representation for the CNN-GRU network in covariance form. The NSCM matrices which are generated for each temporal band are concatenated. This spatio-temporal feature representation is finally adopted as the input for the CNN-GRU network. The size of feature representation is $C \times C \times T$, as the size of NSCM is $C \times C$. C denotes the number of channels and T denotes the size of the temporal band.

To be specific, the raw MI signal is filtered by 8–30 Hz. After that, we segmented the filtered signal between 0.5 s and 2.5 s to 2 s and 4 s after the onset of the cue with 0.1 s sliding window. Here, NSCM is applied to the signal between 0.5 s and 2.5 s to 2 s and 4 s. Consequentially, 16 NSCMs are generated because a sliding window of 0.1 s is applied. In this case, the value of T is 16. Since all temporal bands are set to the same size of 2 s, the amount of information contained in each NSCM is the same. By generating the spatio-temporal feature representation, both spatial information and temporal information can be preserved.

2.2 Classification with CNN-GRU Network

To decode spatio-temporal feature representation, we designed a CNN-GRU network. In the network, two 2-dimensional convolution layers were adopted to handle spatial features, and GRU was utilized further to process temporal information which is sequential feature map output from convolution layers. To be specific, two convolutional layers learn $C \times C$ sized spatial features and one GRU layer learns T time step temporal features. The network configuration is summarized in Table 1.

For the network, we applied two convolutional layers of size $(\mathcal{K} \times \mathcal{K})$ and $((C - \mathcal{K} + 1) \times (C - \mathcal{K} + 1))$, respectively, to learn spatial information from the input. $\mathcal{K}$ is the kernel size, which is set to 3. For all convolutional layers, we adopted bias and rectified linear units (RELU) [26]. The outputs from these two convolutional layers of temporal step size T are put to the GRU layer to learn temporal information. Between last convolutional layer and GRU layer, dropout [27] layers are adopted with a probability of 80%. The final classification is performed from the last GRU layer. We fit the model using Adam-optimizer [28] to optimize the cost. For training, the batch size was set equal to the test set size, which is called the full-batch setting. The performance was obtained when the number of epochs reached 500, and the learning rate was 0.0001.

3 Data Description and Evaluation

3.1 BCI Competition IV_2a Data

We verified the proposed method with BCI Competition IV_2a data [29], which is commonly used for verification of EEG motor imagery studies. The data was

Table 1. Configuration of CNN-GRU network.

Layer	#1 Conv layer	#2 Conv layer	#3 Dropout	#4 GRU
Input size	$C \times C \times T$	$(C - \mathcal{K} + 1) \times (C - \mathcal{K} + 1) \times T$	$1 \times 1 \times T$	$1 \times 1 \times T$
Kernel size	$\mathcal{K} \times \mathcal{K}$	$(C - \mathcal{K} + 1) \times (C - \mathcal{K} + 1)$	-	-
Padding	0	0	–	–
Stride	1	1	–	–
Outputs	128	T	T	# class labels

measured when the subject performed motor imagery tasks according to the cue which are displayed on the monitor. The data set consists of the EEG data collected from 9 subjects, namely (A01–A09). The data consist of 25 channels, which include 22 EEG channels, and 3 EOG channels with a sampling frequency 250 Hz. EOG was not considered in this study. The data were collected on four different motor imagery tasks but only left and right-hand motor imagery tasks are selected for this study. The label values inform which tasks the subjects performed. All data were labeled without exception. The EEG data were sampled 250 Hz and band-pass filtered between 0.5 Hz 100 Hz. To suppress line noise, 50 Hz notch filter was also adopted. The performance of the proposed method was evaluated by accuracy. We followed the common practice in machine learning to partition the data into training and test sets. The total number of 144 trials for two tasks were used as the training and the same number of trials are used for the test set. In this study, the experiments were conducted in the Tensorflow environment on Intel 3.20 GHz Core i5 PC with 24 GB of RAM.

3.2 Baseline Methods

We compared the classification accuracy of our model with baseline methods. CSP [9] and CSSP [11] were employed as the linear methods for the feature extraction method. For the classification, LDA was applied to all linear methods [30,31]. The signal was band-pass filtered between 8 13 Hz (μ band). We also compared our proposed method with the nonlinear methods described by Sturm et al. [18], Sakhavi et al. [21] and Shi et al. [25]. For the Shi et al. [25], 3D-CNN-RNN model was selected for comparison which was reported to exhibit the highest performance in the paper. For comparison, the same pre-processing methods used in the corresponding papers were adopted. To compare with Sturm et al. [18], the signal was band-pass filtered in the range of 9–13 Hz and adopted local-average-reference function, envelope, and baseline correction. To compare with Shi et al. [25], the signal was band-pass filtered in the range of 1–20 Hz and adopted local-average-reference function and baseline correction. The signal for comparisons with Sakhavi et al. [21] was band-pass filtered with a filter bank containing nine subsequential filters (4–8 Hz, 8–12 Hz, ...), with four of them being selected. The first to the fourth were selected, after the subsequential filters are sorted in descending order of the mutual information, as per the corresponding paper. The signal was segmented between 0.5 and 2.5 s after the onset of the cue for all three methods [32,33]. In the paper [25], although the time intervals for segmentation was different since the task of the paper was not classifying motor imagery, we unified them to 0.5–2.5 to make same basis. As a result, the size of the input of the network has changed, but the kernel size has all been set the same as the paper. For all three methods, the learning rate was set to 0.0001, full-batch setting was adopted, and the initial value of the weight was fixed. The final accuracy was determined when the number of iterations of the classifier reached 500, as in the proposed method. Note that in the method used by Sakhavi et al. [21], parameters such as kernel size and the number of hidden nodes are optimized. Hence, the same parameters as in the corresponding paper were used for comparison.

Table 2. Comparison of the proposed method and baseline method with BCI Competition IV_2a Data.

Subjects	Methods					
	CSP [9]	CSSP [11]	Sturm et al. [18]	Sakhavi et al. [21]	Shi et al. [25]	Proposed
A01	79.86	88.89	72.92	75.00	70.83	88.8
A02	49.31	51.39	63.19	63.19	72.22	54.86
A03	97.22	94.44	94.44	78.47	67.36	97.22
A04	59.03	52.08	60.42	77.78	59.72	72.22
A05	59.72	50.69	56.94	82.64	61.81	61.11
A06	66.67	61.81	65.97	70.83	67.36	67.36
A07	63.89	72.22	61.81	80.56	70.14	73.61
A08	93.75	95.83	96.53	86.11	71.53	95.83
A09	86.11	93.06	89.58	75.69	68.06	88.19
Mean	72.84	73.38	73.53	76.60	67.67	77.70

4   Results

We compared the proposed model with baseline methods by obtaining decoding accuracy. Performance was obtained from given training data and test data of the BCI competition IV_2a data.

4.1   Comparison with Baseline Methods

Table 2 represents the performance that were obtained with the BCI Competition IV_2a data. Results of both proposed method and previous linear and nonlinear methods are presented for all subjects. The mean accuracy of the baseline methods were 72.84% ($\pm$16.93), 73.38% ($\pm$19.88), 73.53% ($\pm$15.70), 76.60% ($\pm$6.74), and 67.67% ($\pm$4.32) for CSP [9], CSSP [11], Sturm et al. [18], Sakhavi et al. [21], and Shi et al. [25] respectively. The mean accuracy of the proposed model was 77.70% ($\pm$15.39) across subjects. The proposed method outperformed all baselines methods.

Table 3. Decoding accuracy when using spatial feature representations only

Temp.	Sub.									
	A01	A02	A03	A04	A05	A06	A07	A08	A09	Mean
2.5–4.5	89.58	53.47	96.53	66.67	65.97	70.83	72.92	96.53	84.03	77.39
2.6–4.6	89.58	57.64	95.83	69.44	68.06	65.28	65.97	97.22	84.72	77.08
2.7–4.7	86.81	54.17	97.22	70.14	68.75	67.36	70.14	96.53	86.81	77.55
2.8–4.8	86.81	58.33	95.83	66.67	62.50	64.58	70.83	95.83	88.89	76.70
2.9–4.9	85.42	57.64	95.83	72.22	61.11	70.14	73.61	95.83	85.42	77.47
3.0–5.0	80.56	59.72	95.83	69.44	63.19	64.58	73.61	95.83	81.94	76.08
3.1–5.1	81.94	61.11	95.83	72.22	63.19	65.97	72.92	95.83	81.25	76.70
3.2–5.2	84.03	58.33	94.44	70.14	61.81	66.67	72.92	95.14	81.94	76.16
3.3–5.3	84.03	56.25	93.06	69.44	57.64	64.58	74.31	92.36	81.94	74.85
3.4–5.4	85.42	48.61	93.75	69.44	61.81	66.67	68.75	93.06	81.94	74.38
3.5–5.5	81.94	50.69	92.36	65.97	58.33	66.67	66.67	91.67	80.56	72.76
3.6–5.6	82.64	52.78	92.36	66.67	56.25	63.19	65.97	90.28	75.00	71.68
3.7–5.7	86.11	52.08	88.89	65.97	58.33	60.42	65.97	88.19	66.67	70.29
3.8–5.8	84.72	50.00	88.19	63.89	51.39	59.72	64.58	87.50	64.58	68.29
3.9–5.9	81.94	50.00	88.19	64.58	54.17	60.42	61.11	86.81	66.67	68.21
4.0–6.0	79.17	54.86	88.19	68.06	50.69	59.72	63.19	84.72	63.89	68.06

4.2 Comparison Spatial Feature Representation Only

We investigated whether our proposed method is appropriate. If the performance is enhanced when using only spatial feature representation, there will be no need for the spatio-temporal feature representation. In our proposed method, spatial features maps are extracted through NSCM from the continuous temporal band and they are concatenated. Total of 16 temporal bands were used at 0.1 s intervals from 2.5–4.5 to 4.0–6.0. For comparison, each of these 16 NSCM feature representations was classified using only CNN and then compared to the proposed method with decoding accuracy. In this process, only the GRU layer was excluded.

Table 3 and Fig. 2 shows the results. Table 3 shows detailed decoding accuracy of each temporal band and each subject. In addition, Fig. 2 graphically represents only the average performance of the nine subjects by each temporal band for legibility. In the figure, gray bars represent the average performance of nine subjects in each temporal band, and the black lines represent the performance of the proposed method. Seeing the result, the minimum accuracy was 68.06% and the maximum accuracy was 77.55%. In conclusion, no performance was higher than the 77.70% which is the performance of the proposed method throughout the entire 16 temporal bands.

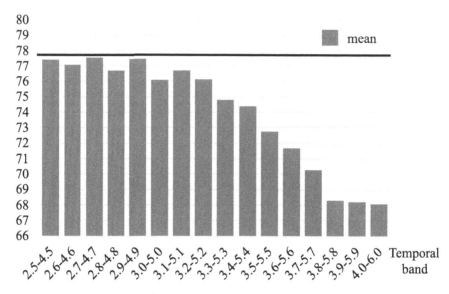

Fig. 2. Average decoding accuracy when using spatial feature representations only. The gray bars are average accuracy of each nine subjects with CNN and the black line indicates the performance of proposed CNN-GRU network.

5   Discussion and Conclusion

In this study, a novel framework that includes spatio-temporal feature representation and corresponding CNN-GRU network was proposed for EEG signal classification. The proposed feature representation can retain structural dependencies of the task-related information of motor imagery based EEG signal. Here, we were able to demonstrate the superiority of the proposed method compared to other methods. Table 2 shows that the proposed method has higher decoding accuracy compared to other methodologies when compared with BCI Competition IV_2a data. In case of Shi *et al.* [25], we compared it with our method as they proposed the mixture model of CNN and RNN network. However, unlike other comparative models, the performance appears to be relatively low since the model was not targeted for the MI classification. Overall, we showed better performance than linear methods as well as nonlinear methods.

We also tried to derive classification results only through spatial feature representation to determine whether the proposed method is meaningful. If the spatial feature representation with the CNN model achieves higher performance than the proposed method, it can be hard to say that the proposed method is useful. For this purpose, we obtained decoding accuracy via CNN without GRU, using only the spatial feature of each temporal band with NSCM. The result was that the performance for each temporal band was not as high as the proposed method at all. This shows that the proposed method that using spatio temporal information at once with the CNN-GRU network is better than simply using spatial feature information.

Generating feature representations by preserving spatial and temporal information of EEG signals has not been adequately addressed in previous CNN-based BCI studies. By preserving spatio-temporal relationships of EEG signals, proposed model has enabled to outperform previous approaches in spatial as well as temporal domains. To deal with temporal information, we adopted GRU networks as well as the CNN, achieving higher performance than using spatial information only. This demonstrated that the proposed method is useful. The proposed feature representation can be applied to other research areas in BCI, such as emotion recognition [34], imagined speech decoding [35,36], BCI assistive application [37,38] or diagnosis [39,40].

References

1. Pfurtscheller, G., Neuper, C.: Motor imagery and direct brain-computer communication. Proc. IEEE **89**(7), 1123–1134 (2001)
2. Chen, Y., Atnafu, A.D., Schlattner, I., Weldtsadik, W.T., Roh, M.C., Kim, H.J., Lee, S.W., Blankertz, B., Fazli, S.: A high-security EEG-based login system with RSVP stimuli and dry electrodes. IEEE Trans. Inf. Forensics Secur. **11**(12), 2635–2647 (2016)
3. Won, D.O., Hwang, H.J., Kim, D.M., Müller, K.R., Lee, S.W.: Motion-based rapid serial visual presentation for gaze-independent brain-computer interfaces. IEEE Trans. Neural Syst. Rehabil. Eng. **26**(2), 334–343 (2018)
4. Lee, M.H., Williamson, J., Won, D.O., Fazli, S., Lee, S.W.: A high performance spelling system based on EEG-EOG signals with visual feedback. IEEE Trans. Neural Syst. Rehabil. Eng. **26**(7), 1443–1459 (2018)
5. Lee, M.H., et al.: EEG dataset and OpenBMI toolbox for three BCI paradigms: an investigation into BCI illiteracy. GigaScience **8**(5), giz002 (2019)
6. Yuan, H., He, B.: Brain-computer interfaces using sensorimotor rhythms: current state and future perspectives. IEEE Trans. Biomed. Eng. **61**(5), 1425–1435 (2014)
7. Pfurtscheller, G., Brunner, C., Schlögl, A., da Silva, F.L.: Mu rhythm (de)synchronization and EEG single-trial classification of different motor imagery tasks. Neuroimage **31**(1), 153–159 (2006)
8. Suk, H.I., Lee, S.W.: Subject and class specific frequency bands selection for multiclass motor imagery classification. Int. J. Imaging Syst. Technol. **21**(2), 123–130 (2011)
9. Ramoser, H., Muller-Gerking, J., Pfurtscheller, G.: Optimal spatial filtering of single trial EEG during imagined hand movement. IEEE Trans. Rehabil. Eng. **8**(4), 441–446 (2000)
10. Blankertz, B., Tomioka, R., Lemm, S., Kawanabe, M., Müller, K.R.: Optimizing spatial filters for robust EEG single-trial analysis. IEEE Signal Process. Mag. **25**(1), 41–56 (2008)
11. Lemm, S., Blankertz, B., Curio, G., Müller, K.R.: Spatio-spectral filters for improving the classification of single trial EEG. IEEE Trans. Biomed. Eng. **52**(9), 1541–1548 (2005)
12. Krauledat, M., Tangermann, M., Blankertz, B., Müller, K.R.: Towards zero training for brain-computer interfacing. PLoS ONE **3**(8), e2967 (2008)

13. Fazli, S., Popescu, F., Danóczy, M., Blankertz, B., Müller, K.R., Grozea, C.: Subject-independent mental state classification in single trials. Neural Netw. **22**(9), 1305–1312 (2009)

14. Kwon, O.Y., Lee, M.H., Guan, C., Lee, S.W.: Subject-independent brain-computer interfaces based on deep convolutional neural networks. IEEE Trans. Neural Networks Learn. Syst. **31**(10), 3839–3852 (2019)

15. Ang, K.K., Chin, Z.Y., Zhang, H., Guan, C.: Mutual information-based selection of optimal spatial-temporal patterns for single-trial EEG-based BCIs. Pattern Recogn. **45**(6), 2137–2144 (2012)

16. Cecotti, H., Graser, A.: Convolutional neural networks for P300 detection with application to brain-computer interfaces. IEEE Trans. Pattern Anal. Mach. Intell. **33**(3), 433–445 (2011)

17. Manor, R., Geva, A.B.: Convolutional neural network for multi-category rapid serial visual presentation BCI. Front. Comput. Neurosci. **9**, 146 (2015)

18. Sturm, I., Lapuschkin, S., Samek, W., Müller, K.R.: Interpretable deep neural networks for single-trial EEG classification. J. Neurosci. Methods **274**, 141–145 (2016)

19. Stober, S., Cameron, D.J., Grahn, J.A.: Using convolutional neural networks to recognize rhythm stimuli from electroencephalography recordings. In: Advances in Neural Information Processing Systems, pp. 1449–1457 (2014)

20. Bashivan, P., Rish, I., Yeasin, M., Codella, N.: Learning representations from EEG with deep recurrent-convolutional neural networks. arXiv preprint arXiv:1511.06448 (2015)

21. Sakhavi, S., Guan, C., Yan, S.: Learning temporal information for brain-computer interface using convolutional neural networks. IEEE Trans. Neural Networks Learn. Syst. **29**(11), 5619–5629 (2018)

22. Bang, J.S., Lee, M.H., Fazli, S., Guan, C., Lee, S.W.: Spatio-spectral feature representation for motor imagery classification using convolutional neural networks. IEEE Trans. Neural Networks Learn. Syst. (2021)

23. LeCun, Y., et al.: Handwritten digit recognition with a back-propagation network. In: Advances in Neural Information Processing Systems, pp. 396–404 (1990)

24. Barachant, A., Bonnet, S., Congedo, M., Jutten, C.: Multiclass brain-computer interface classification by Riemannian geometry. IEEE Trans. Biomed. Eng. **59**(4), 920–928 (2011)

25. Shi, X., Wang, T., Wang, L., Liu, H., Yan, N.: Hybrid convolutional recurrent neural networks outperform CNN and RNN in task-state EEG detection for Parkinson's disease. In: 2019 Asia-Pacific Signal and Information Processing Association Annual Summit and Conference, pp. 939–944. IEEE (2019)

26. Nair, V., Hinton, G.E.: Rectified linear units improve restricted Boltzmann machines. In: Proceedings of the 27th International Conference on Machine Learning, pp. 807–814 (2010)

27. Srivastava, N., Hinton, G., Krizhevsky, A., Sutskever, I., Salakhutdinov, R.: Dropout: a simple way to prevent neural networks from overfitting. J. Mach. Learn. Res. **15**(1), 1929–1958 (2014)

28. Kingma, D.P., Ba, J.: Adam: a method for stochastic optimization. arXiv preprint arXiv:1412.6980 (2014)

29. Tangermann, M., et al.: Review of the BCI competition IV. Front. Neurosci. **6**, 55 (2012)

30. Coyle, D., Satti, A., Prasad, G., McGinnity, T.M.: Neural time-series prediction preprocessing meets common spatial patterns in a brain-computer interface. In:

2008 30th Annual International Conference of the IEEE Engineering in Medicine and Biology Society, pp. 2626–2629. IEEE (2008)

31. Coyle, D.: Neural network based auto association and time-series prediction for biosignal processing in brain-computer interfaces. IEEE Comput. Intell. Magaz. **4**(4) (2009)

32. Lotte, F., Guan, C.: Regularizing common spatial patterns to improve BCI designs: unified theory and new algorithms. IEEE Trans. Biomed. Eng. **58**(2), 355–362 (2011)

33. Ang, K.K., Chin, Z.Y., Wang, C., Guan, C., Zhang, H.: Filter bank common spatial pattern algorithm on BCI competition IV datasets 2a and 2b. Front. Neurosci. **6**, 39 (2012)

34. Kim, S.H., Yang, H.J., Nguyen, N.A.T., Lee, S.W.: AsEmo: automatic approach for EEG-based multiple emotional state identification. IEEE J. Biomed. Health Inform. **25**(5), 1508–1518 (2020)

35. Lee, S.H., Lee, M., Lee, S.W.: Neural decoding of imagined speech and visual imagery as intuitive paradigms for BCI communication. IEEE Trans. Neural Syst. Rehabil. Eng. **28**(12), 2647–2659 (2020)

36. Lee, D.Y., Lee, M., Lee, S.W.: Decoding imagined speech based on deep metric learning for intuitive BCI communication. IEEE Trans. Neural Syst. Rehabil. Eng. **29**, 1363–1374 (2021)

37. Jeong, J.H., Shim, K.H., Kim, D.J., Lee, S.W.: Brain-controlled robotic arm system based on multi-directional CNN-BiLSTM network using EEG signals. IEEE Trans. Neural Syst. Rehabil. Eng. **28**(5), 1226–1238 (2020)

38. Kim, K., et al.: Development of a human-display interface with vibrotactile feedback for real-world assistive applications. Sensors **21**(2), 592 (2021)

39. Zhang, Y., Zhang, H., Chen, X., Lee, S.W., Shen, D.: Hybrid high-order functional connectivity networks using resting-state functional MRI for mild cognitive impairment diagnosis. Sci. Rep. **7**(1), 1–15 (2017)

40. Zhang, Y., et al.: Strength and similarity guided group-level brain functional network construction for MCI diagnosis. Pattern Recogn. **88**, 421–430 (2019)

Planar Motion Estimation for Multi-camera System

Xinlei Qi[1,2], Yaqing Ding[1,2], Jin Xie[1,2], and Jian Yang[1,2(✉)]

[1] PCA Lab, Key Lab of Intelligent Perception and Systems for High-Dimensional Information of Ministry of Education, Nanjing University of Science and Technology, Nanjing, China
{qixinlei,dingyaqing,csjxie,csjyang}@njust.edu.cn
[2] Jiangsu Key Lab of Image and Video Understanding for Social Security, School of Computer Science and Engineering, Nanjing University of Science and Technology, Nanjing, China

Abstract. In this paper, we propose efficient solutions to relative pose estimation with a multi-camera system. We focus on the case where the system navigates under planar motion, and propose two new algorithms: the non-minimal linear 6-point algorithm and the minimal 3-point algorithm. For the 6-point algorithm, we use a simple and easy-to-implement way to avoid the SVD (singular value decomposition) induced degenerate configuration, which happens in the multi-camera system based relative pose estimation. The minimal 3-point algorithm results in a system of polynomials with respect to three unknowns, and we show that it can be converted to solve a univariate polynomial in degree 4. The proposed algorithms are compared with the state-of-the-art methods on both synthetic data and public real-world images. Experimental results show very promising performance in terms of accuracy, robustness and efficiency.

Keywords: Planar motion · Relative pose · Generalized camera model

1 Introduction

Estimating the relative camera motion from the image sequences of a camera or a multi-camera system is one of the basic problems in computer vision and robotics [8]. The relative pose of a monocular camera has been well studied in the literature [2,3,7,18], while the relative motion of a multi-camera system is rarely studied [9,20]. However, in challenging real-world environments, the camera's field of view plays an important role in the camera motion estimation, especially in complex indoor scenes, fisheye lenses or catadioptric cameras are generally used to expand the field of view [1,4]. In addition, multiple cameras can be rigidly coupled to form a multi-camera system. The multi-camera system can provide a wider field of view coverage to better perceive the surrounding

This work was supported by Shanghai Automotive Industry Science and Technology Development Fundation (No. 1917).

environment. Research results show that the wide field of view can improve the accuracy of camera relative pose estimation [17,22], and the multi-camera system can get the true translation scale.

By contrast to the standard pinhole camera, the multi-camera system has a different camera model since it does not have a single projection center. Pless [19] first use a set of unconstrained image rays to replace the image pixels so that a generalized camera model which can represent a multi-camera system is proposed. In this case, the generalized epipolar constraint is also derived. Stewénius *et al.* [20] first introduced the minimal solution for the generalized epipolar constraint using the Gröbner basis technique. Only 6 points are needed to estimate the six degrees of freedom camera motion. However, there are up to 64 possible solutions, which leads to computational complexity and time cosuming to perform robust estimation. Li *et al.* [9] proposed a new linear method to solve the degradation of the generalized camera system in the locally-central or axial case, which overcomes the shortcomings of using the standard SVD method to solve linearly and extended the work of the generalized epipolar constraint. The proposed linear algorithm needs 17 point correspondences. The SVD for solving the linear equations is very efficient, but the large number of samples and sensitivity to noise result in a large number of RANSAC iterations and a very high computational complexity. Since this linear approach has a very high computational complexity and cannot meet the real application requirements, other researchers proposed a lot of solutions to improve the efficiency based on reasonable motion assumptions or using additional sensors. Lee *et al.* [12,13] proposed a two-point algorithm by combining the Ackermann motion model and the planar motion assumption. Liu *et al.* [14] simplified this assumption based on the known vertical direction and proposed a first-order approximation of the rotation matrix in the case of small rotation to simplify the solution process. Ventura *et al.* [21] simplifies the problem by making a first-order approximation of rotation based on the small rotation hypothesis on Stewénius *et al.*'s algorithm. Kneip *et al.* [11] presented an iterative solution based on minimizing the eigenvalues.

In this paper, we study the relative pose estimation with a multi-camera system based on the assumption of planar motion (See Fig. 1). The planar motion assumption is reasonable in real-world scenarios, for example, most indoor robots including sweeping robots, service robots, industrial mobile robots and so on satisfy this assumption. Moreover, such robots are often resource-constrained so that efficient motion estimation algorithms are needed. Therefore, we use the prior knowledge of planar motion to propose two extremely efficient solvers for relative pose estimation with a multi-camera system: the linear 6-point method and the minimal 3-point method. By combining them in the RANSAC [5] sampling scheme, an efficient and robust planar motion estimation can be achieved. The main contributions of this paper are:

1. We propose efficient and robust relative pose estimation methods under planar motion for multi-camera systems.
2. Based on the planar motion assumption, we propose two effective solvers: the linear 6-point solver and the minimal 3-point solver.

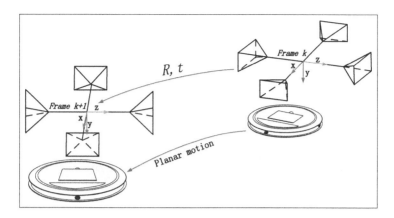

Fig. 1. Illustration of relative pose estimation for a robot with a multi-camera system during planar motion. The unknowns are the transformation parameters between the two frames k and k+1, given by R and t.

3. The proposed methods are analyzed and compared with the existing solvers under different configurations, including computational complexity, robustness to noise, and numerical stability. The real experiments illustrate the usefulness of our methods.

2   Generalized Camera Model

In this section, we briefly describe the generalized camera model. By using the unconstrained image rays instead of the image pixels, the generalized camera model can be formulated, where each ray is represented by the Plücker line. Given K_C and R_C, t_C, which are the internal and external parameters of a camera, then the 6-vector Plücker line of the image ray corresponding to the image pixel (x, y) of the camera can be formulated using two parts: the direction vector $q = R_C K_C^{-1}[x, y, 1]^\top$, and the moment vector $q' = q \times t_C$. If there is a correspondence between pixels (x_m, y_m) in frame m image of generalized camera and pixels (x_n, y_n) in frame n image, this correspondence means that image ray $\langle q_m, \ q'_m \rangle$ and $\langle q_n, \ q'_n \rangle$ corresponding to these pixels must intersect in space. Assuming that the generalized camera moves from frame m to frame n under rotation R and translation t, then the generalized epipolar constraint (GEC) [19] can be expressed as:

$$q_n^\top R q'_m + q_n^\top R[t]_\times q_m + q_n'^\top R q_m = 0. \tag{1}$$

Compared with the traditional epipolar constraint on the pinhole camera, the generalized epipolar constraint can also be written in the form of the following homogeneous 6×6 matrix equation [9]:

$$l_n^{\top} \underbrace{\begin{bmatrix} E & R \\ R & 0 \end{bmatrix}}_{E_G} l_m = 0, \tag{2}$$

where $l_m = \langle q_m, q'_m \rangle$ and $l_n = \langle q_n, q'_n \rangle$ is the corresponding plücker vector of frame m and frame n of the generalized camera, $E = [t]_{\times}R$ is the standard essential matrix, and E_G is the generalized essential matrix.

3 Our Approach

In this section, we give a new formulation of the generalized essential matrix under planar motion, and based on this derivation, we propose a linear 6-point solver and a minimal 3-point solver for the relative pose estimation.

3.1 Generalized Essential Matrix Under Planar Motion

Under planar motion constraint, the rotation has only one degree of freedom. Assuming that the generalized camera rotates around the y-axis (see Fig. 1) and the rotation angle is θ, in the case, the rotation vector can be written as $[0, \theta, 0]^{\top}$. The rotation matrix R_y can be expressed using the Rodrigues' formula:

$$R_y = \begin{bmatrix} \cos\theta & 0 & \sin\theta \\ 0 & 1 & 0 \\ -\sin\theta & 0 & \cos\theta \end{bmatrix}. \tag{3}$$

Since the translation is always zero along the y-axis, we can set α as the direction angle of the translation, and k as the scale factor. Then the translation vector can be written as

$$\tilde{t} = k[\sin\alpha \quad 0 \quad \cos\alpha]^{\top}. \tag{4}$$

Therefore, the skew symmetric matrix $[\tilde{t}]_{\times}$ of the translation vector can be obtained:

$$[\tilde{t}]_{\times} = k \begin{bmatrix} 0 & -\cos\alpha & 0 \\ \cos\alpha & 0 & -\sin\alpha \\ 0 & \sin\alpha & 0 \end{bmatrix}. \tag{5}$$

Based on Eq. (3) and (5), the general essential matrix E_y under plane motion can be formulated as:

$$E_y = [\tilde{t}]_{\times}R_y = k \begin{bmatrix} 0 & -\cos\alpha & 0 \\ \cos(\theta-\alpha) & 0 & \sin(\theta-\alpha) \\ 0 & \sin\alpha & 0 \end{bmatrix}. \tag{6}$$

In this case, the generalized essential matrix for GEC (2) can be expressed as:

$$
E_G = \begin{bmatrix} E_y & R_y \\ R_y & 0 \end{bmatrix} = \begin{bmatrix} 0 & -k\cos\alpha & 0 & \cos\theta & 0 & \sin\theta \\ k\cos(\theta-\alpha) & 0 & k\sin(\theta-\alpha) & 0 & 1 & 0 \\ 0 & k\sin\alpha & 0 & -\sin\theta & 0 & \cos\theta \\ \cos\theta & 0 & \sin\theta & & & \\ 0 & 1 & 0 & & 0 & \\ -\sin\theta & 0 & \cos\theta & & & \end{bmatrix}. \tag{7}
$$

3.2   The Linear 6-Point Algorithm

For the convenience of expressing E_G, we set the non-zero parameter in Eq. (7) as a variable:

$$
E_G = \begin{bmatrix} 0 & e_1 & 0 & e_5 & 0 & e_6 \\ e_3 & 0 & e_4 & 0 & 1 & 0 \\ 0 & e_2 & 0 & -e_6 & 0 & e_5 \\ e_5 & 0 & e_6 & & & \\ 0 & 1 & 0 & & 0 & \\ -e_6 & 0 & e_5 & & & \end{bmatrix}. \tag{8}
$$

In GEC (2), l_m and l_n are two plücker vectors which represent two corresponding rays, respectively. Assume the Plücker vector of one ray is: $l_m = [q_m^\top, \ q_m'^\top]^\top$, where $q_m = [q_{m1}, \ q_{m2}, \ q_{m3}]^\top, q_m' = [q_{m1}', \ q_{m2}', \ q_{m3}']^\top$. And the Plücker vector of the other ray is: $l_n = [q_n^\top, \ q_n'^\top]^\top$, where $q_n = [q_{n1}, q_{n2}, q_{n3}]^\top, q_n' = [q_{n1}', \ q_{n2}', \ q_{n3}']^\top$. Then Eq. (2) can be written in a linear equation with respect to e:

$$
\tilde{q}e^\top = 0, \tag{9}
$$

where

$$
\begin{aligned}
\tilde{q} &= [q_{n1}q_{m2}\ q_{n3}q_{m2}\ q_{n2}q_{m1}\ q_{n2}q_{m3}\ q_{n1}'q_{m1}+q_{n1}q_{m1}'+q_{n3}'q_{m3} \\
&\quad +q_{n3}q_{m3}'\ q_{n1}'q_{m3}+q_{n1}q_{m3}'-q_{n3}'q_{m1}-q_{n3}q_{m1}'\ q_{n2}'q_{m2}+q_{n2}q_{m2}'], \\
e &= [e_1\ \ e_2\ \ e_3\ \ e_4\ \ e_5\ \ e_6\ \ e_7].
\end{aligned}
$$

By stacking the vectors $\tilde{q}$ corresponding to the six pairs of Plücker lines, we can get a system of linear equations:

$$
Ae^\top = 0, \tag{10}
$$

where A is a 6×7 matrix. Equation (10) can be solved using the standard SVD method, and then all the unknowns in E_G can be calculated according to the constraint $e_7 = 1$. However, in practice, we found that the solutions returned by the standard SVD method is not valid, which is only in the form of $(\lambda E_y, \ \lambda R_y + \mu I)$. We can see that the standard essential matrix part E_y is still linear, and the ambiguity only exists in the rotation matrix R_y. The strategy proposed in the 17-point method [9] is adopted here to solve the problem. Since the rotation part R_y provides redundant information, we divide e into into two parts, and only use the essential matrix part E_y to find valid solutions:

$$A[vec(E_y), \ vec(R_y)]^\top = 0, \tag{11}$$

where $vec(E_y) = [e_1 \ e_2 \ e_3 \ e_4]$, and $vec(R_y) = [e_5 \ e_6 \ e_7]$. Instead of using the constraint $\|e\| = 1$ in the standard SVD method, we use the constraint $\|E_y\| = 1$ to solve the system of equations. Hence, the SVD method is used to minimize $Ae^\top$:

$$\|A[vec(E_y), \ vec(R_y)]^\top\| \quad s.t. \ \|E_y\| = 1. \tag{12}$$

Finding a solution that satisfies $\|vec(E_y)\| = 1$ is equivalent to solve:

$$(A_{R_y} A_{R_y}^+ - I) A_{E_y} vec(E_y)^\top = 0, \tag{13}$$

where A_{E_y} and A_{R_y} are the first four columns and the last three columns of the coefficient matrix A corresponding to $vec(E_y)$ and $vec(R_y)$, respectively. $A_{R_y}^+$ is the pseudo-inverse of the matrix A_{R_y}. Then we use the standard SVD method to solve the equation to get all the unknowns in E_y. Finally, the planar motion parameters of the generalized camera are obtained by decomposing E_y: the rotation matrix R_y and the translation vector $\tilde{t}$. Since E_y is homogeneous, the translation vector obtained here is only up to a scale factor, which can be calculated by substituting the rotation matrix R_y into the original generalized epipolar constraint (1).

3.3   The Minimal 3-Point Algorithm

In the above section, we have decribed the linear 6-point algorithm. It is very fast since we only need to solve a system of linear equations. However, this solver needs 6 points, and the number of iterations for RANSAC is usually very large. In order to reduce the necessary points to increase the speed of RANSAC, we propose the minimal 3-point algorithm in this section. By combining Eq. (7) and (8) we obtain the following constraints of E_G:

$$\begin{aligned} e_1 = -k\cos\alpha, \ e_2 = k\sin\alpha, \ e_3 = k\cos(\theta - \alpha), \\ e_4 = k\sin(\theta - \alpha), \ e_5 = \cos\theta, \ e_6 = \sin\theta, \ e_7 = 1. \end{aligned} \tag{14}$$

By eliminating k, α, θ from (14) we can obtain the following constraints with respect to e_i:

$$\begin{aligned} e_5^2 + e_6^2 - e_7^2 = 0, \\ e_1^2 + e_2^2 - e_3^2 - e_4^2 = 0, \\ e_1 e_5 - e_2 e_6 + e_3 e_7 = 0, \\ e_2 e_5 + e_1 e_6 + e_4 e_7 = 0, \\ e_3 e_5 + e_4 e_6 + e_1 e_7 = 0, \\ e_4 e_5 - e_3 e_6 + e_2 e_7 = 0. \end{aligned} \tag{15}$$

Based on Eq. (9), the vector $\tilde{q}$ corresponding to three pairs of plücker lines is used to obtain a 3×7 coefficient matrix. Using SVD or QR decomposition we can calculate four vectors e_x, e_y, e_z, e_w that span the right null space of the matrix, and e can be formulated as:

$$e = xe_x + ye_y + ze_z + we_w, \tag{16}$$

where x, y, z, w are unknown coefficients which need to be found. Since the vector e is homogeneous, we can make $w = 1$. In this case, only the three unknowns of x, y and z are required to be found, and then the unique solution of e can be determined by using the constraint $e_7 = 1$. Now we describe the details for solving x, y and z. Inspired by the five-point method [18], we first substitute (16) into the constraint (15), which results in a system of quadratic equations with respect to x, y, z, and the we use the Gauss-Jordan elimination to obtain the coefficient matrix B_1 based on the following system:

B_1	x^2	y^2	xy	z^2	z	1	x	y
$\langle a \rangle$	1	·	·	·	·	·	[1]	[1]
$\langle b \rangle$		1	·	·	·	·	[1]	[1]
$\langle c \rangle$			1	·	·	·	[1]	[1]
$\langle d \rangle$				1			[1]	[1]
$\langle e \rangle$					1		[1]	[1]
$\langle f \rangle$						1	[1]	[1]

where · denotes a non-zero coefficient term, the blank area represents a coefficient of 0, $[N]$ denotes a polynomial of degree N with respect to the variable z. Since the first three lines of the equation are not needed, Elimination can be chosen to stop three lines earlier in order to reduce the computation complexity. In addition, we construct the following additional equations to do further elimination:

$$\begin{aligned} \langle g \rangle &= \langle d \rangle - z\langle e \rangle, \\ \langle h \rangle &= \langle e \rangle - z\langle e \rangle. \end{aligned} \tag{17}$$

Combining equation$\langle f \rangle$ with Eq. (17), we can get a coefficient matrix B_2 whose elements are polynomials with respect to z:

B_2	1	x	y
$\langle f \rangle$	1	[1]	[1]
$\langle g \rangle$	0	[2]	[2]
$\langle h \rangle$	0	[2]	[2]

Since $[1, x, y]^\top$ is the solution vector of B_2, it means that the system of equations has non-zero solutions, and the determinant of B_2 must vanish.

$$det(B_2) \equiv 0. \tag{18}$$

The determinant of B_2 obtained here is the quartic equation of z, which can be solved in closed form. Then the variables x and y can be found according to the equation system B_2. Finally, the vector e is obtained by Eq. (16), and the motion parameters of the generalized camera are obtained. From the definitions (3) and (4) of the rotation matrix R_y and the translation vector $\tilde{t}$, and using the constraint (14), we can directly derive:

$$R_y = \begin{bmatrix} e_5 & 0 & e_6 \\ 0 & 1 & 0 \\ -e_6 & 0 & e_5 \end{bmatrix}, \quad \tilde{t} = \begin{bmatrix} e_2 \\ 0 \\ -e_1 \end{bmatrix}. \tag{19}$$

4 Experiments

In this section, we compare the proposed methods with the existing algorithms on both synthetic data and real image sequences to show the benefits in terms of computational complexity and accuracy.

In the following experiments, we compare the linear 6-point method (Our-6pt) and the minimal 3-point method (Our-3pt) proposed in Sect.3 with Li-17pt [9], Stewenius-6pt [20], Kneip-8pt [11], Lee-8pt [13], Lee-4pt [13], Liu-4pt [14] and Ventura-6pt [21]. The experiments was tested on the cloud server with Intel(R) Xeon(R) CPU E5-2650 v4 @ 2.20 GHz. All codes are written in C++. The implementation of Li-17pt, Stewenius-6pt and Kneip-8pt are provided by the OpenGV library [10]. Liu-4pt, Ventura-6pt are implemented by the source code provided by the papers [14,21]. Since Lee-8pt and Lee-4pt are not open source code, the algorithm implementation is based on the reproduced paper [13]. Since the two-point method of Lee *et al.* [12] is only applicable to the Ackermann model, it is not compared with this method in this paper.

4.1 Computational Complexity

Table 1 reports the average running time of all algorithms in 10,000 randomized trials. Our-3pt only performs QR decomposition of a 3×7 matrix and Gauss-Jordan elimination of a 6×10 matrix in the calculation process, and finally solves a quaternary equation of one variable. Most of the other solvers need to go through the steps of decomposing large matrices. For example, Stewenius-6pt needs to perform eigenvalue decomposition on a 64×64 matrix, and Li-17pt also needs SVD to decompose a 17×9 matrix during the solution process. And in the end, it is often necessary to solve a higher-order equation to obtain a closed-form solution, such as Ventura-6pt solves the twentieth degree equation through the Sturm sequence, and Lee-4pt needs to solve the eighth degree equation. Therefore, our algorithm greatly reduces the time complexity, which is also verified by the experimental results. It can be seen from Table 1: The running time of the existing fastest algorithm Liu-4pt is more than twice that of Our-3pt. Although our Our-6pt algorithm runs slightly slower than Liu-4pt. But Our-6pt has only one closed-form solution, while Liu-4pt has up to four solutions, and it takes extra time to remove the wrong solution, so the two times are similar when obtaining the only correct motion estimation. And the running time of other methods is dozens to thousands of times that of our algorithm.

Table 1. Efficiency comparison of the proposed algorithm with other existing generalized camera relative position estimation methods.

Algorithm	Time(μs)	Max no. of real solutions	Iterations with inliers (w)				Total trials ($w = 0.5$)
			0.9	0.7	0.5	0.3	
Our-6pt	8.92	1	6	37	292	6315	292
Our-3pt	**1.35**	4	**4**	**11**	**34**	**168**	**136**
Lee-8pt [13]	13.28	1	8	78	1176	70188	1176
Lee-4pt [13]	15.13	8	5	17	71	566	568
Liu-4pt [14]	3.04	4	5	17	71	566	284
Ventura-6pt [21]	129	20	6	37	292	6315	5840
Kneip-8pt [11]	144	1	8	78	1176	70188	1176
Li-17pt [9]	78	1	25	1977	603606	3.56×10^9	603606
Stewenius-6pt [20]	2930	64	6	37	292	6315	18688

In practical applications, in order to achieve robust relative pose estimation, the algorithm is generally embedded in RANSAC or other robust estimation methods to effectively reject outliers. Therefore, the number of iterations (the necessary number of iterations for RANSAC and the number of solutions for the algorithm) is important to consider efficiency. The number of iterations k required in RANSAC is given by $k = \frac{ln(1-p)}{ln(1-w^n)}$, where n is the number of corresponding points required by the algorithm, such as our minimal 3-point method: $n = 3$, w is the probability that the selected corresponding point is inliers, that is, the percentage of inliers in the total, and p is the probability that RANSAC is expected to get an accurate model, where $p = 0.99$. From Table 1, we can see that as the rate of inliers decreases, the iteration times of our method are more advantageous than other algorithms. When a solver obtains multiple solutions, the correct solution needs to be determined. Therefore, the total number of iterations of the algorithm in a robust estimation can be considered as the product of the number of iterations k and the number of solutions. Assuming $w = 0.5$, it can be seen that our method still has obvious advantages in the total number of iterations, which is also proved in actual experiments.

4.2   Experiments on Synthetic Data

In this section, we evaluate the numerical stability and accuracy of each algorithm on the synthetic data of known ground truth. The synthetic data set consists of image point pairs obtained by reprojecting 500 3D points onto a generalized camera that performs planar motion. The generalized camera system used here includes four cameras with a focal length of 800 pixels and a random

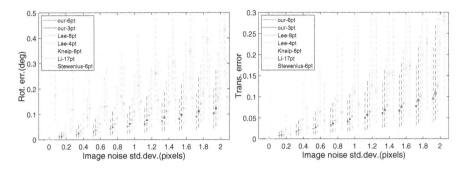

Fig. 2. Comparisons of rotation(unit: degree) and translation(no units) errors of algorithms under different image pixel noise levels

posture 0.5 m from the origin of the viewpoint, and 3D points are randomly sampled within the range of 4 to 8 m from the origin of the viewpoint. We generated 1000 such synthetic datasets with random plane motion, and observed 10 times on each dataset for scenes with added pixel noise and small rotational motion, respectively.

Pixel Noise: In order to measure the accuracy and robustness of our method under different image noise levels, experiments are carried out on different image pixel noises with a standard deviation of 0 to 2.0 pixels and an interval of 0.2 pixels. For each experiment, the planar relative motion of the generalized camera system is randomly selected within the range of rotation $[0.1, 0.5]$ rad, translation scale $[0, 2]$ m, and arbitrary translation direction. The definition of rotation error δ_R and translation error δ_t is as follows:

$$\delta_R = \arccos((\text{trace}(\boldsymbol{R}_{gt}\boldsymbol{R}^\top) - 1)/2),$$
$$\delta_t = 2\|\boldsymbol{t}_{gt} - \boldsymbol{t}\|/(\|\boldsymbol{t}_{gt}\| + \|\boldsymbol{t}\|),$$

where $\boldsymbol{R}_{gt}$ and $\boldsymbol{t}_{gt}$ are ground-truth rotation and translation respectively; $\boldsymbol{R}$ and $\boldsymbol{t}$ are the rotation matrix and translation vector estimated by the algorithms, respectively. The results of 10,000 random trials are shown in Fig. 2. It can be seen that our algorithm is the best in terms of numerical stability and accuracy compared with other methods when the generalized camera is in planar motion. The boxplot shows that our method has the smallest average error and the smallest fluctuation of error. Li-17pt is very sensitive to noise due to a large number of selected samples, so the error increases rapidly as the noise increases. Kneip-8pt is solved by local iteration, and convergence cannot be guaranteed, so the error fluctuation is particularly large.

Small Rotation: The purpose of this test is to compare with some methods based on the hypothesis of small rotation and to check the numerical stability of our method in the case of small rotation. In this test, we add Gaussian noise

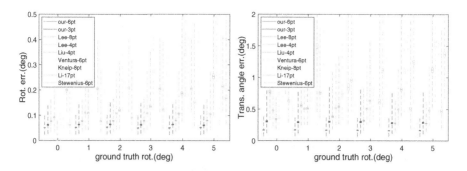

Fig. 3. Comparisons of rotation(unit: degree) and translation(unit: degree) errors of algorithms under different rotation angles at small rotations

with a standard deviation of 1.0 pixels to the observations, and experiment with ground-truth rotation in the range of 0 to 5.0 ° with an interval of 1.0 °, respectively. However, when a generalized camera is in small rotating motion, it can be approximated that it is in pure translation motion. Only uses feature correspondences from a single camera (no cross-camera correspondences), and the generalized polar constraint is degraded, making it impossible to uniquely determine the metric scale of relative motion [12]. Therefore, only the direction of translation is considered for the error of translation, and the translation angle error is defined as: $\xi_t = \arccos((\boldsymbol{t}_{gt}\boldsymbol{t}^\top)/(\|\boldsymbol{t}_{gt}\|\|\boldsymbol{t}\|))$. For each rotation in the range of 0 to 5.0 °, the results obtained by performing 10,000 random experiments in the above manner are shown in Fig. 3. It can be seen that our method is still optimal compared with other methods in small rotational planar motion, and very stable, and will not change with the change of the rotation amplitude. Since `Ventura-6pt` and `Lee-4pt` are based on the hypothesis of small rotation, the error will increase as the rotation amplitude increases.

4.3   Experiments on Real Image Sequences

In this section, we test the performance of our method on the real image sequences KITTI visual odometry dataset [6] and compare it with other existing methods. In the experiment, we regard the two stereo grayscale cameras in the dataset as a generalized multi-camera system, and the video image sequences 0 to 10 with the ground-truth label were used for evaluation. By extracting the SIFT [15] feature points and descriptors of the images, the Flann [16] matching algorithm is applied to obtain about 2400 pairs of feature corresponding points. Since the relative motion between consecutive frames in the sequences is very small, which conforms to the hypothesis of small rotation, the scale of relative motion cannot be solved by using only the feature correspondence in the intra-camera [12]. Therefore, the cross-camera correspondence is used here, that is, four pairs of images are used for feature matching in each frame, and approximately 600 pairs of feature correspondence points are selected for each pair of

Table 2. The average rotation error δ_R(unit: degree) and the average translation error δ_t(no units) of different algorithms on the KITTI sequences, and the average running time T(unit: s) of RANSAC.(Red: First, Orange: Second, Cyan: Third)

Algorithm		seq.00	seq.01	seq.02	seq.03	seq.04	seq.05	seq.06	seq.07	seq.08	seq.09	seq.10
Our-6pt	δ_R	0.0852	0.0674	0.0637	0.0795	0.0329	0.0505	0.0448	0.0528	0.0509	0.0536	0.0542
	δ_t	0.0827	0.3681	0.0498	0.1792	0.0455	0.1109	0.0484	0.2152	0.0958	0.0535	0.0894
	T	0.0377	0.1603	0.0266	0.0181	0.0122	0.0220	0.0248	0.0117	0.0223	0.0446	0.0283
Our-3pt	δ_R	0.1121	0.0964	0.0834	0.1040	0.0531	0.0700	0.0665	0.0755	0.0695	0.0811	0.0705
	δ_t	0.1295	0.5804	0.0758	0.2897	0.0762	0.1554	0.0938	0.2701	0.1443	0.0957	0.1415
	T	0.0088	0.0165	0.0072	0.0071	0.0057	0.0068	0.0077	0.0056	0.0073	0.0101	0.0082
Lee-8pt [13]	δ_R	0.0626	0.0460	0.0488	0.0567	0.0257	0.0425	0.0383	0.0471	0.0408	0.0454	0.0448
	δ_t	0.0599	0.2556	0.0355	0.1039	0.0315	0.1020	0.0396	0.2075	0.0833	0.0420	0.0765
	T	0.0512	0.3991	0.0360	0.0200	0.0179	0.0347	0.0542	0.0186	0.0329	0.0927	0.0478
Lee-4pt [13]	δ_R	0.0888	0.0722	0.0541	0.0787	0.0334	0.0453	0.0489	0.0485	0.0512	0.0518	0.0464
	δ_t	0.0891	0.3843	0.0488	0.2057	0.0471	0.1139	0.0568	0.2201	0.1020	0.0585	0.0900
	T	0.0528	0.1552	0.0377	0.0337	0.0257	0.0356	0.0415	0.0260	0.0375	0.0571	0.0439
Liu-4pt [14]	δ_R	0.1054	0.0737	0.0701	0.0829	0.0333	0.0508	0.0623	0.0666	0.0525	0.0581	0.0481
	δ_t	0.0965	0.3818	0.0536	0.2077	0.0462	0.1189	0.0660	0.2326	0.1056	0.0612	0.0917
	T	0.0172	0.0440	0.0120	0.0118	0.0085	0.0117	0.0135	0.0097	0.0125	0.0178	0.0141
Ventura-6pt [21]	δ_R	0.0889	0.0818	0.0729	0.0989	0.0507	0.0619	0.0627	0.0728	0.0691	0.0677	0.0729
	δ_t	0.0656	0.3215	0.0377	0.1418	0.0358	0.1039	0.0516	0.2189	0.0898	0.0439	0.0788
	T	0.0925	0.6441	0.0833	0.0635	0.0541	0.0755	0.1129	0.0604	0.0793	0.1628	0.0940
Kneip-8pt [11]	δ_R	0.0829	0.0767	0.0697	0.0793	0.0469	0.0650	0.0545	0.0770	0.0641	0.0621	0.0793
	δ_t	0.0592	0.2933	0.0335	0.1134	0.0307	0.1045	0.0397	0.2168	0.0857	0.0398	0.1026
	T	0.0877	1.0161	0.0679	0.0351	0.0380	0.0661	0.1254	0.0418	0.0671	0.1825	0.0914
Li-17pt [9]	δ_R	0.0812	0.1475	0.0741	0.0669	0.0527	0.0636	0.0599	0.0666	0.0622	0.0890	0.0750
	δ_t	0.0547	0.7017	0.0340	0.0697	0.0310	0.1062	0.0432	0.2072	0.0798	0.0591	0.0792
	T	0.8987	1.7836	0.4899	0.5964	0.7489	0.6037	1.0297	0.5802	0.7178	1.1147	0.9120
Stewenius-6pt [20]	δ_R	0.2013	0.1609	0.2745	0.3348	0.0820	0.1652	0.1092	0.1934	0.1772	0.1866	0.2618
	δ_t	0.2064	0.7168	0.1809	0.4592	0.0699	0.2274	0.1261	0.3408	0.2207	0.1926	0.2728
	T	7.8813	16.6187	9.5698	5.3869	1.2817	6.0231	5.6602	3.2866	6.7714	15.0691	13.7905

images. In order to fairly compare the performance of the algorithm itself, we use the standard RANSAC [5] and without apply any optimizations including inlier set refinement, non-linear refinement, bundle adjustment or loop closure, etc. The RANSAC confidence is set to 0.99, and the maximum number of iterations is 10,000. The relationship between the Sampson error [8] corresponding to each point in the camera and the threshold value of 0.1 is checked to realize the screening of inliers or outliers, and the actual number of iterations is dynamically given according to the rate of inliers. Some algorithms are proposed based on the assumption of a known vertical direction, using the roll and pitch angles obtained by ground-truth to align the reference coordinate system of the multi-camera system with the direction of gravity. In order to ensure the fairness of the experiment, the other algorithms also perform the same operation.

As a result of our method is based on the hypothesis of planar motion, but the KITTI dataset and can't well conform to the planar motion hypothesis, it is not our intention to compete with other algorithms in accuracy (unfair to our method). The purpose of this experiment is to qualitatively verify whether our method is applicable to real-world scenarios. Nevertheless, Table 2 shows that although our method is slightly worse than the optimal performance, there is not much difference or even better than some algorithms, and our method still maintains a significant advantage over time. `Stewenius-6pt` has the worst comprehensive performance. On the one hand, the computational complexity is extremely high, and on the other hand, it produces a large number of solutions, which leads to RANSAC can not screen out the correct solutions. Since our method has obvious advantages in computational efficiency, it is very suitable to find a correct inlier set, and then used in subsequent visual odometry for more accurate motion estimation.

5   Conclusion

In this paper, we proposed two different methods for relative pose estimation of multi-camera systems based on the planar motion assumption. This assumption is reasonable and generally feasible. For example, indoor sweeper robots, medical service robots, industrial sorting robots, and so on. Based on the above assumptions, this paper presents the linear 6-point and the minimal 3-point algorithm. By combining them with RANSAC, an efficient and robust planar motion estimation can be achieved. The results of synthetic and real datasets demonstrate the feasibility of our proposed algorithm.

References

1. Bazin, J., Demonceaux, C., Vasseur, P., Kweon, I.: Motion estimation by decoupling rotation and translation in catadioptric vision. Comput. Vision Image Underst. **114**(2), 254–273 (2010). https://doi.org/10.1016/j.cviu.2009.04.006
2. Ding, Y., Yang, J., Kong, H.: An efficient solution to the relative pose estimation with a common direction. In: 2020 IEEE International Conference on Robotics and Automation (ICRA), pp. 11053–11059 (2020). https://doi.org/10.1109/ICRA40945.2020.9196636
3. Ding, Y., Yang, J., Ponce, J., Kong, H.: Minimal solutions to relative pose estimation from two views sharing a common direction with unknown focal length. In: Proceedings of the IEEE/CVF Conference on Computer Vision and Pattern Recognition (CVPR) (2020)
4. Eichenseer, A., Bätz, M., Seiler, J., Kaup, A.: A hybrid motion estimation technique for fisheye video sequences based on equisolid re-projection. In: 2015 IEEE International Conference on Image Processing (ICIP), pp. 3565–3569 (2015). https://doi.org/10.1109/ICIP.2015.7351468
5. Fischler, M.A., Bolles, R.C.: Random sample consensus: a paradigm for model fitting with applications to image analysis and automated cartography. Commun. ACM **24**(6), 381–395 (1981)
6. Geiger, A., Lenz, P., Stiller, C., Urtasun, R.: Vision meets robotics: the kitti dataset. Int. J. Rob. Res. **32**(11), 1231–1237 (2013). https://doi.org/10.1177/0278364913491297
7. Hartley, R.I.: In defense of the eight-point algorithm. IEEE Trans. Pattern Anal. Mach. Intell. **19**(6), 580–593 (1997). https://doi.org/10.1109/34.601246
8. Hartley, R., Zisserman, A.: Multiple View Geometry in Computer Vision, 2nd edn. Cambridge University Press, Cambridge (2003)

9. Li, H., Hartley, R., Kim, J.: A linear approach to motion estimation using generalized camera models. In: 2008 IEEE Conference on Computer Vision and Pattern Recognition, pp. 1–8 (2008). https://doi.org/10.1109/CVPR.2008.4587545

10. Kneip, L., Furgale, P.: Opengv: a unified and generalized approach to real-time calibrated geometric vision. In: 2014 IEEE International Conference on Robotics and Automation (ICRA), pp. 1–8 (2014). https://doi.org/10.1109/ICRA.2014.6906582

11. Kneip, L., Li, H.: Efficient computation of relative pose for multi-camera systems. In: 2014 IEEE Conference on Computer Vision and Pattern Recognition, pp. 446–453 (2014). https://doi.org/10.1109/CVPR.2014.64

12. Lee, G.H., Faundorfer, F., Pollefeys, M.: Motion estimation for self-driving cars with a generalized camera. In: 2013 IEEE Conference on Computer Vision and Pattern Recognition, pp. 2746–2753 (2013). https://doi.org/10.1109/CVPR.2013.354

13. Lee, G.H., Pollefeys, M., Fraundorfer, F.: Relative pose estimation for a multi-camera system with known vertical direction. In: 2014 IEEE Conference on Computer Vision and Pattern Recognition, pp. 540–547 (2014). https://doi.org/10.1109/CVPR.2014.76

14. Liu, L., Li, H., Dai, Y., Pan, Q.: Robust and efficient relative pose with a multi-camera system for autonomous driving in highly dynamic environments. IEEE Trans. Intell. Transp. Syst. **19**(8), 2432–2444 (2018). https://doi.org/10.1109/TITS.2017.2749409

15. Lowe, D.G.: Distinctive image features from scale-invariant keypoints. Int. J. Comput. Vision **60**(2), 91–110 (2004)

16. Muja, M., Lowe, D.G.: Fast approximate nearest neighbors with automatic algorithm configuration. In: In VISAPP International Conference on Computer Vision Theory and Applications, pp. 331–340 (2009)

17. Neumann, J., Fermuller, C., Aloimonos, Y.: Polydioptric camera design and 3D motion estimation. In: 2003 IEEE Computer Society Conference on Computer Vision and Pattern Recognition, 2003. Proceedings, vol. 2, pp. II-294 (2003). https://doi.org/10.1109/CVPR.2003.1211483

18. Nistér, D.: An efficient solution to the five-point relative pose problem. IEEE Trans. Pattern Anal. Mach. Intell. **26**(6), 756–770 (2004). https://doi.org/10.1109/TPAMI.2004.17

19. Pless, R.: Using many cameras as one. In: 2003 IEEE Computer Society Conference on Computer Vision and Pattern Recognition, 2003. Proceedings, vol. 2, pp. II-587 (2003). https://doi.org/10.1109/CVPR.2003.1211520

20. Stewénius, H., Nistér, D., Oskarsson, M., Åström, K.: Solutions to minimal generalized relative pose problems. In: Workshop on Omnidirectional Vision (2005)

21. Ventura, J., Arth, C., Lepetit, V.: An efficient minimal solution for multi-camera motion. In: 2015 IEEE International Conference on Computer Vision (ICCV), pp. 747–755 (2015). https://doi.org/10.1109/ICCV.2015.92

22. Zhang, Z., Rebecq, H., Forster, C., Scaramuzza, D.: Benefit of large field-of-view cameras for visual odometry. In: 2016 IEEE International Conference on Robotics and Automation (ICRA), pp. 801–808 (2016). https://doi.org/10.1109/ICRA.2016.7487210

SARNN: A Spatiotemporal Prediction Model for Reducing Error Transmissions

Yonghui Liang[1], Lu Zhang[2], Yuqing He[1(✉)], Na Xu[2], Mingqi Liu[1], and Jeremy Jianshuo-li Mahr[3]

[1] MOE Key Laboratory of Optoelectronic Imaging Technology and System, School of Optics and Photonics, Beijing Institute of Technology, Beijing 100081, China
yuqinghe@bit.edu.cn

[2] Key Laboratory of Radiometric Calibration and Validation for Environmental Satellites (LRCVES/CMA), National Satellite Meteorological Center, China Meteorological, Administration (NSMC/CMA), Beijing 100081, China

[3] Division of Life Sciences, Rutgers, The State University of New Jersey, Piscataway, NJ, USA

Abstract. Spatiotemporal prediction has become an important research topic in weather forecasting and traffic planning. Due to the cyclic structure for prediction images frame by frame, the error generation and accumulation has often led to blurred images. In this paper, we propose a new end-to-end spatiotemporal attention recurrent neural network (SARNN) to overcome this problem. A new cyclic core mechanism based on long-short term memory (LSTM) is used for extracting the directions of spatial correlation and temporal evolution feature separately. Specifically, an attention mechanism added in temporal direction allows for adaptively choosing highlight input time step of hidden state, instead of decoder just relying on the output of previous time step; a scale change convolution block has been added in the spatial direction to enhance the capability of extraction multi-level semantic features. The validation experiment on Moving-Mnist and KTH dataset demonstrates that SARNN can output more accurate and clearer prediction frames.

Keywords: RNN based model · Spatiotemporal prediction · LSTM · Attention mechanism

1 Introduction

In the past ten years, the recurrent neural networks (RNN) and long short-term memory (LSTM) [1] have achieved great success in the prediction tasks of natural language processing (NLP). Recently, two-dimensional sequence prediction has become a research hotspot, which can be used in weather forecasting [2], traffic planning [3] and autonomous driving cars [4].

The spatiotemporal prediction model has two major tasks: spatial correlations learning and temporal dynamics prediction. To achieve those goals, the fully-connected computation in LSTM is replaced by convolutional operation to obtain the capability of

© Springer Nature Switzerland AG 2022
C. Wallraven et al. (Eds.): ACPR 2021, LNCS 13188, pp. 130–143, 2022.
https://doi.org/10.1007/978-3-031-02375-0_10

spatial feature extraction, and the multi-layer stacked encoder-decoder architecture is adopted to obtain high-level spatial features. A number of models based on this design have achieved state-of-the-art results. However, they often suffer from problems such as huge memory usage, gradient vanishing and frame-by-frame error accumulation. To overcome these problems, a new model with multi-layer stacking encoder-decoder architecture based on the RNN, spatiotemporal attention recurrent neural networks (SARNN) is proposed in this paper. In order to reduce the global prediction error, we have successfully suppressed the prediction error of delivery frame-by-frame. The major innovations of the paper can be summarized as follows.

(1) A new memory state storage separated LSTM (Sep-LSTM) is designed to separate temporal feature extraction from spatial feature, which has fast gradient propagation channel in each respective direction.
(2) To improve the efficiency of model feature extraction ability, a special convolution block (SC-Block) is added between the stack layers which samples down in the encoder and up in the decoder. This pyramid structure can extract multi-level semantic information, reduce memory consumption during training and accelerate prediction speed.
(3) The attention mechanism is extended in two dimensions by the spatiotemporal attention (ST-Attention) structure, which can adaptively highlight input time step of hidden state.

The Moving-Mnist and KTH action datasets are used for validation, and the results show that SARNN has better predicted frames that maintain sharpness with increasing time steps, demonstrating that SARNN suppresses the transmission of errors, and has state-of-the-art performance.

2   Related Work

The spatiotemporal prediction model predicts several future frames by understanding the temporal and spatial characteristics of moving objects and backgrounds in existing video frames.

The CNNs have achieved significant success in computer vision by virtue of their powerful spatial feature extraction capabilities. Oh et al. [5] defined a CNN-based action autoencoder model to predict the next frame of Atari games. Kalchbrenner et al. [6] proposed a video pixel network (VPN) to estimate the discrete joint distribution of the original pixel values in the video, while Wang et al. [7] proposed Eidetic3DLSTM combining 3DCNN and LSTM to improve the performance for both long- and short-term prediction. Compared with CNN, the application of GAN [8] remains in its infancy. Mathieu et al. [9] reconstructed frames with high resolution and high quality through multi-scale networks, and the StackGAN was proposed by Zhang et al. [10] to iteratively generate high quality images.

RNN has many applications in predictive learning. Ranzato et al. [11] used encoded video frames to extend the traditional RNN model into two dimensions, which could only predict one frame. Srivastava et al. [12] developed a LSTM-based encoder-decoder predictive model that accomplished multi-step prediction, but the fully connected LSTM (FC-LSTM) does not easily capture the spatial correlation features. Subsequently, the ConvLSTM was proposed by Shi et al. [13], which replaced the fully connected operation of the LSTM with a convolutional operation. This work also became the basis for subsequent spatiotemporal prediction models. Based on this, PredRNN was proposed by Wang et al. [14], which adding a connection between the top unit at time t and the bottom unit at time $t + 1$, but the ST-LSTM with two memory units had a greater gradient disappearance. Therefore, they proposed PredRNN++ [15], which had a reasonable gradient highway unit to cope with gradient disappearance, but this model had great parameters. Lotter et al. [16] used ConvLSTM for predictive architecture based on predictive coding that the prediction errors could be transmitted over the network. The method proposed by Villegas et al. [17] could allow the separation of background and human motion into different encoders. Li et al. [18] proposed a CostNet with a horizontal and vertical cross-connection, designing Horizon LSTM which could mitigate gradient vanishing. Oliu et al. [19] proposed a new recursive auto-encoder network named FRNN and its hidden states shared between the encoder and decoder, so the hidden states can be used more effectively.

The RNNs have more advantages in predictive learning than the CNNs and the GANs due to their better ability to extract temporal dynamics patterns between frames. The prediction frames of the mainstream models are often gradually blurred due to gradient vanishing, error accumulation and insufficient spatial correlation extraction capability. To solve this problem, we proposed a new spatiotemporal prediction model called SARNN, which had stronger spatial modeling capability, reducing error transmission together with sharper prediction frames.

3 Methods

In this section, we have given a detailed description of SARNN which can be divided into three parts: Sep-LSTM, ST-Attention and SC-Block.

The model inputs are T consecutive frames from a video or picture sequence, where each frame is recorded at all locations in the spatial region donated by an $M \times N$ grid. There are P measurements represented by a tensor $\mathcal{X} \in \mathbb{R}^{P \times M \times N}$ in each frame (e.g. a RGB channel).

The spatiotemporal predictive learning problem is to predict the most probable length-K sequence in the context of the previous length-J sequence including the current observation. It can be expressed as follows:

$$\widehat{\mathcal{X}}_{t+1}, \ldots, \widehat{\mathcal{X}}_{t+K} = \underset{\mathcal{X}_{t+1}, \ldots, \mathcal{X}_{t+K}}{\arg\max} \; p(\mathcal{X}_{t+1}, \ldots, \mathcal{X}_{t+K} | \mathcal{X}_{t-J+1}, \ldots, \mathcal{X}_t) \tag{1}$$

3.1 Sep-LSTM

To solve gradient vanishing of LSTM, a "gradient highway" for the temporal memory state C is established. When the output of the forgetting gate is 1, the update of C is similar to the residual connection in ResNet [20] and the information could flow unimpeded to the next time step.

Inspired by this, we proposed a new loop computing cell called Sep-LSTM. It has two paths to model temporal variation and spatial correlation respectively, suppressing the gradient vanishing by the "gradient highway" and the Sep-LSTM designed as shown in Fig. 1.

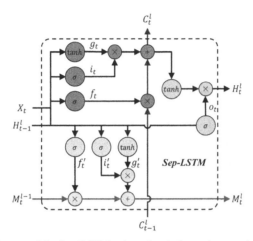

Fig. 1. Schematic diagram of the Sep-LSTM, where the circles and arrows indicate the calculation and memory flow; Green denotes spatial, the green and blue represent the spatial and temporal memories while the gray is on behalf of the fusion of two memories.

The states C and M carry respectively temporal and spatial information for vertical and horizontal transmission, while the state H is a spatiotemporal unit transmitting simultaneously along both horizontal and vertical directions, where the subscript and superscript indicates the number of time steps and the number of stacked layers, respectively.

$$f_t = \sigma(W_{fx} * X_t + W_{fh} * H_{t-1} + b_f)$$
$$i_t = \sigma(W_{ix} * X_t + W_{ih} * H_{t-1} + b_i)$$
$$g_t = \sigma(W_{gx} * X_t + W_{gh} * H_{t-1} + b_g)$$
$$C_t = f_t \odot C_{t-1} + i_t \odot g_t$$
$$f'_t = \sigma(W'_{fx} * X_t + W'_{fh} * H_{t-1} + b'_f)$$
$$i'_t = \sigma(W'_{ix} * X_t + W'_{ih} * H_{t-1} + b'_i)$$
$$g'_t = \sigma(W'_{gx} * X_t + W'_{gh} * H_{t-1} + b'_g)$$
$$M_t = f'_t \odot M_{t-1} + i'_t \odot g'_t$$
$$o_t = \sigma(W_{ox} * X_t + W_{oh} * H_{t-1} + b_o)$$
$$H_t = \tanh(C_t) \odot o_t \tag{2}$$

The memory states C and M are focused on the temporal and spatial models, respectively. The information transmitted by the C flow predicts the trajectory, scale change and internal motions of the moving target from time step $t\text{-}1$ to t. The state M flows only in the same time step, and the multi-layer stacked M can provide multi-level features of the target, which is conducive to the reconstruction of clearer frames. As shown in Eq. 2, the σ is the element-wised sigmoid function, while $*$ and $\odot$ represent the convolution operation and Hadamard product. This equation is kernel of the Sep-LSTM.

3.2 ST-Attention

The RNN based spatiotemporal prediction models usually do not perform well in long-term prediction because of the gradient disappearance together with the frame-by-frame accumulation of prediction errors. For example, if the target is blurred in the prediction frame for the time step t, it will be fed into the network as the input for the next prediction and leads to the increasing degree of blurring.

Therefore, an idea of changing the input of the decoder is presented. It depends on the output of the previous time step, and also adaptively depends on the hidden states of input frames from encoder. Like the attention mechanism [21], it gives more computational resources to the more valuable parts, thus it can fully employ the encoded information at different time steps. Based on this idea, we extend a 2D space for spatiotemporal prediction and propose ST-Attention.

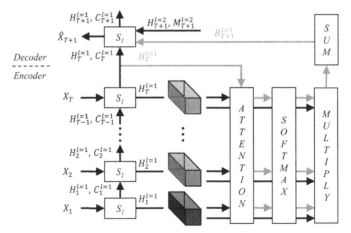

Fig. 2. Schematic diagram of the ST-Attention, where orange arrow indicates the computational flow from the query tensor to the background tensor. Blue, red and black cubes emphasize the hidden states are three-dimension tensor. Arrows which only contact the box indicate that an operation is performed.

The structure is displayed in Fig. 2 and the key equations are shown as follows:

$$B_{T+p}^{l} = softmax\,(H_{T+p-1}^{l} \otimes (H_{1:T}^{l})^{\top}) \cdot H_{1:T}^{l} \qquad (3)$$

where T together with l and p represent the number of the input time steps, layers and predicted time steps, while the symbols $\otimes$ and $\cdot$ stand for the tensor inner product and the scalar multiplication of the tensor and weighted sum.

Firstly, we obtain the hidden state of encoder at each time step. Then we get the attention value of the inner product of hidden state and the query tensor separately. Next, we put the attention value into the softmax function to get the attention weight. Then we get the background tensor B^l_{T+p} by making weighting sum of all encoder hidden states. Finally, we concatenate B^l_{T+p} and H^{l+1}_{T+p} in the channel dimension as the input of the decoder.

3.3 SC-Block

Because we use the Sep-LSTM structure, the separation of the temporal and spatial features are clear, and the spatial features are mainly stored in the state M and H.

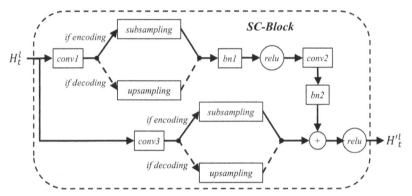

Fig. 3. Schematic diagram of the SC-Block, where solid line indicates the encoding process and the dashed line indicates the decoding process. The branch of conv3 represents the residual connection and the convolutional kernel size is 1×1, which is used mainly to change the number of channels.

Solely considering the convolution operation in the Sep-LSTM unit leads to inadequate extraction of spatial features, which can result in incorrect or ambiguous predictions. So, a spatial scale changed convolutional block (SC-Block) with residual connection is added between layers, as structure shown in Fig. 3.

conv1 and *conv2* are the convolutional layers used to extract the spatial features, while *bn1* and *bn2* together with *relu* are the batch norm layers and the activation function. The convolutional kernel size of *conv3* is 1×1, which is used mainly to change the number of channels. Different from the ordinary residual block, a scale transformation mechanism is introduced to change H and W to half of the original size by down sampling after *conv1* during encoding, and to double H and W by up sampling after conv1 during decoding. With such a structure, it is possible to obtain different levels of semantic information at encoding time and combine the high-level semantic and low-level superficial information at decoding time, so it has a better performance for reconstruction of the image.

Because the images have high complexity, and are better able to extract the spatial features in the images, the multiple SC-Blocks can be stacked between layers. Of course, the up sampling and down sampling only happen in the first SC-Block.

3.4 SARNN

We combine the above three parts to obtain a SARNN structure similar to an "upright sandwich" as shown in Fig. 4, where S and R stand for Sep-LSTM and SC-Block, while the orange line and arrow represent the background state calculation introduced in Sect. 3.2.

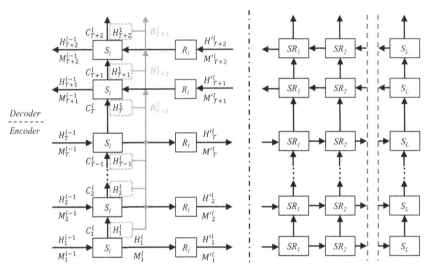

Fig. 4. Left: A base stacking block consisting of a Sep-SLTM and a SC-Block. The orange line indicates the calculation of ST-Attention. We refer to this base block as the SR-Block. Right: SARNN stacked by multiple SR-Blocks. Note that the last layer contains only Sep-LSTM.

SARNN has a strong spatial feature extraction capability in the horizontal direction due to the horizontal "gradient highway" of M in the Sep-LSTM and the residual connectivity in the SC-Block. The vertical ST-Attention allows the decoder of each layer to not only depend on the output of the previous time step, but also adaptively decide to focus on encoding hidden state of input time steps, thus suppressing the transmission of errors when they are generated.

At the same time, low-resolution and semantically strong features are combined with high-resolution and semantically weak features through top-down pathways, This pyramid structure can also accelerate prediction speed. This multilayer stacking structure is particularly suitable for ablation experiments, facilitating our understanding and interpretation of the inner workings of the network.

4   Experiments

In order to verify the proposed model in this paper, we use Pytorch 1.1.0 and a Quadro GV100 GPU with 32 GB memory to train and test SARNN, TrajGRU, ConvLSTM and PredRNN on Moving-Mnist and KTH human action datasets respectively as contrast experiments.

The SARNN consists of four layers of Sep-LSTM with 64 channels each, and there is one SC-Block between every two layers. The ConvLSTM has a three-layer stacking structure with 128, 64, and 64 channels, and the PredRNN uses a four-layer ST-LSTM stacking structure with 64 channels each layer.

We set the convolution kernel size to 5×5 within all recursive cells. All networks training use ADMA optimizer and L2 loss. Batch size is set to 8 for all networks, with an initial learning rate of 0.001. We use the StepLR strategy to decrease learning rate to 0.9 times after every 5 epochs automatically, as well as an early stopping strategy. The patience is set to 10.

4.1   Moving Mnist Dataset

Implementation
We randomly select three handwritten digits from the Mnist dataset and then place them in a 64×64 pixels image grid with random position. First, we give an initial velocity, in which the directions are selected randomly with the unit circle and the time interval between two adjacent frames is set as 0.1. Second, when the digits touch the boundary, we reverse corresponding velocity component. In this experiment, we set 20 consecutive frames as a group, and the first 10 as input together with the last 10 as ground truth. In this way, a dataset which includes 10000 groups of training images and 3000 groups of test images is constructed. In order to assess generation ability, the models trained on Mnist-3 are also applied in Mnist-4.

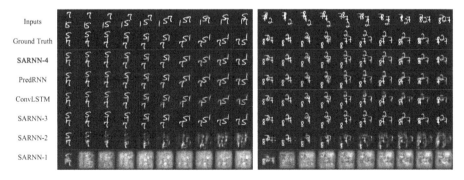

Fig. 5.   Prediction examples on the Moving Mnist-3 (left) and Mnist-4 (right) test set.

Qualitative Analysis
In Fig. 5, on both datasets, the ConvLSTM produces significant defocus and distortion frame by frame. The PredRNN can predict position and shape of numbers accurately

in Mnist-3 but does not perform well in the more complex dataset of Mnist-4. For example, as the two numbers on the left side are overlapping, the upper horizontal line of the digit "7" disappears, the middle of the digit "8" is disconnected and becomes two separate "0". The SARNN performs well on both datasets, which can fully extract high-level features and has better prediction results in the Mnist-4, especially in severe crossover and occlusion. The ablation experiments of the SARNN show that the added stacked layers mainly serve the converge spatial features, where SARNN-x indicates the x-layer stacking structure. This is closely related to the structure of the Sep-LSTM, the result indicating that the Sep-LSTM is indeed able to separate the extraction of spatial and temporal features. In our experiment, the task is simpler and the 3-layer stacking structure can sufficiently extract spatial features, so the performance of 3-layer and 4-layer SARNNs are nearly equal. In complex tasks, the performance can be improved by increasing the number of layers.

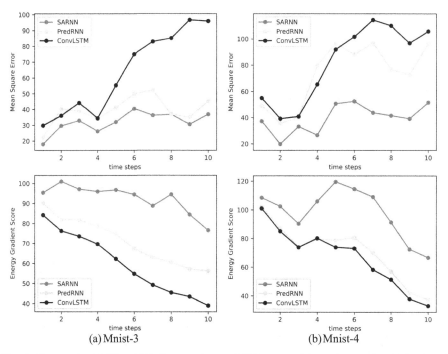

Fig. 6. Frame-wise MSE and EOG comparisons of different models on the Moving Mnist-3 and Moving Mnist-4 test set.

Quantitative Analysis

The mean square error (MSE) and energy of gradient (EOG) [22] are used to evaluate the prediction results objectively. The MSE shows the similarity of the predicted frame to the true value feature (the smaller the better), while the EOG shows the clarity of the predicted frame (the larger the better).

In Fig. 6, the SARNN controls the MSE errors in a range of [18, 40] for the Mnist-3 and [20, 60] for more complex Mnist-4, respectively. The relatively stable MSE and energy gradient trends indicate that the accumulation of predicted frames over time steps simultaneously has properties similar to ground truth and remains sharp. This shows that the error is generated but not propagated over the time step, and also repeats the significant role of the ST-Attention structure. The MSEs of the ConvLSTM and PredRNN have an increasing trend and their energy gradients have a decreasing trend, indicating that the images are distorted and blurred frame by frame with the accumulation of errors.

4.2 KTH Action Dataset

Implementation

The KTH action dataset consists of six types of movements (walking, jogging, running, boxing, hand waving and hand clapping) performed by 25 people, with similar background and fixed camera. The walking, jogging and running datasets are resized to 64 × 64 used bilinear interpolation to improve training efficiency. Referring to the dataset settings in PredRNN [14], a sliding window with the length of 20 is used to choose the data. The first 10 frames are selected as input while the next 10 frames as ground truth, and the step size of the walking dataset is 3 and 20 for others. The people ids 1–16 used as the training dataset and 17–25 as the test. In this way, we constructed 35255 groups of training images and 3832 groups of test images.

Qualitative Analysis

To validate the capability of the SARNN, we carry out a large number of validation experiments on the test dataset. Figure 7 and Fig. 8 show the results in person-25-jogging-d2 dataset and person-20-running-d3 dataset.

TrajGRU, ConvLSTM and PredRNN can predict the position of the moving target accurately, but they both show varying degrees of blurring with the number of frames increasing, and especially in the case of faster target movement and larger movement amplitude. The results of SARNN on both datasets have high accuracy and definition. We also note that SARNN results on person-20-running-d3 show that the hand motion state can still be reconstructed in the case of clothing gradually disappearing, so the SARNN has powerful capabilities when it comes to predicting moving targets. In addition, as shown in the ablation experiments of SARNN, the first layer reconstructs the background information, the second layer predicts the target location, and the third and fourth layers are able to reconstruct the details of the target.

Quantitative Analysis

The structural similarity (SSIM) and EOG is used to objectively evaluate the prediction results. SSIM shows the similarity of the predicted frame to the true value feature and the value of SSIM is between −1 and 1 (the larger the better). In Fig. 9, the SSIM of the SARNN is above 0.75 on both jogging and running datasets, and the EOG indicators is much better than TrajGRU, ConvLSTM and PredRNN. It is able to select the focused coding information adaptively in the low-dimensional feature to high-dimensional feature layer. So even if errors arise in the process of prediction, the impact of error transmission on subsequent predictions can be minimized, and the prediction quality of all frames is finally controlled within a good range.

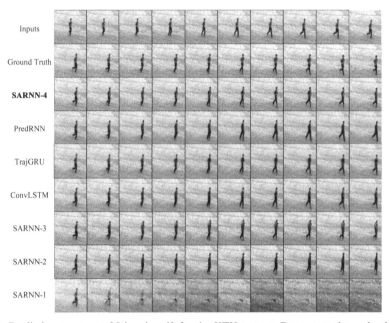

Fig. 7. Prediction on person-25-jogging-d2 for the KTH test set. Represents the scale changed prediction scenario.

Because of the use of a four-layer stacked SARNN structure, four confusion matrices are generated in a single prediction. The attention weights of a certain output frame are used to obtain the joint attention confusion matrix. Based on Fig. 10, in 1–10 and out 1–10 denote the 10 input frames and the 10 predicted frames, respectively.

Color blocks indicate the size of the attention weight: the darker the color, the larger the value. It can be seen that the first prediction frame focuses mainly on the 10th input frame, which could be caused by the close connection between the last input frame and the first output frame. Since all the predictions are based on the first input frame, the other prediction frames focus mainly on it. In addition to that, each prediction frame also focuses on some input frames in different degrees for improving the detail performance. For example, out_8 of the jogging dataset also focuses on in_8, in_9 and in_10 in Fig. 10(a). As shown in Fig. 7, SARNN could consider that out_8 has the most similar target features to in_8, in_9 and in_10, so SARNN models the details of the moving object from the changes of these three frames. As shown in Fig. 9(a), the SSIM of frame 8 are not decreasing and the EOG reaches the highest value, which demonstrate that the ST-Attention gets a sharp frame. Out_4 of the running dataset focuses on in_6 as shown in Fig. 10(b). The SSIM reduction rate of out_4 is small and the EOG reaches the highest value as shown in Fig. 9(b). So, the transmission of errors is reduced by ST-Attention and the clarity of the image is maintained.

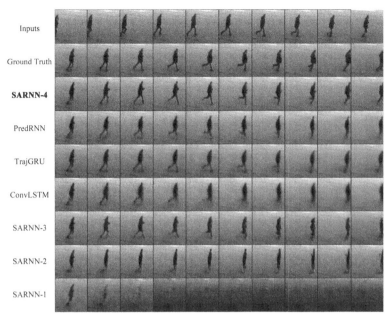

Fig. 8. Prediction on person-20-running-d3 for the KTH test set. Represents the clothing cover-up and fast movement prediction scenario.

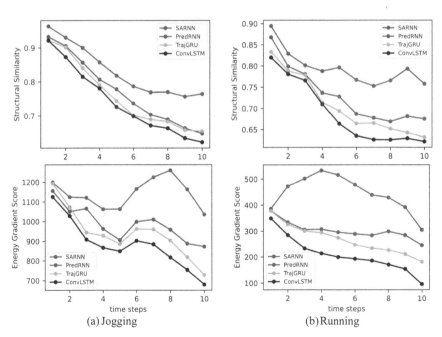

Fig. 9. Frame-wise SSIM and EOG comparisons of different models on the Jogging and Running test set.

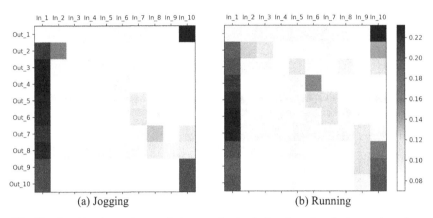

Fig. 10. Combined attention confusion matrix, the darker the color, the larger the value.

4.3 Limitations of SARNN

In the spatiotemporal prediction tasks with fixed camera such as weather forecasting and traffic planning, SARNN has a large fraction of parameters usage to model background which is almost fixed. This slows down the speed of reasoning and processing speed. More importantly, it also limits the learning capability of the true moving target. For example, our model learns to predict six types of human movements at once in KTH dataset, but for few complex running situations, it will gradually become jogging, with clear background every time step.

We will try to using stronger spatial attention mechanisms to solve this problem, which can impose constraints on the partition of the real moving target. Meanwhile, we will use a new loss function to confer different weight of target and background.

5   Conclusions

In this paper, we proposed a new end-to-end spatiotemporal prediction network-SARNN. The focus of our work is to reduce error accumulation and decrease blurring of prediction frames. It extracts spatial correlations in the horizontal direction together with a spatial scale changed convolutional block between each two stack layers to obtain multi-level semantic features. In the vertical direction, the decoder will decide which encoded hidden state of input time steps to be concerned adaptively.

In Moving-Mnist dataset and the KTH dataset, when compared with ConvLSTM and PredRNN, SARNN has better performance. In future work, we will pay more attention to the prediction task with changing background.

Acknowledgments. This work is support by the National Key Research and Development Program of China under Grant No. 2018YFB0504901.

References

1. Ushiku, Y.: Long short-term memory, In: Neural Computation, pp. 1–7 (1997)
2. Klein, B., Wolf, L., Afek, Y.: A dynamic convolutional layer for short range weather prediction. In: Computer Vision and Pattern Recognition, pp. 4840–4848 (2015)
3. Yu, B., Yin, H., Zhu, Z.: Spatio-temporal graph convolutional networks: a deep learning framework for traffic forecasting. In: International Joint Conference on Artificial Intelligence, pp. 3634–3640 (2018)
4. Liang, X., Lee, L., Dai, W., Xing, E.: Dual motion gan for future-flow embedded video prediction. In: International Conference on Computer Vision, pp. 1762–1770 (2017)
5. Oh, J., Guo, X., Lee, H., Lewis, R.: Action-conditional video prediction using deep networks in atari games. In: Neural Information Process System, pp. 2863–2871 (2015)
6. Kalchbrenner, N., Oord, A., Simonyan, K., Danihelka, I., Vinyals, O., Graves, A.: Video pixel networks. In: International Conference on Machine Learning (2016)
7. Wang, Y., Lu, J., Yang, M.H., Li, L.J., Long, M.: Eidetic 3d lstm: A model for video prediction and beyond. In: International Conference on Machine Learning (2018)
8. Goodfellow, I.J., Pouget-Abadie, J., Mirza, M., et al.: Generative adversarial networks. In: Advances in Neural Information Processing Systems, pp: 2672–2680 (2014)
9. Mathieu, M., Couprie, C., Lecun, Y.: Deep multi-scale video prediction beyond mean square error. In: International Conference on Machine Learning, pp: 1–14 (2016)
10. Zhang, H., Xu, T., Li, H.: Stackgan: Text to photo-realistic image synthesis with stacked generative adversarial networks. In: International Conference on Computer Vision, pp. 5908–5916 (2017)
11. Ranzato, M.A., Szlam, A., Bruna, J., Mathieu, M., Collobert, R.: Video (language) modeling: a baseline for generative models of natural videos. In: Eprint Arxiv, pp: 1–15 (2014)
12. Srivastava, R.K., Greff, K., Schmidhuber, J.: Training very deep networks. In: Advances in Neural Information Processing Systems, pp. 2377–2385 (2015)
13. Shi, X., Chen, Z., Wang, H., Yeung, D.Y., Wong, W.K., WOO, W.C.: Convolutional LSTM network: a machine learning approach for precipitation nowcasting. In: Neural Information Process System, pp. 802–810 (2015)
14. Wang, Y., Long, M., et al.: Predrnn: recurrent neural networks for predictive learning using spatiotemporal lstms. In: Neural Information Process System, pp. 879–888 (2017)
15. Wang, Y., Gao, Z., Long, M., Wang, J., Yu, P.: Predrnn++: towards a resolution of the deep-in-time dilemma in spatiotemporal predictive learning. In: International Conference on Machine Learning, pp. 5123–5132 (2018)
16. Lotter, W., et al.: Deep predictive coding networks for video prediction and unsupervised learning. In: International Conference on Learning Representations, pp. 4213–4223 (2016)
17. Villegas, R., Yang, J., et al.: Decomposing motion and content for natural video sequence prediction In: International Conference on Machine Learning, pp. 3560–3569 (2017)
18. Sun, F., Li, S., et al.: Costnet: a concise overpass spatiotemporal network for predictive learning. In: ISPRS International Journal of Geo-Information, pp: 209–220 (2020)
19. Oliu, M., Selva, J., Escalera, S.: Folded recurrent neural networks for future video prediction. In: European Conference on Computer Vision, pp. 716–731 (2018)
20. He, K., Zhang, X., Ren, S., Sun, J.: Deep residual learning for image recognition. In: IEEE Conference on Computer Vision and Pattern Recognition, pp. 770–778 (2016)
21. Luong, M.T., Pham, H., Manning, C.: Effective approaches to attention-based neural machine translation. In: Computer ence, pp: 523–530 (2015)
22. Subbarao, M., Tyan, J.K.: Selecting the optimal focus measure for autofocusing and depth-from-focus. In: Pattern Analysis and Machine Intelligence, pp: 864–870 (1998)

3OFRR-SLAM: Visual SLAM with 3D-Assisting Optical Flow and Refined-RANSAC

Yujia Zhai[1,2,3], Fulin Tang[1,3(✉)], and Yihong Wu[1,3(✉)]

[1] National Laboratory of Pattern Recognition, Institute of Automation,
Chinese Academy of Sciences, Beijing, China
{fulin.tang,yhwu}@nlpr.ia.ac.cn
[2] Institute of Semiconductors, Chinese Academy of Sciences, Beijing, China
[3] University of Chinese Academy of Sciences, Beijing, China

Abstract. To perform navigation or AR/VR applications on mobile devices, SLAM is expected to be with low computational complexity. But using feature descriptors restricts the minimization and lightweight of a SLAM system. In this paper, we propose a lightweight monocular SLAM system called 3OFRR-SLAM, which is precise, fast, and achieves real-time performance on CPU and mobile phones. It integrates a 3D-assisting optical flow tracker, uses a local map to provide prior information for optical flow, and improves the Lucas-Kanade algorithm, which makes data association fast and reliable. To further eliminate outliers of data association, we propose a novel Refined-RANSAC, improving the accuracy of camera pose estimation without taking much extra time cost. We evaluate our system on TUM-RGBD dataset and real-world data. The results demonstrate that our system obtains an outstanding improvement in both speed and accuracy compared with current state-of-the-art methods ORB-SLAM2 and DSO. Moreover, we transplant our system to an android-based smartphone and show the application for augmented reality (AR).

Keywords: Visual localization · Fast tracking · SLAM

1 Introduction

Over the past decades, simultaneous localization and mapping(SLAM) [3] has made rapid progress. With visual SLAM technology getting mature, it has been applied in robotics, unmanned driving and AR/VR widely [25]. Several sensor types can be used as input of visual SLAM, such as monocular cameras [6,13], stereo cameras [24] and RGB-D cameras [9]. In consideration of the low cost and

Supported by National Natural Science Foundation of China under Grant Nos. 62002359, 61836015 and the Beijing Advanced Discipline Fund under Grant No. 115200S001.

easy deployment of the monocular camera, we focus on monocular visual SLAM in this paper.

For visual SLAM, one of the key problems is data association, which has a decisive influence on the efficiency and accuracy of the visual localization and reconstruction [28]. Based on the geometric features of image points, data association methods can be divided into two types. One is to construct data association by calculating specific descriptors of feature points. Although high accuracy and robustness can be obtained, even fast feature descriptors such as ORB [21] may decrease the real-time performance of SLAM systems in the case of high frame rates and high image resolution. The other is to detect corners and utilize sparse optical flow to construct data association. Compared with the first one, it is faster but more likely to cause incorrect feature correspondences. Another mainstream method of data association is the direct method, which directly minimalizes the photometric error by solving a nonlinear optimation instead of relying on geometric features. As it avoids the complex calculation of descriptor matching, it obtains high efficiency. However, the optimization of sliding windows still requires a lot of computing power, which also limits the application of this method on the mobile terminals.

To address these problems, we propose 3OFRR-SLAM, a lightweight and accurate monocular SLAM system, which combines a 3D-assisting optical flow tracker that can give one-to-one correspondences for accurate and fast data association. And to further reject outliers of 3D-2D correspondences obtained from the proposed tracker, we propose a novel Refined-RANSAC method to refine the estimation of camera poses, where we also give a criteria function to choose 3D information with high quality.

The main contributions of this paper are as follows:

– A lightweight monocular visual SLAM system integrates a 3D-assisting optical flow tracker.
– A novel Refined-RANSAC method is proposed to better eliminate outliers. Compared with standard-RANSAC, it makes camera pose estimation more accurate without taking much extra time cost.
– We demonstrate on TUM-RGBD [23] dataset that our system outperforms the state-of-art systems in accuracy and speed, and implement our system on the mobile terminal for visual localization and AR applications.

The rest of this paper is organized as follows. In Sect. 2 we discuss the related work. The framework of the proposed system is shown in Sect. 3. Section 4 provides the details of the tracking thread and the mapping thread is described in Sect. 5. Section 6 provides qualitative and quantitative experimental results. And the conclusions and future work are given in Sect. 7.

2   Related Work

At present, the mainstream visual SLAM methods can be roughly divided into three categories: filter-based visual SLAM, keyframe-based visual SLAM, and direct-based visual SLAM.

Filter-based visual SLAM uses a Gaussian probability model to express the system state at each moment and continuously update it. Davison first proposed MonoSLAM [2], a real-time SLAM system using a monocular camera in 2003. MonoSLAM is implemented using the Extended Kalman Filter (EKF) [27] under a probability framework. The computational complexity of MonoSLAM is very high, which makes it difficult to apply on a large scale. Paz et al. [18] proposed a divide-and-conquer EKF-SLAM method to reduce the amount of calculation. Filter-based visual SLAM has more entangled data association and thus is more easy to drift.

It is proved in [22] that the keyframe-based visual SLAM outperforms filter-based visual SLAM. Klein et al. [10] proposed and open-sourced the first keyframe-based monocular visual SLAM system called PTAM in 2007, and transplanted it to the iPhone 3G in 2009 [11]. A classic two-thread framework is proposed in PTAM, which performs tracking and mapping as two independent tasks in two parallel threads. ORB-SLAM [15] proposed by Mur-Artal et al. in 2015 gets improvement from the FAST features [20] and the ORB [21] descriptors as while as the addition of the loop detection module. They further proposed ORBSLAM2 [16] in 2017, which is an extension from ORB-SLAM.

Visual direct SLAM directly optimizes the photometric error instead of considering the geometric information. It attains better robustness in the case of weak texture and images blurred. DTAM [17] is a dense visual SLAM system based on the direct method proposed in 2011. It constructs a dense depth map of keyframes by minimizing the energy function of the global space specification. DTAM is computationally intensive and requires GPU parallel computing. LSD-SLAM [5] restores the depth values of some pixels in the image to get a semi-dense model, which can run in real time on the CPU and smartphones. DSO [4] is a sparse direct visual odometry, which combines the photometric calibration model to improve the robustness. DSO can also run in real time on the CPU. What's more, SVO [7] and SVO2 [8] are a kind of semi-direct visual odometry and use a combination of feature points and direct methods. In the tracking thread, they extract FAST [20] corners and track them using the direct method while using a depth filter [19] to recover the depths. Since they avoid to calculate a large number of descriptors, they can be extremely fast.

These methods either have entangled data association or use image descriptors to associate data. To make SLAM more lightweight along with better accuracy, we design a visual odometry based on the optical flow, utilizing the information of the local map and the forward poses to optimize and accelerate the optical flow tracking. Besides, we solve the camera pose by the proposed Refined-RANSAC, which is a promotion of Lebeda's LO-RANSAC [12]. But instead of processing the data completely based on randomness without bias, we introduce the information of the local map to give the data points an estimated weight in voting, which makes camera pose estimation more accurate without taking much extra time cost.

3   System Overview

The system overview of 3OFRR-SLAM is shown in Fig. 1. Tracking and reconstructing run in two separate threads. The tracking thread implements the proposed 3D-assisting optical flow tracker to get an accurate estimation of the camera pose for each frame. First we detect FAST corners on the current frame $\mathbf{K_j}$ and get an initial pose prediction from the last frame $\mathbf{K_{j-1}}$. Then we use an improved LK optical flow tracker to reproject the local map into the current frame $\mathbf{K_j}$ with the initial pose to obtain 3D-2D correspondences, and estimate the camera pose with the proposed Refined-RANSAC. The pose will be further optimized by a local BA(bundle adjustment). If the current frame is determined to be a keyframe, we will add it to the keyframe sequence, in which it will be waited to be inserted to the mapping thread.

The mapping thread incrementally reconstructs the 3D structure of the surroundings. Map points will be produced by triangulation with the 2D-2D correspondences found between the current keyframe and its nearst keyframe. Afterwards, a local BA is performed to refine the new reconstructed points and then a global BA will be performed within several selected representative keyframes.

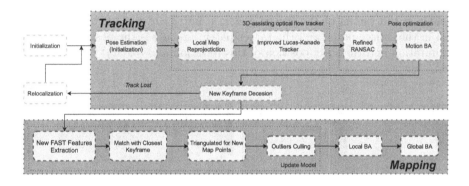

Fig. 1. The framework of 3OFRR-SLAM

4   Tracking

4.1   3D-Assisting Optical Flow Tracker

Those 3D points which may be visible will be chosen to be tracked by the proposed 3D-assisting optical flow tracker to get 3D-2D correspondences.

Considering that the disparity between the reference keyframe and the current frame may be relatively large, the source image patch around $\boldsymbol{m}_{ij}$ and the target image patch around $\boldsymbol{m}_{ic}$ may be quite different and remote. If we directly calculate the optical flow, it could hardly find the right correspondences. Firstly we use LK optical flow to track points between the last frame and the current frame to get an intial pose prediction of the current frame $\mathbf{K_j}$. According to 3D-2D correspondences in the current frame, the initial pose of $\mathbf{K_j}$ can be estimated by solving the PnP problem. Afterwards an affine transformation is performed to correct the source image patch. Then we set the initial search position for the optical flow tracker by projecting the selected 3D points onto the current frame with the predicted initial camera pose. This strategy is a one-to-one correspondence way and thus makes the initial search position closer to the real value, which accelerates the iteration and improves the matching accuracy. That's why we call it the 3D-assisting optical flow tracker. It can be seen in Fig. 2 that the mismatchs of our method are much less than the ordinary LK optical flow.

Starting from the given initial positions, the 3D-assisting optical flow tracker iteratively searches the correspondence of the source patch in the target image by minimizing the sum of squared difference (SSD) between them. For each iteration, the following photometric residual is minimized:

$$\sum_{x=-r}^{r} \sum_{y=-r}^{r} (I(x,y) - J(x + x_0 + dx, y + y_0 + dy))^2$$

$$= \sum_{p=0}^{(2r+1)^2} \left(I(p) - J(p)|_{(x_0+dx, y_0+dy)} \right)^2, \tag{1}$$

where r is the radius of the image patch, I and J are the brightness of each pixel in the source patch and the target patch, (x_0, y_0) is the position after the last iteration and the start position of this iteration and (dx, dy) is the required offset.

(a) The proposed 3D-assisting optical flow tracker

(b) The ordinary LK optical flow

Fig. 2. Performances of optical flow tracker on TUM- RGBD dataset.

To mitigate the influence of lighting variation while speeding up the convergence, unlike the LK optical flow method that modifies the residual representation and introduces new parameters, we adopt a direct method: normalize the source image patch to get $I'(p)$, and the image patch at the beginning of this iteration in the target image is also normalized to get $J'(p)$, then the solution of (dx, dy) can be expressed as:

$$\begin{bmatrix} dx \\ dy \end{bmatrix} = \begin{bmatrix} \sum_p I'_x(p)^2 & \sum_p I'_x(p)I'_y(p) \\ \sum_p I'_x(p)I'_y(p) & \sum_p I'_y(p)^2 \end{bmatrix}^{-1} \\ \cdot \begin{bmatrix} \sum_p I'_x(p)\left(I(p)' - J'(p)|_{(x_0,y_0)}\right) \\ \sum_p I'_y(p)\left(I(p)' - J'(p)|_{(x_0,y_0)}\right) \end{bmatrix},$$

(2)

where (I'_x, I'_y) are the normalized brightness of the source patch.

To further adapt to the situation where the position of the target image patch is greatly different from the predicted patch, we build a 4-level image pyramid and obtain the target position from coarse to fine.

4.2   Refined-RANSAC and Camera Pose Estimation

In order to further improve the accuracy of the pose estimation, we study a novel Refined-RANSAC to remove 2D-3D correspondence outliers.

The standard RANSAC algorithm randomly selects several data elements from the input data set, then repeatedly solves a model that fits the chosen samples. It considers that each data point has an equal confidence when evaluating the estimated model. Therefore, the number of the data elements that the model can fit within a given tolerance is used as the evaluation criteria of model quality. And the model with the most inliers will be returned. This leads to the fact that the performance of standard RANSAC method will decrease rapidly as the outliers ratio increases. And it is very sensitive to the threshold boundaries for dividing inliers and outliers. Meanwhile, the standard RANSAC is based on the assumption that all-inlier samples lead to the optimal solution. However, this assumption has been observed to be not valid in practice as pointed out in [1, 26].

To this end, we propose the Refined-RANSAC to further reject outliers in pose estimation. Compared to the standard RANSAC, the proposed Refined-RANSAC includes two new processes.

1. **Local Optimization**: after a potential model is found by the standard RANSAC, we run an additional local optimization step on it.

2. **Weighted Voting**: data points are assigned with different voting weights in the model evaluation according to their reliability.

We use the past recurrence rate of a map point ω as an index to evaluate the reliability of the map point. The recurrence rate ω is given by:

$$\omega = N'/N,$$

(3)

where N is the number of past frames at which the point can be observed and N' is the number of the times that the map point and its corressponding 2D point stay within inliers after local bundle adjustment. And the score $\mathcal{E}_M$ of a model can be calculated as follows:

$$\mathcal{E}_M = \sum_{i=1} max(\omega \cdot |p_i^m - p_i|, Thr_{error}),$$

(4)

where p_i is the real position of an image point, p_i^m represents the reprojected position of p_i using model M, and Thr_{error} is a given threshold to limit the impact of a single data point.

Algorithm 1. Refined-RANSAC
_____
Require: $\mathcal{I}, \omega, \theta$
 1: $\mathcal{I} \leftarrow$ input samples
 2: $\omega \leftarrow$ the weights of input data
 3: $\theta \leftarrow$ the inlier-outlier error threshold
 4: **for** $k = 1 \rightarrow \mathrm{K}(\mathcal{I})$ **do**
 5:      $\mathcal{S}_k \leftarrow$ randomly drawn minimal sample from $\mathcal{I}$
 6:      $M_k \leftarrow$ model estimated from sample $\mathcal{S}_k$
 7:      $\mathcal{E}_k \leftarrow$ score_model(M_k, ω, θ)
 8:      **if** $\mathcal{E}_k > \mathcal{E}_s^*$ **then**
 9:          $M_s^* \leftarrow M_k; \mathcal{E}_s^* \leftarrow \mathcal{E}_k$
10:          $M_{LO}, \mathcal{E}_{LO} \leftarrow$ run Local Optimization (M_s^*, ω, θ)
11:          **if** $\mathcal{E}_{LO} > \mathcal{E}^*$ **then**
12:              $M^* \leftarrow M_{LO}; \mathcal{E}^* \leftarrow \mathcal{E}_{LO}$
13:              update K
14:          **end if**
15:      **end if**
16: **end for**
17: **return** M^*
_____

The whole process of the proposed Refined-RANSAC is summarized in **Algorithm** 1 and the local optimization step is summarized in **Algorithm** 2. The function $find\_inliers$ evaluates the samples with input model M, and returns the subset of inliers whose errors are smaller than threshold θ. And function $score\_model$ uses the given weights ω and threshold θ to calculate the score $\mathcal{E}$ of the input model M.

As shown in **Algorithm** 1, firstly we execute an outer iteration with a minimal solver to find a potential best model. The minimal solver is used because the input dataset here has not been filtered and may have a relatively larger outlier ratio. Then we run the local optimization phase. As shown in **Algorithm** 2, The samples input here are only chosen from $\mathcal{I}_s$ (the inliers of the model found by a minimal solver under a slightly bigger in-out-threshold). As the sampling is running on so-far-inner data, in this iteration a non-minimal solver can be performed to introduce more information, such as the nonlinear optimization we used.

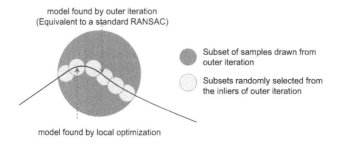

Fig. 3. Schematic of the local optimization

Substantially, the inner local optimization step aims to refine the estimated model by solving the same problem again within a smaller area which is verified to be reliable by the outer interation. Figure 3 is a schematic of the process. The Refined-RANSAC algorithm is very stable and is insensitive to the choice of the inlier-outlier threshold. It offers a significantly better initial value point for bundle adjustment. The quantitative evaluation of the performance of Refined-RANSAC can be seen in Sect. 6, which can be seen in Table 1.

The pose estimation obtained after the Refined-RANSAC solver will be refined further by a non-linear optimizer with 3D-2D correspondences.

Algorithm 2. Local Optimization

Require: $M_s, \omega, \theta, , m_\theta$
1: $M_s \leftarrow$ model estimated by outer iteration
2: $\omega \leftarrow$ the weights of input data
3: $\theta \leftarrow$ the inlier-outlier error threshold
4: $m_\theta \leftarrow$ the threshold multiplier
5: $\mathcal{I}_s \leftarrow$ find_inliers (M_s, θ)
6: **for** $i = 1 \rightarrow iters1$ **do**
7:     $\mathcal{S}_{is} \leftarrow$ sample of size s_{is} randomly drawn from $\mathcal{I}_s$
8:     $M_{is} \leftarrow$ model estimated from $\mathcal{S}_{is}$ by least squares solution
9:     $\theta' \leftarrow m_\theta \cdot \theta$
10:    $\mathcal{I}' \leftarrow$ find_inliers (M_{is}, θ')
11:    $M' \leftarrow$ model estimated by nonlinear optimization on $\mathcal{I}'$
12:    $\mathcal{E}' \leftarrow$ score_model (M', ω, θ')
13:    **if** $\mathcal{E}' > \mathcal{E}'^*$ **then**
14:        $M_s^* \leftarrow M'$
15:    **end if**
16:    $M_r \leftarrow$ the best of M'
17: **end for**
18: **return** the best of M_r, with its inliers

4.3   Relocalization

If the tracking quality is poor for consecutive 5 frames, tracking is assumed to be lost and the relocalization will be performed in the next frame. The relocalization process firstly searches for the 3D-2D correspondences between the global map and current frame through a random forest. Then the camera pose is calculated by EPnP algorithm and the current camera pose is retrieved in the global map.

5   Mapping

The addition of new keyframes brings new information to update the map. We detect FAST feature points on the newly added keyframe and select those further from the observation of existing map points as new features, then search for their correspondences on the nearest keyframes. Matching search is performed along the epipolar line with a cross-check matching method: two feature points are considered to be a valid pair only if they are both the most similar feature points of each other. Once the correspondences are obtained, the new map points can be triangulated.

After updating the model, we perform a local bundle adjustment [14] to optimize the newly reconstructed map. And then a global bundle adjustment is applied. Considering the efficiency of the system in a long image sequence, we select some representative keyframes through the covisible relationship and optimize the map points and the poses of the selected keyframes together.

6   Experiment

We perform experiments on a public dataset and in a real world environment to evaluate the proposed 3OFRR-SLAM system. We carry out all experiments with an Intel Core i7-8750H CPU (12 cores@ 2.20 GHz) and 32 GB RAM. Our system is compared with two state-of-the-art methods: ORB-SLAM2 and DSO. Additionally, we port the proposed system to two applications, including an implementation for augmented reality and an app running on an android mobile device.

Table 1. Localization error of each frame comparison in the TUM RGB-D dataset

| Sequence | 3OFRR-SLAM | | | | ORB-SLAM2 | | DSO | |
| | Standard RANSAC | | Local RANSAC | | | | | |
	ATE (m)	RPE (deg/m)	ATE (m)	RPE (deg/m)	ATE (m)	RPE (deg/m)	ATE (m)	RPE (deg/m)
fr1/xyz	0.0131	0.4912	**0.0083**	**0.4822**	0.0102	0.5256	0.0202	0.9982
fr2/xyz	0.0312	0.7088	0.0318	0.7275	**0.0251**	**0.0242**	0.0416	0.554
fr2/rpy	0.0092	1.3305	**0.0068**	**1.3178**	CNI[1]	CNI	0.0152	2.9585
fr1/desk	0.0201	1.3744	**0.0169**	1.2780	0.0190	**1.2556**	0.0285	1.8569
fr2/desk	0.0362	0.6989	0.0220	0.6875	**0.0116**	**0.2443**	0.0224	0.6899
fr3/long_office	0.0322	0.2366	**0.0275**	**0.2091**	0.0434	0.2334	0.0855	0.7341
fr3/sitting_halfsphere	0.0551	0.9002	0.0379	0.8452	**0.0142**	**0.4266**	0.0410	0.9233
fr3/sitting_xyz	0.0180	0.3170	**0.0176**	**0.3166**	0.0268	0.3646	0.0232	1.3140
fr3/walking_halfsphere	0.1722	2.1220	**0.0990**	**1.8201**	0.1606	3.1870	0.1953	3.2845
fr2/desk_with_person	0.0090	0.3109	**0.0064**	**0.2815**	0.0072	0.2955	0.0288	1.0020
fr3/str_tex_near	0.0575	0.5090	**0.0175**	**0.4732**	0.0188	0.5323	0.0219	1.2091
fr3/str_tex_far	0.0309	0.5466	0.0184	0.5533	**0.0091**	0.2108	0.1056	2.6555
fr3/nostr_tex _near_withloop	0.0303	0.3810	**0.0247**	**0.3099**	0.0262	0.3217	0.0426	0.6713
fr3/nostr_tex_far	0.1022	3.2988	**0.0690**	**2.4750**	AD[2]	AD	0.8522	2.9666

1 CNI: cannot initialize
2 AD:ambiguity detected

6.1   Evaluation on TUM-RGBD Dataset

We evaluate our system on the public TUM-RGBD dataset, which contains indoor sequences from RGBD sensors grouped in several categories and provides the ground truth of the camera pose for each frame. It is widely used to evaluate the SLAM or odometry systems. Since 3OFRR-SLAM is based on a monocular camera, we only use the RGB images as input.

ORB-SLAM2 and DSO are chosen to be the state-of-the-art systems of the feature-based methods and the direct methods respectively. The experimental results of them are obtained by running the open-source codes. To be fair, the ORB-SLAM2 is loop closure-disabled. We run each sequence for 5 times and pick the median result. The camera poses of all frames are recorded.

We adopt absolute trajectory error (ATE) and relative pose error (RPE) to conduct the quantitative evaluation of the system. The ATE directly calculates the difference between the ground-truth and the estimated camera poses, which reflects the overall performance of system. The relative pose error describes the pose difference of two frames during a fixed time interval. It reflects the drift of the system. The Root-Mean-Square Error (RMSE) of ATE and RPE is shown in Table 1, which is calculated by the benchmark tool [29]. It can be seen in Table 1 that our system outperforms ORB-SLAM2 and DSO on most sequences. That benefits from the accurate position from the proposed optical flow tracker, and the subsequent Refined-RANSAC gives a reliable filtering of data associations. The severe jitter and rapid moving on some sequences (such as fr2/xyz) will cause motion blur, and make most of the motion assumptions invalid, which makes optical flow tracking and the direct method performs terrible. But it has relatively little impact on the ORB-SLAM2, which adopts robust ORB feature to get correspondences.

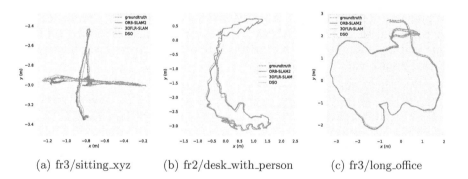

(a) fr3/sitting_xyz   (b) fr2/desk_with_person   (c) fr3/long_office

Fig. 4. Estimated trajectories by 3OFRR-SLAM, ORB-SLAM2 and DSO on TUM-RGBD dataset.

Figure 4 shows the estimated trajectories by our method, ORB-SLAM2 and DSO on three different TUM-RGBD sequences. It can be seen clearly that our estimated trajectories are smoother than those of ORB-SLAM2 and DSO with fewer sudden jumps.

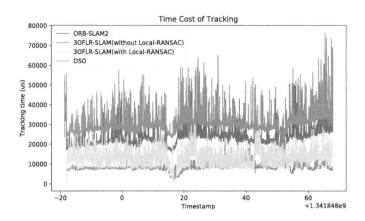

Fig. 5. Tracking timecost of each frame on the sequence fr3/long_office of TUM-RGBD dataset

Running time is an important factor of the performance of the online system. Figure 5 shows the time cost comparisons of our camera pose tracking method with ORB-SLAM2 and DSO on the fr3/long_office sequence. As the proposed method is based on the optical flow, it preserves from the calculation and matching of descriptors adopted in ORB-SLAM2 and the iteratively optimization of the sliding keyframe window adopted in DSO. The reduced computational complexity brings a noticeable speed increase. It can be seen that our speed can generally reach 2-3 times of ORB-SLAM2 and DSO.

6.2 Evaluation of Refined-RANSAC

The proposed Refined-RANSAC brings obvious improvement in terms of accuracy compared to standard RANSAC,which can be seen in Table 1. And Fig. 6 shows that the pose trajectory with Refined-RANSAC is more smooth and closer to the groundtruth.

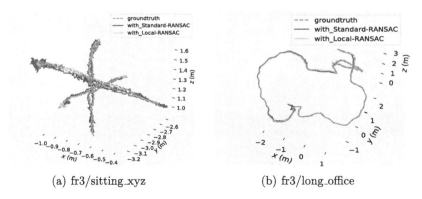

(a) fr3/sitting_xyz   (b) fr3/long_office

Fig. 6. Performances of the proposed Refined-RANSAC compared with standard-RANSAC on TUM- RGBD dataset.

The experiment on TUM-RGBD dataset demonstrates that Refined-RANSAC does not need much extra time cost in contrast to the standard RANSAC. The reason is that more correct inliers can trigger the stopping criterion earlier and the improvement of the initial value can accelerate the convergence of the subsequent optimization. It can be seen in Fig. 5 that the addition of the Refined-RANSAC method does not affect the speed of camera pose tracking, and even speeds up the convergence of pose optimization.

6.3   Application

1) *AR with a Hand-held Camera*

Fig. 7. An implementation for augmented reality: a virtual 3D model of a wine bottle is projected on the desk in the real office scene. Although the camera moves, the bottle remains still stable.

We present a simple AR application with a hand-held monocular camera to exhibit the accuracy and robustness of our system. The performance can be seen in Fig. 7. We add a virtual 3D model of a wine bottle to the real scene in the office and place it on the desk. It can be seen that the red wine bottle on the desk remains stable as the hand-held camera rotates and moves, demonstrating the high visual localization accuracy of our SLAM system.

2) *Implementation on Mobile Device*

As 3OFRR-SLAM is lightweight, we transplant it to mobile devices and test its performance in real-world indoor scene. It can run in real time on a Huawei P9 smartphone, using images 30 Hz and 640 × 480 resolution. Figure 8 shows the performance of the app.

Fig. 8. APP of 3OFRR-SLAM running on a mobile device in a real-world indoor scene, 30 Hz and 640 × 480 resolution images as input.

7   Conclusions and Future Work

In this paper, we propose a lightweight SLAM system that uses optical-flow to solve data association instead of the common-used descriptor-based method or direct method. The system is composed of an improved 3D-assisting optical flow tracker and a novel Refined-RANSAC algorithm that combines the information of the local map to further eliminate the outliers and improve the camera pose estimation. Experiments show that the proposed SLAM system has superior performances in terms of accuracy and speed than state-of-the-art methods. And it is proved that the system we proposed can run in real time on a small mobile terminal. In the future, we will add closure loop detection to deal with large city environments and fuse IMU information to assist visual localization.

References

1. Chum, O., Matas, J., Kittler, J.: Locally optimized RANSAC. In: Michaelis, B., Krell, G. (eds.) DAGM 2003. LNCS, vol. 2781, pp. 236–243. Springer, Heidelberg (2003). https://doi.org/10.1007/978-3-540-45243-0_31
2. Davison, A.J., Reid, I.D., Molton, N.D., Stasse, O.: Monoslam: real-time single camera slam. IEEE Trans. Pattern Anal. Mach. Intell. **29**(6), 1052–1067 (2007)
3. Durrant-Whyte, H., Bailey, T.: Simultaneous localization and mapping: part i. IEEE Robot. Autom. Mag. **13**(2), 99–110 (2006)
4. Engel, J., Koltun, V., Cremers, D.: Direct sparse odometry. IEEE Trans. Pattern Anal. Mach. Intell. **40**(3), 611–625 (2017)
5. Engel, J., Schöps, T., Cremers, D.: LSD-SLAM: large-scale direct monocular SLAM. In: Fleet, D., Pajdla, T., Schiele, B., Tuytelaars, T. (eds.) ECCV 2014. LNCS, vol. 8690, pp. 834–849. Springer, Cham (2014). https://doi.org/10.1007/978-3-319-10605-2_54
6. Engel, J., Sturm, J., Cremers, D.: Semi-dense visual odometry for a monocular camera. In: Proceedings of the IEEE International Conference on Computer Vision, pp. 1449–1456 (2013)
7. Forster, C., Pizzoli, M., Scaramuzza, D.: Svo: fast semi-direct monocular visual odometry. In: 2014 IEEE International Conference on Robotics and Automation (ICRA), pp. 15–22. IEEE (2014)

8. Forster, C., Zhang, Z., Gassner, M., Werlberger, M., Scaramuzza, D.: Svo: semidirect visual odometry for monocular and multicamera systems. IEEE Trans. Robot. **33**(2), 249–265 (2016)
9. Kerl, C., Stuckler, J., Cremers, D.: Dense continuous-time tracking and mapping with rolling shutter RGB-D cameras. In: Proceedings of the IEEE International Conference on Computer Vision, pp. 2264–2272 (2015)
10. Klein, G., Murray, D.: Parallel tracking and mapping for small AR workspaces. In: 2007 6th IEEE and ACM International Symposium on Mixed and Augmented Reality, pp. 225–234. IEEE (2007)
11. Klein, G., Murray, D.: Parallel tracking and mapping on a camera phone. In: 2009 8th IEEE International Symposium on Mixed and Augmented Reality, pp. 83–86. IEEE (2009)
12. Lebeda, K., Matas, J., Chum, O.: Fixing the locally optimized ransac. In: British Machine Vision Conference (2012)
13. Li, X., Ling, H.: Hybrid camera pose estimation with online partitioning for slam. IEEE Robot. Autom. Lett. **5**(2), 1453–1460 (2020)
14. Lourakis, M.I., Argyros, A.A.: SBA: a software package for generic sparse bundle adjustment. ACM Trans. Math. Softw. (TOMS) **36**(1), 1–30 (2009)
15. Mur-Artal, R., Montiel, J.M.M., Tardos, J.D.: Orb-slam: a versatile and accurate monocular slam system. IEEE Trans. Robot. **31**(5), 1147–1163 (2015)
16. Mur-Artal, R., Tardós, J.D.: Orb-slam2: an open-source slam system for monocular, stereo, and RGB-D cameras. IEEE Trans. Robot. **33**(5), 1255–1262 (2017)
17. Newcombe, R.A., Lovegrove, S.J., Davison, A.J.: Dtam: dense tracking and mapping in real-time. In: 2011 International Conference on Computer Vision, pp. 2320–2327. IEEE (2011)
18. Paz, L.M., Jensfelt, P., Tardos, J.D., Neira, J.: EKF slam updates in o (n) with divide and conquer slam. In: Proceedings 2007 IEEE International Conference on Robotics and Automation, pp. 1657–1663. IEEE (2007)
19. Pizzoli, M., Forster, C., Scaramuzza, D.: Remode: Probabilistic, monocular dense reconstruction in real time. In: 2014 IEEE International Conference on Robotics and Automation (ICRA), pp. 2609–2616. IEEE (2014)
20. Rosten, E., Drummond, T.: Machine learning for high-speed corner detection. In: Leonardis, A., Bischof, H., Pinz, A. (eds.) ECCV 2006. LNCS, vol. 3951, pp. 430–443. Springer, Heidelberg (2006). https://doi.org/10.1007/11744023_34
21. Rublee, E., Rabaud, V., Konolige, K., Bradski, G.: Orb: an efficient alternative to sift or surf. In: 2011 International Conference on Computer Vision, pp. 2564–2571. IEEE (2011)
22. Strasdat, H., Montiel, J.M., Davison, A.J.: Visual slam: why filter? Image Vis. Comput. **30**(2), 65–77 (2012)
23. Sturm, J., Engelhard, N., Endres, F., Burgard, W., Cremers, D.: A benchmark for the evaluation of RGB-D slam systems. In: 2012 IEEE/RSJ International Conference on Intelligent Robots and Systems, pp. 573–580. IEEE (2012)
24. Tang, F., Li, H., Wu, Y.: FMD stereo slam: Fusing MVG and direct formulation towards accurate and fast stereo slam. In: 2019 International Conference on Robotics and Automation (ICRA), pp. 133–139. IEEE (2019)
25. Tang, F., Wu, Y., Hou, X., Ling, H.: 3D mapping and 6D pose computation for real time augmented reality on cylindrical objects. IEEE Trans. Circ. Syst. Video Technol. **30**(9), 2887–2899 (2019)

26. Tordoff, B., Murray, D.W.: Guided sampling and consensus for motion estimation. In: Heyden, A., Sparr, G., Nielsen, M., Johansen, P. (eds.) ECCV 2002. LNCS, vol. 2350, pp. 82–96. Springer, Heidelberg (2002). https://doi.org/10.1007/3-540-47969-4_6

27. Welch, G., Bishop, G., et al.: An Introduction to the Kalman Filter (1995)

28. Wu, Y., Tang, F., Li, H.: Image-based camera localization: an overview. Vis. Comput. Ind. Biomed. Art **1**(1), 1–13 (2018). https://doi.org/10.1186/s42492-018-0008-z

29. Zhang, Z., Scaramuzza, D.: A tutorial on quantitative trajectory evaluation for visual (-inertial) odometry. In: 2018 IEEE/RSJ International Conference on Intelligent Robots and Systems (IROS), pp. 7244–7251. IEEE (2018)

Motor Imagery Classification Based on Local Log Riemannian Distance Matrices Selected by Confusion Area Score

Jinhyo Shin and Wonzoo Chung[✉]

Korea University, Seoul 02841, Republic of Korea
{jinhyo,wchung}@korea.ac.kr

Abstract. In this paper, we propose a novel motor imagery (MI) classification method in electroencephalogram (EEG)-based brain-computer interface (BCI) using local log Riemannian distance matrices (LRDM). The proposed method selects optimal local LRDM based on confusion area score which is designed to minimize the overlap between the class-dependent distributions of Riemannian distance between local covariance matrices that are generated from adjacent (local) channels centered on each channel. A feature vector is formed by concatenating vectorized selected local LRDM and used as input to support vector machine (SVM) in order to classify motor imagery. The performance of the proposed method is evaluated using BCI Competition III dataset IVa and BCI Competition IV dataset I. The results confirm performance improvement of the proposed method compared to existing MI classification methods.

Keywords: Brain-computer interface (BCI) · Electroencephalogram (EEG) · Motor imagery (MI) · Local feature · Log Riemannian distance matrix

1 Introduction

Brain-computer interface (BCI) is a system that translates brain signal to command in order to control external devices. Among non-invasive BCI techniques, electroencephalography (EEG), which records the brain wave activity, has been mostly studied and utilized because of its simplicity and good temporal resolution [14]. The event-related desynchronisation (ERD) and event-related synchronisation (ERS) patterns in EEG during motor imagery is used as important features for EEG based BCI.

The common spatial pattern (CSP) is perhaps the most popular feature generation algorithm to capture ERD/ERS for MI classification in EEG-based BCI. CSP designs the optimal spatial filter which maximizes the difference of the variances between two classes by solving a generalized eigenvalue problem based on covariance matrices [15]. Among intensive studies to improve the performance

© Springer Nature Switzerland AG 2022
C. Wallraven et al. (Eds.): ACPR 2021, LNCS 13188, pp. 159–169, 2022.
https://doi.org/10.1007/978-3-031-02375-0_12

of CSP algorithms, recently there have been an approach to localize CSP filters [12,16,17] to prevent overfitting problem of global CSP and reduce the noise contributed from task-irrelevant channels.

Common spatial pattern patch (CSPP) proposed in [16,17] apply CSP to the subsets of channels (patch). With reduced number of parameters to estimate due to the localized covariance matrix, CSPP reduced the risk of overfitting. In [12], locally generated common spatial pattern (LRCSP) is proposed to use local CSPs generated from each individual channel and its neighboring channels (local region) rather than global CSP generated from entire channels and several selection rules for good local regions to improve the overall performance.

On the other hand, there have been an approach to utilize covariance matrices directly to extract features. Since covariance matrices are symmetric positive definite (SPD) matrices, it is natural to consider the geometrical structure of SPD set, which is a Riemannian manifold. In [3] the use of minimum Riemannian distance to Riemannian mean (MDRM) of covariance matrices is proposed. MDRM exhibits comparable performance to the standard CSP. In [3] Riemannian tangent space linear discriminant analysis method (TSLDA) that maps covariance matrices onto the tangent space to apply linear discriminant analysis (LDA) is proposed. TSLDA outperforms standard CSP and MDRM. The additional advantage of this method is that conventional classification algorithms can replace LDA, since the tangent space is Euclidean space.

In this paper, we attempt to exploit the advantage of both local region approach and Riemannian approach to improve MI classification performance. In contrast to the existing Riemannian approach, we utilizes the vectorized log Riemannian distance matrices (LRDM) generated in local region. By using all coefficients of LRDM instead of the norm of LRDM as features, the classification performance has been improved. Furthermore, in order to select the optimal local regions with respect to the local LRDM features, we defined a criterion called confusion area score that computes the smallest normalized difference between averaged Riemann distance to the Riemannian mean and the minimum Riemann distance to the Riemannian mean among two classes. We selected the local regions with empirically determined 20% of the lowest confusion area score and cascaded the LRDM in selected regions. The proposed method is evaluated using BCI Competition III dataset IVa and BCI Competition IV dataset I. The results confirm performance improvement of the proposed method.

This paper is organized as follows. In Sect. 2, local region and local covariance matrix, review of log Riemannian distance matrix, local region selection and forming feature vector are described. Section 3 provides the data and experiments. Section 4 analyzes the results. Finally, Sect. 5 is conclusion.

2   Method

The block diagram in Fig. 1 illustrates the process of the proposed method. Consider a N-channel, spatial-temporal EEG data. First, we define a set of channels for each channel, namely local region, by grouping the channel and its

Training phase

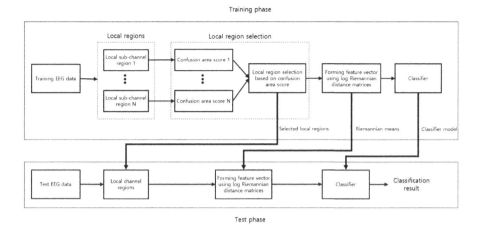

Test phase

Fig. 1. Process of the proposed method

neighbor channels. Second, local regions are selected by a novel criteria, confusion area score. Third, LRDM are generated from the selected local regions and used to form feature vector. Then, the feature vectors are used as input to support vector machine (SVM) classifier.

Note that there are three arrows between the training phase and the test phase in Fig. 1. First, the list of local regions selected in the training phase is saved to select same local regions in the test phase. Second, Riemannian means from the selected local regions, which are obtained in the training phase, are kept in memory and reused to calculate Riemannian distance matrices in the test phase. Third, the trained classifier model is transferred to the test phase to classify test trials.

2.1   Local Region and Local Covariance Matrix

Let $X \in \mathbb{R}^{N \times T}$ denote the bandpass filtered EEG measurement, where N is the number of channel and T is the number of EEG time sample per channel. For each channel $n = 1, ..., N$, we define a set of channels, denoted by $R_n \subset \{1, 2, ..., N\}$, consisting of central channel n and its adjacent channels. The set R_n is termed as a local sub-channel region of n, or shortly the local region n. Let $|R_n|$ denote the number of channels in R_n, it may vary according to the central channel n. The examples in Fig. 2 illustrates for $N = 118$. Note that the local regions are allowed to share channels. Let $X^{(n)} \in \mathbb{R}^{|R_n| \times T}$ denote the EEG data for channels in the local region n. Assume that K trials of training EEG data are available, $X_i \in \mathbb{R}^{N \times T}, i = 1, ..., K$. Since we consider the binary MI classification, each trial belongs to one of the two index sets L_1 and L_2, indicating class 1 and 2 ($L_1 \cap L_2 = \emptyset, L_1 \cup L_2 = \{1, ..., K\}$). Let $X_i^{(n)} \in \mathbb{R}^{|R_n| \times T}$ denote the i-th trial of local region n. The covariance matrix of $X_i^{(n)}$, termed local covariance matrix, is given by:

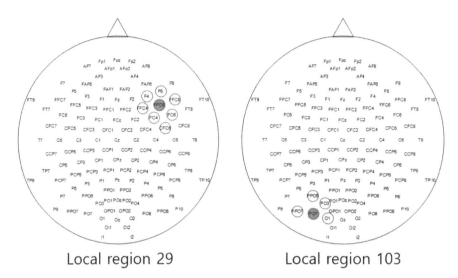

Local region 29   Local region 103

Fig. 2. Examples of local region ($N = 118$). The marked channels indicate local region. The channel filled in red indicates the central channel of local region. (Color figure online)

$$C_i^{(n)} = \frac{1}{T} X_i^{(n)} X_i^{(n)\top} \tag{1}$$

2.2 Review of Log Riemannian Distance Matrix

In this section, we briefly introduce three terminologies in Riemannian manifolds of SPD matrices used in this paper; Riemannian distance, log Riemannian distance matrix and Riemannian mean.

Riemannian Distance. The Riemannian distance between two covariance matrices C_i and C_j is given by [13]:

$$d_R(C_i, C_j) = ||\mathrm{Log}(C_j^{-1/2} C_i C_j^{-1/2})||_F \tag{2}$$

where $|| \cdot ||_F$ is the Frobenius norm and Log is the matrix logarithm operator. For SPD matrix $A = PDP^\top \in \mathbb{R}^{N \times N}$, the matrix logarithm of A is given by [13]:

$$\mathrm{Log}(A) = P \begin{bmatrix} \log d_{11} & \cdots & 0 \\ \vdots & \ddots & \vdots \\ 0 & \cdots & \log d_{NN} \end{bmatrix} P^\top \tag{3}$$

Log Riemannian Distance Matrix. Before introducing log Riemannian distance matrix (LRDM), we first introduce Riemannian distance matrix. The Riemannian distance matrix between two covariance matrices C_i and C_j is given by [6]:

$$\Delta(C_i, C_j) = C_j^{-1/2} C_i C_j^{-1/2} \tag{4}$$

Riemannian distance matrix contains not only information about distance but also directional information in the manifold. The Riemannian distance between C_i and C_j equals the Riemannian distance between the Riemannian distance matrix $D = \Delta(C_i, C_j)$ and the identity matrix I, $d_R(C_i, C_j) = d_R(D, I)$.

The LRDM between C_i and C_j is defined as:

$$\Delta_{log}(C_i, C_j) = \text{Log}(\Delta(C_i, C_j)) \tag{5}$$

Note that LRDM is symmetric but not positive definite. Therefore LRDM lies in Euclidean space.

Riemannian Mean. The Riemannian mean of given covariance matrices $C_i, i = 1, ..., K$ is given by [13]:

$$M = \arg\min_M \sum_{i=1}^{K} d_R^2(C_i, M) \tag{6}$$

Note that there is no closed form solution for mean computation, when $K > 2$. We used the iterative algorithm to obtain Riemannian mean [6,13]:

1. Initialize $M = \frac{1}{K} \sum_{i=1}^{K} C_i$
2. Update M using update Eq. (7)

$$M \leftarrow M^{1/2} \text{Exp}[\frac{1}{K} \sum_{i=1}^{K} \text{Log}(M^{-1/2} C_i M^{-1/2})] M^{1/2} \tag{7}$$

3. Repeat step 2 until convergence or, equivalently, when Eq. 8 is satisfied.

$$|| \sum_{i=1}^{K} \text{Log}(M^{-1/2} C_i M^{-1/2}) ||_F < \epsilon \tag{8}$$

where Exp is the matrix exponential operator. Calculating the exponential of a diagonalizable matrix is similar with Eq. 3. Note that the iterative algorithm uses LRDM.

2.3   Local Region Selection

To select optimal local region of which feature contributes to improve classification performance, we introduce a new criteria, confusion area score based on Riemannian distances.

For a local region n, we computes class-dependent Riemannian means $M_1^{(n)}$ and $M_2^{(n)}$ using Eq. 6. For a class $l \in \{1, 2\}$, let $v_l^{(n)}$ denote the averaged Riemannian distance between $M_l^{(n)}$ and a local covariance matrix which belongs to same class l:

$$v_l^{(n)} = \frac{1}{|L_l|} \sum_{i \in L_l} d_R(C_i^{(n)}, M_l^{(n)}) \tag{9}$$

Let $p_l^{(n)}$ denote the minimum Riemannian distance between $M_l^{(n)}$ and a local covariance matrix which belongs to the other class:

$$p_l^{(n)} = \min_{i \in L_l{}^c} d_R(C_i^{(n)}, M_l^{(n)}) \tag{10}$$

We consider the difference value of $v_l^{(n)} - p_l^{(n)}$ as the overlap between class-dependent distributions of Riemannian distance. The lower the difference value, the smaller the overlap. Note that the difference value can be negative which indicates the class-dependent distributions are well separable. We define the difference value normalized by Riemannian distance between $M_1^{(n)}$ and $M_2^{(n)}$ as the confusion area score:

$$g_l^{(n)} = \frac{v_l^{(n)} - p_l^{(n)}}{d_R(M_1^{(n)}, M_2^{(n)})} \tag{11}$$

For each local region, there are two confusion area score depending on the class. We choose the minimum valued score as the confusion area score of the local region n:

$$g^{(n)} = \min\{g_1^{(n)}, g_2^{(n)}\} \tag{12}$$

Local regions with low confusion area score are expected to generate discriminative feature for MI classification. Finally, we list the confusion area score in ascending order and selected first 20% of listed local regions as optimal local region set. The number 20% is empirically determined. Table 1 shows the classification accuracy by percentage on the BCI Competition III dataset IVa. The numbers in parentheses are those of selected local regions.

Table 1. Classification accuracy by percentage for local region selection on BCI Competition III dataset IVa

Subject	10% (12)	20% (24)	30% (35)	40% (47)
al	**100**	**100**	**100**	**100**
aa	75.89	**78.57**	77.68	**78.57**
av	67.86	**76.02**	**76.02**	73.98
aw	95.09	95.09	**95.54**	92.86
ay	**91.67**	90.08	88.10	85.32
mean	86.10	**87.95**	87.47	86.15

2.4   Forming Feature Vector

For each selected local region, we compute Riemannian mean $M^{(n)}$ using training local covariance matrices $C_i^{(n)}, i = 1, ..., K$. Then, we generate local LRDM $Z_i^{(n)}$ using the Riemannian mean $M^{(n)}$.

$$Z_i^{(n)} = \Delta_{log}(C_i^{(n)}, M^{(n)}) \tag{13}$$

For classification we need a vector representation. Since $Z_i^{(n)}$ is symmetric, it can be represented using only diagonal and upper diagonal elements (the number of meaningful elements is $|R_n|(|R_n| + 1)/2)$ [13]. For symmetric matrix $Z \in \mathbb{R}^{N \times N}$, the vectorization operator is defined as:

$$\text{vec}(Z) = [z_{11} \ \sqrt{2}z_{12} \ \sqrt{2}z_{13} \ ... \ z_{22} \ \sqrt{2}z_{23} \ ... \ z_{NN}]^{\top} \qquad (14)$$

Note that the Euclidean norm of vectorized LRDM equals Riemannian distance.

$$||\text{vec}(Z_i^{(n)})||_2 = d_R(C_i^{(n)}, M^{(n)}) \qquad (15)$$

Finally, we concatenate all vectorized selected local LRDM to form feature vector for classifier.

3   Data and Experiments

The performance of our proposed method is evaluated using BCI Competition III dataset IVa [1] and BCI Competition IV dataset I [4]. The BCI Competition III dataset IVa consists of motor imagery EEG signals for two classes(right hand and foot) recorded from five healthy subjects('al', 'aa', 'aw', 'av' and 'ay') using 118 channels ($N = 118$). 280 trials were provided per subject and 140 trials were equally provided per class. The number of training/test data for each subject is shown in Table 2. Downsampled signals 100 Hz have been used. Detailed information of the dataset can be found in [5].

The BCI Competition IV dataset I was recorded from seven subjects and contains two classes. All subjects performed 200 trials, i.e., 100 trials per class. The EEG signal was recorded from 59 channels ($N = 59$) at a sampling rate of 1000 HzHz and bandpass-filtered between 0.05Hz 200 Hz. We used the downsampled signal 100 Hz.

For the experiments, EEG signal was used from 0.5 to 3 s after the cue and bandpadss filtered with 9-30Hz using the 4th order Butterworth filter.

In order to ensure positive definite matrices, we conducted sanity check for covariance matrices and filter fiftieth trial of subject 'av'. We found that one of the channels recorded fixed value, resulting a non-positive definite matrix. In this study, we use SVM as classifier and feature vectors formed by local LRDM as inputs.

Table 2. The number of training/test data on BCI Competition III dataset IVa

Subject	Training data	Test data
al	224	56
aa	168	112
av	84	196
aw	56	224
ay	28	252

4   Result and Discussion

The performance of the proposed method is compared with R-CSP [10], FBCSP [2], SBRCSP [11], LRCSP [12], MDRM [3] and TSLDA [3], using BCI Competition III dataset IVa. Table 3 shows the classification results of both algorithm for each subject in the perspective of accuracy rate. As shown in Table 3, mean classification accuracy improvements of 14.81%, 7.36%, 4.86%, 3.49%, 8.90% and 1.16% are achieved compared to R-CSP, FBCSP, SBRCSP, LRCSP, MDRM and TSLDA. Except for the subject 'aa', the accuracy is 8.04% lower than SBRCSP, the proposed method yields the highest classification accuracy in all subjects. Especially, for the subjects 'av', 'aw' and 'ay' in the small sample setting (SSS) environment that consists of small training data, the accuracy is significantly improved relative to conventional MI classification method. Figure 3 shows the locations of central channel of local region in the optimal local region set. The number of channels in the optimal local region set for subjects 'al', 'aa', 'av', 'aw' and 'ay' are 32, 31, 50, 38 and 32, respectively.

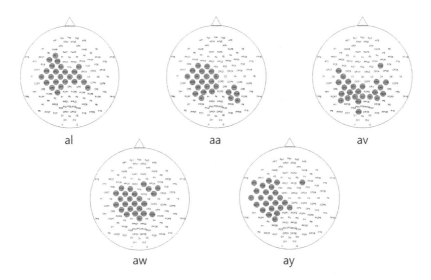

Fig. 3. Central channel location of selected local regions by the proposed method for five subjects

For reliability and robustness, we also evaluate the performance of the proposed method using BCI Competition IV dataset I. Table 4 shows the 10 × 10 cross validation classification accuracy of CSP-TSM [7], SBLFB [18], TFPO-CSP [8], I-DFBCSP [9] and the proposed method. The proposed method shows higher classification accuracy than other MI classification algorithms in this evaluation. CSP-TSM extracts Riemannian tangent space mapping(TSM) features from the spatial filtered EEG signal, fuses it with CSP variance features and performs feature selection. The proposed method solely depends on Riemannian geometry to generate features and to select important feature, and shows higher performance than CSP-TSM. SBLFB utilizes sparse Bayesian learning to extract significant features with a linear discriminant criterion and TFPO-CSP exploits temporal filter parameter optimization to achieve performance improvement. I-DFBCSP uses discriminative filter bank selection based on mutual information. I-DFBCSP shows a mean classification accuracy of 82.3% which is higher than CSP-TSM, SBLFB and TFPO-CSP. However, the proposed method achieves the highest mean classification accuracy.

Table 3. Classification accuracy on BCI Competition III dataset IVa

Subject	R-CSP	FBCSP	SBRCSP	LRCSP	MDRM	TSLDA	Proposed method
al	85.71	98.21	98.21	**100**	98.21	98.21	**100**
aa	74.11	80.36	**86.61**	74.11	65.18	83.04	78.57
av	58.16	61.73	63.78	67.85	68.88	70.41	**76.02**
aw	72.32	88.84	89.05	90.07	77.68	94.20	**95.09**
ay	75.40	73.81	77.78	89.29	85.32	88.10	**90.08**
mean	73.14	80.59	83.09	84.46	79.05	86.79	**87.95**

Table 4. 10 × 10 Cross-validation classification accuracy on BCI Competition IV dataset I

Subject	CSP-TSM	SBLFB	TFPO-CSP	I-DFBCSP	Proposed method
a	88.1 ± 6.6	80.9 ± 9.73	87.5 ± 4.68	85.7 ± 9.26	$\mathbf{92.3 \pm 5.47}$
b	59.1 ± 10.62	58.5 ± 11.12	55 ± 3.26	57 ± 10.74	$\mathbf{69.2 \pm 8.76}$
c	67.9 ± 8.7	66.8 ± 12.53	67.5 ± 7.45	$\mathbf{69 \pm 9.85}$	68.15 ± 7.9
d	84.3 ± 7.9	88.5 ± 7.91	85 ± 8.66	$\mathbf{93.4 \pm 5.57}$	88.3 ± 7.31
e	90.2 ± 5.8	88.4 ± 6.88	87.5 ± 7.17	91.9 ± 6.92	$\mathbf{92.45 \pm 4.99}$
f	85.9 ± 7.1	78.8 ± 11.98	85 ± 4.81	86.6 ± 8.48	$\mathbf{89.6 \pm 7.4}$
g	92.2 ± 5.7	94.1 ± 5.41	92.5 ± 7.2	92.8 ± 5.26	$\mathbf{94.65 \pm 4.95}$
mean	81.1 ± 7.4	79.4 ± 9.36	80 ± 6.18	82.3 ± 8.01	$\mathbf{84.95 \pm 6.68}$

5   Conclusion

We proposed a novel MI classification method exploiting the advantage of both local region approach and Riemannian approach. We generated local regions for each channel and ranked them by confusion area score which is designed using Riemannian distance and Riemannian mean. In order to improve performance, we selected local regions with 20% of the lowest confusion area score. Then, we concatenated the log Riemannian distance matrices in the selected local region. The proposed method substantially outperforms existing methods in terms of classification accuracy on BCI Competition III dataset IVa. For reliability and robustness, the proposed method is also evaluated on BCI Competition IV dataset I and the results confirm performance improvement compared to conventional methods.

Acknowledgements. This work was partly supported by Institute of Information & communications Technology Planning & Evaluation (IITP) grant funded by the Korea government (MSIT) (No. 2017-0-00432, Development Of Non-invasive Integrated BCI SW Platform To Control Home Appliance And External Devices By User's Thought Via AR/VR Interface), Institute for Information & communications Technology Planning & Evaluation (IITP) grant funded by the Korea government (MSIT) (No. 2017-0-00451, Development of BCI based Brain and Cognitive Computing Technology for Recognizing User's Intentions using Deep Learning) and Institute of Information & communications Technology Planning & Evaluation (IITP) grant funded by the Korea government(MSIT) (No. 2019-0-00079, Artificial Intelligence Graduate School Program(Korea University)).

References

1. Data Set IVa for the BCI Competition III. https://www.bbci.de/competition/iii/desc_IVa.html, Accessed 15 July 2017
2. Ang, K.K., Chin, Z.Y., Zhang, H., Guan, C.: Filter bank common spatial pattern (FBCSP) in brain-computer interface. In: 2008 IEEE International Joint Conference on Neural Networks (IEEE World Congress on Computational Intelligence), pp. 2390–2397. IEEE (2008)
3. Barachant, A., Bonnet, S., Congedo, M., Jutten, C.: Multiclass brain-computer interface classification by Riemannian geometry. IEEE Trans. Biomed. Eng. **59**(4), 920–928 (2011)
4. Blankertz, B., Dornhege, G., Krauledat, M., Müller, K.R., Curio, G.: The non-invasive Berlin brain-computer interface: fast acquisition of effective performance in untrained subjects. NeuroImage **37**(2), 539–550 (2007)
5. Blankertz, B., et al.: The BCI competition III: validating alternative approaches to actual BCI problems. IEEE Trans. Neural Syst. Rehabil. Eng. **14**(2), 153–159 (2006)
6. Congedo, M., Sherlin, L.: EEG source analysis: methods and clinical implications. In: Neurofeedback and Neuromodulation Techniques and Applications, pp. 25–433. Elsevier (2011)
7. Kumar, S., Mamun, K., Sharma, A.: CSP-TSM: optimizing the performance of Riemannian tangent space mapping using common spatial pattern for MI-BCI. Comput. Biol. Med. **91**, 231–242 (2017)
8. Kumar, S., Sharma, A.: A new parameter tuning approach for enhanced motor imagery EEG signal classification. Med. Biol. Eng. Comput. **56**(10), 1861–1874 (2018). https://doi.org/10.1007/s11517-018-1821-4
9. Kumar, S., Sharma, A., Tsunoda, T.: An improved discriminative filter bank selection approach for motor imagery EEG signal classification using mutual information. BMC Bioinf. **18**(16), 125–137 (2017)
10. Lu, H., Plataniotis, K.N., Venetsanopoulos, A.N.: Regularized common spatial patterns with generic learning for EEG signal classification. In: 2009 Annual International Conference of the IEEE Engineering in Medicine and Biology Society, pp. 6599–6602. IEEE (2009)

11. Park, S.H., Lee, S.G.: Small sample setting and frequency band selection problem solving using subband regularized common spatial pattern. IEEE Sensors J. **17**(10), 2977–2983 (2017)
12. Park, Y., Chung, W.: BCI classification using locally generated CSP features. In: 2018 6th International Conference on Brain-Computer Interface (BCI), pp. 1–4. IEEE (2018)
13. Pennec, X., Fillard, P., Ayache, N.: A Riemannian framework for tensor computing. Int. J. Comput. Vision **66**(1), 41–66 (2006)
14. Ramadan, R.A., Vasilakos, A.V.: Brain computer interface: control signals review. Neurocomputing **223**, 26–44 (2017)
15. Ramoser, H., Muller-Gerking, J., Pfurtscheller, G.: Optimal spatial filtering of single trial EEG during imagined hand movement. IEEE Trans. Rehabil. Eng. **8**(4), 441–446 (2000)
16. Sannelli, C., Vidaurre, C., Müller, K.R., Blankertz, B.: Common spatial pattern patches-an optimized filter ensemble for adaptive brain-computer interfaces. In: 2010 Annual International Conference of the IEEE Engineering in Medicine and Biology, pp. 4351–4354. IEEE (2010)
17. Sannelli, C., Vidaurre, C., Müller, K.R., Blankertz, B.: Common spatial pattern patches: online evaluation on BCI-naive users. In: 2012 Annual International Conference of the IEEE Engineering in Medicine and Biology Society, pp. 4744–4747. IEEE (2012)
18. Zhang, Y., Wang, Y., Jin, J., Wang, X.: Sparse Bayesian learning for obtaining sparsity of EEG frequency bands based feature vectors in motor imagery classification. Int. J. Neural Syst. **27**(02), 1650032 (2017)

Distance-GCN for Action Recognition

Haetsal Lee[1], Junghyun Cho[2], Ig-jae Kim[2], and Unsang Park[1(✉)]

[1] Sogang University, Seoul 04107, Korea
{HaetsalLee,UnsangPark}@sogang.ac.kr
[2] Korea Institute of Science and Technology, Seoul 02792, Korea
{jhcho,drjay}@kist.re.kr

Abstract. Many skeleton-based action recognition models have been introduced with the application of graph convolutional networks (GCNs). Most of the models suggested new ways to aggregate adjacent joints information. In this paper, we propose a novel way to define the adjacency matrix from the geometrical distance between joints. By combining this method with the formerly used adjacency matrix, we can increase the performances of graph convolution layers with slightly increased computational complexity. Experiments on two large-scale datasets, NTU-60 and Skeletics-152, demonstrate that our model provides competitive performance.

Keywords: Skeleton-based action recognition · Graph convolutional networks (GCNs) · Dynamic adjacency matrix generation

1 Introduction

Video understanding is an important task with many real-world applications. In particular, human action recognition is receiving increasing attention due to its simplicity and various applications in surveillance, elder care, human-computer interfaces, and entertainment systems. RGB video and depth map-based video classification models [7, 29, 30, 34], have been extensively studied recently. While they provide satisfactory performance for general action recognition, they require heavy computational power to be operated. RGB-based models are also affected by noise from various environmental issues such as illumination and background. Moreover, as a lightweight and decent human pose estimator [1, 26] is developed, accessibility to human skeleton data has been made easy. Therefore, instead of using RGB data for action recognition, we focus on skeleton data in this work.

While convolution neural networks (CNNs) successfully perform input data on grid structures such as images, videos, and audio, applying CNNs to graph data is not straightforward. When we focus on fundamental elements of each data type, say pixels on an image, we have a fixed number of 8 neighbors except at corners and edges. On the other hand, there is no fixed number of neighbors. CNNs have kernels that can be applied to grid data. How to aggregate information to extract deep features using CNNs from graph data has been researched extensively over the years [5, 6, 10, 20, 21, 37].

C. Wallraven et al. (Eds.): ACPR 2021, LNCS 13188, pp. 170–181, 2022.
https://doi.org/10.1007/978-3-031-02375-0_13

Especially for human action recognition, many methods for generating pseudoimages from skeleton data have been developed to feed nongrid skeleton graph data as CNN inputs [4,13,18,33]. Colored maps and projecting the temporal trajectory of whole body joints are encoded into a 2D image with three viewpoints [33], rank-pooling [8] is applied along the temporal axis of joints [18], and colormaps are encoded each joint along the temporal axis [4] similar to [33]. The weakness of pseudoimage-based action recognition is that convolutional operations are only applied to neighboring joints, as they are represented as images on a grid. That is, although there are many joint combinations to consider together, only three joints are considered when we convolve with a kernel size of 3. To alleviate this problem, while using VGG [28]-like CNN architectures [16] intermediate layers were modified to swap channel and joint axes from $T \times V \times C$ to $T \times C \times V$. This swapping method leads to significant performance improvement without additional cost, and it shows that nonlocal operation on a wide range of neighboring joints is important for action recognition.

From the above observation, action recognition with graph neural networks (GCNs) has been explored extensively [3,19,24,25,36]. ST-GCN [36], an extension of GCN [14] developed a subset partitioning method to divide neighboring joints into groups in the spatial domain and used a 1D convolutional layer to capture the dynamics of each joint in the temporal domain. A learnable adjacency matrix is made by applying the outer product on intermediate features and combining them [24,25] with the one used in ST-GCN. In [19], they extended the adjacency matrix to temporal directions to capture more comprehensive ranges of spatiotemporal nodes. Inspired by shift CNNs [12,35,38], Shift-CNN plugged the shifting mechanism instead of utilizing the adjacency matrix in aggregating features. From previous research on GCNs in action recognition, we can say that designing an adjacency matrix takes a critical effect on performance.

In this paper, we address the issue of making a more flexible way of generating an adjacency matrix. First, we propose a new distance-based graph convolutional layer that compares geometrical distances between nodes and filters the neighboring nodes with ranges. Second, we propose a jointwise, subsetwise, and channelwise attention mask to focus on important features between nodes. Remarkably, our proposed skeleton action recognition model achieves competitive results on the NTU-60 [23] dataset and outperforms state-of-the-art models on Skeletics-152 [9]. The main contributions of this work are summarized as follows:

(i) We propose a new adjacency matrix generation method by comparing the geometrical distance between nodes with learnable sets of ranges. We experimented with three settings: a) static ranges, which are decided manually from dataset statistics, b) learnable ranges shared between layers, and c) per-layer learnable ranges.

(ii) We propose to use an attention multiplication mask before aggregating subset features, which was just averaged in the previous models.

2   Distance Graph Convolutional Networks

Since graph convolutional networks have been successfully adopted for skeleton-based human action recognition, many variants have been suggested. Some researchers have suggested making a new adjacency matrix. This means partitioning 1-neighbor nodes into three subsets [36], extending concepts of adjacency over many frames [19] and inferring a data-adaptive adjacency matrix. Others suggested inserting new modules attending along each axis of the input tensor [25] or adopting a new temporal module [22]. In this section, we explain how graph convolutional networks (GCNs) work given skeleton data, how to compose the adjacency matrix used for aggregation, and how to convolve the skeleton joints.

2.1   Graph Construction

The skeleton data, which are inferred from depth [26] or RGB [1] images have a natural edge representation which are physical connections between joints. From those joint connectivities, we can define a graph $\mathbb{G} = (\mathbb{V}, \mathbb{E})$, where $\mathbb{V} = \{v_i\}$ as joint coordinates and $\mathbb{E} = \{\lambda(v_i, v_j)\}$ as connectivity between two joint vertices calculated by a rule function λ. Traditional GCNs for action recognition as ST-GCN [36] adopted a binary function as λ, which outputs 1 if two vertices are 1-hop distance and 0 otherwise. Furthermore, among close joints, they divided joints into at most three subsets, i.e., 1, 2, and 3, 'itself', 'close to the center' and 'far from the center', respectively. This kind of subset partitioning strategy can be understood as a shape of the kernel in CNNs. By increasing the number of adjacent sets into three subsets, which are referred to as unilabeling and spatial configuration, the performance of ST-GCN was increased over 50%. From the observed performance improvement of ST-GCN, we devised a new way to partition adjacent vertices depending on the geometrical distance between joints. Figure 1 shows subset partitioning for each suggested strategy visually.

Distance-Based Adjacency. Our method, distance-based adjacency represents a level of connectivity between two joints as geometrical distance. At each layer of distance graph convolution, R sets of start($s_{r,s}$) and end($e_{r,s}$) ranges are defined. The distance normalization function $\bar{d}$ and weight function λ are defined as follows:

$$\lambda(v_i, v_j) = \sigma(\bar{d}_r(v_i, v_j)) \tag{1}$$

$$\bar{d}_r(v_i, v_j) = \begin{cases} \frac{\min(\|v_{ij}\| - s_r, \|v_{ij}\| - e_r)}{2}, & \text{if } s_r \leq \|v_{ij}\| \leq e_r \\ 0, & \text{otherwise} \end{cases} \tag{2}$$

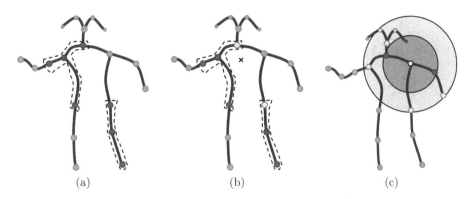

Fig. 1. Proposed adjacency partitioning strategies. From left to right: **(a)** Unilabeling, **(b)** spatial configuration, and **(c)** distance Strategy. The node of interest is highlighted in yellow. The first and second subsets are colored green and purple, respectively. The center of the nodes used for (b) is marked as ✖. Note that our method (c) has no restriction of 1-hop distance on the physical graph differently from (a) and (b). In (c), two different ranges and corresponding included joints are shown in different colors.

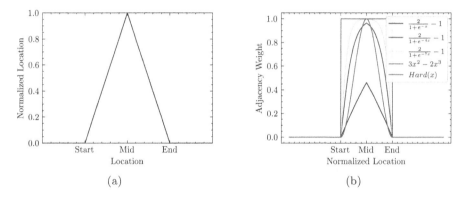

Fig. 2. **(a)** Distance normalization function $\bar{d}$ and **(b)** sets of range activation functions λ. The distance normalization function returns the largest value at the middle of the range. Consequently, the activation function also obtains the largest value at the middle of the ranges.

As shown in Fig. 2, given a range and a distance, the range-activation function λ returns a positive weight of the connection if and only if a distance is in the range and zero elsewhere. We compared the performance of five different types of range-activation functions (4 types of sigmoid functions and binary functions). The results of the comparison are shown in Sect. 3.3.

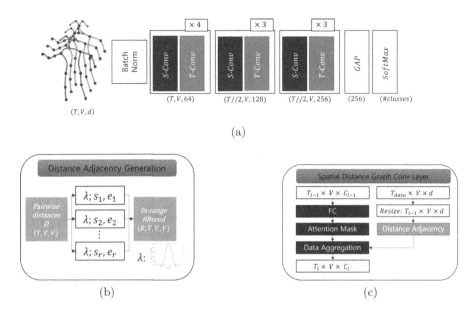

(a)

(b)   (c)

Fig. 3. (a) The whole model of our Distance-GCN. There are three stages of feature channels, and a number of frames are halved as stages change. Kernel size 9 is used for temporal 1D convolution. If there is more than one human, they are averaged in the GAP module. **(b)** Adjacency matrix generation module. It calculates the pairwise distance between joints and weights are calculated by range activation λ with R distance ranges in an elementwise manner. **(c)** The spatial distance convolutional layer obtains not only features from the previous layer but also raw initial coordinates. Raw coordinates are resized to meet the temporal size of input features and passed by (b).

2.2 Graph Convolution

Given a graph G that is constructed with an arbitrary strategy, multiple spatial graph convolutional layers and temporal 1D convolutional layers are applied to the input data $(M \times V \times T \times C)$ to extract high-dimensional complex features. Global average pooling (GAP) is applied over features, and then the *softmax* classifier finalizes the prediction task. For spatial graph convolution, the operation is formulated as the following equation:

$$f_{out}(v_i) = \sum_{v_j \in B(v_i)} f_{in}(v_j) \cdot \lambda(v_i, v_j) \tag{3}$$

2.3 Subset Attention Mask Module

Due to many observed performance improvements with the attention mechanism [11,17,25,27,31,32], we also devised an attention module. To make an attention module as light as possible, we adopted a simple static multiplication mask. Our mask module is a subset, vertex, and channelwise multiplication mask, which results in consistent performance improvements but with almost zero cost and little increase in weight parameters. The shape of our multiplication mask is $R \times 1 \times V \times C$ for features of $R \times T \times V \times C$ where R is the number of distance-based subsets. Ablation study about our attention mask is at Sect. 3.3

2.4   Full Network Architecture

Distance-GCN comprises 10 layers of interleaving spatial distance graph convolutional layers and temporal 1D convolutional layers followed by a global average pooling, and a softmax layer, as shown in Fig. 3a. Spatial convolution layers use a distance adjacency generation module with the start and end of ranges as parameters.

3   Experiment

3.1   Dataset and Experiment Settings

NTU-60. NTU-60 [23] is a dataset with four kinds of modalities: RGB, depth-map, infrared and 3D skeletons. It contains 56,880 samples with 40 subjects, 3 camera views, and 60 actions. There are two official benchmark train-test splits: (1) cross-subject (CS) (2) cross-view (CV). There are also 2D skeletons that are projected to RGB, depth-map, and infrared from 3D, respectively. 3D skeleton data are represented in meter units, and distances between joints range from 0.001 m to 2.32 m with an average of 0.58 m and std of 0.33 m. All the modalities are captured by a Kinects v2 sensor, and 3D skeletons are inferred from a depth-map [26]. Due to the limitations of a depth-map and ToF sensor, some samples have much noise in skeleton coordinates. The lengths of the samples are at most 300 frames, and the number of people in a view is at most 4. We choose the most active 2 people and 300 frames. Samples with fewer than 300 frames or fewer than 2 people are preprocessed with the method used in [25].

Skeletics-152. Skeletics-152 [9] is a skeleton action dataset extracted from the Kinetics700 [2] dataset with the VIBE [15] pose estimator. Because Kinetics-700 has some activities without a person or impossible to classify without the context of what humans interact with, 152 classes out of 700 classes are chosen to build Skeletics-152. Thanks to the good pose estimation performance of the VIBE pose estimator, unlike NTU-60 skeletons, Skeletics-152 samples have much less noise. The number of people appearing in the samples ranges from 1 to 10, with an average of 2.97 and a standard deviation of 2.8. The length of the samples ranges from 25 frames to 300 frames with an average of 237.8 and a standard deviation of 74.72. We choose at most three people in the samples for all the experiments done in this paper. While NTU-60 contains coordinates of skeleton joints in meter units, Skeletics-152 has normalized values in the range $[0, 1]$. The mean distance between the joints is 0.69, and the std is 0.40. Samples with fewer than 300 frames or fewer than 3 people are padded with zeros, and no further preprocessing is performed for training and testing.

Experimental Settings. We use SGD with Nesterov momentum (0.9) and batch size 64 to train the model for 65 epochs. The learning rate is set to 0.1 and multiplied by 0.1 at epochs 45, 55, and 65. Unless otherwise stated, all experiments are trained using 5 subsets (3 for spatial configuration and 2 for distance ranges) for graph convolution.

3.2   Comparisons of Range Activation Functions

As shown in Fig. 2, adjacency weights are decided by range activation functions. We choose functions with ranges only between 0 and 1. In particular, to test binary settings, the $Hard(x)$ function is used but only tested with the static distance setting. We assumed that the function with a smooth gradient had stable results, but as shown in Table 1, $2\sigma(x) - 1$ had the best performance. We suppose that activation functions with sharp gradients help find the optimal distance ranges better with large gradient steps even at the middle of the ranges.

Table 1. Performance of various range activation functions. All the models were trained with the same initial distance ranges.

Range activation	Distance method	Accuracy (%)
$Hard(x)$	Static distance	84.76
$2\sigma(x) - 1$	Per-layer learnable	**88.05**
$2\sigma(4x) - 1$	Per-layer learnable	87.50
$2\sigma(7x) - 1$	Per-layer learnable	87.29
$3x^3 - 2x^2$	Per-layer learnable	86.40
$ReLu(x)$	Per-layer learnable	87.14

3.3   Ablation Study on Distance Graph and Attention Module

Distance Graph. We experimented with conventional subset partitioning strategies, distance partitioning strategies, and combinations of the aforementioned strategies. Table 2 shows the results of experiments. Although for a single partitioning strategy, we used three subsets for spatial strategies and two subsets for distance strategies, with approximately 2/3 of parameters and computation, the per-layer distance strategy shows the best result. For a combination of two partitioning strategies, it is interesting that the best performance is not from combinations of the bests of each strategy. From the above observations, we choose to use combinations of static-spatial and per-layer distance strategies for the following experiments in this paper.

Subset-Channel-Vertex Attention Module. Table 3 shows the impact of our attention module. From experiments, we can find that there are consistent performance improvements after inserting attention modules except for a static spatial graph.

Table 2. Comparisons of combinations of graph convolutional layer subset partitioning strategies on the NTU-60 CS split.

Static spatial	Learnable spatial	Static distance	Learnable distance	Per-layer learnable distance	Accuracy (%)
✓					85.31
	✓				86.35
		✓			85.59
			✓		86.46
				✓	**87.63**
✓	✓				87.16
✓			✓		85.51
✓			✓		86.61
✓				✓	**88.43**
	✓	✓			86.69
	✓		✓		86.84
	✓			✓	**86.86**

Table 3. The impact of the suggested attention mask on sets of graph convolution partitioning strategies tested on NTU-60 CS. The performances of no attention modules are denoted inside parentheses.

Adjacency method	Accuracy (%)
Static spatial	85.31 (86.61)
Learnable spatial	86.35 (86.26)
Static distance	85.59 (84.78)
Learnable distance	86.46 (86.25)
Per-layer distance	87.63 (87.27)

3.4   Comparisons with the State of the Arts

We compare the final model with the state-of-the-art GCN models on both the NTU-60 dataset and Skeletics-152 dataset. The results of these two comparisons are shown in Table 4 and Table 5, respectively.

Table 4. Comparisons of Top-1 accuracy with the state-of-the art methods on the NTU-60 dataset.

Model	CS (%)	CV (%)	Average (%)
AAGCN [25]	90.0	96.2	93.1
MS-G3D [19]	**91.5**	96.2	**93.9**
ShiftGCN [3]	90.7	**96.5**	93.6
Distance-GCN (ours)	91.1	96.2	93.7

Table 5. Comparisons of Top-1 accuracy with the state-of-the art methods on the Skeletics-152 dataset.

Model	Accuracy (%)
MS-G3D [19]	56.39
ShiftGCN [3]	57.01
Distance-GCN (ours)	**64.93**

3.5 Visualization of Learnt Distance Ranges

We visualize the ranges of distance trained on NTU-60 and Skeletics-152. There are ten distance graph convolutional layers in Distance-GCN, and each layer has two range subsets. As shown in Fig. 4, various types of ranges are learned to extract dynamic features of human activity. Considering that skeleton coordinates of Skeletics-152 are normalized, it seems natural that ranges tend to be concentrated in small areas. On the other hand, learned ranges on NTU-60 cover larger areas. It is worth noting that NTU-60 data of skeleton coordinates are slightly noisy, so to compensate for such errors, it might become larger to capture more adjacent joints.

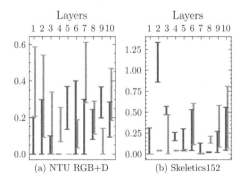

Fig. 4. Visualization of trained ranges for each layer. Green and blue represent the ranges of the first and second subsets, respectively. (Color figure online)

4   Conclusion and Future Work

In this paper, we propose the Distance-GCN, an action recognition network with a new distance-based subset partitioning strategy and attention module. We experimented with various combinations of partitioning strategies and types of range activations. Experimental evaluations on our new model have competitive performances for the NTU-60 dataset and state-of-the-art results on the Skeletics-152 dataset with slight modifications and computational overhead.

The work described in this paper is focused on partitioning schemes only with intraframe joints. We will devise another new method to utilize a learnable partitioning scheme for interframe joints to capture spatiotemporal features.

Acknowledgements. This work was supported by the Institute of Information & communications Technology Planning & Evaluation (IITP) grant funded by the Korea government (MSIT) (No. 2017-0-00162, Development of Human-care Robot Technology for Aging Society, 50%) and the KIST Institutional Program (Project No. 2E31082, 50%).

References

1. Cao, Z., Hidalgo, G., Simon, T., Wei, S.E., Sheikh, Y.: OpenPose: realtime multi-person 2D pose estimation using part affinity fields. IEEE Trans. Pattern Anal. Mach. Intell. **43**(1) (2021). https://doi.org/10.1109/TPAMI.2019.2929257
2. Carreira, J., Noland, E., Hillier, C., Zisserman, A.: A short note on the kinetics-700 human action dataset. arXiv, July 2019. https://arxiv.org/abs/1907.06987v1
3. Cheng, K., Zhang, Y., He, X., Chen, W., Cheng, J., Lu, H.: Skeleton-based action recognition with shift graph convolutional network. In: CVPR, pp. 180–189 (2020). https://doi.org/10.1109/cvpr42600.2020.00026
4. Choutas, V., Weinzaepfel, P., Revaud, J., Schmid, C.: PoTion: pose MoTion representation for action recognition. In: CVPR, pp. 7024–7033 (2018)
5. Defferrard, M., Bresson, X., Vandergheynst, P.: Convolutional neural networks on graphs with fast localized spectral filtering. In: Advances in Neural Information Processing Systems (2016)
6. Duvenaud, D., et al.: Convolutional networks on graphs for learning molecular fingerprints. In: Advances in Neural Information Processing Systems, vol. 2015, January 2015
7. Feichtenhofer, C., Fan, H., Malik, J., He, K.: SlowFast networks for video recognition. CoRR abs/1812.03982 (2018). http://arxiv.org/abs/1812.03982
8. Fernando, B., Gavves, E., Jose Oramas, M., Ghodrati, A., Tuytelaars, T.: Modeling video evolution for action recognition. In: CVPR, pp. 5378–5387. IEEE, June 2015. https://doi.org/10.1109/CVPR.2015.7299176
9. Gupta, P., et al.: Quo Vadis, skeleton action recognition? Int. J. Comput. Vision **129**(7), 2097–2112 (2021). https://doi.org/10.1007/s11263-021-01470-y
10. Henaff, M., Bruna, J., LeCun, Y.: Deep convolutional networks on graph-structured data. CoRR abs/1506.05163 (2015). http://arxiv.org/abs/1506.05163
11. Hu, J., Shen, L., Albanie, S., Sun, G., Vedaldi, A.: Gather-excite: exploiting feature context in convolutional neural networks. In: Advances in Neural Information Processing Systems, vol. 2018, December 2018

12. Jeon, Y., Kim, J.: Constructing fast network through deconstruction of convolution. In: Advances in Neural Information Processing Systems (2018)

13. Ke, Q., Bennamoun, M., An, S., Sohel, F., Boussaid, F.: A new representation of skeleton sequences for 3D action recognition. In: Proceedings - 30th IEEE Conference on Computer Vision and Pattern Recognition, CVPR 2017, January 2017, pp. 4570–4579 (2017). https://doi.org/10.1109/CVPR.2017.486

14. Kipf, T.N., Welling, M.: Semi-supervised classification with graph convolutional networks. In: ICLR, pp. 1–14 (2017)

15. Kocabas, M., Athanasiou, N., Black, M.J.: VIBE: video inference for human body pose and shape estimation. In: Proceedings of the IEEE Computer Society Conference on Computer Vision and Pattern Recognition (2020). https://doi.org/10.1109/CVPR42600.2020.00530

16. Li, C., Zhong, Q., Xie, D., Pu, S.: Co-occurrence feature learning from skeleton data for action recognition and detection with hierarchical aggregation. In: IJCAI, April 2018. http://arxiv.org/abs/1804.06055

17. Liang, L., Cao, J., Li, X., You, J.: Improvement of residual attention network for image classification. In: Cui, Z., Pan, J., Zhang, S., Xiao, L., Yang, J. (eds.) IScIDE 2019. LNCS, vol. 11935, pp. 529–539. Springer, Cham (2019). https://doi.org/10.1007/978-3-030-36189-1_44

18. Liu, M., Yuan, J.: Recognizing human actions as the evolution of pose estimation maps. In: CVPR (2018). https://doi.org/10.1109/cvpr.2018.00127

19. Liu, Z., Zhang, H., Chen, Z., Wang, Z., Ouyang, W.: Disentangling and unifying graph convolutions for skeleton-based action recognition. In: CVPR, pp. 140–149 (2020). https://doi.org/10.1109/cvpr42600.2020.00022

20. Monti, F., Boscaini, D., Masci, J., Rodolà, E., Svoboda, J., Bronstein, M.M.: Geometric deep learning on graphs and manifolds using mixture model CNNs. In: Proceedings - 30th IEEE Conference on Computer Vision and Pattern Recognition, CVPR 2017 (2017). https://doi.org/10.1109/CVPR.2017.576

21. Niepert, M., Ahmad, M., Kutzkov, K.: Learning convolutional neural networks for graphs. In: 33rd International Conference on Machine Learning, ICML 2016, vol. 4 (2016)

22. Obinata, Y., Yamamoto, T.: Temporal extension module for skeleton-based action recognition. In: ICPR (2020). http://arxiv.org/abs/2003.08951

23. Shahroudy, A., Liu, J., Ng, T.T., Wang, G.: NTU RGB+D: a large scale dataset for 3D human activity analysis. In: CVPR, January 2017, pp. 77–85. IEEE, April 2017

24. Shi, L., Zhang, Y., Cheng, J., Lu, H.: Two-stream adaptive graph convolutional networks for skeleton-based action recognition. In: CVPR, pp. 12026–12035, May 2019

25. Shi, L., Zhang, Y., Cheng, J., Lu, H.: Skeleton-based action recognition with multi-stream adaptive graph convolutional networks. IEEE Trans. Image Process. **29**, 9532–9545 (2020). https://doi.org/10.1109/TIP.2020.3028207

26. Shotton, J., et al.: Real-time human pose recognition in parts from single depth images. Commun. ACM **56**(1), 116–124 (2013). https://doi.org/10.1145/2398356.2398381

27. Siegelmann, H.T.: Show, attend and tell: neural image caption generation with visual attention. In: ICML, April 2015. https://arxiv.org/pdf/1502.03044.pdf

28. Simonyan, K., Zisserman, A.: Very deep convolutional networks for large-scale image recognition. In: 3rd International Conference on Learning Representations, ICLR 2015 - Conference Track Proceedings (2015)

29. Tran, D., Bourdev, L., Fergus, R., Torresani, L., Paluri, M.: Learning spatiotemporal features with 3D convolutional networks. In: Proceedings of the IEEE International Conference on Computer Vision (2015). https://doi.org/10.1109/ICCV.2015.510

30. Tran, D., Wang, H., Torresani, L., Ray, J., LeCun, Y., Paluri, M.: A closer look at spatiotemporal convolutions for action recognition. In: CVPR, November 2018. https://doi.org/10.1109/CVPR.2018.00675. http://arxiv.org/abs/1711.11248

31. Vaswani, A., et al.: Attention is all you need. In: NIPS, Neural Information Processing Systems Foundation, December 2017, pp. 5999–6009 (2017)

32. Wang, F., et al.: Residual attention network for image classification. In: Proceedings - 30th IEEE Conference on Computer Vision and Pattern Recognition, CVPR 2017 (2017). https://doi.org/10.1109/CVPR.2017.683

33. Wang, P., Li, W., Li, C., Hou, Y.: Action recognition based on joint trajectory maps with convolutional neural networks. Knowl.-Based Syst. **158**, 43–53 (2018). https://doi.org/10.1016/j.knosys.2018.05.029

34. Wang, P., Li, W., Ogunbona, P., Wan, J., Escalera, S.: RGB-D-based human motion recognition with deep learning: a survey. Comput. Vis. Image Underst. (2018). https://doi.org/10.1016/j.cviu.2018.04.007

35. Wu, B., et al.: Shift: a zero FLOP, zero parameter alternative to spatial convolutions. In: Proceedings of the IEEE Computer Society Conference on Computer Vision and Pattern Recognition (2018). https://doi.org/10.1109/CVPR.2018.00951

36. Yan, S., Xiong, Y., Lin, D.: Spatial temporal graph convolutional networks for skeleton-based action recognition. In: AAAI, pp. 7444–7452 (2018)

37. Zhang, P., Lan, C., Xing, J., Zeng, W., Xue, J., Zheng, N.: View adaptive neural networks for high performance skeleton-based human action recognition. IEEE Trans. Pattern Anal. Mach. Intell. **41**(8), 1963–1978 (2019). https://doi.org/10.1109/TPAMI.2019.2896631. https://arxiv.org/pdf/1804.07453.pdf

38. Zhong, H., Liu, X., He, Y., Ma, Y.: Shift-based primitives for efficient convolutional neural networks. arXiv (2018)

Causal Intervention Learning for Multi-person Pose Estimation

Luhui Yue, Junxia Li, and Qingshan Liu$^{(\boxtimes)}$

B-DAT and CICAEET, School of Automation, Nanjing University of Information
Science and Technology, Nanjing 210044, China
`qsliu@nuist.edu.cn`

Abstract. Most of learning targets for multi-person pose estimation
are based on the likelihood $P(Y|X)$. However, if we construct the causal
assumption for keypoints, named a Structure Causal Model (SCM) for
the causality, $P(Y|X)$ will introduce the bias via spurious correlations
in the SCM. In practice, it appears as that networks may make biased
decisions in the dense area of keypoints. Therefore, we propose a novel
learning method, named Causal Intervention pose Network (CIposeNet).
Causal intervention is a learning method towards solving bias in the
SCM of keypoints. Specifically, under the consideration of causal inference, CIposeNet is developed based on the backdoor adjustment and the
learning target will change into causal intervention $P(Y|do(X))$ instead
of the likelihood $P(Y|X)$. The experiments conducted on multi-person
datasets show that CIposeNet indeed releases bias in the networks.

Keywords: Multi-person pose estimation · Structure Causal Model ·
Biased decision · Causal intervention

1 Introduction

Multi-person pose estimation is an important but challenging task serving for
many application scenarios, such as human-computer interaction [1], person re-
identification [2] and action recognition [3].

Current developments of convolutional neural networks have achieved superior performance in multi-person pose estimation. He et al. [4] propose the Mask
R-CNN for jointly detecting human and localizing keypoints through a single
model. Newell et al. [5] design a novel stacked hourglass network to consolidate
keypoints feature across all scales. Sun et al. [6] propose the High-Resolution Network (HRNet) which fuses multi-stage features from different scales in parallel
and retains the highest resolution at the same time, achieving the state-of-the-art
performance. Almost all of the deep methods lie in designing various structures
to learn the feature representation of keypoints. However, by using HRNet, there
still exist some mistakes. As shown in Fig. 1, some keypoints are missing in the
white circle of predictions, e.g. ankles and knees. It is worth noting that the
missing ones are located in the dense area of keypoints, where HRNet tends to
make biased decisions and thus ignores them in such cases.

© Springer Nature Switzerland AG 2022
C. Wallraven et al. (Eds.): ACPR 2021, LNCS 13188, pp. 182–194, 2022.
https://doi.org/10.1007/978-3-031-02375-0_14

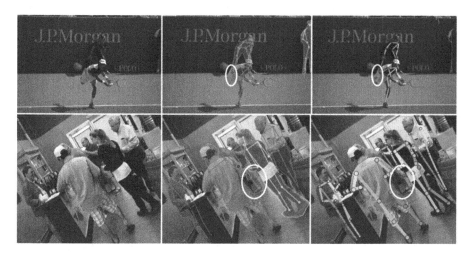

Fig. 1. The mistakes appearing in HRNet. The original image, ground truth and the prediction, denote from the left to the right. The ankle is missing in the white circle of the upper figure while the ankle and the knee are missing in that of lower figure, which indicates that HRNet tends to make biased decisions in the dense area of keypoints and thus ignores ankle.

In this paper, we point out that some networks, such as HRNet, tend to make biased decisions in some situations and propose a novel learning method, named Causal Intervention pose Network (CIposeNet), to release the bias. Under the consideration of causal inference, CIposeNet is developed based on the backdoor adjustment and the learning target changes into causal intervention $P(Y|do(X))$ instead of likelihood $P(Y|X)$, solving bias in the SCM of keypoints. Specifically, the contributions of this work are summarized as follows:

- We find that some networks may tend to make biased decisions in some case and propose the CIposeNet to release the bias in multi-person pose estimation. The theory is based on the assumption of *causalities* [7,8] among keypoints.
- We formulate a Structure Causal Model (SCM) assumption of keypoints, which shows that the class of keypoints is essentially a *confounder* that causes spurious correlations between the keypoints feature and their labels.
- Extensive experiments conducted on multi-person benchmark dataset, MSCOCO keypoint detection dataset, demonstrate that CIposeNet can better release the bias in the network.

2 Related Work

Multi-person Pose Estimation. Multi-person keypoints detection is studied extensively. Compared to single-person scenarios, multi-person pose estimation is relatively challenging due to occlusion and increasingly complex background.

Generally, there are two main solutions to multi-person pose estimation, including bottom-up approaches and top-down methods. Bottom-up approach [9–13] directly localizes all human keypoints and then assembles them into full poses via certain algorithms. DeepCut [12] formulates keypoints association as an Integer Linear Program (ILP). DeeperCut [10] extends the network depth of Deep-Cut via ResNet and further enhances the perfomance of assemble algorithm with image-conditioned pair-wise terms. Cao et al. [9] propose the Part Affinity Fields (PAFs), which assigns the keypoints through vector fields. Newell et al. [11] group the candidate keypoints to a certain human combining the score maps and pixel-wise embeddings. PifPaf [13] detects the keypoints via Part Intensity Field (PIF) and assembles them via the Part Association Field (PAF). Cheng et al. [14] design the HigherHRNet to release the medium and small scale problem in keypoints detection.

Top-down approach [4,6,15,16] interprets the process of detecting keypoints as a two-stage pipeline. It could be summarized that the detect human at first and subsequently feed to the pose estimation network. Papandrou et al. [16] train a network combining the keypoint location and its offset jointly. He et al. [4] propose Mask R-CNN, which detects the bounding box and localizes the keypoints via a unified architecture. Chen et al. [15] design a Cascade Pyramid Network (CPN) which learns the keypoints feature and optimizes the prediction results via two stages. Huang et al. [17] propose the Unbiased Data Processing (UDP) and a new style to encode-decode keypoints. Sun et al. [6] propose the High Resolution Network (HRNet), achieving the state-of-the-art performance, which fuses multi-stage features from different scales in parallel and retains the highest resolution at the same time.

Causal Inference. Causal inference [7,8] is an approach modeling the dependence of data, which aims at inferring how data generation systems behave under conditions changing. Due to causal structure providing the information of distribution and variation, causal inference can be exploited to improve the transferring and generalization ability of a network if the distribution of machine learning changes. Increasing researchers attempt to combine the deep learning with causal inference [18,19] and find the complementary between them. The research is carried out in some semantic scene tasks, including image classification [20,21], reinforcement learning [19,22] and adversarial learning [23,24]. In the task of computer vision, causal inference is mainly exploited as the complementary module of vision, such as visual dialogue [18], image caption [25] and scene graph generation [26]. Wang et al. [27] design the VC R-CNN to learn relationship of classes via causal intervention. Yue et al. [28] apply causal intervention to release the bias in the few shot learning. Tang et al. [26] change the flow of information in the network via counterfactual, leading to more precise predicate of scene graph.

Although current approaches design various structures and reach a better performance, some of them tends to make biased decisions in the dense area of keypoints. Therefore, We propose a novel learning method, named Causal Intervention pose Network (CIposeNet), to release the bias in multi-person pose estimation. The theory is based on the assumption of causalities among keypoints. It is worth noting that CIposeNet is merely an approach to solve bias via causal intervention, which means other alternatives may reach the similar performance as ours.

3 CIposeNet Based Multi-Person Pose Estimation

The first subsection begins with an overview of CIposeNet (Sect. 3.1). The second subsection formulates the causal assumption of keypoints (Sect. 3.2). The third subsection is the backdoor adjustment criterion, which is essentially a causal intervention learning method towards solving bias in the SCM of keypoints (Sect. 3.3).

3.1   Overview

As illustrated in Fig. 2, we summarize the CIposeNet for multi-person pose estimation. CIposeNet takes an image as input and generates feature map from a CNN backbone (e.g. HRNet [6]). Following the standard protocol of multi-person pose estimation, the input is an RGB image of size $3 \times H \times W$. X, Y and D are feature maps extracted from different layers in the network and are fed into three branches. For example, in HRNet, D is selected as the feature maps before 1×1 classification. X is the heatmap of keypoints which can be obtained by the feature maps in the final stage. Y is the final feature map measured by label of keypoints. The do expression is performed on Y and D to produce $\mathbb{E}[g_y(d)]$, where D serving as confounder affects on Y and the effect module is denoted as tensor addition in practice. Finally, X and $\mathbb{E}[g_y(d)]$ are projected to the same space via weight vectors and make final prediction.

3.2   Causal Assumption of Keypoints

In order to deal with the question of causality, we formulate a Structural Causal Model (SCM) [7], which is a way describing the causal assumption of keypoints. Considered that the Y is learned from the feature X and the D is performed as confounder which has influence on both of them. Therefore, the relationship among them can be shown as SCM in left-subfigure of Fig. 3. Specifically, the nodes denote the abstract data variables and the directed edges denote the (functional) causality, $e.g.$, $X \to Y$ denoting that X is the reason and Y is the effect. The right sub-figure describes that all of the keypoints affect on the elbow, where the bounding box in the figure is just used as an indication. There are two main parts in SCM of keypoints.

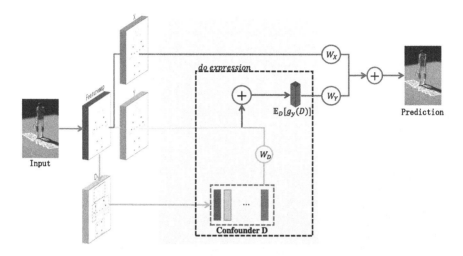

Fig. 2. The overview of CIposeNet. Any CNN-based backbone (*e.g.*, HRNet [6]) can be applied to extract the feature of keypoints. X, Y and D are feature maps extracted from different layers in the network and are fed into three branches. The do expression is performed on Y and D to produce $\mathbb{E}[g_y(d)]$. Finally, X and $\mathbb{E}[g_y(d)]$ are projected to the same space via weight vectors and make final prediction.

(1) $D \to X$. X is defined as the feature representation, denoting the input feature of keypoints. D is confounder defined as cause among observed values. In practice, X and D are feature maps extracted from different layers in the network (e.g. HRNet), where X is the heatmap. In this paper, D is defined as the class of keypoints and can be estimated by the final feature map before 1×1 classification. The connection between D and X denotes the (functional) causality, namely X learned from the D.

(2) $X \to Y \leftarrow D$. Y is defined as prediction feature, denoting the output feature of keypoints. In practice, Y is the label of keypoints in the network (e.g. HRNet). The arrows from X to Y and from D to Y are two (functional) causal connections denoting the flow of information in the network, which indicates that Y is learned by X and D.

3.3   Causal Intervention via Backdoor Adjustment for Keypoints

As shown in Fig. 3 (left), confounder D affects (or causes) X either Y, leading to spurious correlations by only learning from the likelihood $P(Y|X)$, which is expanded via Bayes rules as follows:

$$P(Y|X) = \Sigma_d P(Y|X, d) P(d|X), \tag{1}$$

where $d \in D$ denotes confounder. The connection between confounder D and input feature X introduces the bias via $P(d|X)$, which leads that some networks (e.g. HRNet) make biased decisions in the dense area of keypoints. Therefore,

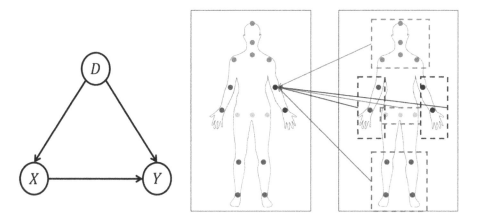

Fig. 3. The causal assumption of keypoints. The left-subfigure denotes a Structural Causal Model (SCM) of keypoints. The right-subfigure describes that all of the keypoints affect on the elbow, where the bounding box in the figure is just used as an indication with avoidance of confusion due to superfluous arrows.

as illustrated in Fig. 4, we propose to break the link of D and X, which is known as the causal intervention in causal inference. Causal intervention can be divided into two types, the randomized controlled trial (RCT) and the backdoor adjustment. RCT is difficult to implement with needing data sample on all condition. Therefore, we usually perform backdoor adjustment instead, denoting as $do - operation$. On the new graph, the causal link between D and X is cut off and the new output is denoted as *causal intervention* $P(Y|do(X))$, which can be expanded via Bayes rules as follows,

$$P(Y|do(X)) = \Sigma_d P(Y|X, d)P(d). \tag{2}$$

Compared with the original form of likelihood, the term $P(d|X)$ changes to the prior $P(d)$ and D no longer influences X. In multi-person pose estimation, causal intervention $P(Y|do(X))$ appears as reassignment of weight on keypoints, which releases biased prediction to a degree. Therefore, the prediction will be more precise based on the $P(Y|do(X))$ in theory.

To implement the theoretical and imaginative causal intervention in Eq. 2, D is approximated to the confounder dictionary $D = [d_1, d_2, \cdots, d_N]$ in the shape of $N \times d$ matrix for practice using, where N is the class of keypoints (e.g. 17 in MSCOCO) and d is the feature dimension of keypoints. Each entry d_i is the channel of feature map denoting i-th keypoint of human. Specifically, given X's keypoits feature x and its class label y. Equation 2 is implemented as $\Sigma_d P(y|x, d)P(d)$. A CNN-based framework can be denoted as function: $P(y|x, d) = f_y(x, d)$, where $f_y(\cdot)$ calculates the heatmap values for N keypoints and the subscript y denotes that $f(\cdot)$ is parameterized by keypoints feature y, motivated by that the prediction for y should be characterized by Y. Therefore, $P(Y|do(X))$ is formulated as follows,

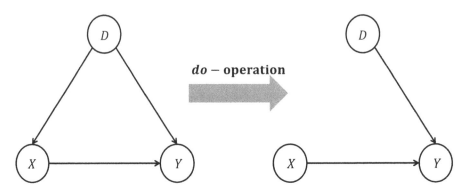

Fig. 4. Causal intervention via backdoor adjustment for keypoints. On the new graph, the causal link between D and X is cut off via $do - operation$.

$$P(Y|do(X)) := \mathbb{E}_d[f_y(x,d)]. \tag{3}$$

The form of the $f(\cdot)$ is various. In this paper, $f(\cdot)$ is selected as linear form, named $f_y(x,d) = W_1 x + W_2 \cdot g_y(d)$, where $W_1, W_2 \in \mathbb{R}^{N \times d}$ are two 1×1 convolution layer and $g_y(d)$ denotes the effect of confounder on input feature. Therefore, Eq. 3 can be derived as follows,

$$\mathbb{E}_d[f_y(x,d)] = W_1 x + W_2 \cdot \mathbb{E}_d[g_y(d)], \tag{4}$$

which denotes Y comes from feature X and confounder D.

To calculate $\mathbb{E}_d[g_y(d)]$, $g_y(d)$ should be computed at first. Under the task of multi-person pose estimation, $g_y(d)$ is the effect of keypoints. Any structure describing the influence of tensor can be utilized as $g_y(d)$. In practise, we have $\mathbb{E}_d[g_y(d)] = \Sigma_d[Y \oplus W_D * D]P(d)$, where $\oplus$ denotes the effect operator and tensor addition is selected in this paper. $P(d)$ is the prior probability of confounder and W_D is a 1×1 convolution layer which maps the dimension of D as the same as Y's. $*$ is the convolution operation. Assuming that keypoints sampling follows uniform distribution, therefore, $P(d) = \frac{1}{N}$, where N is the number of keypoint depending on the dataset.

For example, in HRNet, the variables, $X \in \{x_1, x_2, \cdots, x_N\}$, $Y \in \{y_1, y_2, \cdots, y_N\}$ and $D \in \{d_1, d_2, \cdots, d_N\}$, are selected from the network. X is the heatmap of keypoints which can be obtained by the feature maps in the final stage. It denotes that the relatively specific features of keypoints and enables the network learning increasingly efficient. Y is the feature map measured by label of keypoints, which is adjusted to causal intervention $P(Y|do(X))$ via backdoor adjustment criterion. D can be estimated by the deep semantic feature of keypoints, which is selected as the final feature map before 1×1 classification. The loss of CIposeNet is MSE function, named $\|a - b\|^2$.

4   Experiments

As a result of that mainstream multi-person benchmark is only MSCOCO datatset, we conduct experiments on it to verify to validity of CIposeNet.

4.1   Dataset

The MSCOCO dataset [31] contains over 200,000 images and 250,000 person instances labeled with 17 keypoints. CIposeNet is trained on COCO train2017 dataset, including 57K images and 150K person instances, and evaluate on the val2017 set, containing 5000 images. The standard evaluation metric is based on Object Keypoint Similarity (OKS). Results are reported based on standard average precision (AP) and recall scores (AR).

Table 1. Ablation study of the effect operator. EMAU [29] refers to Expectation-Maximization Attention Unit. Effect operator is not sensitive to the concrete form. Although three types of operators can reach almost the same performance, the parameters and GFLOPS are increased if we employ attention or EMAU.

Variant method	Effect operator	AP	$AP^{.5}$	$AP^{.75}$	AP^M	AP^L	AR
(a)	Attention [30]	75.9	**90.6**	**82.8**	72.0	**82.8**	81.1
(b)	EMAU [29]	75.9	90.4	82.6	72.2	82.7	**81.2**
(c)	Tensor addition	**76.0**	**90.6**	82.7	**72.3**	82.7	81.1

4.2   Ablation Study

The main purpose of ablation study is to clarify that effect operator is not sensitive to the concrete form. In practise, we exploit the tensor addition as effect operator to describe $g_y(d)$, but it's not limited to that. As illustrated in Table 1, three types of effect operators are conducted in CIposeNet, where (a) denotes the attention [30] module. (b) denotes Expectation-Maximization Attention Unit (EMAU) [29] and (c) denotes tensor addition in this paper. Confounder is also presented as channels of feature map in the attention and EMAU, but the effect operator is tensor multiplication. Although three types of operators can reach almost the same performance, the parameters and GFLOPS are greatly increased if we employ attention or EMAU and our laboratory conditions are not allowed CIposeNet to add any other modules in this case. Parameters and GFLOPS are metrics measuring the memory and speed of a model respectively, which is of vital importance for computer. Therefore, we utilize tensor addition operator with less parameters and GFLOPS. If an increasingly complete structure is employed, the better performance of network will be.

Table 2. The results on the MSCOCO validation set. CI refers to CIposeNet.

Method	Back bone	Input size	Params	GFLOPS	AP	$AP^{.5}$	$AP^{.75}$	AP^M	AP^L	AR
Sim. [33]	ResNet -50	256×192	34.0	8.90	70.4	88.6	78.3	67.1	77.2	76.3
Sim. [33]	ResNet -101	256×192	53.0	12.4	71.4	89.3	79.3	68.1	78.1	77.1
Sim. [33]	ResNet -152	256×192	68.6	15.7	72.0	89.3	79.8	68.7	78.9	77.8
Sim. [33]	ResNet -152	384×288	68.6	35.6	74.3	89.6	81.1	70.5	79.7	79.7
HRNet [6]	HRNet -W32	256×192	28.5	7.10	73.4	89.5	80.7	70.2	80.1	78.9
HRNet [6]	HRNet -W32	256×192	28.5	7.10	74.4	90.5	81.9	70.8	81.0	79.8
EM [32]	HRNet -W32	256×192	30.3	7.63	75.0	90.3	82.3	71.7	81.5	80.2
CI	HRNet -W32	256×192	28.5	7.13	**76.0**	**90.6**	**82.7**	**72.3**	**82.7**	**81.1**

Table 3. The results on the MSCOCO test-dev set. CI refers to CIposeNet.

Method	Back bone	Input size	Params	GFLOPS	AP	$AP^{.5}$	$AP^{.75}$	AP^M	AP^L	AR
OpenPose [39]	–	–	–	–	61.8	84.9	67.5	57.1	68.2	66.5
G-RMI [34]	ResNet -101	353×257	42.6	57.0	64.9	85.5	71.3	62.3	70.0	69.7
DGCN [40]	ResNet - 152	641×641	–	–	67.4	88.0	74.4	63.6	73.0	73.2
I.P.R. [35]	ResNet -101	256×256	45.0	11.0	67.8	88.2	74.8	63.9	74.0	–
RMPE [36]	Pyra -Net	320×256	28.1	26.7	72.3	89.2	79.1	68.0	78.6	–
CFN [37]	–	–	–	–	72.6	86.1	69.7	78.3	64.1	–
CPN [38]	ResNet -Inception	384×288	–	–	73.0	91.7	80.9	69.5	78.1	79.0
Sim. [33]	ResNet -152	384×288	68.6	35.6	73.7	91.9	81.1	70.3	80.0	79.0
HRNet [6]	HRNet -W32	256×192	28.5	7.10	73.4	92.3	81.8	69.9	79.2	78.8
EM [32]	HRNet -W32	256×192	30.3	7.63	73.8	**92.3**	82.0	70.4	79.5	79.1
CI	HRNet -W32	256×192	28.5	7.13	**75.0**	**92.3**	**82.3**	**71.6**	**80.8**	**80.1**

4.3   The Results Analysis of CIposeNet

Since the backbone of CIposeNet is selected as HRNet [6], in order to produce a convincing result, the operation on dataset in experiment is motivated by HRNet's. However, the error of flipping in the data processing is corrected via Unbiased Data Processing (UDP) [17], which unifies the metrics between continuous space and discrete one.

Fig. 5. The visualization on MSCOCO dataset. CIposeNet can make more reasonable decisions in the dense area of keypoints.

The results tested on the validation set and test set are reported in Table 2 and Table 3, respectively. As shown in Table 2, CIposeNet achieves **AP76.0%** and **AR81.1%** respectively on MSCOCO validation set. Compared to the performance of **AP74.4%** and **AR79.8%** in HRNet, CIposeNet obtains **AP1.6%** and **AR1.3%** gains respectively, which indicates CIposeNet indeed releases the bias in HRNet. Compared with EMpose [32], CIposeNet obtains **AP1.0%** and **AR0.9%** gains respectively as well. EMpose is a method which exploits Expectation Maximization (EM) mapping to learn the constrains within the related keypoints groups, which is a relatively completed framework with less bias. CIposeNet still obtains gains compared to that, which shows it can make the network make more reasonable decisions. As shown in Table 3, CIposeNet can reach **AP75.0%** and **AR80.1%** respectively on MSCOCO test set. The performance of our method is still stronger than HRNet.

Generally, the larger input size can provide higher resolution for networks, which is beneficial for pixel-level prediciton. However, large input size will lead to high storage overhead. As known from Table 3, the performance of CIposeNet with smaller input size is even greater than the approach of Simple Baseline [33] whose input size is 384 × 288. Compared to EMpose, CIposeNet achieves **AP1.2%** and **AR1.0%** gains respectively. Meanwhile, the parameters and GFLOPS obtain $1.8M$ and 0.5 reduce respectively. The learning targets of methods for multi-person pose estimation compared above are based on the likelihood $P(Y|X)$, which introduces the bias via spurious correlation in the SCM. CIposeNet adjusts the connection in the SCM and releases the bias in the some network via causal intervention $P(Y|do(X))$. The last but not the least, the causal intervention strategy is not a additional part in the CIposeNet. Although it seems that the causal intervention is somewhat incremental in the CIposeNet, it is a strategy to solve the bias in the multi-person estimation in fact, which can be exploited in many biased frameworks. From another perspective, in terms of parameters and GFLOPS compared with HRNet, as shown in Table 2 in Sec. 4.3, the number of parameters of CIposNet is 28.5M, which is as the same as HRNet's. Meanwhile, the GFLOPS of HRNet is 7.10 and that of CIposeNet is 7.13, with a negligible gap between them, which is not in the range of module addition magnitude. Therefore, the contribution of us is not incremental to the previous work. The results of visualization on MSCOCO multi-person pose estimation are reported in Fig. 5 and CIposeNet can make more reasonable decisions in the dense area of keypoints, which prove the validity of CIposeNet furthermore.

5   Conclusion

In this paper, we propose CIposeNet to release the bias in some mainstream networks. The key novelty of CIposeNet is that the learning objective is based on causal intervention, which is fundamentally different from the conventional likelihood. The results on the current multi-person pose estimation dataset proves that CIposeNet can make more reasonable decisions in the dense area of keypoints. In the future, we will design an increasingly complete effect operater structure and lead the network to make more precise predictions.

References

1. Moeslund, T.B., Granum, E.: A survey of computer vision-based human motion capture. Comput. Vision Image Underst. **8**, 231–268 (2001)
2. Chi, S., Li, J., Zhang, S., Xing, J., Qi, T: Pose-driven deep convolutional model for person re-identification. In: ICCV (2017)
3. Wang, C., Wang, Y., Yuille, A.L.: An approach to pose-based action recognition. In: CVPR (2013)
4. He, K., Gkioxari, G., Doll'ar, P., Girshick, R.: Mask r-cnn. In: ICCV (2017)
5. Newell, A., Yang, K., Deng, J.: Stacked hourglass networks for human pose estimation. In: Leibe, B., Matas, J., Sebe, N., Welling, M. (eds.) ECCV 2016. LNCS, vol. 9912, pp. 483–499. Springer, Cham (2016). https://doi.org/10.1007/978-3-319-46484-8_29
6. Sun, K., Xiao, B., Liu, D., Wang, J: Deep high-resolution representation learning for human pose estimation. In: CVPR (2019)
7. Pearl, J., Glymour, M., Jewell, N.P.: Causal Inference in Statistics: A Primer. John Wiley & Sons, Hoboken (2016)
8. Pearl, J.: Interpretation and identification of causal mediation. Psychol. Methods **19**, 459 (2014)
9. Cao, Z., Simon, T., Wei, S.E., et al.: Realtime multi-person 2D pose estimation using part affinity fields. In: CVPR (2017)

10. Insafutdinov, E., Pishchulin, L., Andres, B., Andriluka, M., Schiele, B.: DeeperCut: a deeper, stronger, and faster multi-person pose estimation model. In: Leibe, B., Matas, J., Sebe, N., Welling, M. (eds.) ECCV 2016. LNCS, vol. 9910, pp. 34–50. Springer, Cham (2016). https://doi.org/10.1007/978-3-319-46466-4_3

11. Newell, A., Huang, Z., Deng, J.: Associative embedding: end-to-end learning for joint detection and grouping. arXiv preprint arXiv:1611.05424 (2016)

12. Pishchulin, L., Insafutdinov, E., Tang, S., et al.: Deepcut: joint subset partition and labeling for multi person pose estimation. In: CVPR (2016)

13. Kreiss, S., Bertoni, L., Alahi, A.: Pifpaf: composite fields for human pose estimation. In: CVPR (2019)

14. Cheng, B., Xiao, B., Wang, J., et al.: Higherhrnet: scale-aware representation learning for bottom-up human pose estimation. In: CVPR (2020)

15. Chen, Y., Wang, Z., Peng, Y., et al.: Cascaded pyramid network for multi-person pose estimation. In: CVPR (2018)

16. Papandreou, G., Zhu, T., Kanazawa, N., et al.: Towards accurate multi-person pose estimation in the wild. In: CVPR (2017)

17. Huang, J., Zhu, Z., Guo, F., et al.: The devil is in the details: delving into unbiased data processing for human pose estimation. In: CVPR (2020)

18. Magliacane, S., van Ommen, T., Claassen, T., et al.: Domain adaptation by using causal inference to predict invariant conditional distributions. arXiv preprint arXiv:1707.06422 (2017)

19. Bengio, Y., Deleu, T., Rahaman, N., et al.: a meta-transfer objective for learning to disentangle causal mechanisms. arXiv preprint arXiv:1901.10912 (2019)

20. Chalupka, K., Perona, P., Eberhardt, F.: Visual causal feature learning. arXiv preprint arXiv:1412.2309 (2014)

21. Lopez-Paz, D., Nishihara, R., Chintala, S., et al.: Discovering causal signals in images. In: CVPR (2017)

22. Nair, S., Zhu, Y., Savarese, S., et al.: Causal induction from visual observations for goal directed tasks. arXiv preprint arXiv:1910.01751 (2019)

23. Kocaoglu, M., Snyder, C., Dimakis, A.G., et al.: Causalgan: learning causal implicit generative models with adversarial training. arXiv preprint arXiv:1709.02023 (2017)

24. Kalainathan, D., Goudet, O., Guyon, I., et al.: Sam: structural agnostic model, causal discovery and penalized adversarial learning. arXiv preprint arXiv:1803.04929 (2018)

25. Yang, X., Zhang, H., Cai, J.: Deconfounded image captioning: a causal retrospect. arXiv preprint arXiv:2003.03923 (2020)

26. Tang, K., Niu, Y., Huang, J., et al.: Unbiased scene graph generation from biased training. In: CVPR (2020)

27. Wang, T., Huang, J., Zhang, H.: Visual commonsense r-cnn. In: CVPR (2020)

28. Yue, Z., Zhang, H., Sun, Q.: Interventional few-shot learning. In: NIPS (2020)

29. Li, X., Zhong, Z., Wu, J., et al.: Expectation-maximization attention networks for semantic segmentation. In: ICCV (2019)

30. Wang, X., Girshick, R., Gupta, A., et al.: Non-local neural networks. In: CVPR (2018)

31. Lin, T.-Y., Maire, M., Belongie, S., Hays, J., Perona, P., Ramanan, D., Dollár, P., Zitnick, C.L.: Microsoft COCO: common objects in context. In: Fleet, D., Pajdla, T., Schiele, B., Tuytelaars, T. (eds.) ECCV 2014. LNCS, vol. 8693, pp. 740–755. Springer, Cham (2014). https://doi.org/10.1007/978-3-319-10602-1_48

32. Yue, L., Li, J., Liu, Q.: Body parts relevance learning via expectation-maximization for human pose estimation. In: Multimedia Systems, pp. 1–13 (2021)

33. Xiao, B., Wu, H., Wei, Y.: Simple baselines for human pose estimation and tracking. In: CVPR (2018)

34. Papandreou, G., Zhu, T., Kanazawa, N., et al.: Towards accurate multi-person pose estimation in the wild. In: Proceedings of the IEEE Conference on Computer Vision and Pattern Recognition, pp. 4903–4911 (2017)

35. Sun, X., Xiao, B., Wei, F., et al.: Integral human pose regression. In: Proceedings of the European Conference on Computer Vision (ECCV), pp. 529–545 (2018)

36. Fang, H.S., Xie, S., Tai, Y.W., et al.: RMPE: regional multi-person pose estimation. In: Proceedings of the IEEE International Conference on Computer Vision, pp. 2334–2343 (2017)

37. Huang, S., Gong, M., Tao, D.: A coarse-fine network for keypoint localization. In: Proceedings of the IEEE International Conference on Computer Vision, pp. 3028–3037 (2017)

38. Chen, Y., Wang, Z., Peng, Y., et al.: Cascaded pyramid network for multi-person pose estimation. In: Proceedings of the IEEE Conference on Computer Vision and Pattern Recognition, pp. 7103–7112 (2018)

39. Cao, Z., Hidalgo, G., Simon, T., Wei, S.-E., Sheikh, Y.: OpenPose: realtime multi-person 2D pose estimation using part affinity fields. IEEE Trans. Pattern Anal. Mach. Intell. **43**(1), 172–186 (2021)

40. Qiu, Z., Qiu, K., Fu, J., Fu, D.: DGCN: dynamic graph convolutional network for efficient multi-person pose estimation, pp. 11924–11931 (2020)

Object Detection and Anomaly

Weakly Supervised Salient Object Detection with Box Annotation

Zhentao Jiang[1]([⊠]), Qiang Chen[2,3], Bo Jiang[1], Cong Leng[2,5], and Jian Cheng[2,3,4,5]

[1] Anhui University, Hefei, China
e19201072@stu.ahu.edu.cn, jiangbo@ahu.edu.cn
[2] NLPR, Institute of Automation, Chinese Academy of Sciences, Beijing, China
{qiang.chen,jcheng}@nlpr.ia.ac.cn
[3] School of Artificial Intelligence, University of Chinese Academy of Sciences, Beijing, China
[4] CAS Center for Excellence in Brain Science and Intelligence Technology, Beijing, China
[5] Nanjing Artificial Intelligence Chip Research, Institute of Automation, Chinese Academy of Sciences, Beijing, China
lengcong@airia.cn

Abstract. Box annotation is cost-friendly compared with pixel-wise dense labeling, more stable than scribbles, and contains more object information than image-level labels. However, recent approaches focus on scribble and image-level labels in weakly-supervised salient object detection (WSSOD) while ignoring box annotation. We first identify the reasons for the above ignorance and find the difficulties in describing the saliency and object contour from the box. To deal with the problems, we propose to make full use of box annotation by introducing three supervisions: vector supervision, point supervision, and plane supervision. We obtain the foreground by vector supervision, add constraints on points predictions in the background, and model the boundary information by learning the pair-wise relations in the image plane. Then, we provide a SOD dataset with box annotation and use our method to train the benchmark model on the dataset. At last, we show results on six benchmark datasets of salient object detection. We achieve the current best weakly-supervised performance and comparable performance with fully-supervised state-of-the-arts, suggesting that the gap between the weakly-supervised and fully-supervised salient object detection is closed by box annotation.

Keywords: Salient object detection · Weak supervision · Box annotation

1 Introduction

Salient object detection (SOD) [1] aims to detect the locations attracting human attention. Generally, the high-performance SOD models [2,14] are full-supervised, using pixel-wise mask annotation (as seen in Fig. 1(d)). The pixel-wise annotation is time-consuming and expensive. In this case, some weakly-supervised methods [18,24,26] are proposed to balance the cost and performance by using defective and noisy labels.

Supplementary Information The online version contains supplementary material available at https://doi.org/10.1007/978-3-031-02375-0_15.

(a) Category   (b) Scribble   (c) Box   (d) Pixel-wise

Fig. 1. The same image with different labels. (a) One kind of image-level annotation: category. (b) Scribble annotation with three different ways. (c) Box annotation. (d) Pixel-wise mask annotation.

As shown in Fig. 1 (a, b, c), we list some examples with the different labels, such as category, scribble, and box.

The question is how to choose among the annotations. Through the comparisons between them, we find box annotation is an excellent method. Compared with scribble annotation, box annotation is cheaper and more standard. For image-level annotations, such as category and caption labels, they can not provide specific object information in the image and have only global semantic information. In summary, box annotation is better in the labeling and training process. However, existing methods ignore box annotation and focus on other weak annotations in weakly-supervision salient object detection (WSSOD).

We analyze the reasons for the above ignorance in WSSOD. We identify two main difficulties that affect the application of box annotation: (1) cropping out the box area individually, the task degenerates into an unsupervised salient object detection task, which makes the task more difficult than before; (2) box annotation is not suitable for labeling pixel-level objects due to the difficulty of describing the object contour by four points [26]. Ultimately, the difficulties are caused by the box not providing the clear foreground and sufficient background.

In this paper, we propose to solve the problems by make full use of box annotation to supervised foreground, background, and pixel relations, respectively. To fulfill the goal, we propose three complementary supervisions: vector supervision, point supervision and plane supervision.

The vector supervision is to supervises the foreground from the box. We find almost horizontal and vertical lines have the foreground in the box. Following the idea of the projection term [9], we project the two-dimensional box annotation into two one-dimensional vectors, representing the horizontal and vertical foreground positions. The projection process is shown in Fig. 2. Then we apply the same operation to the predic-tion map and build supervision on the vectors.

We supervise the background by using two points on point supervision. The first point supervises the background outside the box that is the omission of previous vec-tor supervision. As shown in Fig. 2, we show the reconstruction process about vector supervision and point out the missing background area. To avoid a large amount of back-ground information destroying the balance between the foreground and background, we supervise the maximum probability point in the missing area and make the area tend to the background. The second point is used to constrain the background in the box. We assume that there is at least one background area in the box, so we use a minimum probability point to ensure that the background in the box is supervised.

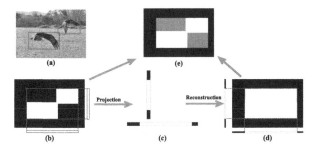

Fig. 2. Illustration of our projection and reconstruction processes. (a) Box annotation. (b) Box mask. (c) Projection vectors. (d) Reconstruction mask. (e) The differences between box mask and reconstruction mask

As their low-dimensional information can not be generalized to high-dimensional information, they have low confidence in a large number of predictions. To spreading their influence in two-dimension, it requires the information on second dimension. However, it is difficult to obtain clean two-dimensional information from weak annotations. Therefore, we turn to the low-level information from the image, such as location and color [8]. Moreover, many pixel-level labels share the phenomenon that neighboring pixels with similar colors are usually annotated with the same label. Relying on these clues, we construct similarity labels between pixels based on the color prior information. Similarly, we generate the corresponding similarity probabilities from the prediction map. We build the plane supervision based on the similarity probabilities and similarity labels, providing two-dimensional guidance for the network learning.

Finally, we provide a SOD dataset with box annotation to supplement the lack of box-labeling in the SOD task and verify the feasibility of our method on the dataset. Combining the three supervisions on point, vector, and plane, we obtain our experimental results by replacing the supervision of OCRNet [22]. Compared with the state-of-the-art weakly-supervised algorithms on six salient object detection benchmarks, our method outperforms the optimal weakly-supervised methods on the evaluation metrics. For fully-supervised models, our results are close to some outstanding fully-supervised models. It demonstrates that box annotation is an excellent choice to replace the pixel-wise label on the salient object detection task. Using box annotation, we reduce the gap between weak supervision and full supervision in salient object detection. Our main contributions:

1) We provide a SOD dataset with box annotation and propose a box-supervised SOD method to fill in the gaps of weakly-supervised salient object detection.
2) We combine the three supervisions on point, vector and plane to overcome two issue in the usage of box annotation.
3) Experimental results on salient object detection benchmarks prove that our methods achieve state-of-the-art weakly-supervised performance.
4) We demonstrate the usefulness of box annotation on the SOD task based on our experimental results.

2 Related Work

Our attention to salient object detection models moves from full supervision to box supervision. As our method uses box annotation in weakly-supervised learning, we mainly discuss weakly-supervised salient object detection and related box-supervised approaches in other pixel-wise supervised tasks.

2.1 Weakly-supervised Salient Object Detection

The fully-supervised salient object detection have achieved high-performance. Some SOD methods attempted to use weak annotations to learn saliency and reduced the cost of hand-labeling. WSS [18] learned saliency from the classification network trained on the image-level label. MWS [24] trained a classification network and a caption network by using category and caption annotations to highlight essential regions as the salient maps. WSSA [26] attempted to get salient maps from scribble labels by a partial cross-entropy loss. However, we find that the box annotation is ignored in the weakly-supervised salient object detection task. In this work, we propose the method to detect salient objects with box supervision, filling in the gap of weakly-supervised salient object detection.

2.2 Box-supervised Pixel-wise Methods

Some methods attempted to use box annotation as weak supervision to train pixel-level models. In the early deep learning time, BoxSup [5] got the initial mask from the box by low-level segmentation algorithms and refined it in training. SDI [10] also relied on low-level segmentation and was the first instance segmentation method under box supervision. Then, BBTP [8] turned to supervise directly from the box, based on Mask R-CNN [7]. It used neighboring pixel pairs to enforce the piece-wise smoothness and set the positive and negative bags to learn the object mask. In Wang's works [9], the projection term might be the first used in box supervision. BoxInst [17] combined the projection term and similar pixel pairs to get good results. For the projection term, it is a very convenient algorithm to distinguish between positive and negative samples as a whole. Although it notices that the foreground exists on most rows and columns inside the box, it ignores that the background also exists inside the box.

3 Approach

This section describes our method by three terms: vector supervision, point supervision, and plane supervision. Vector supervision projects the box annotation into two vectors and spreads the saliency information into the network. Point supervision is used to supplement the background information inside and outside the box. Plane supervision employs the pairwise similarity to obtain the two-dimensional pixel-level information. At last, we combine the three terms to supervise the network during the training process jointly. The whole method is shown in Fig. 3.

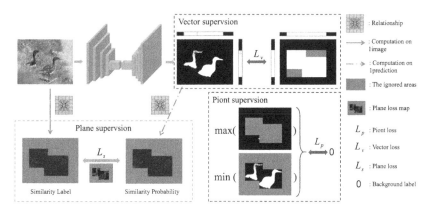

Fig. 3. The overview of our method. We build the vector loss between the prediction vectors and label vectors on vector supervision. We extract the background predictions inside and outside the box and supervise them with point loss. The similarity label and similarity probability are obtained from the pixel-based relationship on the image and prediction and are supervised by plane loss. The ignored areas should not be involved in the calculation, but may be calculated in vector supervision.

3.1   Vector Supervision

Following the projection term [9], we establish vector supervision between the projections of prediction and box mask. The prediction and label are projected onto the x-axis and y-axis vectors. A max-pooling can define the projection operation with each axis. Let $l \in \{0, 1\}^{H \times W}$ be the mask generated by assigning 1 to the area inside the box and 0 to others. We have:

$$l_x = \mathrm{Vect}_x(l) = \max_x(l),$$
$$l_y = \mathrm{Vect}_y(l) = \max_y(l), \tag{1}$$

where Vect_x and Vect_y project $l \in \mathbb{R}^{H \times W}$ to $l_x \in \mathbb{R}^H$ and $l_y \in \mathbb{R}^W$, $\max_x$ and $\max_y$ are the max operations as practical use replaced Vect_x and Vect_y.

Let $\tilde{m} \in (0, 1)^{H \times W}$ be the salient mask from the model prediction, as the foreground probability. Although the salient mask is a non-binary result, we can follow the max pooling operation to implement the projection operation, as Eq.(1). Through this operation, we can obtain the prediction vectors of the x-axis and y-axis from the salient mask. Then we build the loss between the projection vectors of the predicted mask and the ground-truth box mask:

$$
\begin{aligned}
L_v &= L(\mathrm{Vect}_x(\tilde{m}), \mathrm{Vect}_x(l)) + L(\mathrm{Vect}_y(\tilde{m}), \mathrm{Vect}_y(l)) \\
&= L(\max_x(\tilde{m}), \max_x(l)) + L(\max_y(\tilde{m}), \max_y(l)) \\
&= L(\tilde{m}_x, l_x) + L(\tilde{m}_y, l_y),
\end{aligned}
\tag{2}
$$

where we use the Dice loss as $L(:,:)$. The network distinguishes between foreground and background roughly under this supervision.

3.2 Point Supervision

As mentioned before, the gray areas in Fig. 2 and the background inside the box are unsupervised by vector supervision. It leads to the network not clearly distinguishing the background. Therefore, we add point supervision to make up for the omissions.

For the area outside the box without supervision, it is time-consuming to filter out the area individually. If we select all areas outside the box as a supplement, the operation will largely overlap with the previous vector supervision and add redundant calculations. Following the projection idea, we do not need to monitor every position but predict the area's maximum point outside the box as the background projection (the top image of the purple area in Fig. 3). The extract operation is formulated as

$$\tilde{m}_{ob} = \max(\tilde{m}(l = 0)), \tag{3}$$

where $\tilde{m}_{ob}$ is the point of the maximum prediction outside the box. Since we set the background label to 0, we select the point from the area with the label of 0.

The background inside the box is also not under supervision. From our observations, there must be background locations inside the box. However, the network cannot directly distinguish the background and the foreground in the box because vector supervision does not indicate a background inside the box. It is more dependent on the network's association ability, which is to predict the background in the box through the existing background and foreground information. We attempt to give point guidance about the background in the box, using the minimum prediction point as the background projection in the box (the down image of the purple area in Fig. 3). With the guidance, the network can recognize the background more clearly. We set the point as

$$\tilde{m}_{ib} = \min(\tilde{m}(l = 1)), \tag{4}$$

where $\tilde{m}_{ib}$ is the point of the minimum prediction inside the box. Following the label set, we can choose the point from the area in the box.

We get two points from Eq.(3) and Eq.(4). For the task, we expect that the points should fit the setting in the labels. The point loss is formulated as

$$\begin{aligned} L_p &= L(\max(\tilde{m}(l = 0)), 0) + L(\min(\tilde{m}(l = 1)), 0) \\ &= L(\tilde{m}_{ob}, 0) + L(\tilde{m}_{ib}, 0), \end{aligned} \tag{5}$$

where $L(:,:)$ is BCE loss. We treat these two guides as the same contribution.

3.3 Plane Supervision

Due to low-dimensional information provided by previous supervisions, most of the foreground and background predictions in the plane rely on the network's generalization. We adopt plane supervision based on position and color to supplement the pixel-wise information in the box. Since it is difficult for us to obtain each pixel's label from weak annotations, we employ the relationships between pixels as plane supervision. The relationships are modeled from low-level features, such as position and color. Because location information and color information are difficult to weight, we treat all neighborhood locations equally and compute the color similarities.

We set each pixel connected with its all $K \times K - 1$ neighbors by edge e, as shown in the relationship of Fig. 3. For each edge e, we define the color similarity as

$$s_e = S_{\text{img}}(c_i, c_j) = \exp(-\frac{\|c_i - c_j\|}{\sigma^2}), \tag{6}$$

where c_i and c_j are the color vectors of pixel i and pixel j, s_e is the color similarity between the pixel i and pixel j. σ^2 is a hyper-parameter, set to 2.

Then, we define $y_e \in \{0, 1\}$ as the similarity label. We set $y_e = 1$ if $s_e > \tau$, otherwise $y_e = 0$. The threshold τ is a fixed hyper-parameter, set to 0.8.

From the similarity label, we supervise the salient mask from the network. We think if two pixels are similar in color, their predictions should be close. The similarity probability of the pair is defined as

$$
\begin{aligned}
p_e &= S_{\text{pre}}(m_i, m_j) \\
&= \tilde{m}_i \tilde{m}_j + (1 - \tilde{m}_i)(1 - \tilde{m}_j) \\
&= 2\tilde{m}_i \tilde{m}_j - \tilde{m}_i - \tilde{m}_j + 1,
\end{aligned}
\tag{7}
$$

where the foreground predictions of pixel i and pixel j are $\tilde{m}_i$ and $\tilde{m}_j$, p_e is supervised by $y_e = 1$.

In training, we only supervise the similar edges, whose similarity labels are $y_e = 1$. As a result, plane loss is formulated as

$$L_s = -\frac{1}{N} \sum_{e \in l_b} y_e \log p_e, \tag{8}$$

where $e \in l_b$ means the edges in the ground-truth box, N is the number of the positive edges in the ground-truth box, and p_e comes from Eq.(7).

We show an example of the pairwise similarity, such as the pictures in the blue area of the Fig. 3. The left picture shows the supervision that each pixel can obtain and the right picture shows relationships that each pixel learn from network. The plane supervision can be monitored to the object internal area and enable the external background to diffuse into the box.

3.4 Training with Multiple Supervisions

We have these three supervisions, which are not suitable for direct combination according to their meanings. As the core of our supervisions, vector supervision (Eq.(2)) determines most of the prediction orientations. So we intend to highlight its capabilities. However, point supervision will bring the information that belongs to background, which should be restricted during training to prevent the network from falling to the background. We set a dynamic weight to maintain balance:

$$w_p = \beta \frac{\sum\limits_{r_i \in l_x} r_i + \sum\limits_{c_j \in l_x} c_j}{H + W}, \tag{9}$$

where $r_i \in l_x$ and $c_j \in l_x$. We count the number of the foreground in l_x and l_y to dynamically adjust the background loss. β is a hyperparameter and we set it to 0.4.

Finally, our total loss function is defined as

$$L_{bsod} = L_v + w_p L_p + \lambda L_s, \tag{10}$$

where λ is the parameter to constrain plane supervision and we set it to 1.0.

Our total loss function is used to supervise the final prediction map. Therefore, our method does not change the internal structure of the model but only modifies the final supervision process. Our approach can be applied to other fully-supervised saliency models.

4 Experiments

4.1 Setup

Datasets. In order to train our box-supervised salient object detection method, we relabel DUTS train dataset [18] with box annotation. In Fig. 1, we show an example of box annotation. It is worth noting that we do not use a single box as the object detection task, but use multiple boxes to label non-connected areas. Since some images have only a salient target or multiple salient objects close, they have single box. We train our network on our labeled box annotation dataset. Then, we evaluate all the models on six SOD benchmarks: DUTS TEST dateset [18], ECSSD [21], DUT-OMRON [20], PASCAL-S [13], HKU-IS [11], and THUR [3].

Evaluation Metrics. We employ four metrics to evaluate the performance of our method and other salient object detection methods, including Mean Absolute Error(MAE) [4], Mean F-measure(F_β), S-measure(S_m) [6], and mean Intersection of Union(mIoU).

4.2 Implementation Details

Our base model is OCRNet [22] with backbone of HRNet [16], pretrained on ImageNet [15]. All models are trained with our box annotation dataset. Our code is developed from MMSegmentation[1] into salient object detection task and will be released for comparisons. In the training process, we use Stochastic Gradient Descent to optimize our network. The weight decay is 0.0005. The learning rate starts from 0.001 to end with 0.00001, and is decayed according to the ploy learning rate policy, multiplied by $1 - (\frac{iter}{max\_iter})^{power}$ with power = 0.9. The backbone network is initialized with pre-training parameters by default. We train our models for 100K iterations with a training batch size of 8. We apply random flip with 0.5 ratio as data augmentation methods. Notice that, random crop is not suitable for our method.

4.3 Comparisons with the State-of-the-Art

To validate our method, we compare our method with the state-of-the-art SOD methods. The fully-supervised SOD models are PAGRN [27], C2SNet [12], HRSOD [23],

---

[1] https://github.com/open-mmlab/mmsegmentation.

Table 1. Evaluation results of the state-of-the-art approaches and our method on six benchmark datasets. ↓ means the larger is the better; ↑ means the smaller is the better. The best performance in weakly-supervised and unsupervised methods is marked with red color.

Metrics	Full Sup. Methods								Un.	Img.	Scribble	Box
	PAGRN	C2SNet	HRSOD	PFAN	MLMSNet	BASNet	GCPANet	OCRNet	SVF	MWS	WSSA	Ours
	18[27]	18 [12]	19 [23]	19 [28]	19 [19]	19 [14]	20 [2]	20 [22]	17 [25]	19 [24]	20 [26]	21
ECSSD												
MAE ↓	.0610	.0593	.0544	.0472	.0380	.0370	.0348	.0457	.0880	.0964	.0590	.0491
F_β ↑	.8940	.8528	.9023	.8431	.9137	.8796	.9193	.9156	.8085	.8401	.8698	.9085
S_m ↑	.8891	.8817	.8829	.9044	.9097	.9162	.9267	.9091	.8329	.8275	.8655	.8868
mIoU ↑	.7694	.7754	.7843	.8048	.8466	.8557	.8579	.8035	.6616	.6047	.7685	.8121
DUT-OMRON												
MAE	.0709	.0790	.0660	.0415	.0613	.0565	.0563	.0596	.1076	.1087	.0684	.0605
F_β	.7114	.6640	.7079	.7751	.7364	.7556	.7478	.7480	.6090	.6089	.7033	.7511
S_m	.7751	.7798	.7718	.8679	.8177	.8362	.8388	.7934	.7471	.7558	.7848	.7978
mIoU	.5558	.5786	.5666	.7212	.6224	.6995	.6821	.5776	.5107	.4766	.6065	.6276
DUTS-TEST												
MAE ↓	.0561	.0668	.0520	.0412	.0537	.0480	.0382	.0459	–	.0919	.0628	.0481
F_β ↑	.7884	.7141	.7961	.7883	.7817	.7958	.8227	.8343	–	.6883	.7440	.8298
S_m ↑	.8370	.8168	.8272	.8739	.8481	.8650	.8903	.8514	–	.7574	.8022	.8417
mIoU ↑	.6423	.6293	.6543	.7243	.6613	.7405	.7593	.6648	–	.4806	.6294	.7014
HKU-IS												
MAE ↓	.0475	–	.0419	.0354	.0437	.0322	.0309	.0406	–	.0843	.0470	.0392
F_β ↑	.8863	–	.8911	.8742	.8852	.8955	.8985	.9059	–	.8139	.7440	.9001
S_m ↑	.8873	–	.8821	.9133	.9010	.9089	.8205	.8965	–	.8182	.8022	.8823
mIoU ↑	.7531	–	.7729	.8046	.7675	.8321	.8343	.7672	–	.5746	.6294	.7939
PASCAL-S												
MAE ↓	.0894	.0867	.0855	.0655	.0789	.0758	.0623	.0708	.1309	.1330	.0924	.0778
F_β ↑	.7985	.7544	.8008	.8140	.7835	.7710	.8266	.8272	.6953	.7125	.7742	.8262
S_m ↑	.8217	.8263	.8068	.8601	.8486	.8380	.8644	.8477	.7581	.7675	.7974	.8229
mIoU ↑	.6607	.6897	.6651	.7444	.7014	.7354	.7605	.7077	.5554	.5131	.6645	.7056
THUR												
MAE ↓	.0704	–	.0674	.0939	.0680	–	–	.0655	–	.1667	.0772	.0627
F_β ↑	.7287	–	.7402	.6624	.7385	–	–	.7571	–	.7365	.7134	.7598
S_m↑	.8304	–	.8196	.7992	.8345	–	–	.8387	–	.7003	.7999	.8239
mIoU ↑	.6543	–	.6609	.6192	.6917	–	–	.6666	–	.4420	.6423	.6860

Fig. 4. Precision-Recall curves, F-measure curves and IoU curves on DUTS-TEST dataset and ECSSD dataset.

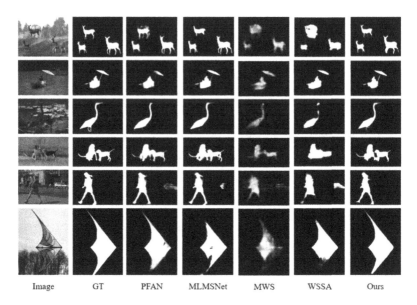

Image   GT   PFAN   MLMSNet   MWS   WSSA   Ours

Fig. 5. Qualitative comparisons of saliency maps. The results are predicted by our method and other state-of-the-art models.

PFAN [28], MLMSNet [19], BASNet [14], GCPANet [2], and OCRNet [22]. The weakly-supervised and unsupervised SOD models are SVF [25], MWS [24], and WSSA [26].

Quantitative. In order to fully demonstrate the excellent performance of our method, we evaluate our model under four metrics and compare them with other full-supervised, weakly-supervised, and unsupervised SOD models. The overall results are shown in Table 1 and Fig. 4.

As demonstrated by the evaluation metrics in Table 1, our method is better than other models in weakly-supervised salient object detection. Evaluated on all datasets, our method outperforms both in terms of object shape description and overall prediction accuracy. Our method is far ahead of current non-fully supervised methods, especially in terms of performance on PASCAL-S [13] and DUTS TEST [18].

As shown in Fig. 4, our results is stable on F-measure curves and IoU curves, and is consistent with the performance in Table 1. It indicates that our results are basically at the ends of the [0, 1] interval and are not sensitive to the threshold of foreground and background division. Therefore, although our method is ahead of other weakly supervised methods on the Precision-Recall curves, it is not as prominent as other curves. In general, our method can clearly distinguish the foreground and the background, has strong confidence in the prediction mask, and will not have vacillating judgments about some areas.

As both the box annotation and the scribble annotation are weak pixel-level labels, we compare and analyze the experimental results from these labels. In terms of annotation, the scribble annotation provides clear foreground and background information, while the box annotation shows vague foreground and partial background. Therefore, the scribble annotation can easily obtain clean salient features, but there is a lot of noise in the box annotation. Based on the current analysis, we believe that the box supervision is more difficult than the scribble supervision. However, we still achieve results that completely outperform it. In terms of methods, our goal is to obtain specially fuzzy guidance from vague information provided by box annotation and to spread the impact of this guidance in the network. This method makes the network more biased towards association capabilities rather than fixed characteristics. The scribble annotation tends to focus more on identifying clear information and generalizing their characteristics. This causes the network to lose a great deal of autonomous association ability during training. Therefore, the generalization of the scribble label on other datasets by the network is not as good as the box label, such as PASCAL-S [13] and THUR [3].

Compared with the fully supervised salient object detection method, our performance is close to MLMSNet [19] and PFAN [28], and exceeds their previous methods. In addition, we show our results with other fully supervised methods through the Precision-Recall curves, F-measure curves and IoU curves in Fig. 4. Compared with our benchmark model OCRNet [22], our box supervised method is close to the results of full supervision on DUT [20], DUTS TEST [18] and HKU-IS [11], without any modifications to the model. But we have a little gap from the result of full supervision on other datasets. Overall, our method bridges the gap between box supervision and full supervision of salient object detection tasks.

Qualitative. We show several predicted maps from different datasets to qualitatively analyze our results, shown in Fig. 5. For the overall approach, our method easily motivates the network to learn the boundary information of the target and then spread this information across the whole image, delineating the foreground and background. This allows the network to focus on the shape characteristics of the object. The prediction of the interior of the target depends on the plane supervision, which comes from the low-level information of the image. Coupled with the guidance on foreground and background provided by our point and vector supervision, our approach achieve effective salient object detection. Moreover, our effect is better than the methods based on scribble annotation [26] and is close to the weakly-supervised methods [19, 28]. In addition, our approach can easily learn the outer edge information of the targets under background interference and show more object details and can clearly show small salient targets, which are more conducive to using our method in reality.

4.4 Ablation Study

Point, Vector and Plane Supervisions. We fixed all hyperparameters in the comparison experiments. We verified the role of dynamic weight on point supervision. Point supervision provides background samples, so when the dynamic weight is not used or is too large, the network will be pulled towards the edge of the object by point supervision and degenerate into edge detection, as shown in the end of Fig. 6 and Table 2. In addition, plane supervision will make the predictions of similar pixels as consistent as possible and does not conflict significantly with point and vector supervisions, so we set its weight to 1.0. Since a pair of pixels with low similarity is likely to be labeled

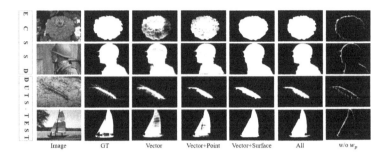

Fig. 6. Qualitative ablation study on different supervisions.

with different categories, a low similarity threshold will introduce a lot of noise. Based on this recognition, we set the similarity threshold to 0.8 and the threshold greater than 0.8 is also allowed.

Table 2. Ablation Study for our losses. Red color is the best.

Vector	Point	Plane	DUTS-TEST			ECSSD		
			MAE ↓	F_β ↑	S_m ↑	MAE ↓	F_β ↑	S_m ↑
✓			.0544	.7847	.8464	.0673	.8717	.8770
✓	✓		.0509	.8191	.8434	.0599	.8984	.8850
✓		✓	.0506	.7949	.8330	.0510	.8810	.8817
✓	✓	✓	.0481	.8298	.8417	.0491	.9085	.8868
✓	w/o w_p	✓	.1390	–	–	.2227	–	–

We analyze our ablation experiments about three supervisions, as shown in Table 2 and Fig. 6. Whether it is quantitative or qualitative analysis, we can note that although point supervision and plane supervision can bring performance improvements, they focus on quite different directions. Point supervision can enhance the network to distinguish between foreground and background by adding background information, just like the performance on F-measure and MAE in Table 2. As shown in Fig. 6, plane supervision can improve the confidence of salient objects globally and make target edges more visible by supplement two-dimensional information. In conclusion, the first issue in the box annotation can be solved by point supervision and vector supervision, and the second issue is more easily overcome by combining the three supervisions.

We also notice that our method performs inconsistently on the S-measure evaluation of DUTS-TEST and ECSSD datasets in Tabel 2. The reason why it happens is that DUTS-TEST dataset pays more attention to the details of the object than ECSSD dataset, as shown in Fig. 6. Since our method relies on the generalization ability of the network when dealing with the details of the target, our method has slight fluctuations on the detailed dataset, which does not affect the significant effect of our method on the entire targets.

Based on these supervisions, our method easily identifies salient objects in images with the box annotation. Our point supervision and vector supervision provide guidance on the foreground and background, which makes the network focus on the shape features of the target. The prediction inside the object depends on the plane supervision, which comes from the low-level information of the image. It has been shown in our extensive experiments that while box annotation does not have the explicit pixel-level information that scribble annotation does, plane supervision provides pixel-level information that the network can refer to and learn from, and allows the guidance to spread across the entire image. By combining the three types of supervision, our method can achieve effective salient target detection.

5   Conclusions

In this paper, we propose a box-supervised salient object detection (SOD) method and provide a box-labeled SOD dataset. Our method proves the feasibility of box annotation in the task of saliency detection. Our method obtains outstanding results through point, vector and plane supervisions. Our method is better than other weakly-supervised saliency models under quantitative and qualitative analysis and is close to the fully-supervised methods. Moreover, our method is end-to-end training and is only used to improve the final supervision process. Our method can be quickly applied to other fully-supervised saliency models.

References

1. Borji, A., Cheng, M.M., Jiang, H., Li, J.: Salient object detection: a benchmark. IEEE Trans. Image Process. **24**(12), 5706–5722 (2015)
2. Chen, Z., Xu, Q., Cong, R., Huang, Q.: Global context-aware progressive aggregation network for salient object detection. In: Proceedings of the AAAI Conference on Artificial Intelligence, vol. 34, pp. 10599–10606 (2020)
3. Cheng, M.M., Mitra, N.J., Huang, X., Hu, S.M.: Salientshape: group saliency in image collections. Vis. Comput. **30**(4), 443–453 (2014)
4. Cong, R., Lei, J., Fu, H., Lin, W., Huang, Q., Cao, X., Hou, C.: An iterative co-saliency framework for RGBD images. IEEE Trans. Cybern. **49**(1), 233–246 (2017)
5. Dai, J., He, K., Sun, J.: Boxsup: exploiting bounding boxes to supervise convolutional networks for semantic segmentation. In: 2015 IEEE International Conference on Computer Vision, pp. 1635–1643 (2015)
6. Fan, D.P., Cheng, M.M., Liu, Y., Li, T., Borji, A.: Structure-measure: a new way to evaluate foreground maps. In: IEEE International Conference on Computer Vision (2017)
7. He, K., Gkioxari, G., Dollár, P., Girshick, R.: Mask R-CNN. In: Proceedings of the IEEE International Conference on Computer Vision, pp. 2961–2969 (2017)
8. Hsu, C.C., Hsu, K.J., Tsai, C.C., Lin, Y.Y., Chuang, Y.Y.: Weakly supervised instance segmentation using the bounding box tightness prior. Adv. Neural. Inf. Process. Syst. **32**, 6586–6597 (2019)

9. Kervadec, H., Dolz, J., Wang, S., Granger, E., Ayed, I.B.: Bounding boxes for weakly supervised segmentation: global constraints get close to full supervision. In: Medical Imaging with Deep Learning, pp. 365–381. PMLR (2020)

10. Khoreva, A., Benenson, R., Hosang, J., Hein, M., Schiele, B.: Simple does it: weakly supervised instance and semantic segmentation. In: Proceedings of the IEEE Conference on Computer Vision and Pattern Recognition, pp. 876–885 (2017)

11. Li, G., Yu, Y.: Visual saliency based on multiscale deep features. In: Proceedings of the IEEE Conference on Computer Vision and Pattern Recognition, June 2015

12. Li, X., Yang, F., Cheng, H., Liu, W., Shen, D.: Contour knowledge transfer for salient object detection. In: Ferrari, V., Hebert, M., Sminchisescu, C., Weiss, Y. (eds.) ECCV 2018. LNCS, vol. 11219, pp. 370–385. Springer, Cham (2018). https://doi.org/10.1007/978-3-030-01267-0_22

13. Li, Y., Hou, X., Koch, C., Rehg, J.M., Yuille, A.L.: The secrets of salient object segmentation. In: 2014 IEEE Conference on Computer Vision and Pattern Recognition, pp. 280–287 (2014)

14. Qin, X., Zhang, Z., Huang, C., Gao, C., Dehghan, M., Jagersand, M.: Basnet: boundary-aware salient object detection. In: Proceedings of the IEEE/CVF Conference on Computer Vision and Pattern Recognition, pp. 7479–7489 (2019)

15. Russakovsky, O., et al.: ImageNet large scale visual recognition challenge. Int. J. Comput. Vis. 115(3), 211–252 (2015). https://doi.org/10.1007/s11263-015-0816-y

16. Sun, K., Xiao, B., Liu, D., Wang, J.: Deep high-resolution representation learning for human pose estimation. In: Proceedings of the IEEE/CVF Conference on Computer Vision and Pattern Recognition, pp. 5693–5703 (2019)

17. Tian, Z., Shen, C., Wang, X., Chen, H.: BoxInst: high-performance instance segmentation with box annotations. In: Proceeding IEEE Conference Computer Vision and Pattern Recognition (2021)

18. Wang, L., Lu, H., Wang, Y., Feng, M., Wang, D., Yin, B., Ruan, X.: Learning to detect salient objects with image-level supervision. In: Proceedings of the IEEE Conference on Computer Vision and Pattern Recognition, pp. 136–145 (2017)

19. Wu, R., Feng, M., Guan, W., Wang, D., Lu, H., Ding, E.: A mutual learning method for salient object detection with intertwined multi-supervision. In: Proceedings of the IEEE/CVF Conference on Computer Vision and Pattern Recognition, pp. 8150–8159 (2019)

20. Yan, Q., Xu, L., Shi, J., Jia, J.: Hierarchical saliency detection. In: 2013 IEEE Conference on Computer Vision and Pattern Recognition, pp. 1155–1162 (2013)

21. Yang, C., Zhang, L., Lu, H., Ruan, X., Yang, M.H.: Saliency detection via graph-based manifold ranking. In: 2013 IEEE Conference on Computer Vision and Pattern Recognition, pp. 3166–3173 (2013)

22. Yuan, Y., Chen, X., Wang, J.: Object-contextual representations for semantic segmentation. In: Vedaldi, A., Bischof, H., Brox, T., Frahm, J.-M. (eds.) ECCV 2020. LNCS, vol. 12351, pp. 173–190. Springer, Cham (2020). https://doi.org/10.1007/978-3-030-58539-6_11

23. Zeng, Y., Zhang, P., Zhang, J., Lin, Z., Lu, H.: Towards high-resolution salient object detection. In: Proceedings of the IEEE/CVF International Conference on Computer Vision, pp. 7234–7243 (2019)

24. Zeng, Y., Zhuge, Y., Lu, H., Zhang, L., Qian, M., Yu, Y.: Multi-source weak supervision for saliency detection. In: Proceedings of the IEEE/CVF Conference on Computer Vision and Pattern Recognition, pp. 6074–6083 (2019)

25. Zhang, D., Han, J., Zhang, Y.: Supervision by fusion: towards unsupervised learning of deep salient object detector. In: Proceedings of the IEEE International Conference on Computer Vision, pp. 4048–4056 (2017)

26. Zhang, J., Yu, X., Li, A., Song, P., Liu, B., Dai, Y.: Weakly-supervised salient object detection via scribble annotations. In: Proceedings of the IEEE/CVF Conference on Computer Vision and Pattern Recognition, pp. 12546–12555 (2020)

27. Zhang, X., Wang, T., Qi, J., Lu, H., Wang, G.: Progressive attention guided recurrent network for salient object detection. In: Proceedings of the IEEE Conference on Computer Vision and Pattern Recognition, pp. 714–722 (2018)
28. Zhao, T., Wu, X.: Pyramid feature attention network for saliency detection. In: Proceedings of the IEEE/CVF Conference on Computer Vision and Pattern Recognition, pp. 3085–3094 (2019)

Foreground-Background Collaboration Network for Salient Object Detection

Fengming Sun, Lufei Huang, Xia Yuan$^{(\boxtimes)}$, and Chunxia Zhao

Nanjing University of Science and Technology, Nanjing 210094, China
{sunfm,lufeihuang714,yuanxia,zhaochx}@njust.edu.cn

Abstract. Saliency object detection has become an active topic in both computer vision and multimedia fields. Though much remarkable progress has been achieved, it is still challenging to predicted saliency maps correctly in complex scenes due to low contrast or huge similarity between salient object and background region. Previous methods only use pixels from foreground objects. As a difference, background pixels are used for salience detection in this research. Specifically, this paper introduce a foreground-background features separation module with the attention mechanism to extract this pair of complementary features. And a spatial feature refinement module was designed to learn the spatial refinement feature. Useing the spatial feature of the low-layer to enhance the foreground and background features, and combine them to generate a final saliency map. Extensive experiments performed on five benchmark datasets demonstrate that the proposed method can achieve satisfactory results on different evaluation metrics compared to other state-of-the-art salient object detection approaches.

Keywords: Saliency object detection · Foreground-background features separation · Attention mechanism · Spatial feature refinement

1 Introduction

Salient object detection (SOD) aims at identifying and locating distinctive objects or regions which attract human attention in natural images. It is a fundamental task in computer vision. In general, SOD is regarded as a prerequisite for some vision tasks, such as object redirection, scene classification, semantic segmentation, and visual tracking.

Traditional methods utilized hand-crafted priors to detect salient objects, e.g., image colors and luminance, center surrounding, and visual contrast. These methods focused on low-level visual features, which makes it difficult to achieve satisfactory results in complex scene images. Compared with these methods, the full convolution network (FCN) based frameworks achieve superior performances by exploiting high-level semantic information.

The deeper network helps extract high-level semantic features. In order to obtain as much salient object semantic information as possible, depth features

© Springer Nature Switzerland AG 2022
C. Wallraven et al. (Eds.): ACPR 2021, LNCS 13188, pp. 212–225, 2022.
https://doi.org/10.1007/978-3-031-02375-0_16

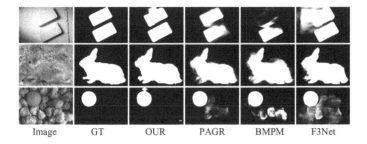

Image   GT   OUR   PAGR   BMPM   F3Net

Fig. 1. Some examples of salient object detection in complex scenes, e.g., low contrast between salient object and background region (the first two rows) or difficult to identify salient object (the third row).

were used for saliency expression. This kind of model achieves good performance but has some defects, such as large number of parameters and loss of spatial information due to the use of full connection layer. Inspired by the semantic segmentation task, the features of different neural network layers are fused to detect salient objects. Because the lower layer of the network can retain more low-level visual features, while the higher layer of the network can extract higher semantic features, the fusion of features of different network layers can not only retain the original low-level spatial information, but also obtain high-level semantic information. Nevertheless, current state-of-the-art works only focus on exploring the foreground objects and pay little attention to the feature embedding of the background region in SOD. This leads to the performance of salient object detection is greatly reduced, especially in complex scenes, e.g., low contrast between salient object and background region or difficult to identify salient object, see Fig. 1 for illustration. modern scenes commonly focus on many similar objects. For these cases, only introducing foreground traps SOD in an unexpected background confusion problem.

To address the above challenges, we propose a foreground background collaboration network to more accurately detect salient objects, namely FBCNet. We argue that the background can assist in the detection of the foreground. The determination of salient object regions largely depends on the spatial context information of the images. To clearly distinguish the foreground and background of images, we design an attention-based foreground-background separation module to extract foreground and background information, respectively. Besides, the high-resolution images can guide the network to segment salient objects more accurately. Therefore, we design a feature refinement module, and integrate the extracted features with foreground and background features to improve the saliency detection results.

To test the proposed model, we evaluate it on five famous salient object detection benchmarks and compare the result with nine approaches. Our main contributions are as follows:

- We present a novel deep network architecture that can extract complementary foreground-background features and predict accurate saliency maps with the guidance of spatial refinement information.
- We design an attention-aware foreground-background separation module to capture foreground and background information. We use the spatial attention mechanism to extract features to obtain informative foreground-background features.
- We propose a spatial feature refinement module and integrate the features into the foreground-background features to predict the salient object.
- Extensive experiments on five SOD datasets show that our model achieves the best performance under different evaluation metrics.

2   Related Work

A plenty of salient object detection approaches have been explored in the past decades. In traditional studies, hand-crafted visual features (e.g. color, texture and contrast) and heuristic prior knowledge were applied to detecting salient objects. Cheng et al. [3] earlier used global contrast to capture salient regions. Yan et al. [22] designed multi-level segmentation model to hierarchically aggregate these saliency features. These hand-crafted features and priors are difficult to obtain the complete salient object information, resulting in the saliency prediction can not be satisfied.

Recently, in the field of salient object detection, the FCN-based model became the mainstream. Different from conventional methods, high-level semantic features can be applied to achieve better results. Liu et al. [11] made a coarse global prediction by automatically learning various global structured saliency cues, and then hierarchically and progressively refined the details of saliency maps step by step via integrating local context information. Wang et al. [17] proposed to augment feedforward neural networks with a novel pyramid pooling module and a multi-stage refinement mechanism, which can capture global context information for saliency detection. Some works propose an integrate the features of different layers to detect salient objects. Zhang et al. [25] proposed a feature aggregating framework to integrate multi-level feature maps into multiple resolutions, then predicted the saliency map in each resolution and fused them to generate the final saliency map. Wei et al. [20] selectively integrate features at different levels and refine multi-level features iteratively with feedback mechanisms to predict salient objects. Zhang et al. [24] proposed a controlled bi-directional passing of features between shallow and deep layers to obtain accurate salient object predictions. Wang et al. [15] progressively polish the multi-level features and employed multiple Feature polishing modules in a recurrent manner, detect salient objects with fine details without any post-processing. Some studies[6] integrated the low-level features with the high-level features through skip connection and extract different scale features to improve the accuracy of predicted salient regions.

The recent research of salient object detection turns to detect pixels that are more challenging to predict, such as the pixels on the edge. Liu et al. [10] used an additional edge dataset for joint training of both edge detection and SOD models. Zhao et al. [27] used the contour as another supervised signal to guide the learning process of bottom features. Feng et al. [5] applied a boundary-enhanced loss to generate sharp boundaries and distinguish the narrow background margins between two foreground areas. Li et al. [8] used a two-branch network to simultaneously predict the contours and saliency maps, which can automatically convert the trained contour detection model to the SOD model. Qin et al. [14] designed a hybrid loss to supervise the training process of SOD on pixel-level, patch-level, and map-level. Chen et al. [2] proposed a boundary-aware network that can learn boundary-wise distinctions between salient objects and background. Wang et al. [18] obtained attention maps from encoded features to focus on the global contexts. Zhang et al. [26] proposed a progressive attention-guided network that used the channel and spatial attention mechanisms to generate attention features for saliency detection. Zhao et al. [28] adopt channel-wise attention for high-level features and spatial attention for low-level features to select effective features and fuse outputs of them to salient detection. Liu et al. [12] proposed global and local attention modules to capture global contexts and local contexts in low-resolution and high-resolution respectively.

These methods are devoted to fully exploiting the foreground feature to detect salient objects, which improved the results of SOD to a certain degree. But most of them only deal with the foreground information of the image and did not focus on background information. Our method learns foreground and background features respectively and uses spatial attention mechanisms to separate foreground-background features.

3   Method

We note that foreground and background have a complementary relationship, and background can be served as supplementary information to detect salient objects. Inspired by that, we propose a foreground-background collaboration network for salient object detection. The network extracts foreground and background features respectively, and accurately detects salient objects with the help of spatial refinement features. Our proposed method mainly consists of two modules: foreground-background separation module and spatial feature refinement module. Details of the proposed approach are described as follows.

3.1   Overview of Network Architecture

As shown in Fig. 2, our model is built on the FCN architecture with ResNeXt101 net [21] as a pretrained model. We feed the input images into the ResNeXt101 net to extract multi-scale backbone features F_1 to F_5 . For the foreground-background separation module, see Fig. 3. We first apply 1×1 convolution on the five feature maps to make them have same channel depth, and upsample F_2, F_3, F_4, and F_5 such that the feature maps have the same resolution. Then, we put the features into the foreground-background separation module respectively

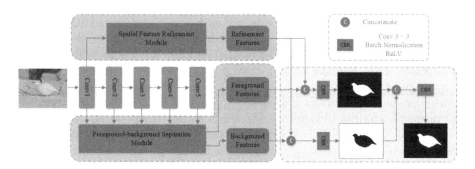

Fig. 2. The overall architecture of the proposed Foreground-Background Collaboration Network. We use ResNeXt101 net to extract multi-scale backbone features, we feed all features into foreground-background separation module to extract foreground features (F_f) and background features (F_b), and feed low-layer features into spatial feature refinement module to obtain spatial features (F_s). F_s is fused into F_f and F_b respectively, and the final salient maps are generated by integrating the fusion features.

and obtain five groups of foreground-background features. The features F_{f_i}, F_{b_i} are computed as:

$$F_{f_i}, F_{b_i} = S(F_i), i \in \{1, \cdots, 5\} \tag{1}$$

Finally, we concatenate them to get the final foreground-background features F_f and F_b computed as:

$$F_f = Cat\left(F_{f_1}, \cdots, F_{f_5}\right) \tag{2}$$

$$F_b = Cat\left(F_{b_1}, \cdots, F_{b_5}\right) \tag{3}$$

For the spatial feature refinement module, we just use backbone features F_1, and feed them into the spatial feature refinement module to get the spatial refinement feature F_s.

After getting the foreground-background features and spatial refinement feature, we use these three groups features to generate the final salient map. The salient map M is computed as:

$$M = f_{conv}\left(f_{conv}\left(F_f, F_s\right), f_{conv}\left(F_b, F_s\right)\right) \tag{4}$$

where f_{conv} represents a concatenating operation and a feature fusing network, consisting of 3×3 convolution layer followed by one ReLU activation function.

3.2   Attention-Aware Foreground-Background Separation Module

Unlike previous methods, we additionally incorporate background information in the SOD. We design an attention-aware foreground-background separation module (FBSM) to distinguish the foreground information and background information.

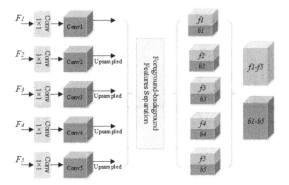

Fig. 3. The structure of the Foreground-background Separation Module (FBSM). The 1×1 convolution used to make multi-scale backbone features F_1 to F_5 have same channel depth, and upsample F_2, F_3, F_4, and F_5 such that the feature maps have the same resolution. Then, these features are separated for the foreground features and background features. Finally, concatenate them to get the final fore-background features F_f and F_b.

Specifically, we use two spatial attention modules to divide features into two branches, as shown in Fig. 4. The use of spatial attention can highlight significant objects and background areas. First, we use one 3×3 convolutional layer to strengthen the combined features, and then we apply two group convolutions to increase receptive field and refine local information. Each convolution group includes two convolution layers with different kernel sizes. Then, we combine them by element-wise addition. After a sigmoid operation, we add it to the original input feature. Finally, we use element-wise multiplication with the original input features to get the feature map filtered by spatial attention. It is worth noting that the receptive fields of foreground target are different from those of background area, usually. We change the size of the convolution kernel in the spatial attention modules which extract foreground features and background features, respectively. In particular, a group of larger convolution kernels are used for the background feature extraction.

We want to distinguish foreground and background information as precisely as possible. Therefore, we further process it to get more public boundary information. We employ a CBR model, consisting of one convolution layer, one batch normalization and one ReLU activation function, to enhance features. Then these features are transformed and fused by multiplication.

To extracts the common parts between foreground features and background features, we put the fused features into another set of spatial attention modules. The spatial attention module here shares the same weight as the previous one. We use element-wise addition to combine them with original features respectively. After multiple feature crossing, foreground features and background features gradually absorb useful information from each other to complement themselves.

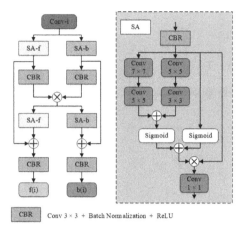

Fig. 4. Inner structure of the FBSM, with designed spatial attention mechanism.

It not only separates the foreground from the background but also sharpens the common information at the boundary.

3.3 Spatial Feature Refinement Module

With the help of the above model, the foreground and the background area can be distinguished roughly. However, the boundary between the salient objects and the background is still not clear enough. To deal with this problem, we design an extra spatial feature refinement module (SFRM) to redistribute difficult pixels at the boundary and refine saliency maps with the use of high resolution spatial features.

As we know, the low-layer features contain more spatial details, and these detailed information can help the network to make more accurate predictions for salient objects. So we extracted refined features from the low-layer.

The salient boundary detection module we proposed is shown in Fig. 5. One 3 × 3 convolutional layer is applied to adapt for the following processing. We used two sets of asymmetric convolutions to extract horizontal and vertical features respectively, and another 3 × 3 convolution is adopted to reinforce the features. We multiply the horizontal and vertical features and add them with the original features. The structure of the residuals can refine the features. We then repeat the previous process with smaller convolution kernels and combine them using element-wise addition to obtain the final spatial refinement feature.

4   Experiments

4.1 Datasets and Evaluation Metrics

We apply our method to five benchmark datasets, which are widely used in saliency detection field, to evaluate its performance: ECCSD [22], DUT-OMRON

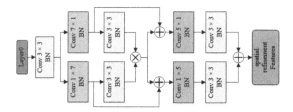

Fig. 5. The structure of the Spatial Feature Refinement Module (SFRM). We use SFRM to extract more spatial information, it consists of two sets of asymmetric convolutions to extract horizontal and vertical features, respectively. Then transformed and fused by multiplication.

[23], HKU-IS [7], PASCAL-S [9], and DUTS-TE [16]. All these datasets are human-labeled with pixelwise ground-truth for quantitative evaluations. We evaluate the performance of the proposed model and compare with other salient object detection methods using three metrics, including precision-recall (PR) curves, F-measure and mean absolute error (MAE). The precision-recall (PR) curves, it is a standard metric to evaluate saliency performance.

The F-measure, denoted as F_β, is an overall performance indicator computed by the weighted harmonic of precision and recall. It is computed as:

$$F_\beta = \frac{\left(1 + \beta^2\right) \times Precision \times Recall}{\beta^2 \times Precision + Recall} \tag{5}$$

Except for PR curve and F-measure, we also calculate the mean absolute error (MAE) to measure the average difference between predicted saliency map and ground truth. It is computed as:

$$MAE = \frac{1}{H \times W} \sum_{i=1}^{H} \sum_{j=1}^{W} |P(i,j) - G(i,j)| \tag{6}$$

4.2 Implementation Details

We utilize the DUTS-TR dataset to train our proposed model. It contains 10533 images with high-quality pixel-wise annotations. We augment the training set by horizontal and vertical flipping and image cropping to relieve the over-fitting problem. We don't use the validation set and train the model until its training loss converges. We use the well-trained ResNeXt network on ImageNet to initialize parameters of feature extraction network. We train our network on four NVIDIA 2080 Ti GPUs for 40K iterations, with a base learning rate at 1e−3, momentum parameter at 0.8 and weight decay at 5e−4, the batch size is set to 16. During the training process, we compute the cross-entropy loss between final predicted saliency map and the ground truth. During the training process, we apply deep supervision mechanism into impose a supervision signal for each saliency output, and thus we can compute the cross-entropy loss between

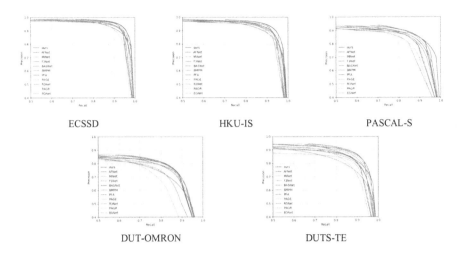

ECSSD   HKU-IS   PASCAL-S

DUT-OMRON   DUTS-TE

Fig. 6. The PR curves of the proposed method with other state-of-the-art methods on five benchmark datasets.

the ground truth and each predicted saliency map, include foreground prediction map, background prediction map and the final predicted saliency map. The total loss of our network is the sum of the loss on all predicted saliency maps. The training process of our model takes about 24 h.

4.3 Comparison with State-of-the-arts

To fully evaluate the effectiveness of the proposed method, 13 state-of-the-art salient object detection methods are introduced to compare, including F3Net [20], MINet [13], EGNet [27], BASNet [14], AFNet [5], PFA [28], BMPM [24], PAGR [26], PAGE [19], R3Net [4], SRM [17], RAS [1] and DSS [6]. For fair comparison, we use their publicly available code with recommended parameters and pretrained models released to test these methods or utilize the saliency maps provided by the authors. For quantitative evaluation, Fig. 6 shows PR curves of our method and other state-of-the-arts. We can see that our proposed method reaches advanced level on all datasets and metrics. Furthermore, we compare our method with other state-of-the-art in term of F-measure and MAE. Table 1 summarizes the numeric comparison on five datasets. The best results are highlighted with red color. It is obvious that F_β of our method achieves the best performance on most of the datasets. As for MAE, our approach is also better compared with the second best results on four datasets expect DUT-OMRON, on which we are the second one.

Figure 7 shows qualitative examples of our result. As can be seen in the figure, our method can well segment the entire objects with fine details in some challenging cases. For images with a low contrast between salient objects and background regions, most existing methods are difficult to detect salient objects completely and accurately as can be seen from the first two rows in Fig. 7.

Table 1. Quantitative comparison with state-of-the-art on five benchmark datasets. The best scores are shown in red and blue,respectively. Our method ranks first or second on these datasets.

Methods	ECSSD		HKU-IS		PASCAL-S		DUT-OMRON		DUTS-TE	
	$F_\beta \uparrow$	MAE $\downarrow$	$F_\beta \uparrow$	MAE $\downarrow$	$F_\beta \uparrow$	MAE $\downarrow$	$F_\beta \uparrow$	MAE $\downarrow$	$F_\beta \uparrow$	MAE $\downarrow$
DSS	0.916	0.053	0.911	0.040	0.829	0.102	0.771	0.066	0.827	0.056
RAS	0.916	0.058	0.913	0.045	0.804	0.105	0.785	0.063	0.831	0.059
SRM	0.910	0.056	0.892	0.046	0.783	0.127	0.707	0.069	0.798	0.059
PFA	0.931	0.038	0.927	0.034	0.856	0.078	0.810	0.064	0.873	0.040
PAGR	0.904	0.061	0.897	0.048	0.815	0.095	0.789	0.070	0.829	0.061
R3Net	0.935	0.040	0.916	0.036	0.845	0.100	0.805	0.063	0.834	0.057
BMPM	0.929	0.044	0.921	0.038	0.860	0.079	0.792	0.063	0.854	0.048
PAGE	0.931	0.042	0.917	0.037	0.853	0.084	0.791	0.062	0.838	0.051
AFNet	0.935	0.041	0.924	0.035	0.868	0.076	0.819	0.057	0.867	0.045
BASNet	0.942	0.037	0.928	0.032	0.861	0.084	0.810	0.063	0.860	0.047
EGNet	0.943	0.040	0.932	0.030	0.866	0.082	0.819	0.061	0.880	0.043
F3Net	0.943	0.033	0.934	0.028	0.865	0.075	0.818	0.062	0.887	0.036
MINet	0.942	0.034	0.933	0.029	0.880	0.073	0.820	0.065	0.880	0.037
Ours	0.944	0.031	0.936	0.027	0.868	0.072	0.820	0.060	0.887	0.035

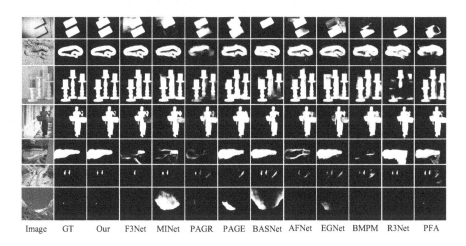

Image   GT   Our   F3Net   MINet   PAGR   PAGE   BASNet   AFNet   EGNet   BMPM   R3Net   PFA

Fig. 7. Qualitative comparisons of the proposed method and the state-of-the-art algorithms in some challenging cases: low contrast, complex background, and multiple (small) salient objects. Apparently, our method is good at dealing with complex scene and producing more accurate saliency maps.

The other rows indicate the robustness of our model when the background is complicated and contains multiple objects.

4.4   Ablation Studies

We begin by investigating the effectiveness of our foreground-background collaboration method. At first, we only use foreground features to detect salient objects. And then, we also explored the effectiveness of the attentiona mechanism, we removed the attentiona mechanism from the foreground-background separation module. From the comparison results shown in Table 2, we can see that the spatial attention mechanism can effectively distinguish foreground and background, and the background can help the network to detect salient targets more accurately. As Fig. 8 shows, we have selected examples where background objects and salient objects can easily be confused, without background features, the network falsely detects some background regions as salient objects.

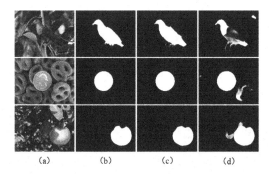

(a)   (b)   (c)   (d)

Fig. 8. Illustration of the effectiveness of the proposed FBSM. From left to right: image, ground truth, the network with F_b, the network without F_b.

Table 2. Ablation study of the model use Foreground-background Separation Module and spatial attention mechanism on DUT-OMRON and DUTS-TE datasets. "base" means only use backbone network features, "w/o F_b" means we predict salient maps without background features, "w/o SA" means FBSM without SA model.

Methods	DUT-OMRON		DUTS-TE	
	$F_\beta \uparrow$	MAE $\downarrow$	$F_\beta \uparrow$	MAE $\downarrow$
Base	0.795	0.070	0.835	0.059
w/o F_b	0.814	0.064	0.878	0.042
w/o SA	0.816	0.064	0.880	0.043
w F_f, F_b	0.817	0.062	0.883	0.039

We then investigate the design of our spatial feature refinement module, as reported in Table 3. The above experiments show the effectiveness of our feature aggregation module in the foreground-background collaboration network for salient object detection. Figure 9 shows the visualization results, the features have more spatial information, which can help to detect salient objects more accurately.

(a)   (b)   (c)   (d)

Fig. 9. Illustration of the effectiveness of the proposed SFRM. From left to right: image, ground truth, the network with SFRM, the network without SFRM.

Table 3. Ablation study of the model use Spatial Feature Refinement Module on DUT-OMRON and DUTS-TE datasets. "w/o" means FBCNet without SFRM.

Methods	DUT-OMRON		DUTS-TE	
	$F_\beta \uparrow$	MAE $\downarrow$	$F_\beta \uparrow$	MAE $\downarrow$
w/o SFRM	0.817	0.062	0.883	0.039
w SFRM	0.820	0.060	0.887	0.035

5 Conclusion

We have introduced a foreground-background collaboration network for salient object detection. Our model takes into account the background features as we believe that the background features can be served as supplementary information to detect salient objects. We propose a foreground-background separation module to extracts foreground and background features respectively, and we design the spatial feature refinement module to extracting more spatial features from the low-layer. These features are fused to detect salient object. The whole network can clearly distinguish the salient object from the background region and accurately segment the salient objects. Experimental results demonstrate that our model demonstrates remarkable saliency object detection performances in both qualitative and quantitative experiments.

References

1. Chen, S., Tan, X., Wang, B., Hu, X.: Reverse attention for salient object detection. In: Proceedings of the European Conference on Computer Vision, pp. 234–250 (2018)
2. Chen, Z., Zhou, H., Xie, X., Lai, J.: Contour loss: boundary-aware learning for salient object segmentation. arXiv preprint arXiv:1908.01975 (2019)
3. Cheng, M.M., Mitra, N.J., Huang, X., Torr, P.H., Hu, S.M.: Global contrast based salient region detection. IEEE Trans. Pattern Anal. Mach. Intell. **37**(3), 569–582 (2014)
4. Deng, Z., et al.: R3net: recurrent residual refinement network for saliency detection. In: Proceedings of the 27th International Joint Conference on Artificial Intelligence, pp. 684–690. AAAI Press (2018)
5. Feng, M., Lu, H., Ding, E.: Attentive feedback network for boundary-aware salient object detection. In: Proceedings of the IEEE/CVF Conference on Computer Vision and Pattern Recognition, pp. 1623–1632 (2019)
6. Hou, Q., Cheng, M.M., Hu, X., Borji, A., Tu, Z., Torr, P.H.: Deeply supervised salient object detection with short connections. In: Proceedings of the IEEE Conference on Computer Vision and Pattern Recognition, pp. 3203–3212 (2017)
7. Li, G., Yu, Y.: Visual saliency based on multiscale deep features. In: Proceedings of the IEEE Conference on Computer Vision and Pattern Recognition, pp. 5455–5463 (2015)
8. Li, X., Yang, F., Cheng, H., Liu, W., Shen, D.: Contour knowledge transfer for salient object detection. In: Proceedings of the European Conference on Computer Vision (ECCV), pp. 355–370 (2018)
9. Li, Y., Hou, X., Koch, C., Rehg, J.M., Yuille, A.L.: The secrets of salient object segmentation. In: Proceedings of the IEEE Conference on Computer Vision and Pattern Recognition, pp. 280–287 (2014)
10. Liu, J.J., Hou, Q., Cheng, M.M., Feng, J., Jiang, J.: A simple pooling-based design for real-time salient object detection. In: Proceedings of the IEEE/CVF Conference on Computer Vision and Pattern Recognition, pp. 3917–3926 (2019)
11. Liu, N., Han, J.: Dhsnet: deep hierarchical saliency network for salient object detection. In: Proceedings of the IEEE Conference on Computer Vision and Pattern Recognition, pp. 678–686 (2016)
12. Liu, N., Han, J., Yang, M.H.: Picanet: learning pixel-wise contextual attention for saliency detection. In: Proceedings of the IEEE Conference on Computer Vision and Pattern Recognition, pp. 3089–3098 (2018)
13. Pang, Y., Zhao, X., Zhang, L., Lu, H.: Multi-scale interactive network for salient object detection. In: Proceedings of the IEEE/CVF Conference on Computer Vision and Pattern Recognition, pp. 9413–9422 (2020)
14. Qin, X., Zhang, Z., Huang, C., Gao, C., Dehghan, M., Jagersand, M.: Basnet: boundary-aware salient object detection. In: Proceedings of the IEEE/CVF Conference on Computer Vision and Pattern Recognition, pp. 7479–7489 (2019)
15. Wang, B., Chen, Q., Zhou, M., Zhang, Z., Jin, X., Gai, K.: Progressive feature polishing network for salient object detection. In: Proceedings of the AAAI conference on artificial intelligence, vol. 34, pp. 12128–12135 (2020)
16. Wang, L., et al.: Learning to detect salient objects with image-level supervision. In: Proceedings of the IEEE Conference on Computer Vision and Pattern Recognition, pp. 136–145 (2017)

17. Wang, T., Borji, A., Zhang, L., Zhang, P., Lu, H.: A stagewise refinement model for detecting salient objects in images. In: Proceedings of the IEEE International Conference on Computer Vision, pp. 4019–4028 (2017)
18. Wang, T., et al.: Detect globally, refine locally: a novel approach to saliency detection. In: Proceedings of the IEEE Conference on Computer Vision and Pattern Recognition, pp. 3127–3135 (2018)
19. Wang, W., Zhao, S., Shen, J., Hoi, S.C., Borji, A.: Salient object detection with pyramid attention and salient edges. In: Proceedings of the IEEE/CVF Conference on Computer Vision and Pattern Recognition, pp. 1448–1457 (2019)
20. Wei, J., Wang, S., Huang, Q.: F^{3}net: fusion, feedback and focus for salient object detection. In: Proceedings of the AAAI Conference on Artificial Intelligence, vol. 34, pp. 12321–12328 (2020)
21. Xie, S., Girshick, R., Dollár, P., Tu, Z., He, K.: Aggregated residual transformations for deep neural networks. In: Proceedings of the IEEE Conference on Computer Vision and Pattern Recognition, pp. 1492–1500 (2017)
22. Yan, Q., Xu, L., Shi, J., Jia, J.: Hierarchical saliency detection. In: Proceedings of the IEEE Conference on Computer Vision and Pattern Recognition, pp. 1155–1162 (2013)
23. Yang, C., Zhang, L., Lu, H., Ruan, X., Yang, M.H.: Saliency detection via graph-based manifold ranking. In: Proceedings of the IEEE Conference on Computer Vision and Pattern Recognition, pp. 3166–3173 (2013)
24. Zhang, L., Dai, J., Lu, H., He, Y., Wang, G.: A bi-directional message passing model for salient object detection. In: Proceedings of the IEEE Conference on Computer Vision and Pattern Recognition, pp. 1741–1750 (2018)
25. Zhang, P., Wang, D., Lu, H., Wang, H., Ruan, X.: Amulet: aggregating multi-level convolutional features for salient object detection. In: Proceedings of the IEEE International Conference on Computer Vision, pp. 202–211 (2017)
26. Zhang, X., Wang, T., Qi, J., Lu, H., Wang, G.: Progressive attention guided recurrent network for salient object detection. In: Proceedings of the IEEE Conference on Computer Vision and Pattern Recognition, pp. 714–722 (2018)
27. Zhao, J.X., Liu, J.J., Fan, D.P., Cao, Y., Yang, J., Cheng, M.M.: Egnet: edge guidance network for salient object detection. In: Proceedings of the IEEE/CVF International Conference on Computer Vision, pp. 8779–8788 (2019)
28. Zhao, T., Wu, X.: Pyramid feature attention network for saliency detection. In: Proceedings of the IEEE Conference on Computer Vision and Pattern Recognition, pp. 3085–3094 (2019)

Attention Guided Multi-level Feedback Network for Camouflage Object Detection

Qiuyan Tang⬤, Jialin Ye⬤, Fukang Chen⬤, and Xia Yuan$^{(\boxtimes)}$⬤

Nanjing University of Science and Technology, Nanjing 210094, China
{qiuyan,119106022037,Fukang,yuanxia}@njust.edu.cn

Abstract. "Camouflage object detection(COD)" refers to identify objects hidden in the surrounding environment, such as oriental scops owl in a tree hole. Nowadays, due to the high similarity between the camouflaged object and its dependent environment, coupled with the lack of large-scale datasets, the research on this task is still very challenging. Current COD models directly send feature maps output by the backbone into the encoding-decoding module and process them equally, which may cause information interference to a certain extent. In addition, regarding the disappearance of the underlying clues in DCNNs, these models have not been well resolved. This article carries out further research based on the existing models and proposes a novel model, AGMFNet. Specifically, we introduce channel attention and spatial attention to obtain more information we need and suppress useless information to avoid information interference. In order to make feature maps integrate better, the Inception module is utilized. Furthermore, the cascade decoding module is further expanded, and we proposed a multi-level feedback module with auxiliary edge information to refine the camouflage image, which can make full use of the high-level features while retaining the low-level clues. After a series of ablation experiments on the introduced modules on the test datasets, all the combinations can improve the performance, which will also help develop camouflage object detection. The code will be available at: https://github.com/baekqiu/AGMFNet-for-COD/

Keywords: Object detection · Camouflage object detection · Multi-level feedback · Attention mechanism · Inception

1 Introduction

According to the theory of evolution put forward by the British biologist Charles Darwin, "It is not the strongest of the species that survive, or the most intelligent, but the one most responsive to change". All creatures in nature are evolving to adapt to the environment in their way. Camouflage is one of these methods.

Studies have shown that biological camouflage in nature is related to human visual perception, similar to salient object detection. On the other hand, salient object detection aims to detect the brightest object in the picture, while COD detects objects embedded in the surrounding environment. Such as pictures

© Springer Nature Switzerland AG 2022
C. Wallraven et al. (Eds.): ACPR 2021, LNCS 13188, pp. 226–239, 2022.
https://doi.org/10.1007/978-3-031-02375-0_17

shown in Fig. 1, the high degree of similarity in color and texture between camouflage creatures in nature and their dependent environment can easily confuse human vision, so we often ignore the existence of camouflage objects. It also means that obtaining high-quality datasets for this task requires a greater price. So COD is more challenging than other object detection.

COD has a wide range of applications, including wild animal protection, medical image segmentation, agricultural pest detection, and so on. In recent years, the research of COD has made rapid progress. Many DCNN-based COD models have been proposed, such as SINet [1], SSDN [2], MCIF-Net [3] etc. However, it is still very difficult to separate camouflage objects accurately from the complex background, as it is even a huge challenge for the human visual system. The defect of general DCNNs is that they have a scale space problem. Specifically, repeated stride and pooling operations in the CNN structure cause the loss of the underlying visual cues and cannot be reconstructed by upsampling operations. Furthermore, multi-scale feature fusion is also crucial. Existing methods directly perform concatation operations on feature maps with different scales generated by the backbone, which will cause feature interference and redundancy, thereby affecting the final result.

To address these challenges, we propose a novel COD model, which is called "Attention Guided Multi-level Feedback Network (AGMFNet)". It achieves competitive experimental results on three datasets according to our experiment. The main contributions of this paper are as follows:

- We further expand the cascaded decoding module and propose a multi-level feedback module that cascades three decoding components to correct and refine the camouflage image progressively. For single decoding component, we convert the result of the previous decoding module into a weight matrix to act on the middle layer feature map obtained from the backbone, which can make better use of the high-level features. At the same time, in order to retain the underlying clues so that the camouflage image has a shaper border, we incorporate edge features into high-level features.
- We introduce channel attention and spatial attention in the model to capture more information of region of interest and suppress low correlation features. It can make feature maps get a better characterization effect.
- Inception module is applied to our network to improve the performance by capturing more effective characteristics from different fields.

2   Related Work

2.1   Generic Object Detection

COD is a kind of generic object detection, and it is also the most challenging object detection currently. For traditional generic object detection algorithms, manual features including color, texture in the object regions are widely used, achieving satisfactory results in a minimal environment. Yet it is almost impossible to detect and recognize objects successfully in a complex environment. With

(a)Moth   (b)Fish   (c)Spider

Fig. 1. Camouflage creatures in nature.

the continuous development of hardware and software facilities, deep learning and neural network have become the most prevalent ways to solve object detection. In 2017, Lin et al. enhanced feature maps from the backbone network to improve the detection accuracy. Specifically, they connected multi-scale feature maps by jump-layer connection. The network they proposed(FPN) has also become a typical structure in follow-up object detection [4]. Based on the FPN, The Google Brain team designed a more optimized structure in conjunction with the current Neural Architecture Search(NAS) in 2019 [5]. As for algorithms based on anchors such as Fast-RCNN [6] and YOLO [7], which may lead to the imbalance of the positive and negative samples, the boom of super parameters and other issues, many scholars began to incorporate the idea of anchor free into the object detection network. Tian et al. proposed a FCOS network, which predicts object pixel-by-pixel [8]; Law et al. took the detection based on the target corner and proposed CornerNet [9]. Based on it, Zhou et al. conducted further research. He transformed object detection into a critical point, detecting the object's centre point, and resulting in a more efficient detection model, CenterNet [10]. It is worth mentioning that Carion et al. integrated Transformer in the NLP field into the object detection field [11]. It not only achieved anchor free strictly but also exceeded the performance of Faster-RCNN.

2.2   Camouflage Object Detection

The traditional camouflage detection algorithms analysed the reasons for the difficulty of camouflage object detection, such as intensity, color, texture and others which have a high similarity between the camouflaged object and the background. Researchers completed this task by manually extracting features. Boult et al. proposed a background subtraction technique using double thresholds [12]. The larger threshold is used to detect certain pixels that belong to the foreground, while the lower threshold is used to detect uncertain pixels. Li et al. realized the camouflage object detection by weighted voting on the intensity and texture after analyzing the difference between the foreground and the background in the low frequency band of the image [13]. However, camouflage object detection using a single feature is quite limited. The corresponding models have not good generalization capability. Harville et al. utilized the depth images as additional information to assist in the detection and segmentation of camouflage objects [14]. Mondal et al. proposed a Modified Probabilistic Neural Network to achieve camouflage object detection by integrating color, texture, shape and other feature elements [15]. Although the combination of various features can effectively improve the detection effect, there are still defects of traditional manual feature extraction: tedious and detection accuracy bottleneck. With the application of DCNN in this field in recent years, a significant breakthrough has been made. Fang et al. proposed a semantic expansion network and made full use of dilated convolution to increase the receptive field [2]. Fan et al. put forward the SINet and reached the SOTA at that time [1]. Lyu et al. first introduced the "rank" to camouflaged object detection, and proposed a triplet tasks learning model to simultaneously localize, segment and rank the camouflaged objects [16]. These methods, however, do not get rid of the limitations of DCNN, that is, the underlying clues will disappear as the network deepens and cannot be reconstructed through upsampling. In our work, we propose a multi-level feedback module with auxiliary edge information. Each module of the cascade takes the middle-level feature map as input, and the edge branch results are utilized as assistance, which can exploit the high-level semantic features more efficiently while retaining the underlying structure information.

So far, the datasets that are widely used for camouflage object detection are COD10K [1], CHAMELEON [17] and CAMO [18]. The large-scale dataset is only COD10K, while CHAMELEON consists of 76 pictures and CAMO consists of 250 pictures for the test. The lack of large-scale datasets limits the research on camouflage object detection.

2.3   Attention Mechanism

Just as its name implies, the attention mechanism is to pay more attention to the information we interest in and suppress other useless information significantly to improve the efficiency and accuracy of visual information processing.

In recent years, significant progress has been made in the research on the combination of deep learning and attention mechanism. Aiming at the problem that the vital information cannot be identified due to the direct information combination, Jaderberg proposed the Spatial Transformer Module [19], which transforms the spatial information in the original picture into another space and retain the key information through the implementation of attention mechanism. Hu et al. started his research from the relationship between characteristic channels and explicitly modeled the interdependence between feature channels. The proposed SENet [20] enables the network to enhance beneficial feature channels selectively and suppress useless feature channels by using global information, thus realizing adaptive calibration of feature channels. Woo et al. further expanded on the basis of SENet and proposed a simple and efficient forward convolutional neural network attention module, CBAM [21]. It inferred the attention map along two separate channel and space and then multiplied them to carry out adaptive feature refinement. Like the SE Module [20], CBAM can be embedded in most mainstream networks at present to improve the feature extraction ability of network models without significantly increasing the amount of computation and the number of parameters. Considering that the convolution unit in CNN only pays attention to the area of kernel size each time, and even if the receptive field becomes big enough in the later period, it is still the operation of local area. In this way, the contribution of other global areas to the current area is ignored. Wang et al. put forward the Non-local Neural Networks [22] to capture the relationship between the long-range, both in the classification of video and image recognition tasks have achieved very good results. Li et al. combined attention mechanism with spatial pyramid structure to extract accurate and dense features [23], and achieved excellent performance in PASCAL VOC 2012 and Cityscapes. Like to [21], we introduce attention mechanism to act on the feature maps generated by the backbone to transfer more attention to regions of our interest. Thereby, we can reduce information redundancy and interference successfully.

3   The Proposed Method

In this section, we will introduce our proposed framework. It consists of two stages, the Attention Guided Capture Module(AGCM) and the Multi-level Feedback Module(MF). The network searches camouflage objects in the AGCM under the guidance of the attention mechanism. In the MF, we take accurate detection and recognition for them with the assistance of the edge branch. As for the backbone network, ResNet-50 is applied. The overall architecture of AGMFNet is illustrated in Fig. 2.

3.1   Attention Guided Capture Module

Attention Mechanism: The model we proposed is based on the ResNet-50 without the final fully connected layer and pooling layer. For an input image, it will generate a set of feature maps with different resolution $(X_i, i = 0, 1, 2, 3, 4)$. Based on SINet[1], this paper considers that the characteristics extracted from different layers contain their own emphasis on the information. For example, the low-layer convolutions contain richer detail information such as edge, contours, locations, the high-layer convolutions have much more semantic information. Referring to the human visual system, which will focus on the target area and ignore other unrelated content naturally, we introduce Spatial Attention(SA)[21] to the low-layer feature maps (X_0, X_1) and Channel Attention (CA)[21] to the higher-layer feature maps (X_2, X_3, X_4). The formula of CA and SA are as follows:

$$X_i(SA) = \sigma \left(f^{7 \times 7} \left([AvgPool(X_i) ; MaxPool(x_i)] \right) \right), i \in [0, 4] \quad (1)$$

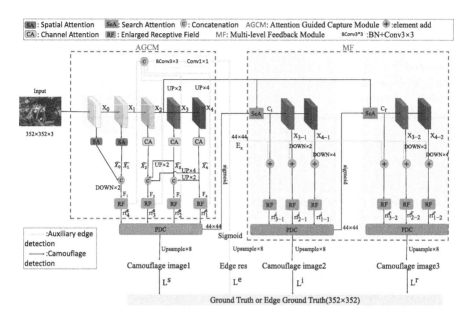

Fig. 2. Structure of the proposed network. PDC means Partial Decoder Component, we utilize it to refine camouflage image progressively, it will be introduced for detail in 3.2.

$$X_i(CA) = \sigma \left(MLP \left(AvgPool \left(X_i \right) \right) + MLP \left(\left(MaxPool \left(X_i \right) \right) \right) \right), i \in [0, 4] \quad (2)$$

X_i is the feature map generated from the backbone. $AvgPool\,(.)$ and $MaxPool\,(.)$ represent average pooling and max pooling separately. The shared MLP is a weight-sharing multi-layer perceptron. $\sigma\,(.)$ is sigmoid function.

Later, we utilize the attention feature $X_i\,(SA)$ or $X_i\,(CA)$ to take a multiplication operation with X_i to obtain feature map after selecting $\hat{X}_i$.

Feature Fusion: We divide feature maps into low-level features, middle-level features, and high-level features. As the lowest feature map, X_0 contains a lot of interference information. Therefore, this branch is not retained in feature fusion, but directly incorporated into the X_1 branch as an auxiliary feature map to provide structural information for the later network. For other feature maps, each branch integrates feature maps of the higher level to enhance its semantic information. The formula is as follows:

$$F_1 = downsample \left(\hat{X}_0 + \hat{X}_1 \right) \quad (3)$$

$$F_2 = \hat{X}_2 + upsample \left(\hat{X}_3 \right) + upsample \left(upsample \left(\hat{X}_4 \right) \right) \quad (4)$$

$$F_3 = \hat{X}_3 + upsample \left(\hat{X}_4 \right) \quad (5)$$

$$F_4 = \hat{X}_4 \qquad\qquad (6)$$

Enlarged Receptive Field: As shown in the Fig. 2, features sent to the PDC are all processed by the RF[24] component for feature enhancement in the whole network. RF contains five parallel branches, and each chapter starts with a 1×1 convolution layer to reduce the channels, followed by the asymmetric convolution and dilated convolution with different dilation rate. RF performs concatenation operation on captured feature maps with varying sizes of receptive fields, which can effectively enhance the representation ability of feature maps.

Auxiliary Edge Detection: As shown in Fig. 2, taking into account that lower-level feature maps preserve better edge information, we resize multi enhanced feature maps to the same resolution as rf_4^s to generate a edge feature map E_x. It will be used as auxiliary information to help obtain the accurate camouflage image in the MF. Moreover, we calculate the loss of the generated edge image and the Edge Ground Truth to participate in the whole training process.

3.2   Multi-level Feedback Module

Existing models are accustomed to sending all the feature maps with different scales obtained from the encoder into the decoder module to produce the desired results. Some decoding layer by layer such as FCN [25], and others fusing all scales feature maps using skip layer connections represented by Amulet [26]. There is also a problem with this. The lowest-layer feature map X_0 also brings a lot of noise and information redundancy, although it contains many detail. The network proposed in this paper refers to the cascade partial decoder, and introduces the deep supervised mechanism to propose a multi-level feedback module. The structure is shown in Fig. 2.

First, in order to capture rich semantic information in high-layers and obtain more accurate camouflage image, our model refines the feature maps twice. In simple terms, after generating a coarse camouflage map(Camouflage image1) which tend to capture much more structural information, on the one hand, we turn it into a weighted matrix and feedback it to the backbone to refine the feature map of the middle layer by using a typical Gaussian filter with standard deviation SeA. Then, for the obtained high-leval feature maps C_i, X_{3-1} and X_{4-1}, we take a elememt add operation to them with the edge feature map E_x to enrich their edge information. So far, we have kept the low-level structure information while using high-level semantic information as efficiently as possible. Later, we send a round of refined features rf_{3-1}^i, rf_{2-1}^i, rf_{1-1}^i to the PDC which is shown in Fig. 3 and so on. On the other hand, we calculate the loss of the resulting camouflage image and the corresponding ground truth, which can supervise the training of the whole network as one part of the entire loss function. Finally, we can obtain feature map complete enough to generate finer camouflage image.

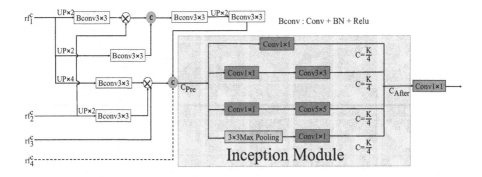

Fig. 3. The structure of the partial decoder component

Secondly, unlike PDC in[1], we consider that although the convolution with the kernel of 3 × 3 can increase the size of filed and transform the feature map to a certain extent in theory. The effect will be somewhat different. By contrast, the Inception Module[27] utilizes four branches with varying sizes of convolution to capture information in different fields respectively, which makes the model have a better characterization effect. We replace the original 3 × 3 convolution layer with the Inception Module. The structure is shown in Fig. 3. In addition, in order to simplify the calculation, we ensure that the number of channels of the input and output feature maps for the Inception Module is consistent. Intuitively, $C_{Pre} \in H \times W \times K$, $C_{After} \in H \times W \times K$, and the channels of the map produced by each branch are $K/4$.

4 Experiment

4.1 Datasets and Evaluation Criteria

COD10K proposed in [1], which consists of 10000 pictures, is the largest and most comprehensive datasets currently used to detect camouflage objects. We train our proposed network on COD10K and CHAMELEON. For the performance of the proposed network, we select four metrics to evaluate it on CAMO, COD10K, CHAMELEON separately, including MAE(Mean Absolute Error), the weighted F_{β}^{ω} [28], S_{α} (Structure-measure) [29], E_{ϕ}(Enhanced-alignment measure) [30].

MAE represents the per-pixel wise difference between the predicted camouflage map and the ground truth. It can reflect the actual situation of the prediction error accurately and intuitively.

$$MAE = \frac{1}{m \times n} \sum_{i=1}^{m} \sum_{j=1}^{n} |\hat{y}_{ij} - y_{ij}| \tag{7}$$

The F_{β}^{ω} proposed in [28] is more reliable and accurate than the traditional F_{β}, and its calculation formula is as follows:

$$F_{\beta}^{\omega} = (1 + \beta^2) \frac{Precision^{\omega} \cdot Recall^{\omega}}{\beta^2 \cdot Precision^{\omega} + Recall^{\omega}} \tag{8}$$

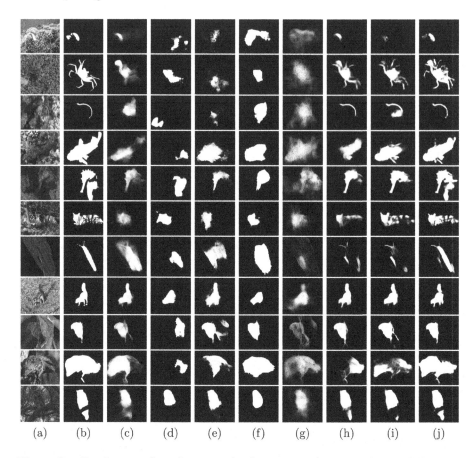

(a)   (b)   (c)   (d)   (e)   (f)   (g)   (h)   (i)   (j)

Fig. 4. Qualitative results of our method, compared with existing GOD and SOD methods. (a)RGB, (B)Ground Truth, (c)FPN, (d)Mask RCNN, (e)UNet++, (f)MSRCNN, (g)PFANet, (h)EGNet, (i)SINet, (j)AGMFNet(ours).

Similar to F_β, β represents the relative importance of $Recall^\omega$ to the $Precision^\omega$. If $\beta_¿1$, $Recall^\omega$ is much more critical; otherwise, it has less influence than $Precision^\omega$.

S_α consists of region-aware and object-aware. It can capture the global structure information of the image and the difference between the foreground and the background, and the formula is as follows:

$$S = \alpha \times S_{object} + (1 - \alpha) \times S_{region} \tag{9}$$

E_ϕ can capture global statistics and local pixel matching information of the image at the same time.

4.2   Implementation Details

The experimental environment of this paper is as follows: Ubuntu20.04, PyTorch3.7.7, TITAN RTX equipped with 24G memory, Inter®Xeon® E5-2680v4 CPU @2.40 GHz × 28. During the training, we select Adam as the optimizer and the attenuation strategy of the learning rate is cosine annealing. In our experiment, we set the batch size is 36, the initial learning rate is 0.0001, and the epoch is 120. The whole training takes about 5h. Furthermore, the size of the input RGB image is resized to $352 \times 352 \times 3$, and the resulting image size is the same.

4.3   Loss Function

Cross entropy describes the distance between the actual output and the expected output. The smaller the value of cross entropy is, the closer the actual output is to the expected output. In the field of object detection, cross entropy is widely used to express the loss function. In this paper, the loss function consists of three parts, it is defined as follows:

$$Loss(total) = L^s + L^i + L^r + L^e \qquad (10)$$

We define the binary cross entropy loss function L^s, L^i, L^r, L^e as:

$$BCE(C,G) = -\frac{1}{N} \sum_{n=1}^{N} [G_n \log(C_n) + (1 - G_n) \log(1 - C_n)] \qquad (11)$$

$N = H \times W$, is the number of all pixel points, n represents a single pixel point. C denotes the camouflage image generated by the single decoding module or the Edge res, and G denotes the corresponding ground truth.

4.4   Comparisons with State-of-the Arts

We compare our model with seven state-of-art methods including FPN[4], MaskR-CNN [31], UNet++ [32], MSRCNN [33], PFANet [34], EGNet [35], SINet [1]. In our comparative experiment, we use the pretrained models provided by the author to take a test for each method.

Qualitative comparisons: As illustrated in Table 1, we take seven qualitative comparison experiments with our proposed network. It can be seen from these data, AGMFNet has had the most dramatic effect than all the competitors. In terms of the MAE, our AGMFNet is improved by 1% on each of the three datasets compared with SINet. For the evaluation F_β^ω, it has an increase of 7.2% on COD10K datasets, 6.5% on CHAMELEON datasets. On CAMO datasets, it is also improved by 4.8%.

Visual comparison: In order to show the superiority of our method more intuitively, we carry out a visual comparison. As shown in Fig. 4. Considering that COD10K is the largest and highest in quality in the three datasets, the samples shown are all from the COD10K and different categories. For the examples listed in Fig. 4, our method obtains the camouflage map with the highest similarity to the corresponding GT. In particular, it has a much sharper boundary, which may be related to the method of the feature fusion and the utilization of edge information.

Table 1. Quantitative evaluation of our method against state-of-the-art methods.

Models	CHAMELEON				CAMO				COD10K			
	$S_\alpha \uparrow$	$E_\phi \uparrow$	$F_\beta^\omega \uparrow$	$M \downarrow$	$S_\alpha \uparrow$	$E_\phi \uparrow$	$F_\beta^\omega \uparrow$	$M \downarrow$	$S_\alpha \uparrow$	$E_\phi \uparrow$	$F_\beta^\omega \uparrow$	$M \downarrow$
FPN	0.794	0.783	0.590	0.075	0.684	0.677	0.483	0.131	0.697	0.691	0.411	0.075
MaskRCNN	0.643	0.778	0.518	0.099	0.574	0.715	0.430	0.151	0.613	0.758	0.402	0.080
UNet++	0.695	0.762	0.501	0.094	0.599	0.653	0.392	0.149	0.623	0.672	0.350	0.086
MSRCNN	0.637	0.686	0.443	0.091	0.617	0.669	0.454	0.133	0.641	0.706	0.419	0.073
PFANet	0.679	0.648	0.478	0.144	0.659	0.622	0.391	0.172	0.636	0.618	0.286	0.128
EGNet	0.848	0.870	0.702	0.050	0.732	0.768	0.583	0.104	0.737	0.779	0.509	0.056
SINet	0.869	0.891	0.740	0.044	0.751	0.771	0.606	0.100	0.771	0.806	0.551	0.051
AGMFNet(ours)	**0.887**	**0.929**	**0.805**	**0.033**	**0.760**	**0.802**	**0.654**	**0.089**	**0.784**	**0.845**	**0.623**	**0.041**

4.5 Ablations

To prove the effectiveness of each module introduced, we conduct a series of ablation studies on three datasets. The results are illustrated in the Table 2.

Table 2. Quantitative evaluation of ablation studies.

Base	CA	SA	Incep	MF	Edge	CHAMELEON				CAMO				COD10K			
						$S_\alpha \uparrow$	$E_\phi \uparrow$	$F_\beta^\omega \uparrow$	$M \downarrow$	$S_\alpha \uparrow$	$E_\phi \uparrow$	$F_\beta^\omega \uparrow$	$M \downarrow$	$S_\alpha \uparrow$	$E_\phi \uparrow$	$F_\beta^\omega \uparrow$	$M \downarrow$
✓						0.869	0.891	0.740	0.044	0.751	0.771	0.606	0.100	0.771	0.806	0.551	0.051
✓	✓					0.873	0.914	0.783	0.039	0.739	0.775	0.621	0.097	0.774	0.833	0.602	0.045
✓		✓				0.883	0.916	0.794	0.035	0.747	0.777	0.622	0.092	0.778	0.831	0.599	0.044
✓			✓			0.872	0.911	0.785	0.038	0.742	0.775	0.621	0.095	0.775	0.832	0.603	0.045
✓					✓	0.881	0.933	0.794	0.034	0.748	0.788	0.628	0.094	0.768	0.829	0.587	0.046
✓	✓	✓				0.878	0.917	0.794	0.034	0.744	0.785	0.627	0.092	0.774	0.833	0.605	0.043
✓	✓	✓	✓			0.883	0.921	0.799	0.034	0.756	0.791	0.638	0.092	0.778	0.833	0.607	0.044
✓	✓	✓	✓	✓		0.885	0.921	0.803	0.034	0.755	0.799	0.648	0.090	0.778	0.833	0.610	0.043
✓	✓	✓	✓	✓	✓	0.887	0.929	0.805	0.033	0.760	0.802	0.654	0.089	0.784	0.845	0.623	0.041

We propose the network AGMFNet based on the SINet, so the ablation experiment is to integrate the introduced modules into SINet in different combinations. According to the results, any combination on all the datasets tested is superior to the base network, which also confirms the effectiveness of these modules. Especially for the SA and the Edge branch, their introduction are of great significance to improving the entire network performance. But in terms of overall performance, AGMFNet is still the most competitive method.

5   Conclusion

In this paper, we carry out further research and experiments based on the SINet, and propose a novel model for camouflage object detection, AGMFNet. We design a multi-level feedback decoding module with auxiliary edge information to make full use of high-level semantic features and lower-level detailed information to refine the camouflage object. Spatial attention, channel attention and inception modules are integrated in our model, and the effectiveness of these modules in improving the performance of the model are proved. Compared with state-of-art methods, AGMFNet has achieved competitive experimental results.

References

1. Dengping, F., Gepeng, J., Guolei, S., Mingming, C., Jianbing, S., Ling, S.: Camouflaged object detection. In: Proceedings of the IEEE Conference on Computer Vision and Pattern Recognition, pp. 2777–2787 (2020). https://doi.org/10.1109/CVPR42600.2020.00285
2. Zheng, F., Xiongwei, Z., Xiaotong, D.: Camouflage people detection via strong semantic dilation network. In: ACM Turing Celebration Conference, pp. 1–7 (2019). https://doi.org/10.1145/3321408.3326662
3. Dong, B., Zhuge, M., Wang, Y., Bi, H., Chen, G.: Towards accurate camouflaged object detection with mixture convolution and interactive fusion. CoRR abs/2101.05687 (2021)
4. TsungYi, L., Piotr, D., Ross, G.: Feature pyramid networks for object detection. In: Proceedings of the IEEE Conference on Computer Vision and Pattern Recognition, pp. 936–944 (2017). https://doi.org/10.1109/CVPR.2017.106
5. Golnaz, G., TsungYi, L., Ruoming, P.: NAS-FPN: learning scalable feature pyramid architecture for object detection. In: Proceedings of the IEEE Conference on Computer Vision and Pattern Recognition, pp. 7036–7045 (2019). https://doi.org/10.1109/CVPR.2019.00720
6. Girshick, R.: Fast R-CNN. In: Proceedings of the IEEE International Conference on Computer Vision, pp. 1440–1448 (2015). https://doi.org/10.1109/ICCV.2015.169
7. Redmon, J., Divvala, S., Girshick, R.: You only look once: unified, real time object detection. In: Proceedings of the IEEE Conference on Computer Vision and Pattern Recognition, pp. 779–788 (2016). https://doi.org/10.1109/CVPR.2016.91
8. Zhi, T., Chunhua, S., Hao, C., Tong, H.: FCOS: fully convolutional one-stage object detection. In: Proceedings of the IEEE International Conference on Computer Vision, pp. 9626–9635 (2019). https://doi.org/10.1109/ICCV.2019.00972
9. Hei, L., Jia, D.: CornerNet: detecting objects as paired keypoints. In: European Conference on Computer Vision, pp. 765–781 (2018). https://doi.org/10.1007/978-3-030-01264-9_45
10. Xingyi, Z., Dequan, W., Philipp, K.: Objects as points. CoRR abs/1904.07850 (2019)
11. Nicolas, C., Francisco, M., Gabriel, S.: End-to-end object detection with transformers. In: European Conference on Computer Vision, pp. 213–229 (2020). https://doi.org/10.1007/978-3-030-58452-8_13

12. Boult, T., Micheals, R., Gao, X., Eckmann, M.: Into the woods: visual surveillance of noncooperative and camouflaged targets in complex outdoor settings. Proc. IEEE **89**(10), 1382–1402 (2001). https://doi.org/10.1109/5.959337

13. Li, S., Florencio, D., Zhao, Y., Cook, C., Li, W.: Foreground detection in camouflaged scenes. In: Proceedings of the IEEE International Conference on Image Processing, pp. 4247–4251 (2017). https://doi.org/10.1109/ICIP.2017.8297083

14. Harville, M., Gordon, G., Woodfill, J.: Foreground segmentation using adaptive mixture models in color and depth. In: Proceedings of IEEE Workshop on Detection and Recognition of Events in Video, pp. 3–11 (2001). https://doi.org/10.1109/EVENT.2001.938860

15. Mondal, A., Ghosh, S., Ghosh, A.: Partially camouflaged object tracking using modified probabilistic neural network and fuzzy energy based active contour. Int. J. Comput. Vision **122**(1), 116–148 (2016). https://doi.org/10.1007/s11263-016-0959-5

16. Yunqiu, L., Jing, Z., Yuchao, D., Aixuan, L., Bowen, L., Nick, B., et al.: Simultaneously localize, segment and rank the camouflaged objects. In: Proceedings of the IEEE Conference on Computer Vision and Pattern Recognition, pp. 11591–11601 (2021)

17. Skurowski, P., Abdulameer, H., Blaszczyk, J., Depta, T., Kornacki, A., Koziel, P.: Animal camouflage analysis: Chameleon database. Unpublished Manuscript (2018)

18. TrungNghia, L., Tam, V., Zhongliang, N., MinhTriet, T., Akihiro, S.: Anabranch network for camouflaged object segmentation, In: Computer Vision and Image Understanding, pp. 45–56 (2019). https://doi.org/10.1016/j.cviu.2019.04.006

19. Max, J., Karen, S., Andrew, Z., Koray.: Spatial transformer networks. In: Neural Information Processing Systems, pp. 2017–2025 (2015)

20. Jie, H., Li, S., Samuel, A., Gang, S., Enhua, W.: Squeeze-and-excitation networks. In: Proceedings of the IEEE Conference on Computer Vision and Pattern Recognition, pp. 7132–7141 (2018). https://doi.org/10.1109/CVPR.2018.00745

21. Sanghyun, W., Jongchan, P., Joonyoung, L., So, K.: CBAM: convolutional block attention module. In: European Conference on Computer Vision, pp. 3–19 (2018). https://doi.org/10.1007/978-3-030-01234-2_1

22. Xiaolong, W., Ross, B., Abhinav, G., Kaiming, H.: Non-local neural networks. In: Proceedings of the IEEE Conference on Computer Vision and Pattern Recognition, pp. 7794–7803 (2018). https://doi.org/10.1109/CVPR.2018.00813

23. Hanchao, L., Pengfei, X., Jie, A., Lingxue, W.: Pyramid attention network for semantic segmentation. In: British Machine Vision Conference, pp. 285–296 (2018)

24. Songtao, L., Di, H., Yunhong, W.: Receptive field block net for accurate and fast object detection. In: European Conference on Computer Vision, pp. 404–419 (2018). https://doi.org/10.1007/978-3-030-01252-6_24

25. Long, J., Shelhamer, E., Darrell, T.: Fully convolutional networks for semantic segmentation. In: IEEE Transactions on Pattern Analysis and Machine Intelligence, pp. 640–651 (2017). https://doi.org/10.1109/TPAMI.2016.2572683

26. Pingping, Z., Dong, W., Huchuan, L., Hongyu, W., Xiang, R.: Amulet: aggregating multi-level convolutional features for salient object detection. In: Proceedings of the IEEE International Conference on Computer Vision, pp. 202–211 (2017). https://doi.org/10.1109/ICCV.2017.31

27. Christian, S., Wei, L., Yangqing, J., Pierre, S., Scott, R., Dragomir, A., et al.: Going deeper with convolutions. In: Proceedings of the IEEE Conference on Computer Vision and Pattern Recognition, pp. 1–9 (2015). https://doi.org/10.1109/CVPR.2015.7298594

28. Ran, M., Lihi, Z., Ayellet, T.: How to evaluate foreground maps. In: Proceedings of the IEEE Conference on Computer Vision and Pattern Recognition, pp. 248–255 (2014). https://doi.org/10.1109/CVPR.2014.39

29. Dengping, F., Mingming, C., Yun, L., Tao, L., Ali, B.: Structure-measure: a new way to evaluate foreground maps. In: Proceedings of the IEEE International Conference on Computer Vision, pp. 4558–4567 (2017). https://doi.org/10.1109/ICCV.2017.487

30. Dengping, F., Cheng, G., Yang, C., Bo, R., Mingming, C., Ali, B.: Enhanced-alignment measure for binary foreground map evaluation. In: Proceedings of the International Joint Conference on Artificial Intelligence, pp. 698–704 (2018). https://doi.org/10.24963/ijcai.2018/97

31. Kaiming, H., Georgia, G., Piotr, D., Ross, G.: Mask R-CNN. In: Proceedings of the IEEE International Conference on Computer Vision, pp. 2980–2988 (2017). https://doi.org/10.1109/ICCV.2017.322

32. Zhou, Z., Rahman, S., Tajbakhsh, N., Liang, J.: UNet++: a nested UNet architecture for medical image segmentation. In: Deep Learning on Medical Image Analysis, pp. 3–11 (2018). https://doi.org/10.1007/978-3-030-00889-5_1

33. Zhaojin, H., Lichao, H., Yongchao, G., Chang, H., Xinggang, W.: Mask scoring R-CNN. In: Proceedings of the IEEE Conference on Computer Vision and Pattern Recognition, pp. 6409–6418 (2019). https://doi.org/10.1109/CVPR.2019.00657

34. Ting, Z., Xiangqian, W.: Pyramid feature attention network for saliency detection. In: Proceedings of the IEEE Conference on Computer Vision and Pattern Recognition, pp. 3085–3094 (2019). https://doi.org/10.1109/CVPR.2019.00320

35. Jiaxing, Z., Jiangjiang, L., Dengping, F., Yang, C., Jufeng, Y., Mingming, C.: EGNet: edge guidance network for salient object detection. In: Proceedings of the IEEE International Conference on Computer Vision, pp. 8778–8787 (2019). https://doi.org/10.1109/ICCV.2019.00887

Confidence-Aware Anomaly Detection in Human Actions

Tsung-Hsuan Wu$^{(\boxtimes)}$, Chun-Lung Yang, Li-Ling Chiu, Ting-Wei Wang,
Gueter Josmy Faure, and Shang-Hong Lai

Department of Computer Science, National Tsing Hua University, Hsinchu, Taiwan
th.wu@mx.nthu.edu.tw

Abstract. Anomaly detection in human actions from video has been a
challenging problem in computer vision and video analysis. The human
poses estimated from videos have often been used to represent the features of human actions. However, extracting keypoints from the video
frames are doomed to errors for crowded scenes and the falsely detected
keypoints could mislead the anomaly detection task. In this paper, we
propose a novel GCN autoencoder model to reconstruct, predict and
group the poses trajectories, and a new anomaly score determined by the
predicted pose error weighted by the corresponding confidence score associated with each keypoint. Experimental results demonstrate that the
proposed method can achieve state-of-the-art performance for anomaly
detection from human action videos.

Keywords: Video anomaly detection · Human pose · GCN ·
Confident scores

1 Introduction

Anomaly detection in human activities from videos is a challenging research
problem that attracts great attention from academia and industry in recent
years. Due to the lack of abnormal data, anomaly detection is usually treated
as an unsupervised task. Since almost all the training data is assumed to be
normal, models are trained to learn the characteristics from the normal data,
such as grouping, reconstructing the data, or predicting the future frames in a
video. Since this skill is only learnt from normal data, it should work badly on
abnormal data so that anomalies can be detected.

Due to the rarity of the abnormal data, anomaly detection is usually treated
as an unsupervised task. With all (or most of) the training data are normal, the
model is asked for learning a "skill" such as grouping [1–3], reconstructing the
data [2–7], or predicting the futures [6–8] of the videos. Since this skill is only

S.-H. Lai—We thank to National Center for High-performance Computing (NCHC)
for providing computational and storage resources.

C. Wallraven et al. (Eds.): ACPR 2021, LNCS 13188, pp. 240–254, 2022.
https://doi.org/10.1007/978-3-031-02375-0_18

learnt from normal data, it might work badly on the anomalies. As a result, the normality can be classified.

Dealing with events in videos, most recent methods focus on the appearance of the time-consecutive images [2,5,6], while the proposed method is focused on the human poses. Human poses are often used in analysis of human behaviors. [9] used pose features to recognize human actions. [10] estimated 3D-poses from 2D-poses. The pose data has the advantage that only the human features are used in the models. However, while extracting the keypoints from the images, the pose estimation may involve large errors for crowded scenes, which makes the follow-up works very difficult. To alleviate this problem, we add the confidence scores into our model so the result will be less sensitive to the errors in keypoint detection.

To classify the normal and the abnormal human actions in the videos, we reconstruct, predict and group the poses trajectories. Considered poses as graphs, our proposed model is based on the graph convolutional networks (GCN), which is recently applied to many deep learning methods on pose data. To group the poses trajectories, we use a multi-centers loss to gather the latent features to their corresponding centers. Moreover, to score the abnormality of the poses, we propose a new method, applying the confident scores, to evaluate the error between the output and the original keypoints.

The main contributions of this work are listed as follows:

- We propose a *temporal poses autoencoder* (TP-AE) framework (Fig. 1) to reconstruct and predict the poses trajectories.
- We propose the multi-centers loss function to cluster the latent features of the poses trajectories.
- We propose a novel anomaly score involving the confidence scores of pose estimation, to reduce the influence brought from the falsely detected keypoints.

2   Related Work

Anomaly Detection on Image Data. Anomaly detection on image data is usually considered as an one-class classification problem. Lukas *et al.* in [1] used a CNN model to gather the features of the normal images to a center and then detected the outliers by the distance between the features and the center. Schlegl *et al.* in [4] used a GAN model so that the generator learnt to construct, from the random latent vectors, the images similar to the normal class, while the abnormal images would not able to be constructed.

Appearance-based Anomaly Detection on Video Data. To detect anomaly events in videos, most of the current works are based on the appearance of the frames. To extract the temporal information, the motion information such as optical flows are often used. Liu *et al.* in [5] used a CNN U-net model to predict the future image from a sequence of frames. To improve the prediction, the intensity difference, gradient difference, optical flows and the GAN structure

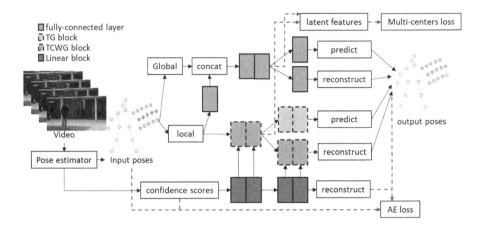

Fig. 1. Architecture of TP-AE model. After the pose estimator evaluates the keypoints and their confidence scores, the poses are separated into global and local information. The yellow pipeline is consisting of fully-connected layers and is to reconstruct and predict the global information. The blue and red parts are the GCN-based layers which reconstruct and predict the local information. The green pipeline, based on linear functions, produces weights to assist the TCWG blocks. The total loss function is composed of the errors of the reconstruction/prediction and the loss of multi-centers clustering.

are also used. Nguyen *et al.* in [6] predicted the optical flow by a single frame. Chang *et al.* in [2] predicted the difference between frames and reconstructed, clustered them in the same time.

Pose-based Anomaly Detection on Video Data. As the appearance-based methods, pose-based anomaly detection also focused on reconstruction or prediction. Morais *et al.* in [7] first separated the poses into global and local information. Then the RNN-based model reconstructed the input poses and predicted the future poses. Based on 1D-CNN, Rodrigues *et al.* in [8] proposed a multi-timescale model to make future and past predictions at different timescales. Markovitz *et al.* in [3] used GCN-based autoencoder to reconstruct the poses trajectories, while the point of this work was the grouping of the latent features by the Dirichlet process mixture model (DPMM). Different from the above error-based anomaly scores, the normality score of each sample was computed by its log probability using the fitted model.

Referring to [7] and [8], our model also reconstructs the inputs and predicts the future pose trajectories, while different from them, we use GCN-based networks and apply confidence scores of the keypoints to the networks and to the computation of anomaly scores. Moreover, we add a loss function to group the pose trajectories unsupervisedly.

3 Proposed Model

In this section, we present the details of our method. As [7] and [8], we estimate the human poses trajectories by applying poses detector and human tracker to the dataset. In addition, we preserve the confidence scores of the keypoints for later usage. To detect anomalies, we first train a model to reconstruct and predict poses on the training videos which contain only normal human behaviors. Then we apply the model to the testing videos to detect anomaly behaviors by the performance of the reconstruction and prediction. Instead of RNN or CNN, our proposed model, temporal poses autoencoder (TP-AE), is based on GCN and applies confidence scores to alleviate the problems of missing nodes. Moreover, to further improve our model, we use the multi-centers SVDD loss function to group the latent vectors. Finally, applying the confidence scores again, we propose a new score to detect anomalies.

3.1 Confidence-weighted Graph Convolution Network

To reduce the influence of the keypoints with low confidence scores, we use the confidence-weighted graph convolution network (CWGCN) [11]. Before we introduce CWGCN, let's recall the function of the classical GCN. For a graph $G = (V, E)$, where V is the set of N vertices and E are the edges, including all the self-loops. Then E induces an adjacency matrix $A \in \{0,1\}^{N \times N}$. Let $X \in \mathbb{R}^{F \times N}$ be the input of the GCN, where F is the dimension of the feature vector of each vertex. Then the output of the GCN is

$$\overline{X} = W X \widetilde{A} , \tag{1}$$

where $W \in \mathbb{R}^{F' \times F}$ is a learnable matrix, F' is the number of features of the next layer, and $\widetilde{A}$ denotes the column normalization of A, that is, for each i, j,

$$\widetilde{A}_{i,j} = \frac{A_{i,j}}{\sum_{k=1}^{N} A_{k,j}} . \tag{2}$$

In (1), we can observe that the output feature vector of the j-th vertex is $\overline{X}_{-,j} = W(X\widetilde{A})_{-,j}$, where

$$(X\widetilde{A})_{-,j} = \frac{1}{\sum_{k=1}^{N} A_{k,j}} \sum_{i=1}^{N} X_{-,i} A_{i,j} \tag{3}$$

is the average of $\{X_{-,i} | (i,j) \in E\}$; in the other words, all the jointed vertices have the same influence on $\overline{X}_{-,j}$.

However, in case some input vertices have lower confidence scores, those unreliable features shouldn't have the same influence as others. Therefore, we take the confidence score as a weight to indicate the influence of each vertex. Let $\{c_i\}_{i=1}^{N}$ be the confidence scores and $C = diag\{c_i\}$. Then the output of the CWGCN is

$$\overline{X} = W X \widetilde{CA} , \tag{4}$$

where $\widetilde{CA}$ denotes the column normalization of CA, that is,

$$\widetilde{CA}_{i,j} = \frac{c_i A_{i,j}}{\sum_{k=1}^{N} c_k A_{k,j}} . \tag{5}$$

In this case, $\overline{X}_{-,j}$ is determined by

$$(X\widetilde{CA})_{-,j} = \frac{1}{\sum_{k=1}^{N} c_k A_{k,j}} \sum_{i=1}^{N} X_{-,i} c_i A_{i,j} , \tag{6}$$

which is the weighted average of $\{X_{-,i} | (i,j) \in E\}$.

3.2   Temporal Confident Weighted Graph Convolution

To consider a single pose $P = \{P_i | 1 \leq i \leq N\}$ as a graph, it is natural to regard the keypoints as vertices and the skeletons as edges, including all the self-loops. However, when things comes to a sequence of poses, various strategies might be taken. Our definition is as follow.

First we define some notations. Let $S \subset N^2$ denote the set of indices of the skeletons of a pose, that is, $(i,j) \in S$ if the i-th and the j-th keypoints are jointed. For a poses trajectory $\{P_t\}_{t=1}^{T} = \{P_{t,i} | 1 \leq t \leq T, 1 \leq i \leq N\}$, we define the temporal poses graph by $TG = (\{P_{t,i}\}, TS)$, where $P_{t,i}$ is the i-th keypoint in the time t and

$$TS = \{(t_1, i, t_2, j) | t_1 \leq T, t_2 \leq T, (i,j) \in S\} . \tag{7}$$

In other words, a keypoint $P_{t_1,i}$ is jointed to every $P_{t_2,j}$ with $(i,j) \in S$, for any t_1 and t_2.

Next, let P^1 and P^2 be two poses trajectories with time-lengths T_1 and T_2, respectively. For further usage, we are going to define the "temporal edges" between P^1 and P^2 by an analogous definition of TS above, that is, the keypoints $P_{t_1,i}^1 \in P^1$ and $P_{t_2,j}^2 \in P^2$ are jointed if $(i,j) \in S$. More specifically, the temporal edges are defined by

$$TE = \{(t_1, i, t_2, j) | t_1 \leq T_1, t_2 \leq T_2, (i,j) \in S\} . \tag{8}$$

Note that the adjacency matrices of TE can be simply derived by A^S, the adjacency matrix of S. First we rearrange the index of the keypoints by

$$P_{t,i} \sim P_{(t-1)*N+i}^{rearrange} . \tag{9}$$

Then if $A_{i,j}^S = 1$, that is, $(i,j) \in S$, we have $P_{(t_1-1)*N+i}^{rearrange}$ and $P_{(t_2-1)*N+j}^{rearrange}$ are jointed for any t_1 and t_2. Therefore, A^{TE}, the adjacency matrix of TE, is a $(T_1 * N)$ by $(T_2 * N)$ matrix generated by repeating A^S $(T_1 \times T_2)$ times. For example, if $N = 3$, $A^S = \begin{pmatrix} 1 & 1 & 0 \\ 1 & 1 & 1 \\ 0 & 1 & 1 \end{pmatrix}$, $T_1 = 2$ and $T_2 = 3$, then

$$A^{TE} = \begin{pmatrix} 1 & 1 & 0 & 1 & 1 & 0 & 1 & 1 & 0 \\ 1 & 1 & 1 & 1 & 1 & 1 & 1 & 1 & 1 \\ 0 & 1 & 1 & 0 & 1 & 1 & 0 & 1 & 1 \\ 1 & 1 & 0 & 1 & 1 & 0 & 1 & 1 & 0 \\ 1 & 1 & 1 & 1 & 1 & 1 & 1 & 1 & 1 \\ 0 & 1 & 1 & 0 & 1 & 1 & 0 & 1 & 1 \end{pmatrix} . \tag{10}$$

Following the above result, if we apply A^{TE} to GCN or CWGCN, the time-lengths of the input trajectory and the output trajectory can be different. This benefits the GCN-based models when doing poses prediction or using an autoencoder architecture. However, it also leads to a problem that the outputs $\overline{X}_{-,(t_1-1)*N+i}$ and $\overline{X}_{-,(t_2-1)*N+i}$ are the same for any t_1 and t_2 since $A^{TE}_{i,(t_1-1)*N+i} = A^{TE}_{i,(t_2-1)*N+i}$, which means the output poses are the same regardless of time.

To correct this problem, we design the *temporal confidence weighted graph convolution network* (TCWGCN) as follows. Let $X \in \mathbb{R}^{F \times T_1 N}$ be the input of the TCWGCN and $C \in \mathbb{R}^{T_1 N}$ be the confidence scores, where F is the number of the input features, T_1 is the input time-length and N is the number of nodes. Let F' be the number of the output features, T_2 be the output time-length. The output of the TCWGCN at the time point t is

$$\overline{X^t} = W^t X \widetilde{CA^{TE}} , \tag{11}$$

where each $W^t \in \mathbb{R}^{F' \times F}$ is a learnable matrix for the time t, $1 \leq t \leq T_2$. In addition, we also define the *temporal graph convolution network* (TGCN) to be the TCWGCN with all scores are replaced by 1.0.

3.3   Network Architecture

As [7], our model first separates each pose into global and local parts. Let B be the bounding box of the pose $P = \{P_i\}_{i=1}^N$. The global information of P is a $4-$dimensional vector $P^G = (w, h, x, y)$ formed by the width w, the height h and the center (x, y) of B. Then the local information P^L is obtained by regularizing P by P^G, that is,

$$P_i^L = (\frac{P_{i,x} - x}{w} + 0.5, \frac{P_{i,y} - y}{h} + 0.5), \tag{12}$$

where $(P_{i,x}, P_{i,y}) = P_i$.

As shown in Fig. 1, the TP-AE model contains 3 pipelines: the global pipeline, the local pipeline and the confidence score pipeline. The global and the local pipelines aim to reconstruct and predict the global and the local information, so each contains one encoder and two decoders. On the other hand, the confidence

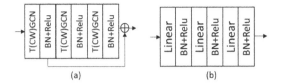

Fig. 2. (a) TCWG and TG block (b) Linear block

score pipeline contains only one encoder and one decoder since the prediction of the confidence scores is unreasonable.

The global encoder and decoders are composed of fully-connected layers, while the local encoder and decoders are composed of TCWG blocks or TG blocks. As shown in Fig. 2 (a), each TCWG block (or TG block) contains three TCWGCNs (or TGCNs). As [10], we use residual blocks, and each TCWGCN is followed by a batch normalization and a ReLU activation. In the encoder, the first TCWGCN in each block may remain or half the time-lengths of the inputs, while in the decoders the first TCWGCN may remain or double the time-lengths.

The confidence score pipeline is almost the same as the local pipeline, except that the TCWGCN's are replaced by linear functions, and there is no residual block (Fig. 2 (b)). As a result, the midterm outputs, as simulated confidence scores, can be passed to all the TCWGCN's in the local pipeline.

3.4 Loss Function

In our model, the total loss function consists of AE-Loss and the multi-centers loss.

The AE-loss is the combination of the loss of pose estimation errors and the loss of the confidence scores. The loss of pose estimation errors is determined by the error between the estimated and the real poses. As [8], the error of a pose is the weighted mean square error

$$e(P) = \sum_{i=1}^{N} \frac{c_i}{\sum_{k=1}^{N} c_K} \left(P_i - \hat{P}_i \right)^2 , \tag{13}$$

where c_i is the i-th confidence score, P_i and $\hat{P}_i$ are the real and the estimated i-th keypoints of P, respectively. Then the loss of pose estimation errors is given by

$$L_p = \frac{1}{|\mathbb{REC}|} \sum_{b \in \mathbb{REC}} e(\hat{P}^b) + \frac{1}{|\mathbb{PRED}|} \sum_{b \in \mathbb{PRED}} e(\hat{P}^b) , \tag{14}$$

where $\mathbb{REC}$ and $\mathbb{PRED}$ are the sets of indices of the reconstructed and the predicted poses.

On the other hand, we use L_2-loss to evaluate the reconstruction loss of the confidence scores L_c.

$$L_c = \frac{1}{|\mathbb{REC}|} \sum_{i=1}^{N} \frac{1}{N} \left(c_i^b - \hat{c}_i^b \right)^2 , \tag{15}$$

Then the AE-loss is

$$Loss_{AE} = \lambda_p L_p + \lambda_s L_c . \tag{16}$$

Consider a pose trajectory as an action, we propose to include unsupervised action grouping to facilitate the detection of abnormal human actions. The classifier, training by the normal actions, should consider the abnormal actions as outliers of all the groups.

Let $\{y_i\}$ denote the latent features extracted by the encoders, and y_i be the vector formed by concatenating the outputs of the local and global encoders. Inspired by the SVDD loss in [1], we define the multi-center loss function by

$$Loss_{mc} = \frac{1}{n} \sum_{i=1}^{n} \min_{1 \leq d \leq D} \| y_i - center_d \|_2 , \tag{17}$$

where $center_d$ is the center of the d-th group and D is the number of groups. From (17), it is obvious that the action x_i is assigned to the d-th group if $center_d$ is the closest center to x_i's latent feature y_i. While minimizing $Loss_{mc}$, all the latent features of the actions belonging to the d-th group would be gathered to $center_d$. As a result, the model would learn to classify the actions.

In the first 20 training epochs, only $Loss_{AE}$ is used to warm up the model. Then all the $\{center_d\}$'s are initialized by applying K-Means on the latent vectors $\{y_i\}$ and they are updated for every 5 epochs. Then the total loss function is defined by

$$Loss_{total} = Loss_{AE} + \lambda_{mc} Loss_{mc} . \tag{18}$$

3.5   Anomaly Detection

Similar to most of the works on anomaly detection of human action videos, we evaluate the accuracy of anomaly detection at frame level. Similar to [7] and [8], the anomaly score of a frame F is the maximum of the anomaly scores for the human poses in this frame, that is,

$$Score(F) = \max_{P_t \in F} score(P_t) . \tag{19}$$

In this paper, $score(P_t)$ is composed of the score of errors, $score_e$, and the score of grouping, $score_g$.

Let $P = \{P_t\}_{t=1}^{T_1+T_2}$ be a pose trajectory, where T_1 and T_2 are the time-lengths of inputs and predictions, respectively, and the pose P_t is composed of the keypoints $\{P_{t,k}\}_{k=1}^{K}$. Let $c_{t,k}$ be the confidence score of $P_{t,k}$, both given by the pose estimator, and let $P_{t,k}^{real}$ denote the "real" location of the k-th keypoint of P_t. In general, lower the confidence score $c_{t,k}$, longer the distance $\|P_{t,k} - P_{t,k}^{real}\|$.

Therefore, we assume that there is a high possibility that $P_{t,k}^{real}$ is lied in a circle with center $P_{t,k}$ and radius $R_{t,k}$, which is inversely proportional to $c_{t,k}$. We call $R_{t,k}$ the *confidence radius* and define it by

$$R_{t,k} = \frac{\beta}{100 * c_{t,k}} . \tag{20}$$

Under this assumption, the error of reconstruction or prediction of $P_{t,k}$ should be ignore during anomaly detection if it is less than $R_{t,k}$.

Moreover, let f denote the TP-AE model and $f(P)$ denote the output of f with input $\{P_t\}_{t=1}^{T_1}$. Since P^{real} is around P, the output $f(P^{real})$ should lie in a neighborhood Nb of $f(P)$, while in case P has detection errors, the distance of $f(P^{real})$ and $f(P)$ could be large. Therefore, a large size of the neighborhood Nb should represent a higher "tolerance" of the reconstruction/prediction errors. Now we use $r_{t,k}$ to simulate the radius of the neighborhood of $f(P)_{t,k}$ and call it the *simulated confident radius*.

To estimate $r_{t,k}$, let $P + R$ be the pose trajectory consisting of the poses

$$P_t + R_t = \{P_{t,k} + (R_{t,k}, R_{t,k})\}_{k=1}^{K} , \tag{21}$$

that is, $P_t + R_t$ is one of the farthest "neighbor" of P and is standing on the border of the region in where P_t^{real} is lied. Therefore, $f(P+R)$ can be considered as the trajectory staying on the border of the above neighborhood. Then $r_{t,k}$ is defined by

$$r_{t,k} = \|f(P + R)_{t,k} - f(P)_{t,k}\|_1 . \tag{22}$$

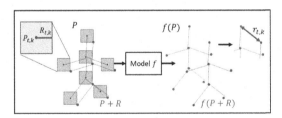

Fig. 3. Confidence radius and simulated confidence radius. After computing the confidence radius of the gray pose trajectory P, the red pose trajectory $P + R$ is one of the farthest "neighbor" of P. Then the simulated confidence radius is given by the distance between $f(P)$ and $f(P + R)$.

Now we define the error of the output $\hat{P}_t$ by

$$e'(\hat{P}_t) = \sum_{k=1}^{K} \frac{\|\hat{P}_{t,k} - P_{t,k}\|_1}{R_{t,k} + r_{t,k}} . \tag{23}$$

In addition, to bridge the gap between the large size pose and small size pose, we normalize the pose error by the pose height $h(P_t)$ as follows:

$$\bar{e}(\hat{P}_t) = \frac{e'(\hat{P}_t)}{h(P_t)} . \tag{24}$$

Thus, the anomaly score of errors of a pose P_t is defined by

$$score_e(P_t) = \frac{1}{|B|} \sum_{b \in B} \bar{e}(\hat{P}_t^b) , \tag{25}$$

where $\{\hat{P}_t^b\}_{b \in B}$ are the reconstructions and the predictions of P_t with the index set B.

On the other hand, since the TP-AE model has learned to group the normal actions by $Loss_{mc}$ (17), an abnormal action can be detected if its latent feature is far away from all the centers. Therefore, the anomaly score of grouping of P_t is defined by

$$score_g(P_t) = \frac{1}{|B|} \sum_{b \in B} \min_{1 \leq d \leq D} \|y_b - center_d\|_2 . \tag{26}$$

Finally, the total anomaly score of pose P_t is given by

$$score(P_t) = \lambda_e score_e(P_t) + \lambda_g score_g(P_t) . \tag{27}$$

4   Experiments

Table 1. Frame-level AUC score of the experiments. * is evaluated by [7]'s open-source code.

	Method	Avenue	ShanghaiTech
Appearance-based	Chang [2]	86.0	73.3
	Liu [5]	84.9	72.8
	Nguyen [6]	**86.9**	–
Pose-based	Morais [7]	81*	73.4
	Rodrigues [8]	82.9	76.0
	Markovitz [3]	–	76.1
	Ours (a)	81.0	**76.6**
	Ours (b)	85.5	69.5

4.1   Data Preparation

In this paper, we experiment with two of the most widely used datasets for anomaly detection tasks, namely the ShanghaiTech Campus [12] and CUHK Avenue datasets [13]. Each of them presents specific challenges due to their singularity. Here, we present a brief introduction to these datasets.

With 13 different scenes and 130 abnormal events spanning over more than 400 videos, the ShanghaiTech Campus dataset [12] contains more realistic scenarios than other anomaly detection datasets making it very challenging for current anomaly detection models. This dataset is known for its diversity but equally important is its complex light conditions and view angles. Also, it includes new, more challenging anomalies such as chasing and brawling.

Smaller than the ShanghaiTech Dataset, the CUHK Avenue Dataset [13] consists of 37 video clips (16 for training and 21 for testing) that were captured on the CUHK campus avenue, hence the name. The training videos only contain normal situations with a few outliers whereas the testing videos contain both normal and abnormal ones. The dataset includes anomalous behaviors such as people running or moving in an unexpected direction as well as challenging settings like slight camera shake.

(a)   (b)

Fig. 4. Examples of the detected anomalies (in the red boxes). (a) In Avenue, the one unnaturally throwing the papers is detected since the model fails to reproduce his pose. (b) In ShanghaiTech, the one riding on the footway is detected since the model fails to adapt his speed. (Color figure online)

To estimate the poses trajectories, [7] first utilized AlphaPose [14–16] to detect poses in the video frames. Then they combined sparse optical flow with the detected skeletons to assign similarity scores between pairs of skeletons in neighboring frames. On the other hand, [8] run a human detector and a multi-target tracker to obtain human trajectories, and run a pose detector to get the poses and the confidence scores.

Different from them, we directly obtain the poses trajectories and the confidence scores by the poses trackers LightTrack [17] or AlphaPose [14–16]. The estimated poses contain 15 keypoints for LightTrack and 17 keypoints for Alpha-Pose. Due to the crowded and staggered people, in some trajectories part of the poses might missing. Therefore, we construct the missing poses and their confidence scores by interpolation.

4.2   Implementation Details

For Avenue dataset, we apply LightTrack, and set the time-lengths $T_1 = 8$ of the input, $T_2 = 4$ of predicted poses, $D = 5$, the number of the groups, and $\lambda_g = 5$. For ShanhhaiTech, we apply AlphaPose, and set $T_1 = T_2 = 4$, $D = 5$ and $\lambda_g = 0.1$. For both dataset, $\lambda_p = \lambda_s = 1$, $\lambda_{mc} = 0.01$, $\beta = 0.1$ and $\lambda_e = 1$. Moreover, before the total AUC of the 12 scenes in ShanhhaiTech is counting, we linearly transform the anomaly scores of frames in a scene so that the lowest anomaly score is 0 and the top 0.5% score becomes 1.

4.3   Results and Discussion

In Table 1, we compare our method with [2,3,5–8]. The scores represent the frame-level AUC.

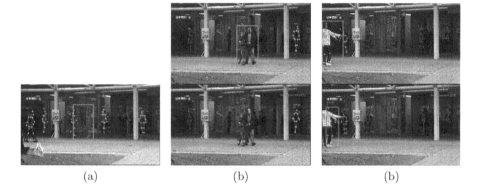

(a)   (b)   (b)

Fig. 5. (a) The running man is a failed case that the pose estimator and the human tracker are failed. (b) The bike is a failed case since our model has no information about it. (c) The dancing man is hard to be considered as anomaly unless he waves arms significantly. The upper images of (b) (c) show the poses given by the pose estimator; the bottom images of (b) (c) show the output poses of our model.

Specially, we present two results for our method. Ours(a) is implemented as mentioned above, while Ours(b) does not use equation (24), that is, the poses errors are not normalized by the poses' heights when computing the anomaly scores, which is similar to the pose-based methods [8] and [8]. In fact, in the Avenue dataset, most of the abnormal people are relatively close to the monitor and have larger sizes. Therefore, (24) will decrease their anomaly scores. As a result, though Ours(a) is more reasonable, it has a lower accuracy of the anomaly detection on Avenue dataset.

[2,5,6] are methods based on the appearance and the optical flows of the frames. By contrast, [3,7,8] and our method are at a disadvantage since there is no information about the abnormal vehicles can be extracted from the human

poses. However, all the pose-based methods perform better on ShanghaiTech and the AUC score of our method is only 1.4 less than [6] on Avenue.

Comparing with previous pose-based methods, our method performs 2.6% better than [8] on Avenue (85.5 vs 82.9), and 0.8% better than [3] on ShanghaiTech (76.6 vs 76.1).

Case Discussion. Fig. 5 shows some failed cases and a hard example.

The anomaly in Fig. 5 (a) is a running man who moves too fast so that the human tracking is failed and since his appearance is a little bit blurred, the pose estimator cannot find him in some frames. As a result, this man is got rid of the pose data in our experiments, so the anomaly detection failed.

The anomaly in Fig. 5 (b) is a man walking a bike. Since he is walking like others and his speed is normal, our model considers his action normal. Therefore, the anomaly detection failed because of lack of information about the bike.

Figure 5 (c) is a hard example. The anomaly is a man dancing in place. Our model detects the anomaly only when he waves his arms. On the other hand, since the appearance is a normal human and his speed is not obvious, it is much more difficult for appearance-based anomaly detection methods, which usually rely on the appearance and the optical flows of the frames.

In conclusion, (a) and (b) shows the weakness of pose-based methods, that is, the abnormal object has to be detected by the pose estimator. On the other hand, (c) shows an advantage of pose-based methods that it helps to find anomalies which are irrelevant to the objects' appearance and speeds. Combining the two types of methods and extracting their respective strengths can be the future research direction.

4.4 Ablation Study

Table 2. AUC of the experiments with/without $loss_{mc}$ and $score_g$, and the experiments of replacing (23) by (13).

Grouping	$score_e$	Avenue	ShanghaiTech
	(13)	76.7	74.0
✓	(13)	77.5	73.3
	(23)	81.1	74.2
✓	(23)	**85.5**	**76.6**

Table 2 depicts the result of the ablation study. We first examine the effect of the multi-center grouping. If the model does not group the latent features, that is, $loss_{mc}$ and $score_g$ are not used, the AUC decreases 4.4% on Avenue and 2.4% on ShanghaiTech.

[8] uses equation (13) to evaluate the anomaly scores from the errors of reconstruction or prediction, so we do the experiments that (23) is replaced by (13). In this case, Table 2 shows that the AUC decrease 8.0% on Avenue and 3.3% on ShanghaiTech.

5 Conclusion

In this work, we present a GCN autoencoder model to reconstruct and predict the pose trajectories in the videos. In this model, we also group the actions by gathering the latent features to the group centers. In addition, we develop the new anomaly score weighted by the confidence radii to detect abnormal human actions. Our experimental results show that we achieve the state-of-the-art accuracy among all the pose-based anomaly detection methods.

References

1. Ruff, L., et al.: Deep one-class classification. In: ICML, vol. 80, pp. 4390–4399. Publisher (2018)
2. Chang, Y., Tu, Z., Xie, W., Yuan, J.: Clustering driven deep autoencoder for video anomaly detection. In: ECCV (2020)
3. Markovitz, A., Sharir, G., Friedman, I., Zelnik-Manor, L., Avidan, S.: Graph embedded pose clustering for anomaly detection. In: The IEEE Conference on Computer Vision and Pattern Recognition (2020)
4. Schlegl, T., Seeböck, P., Waldstein, S.M., Schmidt-Erfurth, U., Langs, G.: Unsupervised anomaly detection with generative adversarial networks to guide marker discovery. In: Niethammer, M., Styner, M., Aylward, S., Zhu, H., Oguz, I., Yap, P.-T., Shen, D. (eds.) IPMI 2017. LNCS, vol. 10265, pp. 146–157. Springer, Cham (2017). https://doi.org/10.1007/978-3-319-59050-9_12
5. Liu, W., Luo, W., Lian, D., Gao, S.: Future frame prediction for anomaly detection - a new baseline. In: The IEEE Conference on Computer Vision and Pattern Recognition (2018)
6. Nguyen, T.N., Meunier, J.: Anomaly detection in video sequence with appearance-motion correspondence. In: The IEEE International Conference on Computer Vision (2019)
7. Morais, R., Le, V., Tran, T., Saha, B., Mansour, M., Venkatesh, S.: Learning regularity in skeleton trajectories for anomaly detection in videos. In: The IEEE Conference on Computer Vision and Pattern Recognition (2019)
8. Rodrigues, R., Bhargava, N., Velmurugan, R., Chaudhuri, S.: Multi-timescale trajectory prediction for abnormal human activity detection. In: The IEEE Winter Conference on Applications of Computer Vision (2020)
9. Yan, S., Xiong, Y., Lin, D.: Spatial temporal graph convolutional networks for skeleton-based action recognition. In: AAAI (2018)
10. Zhao, L., Peng, X., Tian, Y., Kapadia, M., Metaxas, D.N.: Semantic graph convolutional networks for 3D human pose regression. In: IEEE Conference on Computer Vision and Pattern Recognition (2019)
11. Vashishth, S., Yadav, P., Bhandari, M., Talukdar, P.: Confidence-based graph convolutional networks for semi-supervised learning. In: Proceedings of Machine Learning Research, pp. 1792–1801 (2019)

12. Luo, W., Liu, W., Gao, S.: A revisit of sparse coding based anomaly detection in stacked RNN framework. In: ICCV (2017)
13. Lu, C., Shi, J., Jia, J.: Abnormal event detection at 150 FPS in matlab. In: ICCV (2013)
14. Fang, H.-S., Xie, S., Tai, Y.-W., Lu, C.: RMPE: regional multi-person pose estimation. In: ICCV (2017)
15. Li, J., Wang, C., Zhu, H., Mao, Y., Fang, H.-S., Lu, C.: CrowdPose: efficient crowded scenes pose estimation and a new benchmark. arXiv preprint. arXiv:1812.00324 (2018)
16. Xiu, Y., Li, J., Wang, H., Fang, Y., Lu, C.: Pose flow: efficient online pose tracking. In: BMVC (2018)
17. Ning, G., Huang, H.: LightTrack: a generic framework for online top-down human pose tracking. In: The IEEE Conference on Computer Vision and Pattern Recognition Workshops (2020)

Segmentation, Grouping and Shape

1D Self-Attention Network for Point Cloud Semantic Segmentation Using Omnidirectional LiDAR

Takahiro Suzuki[✉], Tsubasa Hirakawa, Takayoshi Yamashita,
and Hironobu Fujiyoshi

Chubu University, 1200 Matsumotocho, Kasugai, Aichi, Japan
{stkin26,hirakawa}@mprg.cs.chubu.ac.jp,
{yamashita,fujiyoshi}@isc.chubu.ac.jp

Abstract. Understanding environment around the vehicle is essential for automated driving technology. For this purpose, an omnidirectional LiDAR is used for obtaining surrounding information and point cloud based semantic segmentation methods have been proposed. However, these methods requires a time to acquire point cloud data and to process the point cloud, which causes the significant positional shift of objects on the practical application scenario. In this paper, we propose a 1D self-attention network (1D-SAN) for LiDAR-based point cloud semantic segmentation, which is based on the 1D-CNN for real-time pedestrian detection of an omnidirectional LiDAR data. Because the proposed method can sequentially process during data acquisition in a omnidirectional LiDAR, we can reduce the processing time and suppress the positional shift. Moreover, for improving segmentation accuracy, we use the intensity as an input data and introduce self-attention mechanism into the proposed method. The intensity enables to consider the object texture. The self-attention mechanism can consider the relationship between point clouds. The experimental results with the SemanticKITTI dataset show that the intensity input and the self-attention mechanism in the proposed method improves the accuracy. Especially, the self-attention mechanism contributes to improving the accuracy of small objects. Also, we show that the processing time of the proposed method is faster than the other point cloud segmentation methods.

Keywords: Point cloud · Semantic segmentation · Self-attention · LiDAR · Autonomous driving

1 Introduction

In automated driving technology, it is essential to understand the environment around the vehicle. For this reason, research on automatic driving has attracted a great deal of attention, and typical functions of driving support systems include detection of objects in the vicinity of the vehicle and path prediction of pedestrians. In particular, object detection is a fundamental method for the automated

ⓒ Springer Nature Switzerland AG 2022
C. Wallraven et al. (Eds.): ACPR 2021, LNCS 13188, pp. 257–270, 2022.
https://doi.org/10.1007/978-3-031-02375-0_19

driving. The object detection can be catetorized into two approaches based on the input data: RGB images from onboard cameras [5,10,14] and 3D point clouds acquired by Light Detection and Ranging (LiDAR) [3,16,17,23].

LiDAR obtains 3D information and intensity by measuring the time it takes for an infrared laser beam to reflect off an object and return. Among several types of LiDAR devices, an omnidirectional LiDAR acquires 3D information in 360° in all directions with the LiDAR as the origin by irradiating the laser toward the surrounding area while rotating.

Many semantic segmentation methods using the omnidirectional LiDAR have been proposed [3,15–19,23]. However, the acquisition of the omnidirectional LiDAR data requires a constant time. In addition to the data acquisition time, considering the processing time for the point clouds, it takes a log time. This causes the significant positional shift of objects and is a crucial problem for the practical automated driving scenario.

In this paper, we propose 1 dimensional self-attention network (1D-SAN), a semantic segmentation method for the omnidirectional LiDAR-based point clouds. The key idea of the proposed method is to process a part of point clouds in the entire 360° point cloud data sequentially. The proposed method is based on 1 dimensional convolutional neural network (1D-CNN) [8], which is a pedestrian detection method for the omnidirectional LiDAR. 1D-CNN regards the distance values obtained from a LiDAR as 1 dimensional waveform data and uses the data for the network input. This enables us to sequentially process the omnidirectional LiDAR data during data acquisition, which can suppress the positional shift of objects. We extend 1D-CNN for semantic segmentation task to deal with multiple object classes. Moreover, we propose to use a reflection intensity values for a network input and to introduce a self-attention mechanism. Since the reflection intensity differs depending onthe material of the object, we can consider the texture of objects. As the self-attention mechanism for 1D waveform data, we propose 1D self-attention block (1D-SAB), which is based on [27]. By introducing 1D-SAB, we can consider the relationship between point clouds. Due to the reflection intensity and 1D-SAB, we can improve the segmentation accuracy while maintaining the sequential process of the omnidirectional LiDAR data. The experimental results with the SemanticKITTI dataset show that the intensity input and the self-attention mechanism in the proposed method improves the accuracy. Especially, the self-attention mechanism contributes to improving the accuracy of small objects. Also, we show that the processing time of the proposed method is faster than the other point cloud segmentation methods.

The contribution of this paper are as follows:

- This paper proposes a point cloud-based semantic segmentation methods.
- The proposed method can process sequentially while acquiring data. Therefore, our method is faster than existing semantic segmentation methods and we can reduce the positional shift.
- The proposed method improves the accuracy of semantic segmentation, especially for small objects by self-attention.

2   Related Work

Many methods using point clouds have been proposed [1,3,4,7–9,11–13,15–26, 28]. These methods can be categorized into three approaches. The first approach treats the point cloud as voxels [11,28]. The second approach is to project the point cloud onto an image and treat it as an image [1,3,4,13,23–25]. And, the third approach is to use the 3D point cloud [1,7,9,12,18–22,26]. In addition to the above approaches, there is a pedestrian vehicle detection using 1D-CNN, which identifies whether the area is a pedestrian area or not sequentially from the process of acquiring data from omnidirectional LiDAR [8]. In this section, we briefly introduce typical methods in the point cloud approach.

2.1   Voxel-Based Method

The voxel-based method first convert a 3D point cloud as a voxel representation. Then, the voxelized point cloud data is input to a network consisting of 3D convolutions to obtain results [28].

In VoxelNet, the 3D point cloud is divided into voxels, and a network for object detection is proposed [28]. Voxelnet is composed of Feature Learning Network (FLN), Convolutional Middle Layers, and Region Proposal Network (RPN). First, the 3D information is divided into equally spaced voxels by FLN, and the shape information in each voxel is obtained. At this time, the feature values of each point in the voxel are also calculated and combined with the feature values of each voxel. Next, 3D convolutional processing is performed using Convolutional Middle Layers to aggregate the features into voxel units. Finally, object regions are detected by RPN.

The voxel-based method is easy to retain the original information of the 3D point cloud, and smooth feature extraction by 3D convolution is possible. It also improves on the sparseness of 3D point clouds by grouping them by voxel, making them easier to handle for each task. However, due to the cubical representation of voxel data, it is computationally expensive and decreases the process speed.

2.2   Image-Based Method

In the image-based method, the 3D point cloud data is first projected into a 2D image. The projected 2D image is then subjected to 2D convolutions, in the same way as a normal images [23].

In SqueezeSeg [23], a network is proposed to project the point cloud data acquired from LiDAR onto a cylinder and treat and process it as an image. By using SqueezeNet to extract features, we have been able to speed up the processing while maintaining the original system. SqueezeNet reduces the number of parameters by introducing the Fire Module into the neural network, and preserves accuracy by performing downsampling backward. SqueezeSeg introduces Fire Deconv to this SqueezeNet and performs upsampling of the feature map. Fire Deconv allows for even faster processing. In addition, the accuracy of segmentation is improved by modifying the labels with a recurrent conditional random field. In summary, SqueezeSeg achieves faster processing while maintaining accuracy with fewer parameters.

By transforming the 3D point cloud as a 2D image, we can apply 2D convolutional process and realize the increase of the process speed. On the other hand, there is a possibility that the original information of the 3D point cloud is missing, for example, a pixel and its neighboring pixels are not the actual neighboring points in the transformed image.

2.3 3D Point Cloud-Based Method

In the 3D point cloud-based method, the point cloud is directly input to the network for processing [16,17]. We input (x, y, z) coordinate information and reflection intensity values of point clouds into a network.

In PointNet [16], a network has been proposed that can be applied to tasks such as three-class classification and segmentation. PointNet is composed of a Spatial Transformer Network (STN), a Classification Network, and a Segmentation Network. First, we reduce the noise for the input point cloud in STN. The next step is to extract the features of each point cloud from the convolution process by Classification Network. After that, Max Pooling is used to extract the overall features and classify them. In the case of segmentation, the overall features extracted by the Classification Network and the local features of each point cloud are combined and input to the Segmentation Network. The convolution process is performed several times again, and segmentation is performed for each point cloud.

PointNet may lack detailed spatial information, and as a result, may not be able to capture the local structure. For this problem, there is PointNet++ [17], which is an improved version of PointNet with higher accuracy. In PointNet++, a network that can capture local features is proposed by applying PointNet hierarchically. In PointNet++, PointNet is used for local feature extraction. It is also possible to extract pseudo local features by inputting neighboring points that have been clustered. This solves the problems of PointNet and improves the accuracy of class classification and segmentation.

In this way, the original information of the 3D point cloud is retained and accurate feature extraction is possible. It also eliminates the computational cost of converting to voxels, etc. On the other hand, processing 3D point clouds as they are requires a huge amount of storage space. The associated computational cost of processing the point cloud is also high, which may result in a reduction in processing speed.

2.4 1D-CNN for Pedestrian Detection

One of the problems with the above mentioned approaches is that the detection process takes a long time. This causes a gap between the detected position and the actual position when it is mounted on a fast-moving object such as an automobile.

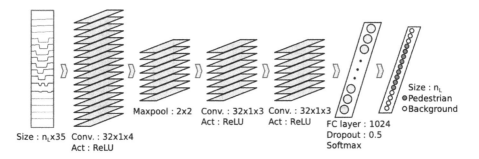

Size : n_Lx35 Conv. : 32x1x4
Act : ReLU
Conv. : 32x1x4
Act : ReLU
Maxpool : 2x2
Conv. : 32x1x3
Act : ReLU
Conv. : 32x1x3
Act : ReLU
FC layer : 1024
Dropout : 0.5
Softmax
Size : n_L
• Pedestrian
○ Background

Fig. 1. The network structure of 1D-CNN. Quote from [8].

To overcome this problem, 1D-CNN [8] has been proposed, which can suppress the positional shift on pedestrian detection problem. For pedestrian detection using 1D-CNN, the distance values obtained from LiDAR are regarded as 1D waveform data for each laser ID, and are sequentially input to 1D-CNN to enable pedestrian detection along with LiDAR rotation. The structure of 1D-CNN is shown in the Fig. 1. The network consists of three convolutional layers and one fully-connected layer. The input data size is $n_L \times 35$, where n_L is the number of laser IDs of LiDAR. Since the average width of a pedestrian is about 7° horizontally, the number of point clouds for 7° is 35, which is the width. During the actual driving of the vehicle, when the number of point clouds for pedestrians is secured with the rotation of LiDAR, they are input to the network sequentially to identify whether they are pedestrians or background. Furthermore, clustering is applied to the point clouds identified as pedestrians to achieve higher accuracy.

This sequential processing along with the rotation of the LiDAR makes it possible to minimize the gap between the detected position of the pedestrian and the actual position even when driving. However, in this method, only pedestrians are detected. In actual automated driving, it is also important to detect objects other than pedestrians. In this paper, therefore, we propose a semantic segmentation method of a omnidirectional LiDAR on the basis of 1D-CNN approach. In addition the distance value, we add the reflection intensity as an input and introduce self-attention mechanism. Because these enable us to consider the texture of each object and the relationship between neighboring point clouds, we can improve the segmentation accuracy while maintaining efficient computational cost.

3 Proposed Method

In this section, we introduce the details of the proposed semantic segmentation method. Figure 2 shows the network structure of our proposed 1 dimensional self-attention network (1D-SAN). We first obtain distance and reflection intensity values from LiDAR and interpolate those missing values. Then, we assume these LiDAR data as 1 dimensional waveform data and concatenate them for channel

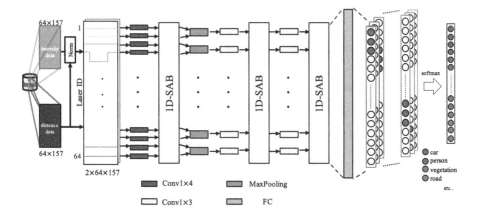

Fig. 2. The network structure of 1D-SAN.

direction. And, we input the processed LiDAR data for 1D-SAN. The 1D-SAN outputs the class probabilities for each waveform data. This process enables us to achieve multi-class classification while maintaining the advantages of 1D-CNN. Moreover The proposed network contains 1 dimensional self-attention blocks (1D-SABs). The 1D-SAB utilizes the relative position between point clouds for weighting process and we can consider the important relationships between the point clouds.

3.1 Network Structure

Here, we describe the detailed network structure of 1D-SAN. As shown in Fig. 2, 1D-SAN consists of three convolutional layers, three 1D-SAB layers, and one fully-connected layer. In all convolutional layers, convolution is performed only in the horizontal direction. The longitudinal size of the input data and the number of output units depend on the number of lasers in the LiDAR. The LiDAR used in this study is 64, because it irradiates 64 lasers. The lateral size is set to 157 points per 30°, which is optimal for semantic segmentation. The number of input channels is two: distance value and intensity.1D convolution of the input data for each laser ID. After each convolutional layer, the data is input to 1D-SAB to take into account the relationship between the point clouds. The features are then combined in the fully-connected layer, and the softmax function calculates the probability of each class for each laser ID in the center of the input data, and outputs the identification results. By doing this sequentially, we can achieve semantic segmentation for all directions.

3.2 Preprocessing Point Cloud Data

The point cloud data is a set of points where the laser beam from the omnidirectional LiDAR is reflected back to the object, and the distance and intensity values can be obtained from the time. However, omnidirectional LiDAR includes scenes where it is difficult to acquire reflected light, such as the sky and specular objects. If the reflected light cannot be obtained, the value at that point cannot be obtained and becomes an outlier, so interpolation of the value at the outlier part is necessary.

In this study, the outliers of the distance values are interpolated with the maximum distance value of 120 assuming that the object is empty when the irradiation angle is 0° or more, and with the corresponding value assuming that the laser hit the ground when the irradiation angle is less than 0°. Similarly, the outliers of the intensity are interpolated with 0.0 when the irradiation angle is more than 0°, and with the average intensity of the ground class such as roads and sidewalks of 0.29 when the irradiation angle is less than 0°. The interpolated distance values and intensities are combined for each laser ID to create waveform data for each laser ID.

3.3   Normalization of Intensity Value

To improve the discrimination accuracy of semantic segmentation, we add the intensity of the object to the input data. The intensity has a is weakened on highly reflective objects such as metal because the light is diffused, and strengthened on less reflective objects such as cloth because the light is returned exactly. Therefore, by adding the intensity as an input to the network, we can expect to identify objects based on their texture. The intensity decreases as the distance to the object increases, and the value returned becomes smaller.

We correct the value by normalizing it with the distance value from LiDAR to suppress the effect of attenuation due to distance. To normalize the intensity, the law of light decay is used. The law of light attenuation states that the intensity of light is inversely proportional to the square of the distance from the light source to the object. We define the normalization of the intensity by distance value as follows:

$$I' = I \times (2 \times d)^2 \tag{1}$$

where I' is the intensity after normalization, I is the intensity before normalization, and d is the distance value obtained from LiDAR. By Eq. (1), it is possible to recover the value attenuated by distance and use the intensity as input.

3.4   1 Dimensional Self-Attention Block (1D-SAB)

Here, we describe the details of 1D-SAB. Figure 3 shows the detailed structure of 1D-SAB. Input the created 1D waveform data into the 1D-SAB for each laser ID. The input data is processed one point at a time, and the Self-Attention of the corresponding point is calculated. When the red value in Fig. 3 is the point of interest for the process, the green is neighborhood 1 and the blue is neighborhood 2. For each neighboring point, we apply pointwise convolution.

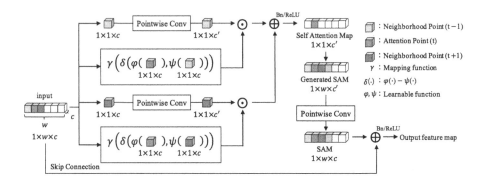

Fig. 3. The detailed structure of 1D-SAB. (Color figure online)

On the other hand, we input the points of interest and neighboring points into the learnable function $\varphi(\cdot)$ and $\psi(\cdot)$. Then the $\varphi(\cdot)$ and $\psi(\cdot)$ are used for the relational function δ, which is defined by

$$\delta\left(\varphi(\cdot), \psi(\cdot)\right) = \varphi(\cdot) - \psi(\cdot). \tag{2}$$

Then, the mapping function $\gamma(\cdot)$ aligns the number of channels with the output of the first process. Then, we calculate the element-wise product with the above mentioned feature by point-wise convolution.

The self-attention map (SAM) is generated by performing this process for neighboring points and summing them up. The generated SAMs are made to have the same number of channels as the input channels by pointwise convolution. To this output, the input data is added as a skip mechanism to form the final output. By using 1D-SAB, we can give a large weight to the important positions among the point clouds and consider the relationship among the point clouds.

4   Experiments

In this section, we evaluate the proposed method. In our experiments, we verify the effectiveness of reflection strength and 1D-SAB for semantic segmentation. We also compare the accuracy with other methods.

4.1   Experimental Summary

Dataset. We use SemanticKITTI [2] for our evaluation. SemanticKITTI is a real-world dataset, which is created based on the KITTI dataset [6] for autonomous driving purposes.

The 3D point cloud data was acquired by HDL-64E. The dataset consists of 22 scenes and the number of frames are 43,000. Among them, 21,000 frames taken in scenes 00 to 10 are used for training and 22,000 frames from scenes 11 to 21 are used for test. In the training set, we use 4,080 frames of scene 08 for validation and the other frames for training.

SemanticKITTI annotates all the point clouds in the KITTI dataset and defines 22 classes, including people, cars, and buildings. People and cars are also classified by the presence or absence of motion. In this study, because dynamic objects are treated in the same way as static objects, we use 19 classes in our experiments.

Comparative Methods. As comparative methods, we use the following methods. To evaluate the effectiveness of reflection intensity and 1D-SAB and the computational time, we compare the performances of the following methods.

- 1D-CNN: We extend the output of the conventional 1D-CNN [8] for predicting probability of 19 classes. Note that it does not use the reflection intensity as an input.
- Ours (w/o SAB): We use the reflection intensity as an input and remove 1D-SAB from the proposed method.
- Ours (w/ SAB): We use both the reflection intensity input and 1D-SAB.

To train these methods, we set the number of training epochs to 20 and the batch size to 24. Cross entropy loss is used as the loss function, and MomentumSGD is used as the optimization method, and the initial learning rate is 0.01. During training, the learning rate is decreased by a factor of 1/2 per epoch.

Moreover, by using test set of SemanticKITTI dataset, we compare the segmentation performance with the following point cloud segmentation methods: PointNet [16], PointNet++ [17], SPGraph [9], and SPLATNet [20].

Evaluation Metrics. We use Intersection over Union (IoU) as an evaluatin metrics IoU measures how well the segmentation result matches the correct label for each point cloud. If the number of point clouds that answered correctly is True Positive (TP), the number of point clouds that predicted the correct class as another class is False Positive (FP), and the number of point clouds that predicted another class as the correct class is False Negative (FN), the IoU can be defined as follows:

$$\text{IoU} = \frac{TP}{TP + FP + FN}. \tag{3}$$

The Mean IoU is used as an overall evaluation metrics. The Mean IoU is obtained by taking the average of the IoU for each class, and it is defined by

$$\text{mIoU} = \frac{1}{C} \sum_{i=1}^{C} \frac{TP}{TP + FP + FN}, \tag{4}$$

where C indicates the number of classes.

Table 1. Evaluation of the effectiveness of the proposed method on SemanticKITTI test set (Sequences 11 to 21). IoU scores are given in percentage (%).

Approach	car	bicycle	motorcycle	truck	othe-vehicle	person	bicyclist	motorcyclist	road	parking	sidewalk	other-ground	building	fence	vegetation	trunk	terrain	pole	traffic sign	mean-IoU
1D-CNN [8]	54.7	0.0	0.0	0.0	0.3	0.0	0.0	0.0	69.6	3.9	39.3	0.0	59.9	20.6	57.9	4.2	40.2	15.0	0.0	19.4
Ours (w/o SAB)	57.1	0.0	0.0	0.3	0.1	0.0	0.0	0.0	**72.6**	10.7	**43.0**	0.0	61.3	17.6	59.9	3.7	42.0	13.9	4.6	20.2
Ours (w SAB)	**58.1**	**3.3**	**2.2**	**4.8**	**3.4**	**6.0**	**10.7**	**0.4**	**72.6**	**16.8**	38.7	**1.2**	**66.9**	**28.4**	**70.7**	**5.5**	**54.7**	**29.7**	**32.2**	**26.6**

Table 2. Quantitative comparison with the other segmentation methods on SemanticKITTI test set (Sequences 11 to 21). IoU Scores are given in percentage (%).

Approach	car	bicycle	motorcycle	truck	othe-vehicle	person	bicyclist	motorcyclist	road	parking	sidewalk	other-ground	building	fence	vegetation	trunk	terrain	pole	traffic sign	mean-IoU
PointNet [16]	46.3	1.3	0.3	0.1	0.8	0.2	0.2	0.0	61.6	15.8	35.7	1.4	41.4	12.9	31.0	4.6	17.7	2.4	3.7	14.6
PointNet++ [17]	53.7	1.9	0.2	0.9	0.2	0.9	1.0	0.0	72.0	**18.7**	41.8	**5.6**	62.3	16.9	46.5	13.8	30.0	6.0	8.9	20.1
SPGraph [9]	**68.3**	0.9	**4.5**	0.9	0.8	1.0	6.0	0.0	49.5	1.7	24.2	0.3	68.2	22.5	59.2	27.2	17.0	18.3	10.5	20.0
SPLATNet [20]	66.6	0.0	0.0	0.0	0.0	0.0	0.0	0.0	70.4	0.8	41.5	0.0	**68.7**	27.8	**72.3**	**35.9**	35.8	13.8	0.0	22.8
Ours (w/o SAB)	57.1	0.0	0.0	0.3	0.1	0.0	0.0	0.0	**72.6**	10.7	**43.0**	0.0	61.3	17.6	59.9	3.7	42.0	13.9	2.4	20.2
Ours (w SAB)	58.1	**3.3**	2.2	**4.8**	**3.4**	**6.0**	**10.7**	**0.4**	**72.6**	16.8	38.7	1.2	66.9	**28.4**	70.7	5.5	**54.7**	**29.7**	**32.2**	**26.6**

4.2 Evaluating the Effectiveness of Intensity

First, we evaluate the effectiveness of intensity and 1D-SAB. Table 1 shows the accuracy comparison between the conventional and the proposed methods on test set of SemanticKITTI.

Comparing 1D-CNN and Ours (w/o SAB), we can see that the mIoU is improved by 0.8 pt. by introducing the reflection intensity. Moreover, we focusing on the IoU of each class. By introducing the reflection intensity, the IoU of 9 out of 19 classes is improved while the IoUs of some classes, e.g., fence and trunk, are decreased even when the intensity is taken into account. This suggests that, depending on the object, the accuracy may not be improved by considering the intensity. On the other hand, it was confirmed that the IoU for car, road, and traffic-sign, which are considered to be important in automated driving, have improved. For the classes with decreasing IoU, the accuracy is almost equal to that of the conventional method. These results show that the introduction of intensity is effective in semantic segmentation.

4.3 Evaluation the Effectiveness of 1D-SAB

Next, we evaluate the effectiveness of 1D-SAB. From Table 1, the mIoU of Ours (w/ SAB) is 26.6%, which is 6.4 pt. higher than that of Ours (w/o SAB). Therefore, it can be said that considering the relationship between point clouds by self-attention mechanism is effective to improve the accuracy of semantic segmentation. In terms of IoU for each class, the introduction of 1D-SAB resulted in the highest IoU for 17 of the 19 classes. In particular, the accuracy for small

other-object   road   vegetation   terrain   motorcycle   unlabeled
truck   sidewalk   building   person   trunk   fence   car   pole

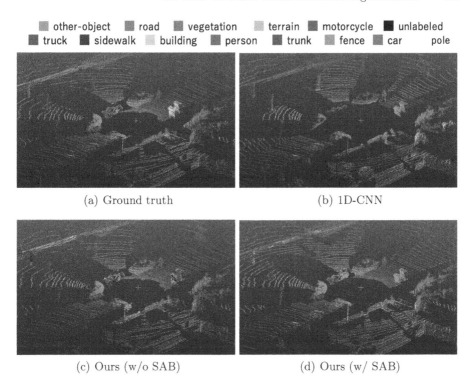

(a) Ground truth

(b) 1D-CNN

(c) Ours (w/o SAB)

(d) Ours (w/ SAB)

Fig. 4. Visualization results on SemanticKITTI test set.

objects such as bicyclist, pole, and traffic-sign has been greatly improved. There-fore, we can say that the use of 1D-SAB, that determines the weights, contributes to the improvement of accuracy, especially for classes with small number of point clouds such as small objects.

4.4 Qualitative Evaluation

Here, we qualitatively evaluate the segmentation results. Figure 4 shows visual-ization results of each methods. As shown in Fig. 4(b), the 1D-CNN recognizes car as vegetation and road as terrian in some parts. Ours (w/o SAB) is able to recognize cars and roads better than 1D-CNN. Moreover, Ours (w/ SAB) is able to recognize objects closer to ground truth, and the recognition accuracy for small objects such as pole and trunk is also improved.

4.5 Comparison of Accuracy with Other Methods

Here, we compare the performance with the other segmentation methods with the test set of SemanticKITTI dataset. A comparison of the accuracy with other methods is shown in Table 2. The proposed method with 1D-SAB has the highest accuracy with mIoU of 26.6%. Focusing on the IoU for each class, the proposed

Table 3. Comparison of processing speed

	PointNet [16]	1D-CNN [8]	Ours (w/o SAB)	Ours (w SAB)
Speed(msec)	208.333	0.0814	0.0888	0.3488

method with 1D-SAB has the highest accuracy in 11 out of 19 classes. In particular, the accuracy for small objects such as fence, pole, and traffic-sign was greatly improved compared to other methods. It can also be seen that the remaining eight classes have almost the same level of accuracy as the other methods. On the other hand, even without 1D-SAB, the mIoU was improved excepting for SPLATNet.

4.6   Comparison of Processing Speed

Finally, we show a comparison of the processing speeds. The speed of PointNet was calculated as the processing time for one rotation of LiDAR data, while the speed of 1D-CNN and the proposed method was calculated as the processing time for a range of data to be processed sequentially. All processing speed measurements were performed using an NVIDIA Quadro RTX 8000.

Table 3 shows that 1D-CNN is the fastest with a frequency of 0.0814 msec. Because the 1D-CNN uses only the distance values and the network structure is also the smallest, the 1D-CNN achieved faster processing time. The model using the intensity as input data, i.e., Ours (w/o SAB), decreased the speed by 0.0074 msec compared to 1D-CNN. The model with 1D-SAB, which had the best accuracy comparison results, significant decreased in speed to 0.3488 msec compared to 1D-CNN and Ours (w/o SAB). Since the omnidirectional LiDAR operates 5 Hz 20 Hz, the proposed method, which can process at a speed of more than 200 msec, can maintain real-time performance.

5   Conclusion

In this paper, we proposed 1 dimensional self-attention network (1D-SAN) for an omnidirectional LiDAR-based point cloud semantic segmentation. The proposed method processes part of LiDAR data and estimate the semantic segmentation results, sequentially, which can reduce the processing time. The proposed method uses the intensity values as an input and introduces self-attention mechanism called 1D-SAB. The experimental results with SemanticKITTI dataset show that the use of intensity value and 1D-SAB improve the accuracy of semantic segmentation while maintaining lower computational time. Especially, 1D-SAB improves the accuracy of small objects.

Our future work includes achieving lower computational costs while maintaining higher accuracy for practical automated driving applications.

References

1. Alonso, I., Riazuelo, L., Montesano, L., Murillo, A.C.: 3D-MiniNet: learning a 2D representation from point clouds for fast and efficient 3D LiDAR semantic segmentation. In: IEEE/RSJ International Conference on Intelligent Robots and Systems (IROS). IEEE (2020)
2. Behley, J., Garbade, M., Milioto, A., Quenzel, J., Behnke, S., Stachniss, C., Gall, J.: SemanticKITTI: a dataset for semantic scene understanding of LiDAR sequences. In: Proceeding of the IEEE/CVF International Conference on Computer Vision (ICCV) (2019)
3. Chen, X., Ma, H., Wan, J., Li, B., Xia, T.: Multi-view 3D object detection network for autonomous driving. In: IEEE Conference on Computer Vision and Pattern Recognition, p. 3 (2017)
4. Cortinhal, T., Tzelepis, G., Aksoy, E.E.: Salsanext: fast, uncertainty-aware semantic segmentation of lidar point clouds for autonomous driving (2020)
5. Dalal, N., Triggs, B.: Histograms of oriented gradients for human detection. In: IEEE Conference on Computer Vision and Pattern Recognition, pp. 886–893 (2005)
6. Geiger, A., Lenz, P., Urtasun, R.: Are we ready for autonomous driving? The KITTI vision benchmark suite. In: Proceeding of the IEEE Conference on Computer Vision and Pattern Recognition (CVPR), pp. 3354–3361 (2012)
7. Hu, Q., et al.: Randla-net: efficient semantic segmentation of large-scale point clouds. In: Proceedings of the IEEE Conference on Computer Vision and Pattern Recognition (2020)
8. Kunisada, Y., Yamashita, T., Fujiyoshi, H.: Pedestrian-detection method based on 1D-CNN during LiDAR rotation. In: The 21st IEEE International Conference on Intelligent Transportation Systems (ITSC) (2018)
9. Landrieu, L., Simonovsky, M.: Large-scale point cloud semantic segmentation with superpoint graphs. In: Proceedings of the IEEE Conference on Computer Vision and Pattern Recognition (2018)
10. LeCun, Y., Boser, B., Denker, J.S., Henderson, D., Howard, R.E., Hubbard, W., Jackel, L.D.: Backpropagation applied to handwritten zip code recognition. Neural Comput. 1(4), 541–551 (1989)
11. Maturana, D., Scherer, S.: Voxnet: a 3D convolutional neural network for real-time object recognition. In: IEEE/RSJ International Conference on Intelligent Robots and Systems, pp. 922–928 (2015)
12. Meyer, G.P., Laddha, A., Kee, E., Vallespi-Gonzalez, C., Wellington, C.K.: Lasernet: an efficient probabilistic 3D object detector for autonomous driving. In: CVPR, pp. 12677–12686. Computer Vision Foundation/IEEE (2019)
13. Milioto, A., Vizzo, I., Behley, J., Stachniss, C.: RangeNet++: fast and accurate LiDAR semantic segmentation. In: IEEE/RSJ International Conference on Intelligent Robots and Systems (IROS) (2019)
14. Papageorgiou, C., Poggio, T.: A trainable system for object detection. Int. J. Comput. Vis. 38(1), 15–33 (2000)
15. Qi, C.R., Liu, W., Wu, C., Su, H., Guibas, L.J.: Frustum pointnets for 3D object detection from RGB-D data. In: IEEE Conference on Computer Vision and Pattern Recognition, pp. 918–927 (2018)
16. Qi, C.R., Su, H., Kaichun, M., Guibas, L.J.: Pointnet: deep learning on point sets for 3D classification and segmentation. In: IEEE Conference on Computer Vision and Pattern Recognition, pp. 77–85 (2017)

17. Qi, C.R., Yi, L., Su, H., Guibas, L.J.: Pointnet++: deep hierarchical feature learning on point sets in a metric space. In: Advances in Neural Information Processing Systems, pp. 5099–5108 (2017)
18. Simon, M., Milz, S., Amende, K., Gross, H.M.: Complex-yolo: real-time 3D object detection on point clouds. arXiv preprint arXiv:1803.06199 (2018)
19. Spinello, L., Luber, M., Arras, K.O.: Tracking people in 3D using a bottom-up top-down detector. In: IEEE Robotics and Automation Society, pp. 1304–1310 (2011)
20. Su, H., Jampani, V., Sun, D., Maji, S., Kalogerakis, E., Yang, M.H., Kautz, J.: SPLATNet: sparse lattice networks for point cloud processing. In: Proceedings of the IEEE Conference on Computer Vision and Pattern Recognition, pp. 2530–2539 (2018)
21. Tatarchenko*, M., Park*, J., Koltun, V., Zhou., Q.Y.: Tangent convolutions for dense prediction in 3D. In: CVPR (2018)
22. Thomas, H., Qi, C.R., Deschaud, J.E., Marcotegui, B., Goulette, F., Guibas, L.J.: Kpconv: flexible and deformable convolution for point clouds. In: Proceedings of the IEEE International Conference on Computer Vision (2019)
23. Wu, B., Wan, A., Yue, X., Keutzer, K.: Squeezeseg: convolutional neural nets with recurrent CRF for real-time road-object segmentation from 3D LiDAR point cloud. In: ICRA (2018)
24. Wu, B., Zhou, X., Zhao, S., Yue, X., Keutzer, K.: Squeezesegv 2: improved model structure and unsupervised domain adaptation for road-object segmentation from a LiDAR point cloud. In: ICRA (2019)
25. Xu, C., et al.: Squeezesegv3: spatially-adaptive convolution for efficient point-cloud segmentation. arXiv preprint arXiv:2004.01803 (2020)
26. Zhang, Y., et al.: Polarnet: an improved grid representation for online lidar point clouds semantic segmentation. In: Proceedings of the IEEE/CVF Conference on Computer Vision and Pattern Recognition (CVPR), June 2020
27. Zhao, H., Jia, J., Koltun, V.: Exploring self-attention for image recognition. In: CVPR (2020)
28. Zhou, Y., Tuzel, O.: Voxelnet: end-to-end learning for point cloud based 3D object detection. In: IEEE Conference on Computer Vision and Pattern Recognition, pp. 4490–4499 (2018)

COMatchNet: Co-Attention Matching Network for Video Object Segmentation

Lufei Huang, Fengming Sun, and Xia Yuan$^{(\boxtimes)}$

Nanjing University of Science and Technology, 210094 Nanjing, China
{lufeihuang714,sunfm,yuanxia}@njust.edu.cn

Abstract. Semi-supervised video object segmentation (semi-VOS) predicts pixel-accurate masks of the target objects in all frames according to the ground truth mask provided in the first frame. A critical challenge to this task is how to model the dependency between the query frame and other frames. Most methods neglect or do not make full use of the inherent relevance. In this paper, we propose a novel network called CO-Attention Matching Network (COMatchNet) for semi-VOS. The COMatchNet mainly consists of a co-attention module and a matching module. The co-attention module extracts frame correlation among the query frame and the previous frame and the first frame. The matching module calculates pixel-level matching scores and finds the most similar regions to preceding frames in the query frame. The COMatchNet integrates two level information and generates fine-grained segmentation masks. We conduct extensive experiments on three popular video object segmentation benchmarks, i.e. DAVIS 2016; DAVIS 2017; YouTube-VOS. Our COMatchNet achieves competitive performance (J&F) of 86.8%, 75.9%, and 81.4% on the above benchmarks, respectively.

Keywords: Co-attention · Pixel-level matching · Video object segmentation

1 Introduction

The aim of Video Object Segmentation (VOS) is to find and segment objects of interest finely from the background throughout a video. According to its supervision type, video object segmentation can be roughly divided into two categories: unsupervised video object segmentation and semi-supervised video object segmentation. In this paper, we focus on the semi-supervised task, which segments the specific objects by referring to the ground truth mask provided in the first frame. This procedure can fit in various challenging fields, including video understanding [9,22,25], object tracking [2,6] and video editing [7].

Early semi-supervised video object segmentation methods [1,3,19] learned the target-specific appearance in evaluation phrase by tuning the pre-trained segmentation network to the first frame. These online fine-tune methods indeed achieved an improved performance, but with a extreme-low inference speed.

© Springer Nature Switzerland AG 2022
C. Wallraven et al. (Eds.): ACPR 2021, LNCS 13188, pp. 271–284, 2022.
https://doi.org/10.1007/978-3-031-02375-0_20

Recently, many works [8,13,14,18,20,24] aiming to avoid online fine-tuning have achieved the balance of performance and run-time. These works can be mainly categorized into matching-based ones and propagation-based ones. Matching-based methods [8,18,24] calculated the pixel-level matching similarity scores between the features of the current query frame and the template frame. These methods segmented pixels in the query frame according to the matching scores directly. These methods were efficient but cannot avoid mismatching problems, because they started from the pixel level and lacked global relevance as the consequence. Propagation-based methods [13,14,20] mainly relied on transmitting the previous information including the masks and the semantic features to the current frame and then integrating this information to generate the prediction mask. There were many ways of fusion, but most of the current methods were based on complex convolution network, which required a large number of parameters. To address the aforementioned problems, some methods were combined with the two methods above and applied the information of the first frame and the previous frame at the same time. Though the use of the first frame and the previous frame can capture the intra-frame features of the target, the simple combination processing strategy may fail to explore the complicated relations between different frames. Therefore, it is difficult to obtain global correlation information of the target.

Due to the above consideration, this paper proposes a novel co-attention matching network (COMatchNet) for semi-supervised video object segmentation. The proposed network adopts a matching mechanism to find the pixels which have the largest similarity with the template frames and designs an effective co-attention module to extract the global correlation to deal with the mismatching problem. Following previous state-of-the-art methods, we match the current frame with the first and the previous frame from the foreground and background, respectively. Before the matching module, we introduce a co-attention module, which receives the three frames mentioned above as input to learn the correlation between frames. The shared features can be extracted from the three frames through fully connected layers. The shared features called co-attention map can help to reduce the mismatching problem in the matching module. The integration of frame-level features relevance and the pixel-level matching scores contributes a lot to achieve better performance than the previous.

Unlike some previous advanced methods, our approach requires no simulated data and no post-processing technologies. And the proposed co-attention matching network (COMatchNet) is trained end-to-end on VOS datasets. We conduct extensive experiments on DAVIS 2016 [15], DAVIS 2017 [16] and YouTube-VOS [23] to verify the efficiency of the components in our model. The COMatchNet shows its advantage on the validation splits of 86.8% (DAVIS 2016), 75.9% (DAVIS 2017), and 81.4% (YouTube-VOS) than other advanced methods while keeping about 5 frames per second (FPS) on a single-object inference. The contributions of this work can be summarized as follows:

- We propose an efficient co-attention module to extract the frame relevance between the query frame and the first and the previous frame. The frames correlation information which can be considered as the common information throughout the video, are able to help relieving the mismatching problem in the matching module.

– We design an end-to-end trainable network, which integrates the frame-level correlation extraction module and the pixel-level matching module. The matching module is the main component to generate the final pixel-level mask, and the co-attention module leads to the final prediction from the video perspective.

– We conduct experiments on three popular video object segmentation benchmarks. The experiment results show that the proposed COMatchNet achieves competitive or even better performance than previous state-of-the-art methods.

2   Related Work

Matching Based VOS Methods. The matching based works [5,8,18,20,24] calculated pixel-level matching scores or semantic feature matching scores between the template frame and the current predicted frame. The matching score was obtained by calculating the pixel space of each pixel in the current predicted frame and responding nearest neighbour pixel in the template frame as the Pixel-Wise Metric Learning adopted in [5]. Some research [7,20] selected the first frame as the template frame because the ground truth mask of the first frame was provided, and the objects in the first frame was the target objects which were supposed to be found in the subsequent frames. [8] proposed a soft matching layer to produce foreground similarity and background similarity between the current and the first frame. However, due to the lack of temporal information, the performance quality of this methods dropped quickly when the appearance of objects in video changed significantly. To solve this problem, other research [18,24] additionally picked the previous frame as the template frame, in considering of the continuity of the video. [18] employed a semantic pixel-wise embedding for global matching (matching between the first and current frames) and local matching (matching between the previous and current frames) to obtain stable prediction. [24] proposed a collaborative foreground-background integration network, which treated the foreground and background information in the first and previous frame equally to effectively handle the mismatching and drifting problem. The above research show that the idea of matching is effective, but the pixel-level matching approaches only consider the correlation between two frames without the full use of the global context in the complete video sequence.

Propagation Based VOS Methods. The propagation based works [13,14,20] resorted to the previous mask or previous feature embedding for better VOS performance. Considering the spatial-temporal consistency of the target objects in a video, the previous information can be used to assist the mask prediction of the current frame. [13] designed a siamese architecture network to stack the first, the previous, and current frames' features during the propagation process. Instead of simply stacking, [20] used a pixel-level matching technique and used the previous frame's mask as the decoder input to receive a more refined prediction mask.

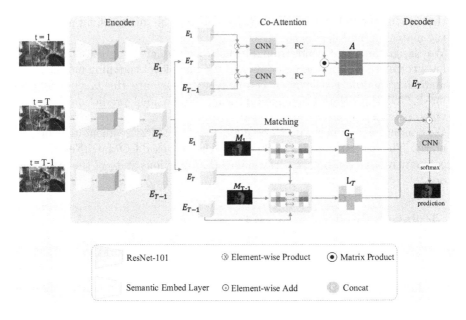

Fig. 1. An overview of the proposed COMatchNet. We first extract the basic semantic features and their semantic embedding vector features by the encoder. The co-attention module is to extract frames correlation features and the matching module is to calculate pixel-wise similarity scores. Then the co-attention map and similarity map and semantic features are fed into the decoder module for the final segmentation.

These approaches made some progress but still suffered from the drifting problem due to the rapid motions or objects occlusions in a video. STMVOS [14] did not explicitly utilize spatio-temporal consistency through mask propagation like the previous propagation-based works. Instead, STMVOS introduced a space-time memory network to save and read previous feature embedding to guide the current mask prediction. The experiments approve that STMVOS outperforms all methods, but STMVOS occupied lots of memory resources due to the stored features and masks. On the other hand, STMVOS relied on considerable simulated data to pre-train the model to boost performance. Without the extensive simulated data, the performance of STMVOS declined significantly. In general, the propagation-based methods cost much memory and computing resource and did not study the correlation from a pixel-level perspective.

Attention Mechanisms. Recently, many works introduced the attention mechanism into the convolution network. In the field of video computer vision, some work [21] applied spatial attention or channel attention to enhancing the representational power of the network. However, both spatial attention and channel attention just focused on the feature enhancement of the single frame without the multi frames. In the field of question answering, [11] designed a co-attention mechanism to extract the common attention information from the features of

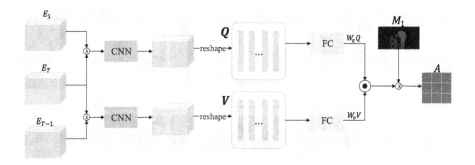

Fig. 2. Illustration of the co-attention module. The semantic embedding vector of the current frame is multiplied by the corresponding vector of the first frame and the previous frame. After convolution layers and reshape operation, the shape of both Q and V is $(H \times W \times C_e, 1)$. Then, Q and V are passed through a fully connected layer with parameter W_q and W_v, respectively, and the calculated result is fused by matrix multiplication. Finally, the result is multiplied by the ground truth of the first frame for the final attention map.

question and the features of image simultaneously. Inspired by the [11], our COMatchNet extracts the shared attention map from multi frames by using the co-attention technique.

3 Method

3.1 Network Overview

Our COMatchNet consists of four parts: an encoder for feature extraction, a co-attention module for correlation extraction, a matching module for pixel matching, and a decoder module for segmentation. An illustration of COMatchNet is shown in Fig. 1.

Encoder. The encoder includes two parts: a DeepLabv3+ [4] architecture to extract semantic features and a semantic embedding layer to extract semantic embedding vector for each pixel p. The DeepLabv3+ adopts the ResNet-101 [4] as the backbone and extracts features which contain appearance and semantic information. The semantic embedding layer generates semantic embedding vector e_p for each pixel p in the learned embedding space. The semantic embedding space makes the features of the same object merge together and makes the features of different objects far away. In practice, the embedding layer is composed of series of depthwise separable convolution and 1*1 convolution and batch normalization.

Co-Attention. We design an effective co-attention module to find and utilize the shared information among the whole video sequence. To save the memory and computation resource, we combine the first frame, i.e., the first frame and

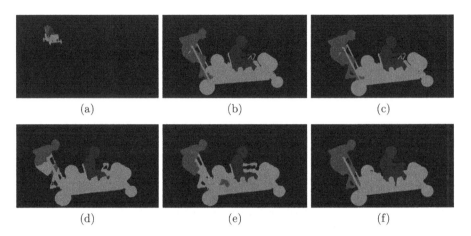

Fig. 3. Qualitative results of co-attention module influence. (a) is the first frame of the query video, (b) is the previous frame of the query frame, and (c) is the query frame. (d) is the prediction mask without first frame in the co-attention module. (e) is the prediction mask without the previous frame in the co-attention module. (f) is our final mask with complete co-attention module.

the previous frame and the current query frame as a complete video. The co-attention module extracts attention map from the whole video and integrates the attention map with the low-level feature of the query frame to emphasize the concerned region.

Matching. The matching module includes two similar submodules: global matching and local matching. The global matching module calculates the distance between the semantic embedding vector of the query frame and the semantic embedding of the first frame. The local matching module calculates the distance between the query frame and the previous frame. By minimizing the two distances, the module finds the similar region with the first frame and the previous frame in the query frame.

Decoder. We first concatenate the matching similarity maps from the match module and the attention maps from the co-attention module in the decoder module. Then, we upsample the scales of the features and fuse them with the low-level backbone feature in the residual connection way to generate the final segmentation mask.

3.2   Co-Attention

Inspired by the hierarchical question-image co-attention for visual question answering [11], which proposed a co-attention mechanism to extract common features between question text and image, we design a parallel co-attention module to extract common features among the query frame and the previous frame and the first frame. Due to the continuity of video, the common features among the three frames in a same video indicates the most attractive region and can help enhancing the representation of features of target object. We design the co-attention module to find the frame correlation from the frame-level perspective instead of pixel-level. To avoid the pixel-level mismatching problem due to the limitation of the receptive field, we adopt the fully connected layer to do the global mapping. And to save the compute resource, we add some convolution layers to reduce the number of channels.

In detail, we first obtain the semantic embedding features of the current frame E_T and the semantic embedding features of the previous frame E_{T-1} and semantic embedding features of the first frame E_1 from the encoder module. The shape of all semantic embedding features is $\mathbb{R}^{H \times W \times C}$. Then, we batch multiply the E_T by the E_{T-1} and E_1, respectively. After two $1 * 1$ convolution layers to decrease the number of channels to C_e and a reshape operation, we obtain the global relevance features Q and the local relevance features V. The shape of both Q and V is $(H \times W \times C_e, 1)$. Then we conduct a fully connected layer to Q and V respectively to extract the features of global frame fields and fuse the two result features by a matrix product. The output of above process is the coarse attention features. Due to the target segmentation objects is been annotated in the ground truth mask of the first frame, we fuse the coarse attention map with the ground truth mask $M_1 \in \mathbb{R}^{H \times W \times C_n}$ by the multiply operation to obtain the final attention map $A \in \mathbb{R}^{H \times W \times C_n}$ where C_n is the objects numbers. The final co-attention map is calculated as the following equation:

$$A = M_1 \times ((W_q(E_T \times E_{T-1}) \odot W_v(E_T \times E_1)) \tag{1}$$

As shown in the Fig. 3 (f), the mismatching problem in the segmentation result with co-attention module has been improved obviously. by contraries, the performance greatly worsen when removing the first frame or the previous frame.

3.3 Matching

We match the current frame with the first frame (global matching) and match the current frame with the previous frame (local matching). We adopt the embedding distance $D_t(p, q)$ designed by [24] to calculate the distance between the pixel p of the current frame T and the pixel q of the template frame t in terms of their responding semantic embedding vector e_p and e_q.

$$D_t(p,q) = \begin{cases} 1 - \frac{2}{1+\exp\left(\|e_p - e_q\|^2 + b_F\right)} & \text{if } q \in F_t \\ 1 - \frac{2}{1+\exp\left(\|e_p - e_q\|^2 + b_B\right)} & \text{if } q \in B_t \end{cases} \tag{2}$$

where F_t and B_t denote the pixel sets of all the foreground objects and background of frame, respectively. b_B and b_F denote trainable background and foreground bias, respectively. Let $F_{t,o} \subseteq F_t$ denotes the set of pixels at time t which belong to object o. Then $B_{t,o} = F_t \setminus F_{t,o}$ denotes the set of background pixels of object o at time t.

Table 1. The quantitative results on DAVIS 2016 validation set. OL denotes using online fine-tuning. SD denotes using extra similated data to pre-train. (Y) denotes using YouTube-VOS for training.

Method	OL	SD	J&F	J	F	Time(s)
OSVOS [3]	✓		80.2	79.8	80.6	50
CINM [1]	✓		84.2	83.4	85.0	700
OnAVOS [19]	✓		85.0	85.7	84.2	13
RGMP [13]		✓	81.8	81.5	82.0	0.14
STMVOS [14]		✓	86.5	84.8	88.1	0.16
VideoMatch [8]			80.9	81.0	80.8	0.32
FEELVOS(Y) [18]			81.7	81.1	82.0	0.45
RANet [20]			85.5	85.5	85.4	0.03
CFBI [24]			86.1	85.3	86.9	0.18
COMatchNet(ours)			**86.8**	**86.3**	**87.2**	0.18
COMatchNet(Y)(ours)			**87.1**	**87.0**	**87.2**	0.18

Global Matching is to find the most similar pixels to the first frame from the current frame. For each ground truth object o, the global foreground matching calculating each pixel p of the current frame T and the pixels of the first frame is,

$$G_{T,o}(p) = \min_{q \in F_{1,o}} D_1(p,q) \tag{3}$$

Local Matching is to find the most similar pixels to the previous frame from the current frame. We denotes $H(p,k)$ as the neighborhood set of pixels which are at k pixels away from p in both x and y directions. $F_{T-1,o}^k = F_{T-1,o} \cap H(p,k)$ denotes the set of pixels of frame $T-1$ which belong to object o or are in the neighborhood $H(p,k)$. The local foreground matching is,

$$L_{T,o}(p) = \begin{cases} \min_{q \in F_{T-1,o}^k} D(p,q) & \text{if } F_{T-1,o}^k \neq \emptyset \\ 1 & \text{otherwise} \end{cases} \tag{4}$$

4 Experiments

4.1 Implement Details

We implement our method with the PyTorch framework and use the ResNet-101 [4], pre-trained on COCO [10], as the backbone for our network. The whole training and evaluating experiments are conducted on four Nvidia TITAN Xp GPUs with 12GB memory. Without any simulated data, we only use the three most famous VOS datasets for training and evaluating: DAVIS 2016 [15] (20 validation videos), DAVIS 2017 [16] (60 train videos and 30 validation videos), and YouTube-VOS [23] (3147 train videos and 507 validation videos). We use flipping, scaling as data augmentations. In the training stage, the frames are

Table 2. The quantitative results on DAVIS 2017 validation set.

Method	OL	SD	J&F	J	F
OSVOS [3]	✓		60.3	56.6	63.9
CINM [1]	✓		70.6	67.2	74.0
OnAVOS [19]	✓		63.6	61.0	66.1
RGMP [13]		✓	66.7	64.8	68.6
STMVOS [14]		✓	71.6	69.2	74.0
VideoMatch [8]			62.4	56.5	68.2
FEELVOS(Y) [18]			71.5	69.1	74.0
RANet [20]			65.7	63.2	68.2
CFBI [24]			74.9	72.1	77.7
COMatchNet(ours)			**75.9**	**73.4**	**78.4**
COMatchNet(Y)(ours)			**79.9**	**77.9**	**81.9**

Table 3. The quantitative results on YouTube-VOS validation set.

Method	OL	SD	Avg	J_{seen}	F_{seen}	J_{unseen}	F_{unseen}
OSVOS [3]	✓		58.8	59.8	54.2	60.5	60.7
e-OSVOS [12]		✓	71.4	71.7	74.3	66.0	73.8
STMVOS [14]		✓	79.4	79.7	84.2	72.8	80.9
CFBI [24]			81.0	80.6	**85.1**	75.2	83.0
COMatchNet(ours)			**81.4**	**80.6**	84.9	**76.0**	**84.2**

uniformly cropped to 465*465. We train our model by the SGD [17] optimizer with a momentum of 0.9 and adopt the bootstrapped cross-entry loss. The batch size is set to 6. After many experiments, we set the initial learning rate of the YouTube-VOS dataset to 0.01 and the DAVIS dataset to 0.006, and dynamically adjust the learning rate during the training process. More details can be found in the https://github.com/huanglf714/COMatchNet.

4.2   Comparing to Other Advanced

Metrics. We adopt three evaluation metrics suggested by [15]: J score, F score, and their average J&F. J score calculates the average IoU between the ground truth mask and the prediction mask. the F score measures the average boundary similarity between the boundary of the ground truth mask and the prediction mask.

Results on DAVIS 2016. As shown in Table 1, we compare our proposed COMatchNet with previous state-of-the-art methods on the DAVIS 2016 validation set and our COMatchNet achieves a J&F mean of 86.8% . The experiment results show our COMatchNet outperforms all of the previous methods.

Table 4. Ablation study on DAVIS 2017 validation set.

	Method	J&F	∇J&F	J	F
0	COMatchNet	**75.9**	–	**73.4**	**78.4**
1	co-attention w/o first frame	71.4	↓ 4.5	68.9	73.8
2	co-attention w/o previous frame	71.7	↓ 4.2	69.4	74.1
3	w/o co-attention	70.1	↓ 5.8	68.8	71.3
4	w/o global matching	74.5	↓ 1.4	71.6	77.5
5	w/o local matching	75.3	↓ 0.6	72.7	77.9

STMVOS achieves 86.5% performance by generating extensive simulated data from static image data to pre-train the model but our model achieves 86.8% performance without any additional train data and post-process tricky. The performance gap (86.8% vs 86.1%) between COMatchNet and CFBI, which only uses pixel-level matching without frame correlation approves the addition of co-attention is effective.

Results on DAVIS 2017. In Table 2, we show the results of all compared methods on the DAVIS 2017 validation set. DAVIS 2017 is more challenging than DAVIS 2016 due to the multi-object scenarios. Our COMatchNet still achieves the best performance. Our COMatchNet achieves a significant performance improvement from 71.6% (STMVOS) to 75.9% without any additional data. The COMatchNet, which only uses the DAVIS train data even outperforms the FEELVOS, which uses both the YouTube-VOS and DAVIS as the train data. As shown in Table 2, on the DAVIS 2017 validation set, our COMatchNet gains the 1.3% performance improvement over CFBI due to the introduction of the co-attention.

Results on YouTube-VOS. Table 3 illustrates the comparison results on the YouTube-VOS 2019 dataset, which is a large-scale multi-object video object segmentation dataset. YouTube-VOS validation data includes some unseen categories in the train data, which can evaluate the generalization ability of different approaches. It can be seen that our proposed COMatchNet achieves better results than other methods on almost all metrics. Our COMatchNet releaizes the best performance with J&F=81.4%. In particular, the performance of COMatchNet for unseen objects is significantly improved compared to other models, which indicates the robustness and generalization ability of our model.

4.3   Ablation Study

We analyze the ablation effect of each component proposed in COMatchNet on the DAVIS 2017 validation set. We only use the DAVIS 2017 training set as training data for these experiments. The qualitative ablation study results is shown in the Table 4.

Fig. 4. Qualitative results of the proposed COMatchNet on VOS scenariors.
The 1-st and 2-nd and 3-rd rows are segmentation masks of the same video in the DAVIS
2017 validation set obtained by three methods. The 4-th row is from the DAVIS 2016
validation set and the 5-th row is from the YouTube-VOS validation set.

Co-Attention. We first analyze the influence of the co-attention module on the
model. In Line 1, we remove the first frame in the co-attention module, which
drops the performance from 75.9% to 71.4%. It is proved significant to join the
first frame to extract the features of the target objects. In Line 2, we demonstrate
the missing of the previous frame degrades the result to 71.7%. Then we further
remove the whole co-attention module and the result drops to 70.1%, which
proves the effectiveness of the co-attention module. These experiments metrics
provide qualitative comparative results about the co-attention module and the
quantitative comparative results is shown in the Fig. 3.

Matching. We also analyze the impact of the matching module on the performance of the model. In Line 4, we only match the current frame with the
previous one, which degrades the result from 75.9% to 74.5%. It demonstrates
that the first frame with the ground truth mask indeed helps boosts the performance. Then in Line 5, we only match the current frame with the first frame.
By doing this, the performance drops to 75.3%. It approves that the features of
the previous frame are useful to predict the mask of the current frame due to
the continuity of video.

In summary, these ablation experiments approve that each component of our
COMatchNet is effective and necessary.

4.4 Qualitative Results

In Fig. 4, we show some qualitative results of our proposed COMatchNet on the
DAVIS 2016, DAVIS 2017, and YouTube-VOS validation datasets. The 1-st and
2-nd and 3-rd rows are segmentation masks of the same video in the DAVIS 2017
validation set obtained by STMVOS [14] and CFBI [24] and our COMatchNet.

The results show that the COMatchNet separates the person and the scooter accurately, but the CFBI mismatches the hand as the scooter. Furthermore, our COMatchNet is influenced less by the surrounding environment, but the STMVOS mismatches the glass of a car parked on the side of the road to the windshield of the scooter. The 4-th row from the DAVIS 2016 validation set demonstrates the COMatchNet is able to segment object which is similar to the background. The 5-th row is from the YouTube-VOS validation set and the segmentation approves the ability of COMatchNet to segmentation multi objects.

5   Conclusion

This paper proposes a novel network for video object segmentation by introducing a co-attention module to extract frame correlation in the video and integrates the frame-level relevance information with the pixel-level matching score information to make our network simple but effective. The proposed network is end-to-end trainable and no need for any simulated data to pretrain or any post-processing technology. Moreover, experiments on three popular video object segmentation benchmarks demonstrate that our COMatchNet achieves outstanding performance than other previous methods.

References

1. Bao, L., Wu, B., Liu, W.: CNN in MRF: video object segmentation via inference in a CNN-based higher-order spatio-temporal MRF. In: Proceedings of the IEEE Conference on Computer Vision and Pattern Recognition, pp. 5977–5986 (2018)
2. Bolme, D.S., Beveridge, J.R., Draper, B.A., Lui, Y.M.: Visual object tracking using adaptive correlation filters. In: 2010 IEEE Computer Society Conference on Computer Vision and Pattern Recognition, pp. 2544–2550. IEEE (2010)
3. Caelles, S., Maninis, K.K., Pont-Tuset, J., Leal-Taixé, L., Cremers, D., Van Gool, L.: One-shot video object segmentation. In: Proceedings of the IEEE Conference on Computer Vision and Pattern Recognition, pp. 221–230 (2017)
4. Chen, L.-C., Zhu, Y., Papandreou, G., Schroff, F., Adam, H.: Encoder-decoder with atrous separable convolution for semantic image segmentation. In: Ferrari, V., Hebert, M., Sminchisescu, C., Weiss, Y. (eds.) ECCV 2018. LNCS, vol. 11211, pp. 833–851. Springer, Cham (2018). https://doi.org/10.1007/978-3-030-01234-2_49
5. Chen, Y., Pont-Tuset, J., Montes, A., Van Gool, L.: Blazingly fast video object segmentation with pixel-wise metric learning. In: Proceedings of the IEEE Conference on Computer Vision and Pattern Recognition, pp. 1189–1198 (2018)
6. Fan, H., et al.: Lasot: a high-quality benchmark for large-scale single object tracking. In: Proceedings of the IEEE/CVF Conference on Computer Vision and Pattern Recognition, pp. 5374–5383 (2019)
7. Girgensohn, A., et al.: A semi-automatic approach to home video editing. In: Proceedings of the 13th Annual ACM Symposium on User Interface Software and Technology, pp. 81–89 (2000)

8. Hu, Y.-T., Huang, J.-B., Schwing, A.G.: VideoMatch: matching based video object segmentation. In: Ferrari, V., Hebert, M., Sminchisescu, C., Weiss, Y. (eds.) ECCV 2018. LNCS, vol. 11212, pp. 56–73. Springer, Cham (2018). https://doi.org/10.1007/978-3-030-01237-3_4

9. Lin, J., Gan, C., Han, S.: TSM: temporal shift module for efficient video understanding. In: Proceedings of the IEEE/CVF International Conference on Computer Vision, pp. 7083–7093 (2019)

10. Lin, T.-Y., Maire, M., Belongie, S., Hays, J., Perona, P., Ramanan, D., Dollár, P., Zitnick, C.L.: Microsoft COCO: common objects in context. In: Fleet, D., Pajdla, T., Schiele, B., Tuytelaars, T. (eds.) ECCV 2014. LNCS, vol. 8693, pp. 740–755. Springer, Cham (2014). https://doi.org/10.1007/978-3-319-10602-1_48

11. Lu, J., Yang, J., Batra, D., Parikh, D.: Hierarchical question-image co-attention for visual question answering. arXiv preprint arXiv:1606.00061 (2016)

12. Meinhardt, T., Leal-Taixé, L.: Make one-shot video object segmentation efficient again. arXiv preprint arXiv:2012.01866 (2020)

13. Oh, S.W., Lee, J.Y., Sunkavalli, K., Kim, S.J.: Fast video object segmentation by reference-guided mask propagation. In: Proceedings of the IEEE Conference on Computer Vision and Pattern Recognition, pp. 7376–7385 (2018)

14. Oh, S.W., Lee, J.Y., Xu, N., Kim, S.J.: Video object segmentation using space-time memory networks. In: Proceedings of the IEEE/CVF International Conference on Computer Vision, pp. 9226–9235 (2019)

15. Perazzi, F., Pont-Tuset, J., McWilliams, B., Van Gool, L., Gross, M., Sorkine-Hornung, A.: A benchmark dataset and evaluation methodology for video object segmentation. In: Proceedings of the IEEE Conference on Computer Vision and Pattern Recognition, pp. 724–732 (2016)

16. Pont-Tuset, J., Perazzi, F., Caelles, S., Arbeláez, P., Sorkine-Hornung, A., Van Gool, L.: The 2017 davis challenge on video object segmentation. arXiv preprint arXiv:1704.00675 (2017)

17. Robbins, H., Monro, S.: A stochastic approximation method. Annals Math. Stat. 400–407 (1951)

18. Voigtlaender, P., Chai, Y., Schroff, F., Adam, H., Leibe, B., Chen, L.C.: Feelvos: fast end-to-end embedding learning for video object segmentation. In: Proceedings of the IEEE/CVF Conference on Computer Vision and Pattern Recognition, pp. 9481–9490 (2019)

19. Voigtlaender, P., Leibe, B.: Online adaptation of convolutional neural networks for video object segmentation. arXiv preprint arXiv:1706.09364 (2017)

20. Wang, Z., Xu, J., Liu, L., Zhu, F., Shao, L.: Ranet: ranking attention network for fast video object segmentation. In: Proceedings of the IEEE/CVF International Conference on Computer Vision, pp. 3978–3987 (2019)

21. Woo, S., Park, J., Lee, J.-Y., Kweon, I.S.: CBAM: convolutional block attention module. In: Ferrari, V., Hebert, M., Sminchisescu, C., Weiss, Y. (eds.) ECCV 2018. LNCS, vol. 11211, pp. 3–19. Springer, Cham (2018). https://doi.org/10.1007/978-3-030-01234-2_1

22. Wu, C.Y., Feichtenhofer, C., Fan, H., He, K., Krahenbuhl, P., Girshick, R.: Long-term feature banks for detailed video understanding. In: Proceedings of the IEEE/CVF Conference on Computer Vision and Pattern Recognition, pp. 284–293 (2019)

23. Xu, N., Yang, L., Fan, Y., Yue, D., Liang, Y., Yang, J., Huang, T.: Youtube-vos: a large-scale video object segmentation benchmark. arXiv preprint arXiv:1809.03327 (2018)

24. Yang, Z., Wei, Y., Yang, Y.: Collaborative video object segmentation by foreground-background integration. In: Vedaldi, A., Bischof, H., Brox, T., Frahm, J.-M. (eds.) ECCV 2020. LNCS, vol. 12350, pp. 332–348. Springer, Cham (2020). https://doi.org/10.1007/978-3-030-58558-7_20

25. Zolfaghari, M., Singh, K., Brox, T.: ECO: efficient convolutional network for online video understanding. In: Ferrari, V., Hebert, M., Sminchisescu, C., Weiss, Y. (eds.) ECCV 2018. LNCS, vol. 11206, pp. 713–730. Springer, Cham (2018). https://doi.org/10.1007/978-3-030-01216-8_43

Unsupervised Domain Adaptive Point Cloud Semantic Segmentation

Yikai Bian, Jin Xie, and Jianjun Qian$^{(\boxtimes)}$

PCA Lab, Key Lab of Intelligent Perception and Systems for High-Dimensional Information of Ministry of Education, School of Computer Science and Engineering, Nanjing University of Science and Technology, Nanjing, China
{yikai.bian,csjxie,csjqian}@njust.edu.cn

Abstract. Domain adaptation for point cloud semantic segmentation is important since manually labeling point cloud datasets for each domain are expensive and time-consuming. In this paper, in order to transfer prior knowledge from the labeled source domain to the unlabeled target domain, we propose a novel domain consistency framework for unsupervised domain adaptive point cloud semantic segmentation. Specifically, in our framework, we construct a multi-level feature consistency model to generate the high quality pseudo labels for the unlabeled target domain. In the constructed feature consistency model, we encourage the labels of feature maps of point clouds at different levels to be as consistent as possible. Based on the generated features with rich geometric structure information, we furthermore impose a feature consistency constraint on the feature memory bank of the source domain and target features to develop a feature bank based cycle association model. Thus, benefiting from the developed cycle association model, we can alleviate the domain gap and learn discriminative features of point clouds for semantic segmentation in the target domain. Extensive evaluations on different outdoor scenarios ("vKITTI to SemanticPOSS" and "SynthCity to SemanticPOSS") and indoor scenarios ("S3DIS to ScanNet") show that our framework achieves state-of-the-art performance.

Keywords: Unsupervised domain adaptation · Point cloud semantic segmentation · Deep learning for visual perception

1 Introduction

LiDAR, as a 3D imaging sensor, is widely used in a variety of 3D environment perception tasks such as 3D point cloud semantic segmentation. Recently, with the development of deep learning techniques and the explosive growth of point cloud data, 3D point cloud semantic segmentation has been receiving more and

This work was supported by the National Science Fund of China under Grant (No. 61876083), Shanghai Automotive Industry Science and Technology Development Foundation (No. 1917).

© Springer Nature Switzerland AG 2022
C. Wallraven et al. (Eds.): ACPR 2021, LNCS 13188, pp. 285–298, 2022.
https://doi.org/10.1007/978-3-031-02375-0_21

more attention. Nonetheless, deep learning based semantic segmentation methods usually require large amount of manually labeled samples. Particularly, the point-level labeling is extremely expensive due to the large amount of manual labors for point cloud semantic segmentation.

One potential solution is to train a network on one labeled dataset (source domain) and generalize it to another unlabeled dataset (target domain), which is commonly referred to as unsupervised domain adaptation (UDA). Different datasets are acquired by different types of 3D sensors in different scenes, even some datasets are synthetic data. Thus, large variations of point cloud distributions between the two domains lead to the domain shift problem, which degrades the semantic segmentation performance in the target point cloud domain.

Recent methods for unsupervised point cloud domain adaptation can be divided into two categories. On one hand, several works aim to reduce domain gap at the input level so that the consistency of data distributions of different domains can be increased. For example, in [19], they focus on generative adversarial networks (GANs) to translate bird-eyes view point cloud images from the source domain to the target domain. Some other methods use completion network [27] or geometric mapping [14] to transfer semantic scans between different LiDAR sensors. Due to complex geometric structures of 3D point clouds, it is a great challenge to obtain consistent inputs for the source and target domains. On the other hand, some works focus on performing feature alignment to alleviate the domain gap. The core idea of these works is to encourage the feature consistency between different domains by minimizing the distribution discrepancy with adversarial learning [23] or domains distance loss [25]. Unfortunately, these methods only consider the global feature alignment and ignore local geometric semantic clues, leading to degraded segmentation performance.

In this paper, we propose a novel framework for unsupervised domain adaptive point cloud semantic segmentation, where we exploit the local geometric structure information of point clouds for feature alignment to alleviate the domain gap. The framework consists of two modules: multi-level feature consistency module and feature bank based cycle association module. Inspired by self-training [12], which is a useful technique for learning knowledge from unlabeled data, we develop a model to facilitate the feature consistency at different levels between two domains with self-produced pseudo labels. We encourage the labels of feature maps of point clouds at different levels to be as consistent as possible. Specifically, we adopt the voting strategy combined with multi-classifiers to produce reliable outputs. Then the outputs serve as the pseudo labels of the target domain data to provide semantic segmentation self-training guidance at different levels. Based on the generated features with rich geometric structure information, the feature bank based cycle association module is proposed to directly align the distributions of the features from the same class between the two domains. Specifically, we stack the features of source points with different local geometric structure information and store them into feature memory bank according to the class labels. Once the feature memory bank is completed, we build cycle association [13] between the features of bank and target features to achieve feature level alignment. Here, we directly minimize their feature discrepancy to alleviate the domain gap and learn discriminative features in target domain. Finally, we verify the effectiveness of our method on different domains with various experiments, including synthetic to real domain scenarios such as "vKITTI to SemanticPOSS" and "SynthCity to SemanicPOSS" and dense to sparse indoor domain scenarios such as "S3DIS to ScanNet".

The main contributions of our paper can be summarized as follows: (i) We propose a novel framework for unsupervised domain adaptive point cloud semantic segmentation; (ii) We propose a multi-level feature consistency module to facilitate the feature consistency of different levels between two domains; (iii) We propose a feature bank based cycle association module to capture abundant source features for efficient feature alignment.

2   Related Work

2.1   Unsupervised Domain Adaptation

Unsupervised domain adaptation focuses on adapting the models from one labeled domain to another unlabeled domain. There are various methods designed for 2D images. Typically, the works on 2D unsupervised domain adaptation can be subdivided into three categories: input level adaptation, feature level adaptation and output level adaptation. Firstly, some methods [15,26] try to address the domain gap problem by matching at the input level to decrease the discrepancy of data distributions of different domains. They attempt to achieve uniformity of visual appearance between domains by image style transfer technologies, e.g., CycleGAN [29]. Secondly, feature level adaptation aims to align the distributions of latent representations. Adversarial learning [4] is a common practice in these methods. Furthermore, PLCA [13] builds the cycle association between source and target pixel pairs. Then they strengthen the connections of association pairs to explicitly reduce the distance between the features from the same class in the two domains. Finally, a group of methods achieve distribution alignment at the output space, where self-constructed pseudo labels [15] are produced to transfer the knowledge from the source domain to the target domain. Moreover, MinEnt [21] and MaxSquare [3] propose different target losses to enforce high prediction certainty on target domain which are also effective methods in output level adaptation.

Relatively, there are few works considering domain adaptation for 3D point clouds. Existing works do not directly process the unordered point cloud data. Wang et al. [23] and Saleh et al. [19] adopt a bird-eyes view to conduct domain adaptive point cloud object detection. Yi et al. [27] voxelize the complete point clouds and use an auxiliary completion network to transfer the semantic labels between different LiDAR sensors. xMUDA [11] proposes cross-modal domain adaptation where the model takes advantage of the respective robustness of point clouds and images in different scenarios. SqueezeSegV2 [25] adopts intensity rendering and geodesic correlation alignment to deal with domain gap problem on point clouds which are projected onto a spherical surface. Achituve et al. [1]

introduce a deformation reconstruction as pretext task to build a self-supervised model, which is applied effectively for domain adaptation.

2.2 Deep Point Cloud Semantic Segmentation

Point cloud semantic segmentation aims to obtain fine-gained semantic information for each point. xMUDA [11] uses SparseConvNet [8] for 3D segmentation, which proposes submanifold sparse convolution networks to process the spatially-sparse voxelized point cloud more efficiently. SqueezeSeg [24] projects point cloud onto a spherical surface in order to use a 2D CNN to predict semantic labels for each point and SqueezeSegV2 [25] is an improved version. Because of variations of point cloud distributions and different 3D sampling patterns, different voxelization and projection methods are required between domains, which may lead to a more serious domain shift problem.

In order to avoid using intermediate representation (*e.g.* spherical, volumetric and multi-view) [10] for point clouds and directly extract semantic context from the unordered point clouds, we focus on a series of point-based networks based on PointNet [18]. GACNet [22] proposes a graph attention convolution to selectively learn local features by dynamically assigning weights to neighboring points. PointNL [5] adopts cascaded non-local module to learn geometric structure information of different neighborhoods. PointWeb [28] builds connections between each point with its neighbors to learn local features. In this work, we select point-based method as our segmentation backbone to build a framework for unsupervised domain adaptive point cloud semantic segmentation.

3 Method

3.1 Overview

Given a labeled source domain $S = \{\mathbf{X}_i^s, \mathbf{Y}_i^s\}_{i=1}^{N_s}$ and an unlabeled target domain $T = \{\mathbf{X}_i^t\}_{i=1}^{N_t}$, we aim to train a semantic segmentation model with the data $\mathbf{X}^s$ with point-level ground truth labels $\mathbf{Y}^s$ of source domain and the unlabeled data $\mathbf{X}^t$ of target domain that can predict accurate point-level labels $\hat{\mathbf{Y}}^t$ for target domain. N_s and N_t denote the number of points in source domain and target domain, respectively. In order to reduce the domain shift, we employ a conjoined architecture with source stream and target stream to learn common feature distribution. Two modules named multi-level feature consistency module and feature bank based cycle association module are proposed to deal with domain adaptation in feature level. In the multi-level feature consistency module, we use source data and the corresponding ground truth labels to train multi classifiers at different levels. Since the target labels cannot be accessed in the unsupervised domain adaptation manner, we adopt a voting strategy to generate different levels of pseudo labels as supervision signals. To further minimize the discrepancy of feature distributions of source domain and target domain, we propose the feature bank based cycle association module. We first build the feature memory

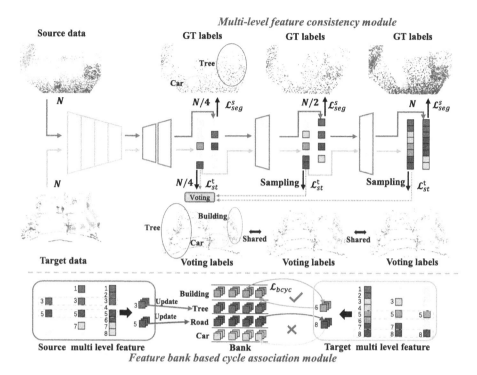

Fig. 1. Illustration of the framework of unsupervised domain adaptive point cloud semantic segmentation. It is a conjoined architecture with two streams. Source data and target data are alternately fed into the model. For multi-level feature consistency module, to enhance the feature consistency at different levels, the features from the source data and target data are both constrained at three levels. While the target labels are generated according to the outputs of three classifiers based on voting strategy. For feature bank based cycle association module, we generate feature memory bank from the source data, and build the cycle association between the memory bank and the target data to minimize the discrepancy of feature distributions in two domains.

bank for each category on the source domain. Then, we construct the cycle association between the feature bank and target features to pull in the feature distance between the source domain and the target domain. As a result, the domain gap can be reduced through the multi-level feature consistency module and the feature bank based cycle association module, thereby improving the segmentation result of the target domain. At test phase, we only input the target point clouds into the network to generate segmentation results. Note that the proposed two modules will be discarded.

3.2 Multi-level Feature Consistency

In order to generate features and semantic segmentation predictions for unordered point clouds, we adopt PointWeb [28] as our segmentation backbone, which is an encoder-decoder architecture with four down sampling and four up sampling modules as shown in Fig. 1. Specifically, given the input point cloud $\mathbf{X} = \{\mathbf{x}_1, \mathbf{x}_2, ..., \mathbf{x}_n\}$ with n points, the down sampling module named Set Abstraction (SA) module uses Farthest Point Sampling (FPS) to select points as sampling centroids, and then applies adaptive feature adjustment module proposed in PointWeb to extract geometric feature with its neighbors. After four down sampling modules, we obtain the abundant features with different local geometric structure information. At up sampling phase, the up sampling module named Feature Propagation (FP) module adopts distance based interpolation and across-level skip links to obtain the up sampling point features. With four up sampling modules, we can get point-wise features for all n points. Then the classifier produces the per-point outputs. We use the point-wise cross entropy loss L_{ce} to train the segmentation model, $i.e.,$

$$L_{ce}(\hat{\mathbf{Y}}, \mathbf{Y}) = -\frac{1}{N} \sum_{i=1}^{N} \sum_{j=1}^{C} \mathbf{Y}_{(i,j)} \log \hat{\mathbf{Y}}_{(i,j)} \tag{1}$$

where $\mathbf{Y}$ is the ground truth semantic label of N points, $\hat{\mathbf{Y}}$ is the output for input point clouds and C is the number of classes.

Self-training methods [1] have been proved to be effective for learning general features from the unlabeled data. Benefiting from the hierarchical structure, we exploit a multi-level feature semantic consistency task for target domain. Once we obtain multi-level features which contain local geometric structure information at different scales, we build another two classifiers after the second and third FP modules to generate multi-level outputs on m and k sampling centroid points selected by FPS at down sampling phase. For the source domain, there exists the point-wise labels for all input points. Therefore, with the outputs $\hat{\mathbf{Y}}^{s1}$ for the m centroid points, outputs $\hat{\mathbf{Y}}^{s2}$ for the k centroid points and outputs $\hat{\mathbf{Y}}^{s3}$ for all n points, we can train the model with the following training loss:

$$L_{seg}^{s} = L_{ce}(\hat{\mathbf{Y}}^{s1}, \mathbf{Y}^{s1}) + L_{ce}(\hat{\mathbf{Y}}^{s2}, \mathbf{Y}^{s2}) + L_{ce}(\hat{\mathbf{Y}}^{s3}, \mathbf{Y}^{s3}) \tag{2}$$

where $\mathbf{Y}^{s3}$ is the complete source ground truth labels and $\mathbf{Y}^{s1}$, $\mathbf{Y}^{s2}$ are sampled from $\mathbf{Y}^{s3}$ according to the index of corresponding centroids.

We then construct a self-training loss with the same architecture for the unlabeled data in target domain. The loss is motivated by the fact that the model can produce multi-level consistent outputs inspired by Eq. (2) and the source data and target data share the same model. Although there is no label available for target domain, we can use the outputs of different levels from the target data to produce pseudo labels, which provide a way to optimize the model with the unlabeled target domain. Specifically, we focus on the selected m centroid points $\mathbf{X}^{t1} = \{\mathbf{x}_1^{t1}, \mathbf{x}_2^{t1}, ..., \mathbf{x}_m^{t1}\}$ at the second FP module which have features of different levels to produce pseudo labels. We leverage the three classifiers to produce the corresponding outputs $\hat{\mathbf{Y}}^{t1}$, $\hat{\mathbf{Y}}^{t2}$ and $\hat{\mathbf{Y}}^{t3}$. Then we extract reliable pseudo labels $\mathbf{Y}^*$ for the m selected points based on the voting strategy in Eq. (3) where c is the index of classes and i indicates the index of m points

$$\mathbf{Y}^*_{(i,c)} = \begin{cases} 1, & \textit{if } c = \arg\max_c \hat{\mathbf{Y}}^{t1}_i \\ & \textit{and } c = \arg\max_c \hat{\mathbf{Y}}^{t2}_i \\ & \textit{and } c = \arg\max_c \hat{\mathbf{Y}}^{t3}_i \\ 0, & \textit{otherwise} \end{cases} \tag{3}$$

Once we get the dynamically generated pseudo labels, we construct the self-training loss, which is given by:

$$L^t_{st} = L_{ce}(\hat{\mathbf{Y}}^{t1}, \mathbf{Y}^*) + L_{ce}(\hat{\mathbf{Y}}^{t2}, \mathbf{Y}^*) + L_{ce}(\hat{\mathbf{Y}}^{t3}, \mathbf{Y}^*) \tag{4}$$

We rely on the above proposed loss to complete the self-training architecture. By conducting the voting strategy on the outputs from different levels, we can generate more reliable pseudo labels for unlabeled target domain. In this way, the model simultaneously trained on the source and target data with the consistent source ground truth labels and target pseudo labels at three levels. The model obtains a way to learn the common feature representation for both domains, which is proved to be effective for the domain adaptation.

3.3 Feature Bank Based Cycle Association

As mentioned above, feature level alignment has been widely employed to construct domain adaptation methods [4,13,25]. Based on the hierarchical structure and generated features with different geometric structure information, we further minimize the discrepancy of feature distributions between the source domain and target domain through feature bank based cycle association module.

We first revisit the point-level cycle association [13]. Given the feature $\mathbf{f}_i$ of a certain source domain point, we find its nearest neighbor feature $\mathbf{f}_j$ in target feature space, where $\mathbf{f}_j$ represents the feature of j-th point in the target domain. Similarly, we could in turn select the feature $\mathbf{f}_k$ of the point in source domain, which is the nearest neighbor feature of $\mathbf{f}_j$. The cycle consistency is satisfied when the source points i and k belong to the same semantic class. Once the cycle association is built, we use the feature distance loss function for associated point pairs to minimize their feature discrepancy.

We argue that directly applying the above method to our unsupervised domain adaptive point cloud semantic segmentation model may cause the biased feature alignment, especially when the input point clouds are split into blocks before being fed into the model. The reason lies in the class sparsity of the input point clouds at the training phase, where the samples of the same class in the source and target domains are difficult to appear in the same iteration. This problem impedes the feature level alignment between the features from the same class in the two domains.

To effectively address the problem, we generate feature representation memory bank for each class to deal with the misalignment of class distributions of the source and target domains. Firstly, we stack the features $\mathbf{F}^1$, $\mathbf{F}^2$ and $\mathbf{F}^3$

Algorithm 1 The process of building the feature bank

Input: The source domain data $S = \{\mathbf{X}_i^s, \mathbf{Y}_i^s\}_{i=1}^{N_s}$
Output: The feature bank $\mathcal{B}$ with C classes

1: **for** epochs 1, 2, 3,..., MAXEPOCH **do**
2:     **for** iterations 1, 2, 3,..., MAXITER **do**
3:         Sample one batch of source data from S
4:         Select the correctly predicted points P_s with Eq. (3) for data
5:         Produce multi-level feature representation $\mathbf{F}^{ml}$ for P^s
6:         **for** each $\mathbf{f}^{ml} \in \mathbf{F}^{ml}$ **do**
7:             Set c as the predicted class for $\mathbf{f}^{ml}$
8:             **if** $\mathcal{B}_c$ is full with b features **then**
9:                 Replace the oldest feature in $\mathcal{B}_c$.
10:            **else**
11:                Push the $\mathbf{f}^{ml}$ into $\mathcal{B}_c$ of bank

---

of different levels of m selected points mentioned in Sect. 3.2 to produce an integrated multi-level feature representation $\mathbf{F}^{ml}$, where $\mathbf{F}^{ml} = \mathbf{F}^1 \oplus \mathbf{F}^2 \oplus \mathbf{F}^3$ and $\oplus$ denotes the concatenation operation. So that the feature $\mathbf{F}^{ml}$ will have different geometric structure information. Benefiting from the stacked abundant features, we can build more reliable cycle association. Secondly, we select the correctly classified source points and store the corresponding integrated feature into the bank according to class label. For an empty feature bank, the bank will be continuously filled with the source features in every iteration. Once the bank is full, the features in the bank will be updated according to First In First Out (FIFO) method. We provide the algorithm of the process of building the feature bank in Algorithm 1. Mathematically, the bank can be written as:

$$
\mathcal{B} = \begin{bmatrix} \mathbf{f}_{(1,1)}^{bank} & \mathbf{f}_{(2,1)}^{bank} & \cdots & \mathbf{f}_{(b,1)}^{bank} \\ \mathbf{f}_{(1,2)}^{bank} & \mathbf{f}_{(2,2)}^{bank} & \cdots & \mathbf{f}_{(b,2)}^{bank} \\ \vdots & \vdots & \ddots & \vdots \\ \mathbf{f}_{(1,c)}^{bank} & \mathbf{f}_{(2,c)}^{bank} & \cdots & \mathbf{f}_{(b,c)}^{bank} \end{bmatrix}, \ \mathbf{f}_{(i,j)}^{bank} \in \mathbf{F}^{ml} \tag{5}
$$

where c is semantic class label and b is the size of memory bank for each class.

Finally, based on the bank of source features, we build cycle association between the bank features and the target features to achieve the feature level alignment. For example, starting from each bank feature $\mathbf{f}_i^{bank}$ in $\mathcal{B}$, we find its nearest neighbor feature $\mathbf{f}_p^{ml}$ in target features and in turn select the nearest neighbor feature $\mathbf{f}_{p'}^{bank}$ in bank. We explore loss function defined in Eq. (6) to minimize the discrepancy between associated P feature pairs where the starting feature and ending feature belong to the same class.

$$
L_{bcyc} = - \sum_{p=1}^{P} \left\| \mathbf{f}_p^{ml} - \mathbf{f}_{p'}^{bank} \right\|_1, \ \mathbf{f}_{p'}^{bank} \in \mathcal{B} \tag{6}
$$

3.4   Training

In point cloud unsupervised domain adaptation, only the source point clouds with its point-level labels and target point clouds are available. Following the xMUDA [11], our method is a two-stage method. At the first stage, the source data and target data are iteratively fed into the model, where the source data is used to train the model with L^s_{seg} at three levels and build a source concatenate feature representation memory bank $\mathcal{B}$. Only several selected points in target data are used for self-training with L^t_{st}. Then we build cycle association between feature memory bank $\mathcal{B}$ of the source domain and target concatenate features. Once the association pairs are built, we use L_{bcyc} to align feature distributions from the same class between the two domains. With the proposed modules, our loss function at the first stage can be formulated as:

$$L = L^s_{seg} + \lambda_1 L^t_{st} + \lambda_2 L_{bcyc} \tag{7}$$

where λ_1 and λ_2 are trade-off parameters which are set empirically.

At the second stage, we fix the model parameters to produce point-level pseudo labels $\mathbf{Y}^{pl}$ for all target points according to the predicted class probability with high confidence. Therefore, we can explore the point-level supervision signals for target data training, which is complementary to our proposed modules. Given the offline produced pseudo labels, we reinitialize the model and train it with the sum of Eq. (7) and Eq. (8), where the Eq. (8) is pseudo label segmentation loss formulated as:

$$L^t_{pl} = L_{ce}(\hat{\mathbf{Y}}^{t1}, \mathbf{Y}^{pl1}) + L_{ce}(\hat{\mathbf{Y}}^{t2}, \mathbf{Y}^{pl2}) + L_{ce}(\hat{\mathbf{Y}}^{t3}, \mathbf{Y}^{pl3}) \tag{8}$$

4   Experiments

4.1   Implementation Details

We leverage the official PyTorch [17] implementation for PointWeb [28] as our base architecture. PointWeb takes a batch of point clouds as input and predicts point-wise semantic labels. Empirically, the size of bank b for each class is set to 32 for indoor datasets and 64 for outdoor datasets. The parameters λ_1 and λ_2 are set to 0.1 and 0.01. To train our model, we use a single TITAN RTX GPU and the batch size is set to 8 in all experiments. Stochastic Gradient Descent (SGD) is used to optimize the segmentation network, where the initial learning rate is 0.05 for vKITTI→SemanticPOSS and S3DIS→ScanNet. For SynthCity→SemanticPOSS, the initial learning rate is 0.005. Following the PointWeb [28], the momentum and weight decay are set to 0.9 and 0.0001, respectively.

4.2   Datasets

vKITTI→SemanticPOSS. The vKITTI [7] dataset contains 6 different sequences of synthetic outdoor scenes. There are 13 semantic classes (including tree, building, road, etc.) with point-level labels, but we use 6 classes in common with SemanticPOSS [16], which are listed in Table 1. SemanticPOSS is a real-word point cloud semantic segmentation dataset collected in dynamic driving scenarios. It contains 2988 LiDAR scans with point-level labels of 14 classes. For experiments, the sequences 00~04 are used for training and the sequences 05 is used as validation set for evaluation. During the training, the points are split into blocks of 15 m × 15 m and each block contains 4096 points.

Table 1. The segmentation performance comparison of adapting vKITTI→ Semantic-POSS on 6 common classes

Model	Plants	Building	Road	Trafficsign	Pole	Car	mIoU
Source Only	57.4	58.2	75.3	16.5	17.7	42.5	44.6
MinEnt [21]	55.6	64.2	73.8	**17.5**	16.1	48.1	45.9
MaxSquare [3]	56.9	67.7	71.8	15.9	15.1	50.3	46.3
ADDA [20]	62.4	73.7	79.3	16.1	23.0	44.5	49.8
xMUDA [11]	62.2	74.8	77.3	15.5	27.5	49.9	51.2
Ours	**63.8**	**76.6**	**82.9**	13.1	**33.9**	**55.6**	**54.3**

Table 2. The segmentation performance comparison of adapting SynthCity→ Semantic POSS on 5 common classes

Model	Plants	Building	Road	Pole	Car	mIoU
Source Only	39.9	57.1	77.2	11.4	18.7	40.9
MinEnt [21]	49.2	58.0	74.5	5.8	30.1	43.5
MaxSquare [3]	47.6	62.4	78.7	4.0	32.6	45.0
ADDA [20]	41.1	59.5	76.3	9.2	27.5	42.7
xMUDA [11]	40.5	61.2	83.2	**26.0**	30.3	48.3
Ours	**55.5**	**67.8**	**85.0**	5.0	**34.5**	**49.6**

SynthCity→SemanticPOSS. The synthetic dataset SynthCity [9] contains 367.9M annotated point clouds from 9 areas, every point is labeled from one of 9 semantic classes (including car, road, etc.). The 5 common classes are used for domain adaptation, which are listed in Table 2. The scenes are divided into blocks of size 10 m × 10 m for training. The SemanciPOSS serves as target domain in domain adaptation.

S3DIS→ScanNet. The S3DIS [2] dataset is an indoor colored point cloud dataset generated by Matterport scanner, which contains 3D coordinates and RGB color values. There are 271 rooms in 6 different areas where each point is labeled from one of 13 semantic classes. The ScanNet [6] dataset contains 1513 indoor point cloud scenes, which is split into 1201/312 for training and testing. All points are annotated with 20 semantic classes. However, we use 8 classes in common with S3DIS, which are listed in Table 3. We select S3DIS as source domain and ScanNet as target domain. To prepare the training data, the points are split into blocks with size of 1.5 m × 1.5 m and each block contains 8192 points.

Table 3. The segmentation performance comparison of adapting S3DIS→ScanNet on 8 common classes

Model	Floor	Wall	Window	Door	Table	Chair	Sofa	Bookshelf	mIoU
Source Only	90.4	67.9	11.7	12.1	45.4	48.4	38.7	30.8	43.2
MinEnt [21]	92.0	77.5	9.1	14.0	42.9	47.3	35.1	36.3	44.3
MaxSquare [3]	90.9	72.1	11.9	13.9	43.9	47.3	38.3	30.9	43.6
ADDA [20]	90.1	74.9	14.7	12.0	37.9	43.2	33.7	33.8	42.5
xMUDA [11]	93.4	74.1	8.5	8.0	**61.6**	**63.4**	**42.5**	**47.1**	49.8
Ours	**94.4**	**82.4**	**18.0**	**15.2**	52.9	60.1	41.0	44.7	**51.0**

Table 4. Ablation study on S3DIS→ScanNet

Model	Floor	Wall	Window	Door	Table	Chair	Sofa	Bookshelf	mIoU
Source Only	90.4	67.9	11.7	12.1	45.4	48.4	38.7	30.8	43.2
Ours (PL)	92.3	68.7	17.9	12.1	48.8	52.0	**45.9**	33.6	46.4
Ours (M)	93.3	79.4	10.7	**16.1**	48.8	52.6	37.1	32.7	46.3
Ours (M+B)	93.6	80.0	14.1	15.2	50.1	55.8	38.3	37.6	48.1
Ours (M+B+PL)	**94.4**	**82.4**	**18.0**	15.2	**52.9**	**60.1**	41.0	**44.7**	**51.0**

4.3 Performance Comparison

We report the quantitative segmentation results of our method for the vKITTI→ SemanticPOSS in Table 1 with mean Intersection over Union (mIoU), the SynthCity → SemanticPOSS in Table 2, and the S3DIS→ScanNet in Table 3. Specifically, the performance is assessed on different common classes between different domain adaptation scenarios. The "Source Only" means the model is trained on source data only with the original PointWeb and then directly tested on the target data. As shown in Table 1, 2 and 3, our method achieves state-of-the-art performance on all three domain scenarios.

We compare against a serial of general UDA methods including: entropy minimization (MinEnt)[21], MaxSquare [3] and Adversarial Discriminative Domain Adaptation (ADDA) [20]. We adapt the published implementations of the above methods to our settings for fair comparison. The recent method [27] requires real world LiDAR sequences to obtain the complete 3D surfaces, which is incompatible with synthetic datasets and indoor datasets. Thus, it limits the reproducibility. Beyond that, we compare with the 3D modal part of xMUDA [11], which brings an impressive adaptation effect on all scenarios. As shown in Table 1, 2 and 3, our method gains a better performance than the above methods. Benefiting from the proposed multi-level feature consistency module and feature bank based cycle association module, the model can successfully transfer domain knowledge from source to target domains. However, the unbalanced point number between different classes leads to performance degradation on low-density classes (*i.e.*, traffic sign and pole).

Finally, visual results are shown in Fig. 2. Due to the domain gap problem, the model trained on source data only produces ambiguous predictions on target data. Specifically, as shown in the source only result at the fifth row of Fig. 2, there are large amounts of visible noisy results in the floor points. The proposed modules provide multi-level information and direct feature alignment, which can effectively alleviate the domain adaptation problem and improve the segmentation performance of target domain.

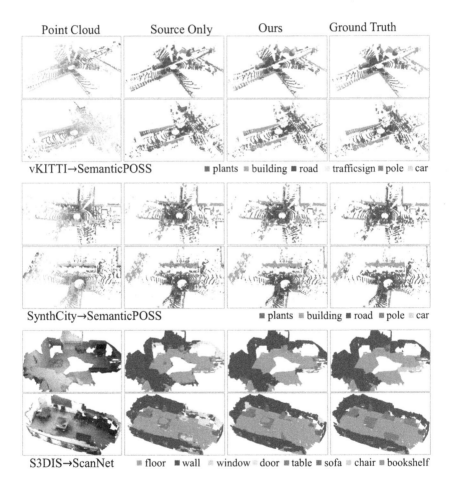

Fig. 2. Visualization results on the three adaptation scenarios. The results of vKITTI→SemanticPOSS are exhibited in the top two rows, the middle two rows show the results of SynthCity→SemanticPOSS and the bottom two rows are the results of S3DIS→ScanNet

4.4   Ablation Study

We conduct ablation studies on S3DIS→ScanNet. The results are shown in Table 4, where M denotes the multi-level feature consistency module, B denotes the feature bank based cycle association module. We set the pseudo-labeling (PL) method as our baseline, where the model is trained on source data only with the original PointWeb [28] and then produces pseudo labels for the second stage training. In general, both the module M and module B achieve impressive results in the S3DIS→ScanNet domain scenarios. As shown on the third row in Table 4, our multi-level feature consistency module brings 3.1% improvements on S3DIS→ ScanNet. Quantitatively, the module B brings another 1.8% improvements on S3DIS→ ScanNet. It can be clearly seen that the module B can further alleviate the domain gap. The reason lies in that with the feature memory bank, the reliable cycle association constraint can effectively align the class-wise feature distributions. The two-stage method with pseudo labels is a common strategy in domain adaptation. We empirically select the most confident prediction class of all points as pseudo labels for target domain, which is same to xMUDA [11]. As shown in Table 4, we observe that our proposed modules and PL are complementary and the fusion model of the proposed two modules gains the state-of-the-art performance on all three domain scenarios.

5   Conclusion

In this paper, we proposed a novel framework for point cloud unsupervised domain adaptive semantic segmentation which directly processes unordered point cloud data. Specifically, we proposed two modules named multi-level feature consistency module and feature bank based cycle association module to alleviate the domain gap. At first training stage, the model with the proposed two modules gained an impressive segmentation performance on target domain. Furthermore, the second training stage with pseudo labels of data of target domain further reduced the domain discrepancy. Experimental results demonstrated that our method can achieve state-of-the-art performance on outdoor domains (vKITTI→SemanticPOSS and SynthCity→SemanticPOSS) and indoor domains (S3DIS→ScanNet).

References

1. Achituve, I., Maron, H., Chechik, G.: Self-supervised learning for domain adaptation on point clouds. In: WACV (2021)
2. Armeni, I., et al.: 3D semantic parsing of large-scale indoor spaces. In: CVPR (2016)
3. Chen, M., Xue, H., Cai, D.: Domain adaptation for semantic segmentation with maximum squares loss. In: ICCV (2019)
4. Chen, Y.C., Lin, Y.Y., Yang, M.H., Huang, J.B.: Crdoco: pixel-level domain transfer with cross-domain consistency. In: CVPR (2019)
5. Cheng, M., Hui, L., Xie, J., Yang, J., Kong, H.: Cascaded non-local neural network for point cloud semantic segmentation. In: IROS (2020)

6. Dai, A., Chang, A.X., Savva, M., Halber, M., Funkhouser, T., Nießner, M.: Scannet: richly-annotated 3D reconstructions of indoor scenes. In: CVPR (2017)
7. Gaidon, A., Wang, Q., Cabon, Y., Vig, E.: Virtual worlds as proxy for multi-object tracking analysis. In: CVPR (2016)
8. Graham, B., Engelcke, M., Van Der Maaten, L.: 3D semantic segmentation with submanifold sparse convolutional networks. In: CVPR (2018)
9. Griffiths, D., Boehm, J.: Synthcity: a large scale synthetic point cloud. arXiv preprint arXiv:1907.04758 (2019)
10. Guo, Y., Wang, H., Hu, Q., Liu, H., Liu, L., Bennamoun, M.: Deep learning for 3D point clouds: a survey. TPAMI **43**, 4338–4364 (2020)
11. Jaritz, M., Vu, T.H., Charette, R.D., Wirbel, E., Pérez, P.: xmuda: cross-modal unsupervised domain adaptation for 3D semantic segmentation. In: CVPR (2020)
12. Jing, L., Tian, Y.: Self-supervised visual feature learning with deep neural networks: a survey. TPAMI **43**, 4037–4058 (2020)
13. Kang, G., Wei, Y., Yang, Y., Zhuang, Y., Hauptmann, A.G.: Pixel-level cycle association: a new perspective for domain adaptive semantic segmentation. arXiv preprint arXiv:2011.00147 (2020)
14. Langer, F., Milioto, A., Haag, A., Behley, J., Stachniss, C.: Domain transfer for semantic segmentation of lidar data using deep neural networks. In: IROS (2020)
15. Li, Y., Yuan, L., Vasconcelos, N.: Bidirectional learning for domain adaptation of semantic segmentation. In: CVPR (2019)
16. Pan, Y., Gao, B., Mei, J., Geng, S., Li, C., Zhao, H.: Semanticposs: a point cloud dataset with large quantity of dynamic instances. In: IV (2020)
17. Paszke, A., et al.: Automatic differentiation in pytorch (2017)
18. Qi, C.R., Su, H., Mo, K., Guibas, L.J.: Pointnet: deep learning on point sets for 3D classification and segmentation. In: CVPR (2017)
19. Saleh, K., et al.: Domain adaptation for vehicle detection from bird's eye view lidar point cloud data. In: ICCV Workshop (2019)
20. Tzeng, E., Hoffman, J., Saenko, K., Darrell, T.: Adversarial discriminative domain adaptation. In: CVPR (2017)
21. Vu, T.H., Jain, H., Bucher, M., Cord, M., Pérez, P.: Advent: adversarial entropy minimization for domain adaptation in semantic segmentation. In: CVPR (2019)
22. Wang, L., Huang, Y., Hou, Y., Zhang, S., Shan, J.: Graph attention convolution for point cloud semantic segmentation. In: CVPR (2019)
23. Wang, Z., et al.: Range adaptation for 3D object detection in lidar. In: ICCV Workshop (2019)
24. Wu, B., Wan, A., Yue, X., Keutzer, K.: Squeezeseg: convolutional neural nets with recurrent crf for real-time road-object segmentation from 3D lidar point cloud. In: ICRA (2018)
25. Wu, B., Zhou, X., Zhao, S., Yue, X., Keutzer, K.: Squeezesegv 2: improved model structure and unsupervised domain adaptation for road-object segmentation from a lidar point cloud. In: ICRA (2019)
26. Yang, Y., Soatto, S.: FDA: Fourier domain adaptation for semantic segmentation. In: CVPR (2020)
27. Yi, L., Gong, B., Funkhouser, T.: Complete & label: a domain adaptation approach to semantic segmentation of lidar point clouds. arXiv preprint arXiv:2007.08488 (2020)
28. Zhao, H., Jiang, L., Fu, C.W., Jia, J.: Pointweb: enhancing local neighborhood features for point cloud processing. In: CVPR (2019)
29. Zhu, J.Y., Park, T., Isola, P., Efros, A.A.: Unpaired image-to-image translation using cycle-consistent adversarial networks. In: ICCV (2017)

Towards the Target: Self-regularized Progressive Learning for Unsupervised Domain Adaptation on Semantic Segmentation

Jui Chang, Yu-Ting Pang, and Chiou-Ting Hsu[✉]

National Tsing Hua University, Hsinchu, Taiwan
cthsu@cs.nthu.edu.tw

Abstract. Unsupervised domain adaptation for semantic segmentation aims to transfer the knowledge learned from a labeled synthetic source domain to an unlabeled real-world target domain. The main challenge lies in the difference between the two domains, i.e., the so-called "domain gap". Although the two domains are supposed to share the same set of class labels, the semantics encoded by the source labels are not always consistent with those of the target data. Some recent efforts have been taken to explore the domain-specific semantics by conducting a within-domain adaptation using the predicted pseudo labels of the target data. The quality of the pseudo labels is therefore essential to the within-domain adaptation. In this paper, we propose a unified framework to progressively facilitate the adaptation towards the target domain. First, we propose to conduct the cross-domain adaptation through a novel source label relaxation. The relaxed labels offer a good trade-off between the source supervision and the target semantics. Next, we propose a dual-level self-regularization to regularize the pseudo-label learning and also to tackle the class-imbalanced issue in the within-domain adaptation stage. The experiment results on two benchmarks, i.e., GTA5→Cityscapes and SYNTHIA→Cityscapes, show considerable improvement over the strong baseline and demonstrate the superiority of our framework over other methods.

Keywords: Unsupervised domain adaptation · Semantic segmentation · Progressive learning · Label relaxation · Self-regularization · Class imbalance

1 Introduction

Semantic segmentation aims to classify each pixel of an image into a semantic class and is essential to many applications such as autonomous driving and image editing. With large-scale labeled datasets, recent deep-learning based methods

---

J. Chang and Y-T Pang—Contributed equally.

© Springer Nature Switzerland AG 2022
C. Wallraven et al. (Eds.): ACPR 2021, LNCS 13188, pp. 299–313, 2022.
https://doi.org/10.1007/978-3-031-02375-0_22

Fig. 1. Issue of inconsistent semantics: (a) the label "bus" in the source domain; (b) the label "train" in the target domain; (c) the predicted result of (b) by the model trained under source label supervision; (d) the prediction of (b) by the model trained with the proposed source label relaxation; and (e) the ground truth label of (b).

have achieved remarkable performance [8–10,21,28]. However, because pixel-wise image labeling is time- and labor-consuming, computer synthetic data offer an alternative solution to generate large scale and labeled datasets. To reduce the gap between synthetic and real-world data, unsupervised domain adaptation (UDA) has been proposed to transfer the knowledge learned from synthetic images and labels (source domain) to the unlabeled real-world scenes (target domain). The domain gap, stemming from the different domain-specific image textures, illumination conditions, or spatial layouts, may severely degrade the performance of the target domain [7]. Many efforts have focused on narrowing the domain gap via different techniques, such as adversarial training [2,4,13,17,24, 25,27], self-training [11,15,20,33,34] and consistency regularization [22,23,29].

Most UDA methods [7,11,12,14,17,23,24,26,30,33,34], although adopt different adaptation methodologies, stick to the supervision of the source labels to maintain the task capability. The ground truth labels inherently capture the semantics of the source domain and are indispensable to the supervised learning. Nevertheless, due to the domain gap, the source labels may not always provide a "ground truth" for the target domain. We use an example to illustrate this issue. As shown in Fig. 1 (a) and (b), the "bus" in the computer synthetic domain GTA5 [18] is visually similar to the "train" in the real-world domain Cityscapes [3]. If we keep using the source labels "bus" and "train" to supervise the model training for the corresponding classes, as shown in Fig. 1 (c), we tend to swing away from the true semantics of "train" in the target domain and wrongly predict it to be "bus". We refer to this issue as semantic inconsistency between the two domains.

To facilitate the adaptation towards the target domain, some recent methods introduce the idea of within-domain adaptation [15,16,20,27] to alleviate the semantic inconsistency. In these methods, the adaptation is conducted in two stages. First, a model is developed via the cross-domain adaptation and is then used to generate the pseudo labels for the target data. Next, the within-domain adaptation is performed to adapt the model by only referring to the target data and their pseudo labels. Notably, because neither source data nor source labels are involved in the within-domain adaptation, the prediction results heavily rely on the pseudo labels. However, due to the domain gap, the pseudo labels tend to be biased towards the semantics of source domain and may mislead the within-domain adaptation. Moreover, because the class distributions are independently imbalanced across the two domains, the class-imbalanced situation may further deteriorate the quality of pseudo labels. Different forms of regularization [15, 16, 20, 27] have been proposed to tackle the noisy pseudo-label issue.

In this paper, to address these two issues, i.e., semantic inconsistency and noisy pseudo labels, we propose a novel adaptation framework to progressively lead the existing cross-domain adaptation methods towards the target domain. First, to alleviate the semantic inconsistency during the cross-domain adaptation, we propose to relax the supervision of source labels to better accommodate both the reliable source semantics and the unknown target semantics. Instead of using the pixel-wise source labels, we use the patch-level labels to loosen the source supervision. To accommodate the target semantics, we include the target domain knowledge predicted by the pre-trained model into the source supervision. The example in Fig. 1 shows that, the model trained with the source label relaxation correctly predicts most of the "train" pixels (Fig. 1 (d)), whereas the model trained without the label relaxation wrongly predicts some of the "train" pixels into "bus" (Fig. 1 (c)). Second, to tackle the noisy pseudo labels and the class-imbalanced issue during the within-domain adaptation, we propose a dual-level self-regularization to constrain the pseudo-label learning in both the pixel-level and the image-level. In the pixel-level regularization, instead of using the hard pseudo labels [27] to supervise the model, we use soft pseudo labels to limit the impact of inaccurate pseudo labels. In the image-level regularization, we encourage the prediction of each image to follow a class-balanced prior distribution to rectify the class-imbalanced situation.

We summarize our contributions as follows:

- We propose a novel source label relaxation for cross-domain adaptation to release the model from being stuck in the source semantics.
- We introduce a dual-level self-regularization to tackle the noisy pseudo labels and the class-imbalanced situation for within-domain adaptation.
- The two proposed mechanisms are unified in a novel learning framework to progressively guide the adaptation towards the target domain.
- Experiment results show that the proposed framework effectively improves the baseline method with a considerable margin on two benchmarks qualitatively and quantitatively.

2   Related Work

Semantic segmentation is a task to assign the semantic label to every pixel in an image. Due to the labeling costs, many researchers [11, 20, 24–27, 33, 34] focused on unsupervised domain adaptation (UDA) to adapt the model from one domain to another without extra labeling costs.

Adversarial Cross-Domain Adaptation. Adversarial training [13,17,24–27] is one of the most popular UDA approaches for semantic segmentation. To reduce the domain discrepancy, the segmentation network is trained to learn domain invariant features to fool the discriminator. For example, in AdaptSegNet [24], a binary discriminator is employed in the output-level to global-wisely align the marginal distributions of the two domains. In CLAN [13], an adaptive cross-domain alignment is further performed through a co-training framework. Also, benefit from the binary discriminator, the authors in PatchAlign [25] conducted the patch-wise adversarial alignment in the output-level. In WeakSegDA [17], the authors proposed to align the conditional distributions of the two domains through a group of category-wise discriminators. Recently, in FADA [27], the binary discriminator is extended to the class-level discriminator by incorporating the category information into the cross-domain adversarial alignment.

Self-supervised Cross-Domain Adaptation. Instead of using an extra discriminator for adversarial training, the self-training based methods, through alternating the pseudo-label updating and the model fine-tuning, indirectly reduce the domain discrepancy. Most of the previous methods [11,33,34] focused on the pseudo-label generation and explored different regularization terms to handle the noisy labels during fine-tuning the model. In BDL [11], a fixed threshold is used to select the high confident pixels as the pseudo labels. In CBST [34], the class-wise threshold is proposed to moderate the class-imbalanced issue caused by the fixed threshold selection; in CRST [33], a regularization term is further proposed to encourage the smoothness on the network outputs. Some recent methods [24,26,33,34] proposed to jointly combine the self-training with consistency regularization [14,23] and the curriculum learning [12,30]. However, because most of them are developed under the supervision of source labels, the adaptation is guided towards the source semantics but is oblivious to the target semantics. To address the semantic inconsistency problem, instead of strictly sticking to the supervision of the source labels, we propose to include the target domain knowledge to relax the source supervision.

Within-Domain Adaptation. To further facilitate learning the target semantics, some methods [15,16,20,27,31,32] conducted the within-domain adaptation by using the pre-trained UDA model to obtain the pseudo labels of target data and then re-training a new model in terms of these pseudo labels. However, because the pseudo labels are not entirely reliable, re-training a model under the supervision of noisy labels inevitably results in performance drop. Moreover, the class-imbalanced issue, if not taken care of, may further deteriorate the performance. Therefore, different regularization terms [15,20,31,32] have been developed and included into the within-domain adaptation. In IAST [15], the model regularization [33] is applied to regularize the high-confidence pixels while minimizing the prediction entropy of the other pixels. In TPLD [20], the bootstrapping loss is combined with the self-training to prevent over-fitting on the low-confident pixels within the high confident images. In R-MRNet [31], instead of using the widely adopted thresholding strategies, the authors introduced an uncertainty regularization, through exploring the discrepancy between auxiliary and primary classifiers, to rectify the noisy pseudo labels. In this paper, different from the previous methods, we do not focus on the pixel-level regularization alone. We design a two-level regularization on the soft pseudo labels to explicitly handle the noisy pseudo-label issue and include a class-balanced prior to tackle the class-imbalanced situation.

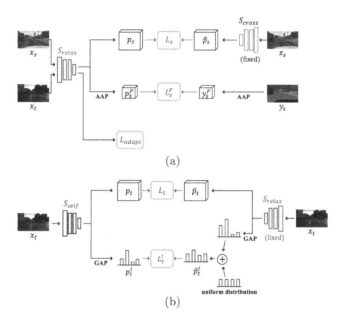

Fig. 2. The proposed progressive adaptation framework. (a) Cross-domain adaptation with source label relaxation. (b) Within-domain adaptation with dual-level self-regularization. **AAP** denotes the adaptive average pooling, and **GAP** denotes the global average pooling.

3   Proposed Method

Under the UDA setting, given the source domain data $X_s = \{x_s\}$ with the corresponding source lables $Y_s = \{y_s\}$ and the unlabeled target domain data $X_t = \{x_t\}$, assuming both domains share the same semantic class labels $\{1, 2, ..., K\}$, the goal is to learn a semantic segmentation model to predict the pixel-level labels for the target domain data.

We propose a progressive adaption framework developed upon existing cross-domain adaptation methods and aim to further adapt the semantic segmentation model towards the target domain. As shown in Fig. 2, the proposed framework includes three segmentation networks, S_{cross}, S_{relax} and S_{self}, all developed using the same network architecture. S_{cross} is a pre-trained UDA model obtained from the cross-domain adaptation baseline method. Using the model S_{cross}, we first perform the cross-domain adaptation to train the model S_{relax} under the proposed source label relaxation. Next, we perform the within-domain adaptation to train the model S_{self} with the proposed dual-level self-regularization.

In Sect. 3.1, we describe the baseline model of S_{cross} adopted in this work. Detail of the proposed source label relaxation and dual-level self-regularization will be given in Sects. 3.2 and 3.3, respectively.

3.1   Baseline for Cross-Domain Adaptation

We adopt the adversarial-training framework [27] as our cross-domain adaptation baseline to develop the model S_{cross}. Two loss terms: L_{gt} and L_{adapt}, are included here. The segmentation loss L_{gt} is formulated by the pixel-wise cross entropy on the source domain:

$$L_{gt} = -\sum_{h,w} \sum_{k \in K} y_s(h, w, k) \, \log(p_s(h, w, k)). \tag{1}$$

As to the adaptation loss L_{adapt}, we follow the framework [27] and include a discriminator loss L_d and an adversarial loss L_{adv} to formulate L_{adapt}. Please refer to [27] for more details.

3.2   Source Label Relaxation for Cross-Domain Adaptation

We use the pre-trained model S_{cross} to initialize the network S_{relax} and then fine-tune S_{relax} using the following label relaxations.

Target-Aware Pixel-Level Relaxation. As mentioned in Sect. 1, the source label Y_s, although indicates the ground truth of the source domain, is oblivious to the target semantics. On the other hand, the cross-domain model S_{cross}, which has been trained to narrow the domain gap, implicitly learns to capture the target semantics along with the labeled source data. We use an example to illustrate our motivation. As shown in Fig. 3, the "bus" class in the computer synthetic domain GTA5 [18] is visually similar to the "train" class in the real-world domain Cityscapes [3]. If we use the pre-trained UDA model S_{cross} from FADA [27] to predict the source image, the result in Fig. 3 (b) shows that most of the "bus" pixels are predicted as "train". This observation suggests that, the labels predicted by S_{cross} better reflect the target semantics than the original ground truth label Y_s.

Therefore, we propose performing the cross-domain adaptation to train the model S_{relax} using the relaxed source labels. We replace the original source supervision Y_s by the soft prediction map $\tilde{p}_s$ obtained from S_{cross} and reformulate the pixel-wise cross entropy loss by:.

$$L_s = -\sum_{h,w} \sum_{k \in K} \tilde{p}_s(h, w, k) \, \log p_s(h, w, k), \tag{2}$$

$$\begin{array}{ccc} \text{(a)} & \text{(b)} & \text{(c)} \end{array}$$

Fig. 3. An example of the target semantics captured by the UDA model S_{cross}. (a) The label "bus" in the source domain; (b) the prediction p_s of (a) by S_{cross}; and (c) the source label y_s of (a).

where $\tilde{p}_s$ and p_s denote the soft prediction maps of X_s obtained from S_{cross} and S_{relax}, respectively.

Source-Attentive Patch-Level Relaxation. The quality of the prediction map $\tilde{p}_s$ highly depends on the pre-trained model S_{cross} as well as the domain gap. To seek a good trade-off between the source supervision and the target-aware supervision, we further include a relaxed source supervision into the model training. Specifically, because the pixel-wise prediction tends to be noisy and discontinuous, we replace the pixel-level labels with patch-level labels to train the model. We use the adaptive average pooling to construct the patch-level labels y_s^P and the soft predictions p_s^P from y_s and p_s, respectively:

$$y_s^P(u, v, k) = avg_{(h,w)\in patch}(y_s(h, w, k)), \tag{3}$$

and

$$p_s^P(u, v, k) = avg_{(h,w)\in patch}(p_s(h, w, k)), \tag{4}$$

where u, v denote the patch indices. The patch-level cross-entropy loss is then formulated by:

$$L_s^P = -\sum_{u,v}\sum_{k\in K} y_s^P(u, v, k) \, \log p_s^P(u, v, k). \tag{5}$$

3.3 Dual-Level Self-regularization for Within-Domain Adaptation

Once obtaining the model S_{relax}, we next need to learn a new model S_{self} through the within-domain adaptation without referring to the source data. As mentioned before, due to the domain gap, the pseudo labels generated by S_{relax} are not always reliable. Furthermore, because the class distributions are not balanced in both domains, the class-imbalanced situation may further deteriorate the quality of pseudo labels. To alleviate this noisy pseudo-label issue, we propose to regularize the learning in both pixel-level and image-level via the dual-level self-regularization.

Pixel-Level Self-regularization. Instead of using the hard pseudo labels as supervision [27], we adopt soft pseudo labels to lessen the impact of inaccurate predictions. For each target image x_t, we obtain the soft predictions $\tilde{p}_t$ and p_t from the models S_{relax} and S_{self}, respectively, and define the pixel-level self-regularization loss by:

$$L_t = -\sum_{h,w} \sum_{k \in K} \tilde{p}_t(h, w, k) \ \log p_t(h, w, k). \tag{6}$$

Image-Level Self-regularization. The issue of rare classes remains a big challenge in semantic segmentation. Limited by lack of training samples, rare classes tend to be poorly predicted or wrongly classified to the dominant classes. To tackle the class-imbalanced issue, we use a class-balanced prior $\tilde{p}_t^I$ to adapt the class distribution of the pixel-level prediction p_t. First, we employ a global average pooling layer to calculate the overall class distribution on p_t by:

$$p_t^I(k) = \frac{1}{HW} \sum_{(h,w) \in p_t} p_t(h, w, k), \tag{7}$$

where H and W denote the height and the width of the image x_t, respectively.

Next, we construct the class-balanced prior $\tilde{p}_t^I$ through combining the prediction $\tilde{p}_t$ with the uniform distribution by:

$$\tilde{p}_t^I(k) = \frac{1}{2K}(1 + K * \frac{1}{HW} \sum_{(h,w) \in \tilde{p}_t} \tilde{p}_t(h, w, k)). \tag{8}$$

In Eq. (8), by linear combining $\tilde{p}_t$ with the uniform distribution, we increase the probabilities of the rare classes while suppressing those of the dominant classes within $\tilde{p}_t^I$. Finally, we define the image-level self-regularization term by:

$$L_t^I = -\sum_{k \in K} \tilde{p}_t^I(k) \ \log p_t^I(k). \tag{9}$$

Objectives and Optimization. The overall optimization function in our proposed self-regularized progressive framework is formulated as:

$$\min_{S_{cross}} L_{gt} + L_{adapt}, \tag{10}$$

$$\min_{S_{relax}} L_s + \lambda_s^P L_s^P + L_{adapt}, \tag{11}$$

and

$$\min_{S_{self}} L_t + \lambda_t^I L_t^I. \tag{12}$$

First, in Eq. (10), we conduct the cross-domain adaptation by using FADA [27] to train the model S_{cross}. Then, in Eq. (11), we fine-tune the model S_{relax}

Table 1. Comparison on GTA5→Cityscapes. The 12 rare classes [13] are highlighted in red, and R-mIoU is the mean of IoU of these rare classes. FADA† indicates that using the hard pseudo labels as supervision during the within-domain adaptation of FADA.

Method	Road	SW	Build	Wall	Fence	Pole	TL	TS	Veg.	Terrain	Sky	Person	Rider	Car	Truck	Bus	Train	Motor	Bike	mIoU	R-mIoU
Source only [24]	75.8	16.8	77.2	12.5	21.0	25.5	30.1	20.1	81.3	24.6	70.3	53.8	26.4	49.9	17.2	25.9	6.5	25.3	36.0	36.6	22.6
AdaptSegNet [24]	86.5	36.0	79.9	23.4	23.3	23.9	35.2	14.8	83.4	33.3	75.6	58.5	27.6	73.7	32.5	35.4	3.9	30.1	28.1	42.4	26.0
ADVENT [26]	89.9	36.5	81.6	29.2	25.2	28.5	32.3	22.4	83.9	34.0	77.1	57.4	27.9	83.7	29.4	39.1	1.5	28.4	23.3	43.8	26.8
CBST [33]	91.8	53.5	80.5	32.7	21.0	34	28.9	20.4	83.9	34.2	80.9	53.1	24.0	82.7	30.3	35.9	16.0	25.9	42.8	45.9	28.8
CRST [33]	91.0	**55.4**	80.0	33.7	21.4	37.3	32.9	24.5	85.0	34.1	80.8	57.7	24.6	84.1	27.8	30.1	26.9	26.0	42.3	47.1	30.1
PyCDA [12]	90.5	36.3	84.4	32.4	29.0	34.6	36.4	31.5	**86.8**	37.9	78.5	62.3	21.5	85.6	27.9	34.8	18.0	22.9	**49.3**	47.4	31.3
PatchAlign [25]	92.3	51.9	82.1	29.2	25.1	24.5	33.8	33.0	82.4	32.8	82.2	58.6	27.2	84.3	33.4	46.3	2.2	29.5	32.3	46.5	29.1
IntraDA [16]	90.6	36.1	82.6	29.5	21.3	27.6	31.4	23.1	85.2	**39.3**	80.2	59.3	29.4	86.4	33.6	**53.9**	0.0	32.7	37.6	46.3	30.0
FADA [27]	87.0	37.6	83.3	36.9	25.3	30.9	35.3	21.0	82.7	36.8	83.1	58.3	34.1	83.3	31.5	35.0	24.4	**34.3**	32.1	46.9	31.5
FADA† [27]	90.4	49.6	**85.6**	**40.9**	**30.1**	35.9	**42.5**	26.1	86.7	37.1	85.2	63.7	37.5	84.9	28.6	42.9	8.0	23.6	36.9	49.2	32.5
Label Relaxation	90.0	43.3	83.9	38.7	24.8	30.1	35.5	20.4	82.9	36.5	85.3	58.5	34.3	84.1	36.9	42.3	**33.0**	29.4	23.6	48.1	32.1
Self-regularization	**92.6**	53.9	**85.6**	34.5	23.1	**38.8**	**42.5**	**28.2**	85.2	36.5	**87.4**	**65.9**	**39.9**	**86.7**	**37.7**	42.7	32.6	30.7	33.1	**51.4**	**35.0**

under source label relaxation. Finally, in Eq. (12), we use the pseudo labels generated by S_{relax} to train the model S_{self}.

4 Experiment

4.1 Datasets and Evaluation Metrics

We evaluate our method by adapting from the synthetic datasets **GTA5** [18] and **SYNTHIA** [19] into the real-world dataset **Cityscapes** [3]. That is, the synthetic dataset is treated as the source domain and the real-world dataset is set as the target domain. **GTA5** [18] contains 24966 pixel-wisely annotated synthetic urban images labeled with 33 classes, where only 19 classes co-existing in **Cityscapes** are used in the experiments. **SYNTHIA** [19] contains 9400 synthetic images labeling with 16 classes, where all the 16 classes and the 13 sub-classes [27] are evaluated in our experiments. **Cityscapes** contains 2975 unlabeled real-world images for training and 500 validation images for evaluation. The performance is evaluated using the intersection-over-union (IoU) [5] of each class and the mean of all classes (mIoU).

4.2 Implementation Details

We use FADA [27] as our pre-trained model S_{cross} and develop the three segmentation networks (i.e., S_{cross}, S_{relax} and S_{self}) based on Deeplab-V2 [1] with ResNet-101 [6]. We follow the same settings in [27] and use Stochastic Gradient Descent (SGD) optimizer and Adam optimizer to train the segmentation networks and the discriminators, respectively. The learning rate is set by the same poly policy as in [27] and is initialized as 2.5×10^{-4} and 10^{-4}, respectively. The hyper-parameters λ_s^P and λ_t^I are set as 1.0 and 0.01, respectively. The patch size for L_s^P is set as 32×64.

Table 2. Comparison on SYNTHIA→Cityscapes. mIoU* is the average of the 13 sub-classes (i.e., the classes without *), and FADA† uses the hard pseudo labels as the supervision for the within-domain adaptation.

Method	Road	SW	Build	Wall*	Fence*	Pole*	TL	TS	Veg.	Sky	PR	Rider	Car	Bus	Motor	Bike	mIoU	mIoU*
Source only [24]	55.6	23.8	74.6	9.2	0.2	24.4	6.1	12.1	74.8	79.0	55.3	19.1	39.6	23.3	13.7	25.0	33.5	38.6
AdaptSegNet [24]	79.2	37.2	78.8	10.5	0.3	25.1	9.9	10.5	78.2	80.5	53.5	19.6	67.0	29.5	21.6	31.3	39.5	45.9
CRST [33]	67.7	32.2	73.9	10.7	**1.6**	**37.4**	**22.2**	**31.2**	80.8	80.5	60.8	**29.1**	82.8	25.0	19.4	**45.3**	43.8	50.1
IntraDA [16]	84.3	37.7	79.5	5.3	0.4	24.9	9.2	8.4	80.0	84.1	57.2	23.0	78	38.1	20.3	36.5	41.7	48.9
FADA [27]	81.3	35.1	80.8	9.6	0.2	26.8	9.1	17.8	82.4	81.5	49.9	18.8	78.9	33.3	15.3	33.7	40.9	47.5
FADA† [27]	84.5	40.1	**83.1**	4.8	0.0	34.3	20.1	27.2	84.8	84.1	53.5	22.6	**85.4**	**43.7**	**26.8**	27.8	45.2	52.5
Label Relaxation	89.9	46.1	81.1	11.4	0.5	26.3	12.4	14.6	81.9	83.8	50.9	18.6	79.2	32.9	14.6	31.8	42.3	49.1
Self-regularization	**92.0**	**51.7**	83.0	**14.0**	0.0	35.1	6.7	15.0	**85.1**	**84.3**	**62.2**	25.4	84.7	40.3	21.9	41.9	**46.5**	**53.4**

4.3 Comparisons

GTA5 → Cityscapes. Table 1 shows the comparisons with the other UDA methods [12,16,24–27,33,34] when adapting from GTA5 to Cityscapes. Note that, all these methods adopt the same backbone (ResNet-101) as ours for the segmentation network. In comparison with the baseline FADA [27], the proposed source label relaxation, by accommodating both the source and target semantics, achieves +1.2% improvement on mIoU and especially has significant improvement on the "Bus" (+7.3%) and "Train" (+8.6%) classes. Moreover, the proposed dual-level self-regularization effectively regularizes the pseudo-label learning for the within-domain adaptation and achieves 51.4% and 35.0% of mIoU and R-mIoU, respectively. To sum up, the proposed method achieves substantial improvement of +14.8% mIoU and +12.4% R-mIoU over the Source only method [24], has +4.5% mIoU and +3.5% R-mIoU improvement over the baseline [27], and also outperforms the other UDA methods [12,16,24–27,33,34].

SYNTHIA → Cityscapes. Table 2 shows the comparisons with the other methods [16,24,27,34] when adapting from SYNTHIA to Cityscapes. We follow the setting of FADA [27] and show the mean of IoU for all the 16 classes (i.e., mIoU) and the 13 sub-classes (i.e., mIoU*) for comparison. The proposed method achieves 46.5% of mIoU and 53.4% of mIoU*, respectively. In comparison with the baseline FADA [27], the proposed source label relaxation has +1.4% and +1.6% improvement of mIoU and mIoU*, respectively. Moreover, unlike in [27], which uses the hard pseudo labels for within-domain adaptation (i.e., the "self-distillation" in [27]), the proposed dual-level self-regularization further improves the baseline with +5.6% of mIoU.

4.4 Ablation Study

In Table 3, we verify the effectiveness of each component in the proposed method and compare the overall framework with the baseline [27]. We present the results on GTA5 → Cityscapes.

Effectiveness of Source Label Relaxation. In the upper part of Table 3, with the target-aware pixel-level relaxation (i.e., L_s), we improve the baseline

Table 3. Ablation study of the proposed source label relaxation and dual-level self-regularization for cross-domain adaptation and within-domain adaptation, respectively.

Method			Loss			mIoU	R-mIoU
Cross-domain adaptation	Baseline		-			46.9	31.5
	Label relaxation		L_s	L_s^P			
	✓		✓			47.7	31.7
	✓		✓	✓		48.1	32.1
Within-domain adaptation	Init		L_{hard}	L_t	L_t^I		
	S_{cross}	S_{relax}					
	✓		✓			49.2	32.5
		✓	✓			50.3	33.6
	✓			✓		50.6	33.7
		✓		✓	✓	51.4	35.0

from 46.9% to 47.7% of mIoU. When further including the source-attentive patch-level relaxation (i.e., L_s^P), we have performance improvement from 47.7% to 48.1%. These improvements demonstrate that the proposed source label relaxation indeed incorporates the target semantics into the source label supervision and effectively alleviates the semantic inconsistency in the cross-domain adaptation.

Effectiveness of Dual-Level Self-regularization. The second part of Table 3 demonstrates the effectiveness of the dual-level self-regularization. The term L_{hard} indicates that, under the same training strategy, the hard pseudo labels are used for the within domain adaptation. The hard pseudo labels, due to the domain gap, are inherently noisy; therefore, the within-domain adaptation only achieves little improvement. Once including the pixel-level regularization L_t, we increase the adaptation performance from 48.1% to 50.6%. When further including the image-level regularization L_t^I to balance the class distribution, we boost the performance from 50.6% to 51.4% of mIoU. The performance improvement on R-mIoU (+1.3%) also verifies the effectiveness of the proposed class-balanced prior.

Effectiveness of the Proposed Progressive Framework. To sum up, under the same training strategy, the proposed source label relaxation significantly alleviates the semantic inconsistency during the cross-domain adaptation and outperforms the baseline [27] with a considerable margin from 49.2% to 50.3% of mIoU. Furthermore, the proposed dual-level self-regularization effectively regularizes the pseudo labels in the within-domain adaptation and improves the overall mIoU from 50.3% to 51.4%.

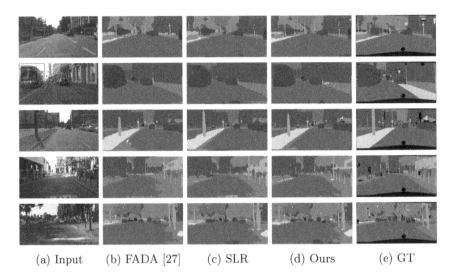

(a) Input   (b) FADA [27]   (c) SLR   (d) Ours   (e) GT

Fig. 4. Visual comparisons on GTA5→Cityscapes: (a) the target images; (b) the baseline method [27]; (c) the proposed source label relaxation (SLR); (d) the progressive learning framework; and (e) the ground truth (GT).

Visualization. Figure 4 shows some examples for visual comparisons. When including the proposed source label relaxation (SLR) in the baseline [27], we alleviate the semantic inconsistency during cross-domain adaptation and much improve the prediction on the "train" class (Fig. 4 (c)). When further resolving the noisy pseudo-label and class-imbalanced issue, we increase the overall prediction accuracy and especially boost the performance on rare classes (Fig. 4 (d)), such as "Train", "Traffic sign", "Bike" and "Person" and "Bus".

5   Conclusion

This paper proposes a progressive learning framework for unsupervised domain adaptation on semantic segmentation. We specifically address the issues of semantic inconsistency and noisy pseudo labels during the adaptation stages. First, we propose a source label relaxation to guide the cross-domain adaptation towards the unknown target domain. Next, we propose a dual-level self-regularization to regularize the pseudo-label learning during the within-domain adaptation. The overall framework readily tackles the issues of inconsistent semantics, noisy pseudo labels, and imbalanced class distribution. Experiment results demonstrate that the proposed framework successively improves the baseline with a considerable margin and outperforms many previous methods.

References

1. Chen, L.C., Papandreou, G., Kokkinos, I., Murphy, K., Yuille, A.L.: Deeplab: semantic image segmentation with deep convolutional nets, atrous convolution, and fully connected crfs. IEEE Trans. Pattern Anal. Mach. Intell. **40**(4), 834–848 (2018). https://doi.org/10.1109/TPAMI.2017.2699184

2. Chen, Y.H., Chen, W.Y., Chen, Y.T., Tsai, B.C., Frank Wang, Y.C., Sun, M.: No more discrimination: cross city adaptation of road scene segmenters. In: Proceedings of the IEEE International Conference on Computer Vision, pp. 1992–2001 (2017)

3. Cordts, M., et al.: The cityscapes dataset for semantic urban scene understanding. In: Proceedings of the IEEE Conference on Computer Vision and Pattern Recognition, pp. 3213–3223 (2016)

4. Du, L., et al.: SSF-DAN: separated semantic feature based domain adaptation network for semantic segmentation. In: Proceedings of the IEEE International Conference on Computer Vision, pp. 982–991 (2019)

5. Everingham, M., Eslami, S.A., Van Gool, L., Williams, C.K., Winn, J., Zisserman, A.: The pascal visual object classes challenge: a retrospective. Int. J. Comput. Vis. **111**(1), 98–136 (2015)

6. He, K., Zhang, X., Ren, S., Sun, J.: Deep residual learning for image recognition (2015)

7. Hoffman, J., et al.: Cycada: cycle-consistent adversarial domain adaptation. In: International Conference on Machine Learning, pp. 1989–1998. PMLR (2018)

8. Hou, Q., Zhang, L., Cheng, M.M., Feng, J.: Strip pooling: rethinking spatial pooling for scene parsing. In: Proceedings of the IEEE/CVF Conference on Computer Vision and Pattern Recognition, pp. 4003–4012 (2020)

9. Huang, Z., Wang, X., Huang, L., Huang, C., Wei, Y., Liu, W.: CCNet: criss-cross attention for semantic segmentation. In: Proceedings of the IEEE/CVF International Conference on Computer Vision, pp. 603–612 (2019)

10. Li, X., Zhong, Z., Wu, J., Yang, Y., Lin, Z., Liu, H.: Expectation-maximization attention networks for semantic segmentation. In: Proceedings of the IEEE/CVF International Conference on Computer Vision, pp. 9167–9176 (2019)

11. Li, Y., Yuan, L., Vasconcelos, N.: Bidirectional learning for domain adaptation of semantic segmentation. In: Proceedings of the IEEE Conference on Computer Vision and Pattern Recognition, pp. 6936–6945 (2019)

12. Lian, Q., Lv, F., Duan, L., Gong, B.: Constructing self-motivated pyramid curriculums for cross-domain semantic segmentation: a non-adversarial approach. In: Proceedings of the IEEE International Conference on Computer Vision, pp. 6758–6767 (2019)

13. Luo, Y., Zheng, L., Guan, T., Yu, J., Yang, Y.: Taking a closer look at domain shift: category-level adversaries for semantics consistent domain adaptation. In: Proceedings of the IEEE/CVF Conference on Computer Vision and Pattern Recognition (CVPR) (June 2019)

14. Ma, H., Lin, X., Wu, Z., Yu, Y.: Coarse-to-fine domain adaptive semantic segmentation with photometric alignment and category-center regularization (2021)

15. Mei, K., Zhu, C., Zou, J., Zhang, S.: Instance adaptive self-training for unsupervised domain adaptation (2020)

16. Pan, F., Shin, I., Rameau, F., Lee, S., Kweon, I.S.: Unsupervised intra-domain adaptation for semantic segmentation through self-supervision. In: Proceedings of the IEEE/CVF Conference on Computer Vision and Pattern Recognition, pp. 3764–3773 (2020)

17. Paul, S., Tsai, Y.-H., Schulter, S., Roy-Chowdhury, A.K., Chandraker, M.: Domain adaptive semantic segmentation using weak labels. In: Vedaldi, A., Bischof, H., Brox, T., Frahm, J.-M. (eds.) ECCV 2020, Part IX. LNCS, vol. 12354, pp. 571–587. Springer, Cham (2020). https://doi.org/10.1007/978-3-030-58545-7_33

18. Richter, S.R., Vineet, V., Roth, S., Koltun, V.: Playing for data: ground truth from computer games. In: Leibe, B., Matas, J., Sebe, N., Welling, M. (eds.) ECCV 2016, Part II. LNCS, vol. 9906, pp. 102–118. Springer, Cham (2016). https://doi.org/10.1007/978-3-319-46475-6_7

19. Ros, G., Sellart, L., Materzynska, J., Vazquez, D., Lopez, A.M.: The synthia dataset: a large collection of synthetic images for semantic segmentation of urban scenes. In: Proceedings of the IEEE Conference on Computer Vision and Pattern Recognition, pp. 3234–3243 (2016)

20. Shin, I., Woo, S., Pan, F., Kweon, I.S.: Two-phase pseudo label densification for self-training based domain adaptation. In: Vedaldi, A., Bischof, H., Brox, T., Frahm, J.-M. (eds.) ECCV 2020, Part XIII. LNCS, vol. 12358, pp. 532–548. Springer, Cham (2020). https://doi.org/10.1007/978-3-030-58601-0_32

21. Takikawa, T., Acuna, D., Jampani, V., Fidler, S.: Gated-SCNN: gated shape CNNs for semantic segmentation. In: Proceedings of the IEEE/CVF International Conference on Computer Vision, pp. 5229–5238 (2019)

22. Tang, S., Tang, P., Gong, Y., Ma, Z., Xie, M.: Unsupervised domain adaptation via coarse-to-fine feature alignment method using contrastive learning (2021)

23. Tranheden, W., Olsson, V., Pinto, J., Svensson, L.: DACS: domain adaptation via cross-domain mixed sampling. In: Proceedings of the IEEE/CVF Winter Conference on Applications of Computer Vision (WACV), pp. 1379–1389 (January 2021)

24. Tsai, Y.H., Hung, W.C., Schulter, S., Sohn, K., Yang, M.H., Chandraker, M.: Learning to adapt structured output space for semantic segmentation. In: Proceedings of the IEEE Conference on Computer Vision and Pattern Recognition, pp. 7472–7481 (2018)

25. Tsai, Y.H., Sohn, K., Schulter, S., Chandraker, M.: Domain adaptation for structured output via discriminative patch representations. In: Proceedings of the IEEE International Conference on Computer Vision, pp. 1456–1465 (2019)

26. Vu, T.H., Jain, H., Bucher, M., Cord, M., Pérez, P.: Advent: adversarial entropy minimization for domain adaptation in semantic segmentation. In: Proceedings of the IEEE Conference on Computer Vision and Pattern Recognition, pp. 2517–2526 (2019)

27. Wang, H., Shen, T., Zhang, W., Duan, L.-Y., Mei, T.: Classes matter: a fine-grained adversarial approach to cross-domain semantic segmentation. In: Vedaldi, A., Bischof, H., Brox, T., Frahm, J.-M. (eds.) ECCV 2020, Part XIV. LNCS, vol. 12359, pp. 642–659. Springer, Cham (2020). https://doi.org/10.1007/978-3-030-58568-6_38

28. Yuan, Y., Chen, X., Wang, J.: Object-contextual representations for semantic segmentation. arXiv preprint arXiv:1909.11065 (2019)

29. Zhang, P., Zhang, B., Zhang, T., Chen, D., Wang, Y., Wen, F.: Prototypical pseudo label denoising and target structure learning for domain adaptive semantic segmentation. arXiv preprint arXiv:2101.10979 2, 1 (2021)

30. Zhang, Y., David, P., Foroosh, H., Gong, B.: A curriculum domain adaptation approach to the semantic segmentation of urban scenes. IEEE Trans. Pattern Anal. Mach. Intell. **42**, 1823–1841 (2019)

31. Zheng, Z., Yang, Y.: Rectifying pseudo label learning via uncertainty estimation for domain adaptive segmentation. Int. J. Comput. Vis. **129**, 1106–1120 (2020)

32. Zheng, Z., Yang, Y.: Unsupervised scene adaptation with memory regularization in vivo (2020)
33. Zou, Y., Yu, Z., Liu, X., Kumar, B., Wang, J.: Confidence regularized self-training. In: Proceedings of the IEEE International Conference on Computer Vision, pp. 5982–5991 (2019)
34. Zou, Y., Yu, Z., Vijaya Kumar, B., Wang, J.: Unsupervised domain adaptation for semantic segmentation via class-balanced self-training. In: Proceedings of the European Conference on Computer Vision (ECCV), pp. 289–305 (2018)

TFNet: Transformer Fusion Network for Ultrasound Image Segmentation

Tao Wang[1], Zhihui Lai[1,2(✉)], and Heng Kong[3]

[1] Computer Vision Institute, College of Computer Science and Software Engineering, Shenzhen University, 518060 Shenzhen, China
lai_zhi_hui@163.com
[2] Shenzhen Institute of Artificial Intelligence and Robotics for Society, Shenzhen, China
[3] Department of Breast and Thyroid Surgery, Baoan Central Hospital of Shenzhen, The Fifth Affiliated Hospital of Shenzhen University, Shenzhen 518102, Guangdong, China

Abstract. Automatic lesion segmentation in ultrasound helps diagnose diseases. Segmenting lesion regions accurately from ultrasound images is a challenging task due to the difference in the scale of the lesion and the uneven intensity distribution in the lesion area. Recently, Convolutional Neural Networks have achieved tremendous success on medical image segmentation tasks. However, due to the inherent locality of convolution operations, it is limited in modeling long-range dependency. In this paper, we study the more challenging problem on capturing long-range dependencies and multi-scale targets without losing detailed information. We propose a Transformer-based feature fusion network (TFNet), which fuses long-range dependency of multi-scale CNN features via Transformer to effectively solve the above challenges. In order to make up for the defect of Transformer in channel modeling, will be improved by joining the channel attention mechanism. In addition, a loss function is designed to modify the prediction map by computing the variance between the prediction results of the auxiliary classifier and the main classifier. We have conducted experiments on three data sets, and the results show that our proposed method achieves superior performances against various competing methods on ultrasound image segmentation.

Keywords: Ultrasound image segmentation · Transformer · Feature fusion

1 Introduction

An accurate breast lesion segmentation from the ultrasound images helps the early diagnosis of cancer. However, due to the feat that scale of tumor lesions in different periods is significantly different, the intensity distribution of the lesion area is not uniform, and there are fuzzy and irregular boundaries in ultrasound, so it is a challenging task to accurately segment the lesion area from

© Springer Nature Switzerland AG 2022
C. Wallraven et al. (Eds.): ACPR 2021, LNCS 13188, pp. 314–325, 2022.
https://doi.org/10.1007/978-3-031-02375-0_23

ultrasound images. Early attempts, such as [17,21], were mainly based on hand-made features to detect the boundaries of breast lesions, but these methods have limit accuracy and are not suitable for more complex situations. Convolutional neural networks (CNN) has been widely used in computer vision, and has achieved excellent performance in medical image segmentation. Especially, UNet [15] based on encoder-decoder structure and its variants networks like [14], UNet++ [25], VNet [11], ResUNet [22] KiUNet [18] and UNet3+ [8] have achieved tremendous success in a wide range of medical applications.

Despite the excellent performance of convolutional neural network, due to the inherent inductive bias of convolution operation, the CNN-based method lacks the modeling ability of long-range dependency. Ultrasound images are often quite different in texture, shape and size, so long-range dependency is necessary. In order to overcome this limitation, some works introduce attention mechanism [12,16,20,23] or use atrous convolution [3,6] to make up for this defect. Recently, transformer [19], designed for sequence-to- sequence prediction, has become an alternative structure of convolutional neural network. Unlike prior CNN-based methods, transformer has strong performance in modeling global context based on self attention mechanism. With large-scale data for training, some pure transformer network models, such as ViT [5], Swin-Transformer [9], have achieved or even surpassed the performance of CNN. However, the pure transformer model often needs large data sets for training in order to achieve better performance, while the number of medical image data is very small. Some researchers are working on combining the CNNs with Transformers to create a hybrid structure. For example, TransUnet [2] utilizes CNNs to extract low-level features, which are then passed through transformer to model global interaction, and finally achieves better performance.

In this paper, we study the more challenging problem of capturing long-range dependencies and multi-scale targets without losing detailed information. We have explored and proposed our method to solve the problem. CNN has a strong ability to capture local details, and because the existing CNN is usually designed as a pyramid structure, the receptive field increases gradually with the deepening of network layers. For small targets, the shallow features contribute more, while for large targets, the deep features contribute more. Therefore, we consider combining the advantages of CNN with transformer and apply transformer to CNN feature fusion, that is to use transformer to model CNN multi-scale features with long-distance dependency, and then perform feature fusion. In addition, the existing transformer structure lacks the ability to weight channel information, so we will improve the transformer structure and add channel attention mechanism. In order to accurately predict the details of the ultrasound images, in addition to fusing the shallow feature information into the up sampling stage by using the jump link, we add an auxiliary classifier, which is different from the deep supervision method to modify the details of the prediction results.

In summary, the contributions of us are as follows: (1) we propose a transformer feature fusion module and designs a novel deep neural network called TFNet, (2) we propose a MultiHead channel attention mechanism and use it in transformer block to improve its channel modeling ability, (3) this paper designs a loss function based on KL distance to correct the details of the predicted targets.

2   Method

The overall architecture of the proposed method is presented in Fig. 1(a). For an input image, four levels of features $\{f_i, i = 1, ..., 4\}$ can be extracted from CNN backbone network. We divide fifeatures into low-level features (f_1) and high-level features (f_2, f_3, f_4). High-level features contain more image semantic information of multi-scale targets due to the different receptive field. First, high-level features are fused together using our proposed Transformer Fuse Module (TFM). Therefore, high-level features can enhance the long-distance dependency modeling and obtain the features fused with multi-scale targets. Then, the above features are decoded by two-step upsampling using 3×3 convolution and linear interpolation. In the first step, we fuse the low-level features via skip connection to make up for details information. Inspired by [24], we add an auxiliary classifier in f_3 features. The loss function between the prediction results of the auxiliary classifier and the main classifier is established to correct the details of the prediction results. The components in our method: TFM, MCA and $\mathcal{L}_{KL}$ will be elaborated as follows.

2.1   Transformer Fuse Module

As shown in Fig. 1(b), TFM receives three different scales of high-level feature inputs. For each high-level features $f_i \in \mathbb{R}^{H \times W \times C}$, we first divide it into several patches, embed them into vector sequences $z_0^i \in \mathbb{R}^{(H'W') \times D}$ $(where\, W' = W/P_i, H' = H/P_i, P_i$ is the size of the patch. The P_i for f_2, f_3, f_4 were set to 4, 2, 1) and add conditional position encoding, see Eq. (2). Then, z_0^i is transformed by Transformer Block into $z_{sc}^i \in \mathbb{R}^{(H'W') \times D}$ (Eq. (3)) and reshape it to get $f_{sc}^i \in \mathbb{R}^{H' \times W' \times D}$. Finally, the fusion features is as follows:

$$f_{sc} = \sigma(Conv(Concat[f_{sc}^2, f_{sc}^3, f_{sc}^4])) \tag{1}$$

where $f_{sc} \in \mathbb{R}^{H' \times W' \times D}$, $Conv$ is 3×3 convolution operation and σ donates ReLU activation function. Next, we will introduce the design of each part of TFM.

Patch and Position Embedding. We reshape the feature $f \in \mathbb{R}^{H \times W \times C}$ into a sequence of flattened patches $x_p \in \mathbb{R}^{P^2 \times C}$ and embed them into a D-dimensional space using a learnable linear projection. In our method, we set $D = 256$ to reduce the amount of subsequent computation.

To encode the patch spatial information, we use the conditional position encoding (CPE) [4] which are added to the patch embeddings to retain positional information as follows:

$$z_0 = [x_p^1 E; x_p^2 E; \cdots ; x_p^N E] + E_{pos} \qquad (2)$$

where $E \in \mathbb{R}^{(P^2 \times C) \times D}$ is the patch embedding projection, and $E_{pos} \in R^{N \times D}$ denotes the conditional position encoding which is generated by position encoding generator. CPE is dynamically generated and conditioned on the local neighborhood of the patchs. Compared with position encoding, CPE can keep the desired translation-invariance, resulting in improved prediction accuracy.

Transformer Block. The structure of a Transformer Block is illustrated in Fig. 1(c), which consists of two main parts. The first part models the long-range dependency of the input sequences, and the second part learns the weight of the channel. For the sequences z_0^i embedded from high-level features f_i, the transformation of Transformer Block is defined:

$$
\begin{aligned}
\hat{z}_s^i &= MSA(LN(z_0^i)) + z_0^i \\
z_s^i &= MLP(LN(\hat{z}_s^i)) + \hat{z}_s^i \\
\hat{z}_{sc}^i &= MCA(LN(z_s^i)) + z_s^i \\
z_{sc}^i &= MLP(LN(\hat{z}_{sc}^i)) + \hat{z}_{sc}^i
\end{aligned} \qquad (3)
$$

where $LN(\cdot)$ denotes the layer normalization operator and z_0^i is the encoded representation of f_i. $MSA(\cdot)$ is MultiHead Self-Attention and $MCA(\cdot)$ is our proposed MultiHead Channel-Attention.

MultiHead Self-Attention. We use the vanilla Multi-Head Self-Attention to model long-range dependency of features, which is defined as follows:

$$
\begin{aligned}
Attention(Q, K, V) &= SoftMax(\frac{QK^T}{\sqrt{d}})V \\
MSA(z) &= Concat(Head_s^i(z), \ldots, Head_s^h(z))W^O \\
Head_s^i(z) &= Attention(zW_i^Q, zW_i^K, zW_i^V)
\end{aligned} \qquad (4)
$$

where queries $Q_i = zW_i^Q$, keys $K_i = zW_i^K$ and values $V_i = zW_i^V$ are all projections computed from the input z. The projection matrices $W_i^Q, W_i^K, W_i^V \in \mathbb{R}^{D \times d}$ and $W^O \in \mathbb{R}^{hd \times D}$ are learnable.

MultiHead Channel-Attention. MSA in transformer lacks ability of channel-attention modeling. Based on the inductive bias of MSA, we improved SENet [7] and designed MultiHead Channel-Attention, as follows:

$$
\begin{aligned}
MCA(z) &= \sigma(W^e(ReLU(Head_c^i(z) + \cdots + Head_c^h(z))))z \\
Head_c^i(z) &= W_i^s(MaxPool(z) + AvgPool(z))
\end{aligned} \qquad (5)
$$

We first use average pooling and max pooling for each position of all patch sequences and sum them and then map the results to the low dimensional space via a learnable projection $W^s \in \mathbb{R}^{D \times D/r}(r = 16)$. After calculating multiple such projections and adding the results, the original dimension is restored via another learnable projection $W^e \in \mathbb{R}^{D/r \times D}$. Finally, the learned channel weight vector is multiplied by each patch.

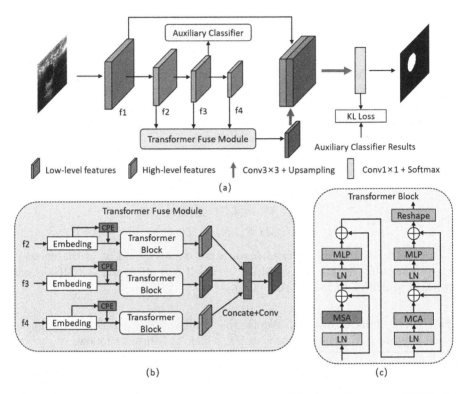

Fig. 1. (a) The main architecture diagram of TFNet. (b) The architecture of TFM. (c) Implementation details of the Transformer Block, which consists of two Transformer blocks. MSA and MCA are multi-head self attention modules and multi-head channel attention modules respectively.

2.2   Loss Function

We add an auxiliary classifier to the f_3 feature. Inspired by [24], the prediction results of the two classifiers are often very different for the targets which are difficult to predict. Therefore, we hope to modify the prediction results of the model through auxiliary classifier. Different from deep supervision, we establish the relationship between the prediction results of the auxiliary classifier and the main classifier by the following loss function:

$$\mathcal{L}_{KL} = \alpha(D_{kl}(p, \overline{p}) + D_{kl}(p_{aux}, \overline{p})) \tag{6}$$

where p is the prediction result of the main classifier, p_{aux} is the prediction result of the auxiliary classifier and $\bar{p} = softmax(p + \gamma \cdot p_{aux}), \gamma = 0.5$. $D_{kl}(P, Q) = \sum_i P(i) \log(P(i)/Q(i))$ donates KL distance. α is the scaling parameter, we set $\alpha = 1/(H \times W)$, H and W are the size of the predicted results.

We hope to reduce the distance between the prediction results of two classifiers by klloss, so as to reduce the area of the uncertain region. Our final loss function is:

$$\mathcal{L}_{total} = \mathcal{L}_{CE} + \lambda \mathcal{L}_{KL}$$
$$\mathcal{L}_{CE} = -\sum_{i=1}^{N} y^i log p^i + (1 - y^i) log(1 - p^i) \tag{7}$$

where $\mathcal{L}_{CE}$ is cross entropy loss function, y is the targets and N is the number of pixels of y. λ is a hyper parameter. In our experiment, we set $\lambda = 0.1$.

3 Experiments

3.1 Datasets

We evaluate our proposed method on three datasets, including two public benchmark datasets BUSI [1], DDTI [13] and our collected dataset. BUSI collected 780 images from 600 female patients, with 437 benign cases, 210 benign masses, and 133 normal cases. In our experiments, we remove images of normal cases as benchmark data, and adopt the three-fold cross-validation to test each model. Another benchmark dataset DDTI contains the analysis of 347 thyroid ultrasound images, performed by two experts in 299 patients with thyroid disorders. We remove some images marked with damage and crop the images containing multiple nodules. We adopt four-fold cross validation on the 637 images to test each model.

Our collected dataset has 982 clinical breast ultrasound images in total from 500 patients. We follow the widely-used annotation procedure of the medical image segmentation for annotating breast lesions. Each image was annotated under the guidance of two experienced physicians. The final ground-truths were reached after several rounds of inspections. We also adopt the four-fold cross-validation to test each segmentation method on this.

3.2 Experimental Settings

Evaluation Metrics. We adopt five metrics to quantitatively compare different methods on the lesion segmentation. They are Dice coefficient (denoted as DSC), Jaccard index (denoted as Jaccard), Recall, Precision and Specificity.

Training Parameters. In order to ensure the fairness of the experiment, each model uses ResNet50 as the backbone network. We initialize the parameters of the backbone network using the pre-trained weights on ImageNet while other parameters of the model are initialized randomly. The input images are uniformly resized to a size of 256×256, and then random clipping, random flip, pad and normalization are used for image enhancement. We use SGD algorithm to optimize the network with a momentum of 0.9, a weight decay of 0.0005 and 40000 iterations. The initial learning rate is set to 0.01, the minimum learning rate is set to 0.0001, and then the polynomial annealing algorithm is used to reduce the learning rate. We implement the network using PyTorch library and train our network on a single NVIDIA RTX 2080Ti GPU with the batch size set to 16.

3.3   Results

We conduct main experiments on three ultrasound image dataset by comparing our TFNet with four previous methods: FCN [10]; UNet [15]; UNet++ [25] and DeepLabV3+ [3].

Table 1 shows the average results of the proposed method based on a cross validation. The experimental results show that our TFNet is superior to other methods in different evaluation metrics. Note that our method performs better on busi dataset. This is because there are a large number of targets with high echo and rugged boundary in BUSI dataset, and the distribution of small, medium and large targets is relatively uniform, which is consistent with the motivation of our proposed method. On the contrary, the boundary of the target in ddti dataset is more smooth, and the scale of target is mostly small. In this case, the improvement effect of our method is relatively less than in other dataset.

Besides, We add a set of vanilla UNet (UNet*) experimental results to compare the effect of the pre-trained backbone network. After replacing the encoder of UNet with ResNet50 network with pre-trained weights, the performance is improved significantly (DSC increases by 2.8%). Therefore, we choose a strong backbone network in the experiment to exclude the influence of CNN feature extraction ability for fair experimental comparison.

3.4   Analysis

Ablation Study. To verify the effectiveness of the principal components of our network: MCA, $\mathcal{L}_{KL}$, and TFM in our network. And the ablation study experiments are conducted on BUSI dataset. The baseline (first row of Table 1) is constructed by removing both components from our network. The first row represents the benchmark architecture of TFNet with TFM and $\mathcal{L}_{KL}$ removed. The second line represents fusion using downsampling feature alignment. MSA donates the TFM only uses MSA, see Fig. 1(c) left. MSA donates the TFM only uses MCA, see Fig. 1(c) right. $\mathcal{L}_{KL}$ donates our KL loss function. The last line shows the result of replacing $\mathcal{L}_{KL}$ with deep supervision.

Table 1. Quantitative results on BUSI, DDTI and our datasets of the TFNet, FCN [10], UNet [15], UNet++ [25] and DeepLabV3+ [3]. Each numerical value represents the average result (%± standard deviation) of k-fold cross validation. UNet* donates the original UNet network without ResNet50.

	Method	DSC %	Jaccard %	Recall %	Precision %	Specificity %
BUSI	UNet*	71.5 ± 5.3	55.8 ± 6.4	77.0 ± 11.0	67.2 ± 3.5	96.7 ± 2.4
	FCN	73.3 ± 5.1	58.0 ± 5.8	78.6 ± 11.4	69.2 ± 2.2	97.9 ± 1.4
	UNet	74.3 ± 5.5	59.3 ± 6.8	78.5 ± 12.8	72.3 ± 2.9	97.7 ± 1.8
	UNet++	75.1 ± 5.5	60.3 ± 6.9	79.2 ± 10.9	71.4 ± 3.2	97.9 ± 1.3
	DeepLabV3+	74.8 ± 6.1	60.0 ± 7.6	77.3 ± 9.8	73.2 ± 8.0	97.5 ± 1.0
	TFNet (Ours)	**77.3 ± 5.5**	**63.0 ± 7.0**	**79.5 ± 11.1**	**75.5 ± 2.3**	**98.1 ± 1.1**
DDTI	FCN	82.7 ± 1.1	70.6 ± 1.6	87.8 ± 1.6	78.3 ± 2.7	**98.1 ± 0.3**
	UNet	83.4 ± 1.0	71.5 ± 1.5	85.7 ± 3.1	81.4 ± 3.0	97.5 ± 0.6
	UNet++	83.0 ± 1.8	71.0 ± 2.6	**87.4 ± 1.2**	79.1 ± 3.0	98.0 ± 0.2
	DeepLabV3+	83.8 ± 1.3	72.2 ± 1.9	84.9 ± 1.2	82.7 ± 2.2	97.5 ± 0.3
	TFNet (Ours)	**84.6 ± 1.7**	**73.2 ± 2.5**	86.6 ± 1.7	**83.2 ± 2.6**	97.8 ± 0.3
Ours	FCN	85.2 ± 1.6	74.2 ± 2.4	85.4 ± 2.2	84.9 ± 1.7	98.0 ± 0.4
	UNet	87.0 ± 1.5	77.1 ± 2.3	88.2 ± 3.4	85.9 ± 1.0	98.2 ± 0.5
	UNet++	86.8 ± 1.6	76.8 ± 2.6	87.9 ± 1.6	85.8 ± 1.9	98.4 ± 0.2
	DeepLabV3+	86.3 ± 2.2	75.9 ± 3.3	85.0 ± 2.1	87.6 ± 4.1	97.9 ± 0.5
	TFNet (Ours)	**87.9 ± 1.4**	**78.4 ± 2.1**	**88.2 ± 1.7**	**87.7 ± 1.6**	**98.5 ± 0.2**

Table 2. Quantitative results of ablation study on BUSI dataset.

Fuse	MSA	MCA	$\mathcal{L}_{KL}$	Parameters (M)	DSC %	Jaccard %
				23.89	74.2 ± 6.4	59.9 ± 7.4
✓				–	74.8 ± 6.1	60.5 ± 7.2
✓	✓			29.94	76.1 ± 5.1	61.9 ± 6.8
✓	✓	✓		31.53	77.0 ± 4.8	62.6 ± 6.5
✓	✓	✓	✓	33.89	**77.3 ± 5.5**	**63.0 ± 7.0**
✓	✓	✓	DSV	–	77.1±5.5	62.5±7.2

Table 2 shows the comparison results of our method with different components. Compared the first line with the second line, the performance of multi-scale feature fusion strategy will be improved, which shows that feature fusion is useful for dataset with multi-scale targets. When using TFM with MSA only, we can see that learning the long-range dependency has a superior performance(DSC increases by 2.9%). 'MSA + MCA' have better performance than MSA, showing that our proposed MCA introduces channel attention into transformer block, which helps capture the dependence between channels. In addition, $\mathcal{L}_{KL}$ can improve the performance of the model, and the effect is better than deep supervision.

We also compare the number of parameters required by each component. When we add TFM module, the number of parameters increases significantly, which is caused by patch embedding. Note that $\mathcal{L}_{KL}$ increases the number of parameters because it adds an auxiliary classifier, which can be ignored in the model inference stage.

Table 3. Comparison of the parameters and MACs between our model and the existing model. The first row represents the backbone network ResNet50.

Method	Backbone	Parameters (M)	MACs (G)
–		23.52	5.70
FCN		47.12	7.12
UNet	ResNet50	43.91	20.25
UNet++		61.31	69.82
DeepLabV3+		**26.70**	9.51
TFNet		31.53	**6.92**

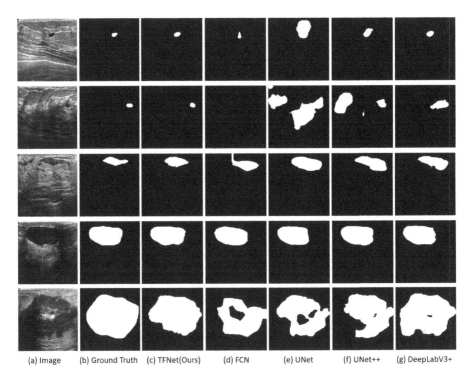

(a) Image   (b) Ground Truth   (c) TFNet(Ours)   (d) FCN   (e) UNet   (f) UNet++   (g) DeepLabV3+

Fig. 2. Visual comparison of the lesion segmentation maps produced by different methods. (a) ultrasound images; (b) ground truths; (c)–(g) are segmentation results by TFNet, FCNN, UNet, UNet++ and DeepLabV3+.

Table 3 shows the comparison of the parameters and MACs between our proposed model and the comparison models. The first row represents the backbone network ResNet50. Our TFNet needs a little more parameters than DeeplabV3+ and less than other models. Our TFNet needs less MACs than other methods.

Visualizations. Figure 2 shows some examples of segmentation results from different cases. We select the small, medium and large scale sample images, as well as the typical images with high echo and serious background influence for visualization. For multi-scale targets, our method shows good segmentation results. Among the comparison method, DeeplabV3+ has better effect on multi-scale target prediction because of the mechanism of ASPP module. UNet, UNet++ and FCN tend to neglect breast lesion details or wrongly classify non-lesion regions as breast lesions into their predicted segmentation maps. For the image with high echo, our method can segment the whole target accurately, while other methods show the phenomenon of internal cavity (the fifth line). This is because our method can capture long-range information. For the images with serious background influence (the second line), the prediction results have a large deviation, and our proposed $\mathcal{L}_{KL}$ can increase the penalty in this case and obtain better results.

4   Conclusion

In this work, in order to solve the problems of large difference in the scale of lesions, uneven intensity distribution in the lesion area, and difficult to distinguish the details in ultrasound images, we propose a feature fusion method using transformer and apply it to ultrasonic image segmentation task. TFNet achieves better performance and faster reasoning speed without using transformer pre-training weights. We design a multi channel attention mechanism to improve the transformer block and enhance its modeling ability on channels. An auxiliary loss function based on KL distance is proposed to correct the detailed information in the prediction results. In our experiments, this loss function is superior to the methods using deep supervision and can transplant to any existing network. In the future, we will study how to improve the multi-head self-attention mechanism to further improve the performance.

Acknowledgement. This work was supported in part by the Natural Science Foundation of China under Grant 61976145 and Grant 61802267, and in part by the Shenzhen Municipal Science and Technology Innovation Council under Grants JCYJ20180305124834854 and JCYJ20190813100801664.

References

1. Al-Dhabyani, W., Gomaa, M., Khaled, H., Fahmy, A.: Dataset of breast ultrasound images. Data Brief **28**, 104863 (2020)

2. Chen, J., et al.: TransUnet: transformers make strong encoders for medical image segmentation. arXiv preprint arXiv:2102.04306 (2021)

3. Chen, L.-C., Zhu, Y., Papandreou, G., Schroff, F., Adam, H.: Encoder-decoder with atrous separable convolution for semantic image segmentation. In: Ferrari, V., Hebert, M., Sminchisescu, C., Weiss, Y. (eds.) ECCV 2018, Part VII. LNCS, vol. 11211, pp. 833–851. Springer, Cham (2018). https://doi.org/10.1007/978-3-030-01234-2_49

4. Chu, X., et al.: Conditional positional encodings for vision transformers. arXiv preprint arXiv:2102.10882 (2021)

5. Dosovitskiy, A., et al.: An image is worth 16x16 words: transformers for image recognition at scale. arXiv preprint arXiv:2010.11929 (2020)

6. Gu, Z., et al.: CE-Net: context encoder network for 2D medical image segmentation. IEEE Trans. Med. Imaging **38**(10), 2281–2292 (2019)

7. Hu, J., Shen, L., Sun, G.: Squeeze-and-excitation networks. In: Proceedings of the IEEE Conference on Computer Vision and Pattern Recognition, pp. 7132–7141 (2018)

8. Huang, H., et al.: UNet 3+: a full-scale connected UNet for medical image segmentation. In: ICASSP 2020–2020 IEEE International Conference on Acoustics, Speech and Signal Processing (ICASSP), pp. 1055–1059. IEEE (2020)

9. Liu, Z., Let al.: Swin transformer: hierarchical vision transformer using shifted windows. arXiv preprint arXiv:2103.14030 (2021)

10. Long, J., Shelhamer, E., Darrell, T.: Fully convolutional networks for semantic segmentation. In: Proceedings of the IEEE Conference on Computer Vision and Pattern Recognition, pp. 3431–3440 (2015)

11. Milletari, F., Navab, N., Ahmadi, S.A.: V-Net: fully convolutional neural networks for volumetric medical image segmentation. In: 2016 Fourth International Conference on 3D Vision (3DV), pp. 565–571. IEEE (2016)

12. Oktay, O., et al.: Attention u-net: learning where to look for the pancreas. arXiv preprint arXiv:1804.03999 (2018)

13. Pedraza, L., Vargas, C., Narváez, F., Durán, O., Muñoz, E., Romero, E.: An open access thyroid ultrasound image database. In: 10th International Symposium on Medical Information Processing and Analysis, vol. 9287, p. 92870W. International Society for Optics and Photonics (2015)

14. Rampun, A., Jarvis, D., Griffiths, P., Armitage, P.: Automated 2D fetal brain segmentation of MR images using a deep U-Net. In: Palaiahnakote, S., Sanniti di Baja, G., Wang, L., Yan, W.Q. (eds.) ACPR 2019, Part II. LNCS, vol. 12047, pp. 373–386. Springer, Cham (2020). https://doi.org/10.1007/978-3-030-41299-9_29

15. Ronneberger, O., Fischer, P., Brox, T.: U-Net: convolutional networks for biomedical image segmentation. In: Navab, N., Hornegger, J., Wells, W.M., Frangi, A.F. (eds.) MICCAI 2015, Part III. LNCS, vol. 9351, pp. 234–241. Springer, Cham (2015). https://doi.org/10.1007/978-3-319-24574-4_28

16. Roy, A.G., Navab, N., Wachinger, C.: Concurrent spatial and channel 'squeeze & excitation' in fully convolutional networks. In: Frangi, A.F., Schnabel, J.A., Davatzikos, C., Alberola-López, C., Fichtinger, G. (eds.) MICCAI 2018, Part I. LNCS, vol. 11070, pp. 421–429. Springer, Cham (2018). https://doi.org/10.1007/978-3-030-00928-1_48

17. Shan, J., Cheng, H.D., Wang, Y.: A novel automatic seed point selection algorithm for breast ultrasound images. In: 2008 19th International Conference on Pattern Recognition, pp. 1–4. IEEE (2008)

18. Valanarasu, J.M.J., Sindagi, V.A., Hacihaliloglu, I., Patel, V.M.: KiU-Net: towards accurate segmentation of biomedical images using over-complete representations. In: Martel, A.L., et al. (eds.) MICCAI 2020, Part IV. LNCS, vol. 12264, pp. 363–373. Springer, Cham (2020). https://doi.org/10.1007/978-3-030-59719-1_36
19. Vaswani, A., et al.: Attention is all you need, pp. 5998–6008 (2017)
20. Wang, X., Girshick, R., Gupta, A., He, K.: Non-local neural networks. In: Proceedings of the IEEE conference on computer vision and pattern recognition. pp. 7794–7803 (2018)
21. Xian, M., Zhang, Y., Cheng, H.D.: Fully automatic segmentation of breast ultrasound images based on breast characteristics in space and frequency domains. Pattern Recognit. **48**(2), 485–497 (2015)
22. Xiao, X., Lian, S., Luo, Z., Li, S.: Weighted Res-UNet for high-quality retina vessel segmentation. In: 2018 9th International Conference on Information Technology in Medicine and Education (ITME), pp. 327–331. IEEE (2018)
23. Xue, C., et al.: Global guidance network for breast lesion segmentation in ultrasound images. Med. Image Anal. **70**, 101989 (2021)
24. Zheng, Z., Yang, Y.: Rectifying pseudo label learning via uncertainty estimation for domain adaptive semantic segmentation. Int. J. Comput. Vis. **129**(4), 1106–1120 (2021)
25. Zhou, Z., Rahman Siddiquee, M.M., Tajbakhsh, N., Liang, J.: UNet++: a nested U-Net architecture for medical image segmentation. In: Stoyanov, D., et al. (eds.) DLMIA/ML-CDS -2018. LNCS, vol. 11045, pp. 3–11. Springer, Cham (2018). https://doi.org/10.1007/978-3-030-00889-5_1

Spatial Pyramid-based Wavelet Embedding Deep Convolutional Neural Network for Semantic Segmentation

Jin Liu, Yazhou Liu$^{(\boxtimes)}$, and Quansen Sun

The School of Computer Science and Engineering, Nanjing University of Science and Technology, Nanjing 210094, China
yazhouliu@njust.edu.cn

Abstract. To reduce the amount of calculation and expand the receptive field, the deep convolutional neural network needs to downsample the feature map. In the process of downsampling, high-frequency information is discarded. This part of information plays an important role in the pixel-by-pixel recognition of the image. At the same time, due to the discarding of high-frequency information, subsequent upsampling is an ill-conditioned process, and high-frequency information cannot be restored. To solve this problem, wavelet embedding network is proposed. The structure proposed in this paper embeds the wavelet transform. In the process of reducing the feature map to enlarge the receptive field, high-frequency information will not be lost. The subsequent use of inverse wavelet transform to enlarge the feature map can avoid the loss of information to the greatest extent. At the same time, the spatial pyramid structure is used to build the network to better integrate the multi-scale information of the image.

This paper makes predictions on large public data sets such as Cityscapes and Pascal VOC 2012, and compares with the current advanced methods to prove its effectiveness.

Keywords: Semantic segmentation · 2D DWT/2D IDWT · Spatial pyramid

1 Introduction

Semantic segmentation is an essential branch in computer vision and is widely used in many fields such as biomedicine [1, 2] and autonomous driving [3–6]. With the development of deep learning, deep convolutional neural networks (CNN) have become the mainstream method for solving such tasks. Fully Convolutional Network (FCN) [7] based on AlexNet [8], an image classification network, upsampling with deconvolution layer to restore the resolution of the image, thus achieving end-to-end fully convolutional semantic segmentation. Many subsequent works are based on FCN.

CNN has shown outstanding performance in the field of semantic segmentation. However, it has a well-known disadvantage. In order to expand the receptive field and reduce the amount of calculation, CNN needs to downsampling. Max pooling is commonly used. It only retains the low-frequency part of the feature map, resulting in

© Springer Nature Switzerland AG 2022
C. Wallraven et al. (Eds.): ACPR 2021, LNCS 13188, pp. 326–337, 2022.
https://doi.org/10.1007/978-3-031-02375-0_24

the loss of high-frequency information. Therefore, in the up-sampling, since the high-frequency information has been discarded, it cannot be restored. Moreover, the missing high-frequency information does not participate in the subsequent feature extraction.

Commonly used upsampling methods are bilinear interpolation and deconvolution, both of which cannot restore the lost information. Bilinear interpolation estimates the value between feature points through linear operations. It is characterized by simple operations but inaccurate. It will smooth some transitions, and these transitions may be important feature information. Deconvolution first expands the size of the feature map through padding and then convolves. Strictly speaking, deconvolution can only restore the size of the feature map but cannot restore the feature map information.

When upsampling, to improve the accuracy, some methods have been proposed. Unpooling [9] uses max pooling for down-sampling and records the position of the retained pixels to guide the up-sampling. PixelShuffle [10] obtains the feature map through convolution and then converts the channel information into spatial information through periodic shuffling to obtain a higher resolution feature map. This method requires additional network training, and this heuristic method is not accurate at a low cost, so it is generally not used in pixel restoration for semantic segmentation. However, these methods cannot solve the problem fundamentally. The essential reason for this problem is the loss of information during downsampling. For this common problem, this paper proposes a Spatial Pyramid-based Wavelet (SPW) embedding deep convolutional structure, which integrates wavelet transform into CNN. The wavelet transform is used for down-sampling to preserve the low-frequency and high-frequency information of the image. In the subsequent up-sampling process, the inverse wavelet transform is used to enlarge the feature map, which avoids the loss of information to the greatest extent.

SPW can be easily inserted into the CNN architecture. Thanks to its structural characteristics, SPW can well retain detailed information. The main contributions of this paper are as follows:

1) This article explains the advantages of 2D DWT and 2D IDWT. On this basis, we promoted down-sampling and up-sampling strategies, embedding wavelet transform into CNN.
2) This paper uses wavelet transform embedding structure, inverse wavelet transform embedding structure, and horizontal pyramid connection to build a semantic segmentation network. This dense structure avoids the loss of information to the greatest extent, and at the same time, it can integrate multi-scale information excellently.
3) Experiments on Cityscapes and Pascal VOC 2012 show that the method proposed in this paper is effective on semantic segmentation tasks. It has an excellent performance in terms of calculation and memory overhead.

2 Related Work

2.1 Semantic Segmentation

FCN realizes the end-to-end semantic segmentation task, which is the basis of the follow-up work. For this intensive classification task, detailed information is essential, and many efforts have been made to preserve the detailed information of the image. [7]

uses deconvolution to try to learn information from low-resolution feature maps for upsampling. In the process of downsampling using max pooling, SegNet [9] records the positions of the reserved pixels to guide upsampling. RefinNet [11] introduces a multi-path refinement network, which uses residual long-distance connections to achieve higher resolution predictions.

Another attempt is to fuse multi-scale information. U-Net [12] adds a horizontal connection between the down-sampling path and the up-sampling path. Deeplabv2 [13] proposes the ASPP module, which is composed of dilated convolutions with different rates. To obtain more detailed information, Deeplabv3+ [14] integrates the underlying feature maps for decoding. SpyGR [15] uses graph reasoning and spatial pyramid structure to capture contextual information.

2.2 Wavelet Transform

In order to increase the receptive field, the scale of the feature map needs to be shrunk. Compared with methods such as max pooling, wavelet transform can save more information when shrinking the feature map. [16] embeds wavelet transform and wavelet inverse transform into CNN, builds a dense, deep neural network, uses it for image denoising tasks, and obtains better results than U-net. [17] uses wavelet transform to decompose the original image into low-frequency images and high-frequency images and uses deep convolution neural network to predict a series of parameters that can convert low-frequency images into high-frequency images. These parameters are independent of the category. The image's original resolution can be restored by inverse wavelet transform of the known low-frequency image and predicted high-frequency image. [18] simply replaces the original pooling layer with wavelet transform and compares it with other pooling strategies. It is found that on some data sets, wavelet pooling has better performance. [19] replaces some layers in CNN with wavelet transform and conducts comparative experiments. The experimental results show that replacing the network layer near max pooling will achieve better results, indicating that the embedding position of wavelet transforms greatly influences accuracy.

The wavelet embedding module proposed in this paper is composed of wavelet transform and convolution operation. It has the functions of reducing the feature map and feature extraction and has found a better combination structure through a large number of comparative experiments.

2.3 Multi-scale Fusion

As we all know, deep convolutional networks have better semantic information, while shallow convolutional networks have better detailed information. Both types of information play a key role in image recognition tasks. Therefore, in order to achieve a better recognition effect, multi-scale fusion is required. Feature Pyramid Network (FPN) [20] allows feature maps of different sizes to be responsible for predicting objects of different sizes and fuse high-level feature maps with low-level feature maps so that low-level feature maps have good semantic features. Liu et al. proposed Feature Pyramid Grid (FPG)

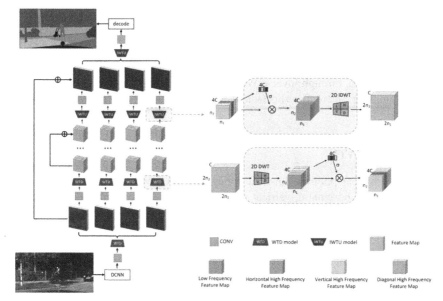

Fig. 1. Structure of SPW. Different colors are used to represent the frequency information relative to the feature map (green - low frequency, red - horizontal high frequency, yellow - vertical high frequency, blue - diagonal high frequency). The WTD module can retain high-frequency and low-frequency information while shrinking the feature map. When the IWTU module expands the feature map, high-frequency and low-frequency information will not be lost. Therefore, the output feature map of SWP contains the low-frequency and high-frequency information of the input feature map. The feature maps obtained by WTD and IWTU are grouped and concated according to frequency to construct a spatial pyramid, which is used to fuse multi-scale information. At the same time, this structure maintains the frequency distribution characteristics of the feature map, which is beneficial to improve the accuracy of the 2D DWT. (Color figure online)

[21] based on it. It is a deep multi-path feature pyramid. The feature scale-space it represents is used as a regular parallel path grid, fused by two-way horizontal connections. In the case of similar calculations, better recognition accuracy is achieved.

Deeplabv2 [13] adopts the ASPP structure and uses dilated convolutions of different rates for feature extraction to obtain feature maps of different receptive field sizes and fuse multi-scale information. Compared with the single-scale Deeplabv1 [22], the performance is significantly improved.

The purpose of multi-scale fusion is to obtain more effective information, but FPN will lose part of the information in down-sampling and up-sampling. The expanded convolution used in ASPP may also lose some essential details in its rough extraction process. Compared with these structures, the pyramid structure proposed in this paper is embedded with wavelet transform. In the process of reducing the feature map to increase the receptive field, high-frequency information will not be lost, and the inverse wavelet transform is used to enlarge the feature map to avoid the loss of information to the greatest extent. The structure of this article can maximize the advantages of the pyramid structure.

3 Spatial Pyramid-based Wavelet (SPW) Embedding Deep Convolutional Structure

The SPW proposed in this paper uses Wavelet Transform Down-sampling (WTD) module for up-sampling, through Inverse Wavelet Transform Up-sampling (IWTU) module for down-sampling, and realizes horizontal connection through spatial pyramid structure (see Fig. 1).

3.1 WTD and IWTU

Compared with mean pooling, down-sampling with 2D DWT can retain high-frequency information in the horizontal, vertical, and diagonal directions, but mean pooling can only retain the low-frequency information of the image. [23] have used systematic experiments to prove that although the high-frequency information of the image is not easy to detect to the human eye, it is crucial information for CNN to recognize. Unlike the traditional down-sampling process, the wavelet transform is reversible. In this paper, a symmetrical up-sampling and down-sampling modules are designed using the reversible characteristics of wavelet transform. Using wavelet transform for down-sampling, the low-frequency and high-frequency information of the feature map is preserved, and the subsequent up-sampling process uses wavelet inverse transform to restore the resolution of the feature map very well. At the same time, we set a learnable weight parameter to weight the feature map of each frequency.

This paper uses the reversible characteristics of wavelet transform to build a symmetrical up-sampling (WTD) and down-sampling (IWTU) module, which is composed of wavelet transform and convolution operation (see Fig. 1).

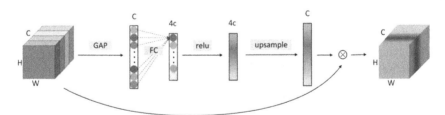

Fig. 2. Wavelet self-attention module. Given the averaged feature map obtained from GAP (Global Average Pooling), the fully connected layer generates *4c* parameters, corresponding to the four frequencies. Then up-sampling expands the number of channels to the original size, and multiplies the original feature map after nonlinear activation.

Wavelet Transform Down-Sampling (WTD) Module
The convolution operation is used to realize fast discrete wavelet transform, and the input feature map $\mathbf{X} \in \mathbb{R}^{C \times 2n_1 \times 2n_2}$ is decomposed into four feature maps $\mathbf{Y}^j \in \mathbb{R}^{C \times n_1 \times n_2}$ $\{j = l, h, v, d\}$, namely low frequency, vertical high frequency, horizontal high frequency and

diagonal high frequency feature maps. We use low-frequency and high-frequency filters in the horizontal and vertical directions, respectively.

$$\mathbf{Y}^l(n_1, n_2) = \lambda^l\Big[\mathbf{X} * \mathbf{h}_L^1(2n_1)\Big] * \mathbf{h}_L^2(2n_2) \tag{1}$$

$$\mathbf{Y}^h(n_1, n_2) = \lambda^h\Big[\mathbf{X} * \mathbf{h}_L^1(2n_1)\Big] * \mathbf{h}_H^2(2n_2) \tag{2}$$

$$\mathbf{Y}^v(n_1, n_2) = \lambda^v\Big[\mathbf{X} * \mathbf{h}_H^1(2n_1)\Big] * \mathbf{h}_L^2(2n_2) \tag{3}$$

$$\mathbf{Y}^d(n_1, n_2) = \lambda^d[\mathbf{X} * \mathbf{h}_H^1(2n_1)] * \mathbf{h}_H^2(2n_2) \tag{4}$$

$\mathbf{h}_k^i$ means filters, where $i = \{1, 2\}$ refers to filtering in the horizontal and vertical directions, and $k = \{H, L\}$ refers to low-frequency and high-frequency filters. During training, the default initialization parameters are used, and then the parameters are updated with gradient descent. $\lambda^j \{j = l, h, v, d\}$ are learnable weight parameters, used to weight the feature map for each frequency.

Inverse Wavelet Transform Up-Sampling (IWTU) Module
The inverse wavelet transform is used to realize the restoration of the feature map pixels, because the low-frequency and high-frequency information of the feature map is completely retained in the down-sampling process. The up-sampling process in this paper is not only the restoration of the feature map scale, but also the restoration of information.

$$\mathbf{X}(2n_1, 2n_2) = \gamma^l\Big[\mathbf{Y}^l * \mathbf{h}_L^1(n_1)\Big] * \mathbf{h}_L^2(n_2) + \gamma^h\Big[\mathbf{Y}^h * \mathbf{h}_L^1(n_1)\Big] * \mathbf{h}_H^2(n_2) +$$
$$\gamma^v\Big[\mathbf{Y}^v * \mathbf{h}_H^1(n_1)\Big] * \mathbf{h}_L^2(n_2) + \gamma^d\Big[\mathbf{Y}^d * \mathbf{h}_H^1(n_1)\Big] * \mathbf{h}_H^2(n_2) \tag{5}$$

$\gamma^j\{j = l, h, v, d\}$ are learnable weight parameters, used to weight the feature map for each frequency.

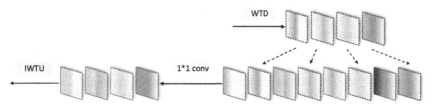

Fig. 3. Spatial pyramid structure. Given the averaged feature map obtained from WTD, combine with the current feature map according to different frequency groups, and use 1 * 1 convolution for feature fusion. Note that the convolution is a grouped convolution with group = 4, which well maintains the original frequency characteristics.

The parameters λ and γ are learned by wavelet sub-attention module (see Fig. 2). Take the parameter λ as an example. First, use GAP on each channel of the input feature map $\mathbf{x} = \{ \mathbf{x}_1, \mathbf{x}_2...\mathbf{x}_C \}$ of dimension $C \times H \times W$ to obtain a series of input parameters $\mathbf{y} = \{ y_1, y_2...y_C \}$, which contain the global information of each channel.

$$y_c = \frac{1}{H \times W} \sum_{i=1}^{H} \sum_{j=1}^{W} \mathbf{x}_c(i,j) \tag{6}$$

In order to obtain the weight of each frequency feature map, a fully connected operation is performed on $\mathbf{y} = \{ y_1, y_2...y_C \}$, and the channel dimension is converted to $4c$. Because the channel dimension is greatly reduced, our full connection does not increase too many parameters and calculations. Then use the relu activation function for non-linear activation, and up-sample to restore the number of channels.

$$\lambda = \text{up - sampling}(\text{relu}(\mathbf{W} \cdot \mathbf{y})) \tag{7}$$

Where $\mathbf{W} \in \mathrm{R}^{4c \times C}$, $\lambda = \{ \lambda_1, \lambda_2...\lambda_C \}$.

3.2 Spatial Pyramid Structure

The spatial pyramid structure used in this article is different from the general pyramid structure. Insert the feature map group obtained by WTD into the feature map of the same size obtained by IWTU. This can not only fully integrate multi-scale information but also maintain the frequency distribution after 2D DWT operation, making the subsequent execution of 2D IDWT more accurate. After that, the 1 * 1 convolution is used for information fusion, and the number of layers of the feature map is reduced to half. Therefore, the pyramid structure does not increase the number of feature layers for subsequent feature extraction, and the additional overhead is insignificant (see Fig. 3).

4 Experiment

4.1 Implementation Details

This paper verifies the performance of SPW on Pascal VOC 2012 and cityscapes. The Resnet101 model pre-trained on ImageNet is used as the backbone, and the 2048-layer feature map obtained from Resnet101 is fused with 1 * 1 convolution to obtain a 512-layer feature map as the input of SPW. The experiment uses a polynomial learning rate. Set an initial learning rate, the learning rate after each iteration is multiplied by $(1 - iter/total\_iter)^{0.9}$. The momentum and weight decay coefficients are set to 0.9 and 0.0001, respectively. The initial learning rate of Pascal VOC 2012 and cityscapes are both set to 0.007. In this paper, general scaling, cropping, and flipping strategies are used for data enhancement. The input size of Cityscapes is set to 769×769, and the other data sets are set to 512×512. For evaluation, the average IoU metric is used as a unified metric. This paper uses a cubic symmetric wavelet transform embedding module and a wavelet inverse transform embedding module stacking network and uses a spatial pyramid to connect horizontally.

4.2 Ablation Experiment

Perform ablation experiments on Cityscapes to explore the contribution of each part of SPW to performance. In order to conduct a comparative study, Resnet101 is used as the backbone. IWTU is dependent on WTD, and the horizontal pyramid connection is based on WTD and IWTU modules. The results of the comparative experiment are shown in Table 1.

Table 1. Ablation experiments on Cityscapes testing set. WTD means WTD module, **IWTU** means adding IWTU module, and **pyramid** represents pyramid structure.

Dilated FCN	WTD	IWTU	pyramid	mIoU
√				77.4
√	√			79.1
√	√	√		79.8
√	√	√	√	81.0

It can be seen from the experimental results that each part of SPW contributes to performance. Combination of thereof so that the entire structure has good properties.

It can be seen from the comparison graph of segmentation results (see Fig. 4) that since the SWP structure proposed in this paper can save the low-frequency and high-frequency information of the feature map, our model has better performance at the edge details than the baseline.

4.3 Comparison with the State-Of The-Arts

Results on Cityscapes

Compare the method proposed in this article with the existing methods on Cityscapes. Cityscapes dataset contains 5,000 images with pixel-level labels and 20,000 images.

with rough annotations, which involve 19 categories of objects and things. Each image has 2048 × 1024 pixels. To be noted, only 5000 finely labeled images are used in this work, which are divided into 2975/500/1525 images for training, verification, and testing. To be fair, this experiment use ResNet-101 as the backbone to train SPW, and the output stride is 8. The training model is for 40 epoch iterations, and the batch size is set to 8. In the test, multi-scale (0.75, 1.0, 1.25, 1.5, 1.75) and flipping are used for image enhancement. Then submit the prediction to the official evaluation server, and the experimental results are shown in Table 2. It can be seen that compared with the current advanced methods, SPW has shown advantages in most categories.

Results on Pascal VOC 2012

Compare the method proposed in this paper with the existing methods on Pascal VOC 2012. This work is compared with Deeplabv3+ and DANet, which also use the pyramid structure to fuse multi-scale information and reach the current advanced level. It is found

Table 2. Per-class results on Cityscapes testing set. Best results are marked in bold. It is shown that SPW achieves the highest performance in most categories. To be noted, only 5000 finely labeled images are used.

Method	mIoU	road	swalk	build	wall	fence	pole	tlight	sign	veg	terrain	sky	person	rider	car	truck	bus	train	motor	bike
RefineNet [11]	73.6	98.2	83.3	91.3	47.8	50.4	56.1	66.9	71.3	92.3	70.3	94.8	80.9	63.3	94.5	64.6	76.1	64.3	62.2	70.0
GCN[24]	76.9	–	–	–	–	–	–	–	–	–	–	–	–	–	–	–	–	–	–	–
DUC[25]	77.6	98.5	85.5	92.8	58.6	55.5	65	73.5	77.9	93.3	72	95.2	84.8	68.5	95.4	70.9	78.8	68.7	65.9	73.8
SAC[26]	78.1	**98.7**	86.5	93.1	56.3	59.5	65.1	73.0	78.2	93.5	**72.6**	**95.6**	85.9	70.8	95.9	71.2	78.6	66.2	67.7	76.0
PSPNet[27]	78.4	–	–	–	–	–	–	–	–	–	–	–	–	–	–	–	–	–	–	–
AAF[28]	79.1	98.5	85.6	93.0	53.8	59.0	65.9	75.0	78.4	**93.7**	72.4	**95.6**	86.4	70.5	95.9	73.9	82.7	76.9	68.7	76.4
PSANet[29]	80.1	–	–	–	–	–	–	–	–	–	–	–	–	–	–	–	–	–	–	–
Dense ASPP[30]	80.6	**98.7**	**87.1**	93.4	60.7	62.7	65.6	**74.6**	78.5	93.6	72.5	95.4	**86.2**	**71.9**	**96.0**	78.0	**90.3**	80.7	69.7	76.8
GloRe[31]	80.9	–	–	–	–	–	–	–	–	–	–	–	–	–	–	–	–	–	–	–
SPW	**81.0**	98.1	85.3	**93.7**	**61.4**	**66.6**	**70.1**	74.3	**83.0**	93.2	64.2	95.2	85.2	69.1	**96.0**	**78.1**	89.5	**81.1**	**73.1**	**80.7**

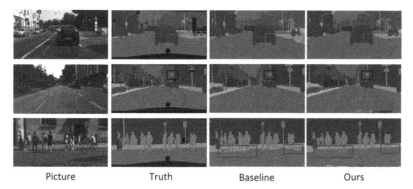

Picture   Truth   Baseline   Ours

Fig. 4. The segmentation effect of the baseline and SWP model. Compared with baseline, the SWP model has better performance at the edge details.

that SPW has advantages on different backbones, especially compared with DANet, it has advantages in performance. DANet is a semantic segmentation network based on dual self-attention in channels and spaces, and its time and memory overhead are much greater than SPW (Table 3).

Table 3. Segmentation results on Pascal VOC 2012. Compared with the current advanced methods with similar structures, SPW has advantages on different backbones.

Method	Backbone	mIoU(%)
Deeplabv3+	Res50	77.7
DANet	Res50	79.0
SPW	**Res50**	**79.1**
Deeplabv3+	Res101	79.4
DANet	Res101	80.4
SPW	**Res101**	**80.7**

5 Conclusion

Taking advantage of the mutual inverse transform characteristics of 2D DWT and 2D IDWT and their own good characteristics, this paper proposes a wavelet embedding deep convolutional neural network and builds a symmetrical up-sampling module. In the process of reducing the feature map to increase the receptive field, and subsequently increasing the feature map, the loss of information can be avoided to the greatest extent. Using the spatial pyramid structure for horizontal connection, the original feature map structure is well maintained, and the multi-scale information of the image is integrated. Experiments show that each part of the module contributes to the improvement of performance. And the method proposed in this paper is superior to the existing methods in accuracy, but still has advantages in time and space consumption.

References

1. Li, B., Chenli, C., Xu, X., Jung, T., Shi, Y.: Exploiting computation power of blockchain for biomedical image segmentation. In: Computer Vision and Pattern Recognition, pp. 4321–4330 (2019)
2. Zhou, Z., Rahman Siddiquee, M.M., Tajbakhsh, N., Liang, J.: UNet++: a nested U-net architecture for medical image segmentation. In: Stoyanov, D., et al. (eds.) DLMIA ML-CDS 2018 2018. LNCS, vol. 11045, pp. 3–11. Springer, Cham (2018). https://doi.org/10.1007/978-3-030-00889-5_1
3. Wang, Q., Gao, J., Li, X.: Weakly supervised adversarial domain adaptation for semantic segmentation in urban scenes. IEEE Trans. Image Process. 28(9), 4376–4386 (2019)
4. Zhou, B., Schwarting, W., Rus, D., Alonso-Mora, J.: Joint multi-policy behavior estimation and receding- horizon trajectory planning for automated urban driving. In: International Conference on Robotics and Automation (ICRA) (2018)
5. Albrecht, S.V., et al.: Interpretable goal-based prediction and planning for autonomous driving. In: International Conference on Robotics and Automation (ICRA) (2020)
6. Li, X., Zhao, Z., Wang, Q.: ABSSNet: attention-based spatial segmentation network for traffic scene understanding. IEEE Trans. Cybernet. PP, 1–11 (2021)
7. Shelhamer, E., Long, J., Darrell, T.: Fully convolutional networks for semantic segmentation. IEEE Trans. Pattern Anal. Mach. Intell. 39(4), 640–651 (2017)
8. Krizhevsky, A., Sutskever, I., Hinton, G.E.: ImageNet classification with deep convolutional neural networks. Commun. ACM 60(6), 84–90 (2017)
9. Badrinarayanan, V., Kendall, A., Cipolla, R.: SegNet: a deep convolutional encoder-decoder architecture for image segmentation. IEEE Trans. Pattern Anal. Mach. Intell. 39(12), 2481–2495 (2017)
10. Shi, W., et al.: Real-time single image and video super-resolution using an efficient sub-pixel convolutional neural network. In: Computer Vision and Pattern Recognition (2016)
11. Lin, G., et al.: RefineNet: multi-path refinement networks for high-resolution semantic segmentation (2016)
12. Ronneberger, O., Fischer, P., Bro, T.: U-Net: convolutional networks for biomedical image segmentation. In: Computer Vision and Pattern Recognition (2015)
13. Chen, L., et al.: DeepLab: semantic image segmentation with deep convolutional nets, atrous convolution, and fully connected CRFs. IEEE Trans. Pattern Anal. Mach. Intell. 40(4), 834–848 (2018)
14. Chen, L.-C., Zhu, Y., Papandreou, G.: Encoder-decoder with atrous separable convolution for semantic image segmentation. In: Computer Vision and Pattern Recognition (2018)
15. Li, X., et al.: Spatial pyramid based graph reasoning for semantic segmentation. In: Computer Vision and Pattern Recognition (2020)
16. Liu, W., Yan, Q., Zhao, Y.: Densely self-guided wavelet network for image denoising. In: Computer Vision and Pattern Recognition (2020)
17. Xiao, M., et al.: Invertible image rescaling. In: Vedaldi, A., Bischof, H., Brox, T., Frahm, J.-M. (eds.) ECCV 2020. LNCS, vol. 12346, pp. 126–144. Springer, Cham (2020). https://doi.org/10.1007/978-3-030-58452-8_8
18. Williams, T., Li, R.: Wavelet pooling for convolutional neural networks. In: International Conference on Learning Representations (2018)
19. Cotter, F.B.: Uses of Complex Wavelets in Deep Convolutional Neural Networks. University of Cambridge (2019)
20. Lin, T.Y., Dollár, P., Girshick, R., He, K., Hariharan, B., Belongie, S.: Feature pyramid networks for object detection. In: Computer Vision and Pattern Recognition (2017)
21. Chen, K., et al.: Feature pyramid grids. In: Computer Vision and Pattern Recognition (2020)

22. Chen, L.C., Papandreou, G., Kokkinos, I., Murphy, K., Yuille, A.L.: Semantic image segmentation with deep convolutional nets and fully connected CRFs. In: International Conference on Learning Representations (2015)
23. Wang, H., et al.: High frequency component helps explain the generalization of convolutional neural networks (2019)
24. Peng, C., et al.: Large kernel matters -- improve semantic segmentation by global convolutional network (2017)
25. Wang, P., et al.: Understanding convolution for semantic segmentation. In: Conference on Applications of Computer Vision, pp. 1451–1460 (2018)
26. Zhang, R., et al.: Perspective-adaptive convolutions for scene parsing. IEEE Trans. Pattern Anal. Mach. Intell. **42**(4), 909–924 (2020)
27. Zhao, H., Shi, J., Qi, X., Wang, X., Jia, J.: Pyramid scene parsing network. In: Computer Vision and Pattern Recognition, pp. 6230–6239 (2017)
28. Ke, T.-W., Hwang, J.-J., Liu, Z., Yu, S.X.: Adaptive affinity fields for semantic segmentation. In: Ferrari, V., Hebert, M., Sminchisescu, C., Weiss, Y. (eds.) ECCV 2018. LNCS, vol. 11205, pp. 605–621. Springer, Cham (2018). https://doi.org/10.1007/978-3-030-01246-5_36
29. Zhao, H., Zhang, Y., Liu, S., Shi, J., Loy, C., Lin, D., Jia, J.: PSANet: Point-wise Spatial Attention Network for Scene Parsing. In: Ferrari, Vittorio, Hebert, Martial, Sminchisescu, Cristian, Weiss, Yair (eds.) ECCV 2018. LNCS, vol. 11213, pp. 270–286. Springer, Cham (2018). https://doi.org/10.1007/978-3-030-01240-3_17
30. Yang, M., Yu, K., Zhang, C., Li, Z., Yang, K.: DenseASPP for semantic segmentation in street scenes. In: Computer Vision and Pattern Recognition, pp. 3684–3692 (2018)
31. Chen, Y., Rohrbach, M., Yan, Z., Shuicheng, Y., Feng, J., Kalantidis, Y.: Facebook AI, Graph-based global reasoning networks. arXiv preprint arXiv:1811.12814 (2018)
32. Fu, J., et al.: Dual attention network for scene segmentation. arXiv preprint arXiv:1809.02983, 2018

CFFNet: Cross-scale Feature Fusion Network for Real-Time Semantic Segmentation

Qifeng Luo, Ting-Bing Xu, and Zhenzhong Wei[✉]

Key Laboratory of Precision Opto-Mechatronics Technology, Ministry of Education, School of Instrumentation and Optoelectronic Engineering, Beihang University, Beijing, China
{luoqifeng,tingbing_xu,zhenzhongwei}@buaa.edu.cn

Abstract. Despite deep learning based semantic segmentation methods have achieved significant progress, the inference speed of high-performance segmentation model is harder to meet the demand of various real-time applications. In this paper, we propose an cross-scale feature fusion network (CFFNet) to harvest the compact segmentatiHon model with high accuracy. Specifically, we design a novel lightweight residual block in backbone with increasing block depth strategy instead of inverted residual block with increasing local layer width strategy for better feature representative learning while reducing the computational cost by about 75%. Moreover, we design the cross-scale feature fusion module which contains three path to effectively fuse semantic features with different resolutions while enhancing multi-scale feature representation via cross-edge connections from inputs to last path. Experiments on Cityscapes demonstrate that CFFNet performs agreeably on accuracy and speed. For 2048 × 1024 input image, our model achieves 81.2% and 79.9% mIoU on validation and test sets at 46.5 FPS on a 2080Ti GPU.

Keywords: Semantic segmentation · Lightweight network · Feature fusion · Real-time

1 Introduction

Semantic segmentation is a basic computer vision task that classifies all pixels of image, which is widely used in virtual reality, autonomous driving and robotics. However in many application scenarios, models are required to satisfy real-time capability, at least 30 FPS. Our research is oriented to real-time semantic segmentation task, aiming to improve the model speed and accuracy at the same time.

This article was funded by "the National Science Fund for Distinguished Young Scholars of China" under Grant No. 51625501, and "Aeronautical Science Foundation of China" under Grant No. 201946051002.
Q. Luo, T.-B. Xu—Equal contribution.

Deep semantic segmentation models often have a powerful backbone with sufficient depth and width (channel numbers) to effectively extract features, such as HRNet [26], Nvidia-seg [25] and DANet [4]. Although these models have achieved considerable segmentation accuracy, their parameters and calculations are enormous which cannot satisfy the requirement of real-time inference speed. To improve inference speed, depthwise separable convolutions based models have been proposed. MobileNetV2 [20] proposes inverted residual block to construct backbone network. Inverted residual block uses linear bottleneck and 6 times channel expansion to achieve better performance than MobileNetV1 [10]. However, due to the limited inference speed of inverted residual block, the whole high computational cost hinder model from applications on real-time semantic segmentation. To obtain better balance between accuracy and speed, we design the lightweight residual block, which increases the depth of residual block by added linear layer moderately, instead of increasing the width.

In addition, semantic segmentation need to fuse detailed information in shallow layers and semantic information in deep layers. Many semantic models have designed multi-scale feature fusion modules. For example, HRNet [26] segmentation model adopt multi-path structure to fuse feature maps with different resolutions at the tail of the model. However the high-resolution path will take up too much memory and computational resources that limits inference speed. Encoder-decoder structure [1] has an up-bottom path for down-sampling to assemble context information and a bottom-up path for up sampling which fuses the deep semantic information to the shallow layer through up-sampling path. However, single direction semantic information dissemination cannot make full use of the characteristic information of various scales of the backbone network.

Based on above analysis, we use depthwise separable convolutions to build the lightweight network to reduce computational cost for inference speed, and use the cross-scale features propagation mechanism to fuse detailed information and semantic information. Our contributions are summarized as follows:

- we present an cross-scale feature fusion network (CFFNet) to obtain the compact segmentation model with higher accuracy.
- we design a novel lightweight residual block in backbone with increasing residual block depth strategy instead of the inverted residual block with increasing local layer width strategy for better feature representative learning. Compared with inverted block, lightweight residual block reduces computational cost by about 75%.
- We design a novel cross-scale feature fusion module, which uses dual-direction mechanism and cross connections from inputs to last path to fuse semantic features with different resolutions.
- Our segmentation model achieves impressive results on Cityscapes set. Specifically, it obtains 81.2% mIoU and 79.9% mIoU on Cityscapes val and test set at 46.5 FPS for 2048 × 1024 input by using single 2080Ti GPU.

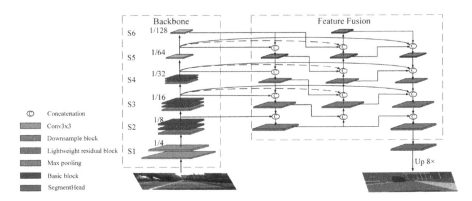

Fig. 1. Model architecture. There are two components: backbone in the red dashed box, cross-scale feature fusion module in the purple dashed box. (Color figure online)

2   Related Work

Real-Time Semantic Segmentation. It expects higher accuracy and faster inference speed for real-time semantic segmentation tasks. ENet [17] uses an asymmetric endoer-decoder structure to imporve inference speed, and uses dilated convolution to increase the receptive field for accuracy. ICNet [30] uses parallel multi-resolution input to obtain multi-scale features for accuracy, yet the speed is just 30 FPS. CABiNet [11] introduces an attention mechanism with dual branch structure, and one path is high-resolution to maintain detailed information and the other is used to extract semantic features. However, inference speed is limited by high-resolution path. MSFNet [22] achieves a better accuracy by using a lightweight backbone and edge supervision, but the computational cost is large.

Multi-scale Feature Fusion. Feature maps of different depths and scales contain different detailed or semantic informations, an efficient feature fusion module will bring better performance [11,24]. Detailed informations are located at shallow layers, while semantic informations are located at depth layers generally. HRNet [26] maintains high-resolution streams and generates low-resolution streams in parallel, to generate multi-scale feature maps and exchanges information between them. Nvidia-seg [25] proposes a multi-scale attention module to perform feature fusion of scale 0.5, 1.0, 2.0 to learn the relative attention masks. MSFNet [22] developes Spatial Aware Pooling (SAP) that uses different size poolings and strides to obtain large receptive fields, and concatenate SAP features of different scales, so that both rich spatial detailed and contextual informations can be obtained.

Residual Block with Depthwise Separable Convolutions. Compared with standard convolution, depthwise separable convolution can acquire a significant speed improvement. Many models have proposed different residual blocks based on depthwise separable convolutions to improve speed and accuracy [2,7,14,20,29]. Xception [2] replaces Inception block of InceptionNetV3 [23] with depth separable convolutions.They show that performance of activation function only after pointwise convolution is the best. MobileNetV2 [20] proposed a novel

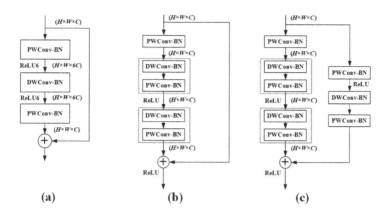

Fig. 2. Residual blocks. (a) is the inverted residual block. (b) is our lightweight residual block. A depthwise convolution and a pointwise convolution compose a depthwise separable (yellow cube) convolution [20]. (c) is downsample block which stride of first 3×3 depthwise conv and the branch path are 2. (Color figure online)

bottleneck named inverted residual block where shortcut connection is between thin bottleneck layers and intermediate layer using depthwise convolutions to filter features as a source of nonlinearity. Zhang *et al.* [29] propose ShuffleNetunit to improve the utilization of features by using channel split and shuffle operations. Subsequently, Zhang *et al.* [14] redesign shuffleNet unit, standardized split and shuffle operations, which further improves inference speed.

3   Methodology

3.1   Architecture

As shown in Fig. 1, Cross-scals feature fusion network includes two compositions: backbone network and cross-scale feature fusion network. Backbone network is divided into 6 stages. The S1 stage uses two 3×3 standard convolutions with stride 2 to output feature maps with 1/4 resolution of input. As feature maps of shallow layers have the characteristics of high resolution and a small number of channel, the performance of standard convolution is suitable choice. The S2−S4 stages have the same structure: a down-sample block as Fig. 2(c) and two lightweight residual blocks as Fig. 2(b). The S5 and S6 are max pooling layers with kernel size = 3, stride = 2. Resolution of final feature maps is 1/128 of the input image, with a sufficiently large receptive field. The output of stages S2−S6 are transmitted to cross-scale feature fusion module (Sect. 3.3). The segment head is the same as BiseNetV2 [28].

3.2   Lightweight Residual Block

Depthwise separable convolution is generally composed of a depthwise convolution and a pointwise convolution (1×1 standard convolution), which is often

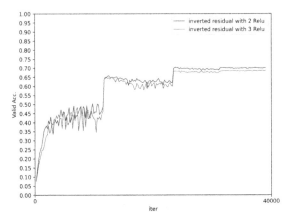

Fig. 3. Accuracy of MobileNetV2 networks with different number of activation functions in inverted residual block.

used to replace standard convolution for lightweight networks [2, 14, 20, 29]. As MobilNetV2 [20] expresses, assuming input tensor size $h_i \times w_i \times d_i$, output tensor size $h_i \times w_i \times d_j$, convolutional kernel size $K \subset \mathcal{R}^{k \times k \times d_i \times d_j}$, computational cost of standard convolutional layers is $h_i \times w_i \times d_i \times d_j \times k \times k$. Computational cost of depthwise separable convolution is the sum of depthwise convolution and 1×1 pointwise convolution $h_i \times w_i \times d_i(k^2 + d_j)$. If kernel size k = 3, the computational cost is about 8–9 times less than that of standard convolutions with a small reduction of accuracy [20].

Based depthwise separable convolution, MobileNetV2 [20] purposes inverted residual block as shown in Fig. 2(a). Inverted residual block uses pointwise convolution to expand the channels by 6 times, then following 3×3 depthwise convolution. Finally linear bottleneck (1×1 convolution without active function) reduces channels to output. Inverted residual block of MobileNetV2 benefits from the following two points:

1. Linear bottleneck layers reduce loss produced by nonlinearity. Activational function will cause feature loss due to its characteristics, though it can give networks non-linear representation ability. Network constructed by depthwise separable convolutions uses more convolutional layers than that constructed by standard convolutions. The activation function used at each convolution will bring a negative impact on performance of network. Based on MobileNetV2 network, we explores the influence of activation function for performance on cifar-100 dataset. We just change the number of activation functions in inverted residual block while training settings and network structure are the same. As shown in Fig. 3, adding ReLu activation function after linear bottleneck layers significantly reduces network performance.

2. Channel expansion enhances feature representation capability of local network. Representation capability of based depthwise separable convolutions networks is limited by depth and width. Although output channels of inverted

residual block is low-demensional, intermediate channel dimensions are sepanded by 6 times, which means width of network increased, so it increases the representation ability of local network. Compared with linear transformation of the lower-dimensional space, this kind of dimensionality expansion and then the dimensionality reduction operation can capture the manifold of interest embedded in the low-dimensional space.

Although inverted residual achieved better performance, it also increased computational cost. According to the 6 times channel expansion in MobileNetV2, assuming that size of the input and output feature maps are the same, the total number of multiply add required of inverted residual is

$$h \times w \times c' \times t(c' + k^2 + c'') \tag{1}$$

where h, w, c', c'', t, k are height and width of feature map, input and output channels, expansion factor and kernel size. The computational cost is 6 times of no expansion block, which is not cost-effective. Inverted residual blocks increase local width of network to improve performance. However, the depth of lightweight network is also insufficient. The performance can be improved by appropriately increasing the width of residual block. Based on the above, we propose lightweight residual module as shown in Fig. 2(b), which is composed of a linear bottleneck and two depthwise separable convolutions. Xception demonstrated that no intermediate activations lead to both faster convergence and better final performance, and ours follows that. The computation of lightweight residual block is

$$h \times w \times c' \times (c' + k^2 + c' + k^2 + c'') \tag{2}$$

We can get the ratio of computation between lightweight residual block and inverted residual block as:

$$\begin{aligned} &\frac{h \times w \times c' \times (c' + k^2 + c' + k^2 + c'')}{h \times w \times c' \times t(c' + k^2 + c'')} \\ &= \frac{2c' + 2k^2 + c''}{t(c' + k^2 + c'')} \end{aligned} \tag{3}$$

Assuming that input and output channels $c' = c'' > 100$, general $k = 3 << 100$, so the ratio is approximately 0.25, which is beneficial for real-time semantic segmentation. Our ablation experiment of lightweight residual block and inverted residual block indicates the advantages.

3.3   Cross-scale Feature Fusion Module

For semantic segmentation networks, feature fusion addresses to aggregate context features and detailed features of different resolutions at different depths. For inputs of features with different resolutions, feature fusion goal is to find a transformation f to output new features : $P^{out} = f(P^{in})$ [20]. For convolutional networks, it has two methods to fuse multi-scale features:

$$P_i^{out} = conv(P_i^{in} + resize(P_j^{out})) \tag{4}$$

$$P_i^{out} = conv(cat(P_i^{in}, resize(P_j^{out}))) \tag{5}$$

Equation 4 fuses features through element-wise additon operations. The addition operation needs to keep the multi-scale features with the same size of channels. However, semantic features of depth layers is required more channels to represent than that of detailed features of shallow layers. The channels of multi-scale features reshaped the same size will loss semantic information. Equation 5 can maintain multi-scale features maps characteristics, and parameterize different features by convolution to generate new feature maps which has more powerful representation. Our ablition experiment of the two methods indicates Eq. 5 achieves better performance.

Recently abundant multi-scale feature propagation methods has been proposed for semantic segmentation, object detection, instance segmentation and other vision tasks. Based on PANet [13] and NAS-FPN [6], EfficentDet [24] proposes a cross-scale feature fusion module named BiFPN, which regards a bidirectional (top-down & bottom-up) path as a feature network layer. EfficentDet repeats multi BiFPNs for better performance. However, for real-time semantic segmentation, repeated use of bidirectional path will significantly increase the computational cost, especially with high resolution size feature maps. Because of this, the feature fusion module we designed only contains two top-down and one bottom-up paths as Fig. 1. As the fusion module is not repeated, just added edges (dotted edges) from inputs to the bottom-up in BiFPN is not beneficial for accuracy. So, we add edges from inputs of multi-scale to the same scale of last top-bottom path. We explore the performance of adding different edges in the ablation experiment, and the results show that only edges from inputs to last up-bottom path has the best performance.

4   Experiments

4.1   Datasets

Cityscapes. Cityscapes [3] dataset contains street scene images of 50 different cities, including 5,000 finely labeled images and 19,998 coarsely labeled images, all with resolution size of 2048×1024. We use finely labeled images to train and test. According to Cityscapes standard, training set contains 2,975 images, validation set contains 500 images, test set contains 1,525 images, and 19 labeled categories are used for training and evaluation. Bisedes, 19,998 autolabeled images of Cityscapes coarse set also are used for train [25].

4.2   Implementation Details

Cityscapes Set Train Settings: Train on Cityscapes is divided into two steps:
Step 1: The stochastic gradient descent optimizer (SGD) algorithm with 0.9 momentum and 0.0005 weight decay is used to train CCFNet. The poly learning

policy with power of 0.9 which initial rate is set to $1.5e^{-3}$. For data augmentation, horizontally flipping and randomly scaling in the range of 0.25 to 2.0 are included. Bisedes, input datas are randomly cropped into 512×1024 for training following BiSeNetV2 [28]. We adopt 24 batch size and 150k iterations to train Cityscapes datasets. If autolabeled images set is used, iterations are 210K.

Step 2: The initial rate is set to $5e^{-4}$, and iterations is 100K. The range of randomly scaling is 0.5 to 2. While input images are randomly cropped into 1024×1024 with batch size 6. Other parameters of training is the same as Step 1. All models are trained on two 2080Ti GPUs.

The loss function is online hard example mining (OHEM) [21]. Any pretrained model on imagenet is not used to initialize network.

Inference Speed Measurement: One GTX 2080Ti GPU is used to measure the speed of inference by setting batch size to 1. The input resolution size for test is 2048×1024. The speed is average results of network running 500 times.

Table 1. Parameters and FLOPs analysis

Model	Input size	Params	GFLOPs
ESPNet [15]	1024×512	0.4M	–
Fast-SCNN [18]	2048×1024	1.1M	–
SwiftNetRN-18 [16]	2048×1024	11.8M	104
SegNet [1]	640×360	29.5M	286
ICNet [30]	2048×1024	26.5M	28.3
ERFNet [19]	1024×512	20.0M	27.7
BiSeNet2 [27]	1536×768	49.0M	55.3
MSFNet [22]	1024×512	–	96.8
DDRNet-23-Slim [9]	2048×1024	5.7M	36.3
DDRNet-23 [9]	2048×1024	21.1M	143.1
CFFNet (ours)	2048×1024	8.9M	54.2

4.3 Parameters and FLOPs

For real-time semantic segmentation models, parameters and FLOPs are important evaluation criterions. We choose models with parameter below 50M for comparison as shown in Table 1. Our model has only 8.9M parameters with resolution 2048×1024 of input image and computational cost of it 54.2 GFLOPs. Compared with models with parameters less than 8M , our model has no advantages in terms of computational cost, while the accuracy is superior(Sec. 4.4). For models with parameters more than 8M, GFLOPs and parameters of CFFNet show better performance. Compared with SwiftNetRN-18, our model parameters and computation are 2.9M and 49.8 GFLOPs less than it, respectively. Although BiSeNetV2 [28] has a similar computational cost to our model, its input size is

Table 2. Accuracy and speed analysis of ciytscapes

Model	Input size	MIoU		FPS
		Val	Test	
ICNet [30]	2048 × 1024	–	69.5%	30.0
SwiftNetRN-18 [16]	2048 × 1024	74.5%	74.4%	39.9
BiSeNet2 [27]	1536 × 768	74.8%	74.7%	65.5
MSFNet [22]	1024 × 512	–	7.1%	41.0
ABiNet [11]	2048 × 1024	76.6%	75.9%	76.5
DDRNet-23-slim [9]	2048 × 1024	77.8%	77.4%	108.8
DDRNet-23 [9]	2048 × 1024	79.5%	79.4%	38.5
CFFNet-1 (ours)	2048 × 1024	78.1%	–	46.5
CFFNet-2 (ours)	2048 × 1024	78.6%	–	46.5
CFFNet-1* (ours)	2048 × 1024	80.3%	78.9%	46.5
CFFNet-2* (ours)	2048 × 1024	**81.2%**	**79.9%**	46.5

only 0.75 times of ours. DDRNet series networks are dual-path modules, and DDRNet-23-slim acquires a exceptional balance of accuracy and speed. But if performance is increased by expanding channels, the parameters and computational cost will increase significantly because of the high-resolution path, like DDRNet-23, which parameters has increased by 2.5 times, and computation cost has increased by 2.9 times. Our CFFNet just has 37.9% GFLOPS and 44.1% parameters of DDRNet-23 to achieve approximate performance.

4.4 Accuracy and Speed

The accuracy and speed comparison with other models is presented in Table 2 on the Ciytscapes validation and test sets. The CFFNet-1 means just step 1 for training, and CFFNet-2 is trained with step 1 and 2. The stars means autolabeled image set [25] used to train together.

It can be observed from Table 3 that CFFNet outperforms porposed models for real-time semantic segmentation and achieve mIoU scores of 80.1% and 79.9% on validation and test sets respectively. Inference speed of CFFNet is comparable to MSFNet, but accuracy is 2.8% mIoU higher than them respectively. Bisedes, it runs similar to BiSeNetV2 [28], but achieves 5.2% mIoU gain on test set. DDRNet is pretrained on imagenet to achieve the state-of-the-art results, but the inference speed of our model is faster than it. As shown in Table 2, our train strategy can get performance improvement by 0.5% mIoU on validation set of Cityscapes. And if autolabeled set is used, accuracy is improved by 0.9% and 1% on validation and test set of Cityscapes.

4.5 Compare of Residual Blocks

This experiment explores performance of lightweight residual block and other residual block, such as MobileNetV2 [20], ShuffleNetV2 [14], GhostNet [7],

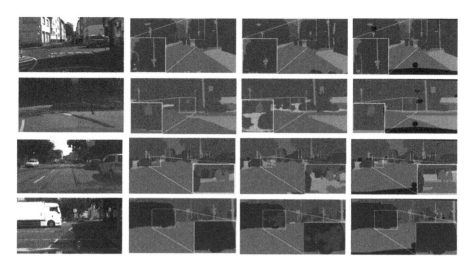

Fig. 4. Visualization results on The Cityscapes validation set. The first row are input images, the second row are CFFNet with solid edges, the third row are CFFNet without any skip edges , the last row are ground truth.

Table 3. Compare of residual blocks.

Model	MIoU	GFLOPs	Params	Speed
Lightweight residual	78.1%	10.1	2.2M	21.5 ms
MobileNetV2 block [20]	77.9%	40.0	8.4M	36.3 ms
ResNet block [8]	77.5%	58.1	12.4M	24.3 ms
GhostNet block [7]	76.5%	3.5	22.8M	22.6 ms
Res2Net block [5]	76.4%	3.6	0.76M	19.3 ms
VovNet block [12]	76.3%	156.5	33.4M	46.4 ms
ShuffleNetV2 block [14]	75.4%	1.7	0.36M	18.1 ms

ResNet [8], Res2Net [5]. We construct backbone of CFFNet with different residual block(dark blue cube in Fig. 1). Model is trained according to step 1 with cityscapes train set. Figure 5 shows train loss of different networks. Lightweight residual block can achieve the lowest loss value. Evaluation results on cityscapes val set, GFLOPs, parameters and speed of networks is shown in Table 3. GFLOPs and parameters are just counted by different residual blocks (dark blue cube). Segmentation accuracy of lightweight residual is slightly higher than that of inverted residual block. However, GFLOPs and parameters of lightweight residual block are 25% of inverted residual block as Sect. 3.3 describes. Resnet blocks have achieved 77.5% MIoU, though parameters and GFLOPs are much larger than that of lightweight residual block. Besides, all other residual blocks in Table 3 is designed based on feature reuse. Because of structure of them is different, GFLOPs and parameters is not the same. However segmentation accuracy is

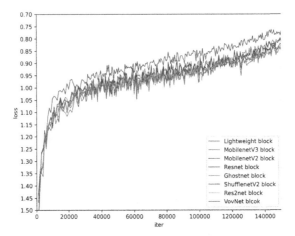

Fig. 5. Train loss of CCFNet with different residual blocks.

close. For cross scale feature fusion structure, it is necessary that different scales contain as many different feature as possible for produce new fusion features, but feature reuse will cause local fusion, which will result in the inclusion of similar features at different scales, thereby reducing ability for feature fusion.

Table 4. Compare of cross-scale connections

Model	Baseline	Baseline with dotted edges	Baseline with solid edges	Baseline with all edges	MIoU
1	✓				77.2%
2	✓	✓			77.6%
3	✓		✓		**78.1%**
4	✓			✓	77.3%

4.6   Ablation Study

Ablation Experiment of Cross-scale Connections. We analyze the effect of cross-scale feature fusion on Cityscapes validation set. Baseline is defined as the feature fusion module without horizontal edge. In addition to baseline, there are three type of horizontal skip edge cases discussed: (a) only solid edge (b) only dotted edge (c) both solid and dotted edges as shown in Fig. 1. Table 4 shows that baseline added the solid edges from input to the last path can abtain better performance from 77.2% to 78.1%. As shown in Fig. 4, compare with no skip-connections, for boundary detail and fine-grained objects, cross-scale feature fusion module can attend these informations at multi-scale.

Table 5. Compare of fusion methods

Model	MIoU	Speed	Params	GFLOPs
Addition	77.4%	20.6 ms	5.9M	47.7
Concatenation	78.1%	21.5 ms	8.9M	54.2

Ablation Experiment of Fusion Methods. We compare the fusion performance of the Eq. 4 and Eq. 5. The outputs of backbone reshape the same channels before features fusion with Eq. 4. And outputs of nodes in feature fusion module have the same channels as 128. As shown in Table 5, parameters and computional cost of Eq. 4 is obviously less than that of Eq. 5, while layers to reshape input channels is added between backbone and cross-scale feature fusion module. GFLOPs and parameters of Eq. 4 are less than Eq. 5, and has advantage of speed 0.9s. However, Eq. 5 can exploit more multi-scale features to improve accuracy, MIoU of it is 0.7% well than Eq. 4.

Table 6. SE and Dilated convolutions ablation

Model	Baseline	SE block	Dilated conv	MIoU
1	✓			77.6%
2	✓		✓	77.8%
3	✓	✓		77.9%
4	✓	✓	✓	**78.1%**

Ablation Experiment of SE and Dilated Convolutions. We adds SE block and dilated convolutions at lightweight residual block of backbone. SE block follows the first depthwise convolution and all of lightweight residual blocks use SE block. The dilated convolutions are just added to the second lightweight residual blocks of each stage, which are located in the first depthwise convolutions in lightweight residual blocks. Baseline is defined as the network without any SE block and dilated convolutions. Results in Table 6 suggests that SE module and dilated convolutions can improve performance of scene parsing, from 77.5% to 78.1% mIoU.

5   Conclusion

In this paper, we propose a novel lightweight model to address the challenge of real-time semantic segmentation which improves the performance and inference speed.We introduce a residual block based on depthwise convolutions and pointwise convolutions. The ablation experiments show that lightweight residual block obtains gratifying balance between accuracy and speed. And cross-scale feature fusion module captures multi-scale information by cross-edges connections which can make full use of features of different scales. Experiments demonstrate that our CFFNet has achieved a new state-of-the art for real-time semantic segmentation.

References

1. Badrinarayanan, V., Kendall, A., Cipolla, R.: SegNet: a deep convolutional encoder-decoder architecture for image segmentation. IEEE Trans. Pattern Anal. Mach. Intell. **39**, 2481–2495 (2017)
2. Chollet, F.: Xception: deep learning with depthwise separable convolutions. In: 2017 IEEE Conference on Computer Vision and Pattern Recognition, 21–26 July, Honolulu, HI, USA (2017)
3. Cordts, M., et al.: The cityscapes dataset for semantic urban scene understanding. In: 2016 IEEE Conference on Computer Vision and Pattern Recognition, Las Vegas, NV, USA, June 27–30 (2016)
4. Fu, J., et al.: Dual attention network for scene segmentation. In: IEEE Conference on Computer Vision and Pattern Recognition, 16–20 June, Long Beach, CA, USA (2019)
5. Gao, S., Cheng, M.M., Zhao, K., Zhang, X., Yang, M.H., Torr, P.H.S.: Res2net: a new multi-scale backbone architecture. IEEE Trans. Pattern Anal. Mach. Intell. **43**, 652–662 (2021)
6. Ghiasi, G., Lin, T.Y., Pang, R., Le, Q.V.: NAS-FPN: learning scalable feature pyramid architecture for object detection. IIn: 2019 IEEE/CVF Conference on Computer Vision and Pattern Recognition (CVPR), pp. 7029–7038 (2019)
7. Han, K., Wang, Y., Tian, Q., Guo, J., Xu, C., Xu, C.: GhostNet: more features from cheap operations. In: 2020 IEEE/CVF Conference on Computer Vision and Pattern Recognition, pp. 1577–1586 (2020)
8. He, K., Zhang, X., Ren, S., Sun, J.: Deep residual learning for image recognition. In: 2016 IEEE Conference on Computer Vision and Pattern Recognition (CVPR), pp. 770–778 (2016)
9. Hong, Y., Pan, H., Sun, W., Jia, Y., et al.: Deep dual-resolution networks for real-time and accurate semantic segmentation of road scenes. arXiv preprint arXiv:2101.06085 (2021)
10. Howard, A.G., et al.: MobileNets: efficient convolutional neural networks for mobile vision applications. arXiv preprint arXiv:1704.04861 (2017)
11. Kumaar, S., Lyu, Y., Nex, F., Yang, M.Y.: Cabinet: efficient context aggregation network for low-latency semantic segmentation. arXiv preprint arXiv:2011.00993, 13 2020
12. Lee, Y., Hwang, J., Lee, S., Bae, Y., Park, J.: An energy and GPU-computation efficient backbone network for real-time object detection. In: 2019 IEEE/CVF Conference on Computer Vision and Pattern Recognition Workshops (CVPRW), pp. 752–760 (2019)
13. Liu, S., Qi, L., Qin, H., Shi, J., Jia, J.: Path aggregation network for instance segmentation. In: 2018 IEEE/CVF Conference on Computer Vision and Pattern Recognition, pp. 8759–8768 (2018)
14. Ma, N., Zhang, X., Zheng, H., Sun, J.: Shufflenet V2: practical guidelines for efficient CNN architecture design. In: 2018–15th European Conference, Munich, Germany, September 8–14, Proceedings, Part XIV. vol. 11218 (2018)

15. Mehta, S., Rastegari, M., Caspi, A., Shapiro, L.G., Hajishirzi, H.: Espnet: efficient spatial pyramid of dilated convolutions for semantic segmentation. In: 2018–15th European Conference, Munich, Germany, September 8–14, Proceedings, Part X. vol. 11214 (2018)

16. Oršic, M., Krešo, I., Bevandic, P., Šegvic, S.: In defense of pre-trained imagenet architectures for real-time semantic segmentation of road-driving images. In: 2019 IEEE/CVF Conference on Computer Vision and Pattern Recognition (2019)

17. Paszke, A., Chaurasia, A., Kim, S., Culurciello, E.: Enet: a deep neural network architecture for real-time semantic segmentation. arXiv preprint arXiv:1606.02147 (2016)

18. Poudel, R.P.K., Liwicki, S., Cipolla, R.: Fast-SCNN: fast semantic segmentation network. In: 30th British Machine Vision Conference, 9–12 September, Cardiff, UK (2019)

19. Romera, E., Alvarez, J.M., Bergasa, L.M., Arroyo, R.: ERFNet: efficient residual factorized convnet for real-time semantic segmentation. IEEE Trans. Intell. Transp. Syst. **19**(1), 263–272 (2018)

20. Sandler, M., Howard, A.G., Zhu, M., Zhmoginov, A., Chen, L.: Mobilenetv 2: inverted residuals and linear bottlenecks. In: 2018 IEEE Conference on Computer Vision and Pattern Recognition, 18–22 June, Salt Lake City, UT, USA (2018)

21. Shrivastava, A., Gupta, A., Girshick, R.: Training region-based object detectors with online hard example mining. In: 2016 IEEE Conference on Computer Vision and Pattern Recognition, Los Alamitos, CA, USA . IEEE Computer Society (2016)

22. Si, H., Zhang, Z., Lu, F.: Real-time semantic segmentation via multiply spatial fusion network. In: 31st British Machine Vision Conference 2020, 2020, 7–10 September, 2020, Virtual Event, UK (2020)

23. Szegedy, C., Vanhoucke, V., Ioffe, S., Shlens, J., Wojna, Z.: Rethinking the inception architecture for computer vision. In: 2016 IEEE Conference on Computer Vision and Pattern Recognition, pp. 2818–2826 (2016)

24. Tan, M., Pang, R., Le, Q.V.: EfficientDet: scalable and efficient object detection. In: 2020 IEEE/CVF Conference on Computer Vision and Pattern Recognition, 13–19 June, Seattle, WA, USA (2020)

25. Tao, A., Sapra, K., Catanzaro, B.: Hierarchical multi-scale attention for semantic segmentation. arXiv preprint arXiv:2005.10821 (2020)

26. Wang, J., et al.: Deep high-resolution representation learning for visual recognition. IEEE Trans. Pattern Anal. Mach. Intell. **10**, 3349–3364 (2020)

27. Yu, C., Wang, J., Peng, C., Gao, C., Yu, G., Sang, N.: BiSeNet: bilateral segmentation network for real-time semantic segmentation. In: European Conference on Computer Vision (2018)

28. Yu, C., Gao, C., Wang, J., Yu, G., Shen, C., Sang, N.: Bisenet v2: bilateral network with guided aggregation for real-time semantic segmentation. arXiv preprint arXiv:2004.02147 (2020)

29. Zhang, X., Zhou, X., Lin, M., Sun, J.: ShuffleNet: an extremely efficient convolutional neural network for mobile devices. In: 2018 IEEE Conference on Computer Vision and Pattern Recognition, 18–22 June, Salt Lake City, UT, USA (2018)

30. Zhao, H., Qi, X., Shen, X., Shi, J., Jia, J.: ICNet for real-time semantic segmentation on high-resolution images. In: Proceedings of the European Conference on Computer Vision (2018)

Semantic Segmentation and Depth Estimation with RGB and DVS Sensor Fusion for Multi-view Driving Perception

Oskar Natan[1,2]([⊠]) [iD] and Jun Miura[1] [iD]

[1] Department of Computer Science and Engineering,
Toyohashi University of Technology, Aichi 441-8580, Japan
{oskar.natan.ao,jun.miura}@tut.jp
[2] Department of Computer Science and Electronics, Universitas Gadjah Mada,
Yogyakarta 55281, Indonesia
oskarnatan@ugm.ac.id

Abstract. In this research, we present a novel deep multi-task learning model to handle the perception stage of an autonomous driving system. The model leverages the fusion of RGB and dynamic vision sensor (DVS) images to perform semantic segmentation and depth estimation in four different perspectives of view simultaneously. As for the experiment, CARLA simulator is used to generate thousands of simulation data for training, validation, and testing processes. A dynamically changing environment with various weather conditions, daytime, maps, and non-player characters (NPC) is also considered to simulate a more realistic condition with expecting a better generalization of the model. An ablation study is conducted by modifying the network architecture to evaluate the influence of the sensor fusion technique. Based on the test result on 2 different datasets, the model that leverages feature maps sharing from RGB and DVS encoders is performing better. Furthermore, we show that our model can inference faster and have a comparable performance against another recent model. Official implementation code is shared at https://github.com/oskarnatan/RGBDVS-fusion.

Keywords: Sensor fusion · Semantic segmentation · Depth estimation · Multi-task learning · Driving perception

1 Introduction

An autonomous driving system contains a lot of important elements, either on the hardware side or software side [10]. Specifically, on the software side, there are four main stages that must be considered to achieve a fully autonomous driving operation, there are environment perception, localization, planning, and control [14]. As the first stage, perception has always been a challenging task in developing the foundation of the complex autonomous driving system. The system needs to understand what kinds of objects are showing up on cameras

© Springer Nature Switzerland AG 2022
C. Wallraven et al. (Eds.): ACPR 2021, LNCS 13188, pp. 352–365, 2022.
https://doi.org/10.1007/978-3-031-02375-0_26

and their relative distance from the ego vehicle. Once the necessary information is ready, another task such as localization, path planning, and actuator control can be done. An autonomous driving vehicle is usually equipped with several sensors, mainly RGB cameras to capture multiple views of surroundings [11]. When it comes to computer vision problems, deep learning algorithm, especially convolutional neural network (CNN) has been proofed as the state-of-the-art by plenty of research [23]. For instance, a CNN-based hierarchical multi-scale attention model [26] improved by Borse et al. [1] is currently holding the highest intersection over union (IoU) score of 85.6% in performing semantic segmentation on a well-known autonomous driving dataset Cityscapes [5]. Another example comes from the depth estimation task which is related to the estimation of relative distance on each pixel of an image. Ranftl et al. [20] currently hold the best depth estimation performance on NYU-Depth V2 dataset [17] with root mean squared error of 0.357. Therefore, it would be the right decision if CNN is used as the main algorithm to deal with various perception tasks.

Currently, there are plenty of important tasks in the field of autonomous driving perception such as semantic segmentation and depth estimation as mentioned earlier. Developing a single-task deep learning model to handle each task can be costly and inefficient [30]. Instead of split the task, we develop multi-task learning (MTL) model that follows an encoder-decoder fashion with additional skip connections to deal with multiple perception tasks simultaneously. Then, another challenge comes from multi-input and multi-modal processing where multiple data need to be processed together to achieve a better understanding. To address this issue, a sensor fusion technique can be adopted where various sensors are deployed to provide more various data in representing the environmental condition [7]. In this research, we placed 8 sensors composed of RGB and DVS cameras in 4 different positions on the ego vehicle to capture front (F), left (L), right (R), and back (B) views. DVS sensors are used to support RGB cameras in providing more information as it is susceptible to illumination variations, especially during night time [16]. With various data modalities taken as inputs, the model is expected to perform better in a dynamically changing environment. In this research, the model is developed entirely from scratch without transfer learning from any pre-trained models so that the architecture is highly customizable. Moreover, we conduct the experiment on 2 different datasets gathered from CARLA simulator [6] to strengthen our findings. Based on the aforementioned approaches, the novelty of this research can be listed in the following points.

– We present a deep MTL model that has input-specified encoders and task-specified decoders. The model processes and fuses multiple inputs of RGB and DVS images to perform multiple views of semantic segmentation and depth estimation in one forward pass. Since the model is developed entirely from scratch, the architecture is highly extendable to retrieve more inputs.
– We study the influence of sensor fusion between RGB and DVS cameras. Based on the ablation experiment, our model gains more improvement when both RGB and DVS images are fused. Moreover, we also perform a compara-

tive study with another recent MTL model to clarify their performance based on the metric score and inference speed.

2   Related Work

To date, a lot of research in driving perception has been done. In this section, we explain several kinds of related research which are also inspiring our works.

2.1   Deep Multi-task Learning

In deep learning, the process of learning to perform several tasks simultaneously is called multi-task learning. MTL aims to leverage shared feature maps during the training process to boost the performance of each task [21]. There is plenty of studies in the MTL area that is applied to the autonomous driving vehicle problems such as conducted by Teichmann et al. [27] where a deep learning model called MultiNet is used to perform several perception tasks such as road segmentation, vehicle detection, and street classification simultaneously. The model works well, however, it needs improvement in recognizing more crucial and various objects on the road. Kocić et al. [12] presented a network architecture called J-Net that processes RGB images to perform various control tasks such as controlling the steering wheel, speed, brake, etc. However, the simulation condition still needs to be improved to test the model generalization. These issues are solved by Cipolla et al. [4] where they develop a semantic segmentation model to recognize more various kinds of objects in Cityscapes dataset [5]. It also performs instance segmentation and depth estimation by creating a branch of task-specified decoder for each task. However, it would be better if the model can take multiple inputs with multiple data modalities so that it can be applied to multi-view systems for a better understanding.

2.2   Sensor Fusion in Deep Learning

A study of multiple inputs processing on an autonomous driving perception model has been done by Hane et al. [9] where several cameras are placed in several different positions on the ego vehicle. Therefore, the model will have a better capability in understanding the environmental condition. Although it has more views of RGB images, the model may still fail during nighttime or heavy rain due to poor illumination conditions. Thus, it needs to be combined with another kind of sensor such as a DVS camera as an alternative in providing surrounding information, especially in performing an active perception [16,29]. Hence, the idea of using the DVS camera can also be adopted in solving an autonomous driving perception problem. To handle various data modalities, Nobis et al. [18] have shown that a deep learning model can be used to process multiple sensor data by fusing extracted feature maps from each input modality. Nobis et al. develop an object detection model called CameraRadarFusionNet (CRF-Net) that processes camera and radar data to get a better result on nuScene dataset

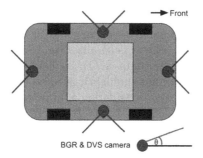

Fig. 1. Sensor placement on the ego vehicle. Four pairs of RGB and DVS cameras are mounted in 4 different positions. The camera's vertical angle of view θ is set to 20° to catch a better view of the surroundings. The red lines on each camera represent the horizontal field of view which is set to 90°.

[2]. CRF-Net provides a specific encoder for each input data and fuses extracted feature maps into the Feature Pyramid Network [15] to perform bounding boxes regression and classification in one forward pass.

In this research, we consider adopting several ideas shown in the aforementioned research. First, we utilize DVS cameras to provide more information as it is more robust against poor illumination problem [16,29]. However, instead of being used to replace RGB cameras, DVS cameras are utilized as support sensors. Therefore, we also adopt the idea of sensor fusion shown by Nobis et al. [18], especially on its strategy in providing an input-specified encoder to process each input modality and fuse them several times at several points in the architecture. Finally, we adopt the task-specified decoder inspired by Cipolla et al. [4] to create two branches of decoders that perform semantic segmentation and depth estimation simultaneously. Hence, a complete deep learning model that processes and fuses multiple inputs to perform multiple tasks can be achieved.

3   Methodology

In this section, we describe the generation of simulation data using CARLA simulator with a lot of settings on weather conditions, NPCs, sensors, and many more. Finally, the network architecture is explained along with hyperparameter tuning and experiment setup including the loss and metric formulation.

3.1   Dataset and Input/Output Representation

In this research, CARLA simulator[6] is used to generate thousands of simulation data for training, validation, and testing sets retrieved from F, L, R, B views of the ego vehicle as shown in Fig. 1. Various kinds of weather conditions (sunny, rainy, foggy, cloudy) and day times (morning, noon, evening, night) are considered to vary the simulation conditions. Besides that, we also use 2 different CARLA maps to ensure the fairness of model validation and testing. Then, numerous pedestrians and other vehicles such as cars, trucks, bikes, and motorcycles are also spawned to simulate more realistic conditions. Therefore, the model is expected to have a better generalization.

As for the model inputs/outputs (I/O), both RGB and DVS images along with their semantic segmentation and depth estimation ground truths. To evaluate the model performance with considering a fair experimental study, we create 2 different sets of data named set A and B which are taken from 2 different CARLA maps named town01 and town02. Based on the CARLA documentation, town01 and town02 are different but have similar characteristics. Therefore, we can make a fair experiment by separating the training set from validation and testing sets completely by differentiating the map. In set A, 4000 pairs of I/O from town01 are used for training, 1000 pairs of I/O from town02 for validation and another 1000 pairs of I/O from different regional areas in town02 are used for testing. Meanwhile, in set B, we retrieve the same amount and ratio of data but with a different map configuration where town02 is used for training, and town01 is for validation and testing. With this scenario, a fair experiment can be achieved where the road situation for each set are totally different.

During the data generation process, we retrieve RGB images as $I_{RGB} \in \mathbb{R}^{128 \times 128 \times 3}$ which represent the height, width, and RGB channels with 8-bit value on each pixel. Meanwhile, the original form of DVS images are arrays $A_{DVS} \in \mathbb{R}^{N \times 4}$ which represents the total N number of 4-elements 1D array retrieved in one simulation step. The element for each array is composed of timestamp, x-position, y-position, and polarization. The timestamp is used for data synchronization with RGB images and ground truths. Then, the x and y-position show the pixel location considered to have a brightness change. The x,y-position has a maximum range of 128. Meanwhile, the polarization can be positive or negative based on the brightness change. Depends on how many pixels are changing, the total number of N can be different for each DVS array A_{DVS}. Thus, in order to fix the number of array elements in A_{DVS} and also to match with the input layer of the network architecture, we pre-process DVS arrays to be DVS images $I_{DVS} \in \mathbb{R}^{128 \times 128 \times 2}$ which represent the height, width, and polarization channels. The x,y-position takes place on the height and width of I_{DVS}, while the polarization takes place on the channel where the first channel is used for positive polarization and the second channel is used for negative polarization. We set the pixel that has polarization to have a full 8-bit value and otherwise 0. Mathematically, it can be written as in (1).

$$I_{DVS_i} = \begin{cases} 255 & \text{if } I_{DVS_i} \text{ is polarized} \\ 0 & \text{otherwise,} \end{cases} \tag{1}$$

where I_{DVS_i} is the positive or negative polarization of i_{th} pixel of the DVS image I_{DVS}. As for ground truths, semantic segmentation images are retrieved from the CARLA simulator following the RGB color pallets in the cityscapes dataset [5]. We use 6 classes of objects (poles, road, road lanes, sidewalks, pedestrian, vehicles) that are considered as important objects in the area of driving perception. We handled the semantic segmentation mask for each class by separating each unique colormap in $I_{segmentation} \in \mathbb{R}^{128 \times 128 \times 3}$ and store them into a tensor $I_{mask} \in \mathbb{R}^{128 \times 128 \times 6}$ where each element has the value of 0 or 1 depends on what kind of semantic class appear on each pixel in $I_{segmentation}$.

Meanwhile, the ground truth of the depth estimation task can be obtained by simply read the logarithmic depth images as $I_{depth} \in \mathbb{R}^{128 \times 128 \times 1}$ which represent the height, width, and 1 channel of 8-bit logarithmic depth value. For the training purpose, each element in all input and output tensors are normalized between 0 to 1 so that each element will have the same influence. Finally, the channel for each input and output tensors are moved to the first axis as needed by PyTorch deep learning framework [19]. Therefore, RGB and DVS inputs size become $(3 \times 128 \times 128)$ and $(2 \times 128 \times 128)$ respectively. Meanwhile, semantic segmentation and depth estimation outputs size become $(6 \times 128 \times 128)$ and $(1 \times 128 \times 128)$ respectively.

3.2   Network Architecture

As mentioned in the previous subsection, we use PyTorch deep learning framework [19] to build the model along with other python packages. The visualization of the model architecture can be seen in Fig. 2. The model is following the encoder-decoder style [28] with additional skip connections inspired from UNet paper [22]. Each feature map in both RGB and DVS encoders is connected to its symmetric feature maps in both depth estimation and semantic segmentation encoders. With this configuration, each encoder can act as a supporter for one another. For example, when the illumination is very poor (e.g. night) and RGB cameras are failed to capture enough information of the surroundings, the network can learn how to leverage extracted information mainly from the DVS encoder. On the other hand, when the car is not moving (e.g. at the crossroads) and there is no enough information as the brightness change is very rare, the network can learn how to rely more on the RGB encoder. In this architecture, each convolutional block on encoder and decoder has 2 times of $((3 \times 3)$ convolutional layer + batch normalization + ReLU activation). Meanwhile, each convolutional block on the bottlenecks has 3 times of them to extract more information from all views concatenation. Then, they are followed by (2×2) max-pooling on the encoder side and (2×2) bilinear upsampling on the decoder side. To deal with the overfitting issue, several dropout layers with $p = 0.5$ are placed on the bottleneck [24]. Finally, a pointwise (1×1) convolutional layer is used to reduce the channel number of feature maps to match with the ground truth size. Then, it is followed by a sigmoid activation for semantic segmentation and a ReLU activation for depth estimation.

In order to discover the advantage of sensor fusion on an MTL model, an ablation study is performed during the experiment. First, we remove the DVS input block (blue) so that the model only processes RGB images to perform semantic segmentation and depth estimation. We refer to this model as A0 where only RGB images are fed into the network. Then, on the second model named A1, DVS inputs are added so that the model is processing 4 pairs of RGB and DVS images. Furthermore, feature maps from DVS encoders are concatenated to the semantic segmentation and depth estimation decoders as well as feature maps from RGB encoders.

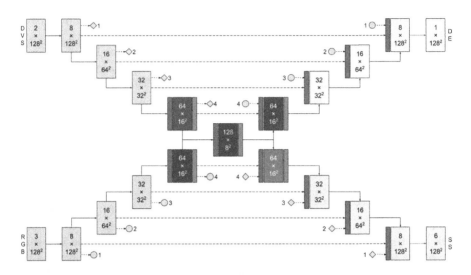

Fig. 2. Network architecture. Blue and green boxes represent the inputs and feature maps for each view (F, L, R, B). Dark blue and dark green boxes are the concatenation across all views, while the dark red box is the concatenation of all feature maps. Then, grey and yellow boxes represent feature maps and outputs for each view of depth estimation (DE) and semantic segmentation (SS). 5 boxes in the center are considered as bottlenecks where a dropout layer (purple) is applied for each. Dark grey and dark yellow boxes are the specific bottlenecks for each task. Solid lines represent the convolution block, while dashed lines represent the skip connection and concatenation (orange boxes). Each dashed line is connecting the feature map on encoders with its symmetric feature map on decoders. Denoted with numbered small blue squares and green circles, both encoders are used to support both tasks decoders. Finally, red lines represent the final pointwise convolution followed with an activation function. (Color figure online)

3.3 Experiment Setup

We set the batch size to 16 so that there will be 250 steps of weights update in one epoch. Kaiming initialization method [8] is used to initialize entire model weights so that the model can be converged faster. Then, a standard Stochastic Gradient Descent (SGD) [25] with momentum $\beta = 0.9$ is used to train the model. For semantic segmentation loss, pixel-wise binary cross-entropy (BCE) (2) combined with dice loss (3) are calculated together to allow loss diversity.

$$\mathcal{L}_{BCE} = \frac{1}{4} \sum_{t=1}^{4} -\frac{1}{N} \sum_{i=1}^{N} y_{ti} \times log(\hat{y}_{ti}) + (1 - y_{ti}) \times log(1 - \hat{y}_{ti}) \qquad (2)$$

$$\mathcal{L}_{dice} = \frac{1}{4} \sum_{t=1}^{4} 1 - \frac{2|\hat{y}_t \cap y_t|}{|\hat{y}_t| + |y_t|} \qquad (3)$$

We average all losses from all views (F, L, R, B). N is total elements in the predicted output tensor of task t (denoted with $\hat{y}_t$) which is the same as the ground truth y_t with the size of $(6 \times 128 \times 128)$. Meanwhile, y_{ti} is ground-truth value of ith pixel in y_t and $\hat{y}_{ti}$ is predicted value of ith pixel in $\hat{y}_t$ after sigmoid activation. Then, as for the depth estimation loss, Huber loss (4) is used since it has some benefits compared to mean absolute error (MAE) that constantly have a large gradient and mean squared error (MSE) which is not robust against outliers. Huber loss is suitable for any regression-based task as it curves around the minima and is robust against outliers.

$$\mathcal{L}_{huber} = \frac{1}{4} \sum_{t=1}^{4} \frac{1}{N} \sum_{i=1}^{N} z_{ti}, \tag{4}$$

where z_{ti} is given by (5).

$$z_{ij} = \begin{cases} 0.5(\hat{y}_{ij} - y_{ij})^2 & \text{if } |\hat{y}_{ij} - y_{ij}| < \alpha \\ \alpha(|\hat{y}_{ij} - y_{ij}| - 0.5\alpha) & \text{otherwise} \end{cases} \tag{5}$$

Similar to the semantic segmentation, y_{ti} is the ground truth value of ith pixel in y_t and $\hat{y}_{ti}$ is the predicted value of ith pixel in $\hat{y}_t$ after ReLU activation. However, the size of $\hat{y}_t$ and y_t is only $(1 \times 128 \times 128)$ since there is only 1 channel containing the normalized logarithmic depth value. Then, we set $\alpha = 0.5$ as the threshold for Huber loss to start to curve around the minima. Finally, the total loss can be calculated as in (6).

$$\mathcal{L}_{total} = (\mathcal{L}_{BCE} + \mathcal{L}_{dice}) + 1.5 \times \mathcal{L}_{huber} \tag{6}$$

Huber loss is weighted with a constant of 1.5 to balance the huge value computed by the semantic segmentation loss function which is composed of BCE and dice loss. Therefore, the model is expected to not losing its learning focus on the depth estimation task. During the training process, weight decay w_d is also used to penalize the model complexity and to prevent overfitting [13]. Thus, the final total loss can be calculated as in (7).

$$\mathcal{L}_{total} = \mathcal{L}_{total} + w_d \times \Sigma w^2, \tag{7}$$

The sum-squared of all model weights (Σw^2) can be very large. Thus, we set a small value of $w_d = 0.0001$ so that it will not affect the total loss too much, as we want the model to learn more from depth estimation and semantic segmentation losses. In order to evaluate model performance, we also compute metric functions composed by average IoU (8) and average MAE (9).

$$IoU = \frac{1}{4} \sum_{i=1}^{4} \frac{|\hat{y}_t \cap y_t|}{|\hat{y}_t| \cup |y_t|} \tag{8}$$

$$MAE = \frac{1}{4} \sum_{i=1}^{4} \frac{1}{N} \sum_{i=1}^{N} |\hat{y}_{ti} - y_{ti}| \tag{9}$$

As shown in (8) and (9), the IoU and MAE are averaged over all views which means that we evaluate the model performance globally. Finally, we also average the loss and metric on all batches for both training and validation sets on each epoch to monitor and evaluate the model performance. In accordance with the fast and smooth update of the model weights, we set the initial learning rate $\eta_0 = 0.1$ and reduce it by half gradually if the validation total metric (TM) (10) is not decreasing in 5 epochs in a row. The learning rate reduction will stop if it hits the minimum learning rate of $\eta_{min} = 0.00001$.

$$TM = MAE + (1 - IoU)$$ (10)

To prevent unnecessary computational cost, an early stopping strategy is used to stop the training process if there is no drop in the validation total metric in 35 epochs in a row. Therefore, the total epochs might be different for each model.

4   Result and Discussion

In this section, an ablation study is performed to study the effect of adding DVS images as the model inputs. In this study, we create 2 different model variants where the first one only takes RGB images (A0) while the other one takes both RGB and DVS images (A1) as described in Subsect. 3.2. Then, to clarify the model performance, we also conduct a comparative study against another MTL model named W-Net [3] that performs the same tasks. Since there are 4 views around the ego vehicle, we create a W-Net model for each view. The evaluation is conducted by comparing metric scores on the validation and testing set as described in Subsect. 3.3. Moreover, we also compare the inference speed to strengthen our justification. Finally, as the qualitative study, we provide several samples of inference results on both test sets.

4.1   Performance Gain by Sensor Fusion

RGB images are usually used as the only input when dealing with semantic segmentation and depth estimation tasks. However, in this research, we study the influence of providing DVS images as the input and fused together with RGB images in the network architecture to leverage the extracted information. As mentioned in Subsect. 3.2, in order to evaluate the contribution of DVS images, we first remove the DVS input block on the Fig. 2 and named the model as A0 model, then compare its performance with the A1 model that has both RGB and DVS input blocks on its architecture. To perform fair testing and comparison, we use 2 different datasets as described in Subsect. 3.1. The comparison of validation total metric, semantic segmentation IoU, and depth estimation MAE on set A and set B can be shown in Fig. 3. The A1 model has a lower total metric score compared to the A0 model on both validation sets. During the validation process, the A1 model has the record of the lowest validation TM of 0.148 (set A) and 0.190 (set B).

Based on the inference result on testing sets shown in Table 1, the A1 model also has lower TM scores of 0.188 (set A) and 0.186 (set B). Considering that the A1 model has a better score in all validation and testing sets, it can be said that DVS is giving a positive influence on the model performance. However, as a result of having more encoders to process DVS data, the A1 model inference slower than the A0 model with an FPS rate of around 83 to 84. Meanwhile, the qualitative result can be seen in Fig. 4 where both A0 and A1 models are deployed in the night (test set B: town01, left) and cloudy day (test set A: town02, right). The A1 model seems to have a better result compared to the A0 model. The A1 model is more stable in segmenting rare objects such as poles and the small appearance of surrounding vehicles, especially during a poor illumination condition (night) as it can leverage the information provided by the DVS. However, both model seems comparable in the depth estimation task.

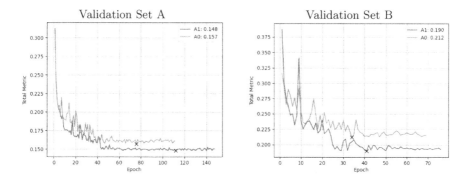

Fig. 3. Performance comparison during validation process Note: Black × mark means the best score among all epochs.

Table 1. Model performance comparison on test sets

Dataset	Model	TM Score	Depth MAE	Segm. IoU	FPS
Test A	A0	0.196 ± < 0.001	**0.056 ± <0.001**	0.860 ± <0.001	**100**
	A1	0.188 ± < 0.001	0.059 ± <0.001	0.871 ± <0.001	83
	W-Net[3]	**0.166 ± < 0.001**	0.057 ± <0.001	**0.891 ± <0.001**	58
Test B	A0	0.193 ± < 0.001	0.038 ± <0.001	0.845 ± <0.001	**104**
	A1	**0.186 ± < 0.001**	**0.035 ± <0.001**	**0.849 ± <0.001**	84
	W-Net[3]	0.220 ± 0.001	0.038 ± <0.001	0.818 ± <0.001	57

The uncertainty on each prediction score is measured by calculating the variance over 1000 inference results. Meanwhile, the speed test is conducted on the same NVIDIA RTX 3090 with batch size = 1 and calculated in frame per second (FPS). The FPS difference on both datasets is caused by the fluctuating GPU condition.

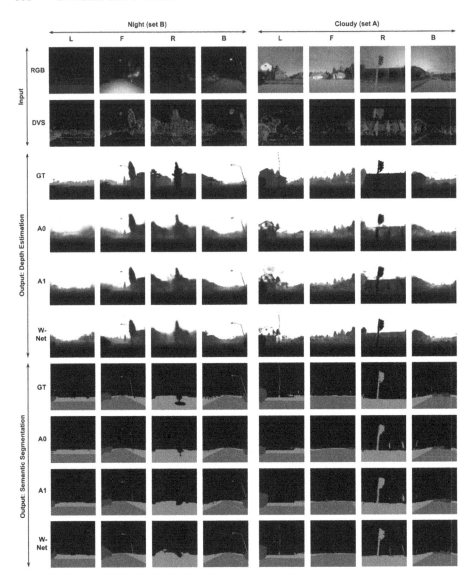

Fig. 4. Inference on test images. Note: F (front); L (left); R (right); B (back); GT (ground truth).

4.2   Comparison with Another Model

As mentioned in Sect. 1, a further comparative study against another MTL model is conducted to clarify the model performance. In this research, we compare our model with W-Net [3] which is composed of 2 serially connected UNet models [22]. W-Net uses its first UNet block to perform semantic segmentation first. Then, the prediction is concatenated with the RGB image as the input for the second UNet block to perform depth estimation. Therefore, W-Net is able to perform both semantic segmentation and depth estimation simultaneously in one forward pass. For a fair comparison, we follow the training configuration described in the W-Net paper to train the model using our datasets. Following the mathematical formulas described in Subsect. 3.3, the comparison of metric scores can be seen in Table 1. To be noted, the metric score is averaged across all views as there are 4 independent W-Net models in total.

Based on Table 1, both A1 and W-Net models can be said to be comparable to each other. On test set A, W-Net performs better than the A1 model with a lower TM score of 0.166. Meanwhile, on test set B, the A1 model is surpassing W-Net with a lower TM score of 0.186. Then, as shown in Fig. 4, W-Net seems to have a better result, especially when the illumination is enough (set A) as it has much more layers compared to the A1 model. W-Net can estimate and segment very thin objects such as light poles on both left images of depth estimation and semantic segmentation. However, in the term of inference speed, A1 model is still better with an FPS rate of more than 80 on both datasets. Meanwhile, W-Net only achieves an FPS rate of below 60 when tested with the same device. Therefore, even though the TM score is comparable, it can be said that a single A1 model is more preferable as it can perform faster inference compared to the combination of 4 W-Net models.

5   Conclusion and Future Work

In this research, we discover the usefulness of the sensor fusion of RGB and DVS cameras by comparing 2 model variants: A0 (without DVS) and A1 (with DVS). Then, a comparative study against another model named W-Net is conducted to clarify the model performance.

Based on the ablation study, we conclude that fusing both RGB and DVS images will boost the overall model performance since the model can take more distinctive information from both RGB and DVS encoders. From the test result on both datasets, the total metric scores are constantly lowered from 0.196 to 0.188 (set A) and 0.193 to 0.186 (set B). Moreover, the A1 model can deal with a poor illumination issue compared to the A0 model that fails to segment surrounding vehicles correctly. Considering that the A1 model is gaining more improvement, it can be said that taking both RGB and DVS images is better to get a more clear scene understanding. Furthermore, the A1 model still maintains to has comparable performance compared with the combination of 4 W-Net models. Considering the further model deployment, the A1 model is more preferable as it can inference faster with an FPS rate above 80.

In the future, the research can be extended to study the network architecture modification, especially on its convolutional blocks. There are plenty of well-known convolutional blocks that are able to improve the model performance further. Then, a study on loss function formulation is also an interesting study, especially in dealing with rare objects issue.

References

1. Borse, S., Wang, Y., Zhang, Y., Porikli, F.: InverseForm: a loss function for structured boundary-aware segmentation. In: Proceedings of the IEEE/CVF Conference on Computer Vision and Pattern Recognition, pp. 5901–5911 (2021)
2. Caesar, H., et al.: nuScenes: a multimodal dataset for autonomous driving. In: Proceedings of the IEEE/CVF Conference on Computer Vision and Pattern Recognition, pp. 11618–11628 (2020)
3. Cantrell, K., Miller, C., Morato, C.: Practical depth estimation with image segmentation and serial U-Nets. In: Proceedings of the International Conference on Vehicle Technology and Intelligent Transport Systems, pp. 406–414 (2020)
4. Cipolla, R., Gal, Y., Kendall, A.: Multi-task learning using uncertainty to weigh losses for scene geometry and semantics. In: Proceedings of the IEEE/CVF Conference on Computer Vision and Pattern Recognition, pp. 7482–7491 (2018)
5. Cordts, M., et al.: The cityscapes dataset for semantic urban scene understanding. In: Proceedings of the IEEE/CVF Conference on Computer Vision and Pattern Recognition, pp. 3213–3223 (2016)
6. Dosovitskiy, A., Ros, G., Codevilla, F., Lopez, A., Koltun, V.: CARLA: an open urban driving simulator. In: Proceedings of the Annual Conference on Robot Learning, pp. 1–16 (2017)
7. Fayyad, J., Jaradat, M.A., Gruyer, D., Najjaran, H.: Deep learning sensor fusion for autonomous vehicle perception and localization: a review. Sensors **20**(15) (2020)
8. He, K., Zhang, X., Ren, S., Sun, J.: Delving deep into rectifiers: surpassing human-level performance on imagenet classification. In: Proceedings of the IEEE/CVF International Conference on Computer Vision, pp. 1026–1034 (2015)
9. Häne, C., et al.: 3D visual perception for self-driving cars using a multi-camera system: calibration, mapping, localization, and obstacle detection. Image Vision Comput. **68**, 14–27 (2017)
10. Kato, S., Takeuchi, E., Ishiguro, Y., Ninomiya, Y., Takeda, K., Hamada, T.: An open approach to autonomous vehicles. IEEE Micro **35**(6), 60–68 (2015)
11. Khatab, E., Onsy, A., Varley, M., Abouelfarag, A.: Vulnerable objects detection for autonomous driving: a review. Integration **78**, 36–48 (2021)
12. Kocic, J., Jovicic, N., Drndarevic, V.: An end-to-end deep neural network for autonomous driving designed for embedded automotive platforms. Sensors **19**(9) (2019)
13. Krogh, A., Hertz, J.A.: A simple weight decay can improve generalization. In: Proceedings of the International Conference on Neural Information Processing Systems, pp. 950–957 (1991)
14. Levinson, J., et al.: Towards fully autonomous driving: systems and algorithms. In: Proceedings of the IEEE Intelligent Vehicles Symposium, pp. 163–168 (2011)
15. Lin, T.Y., Dollár, P., Girshick, R., He, K., Hariharan, B., Belongie, S.: Feature pyramid networks for object detection. In: Proceedings of the IEEE/CVF Conference on Computer Vision and Pattern Recognition, pp. 936–944 (2017)
16. Munir, F., Azam, S., Jeon, M., Lee, B.G., Pedrycz, W.: LDNet: end-to-end lane marking detection approach using a dynamic vision sensor. IEEE Trans. Intell. Transp. Syst. 1–17 (2021)
17. Nathan, S., Derek, H., Pushmeet, K., Rob, F.: Indoor segmentation and support inference from RGBD images. In: Proceedings of the European Conference on Computer Vision, pp. 746–760 (2012)

18. Nobis, F., Geisslinger, M., Weber, M., Betz, J., Lienkamp, M.: A deep learning-based radar and camera sensor fusion architecture for object detection. In: Proceedings of the Sensor Data Fusion: trends, Solutions, Applications, pp. 1–7 (2019)
19. Paszke, A., et al.: PyTorch: an imperative style, high performance deep learning library. In: Advances in Neural Information Processing Systems, vol. 32, pp. 8024–8035 (2019)
20. Ranftl, R., Bochkovskiy, A., Koltun, V.: Vision transformers for dense prediction. ArXiv (2021). https://arxiv.org/abs/2103.13413
21. Ravoor, P.C., Sudarshan, T.S.B.: Deep learning methods for multi-species animal re-identification and tracking - a survey. Comput. Sci. Rev. **38**, 100289 (2020)
22. Ronneberger, O., Fischer, P., Brox, T.: U-Net: convolutional networks for biomedical image segmentation. In: Proceedings of the International Conference on Medical Image Computing and Computer-Assisted Intervention, pp. 234–241 (2015)
23. Shekhar, H., Seal, S., Kedia, S., Guha, A.: Survey on applications of machine learning in the field of computer vision. In: Emerging Technology in Modelling and Graphics, pp. 667–678 (2020)
24. Srivastava, N., Hinton, G., Krizhevsky, A., Sutskever, I., Salakhutdinov, R.: Dropout: a simple way to prevent neural networks from overfitting. J. Mach. Learn. Res **15**(56), 1929–1958 (2014)
25. Sutskever, I., Martens, J., Dahl, G., Hinton, G.: On the importance of initialization and momentum in deep learning. In: Proceedings of the International Conference on Machine Learning. pp. 1139–1147 (2013)
26. Tao, A., Sapra, K., Catanzaro, B.: Hierarchical multi-scale attention for semantic segmentation. ArXiv (2020). https://arxiv.org/abs/2005.10821
27. Teichmann, M., Weber, M., Zollner, M., Cipolla, R., Urtasun, R.: MultiNet: real-time joint semantic reasoning for autonomous driving. In: Proceedings of the IEEE Intelligent Vehicles Symposium, pp. 1013–1020 (2018)
28. Ye, J.C., Sung, W.K.: Understanding geometry of encoder-decoder CNNs. In: Proceedings of the International Conference on Machine Learning, pp. 7064–7073 (2019)
29. Yousefzadeh, A., Orchard, G., Gotarredona, T.S., Barranco, B.L.: Active perception with dynamic vision sensors. Minimum saccades with optimum recognition. IEEE Trans. Biomed. Circuits Syst. **12**(4), 927–939 (2018)
30. Zhang, Y., Yang, Q.: A survey on multi-task learning. IEEE Trans. Knowl. Data Eng. (early access) (2021)

ARTSeg: Employing Attention for Thermal Images Semantic Segmentation

Farzeen Munir[(✉)], Shoaib Azam, Unse Fatima, and Moongu Jeon

School of Electrical Engineering and Computer Science, Gwangju Institute of Science
and Technology, Gwangju, South Korea
{farzeen.munir,shoaibazam,mgjeon}@gist.ac.kr, unse.fatima@gm.gist.ac.kr

Abstract. The research advancements have made the neural network algorithms deployed in the autonomous vehicle to perceive the surrounding. The standard exteroceptive sensors that are utilized for the perception of the environment are cameras and Lidar. Therefore, the neural network algorithms developed using these exteroceptive sensors have provided the necessary solution for the autonomous vehicle's perception. One major drawback of these exteroceptive sensors is their operability in adverse weather conditions, for instance, low illumination and night conditions. The useability and affordability of thermal cameras in the sensor suite of the autonomous vehicle provide the necessary improvement in the autonomous vehicle's perception in adverse weather conditions. The semantics of the environment benefits the robust perception, which can be achieved by segmenting different objects in the scene. In this work, we have employed the thermal camera for semantic segmentation. We have designed an attention-based Recurrent Convolution Network (RCNN) encoder-decoder architecture named ARTSeg for thermal semantic segmentation. The main contribution of this work is the design of encoder-decoder architecture, which employ units of RCNN for each encoder and decoder block. Furthermore, additive attention is employed in the decoder module to retain high-resolution features and improve the localization of features. The efficacy of the proposed method is evaluated on the available public dataset, showing better performance with other state-of-the-art methods in mean intersection over union (IoU).

Keywords: Thermal image · Semantic segmentation · Recurrent convolution neural network · Attention

1 Introduction

The last three decades have shown significant technological advancements that reflects the development of efficient sensors. The applicability of these sensors in the autonomous vehicle ensures its safe and secure services to the urban

© Springer Nature Switzerland AG 2022
C. Wallraven et al. (Eds.): ACPR 2021, LNCS 13188, pp. 366–378, 2022.
https://doi.org/10.1007/978-3-031-02375-0_27

environment, as indicated by SOTIF-ISO/PAS-21448[1]. Keeping safety as a priority in autonomous vehicles, perception of the environment play a critical role along with localization, planning and control module [1–3]. In the context of perception, the most common exteroceptive sensors that are being deployed are cameras (visible spectrum) and Lidar. The utilization of these sensor modalities provides the necessary perception for the autonomous vehicle. However, these sensors have limitations in adverse weather conditions at night and low illumination environments. For instance, cameras (visible spectrum) are operated in the visible spectrum domain and provide an in-depth understanding of the environment. Still, environmental conditions like sun-glare, low illumination affect the camera result, thus yielding low performance in perception algorithms. On the other hand, as a surrogate to 2D information from cameras, Lidar gives the 3D information about the environment. Lidar provides 3D information of the environment by making a point cloud map by projecting nearly thousands of laser beams to the environment. Besides, Lidar effectiveness in providing the detailed 3D representation of the environment, its expensive cost and limitation in adverse weather conditions are the prime concern of its detriment. On the other hand, thermal cameras, contrary to cameras (visible-spectrum) and Lidar, enable the perception algorithms to be utilized in adverse weather conditions, such as at night or low illumination environmental conditions [4].

Thermal cameras operate in the infrared domain and capture the infrared radiation emitted by the different entities in the environment having the temperature above absolute zero [6]. This property of the thermal camera makes it an optimal solution to be included in the sensor suite of the autonomous vehicle for the perception of the environment in low illumination and night conditions. Furthermore, besides thermal cameras applicability in adverse weather conditions, the affordability of thermal cameras gives the potential to be utilized in different perception tasks for the autonomous vehicle. These perception tasks involve different computer vision applications such as object detection [7,8], visual tracking [9] and person re-identification [10]. In order to determine the semantics of environment for the scene understanding for the autonomous vehicle, semantic segmentation plays a vital role in the perception of the autonomous vehicle. The capacity of thermal cameras to operate at night and low illumination conditions motivate to use of the thermal camera for semantic segmentation and investigate the semantic segmentation problem using the thermal cameras.

In computer vision, semantic segmentation provides an in-depth understanding of the scene by employing a semantic label to each pixel in the image. Despite traditional machine learning approaches used to tackle semantic segmentation problems, deep learning approaches gain unprecedented success. For instance, most of these deep learning techniques (convolutional neural networks) are applied using the RGB images for semantic segmentation. Thermal cameras provide the grey-scale image that benefits the neural networks employed on thermal images for different computer vision tasks.

---

[1] https://www.daimler.com/innovation/case/autonomous/safety-first-for-automated-driving-2.htm.

This work explores the thermal image segmentation problem by designing a novel encoder-decoder architecture called ARTSeg. The encoder consists of a residual recurrent convolution block accompanied by a max-pooling layer. The encoder outputs a latent representation of features which is fed to the decoder. The decoder incorporates additive attention from the residual connections from the encoder. The ARTSeg is evaluated on a public dataset and compared with state-of-the-art methods. The main contributions of this work are as follows:

1. We have designed a novel encoder-decoder architecture using a residual recurrent convolution neural network.
2. We have employed the additive attention mechanism to enhance the localization of encoded features. Further, no post-processing steps are used because of utilizing the attention for the thermal image segmentation.
3. The proposed method's efficacy is performed on available public datasets shows better performance in terms of average accuracy and intersection over the union in contrast to state-of-the-art methods.

The rest of the paper is organized as follows: Sect. 2 explains the related work. The proposed method is described in the Sect. 3. Section 4 illustrate the experimentation and results for the proposed method. Finally, Sect. 5 concludes the paper.

2   Related Work

The concept of semantic segmentation plays a critical role in the robust perception of the environment for autonomous driving. Deep neural networks, especially convolution neural networks, are mostly used for semantic segmentation using RGB cameras as a sensor modality. The early state-of-the-art method that is employed for the semantic segmentation is Fully Convolutional Network (FCN) proposed by [5]. In FCN, the fully connected layers are replaced with the convolutional layers to output the full resolution maps for the semantic segmentation using the backbone network of VGG16 [23], and GoogleNet [11] architectures, respectively.

In literature, the encoder-decoder architecture is also used for semantic segmentation. In the encoder-decoder architecture, the features are encoded to give the latent representation and then decoded to provide the object details and spatial resolution. [22] have proposed the encoder-decoder architecture named SegNet. The encoder network consists of convolutional layers adopted from the VGG16 [23] network to learn the encoded representation followed by batch-normalization, rectified linear unit (ReLU) units and max-pooling layers. The decoder follows the same encoder architecture for upsampling the encoded features for semantic segmentation. Similarly, using the encoder-decoder architecture, the encoder of the network is improved by using image pyramids [28,29], conditional random fields [28], spatial pyramid pooling [28] and atrous convolution [30,31]. There is a trade-off between accuracy and speed; in literature, some research is focused on improving the inference speed using the encoder-decoder architecture; for instance, [13] have proposed the encoder-decoder architecture ENet that is optimized for the fast inference speed for semantic segmentation. In order to retain the feature generalization, skip connections have been introduced for the semantic segmentation as proposed by UNet [12].

Besides, using the single sensor modality, for instance, RGB images, in literature, the fusion of thermal and visible-spectrum RGB domain is also investigated for semantic segmentation. [15] have proposed FuseNet for the semantic segmentation by incorporating the fusion of visible-spectrum RGB domain with the thermal domain. Similarly, MFNet [19] and RTFNet [21] networks follows the encoder-decoder architecture for the semantic segmentation using the fusion of RGB and thermal data. [20] have proposed the FuseSeg using the Bayesian fusion theory for the semantic segmentation using both RGB and thermal data. In addition to the fusion techniques, some research is focused on multi-spectral domain adaptation [32–34].

In contrast to the literature review, we have designed a novel encoder-decoder architecture using the residual recurrent convolution layers followed by an attention mechanism to retain the feature generalization for semantic segmentation. Furthermore, we have explicitly used the thermal data for the semantic segmentation without employing the fusion or domain adaption techniques in this work.

3   Methods

This section presents the proposed method for the thermal image segmentation, as illustrated in Fig. 1. The proposed method is composed of encoder-decoder architecture. The encoder module of the proposed method contains the residual recurrent convolution block (RRCNN) followed by the max-pooling layer. The residual recurrent convolutional block is comprised of recurrent convolutional layers and skip connections from the encoder to decoder module. The encoder module of the architecture receives the thermal image as input and generates the encoded feature representation for the input image. Suppose x_l represent the input image at the lth layer of the residual recurrent convolutional block, and a pixel is located at (u, v) at the input image on the p feature map of the recurrent convolution layer, then the output o_{uvp} is expressed in Eq. 1.

$$o^l_{uvp} = (w^f_p)^T * x^f_l(u, v)(t) + (w^r_p)^T * x^r_l(u, v)(t - 1) + b_p, \qquad (1)$$

where w^f_p and w^r_p are the weights of convolutional and recurrent convolutional layer respectively and b_p is the bias of the network. The inputs to the convolution and l^{th} layer recurrent convolutional layer are represented as $x^f_l(u, v)(t)$ and $x^r_l(u, v)(t-1)$ respectively. In Fig. 1 the recurrent convolution layer are represented in the RRCNN block with the "arrow" indicating the recurrence. The output of the recurrent convolutional layer is batch-normalized, and fed to the rectified linear activation function (ReLU) as shown in Eq. 2.

$$\mathfrak{F}(\mathbf{x_1}, \boldsymbol{w_l}) = f(o^l_{uvp}(t))) = max(0, o^l_{uvp}(t)), \qquad (2)$$

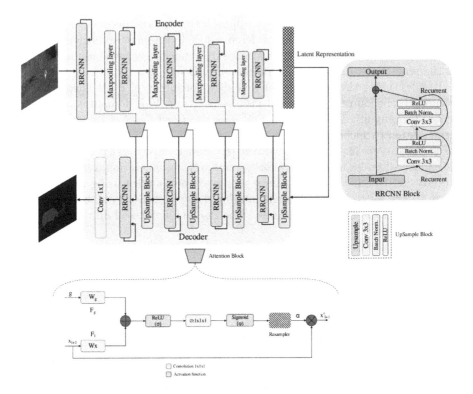

Fig. 1. The overall framework of ARTSeg Network consists of an encoder-decoder architecture.

$\mathfrak{F}(\mathbf{x_l}, \boldsymbol{w_l})$ represents the outcome of the activation function from the lth layer recurrent convolutional network. This is summed with the input x_l in residual to give us the output of RRCNN block as expressed as Eq. 3.

$$x_{l+1} = x_l + \mathfrak{F}(\mathbf{x_l}, \boldsymbol{w_l}), \tag{3}$$

where x_{l+1} represent the outcome from the RRCNN block.

The decoder module follows the same architecture of the encoder module with the addition of Upsample block and additive attention in the skip connections. The decoder includes the same RRCNN block as the encoder module, but the RRCNN module is used to upsampling the encoded features. Figure 1 shows the decoder module with attention block. The output of the attention is calculated by the element-wise multiplication of attention coefficient and input feature maps from as shown in Eq. 4.

$$x'_{l+1} = x_{l+1} \cdot \alpha, \tag{4}$$

The purpose of the attention module is to focus on the salient region for the thermal image segmentation. Mathematically, the attention of the network is given by Eq. 5. The term g represents the vector taken from the lowest layer of the network. The detailed architecture is presented in Table 1.

Table 1. The detailed architecture of the proposed ARTSeg

	Layer	Output size
	Input data	
Encoder	RRCNN-1 block	32 * 256 * 256
	Max pooling	32 * 128 * 128
	RRCNN-2 block	64 * 128 * 128
	Max pooling	64 * 64 * 64
	RRCNN-3 block	128 * 64 * 64
	Max pooling	128 * 32 * 32
	RRCNN-4 block	256 * 32 * 32
	Max pooling	256 * 8 * 8
	RCNN-5 block	256 * 8 * 8
Decoder	Up-Block	128 * 32 * 32
	Attention Module	256 * 32 * 32
	RRCNN-4 block	128 * 32 * 32
	Up-Block	128 * 64 * 64
	Attention Module	256 * 64 * 64
	RRCNN-3 block	128 * 64 * 64
	Up-Block	64 * 128 * 128
	Attention Module	128 * 128 * 128
	RRCNN-2 block	64 * 128 * 128
	Up-Block	32 * 256 * 256
	Attention Module	64 * 256 * 256
	RRCNN-1 Block	32 * 256 * 256
Output	Conv 1X1	5 * 256 * 256

$$s_{att}^l = \phi^T(\sigma(W_x^T x_{l+1}^i + W_g^T g^i + b_g)) + b_\phi,$$
$$\alpha^l = \varphi(s_{att}^l(x_{l+1}^i, g^i; \Theta_{att})),$$
(5)

where σ and φ represent ReLU and sigmoid activation function respectively. The W_x and W_g shows the linear transformation for the attention network. In addition, the Upsample block includes an upsampling layer followed by convolutional layer, batch normalization and the ReLU activation unit. The semantic segmentation output is obtained by placing the final convolution layer of kernel size 1×1 at the final RRCNN block in the decoder layer.

4   Experimentation and Results

This section explains the experimentation and results of the proposed method. The performance of the proposed method is evaluated on the available public dataset [19]. The efficacy of the proposed method is compared with the state-of-the-art methods for thermal image semantic segmentation. For the evaluation, we have adopted the standard metrics: Average class accuracy and mean Intersection over Union (IoU). The following section discusses the details of experimentation and results.

4.1   Thermal Semantic Segmentation Dataset

We have utilized the available public dataset for thermal image segmentation provided by [19]. The dataset is comprised of thermal and visible-spectrum RGB images. The dataset is collected using the InfRec R500 thermal camera, simultaneously capturing the thermal spectrum and visible spectrum images. The range of the thermal spectrum for collecting the images is $814\,\mu$m, giving the images of resolution 480×640. However, the field of view of the visible-spectrum image and the thermal image is not identical. The visible spectrum images have a horizontal field of view of $100°$; besides, the thermal spectrum images have a horizontal field of view of $32°$. In order to align the thermal and RGB spectrum images, the RGB images are cropped and resized. The dataset provides the semantic labels for the urban environment and is classified into nine classes: bicycle, person, car, curve, car_stop, color_cone, guardrail, and background. The dataset has 1569 images pairs of RGB and thermal altogether. There are 820 image pairs recorded during the daytime and 749 recorded at nighttime. The dataset is split into the training set and testing set. The testing set is further split into the day and nighttime groups. The number of images in each group is shown in Table 2.

Table 2. The number of images in training and testing split of the dataset.

Dataset	Training set	Testing set
Day & Night time	784	393
Day time	–	205
Night time	–	188

4.2   Training Details

The proposed method ArtSeg is implemented using Pytorch deep learning library. In training the proposed method, no pre-processing step is performed on the input images. The proposed network ArtSeg is trained from scratch in an end-to-end manner and does not employ any pre-trained weights. The network is trained for a total of 500 epochs on Nvidia RTX 3090 having 24 GB memory. The cross-entropy loss function is used for training the network given by Eq. 6.

$$Loss = -\frac{1}{M}\sum_{j=1}^{M}\sum_{c=1}^{C} S_{c,j}\ln(\hat{S}_{c,j}) \tag{6}$$

Table 3. Comparison of the evaluation results of ARTSeg with other state-of-the-art methods on the test set consisting of Day and Night time images. The Class Accuracy (%), Avg.Acc (%) and *IOU* (%) are the evaluation metrics. "-" indicates that the value is not available.

Model	Background	Car	Pedestrian	Bike	Curve	Car stop	Guardrail	Color cone	Bump	Avg.Acc	IOU
SegNet [19]	96.90	83.30	72.10	76.80	58.30	31.90	0.00	0.00	63.90	53.70	58.30
SegNet_4ch [19]	96.10	89.00	82.30	0.00	61.40	21.70	0.00	0.00	86.70	48.60	50.40
ENet [19]	88.50	58.60	42.70	24.70	30.10	18.10	0.30	45.80	23.00	37.00	44.90
MFNet [19]	96.80	82.90	85.20	74.20	61.50	27.30	0.00	60.70	43.30	59.10	64.90
FuseSeg [20]	–	93.10	81.40	78.50	68.40	29.10	63.70	55.80	66.64	70.60	54.50
RTFNet [21]	–	93.00	79.30	76.80	60.70	38.50	0.00	45.50	74.70	63.10	53.20
ARTSeg (Our)	**97.10**	**94.76**	**86.66**	**79.20**	**71.25**	**49.69**	**65.21**	**58.11**	64.28	**74.03**	**68.80**

where M is the total number of pixels in the ground truth label image, C is the number of classes, in this case, 9. $S_{c,j}$ denotes the ground truth class label of each pixel, and $\hat{S}_{c,j}$ denotes the predicted class of each pixel. We have used Adam optimizer for training the ARTSeg network with the weight decay of 1×10^{-4}; epsilon of 1×10^{-8} and learning rate of 5×10^{-4}. The learning rate schedule policy given by the Eq. 7 is used to update the learning rate.

$$LR = LR_{initial} \times (\frac{1 - epoch}{epochs_{total}})^p, \tag{7}$$

The p is set to 0.9. The network is trained for 100 epochs. All the parameter values are chosen empirically through grid search. These parameters are kept constant in all the experiments. Moreover, training data is augmented using the flip technique.

4.3 Evaluation Metrics

In order to evaluate the performance of the proposed network, two evaluation metrics are selected. The Average class accuracy and mean Intersection over Union (IoU). The Average class accuracy is expressed as

Table 4. Quantitative analysis of ARTSeg with other state-of-the-art methods for day time and night time test set. The evaluation is performed using Avg.acc (%) and *IoU* (%) metrics.

Methods	Day time		Night time	
	Avg.Acc(%)	$IOU(\%)$	Avg.Acc(%)	$IOU(\%)$
SegNet [19]	46.10	48.80	54.00	55.20
SegNet_4ch [19]	50.50	51.10	50.50	51.10
MFNet [19]	47.70	57.40	63.50	62.10
FuseSeg [20]	62.10	47.80	67.30	54.60
RTFNet [21]	60.00	45.80	60.70	54.80
ARTSeg (Our)	**65.58**	**64.08**	**70.85**	**65.56**

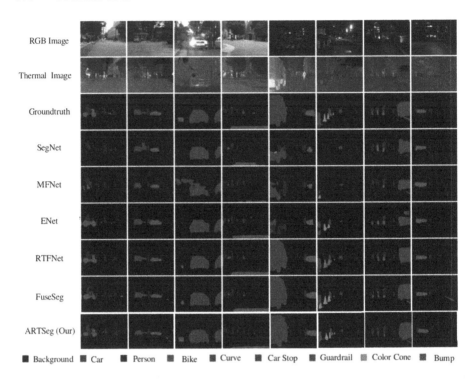

Fig. 2. The qualitative comparison between ARTSeg and other state-of-the-art methods for semantic segmentation on thermal image dataset.

$$Avg.Acc = \frac{1}{N} \sum_{i=1}^{N} \frac{TP_i}{TP_i + FN_i}, \tag{8}$$

where N is number of classes. TP is true positive rate $(TP_i = \sum_{m=1}^{M} p_{ii}^m)$ and FN is false negative rate $(FN_i = \sum_{m=1}^{M} \sum_{j=1, j \neq i}^{N} p_{ij}^m)$. The IoU is expressed as

$$IoU = \frac{1}{N} \sum_{i=1}^{N} \frac{TP_i}{TP_i + FN_i + FP_i}, \tag{9}$$

here FP is define as false positive rate $(FP_i = \sum_{m=1}^{M} \sum_{j=1, j \neq i}^{N} p_{ji}^m)$. The p_{ii} corresponds to the correct number of pixels classified for class i having the same class i in the frame m, whereas p_{ji} represents the number incorrectly classified pixel of class j as class i in the frame m. Similarly, the number of incorrectly classified pixel of class i as class j is represented by p_{ij} in the frame m.

4.4 Results

The thermal image semantic segmentation dataset is benchmarked on existing techniques, including MFRNet [19], FuseSeg [20], SegNet [22] and RTFNet [21].

Image segmentation using thermal images is an emerging research direction in contrast to RGB image segmentation; given this, a few techniques have been employed in the literature for thermal image segmentation. The MFRNet, FuseSeg and RTFNet have fused the information from the visible spectrum and thermal spectrum images. However, SegNet uses only thermal images for predicting semantic segmentation. The proposed network ARTSeg is trained on only thermal images. The evaluation of ARTSeg in comparison to the algorithms as mentioned earlier is shown in Table 3. The Table shows the Accuracy measure of each class and Avg.Acc and IoU over all classes for both day and night time. However, Table 4 shows the evaluation of the methods for daytime and nighttime separately for all classes. ARTSeg has outperformed all existing methods and achieved an improvement 3.43% on Avg.Acc and 3.9% in IoU scores in comparison to FuseSeg. Figure 2 manifests the qualitative results of the proposed ARTSeg algorithm with other methods. In addition, we have also investigated the effect of using different backbone networks to extract the features for the encoder of the ARTSeg network.

Table 5. Quantitive analysis of ARTSeg with different backbone networks. The evaluation is performed using Avg.acc (%) and IOU (%) metrics on day and night time test set.

Methods	DayTime		NightTime	
	Avg.Acc(%)	IOU (%)	Avg.Acc(%)	IOU(%)
ARTSeg-VGG16	54.21	46.80	59.12	48.20
ARTSeg-ResNet-18	57.50	47.60	61.89	51.10
ARTSeg-ResNet-50	63.25	55.40	65.50	57.23
ARTSeg-MobileNetv2	59.45	49.89	60.10	50.80
ARTSeg-DenseNet	58.41	49.50	59.45	49.34
ARTSeg-ShuffleNet	62.58	58.18	66.85	59.56
ARTSeg (Our)	**65.58**	**64.08**	**70.85**	**65.56**

We utilize six different backbone network including VGG16 [23], ResNet-18 [24], ResNet-50 [24], MobileNetV2 [25], ShuffleNet [26] and DenseNet [27]. The thermal image is input to the backbone network. The encoded features are then passed to the decoder module. The backbone networks are trained with pretrained weights. The Table 5 shows the quantitative results with the backbone networks. The results using different backbone networks in the encoder module do not show any significant improvement compared to ARTSeg.

5   Conclusion

In this research article, we proposed ARTSeg, a novel encoder-decoder architecture for thermal image semantic segmentation. The ARTSeg introduces residual recurrent convolution block in the encoder, followed by a decoder that utilizes additive attention in skip connection to refine full resolution detection. The ART-Seg is evaluated on the public dataset in terms of Avg.Acc and IoU. In comparison to other state-of-the-art methods, ARTSeg has a higher Avg.Acc (74.03%) and IoU (68.80%).

The inclusion of the thermal camera in the autonomous driving stack provide help to understand the surroundings in low illumination conditions. In future work, we aim to fuse information from the thermal camera and Lidar to improve the autonomous vehicle's perception.

Acknowledgement. This work was partly supported by the ICT R&D program of MSIP/IITP (2014-3-00077, Development of global multitarget tracking and event prediction techniques based on real-time large-scale video analysis), National Research Foundation of Korea (NRF) grant funded by the Korea Government (MSIT) (No. 2019R1A2C2087489), Ministry of Culture, Sports and Tourism (MCST), and Korea Creative Content Agency (KOCCA) in the Culture Technology (CT) Research & Development (R2020070004) Program 2021.

References

1. Azam, S., Munir, F., Sheri, A.M., Kim, J., Jeon, M.: System, design and experimental validation of autonomous vehicle in an unconstrained environment. Sensors **20**(21), 5999 (2020)
2. Munir, F., Azam, S., Hussain, M.I., Sheri, A.M. and Jeon, M.: Autonomous vehicle: the architecture aspect of self driving car. In: Proceedings of the 2018 International Conference on Sensors, Signal and Image Processing, pp. 1–5, October 2018
3. Azam, S., Munir, F. and Jeon, M.: Dynamic control system design for autonomous car. In: VEHITS, pp. 456–463 (2020)
4. Rosique, F., Navarro, P.J., Fernández, C., Padilla, A.: A systematic review of perception system and simulators for autonomous vehicles research. Sensors **19**(3), 648 (2019)
5. Long, J., Shelhamer, E., Darrell, T.: 'Fully convolutional networks for semantic segmentation. In: Proceedings of the IEEE Conference on Computer Vision and Pattern Recognition, pp. 3431–3440 (2015)
6. Vollmer, M., Möllmann, K.P.: Infrared Thermal Imaging: Fundamentals, Research and Applications. Wiley, Weinheim (2017)
7. Hwang, S., Park, J., Kim, N., Choi, Y., So Kweon, I.: Multispectral pedestrian detection: Benchmark dataset and baseline. In: Proceedings of the IEEE Conference on Computer Vision and Pattern Recognition pp. 1037–1045 (2015)
8. Xu, D., Ouyang, W., Ricci, E., Wang, X., Sebe, N.: Learning cross-modal deep representations for robust pedestrian detection. In: Proceedings of the IEEE Conference on Computer Vision and Pattern Recognition, pp. 5363–5371 (2017)
9. Li, C., Zhu, C., Huang, Y., Tang, J., Wang, L.: Cross-modal ranking with soft consistency and noisy labels for robust RGB-T tracking. In: Ferrari, V., Hebert, M., Sminchisescu, C., Weiss, Y. (eds.) ECCV 2018. LNCS, vol. 11217, pp. 831–847. Springer, Cham (2018). https://doi.org/10.1007/978-3-030-01261-8_49
10. Wu, A., Zheng, W.S., Yu, H.X., Gong, S., Lai, J.: RGB-infrared cross-modality person re-identification. In: Proceedings of the IEEE International Conference on Computer Vision, pp. 5380–5389 (2017)

11. Szegedy, C., et al.: Going deeper with convolutions. In: Proceedings of the IEEE Conference on Computer Vision and Pattern recognition, pp. 1–9 (2015)

12. Ronneberger, O., Fischer, P., Brox, T.: U-Net: convolutional networks for biomedical image segmentation. In: Navab, N., Hornegger, J., Wells, W.M., Frangi, A.F. (eds.) MICCAI 2015. LNCS, vol. 9351, pp. 234–241. Springer, Cham (2015). https://doi.org/10.1007/978-3-319-24574-4_28

13. Paszke, A., Chaurasia, A., Kim, S., Culurciello, E.: ENet: a deep neural network architecture for real-time semantic segmentation. arXiv preprint arXiv:1606.02147 (2016)

14. Song, S., Lichtenberg, S.P., Xiao, J.: Sun RGB-D: a RGB-D scene understanding benchmark suite. In: Proceedings of the IEEE Conference on Computer Vision and Pattern Recognition, pp. 567–576 (2015)

15. Hazirbas, C., Ma, L., Domokos, C., Cremers, D.: FuseNet: incorporating depth into semantic segmentation via fusion-based CNN architecture. In: Lai, S.-H., Lepetit, V., Nishino, K., Sato, Y. (eds.) ACCV 2016. LNCS, vol. 10111, pp. 213–228. Springer, Cham (2017). https://doi.org/10.1007/978-3-319-54181-5_14

16. Yu, C., Wang, J., Peng, C., Gao, C., Yu, G., Sang, N.: Learning a discriminative feature network for semantic segmentation. In: Proceedings of the IEEE Conference on Computer Vision and Pattern Recognition, pp. 1857–1866 (2018)

17. Qiao, Y., Wei, Z., Zhao, Y.: Thermal infrared pedestrian image segmentation using level set method. Sensors 17(8), 1811 (2017)

18. Li, C., Xia, W., Yan, Y., Luo, B., Tang, J.: Segmenting objects in day and night: Edge-conditioned CNN for thermal image semantic segmentation. IEEE Trans. Neural Networks Learn. Syst. 32, 3069–3082 (2020)

19. Ha, Q., Watanabe, K., Karasawa, T., Ushiku, Y., Harada, T.: MFNet: towards real-time semantic segmentation for autonomous vehicles with multi-spectral scenes. In: 2017 IEEE/RSJ International Conference on Intelligent Robots and Systems (IROS), pp. 5108–5115. IEEE (2017)

20. Sun, Y., Zuo, W., Yun, P., Wang, H., Liu, M.: FuseSeg: semantic segmentation of urban scenes based on RGB and thermal data fusion. IEEE Trans. Autom. Sci. Eng. 18, 1000–1011 (2020)

21. Sun, Y., Zuo, W., Liu, M.: Rtfnet: Rgb-thermal fusion network for semantic segmentation of urban scenes. IEEE Robot. Autom. Lett. 4(3), 2576–2583 (2019)

22. Badrinarayanan, V., Kendall, A., Cipolla, R.: Segnet: a deep convolutional encoder-decoder architecture for image segmentation. IEEE Trans. Pattern Anal. Mach. Intell. 39(12), 2481–2495 (2017)

23. Simonyan, K., Zisserman, A.: Very deep convolutional networks for large-scale image recognition. arXiv preprint arXiv:1409.1556 (2014)

24. He, K., Zhang, X., Ren, S., Sun, J.: Deep residual learning for image recognition. In: Proceedings of the IEEE Conference on Computer Vision and Pattern Recognition, pp. 770–778 (2016)

25. Sandler, M., Howard, A., Zhu, M., Zhmoginov, A., Chen, L.-C.: Mobilenetv2: inverted residuals and linear bottlenecks. In: Proceedings of the IEEE Conference on Computer Vision and Pattern Recognition, pp. 4510–4520. 2018

26. Ma, N., Zhang, X., Zheng, H.-T., Sun, J.: ShuffleNet V2: practical guidelines for efficient CNN architecture design. In: Ferrari, V., Hebert, M., Sminchisescu, C., Weiss, Y. (eds.) Computer Vision – ECCV 2018. LNCS, vol. 11218, pp. 122–138. Springer, Cham (2018). https://doi.org/10.1007/978-3-030-01264-9_8

27. Huang, G., Liu, Z., Weinberger, K.Q.: Densely connected convolutional networks. CoRR abs/1608.06993 (2016). arXiv preprint arXiv:1608.06993 (2016)

28. Chen, L.C., Papandreou, G., Kokkinos, I., Murphy, K., Yuille, A.L.: Deeplab: semantic image segmentation with deep convolutional nets, atrous convolution, and fully connected CRFS. IEEE Trans. Pattern Anal. Mach. Intell. **40**(4), 834–848 (2017)
29. Chen, L.C., Yang, Y., Wang, J., Xu, W., Yuille, A.L.: Attention to scale: scale-aware semantic image segmentation. In: Proceedings of the IEEE Conference on Computer Vision and Pattern Recognition, pp. 3640–3649 (2016)
30. Chen, L.C., Papandreou, G., Schroff, F., Adam, H.: Rethinking atrous convolution for semantic image segmentation. arXiv preprint arXiv:1706.05587 (2017)
31. Wang, P., et al.: Understanding convolution for semantic segmentation. In: 2018 IEEE Winter Conference on Applications of Computer Vision (WACV), pp. 1451–1460. IEEE, March 2018
32. Kim, Y.H., Shin, U., Park, J., Kweon, I.S.: MS-UDA: multi-spectral unsupervised domain adaptation for thermal image semantic segmentation. IEEE Robot Autom. Lett. **6**, 6497–6504 (2021)
33. Tsai, Y.H.: Learning to adapt structured output space for semantic segmentation. In: Proceedings of the IEEE Conference on Computer Vision and Pattern Recognition, pp. 7472–7481 (2018)
34. Kim, M., Byun, H.: Learning texture invariant representation for domain adaptation of semantic segmentation. In: Proceedings of the IEEE/CVF Conference on Computer Vision and Pattern Recognition, pp. 12975–12984 (2020)

Robust Frequency-Aware Instance Segmentation for Serial Tissue Sections

Guodong Sun[1,2], Zejin Wang[1,2], Guoqing Li[1(✉)], and Hua Han[1,2,3(✉)]

[1] National Laboratory of Pattern Recognition, Institute of Automation,
Chinese Academy of Sciences, Beijing, China
{sunguodong2019,wangzejin2018,guoqing.li,hua.han}@ia.ac.cn
[2] School of Artificial Intelligence, School of Future Technology, University of Chinese
Academy of Sciences, Beijing, China
[3] CAS Center for Excellence in Brain Science and Intelligence Technology,
Shanghai, China

Abstract. Serial tissue sections are widely used in imaging large tissue volumes. Navigating to each section is indispensable in the automatic imaging process. Nowadays, the locations of sections are labeled manually or semi-manually. Sections are similar and the border is indiscernible if they stick together, which makes it difficult to locate the sections automatically. In this paper, we present frequency-aware instance segmentation framework (FANet), which can extract shape and size information of sections very well. Firstly, FANet uses discrete cosine transform (DCT). Secondly, each channel extracts an specific frequency component of themselves. Frequency components from all channels is taken as the multi-frequency description of feature map and finally used to model the channel attention. Additionally, we propose a dataset about the serial sections as benchmark, which contains 2708 images in training set and 1193 images in validation set. Experimental results on the benchmark demonstrate our FANet achieves superior performance compared with the current methods. Our code and dataset will be made public.

Keywords: Serial sections · Instance segmentation · Computer vision

1 Introduction

Serial tissue sections offer superlative opportunities to ascertain biological tissues in three dimensions. A series of methods are proposed to image the serial sections. As a pioneering work, Micheva et al. [23] proposes array tomography(AT), which "array" means arranging serial ultrathin tissue sections in spatial array on a planar solid surface, while "tomography" means imaging the two-dimensional sections to capture of three-dimensional structure using microscope [29]. Therefore, many works combined AT with electron microscope to explore fine details in large tissue volumes [10,18,24,28,30,32], including serial-section transmission electron microscopy (ssTEM) [4,9] and scanning electron microscopy (SEM)

© Springer Nature Switzerland AG 2022
C. Wallraven et al. (Eds.): ACPR 2021, LNCS 13188, pp. 379–389, 2022.
https://doi.org/10.1007/978-3-031-02375-0_28

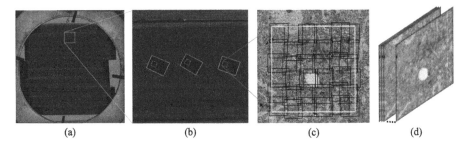

(a)	(b)	(c)	(d)

Fig. 1. The imaging process of ATUM-SEM. (a) is the image that silicon wafer which tape strips with sections are adhered to is on SEM stage. (b) is the enlarged view of the blue box of (a). The quadrangle is sections' contour, and the red rectangle is ROI on each section. (c) is SEM imaging ROI on a section. Each yellow square is the field of view (FOV) that SEM image the section once. (d) is sequentially stacking the ROIs on each section to get the 3D structure.

[2,17]. Especially, SEM with its imaging method fits well with AT, thus it is most often used with AT. Automatic Tape-collecting UltraMicrotome SEM (ATUM-SEM) is the combination of SEM and AT, using ultramicrotome to cut tissue volumes in ultrathin sections and automatically collecting the sections on tape in sequence. The tape is cut in strips and adhered to silicon wafers which is loaded on SEM stage to be imaged. Then, SEM images hundreds of sections' same region (ROI) on the wafer automatically , as illustrated/shown in Fig. 1. In order to accomplish the automation of the imaging process on a wafer, researchers firstly take an image (wafer image) of the wafer, which has hundreds sections on and secondly label the contour of sections which contains ROI and satisfy the condition of imaging, then map wafer image coordinate to SEM stage physical coordinate. Therefore, after setting up the ROI on one section, SEM can navigate to ROIs on every section accurately. Nowadays, the contour of each section is labeled manually or semi-manually [11]. As the volume of tissue that researchers want to explore becoming larger, the number of sections become to tens of thousands [28,32] that requires a lot of people and time to label. Besides, on account of the uncertainty in section preparation processes such as cutting and collecting, the sections on the wafer could be damaged, contaminated with dust or stick together (as shown in Fig. 2), bringing difficulty to label sections automatically.

To detect the contour of every section automatically, we accomplish this task using instance segmentation of sections on wafer image, which can segment each section in pixel level and classify the section abnormal or not. In recent years, instance segmentation task has been rapidly improved benefiting from convolutional neural networks (CNNs). Among them, , Mask R-CNN [12] is the dominant framework in this task as a two-stage method. Mask R-CNN incorporates the advantages of Faster R-CNN [26] and FCN [22], in consideration of the bounding-boxes, classification and masks for each objects simultaneously. Each bounding-box of an object is used to crop the feature maps using ROIAlign to

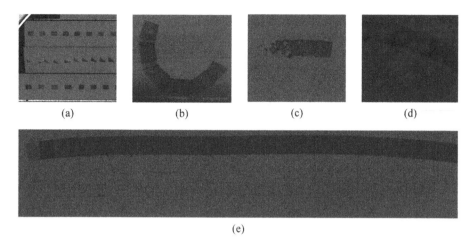

(a)   (b)   (c)   (d)

(e)

Fig. 2. Some exceptional situations of sections on wafer. (a) incomplete sections resulting from the replacement of diamond knife (b) fold sections stick to good sections. (c) damaged sections. (d) contaminated with dust. (e) sections stick together and the three sections on the far left are incomplete.

get the ROI. Then FCN perform semantic segmentation to these ROIs. Many works [6,16,21] which have top performance on COCO [20] benchmark dataset are based on Mask R-CNN. However, different from the objects in natural image, the sections in the same wafer image are significantly similar to each other (e.g. in Fig. 2, between the good sections or the incomplete and good sections). In addition, if the sections stick together, the boundary between sections is difficult to identify. Moreover, there is little difference between the sections of each category, especially incomplete sections sometimes (Fig. 2(e)). Therefore, the performance of these works on wafer image could be sub-optimal, such as incorrect category or boundary. To better distinguish the different categories of sections and identify the boundary between the stick sections more accurately, inspired by [25], we propose a robust frequency-aware network (FANet) which uses multiple frequency components of feature map to model channel attention. FANet aggregates multiple frequency components efficiently and pools frequency information of the feature map. We apply discrete cosine transform (DCT) to feature map and convert it to frequency domain. Then we choose several specific frequency components as a multi-spectral description for feature map. Finally, the frequency components are used as feature map channel importance weight to let network take more attention on important information. Finally, we propose a dataset of wafer image and use it as the benchmark. Experimental results demonstrate that FANet achieves state-of-the-art performance on the benchmark.

In brief, the contributions of this paper are summarized as follows:

- We propose a robust method, FANet, which uses multiple frequency components to take channel attention more efficiently for take instance segmentation on wafer image.

- We propose a dataset of wafer image as benchmark which contains different conditions of sections as more as we can find, comprised of 2708 images as training set and 1193 images as validation set.
- Experiments results on the benchmark demonstrate FANet achieves state-of-the-art performance.

This paper is organized as follows. Section 2 briefly introduces the related work about instance segmentation. Section 3 presents the proposed method. Section 4 shows the experimental results on the benchmark. Finally, the conclusion is in Sect. 5.

2   Related Work

2.1   Instance Segmentation

Instance segmentation aims at predicting the mask and classification score for each object. Nowadays, the two-stage method Mask R-CNN is still the dominant framework which applies Faster R-CNN to get the bounding-boxes of instances and uses FCN to predict the mask of each instance on the feature map cropped according to the bounding-boxes. [6] combines Cascade R-CNN [5] with Mask R-CNN and interweaves detection and segmentation joint. [21] uses FPN features [19] to enriching the ROI feature. And [16] adds a MaskIOU head to learn the segmentation score. Besides, one-stage methods for instance segmentation are faster than two-stage methods conceptually. [8] takes this task into fully convolutional by predicts position-sensitive score maps. YOLACT [3] uses mask coefficients to distinguish mask for each object on the original mask. Due to the weak accuracy of one-stage method, our method is based on two-stage.

2.2   Channel Attention Mechanism

To date, channel attention mechanism has been widely used in CNNs and achieved satisfactory performance. SENet [15] uses GAP and fully connected layers to get the channel importance weight. And ECANet [31] uses local one-dimensional convolution instead of fully connected to reduce the redundancy. FcaNet [25] states that using GAP to get channel importance weight loses much useful information on feature channels. So it introduces DCT to get more information from different frequency components. However, FcaNet down-samples feature map before calculating frequency components, which much information does not be transformed into frequency domain. And FANet we proposed directly uses DCT to transform information into frequency domain, which can get all the information of specific frequency components. Therefore, FANet can take more information to model channel attention.

3   Method

In this section, we first introduce the DCT frequency on feature map. Then, we elaborate our proposed method FANet and explain why it aggregates multiple frequency components more efficiently and pools more frequency information.

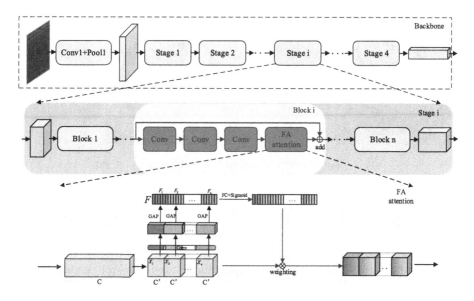

Fig. 3. The architecture of FANet. Frequency aware channel attention is placed in every block. First the input feature map is divided into n parts averagely. Then every channel of feature map in the same part calculates one specific frequency component. The frequency components of all channels are concatenated to a vector F. After FC and Sigmoid, F is used to weighting the Feature map as modeling channel attention. Best viewed in color. (Color figure online)

3.1 DCT Frequency on Feature Map

Generalized from one-dimensional (1D) DCT fefinition [1], two-dimensional (2D) DCT can be written as:

$$f_{h,w} = \sum_{u=0}^{H-1} \sum_{v=0}^{W-1} x_{u,v} \cos(\frac{(2u+1)h\pi}{2H}) \cdot \cos(\frac{(2v+1)w\pi}{2W}), \tag{1}$$
$$s.t. \quad h \in \{0, 1, ..., H-1\}, w \in \{0, 1, ..., W-1\},$$

where $f_{h,w}$ is the frequency component (h, w) on the 2D DCT frequency spectrum $f \in \mathbb{R}^{H \times W}$, $x_{u,v}$ is the pixel value on (u, v) of input $x \in \mathbb{R}^{H \times W}$, H and W are the height and width of x respectively. The inverserse 2D DCT can be written as:

$$x_{u,v} = \sum_{h=0}^{H-1} \sum_{w=0}^{W-1} f_{h,w} \cos(\frac{(2u+1)h\pi}{2H}) \cdot \cos(\frac{(2v+1)w\pi}{2W}), \tag{2}$$
$$s.t. \quad u \in \{0, 1, ..., H-1\}, v \in \{0, 1, ..., W-1\},$$

Equations 1 and 2 remove some constant normalization factors, and this has no effect on the results in this work. As we can see in Eq. 2, every pixel value of

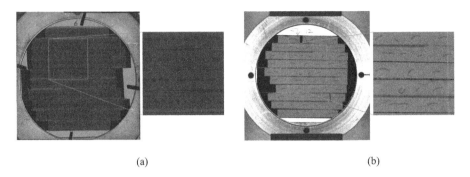

(a)   (b)

Fig. 4. Wafer images in dataset. (a) The SCN region of the rat brain (b) Zebrafish whole brain.

the input contains information from all the frequency components. If only use the lowest frequency component of input, h and w are 0 in Eq. 1, we have:

$$
\begin{aligned}
f_{0,0} &= \sum_{u=0}^{H-1} \sum_{v=0}^{W-1} x_{u,v} \cos(\frac{(2u+1) \cdot 0}{2H}) \cdot \cos(\frac{(2v+1) \cdot 0}{2W}) \\
&= \sum_{u=0}^{H-1} \sum_{v=0}^{W-1} x_{u,v} \\
&= GAP(x) \cdot HW
\end{aligned}
\tag{3}
$$

Thus, GAP, which conventional channel attention approaches [15,31] applies to calculate channel importance weight, only differ one constant scaling factor from the lowest frequency component of input. The information from other frequency components is discard. However, deep networks are redundant [14,33]. It is possible that different channels get the same information using GAP. Therefore, as the different frequency components contain different information, utilizing more frequency components may extract more information to model channel attention.

3.2 FANet

From the analysis illustrated in Sect. 3.1, conventional channel attention only utilizes the lowest frequency component information of input, which is inadequate. Therefore, as shown in Fig. 3, we propose the Frequency-Aware network (FANet), which generalizes the channel attention to more frequency components and models more information in channel attention.

Given a feature map as input $X \in \mathbb{R}^{C \times H \times W}$, we first divide it into n parts averagely along the channel dimension and every part is denoted as $X_i \in \mathbb{R}^{C' \times H \times W}, i \in \{0, 1, ..., n-1\}, C' = \frac{C}{n}$. In X_i, each channel of feature map are calculated a specific frequency component (h_i, w_i), which can be written as :

Table 1. Specific frequency components.

(h_i, w_i)			
(0, 0)	(0, 1)	(6, 0)	(0, 5)
(0, 2)	(1, 0)	(1, 2)	(4, 0)
(5, 0)	(1, 6)	(3, 0)	(0, 4)
(0, 6)	(0, 3)	(3, 5)	(2, 2)

$$f^j_{h_i,w_i} = \sum_{u=0}^{H-1} \sum_{v=0}^{W-1} X^j_i \cos(\frac{(2u+1)h_i\pi}{2H}) \cos(\frac{(2v+1)w_i\pi}{2W}), \tag{4}$$

in which $X^j_i \in \mathbb{R}^{H \times W}, j \in \{0, 1, ..., C'-1\}$, is one of the channel of X_i. All the $f^j_{h_i,w_i} \in \mathbb{R}, j \in \{0, 1, ..., C'-1\}$ of X_i form a C'-dimensional vector $F_i \in \mathbb{R}^{C'}$. For the whole input X, All F_i are concatenated as F:

$$F = cat([F_0, F_1, ..., F_{n-1}]), \tag{5}$$

In which $F \in \mathbb{R}^C$ is the vector containing specific frequency components information of X. Finally, the whole channel importance weight for modeling channel attention of X is obtained as:

$$att = sigmoid(fc(F)), \tag{6}$$

In which $att \in \mathbb{R}^C$. Therefore, from Eqs. 5 and 6, utilizing att to weight X in the channel dimension introduces multiple frequency components information to model the channel attention of X.

As shown in Eq. 2, every pixel of the input contains all the frequency components information. FANet applies DCT to all the pixel of input, which can extract all information of one specific frequency component and model channel attention more efficiently and accurately. Besides, in view of the redundant information of feature map, the channels between feature map are likely to contain the same information. It is believable that each part contains much information of whole feature map. Therefore, obtaining a specific frequency component information from one part is sufficient, which reduces the complexity and size of the method.

4   Experiments

In this section, we first introduce the proposed dataset. Then elaborate on the details of our experiments on the dataset.

4.1   Dataset

To train and evaluate the models, we propose a dataset of wafer image as the benchmark. We choose two biological tissue sections which are suprachiasmatic

Table 2. Instance segmentation results of different methods on wafer image dataset.

Method	Backbone	Detector	AP	AP_{50}	AP_{75}	AP_s	AP_m	AP_L
ResNet [13]	ResNet-34 [13]	Mask R-CNN [12]	34.5	45.1	39.2	27.1	37.5	**28.3**
SENet [15]			38.0	**52.5**	41.1	29.7	42.6	24.2
FcaNet [25]			36.8	48.9	44.2	29.9	40.5	26.5
FANet(ours)			**38.1**	50.9	**45.0**	**36.8**	**43.2**	25.7
ResNet [13]	ResNet-50 [13]		37.7	49.4	**46.5**	26.1	41.6	**32.7**
SENet [15]			38.3	51.4	44.3	27.9	43.5	25.9
FcaNet [25]			38.6	50.1	44.8	**33.3**	44.5	25.3
FANet(ours)			**40.1**	**51.5**	45.7	27.4	**45.8**	24.6
ResNet [13]	ResNet-34 [13]	Mask Scoring R-CNN [16]	37.4	48.4	43.7	**35.0**	39.6	**31.7**
SENet [15]			38.2	50.4	44.9	34.4	43.5	26.1
FcaNet [25]			38.4	50.4	45.3	33.8	44.1	26.2
FANet(ours)			**39.7**	**52.8**	**46.2**	33.6	**45.0**	26.5
ResNet [13]	ResNet-50 [13]		38.9	50.4	47.4	31.2	44.0	24.2
SENet [15]			43.7	56.8	49.3	34.3	49.1	28.8
FcaNet [25]			44.9	58.2	**53.4**	**34.7**	51.6	28.6
FANet(ours)			**46.6**	**60.0**	52.9	33.7	**53.4**	**29.2**

nucleus (SCN) region of the rat brain and Zebrafish whole brain to improve the generalization and robustness of the model. As shown in Fig. 4, these two biological tissue sections have a big difference. After consulting a lot of experts, we identify three most common anomalistic situation of sections, which are incomplete, fold and damaged (Fig. 2). Therefore, there are four classes of sections in the dataset, which are good section and three kinds of bad section. Because of the original wafer images are much large, which are usually more than 10K × 10K pixels, we crop the wafer images into sub-images (1024 × 1024) with overlap of 10%. Finally, the sub-images are randomly divided into training set and validation set. The training set contains 2708 sub-images and validation set is 1193, and both of them contain the two biological tissue sections. All experiments are conducted on the dataset as benchmark.

4.2 Implementation Details

We evaluate the performance of the proposed FANet with ResNet-34 and ResNet-50 [13] as backbone models. Experiments are implemented in mmdetection [7]. The data augmentation except image scale and hyper-parameter are followed [7]. The input image scale is 1024. The models are trained using stochastic gradient descent (SGD) with momentum of 0.9, a weight decay of 0.0001 and batch size of 8 per GPU. The training epoch is 36 and learning rate is 0.01 with warmup iters of 2000. The learning rate is reduced by a factor of 10 at epoch 24 and 34.

All models are trained with one Tesla P40 GPU.

4.3 the Specific Frequency Components

Because of the limitations of experimental conditions, we follow the experiment results in [25]. The two-dimensional DCT frequency space is divided into 7×7 parts. Using one frequency component each time, it still has a competitive performance on ImageNet [27]. Finally, we choose 16 frequency components (Table 1) with top-16 highest performance in the total 49 experiments results.

4.4 Instance Segmentation on the Benchmark

To evaluate our method on the benchmark, we use Mask R-CNN [12] and Mask Scoring R-CNN [16]. FcaNet [25] and FANet are used the same 16 frequency components. As shown in Table 2, our method has a superior performance. Especially compared with FcaNet, FANet could outperform it by 1.3%–1.7% in terms of mAP, which indicates our method aggregates multiple frequency components more efficiently.

5   Conclusions

In this paper, we propose a robust channel attention mechanism using multi frequency components, named FANet, which is utilized to detect the tissue sections on wafer images. Besides, we propose a dataset of wafer images as benchmark and FANet has a superior performance. With satisfying performance, FANet can reduce much people and time to label the sections. In the future work, we will further collect wafer images of different biological tissue, evaluate FANet and improve it.

Acknowledgement. This research was funded by CAS Key Technology Talent Program (No. 292019000126 to X.C.)

References

1. Ahmed, N., Natarajan, T., Rao, K.R.: Discrete cosine transform. IEEE Trans. Comput. **100**(1), 90–93 (1974)
2. Bogner, A., Jouneau, P.H., Thollet, G., Basset, D., Gauthier, C.: A history of scanning electron microscopy developments: Towards "wet-stem" imaging. Micron **38**(4), 390–401 (2007)
3. Bolya, D., Zhou, C., Xiao, F., Lee, Y.J.: Yolact: real-time instance segmentation. In: Proceedings of the IEEE/CVF International Conference on Computer Vision, pp. 9157–9166 (2019)
4. Briggman, K.L., Bock, D.D.: Volume electron microscopy for neuronal circuit reconstruction. Curr. Opin. Neurobiol. **22**(1), 154–161 (2012)
5. Cai, Z., Vasconcelos, N.: Cascade R-CNN: delving into high quality object detection. In: Proceedings of the IEEE Conference on Computer Vision and Pattern Recognition, pp. 6154–6162 (2018)

6. Chen, K., et al.: Hybrid task cascade for instance segmentation. In: Proceedings of the IEEE/CVF Conference on Computer Vision and Pattern Recognition, pp. 4974–4983 (2019)
7. Chen, K., et al.: MMDetection: open mmlab detection toolbox and benchmark. arXiv preprint arXiv:1906.07155 (2019)
8. Dai, J., He, K., Li, Y., Ren, S., Sun, J.: Instance-sensitive fully convolutional networks. In: Leibe, B., Matas, J., Sebe, N., Welling, M. (eds.) ECCV 2016. LNCS, vol. 9910, pp. 534–549. Springer, Cham (2016). https://doi.org/10.1007/978-3-319-46466-4_32
9. Denk, W., Briggman, K.L., Helmstaedter, M.: Structural neurobiology: missing link to a mechanistic understanding of neural computation. Nat. Rev. Neurosci. **13**(5), 351–358 (2012)
10. Harris, K.M., Perry, E., Bourne, J., Feinberg, M., Ostroff, L., Hurlburt, J.: Uniform serial sectioning for transmission electron microscopy. J. Neurosci. **26**(47), 12101–12103 (2006)
11. Hayworth, K.J., Morgan, J.L., Schalek, R., Berger, D.R., Hildebrand, D.G., Lichtman, J.W.: Imaging atum ultrathin section libraries with wafermapper: a multiscale approach to em reconstruction of neural circuits. Front. Neural Circ. **8**, 68 (2014)
12. He, K., Gkioxari, G., Dollár, P., Girshick, R.: Mask R-CNN. In: Proceedings of the IEEE International Conference on Computer Vision, pp. 2961–2969 (2017)
13. He, K., Zhang, X., Ren, S., Sun, J.: Deep residual learning for image recognition. In: Proceedings of the IEEE Conference on Computer Vision and Pattern Recognition, pp. 770–778 (2016)
14. He, Y., Zhang, X., Sun, J.: Channel pruning for accelerating very deep neural networks. In: Proceedings of the IEEE International Conference on Computer Vision, pp. 1389–1397 (2017)
15. Hu, J., Shen, L., Sun, G.: Squeeze-and-excitation networks. In: Proceedings of the IEEE Conference on Computer Vision and Pattern Recognition, pp. 7132–7141 (2018)
16. Huang, Z., Huang, L., Gong, Y., Huang, C., Wang, X.: Mask scoring R-CNN. In: Proceedings of the IEEE/CVF Conference on Computer Vision and Pattern Recognition, pp. 6409–6418 (2019)
17. Joy, D.C.: The theory and practice of high-resolution scanning electron microscopy. Ultramicroscopy **37**(1–4), 216–233 (1991)
18. Kasthuri, N., et al.: Saturated reconstruction of a volume of neocortex. Cell **162**(3), 648–661 (2015)
19. Lin, T.Y., Dollár, P., Girshick, R., He, K., Hariharan, B., Belongie, S.: Feature pyramid networks for object detection. In: Proceedings of the IEEE Conference on Computer Vision and Pattern Recognition, pp. 2117–2125 (2017)
20. Lin, T.-Y., et al.: Microsoft COCO: common objects in context. In: Fleet, D., Pajdla, T., Schiele, B., Tuytelaars, T. (eds.) ECCV 2014. LNCS, vol. 8693, pp. 740–755. Springer, Cham (2014). https://doi.org/10.1007/978-3-319-10602-1_48
21. Liu, S., Qi, L., Qin, H., Shi, J., Jia, J.: Path aggregation network for instance segmentation. In: Proceedings of the IEEE Conference on Computer Vision and Pattern Recognition, pp. 8759–8768 (2018)
22. Long, J., Shelhamer, E., Darrell, T.: Fully convolutional networks for semantic segmentation. In: Proceedings of the IEEE Conference on Computer Vision and Pattern Recognition, pp. 3431–3440 (2015)
23. Micheva, K., Smith, S.: Array tomography: a new tool for imaging the molecular architecture and ultrastructure of neural circuits. Neuron **55**(1), 25–36 (2007)

24. Morgan, J.L., Berger, D.R., Wetzel, A.W., Lichtman, J.W.: The fuzzy logic of network connectivity in mouse visual thalamus. Cell **165**(1), 192–206 (2016)
25. Qin, Z., Zhang, P., Wu, F., Li, X.: Fcanet: frequency channel attention networks. arXiv preprint arXiv:2012.11879 (2020)
26. Ren, S., He, K., Girshick, R., Sun, J.: Faster R-CNN: towards real-time object detection with region proposal networks. Adv. Neural. Inf. Process. Syst. **28**, 91–99 (2015)
27. Russakovsky, O., et al.: Imagenet large scale visual recognition challenge. Int. J. Comput. Vision **115**(3), 211–252 (2015)
28. Shapson-Coe, A., et al.: A connectomic study of a petascale fragment of human cerebral cortex. bioRxiv (2021)
29. Smith, S.J.: Q&A: array tomography. BMC Biol. **16**(1), 1–18 (2018)
30. Takemura, S.V., et al.: A visual motion detection circuit suggested by drosophila connectomics. Nature **500**(7461), 175–181 (2013)
31. Wang, Q., Wu, B., Zhu, P., Li, P., Zuo, W., Hu, Q.: ECA-Net: efficient channel attention for deep convolutional neural networks. In: 2020 IEEE CVF Conference on Computer Vision and Pattern Recognition (CVPR). IEEE (2020)
32. Yin, W., et al.: A petascale automated imaging pipeline for mapping neuronal circuits with high-throughput transmission electron microscopy. Nat. Commun. **11**(1), 1–12 (2020)
33. Zhuang, Z., et al.: Discrimination-aware channel pruning for deep neural networks. arXiv preprint arXiv:1810.11809 (2018)

Joint Semantic Segmentation and Edge Detection for Waterline Extraction

Yuhang Chen[1,2(✉)], Bolin Ni[1,2], Gaofeng Meng[1,2,3], and Baoyin Sha[4]

[1] National Laboratory of Pattern Recognition, Institute of Automation,
Chinese Academy of Sciences, Beijing 100190, China
chenyuhang2019@ia.ac.cn
[2] School of Artificial Intelligence, University of Chinese Academy of Sciences,
Beijing 100049, China
[3] Centre for Artificial Intelligence and Robotics,
HK Institute of Science and Innovation, Chinese Academy of Sciences,
Beijing, China
[4] Coal Science and Technology Research Institute Co., Ltd., Beijing 100013, China

Abstract. Automatic water gauge reading is very important for cargo weighting in ocean transportation. In this process, accurate waterline extraction is an important yet challenging step. Waterline extraction is subjected to many environmental interference factors, e.g., bad illumination, bad weather conditions, ambiguous contours of water stain, etc. In this paper, we propose a joint multitask based deep model for accurate waterline extraction. The proposed model consists of two main branches. One branch is used to extract high-level contextual information. The other branch rooted in shallow layers is used to extract low-level detail features. The two branches are later coupled with each other to co-supervise the estimation of waterline. Our model works well on various conditions, such as uneven light, serious reflections, etc. We also introduce a new benchmark dataset for waterline extraction. This dataset consists of 360 pictures extracted from 69 videos collected in several actual ports. Furthermore, sufficient experiments show that our model is effective on the introduced dataset and outperforms the state-of-the-art methods.

Keywords: Waterline extraction · Joint multitask · Co-supervise · Benchmark dataset

1 Introduction

Ocean transportation is an important way of cargo freight. Its biggest advantage is the large cargo capacity and low transportation cost. The weight of the cargo needs to be calculated every time before the cargo is transported. At present, the weight of the cargo is calculated by reading ship's water gauge. The most important step is accurately extracting waterline. 1 cm of reading error will cause several tons difference in the weight of the cargo. Therefore, it is important to improve the accuracy of waterline extraction.

© Springer Nature Switzerland AG 2022
C. Wallraven et al. (Eds.): ACPR 2021, LNCS 13188, pp. 390–400, 2022.
https://doi.org/10.1007/978-3-031-02375-0_29

At present, The methods of waterline extraction mainly include manual observation, ultrasonic measurement and detection method based on image processing. Manual observation method needs to observe six values of midship, bow and stern on both sides of the ship. Due to the influence of the sea condition and the high subjectivity of manual reading, there are large uncontrollable factors in the error of water gauge reading. The ultrasonic measurement method calculates the water gauge by measuring the distance from the ship's deck to the water surface, but the ultrasonic propagation speed is easily affected by external factors such as air density, and the precision is only 0.1 m.

Since the Sobel [12] operator, many edge detectors like Canny [1] have been proposed and being used to extract waterline. For these classic methods, the input image usually needs to be grayed and binarized. This process is easily affected by factors such as weather, waves, mottled hulls, etc. Therefore, this type of method has poor robustness and is difficult to adapt to complex and changeable sea condition. Recently, semantic segmentation method based on deep learning has been proposed. Specifically, fully convolutional network [10] (FCN) have made remarkable progress. DeepLabV2 [2] proposed atrous spatial pyramid pooling module with multi-scale dilation convolutions to aggregate contextual information. PSPNet [19] introduces a pyramid pooling module to enhance contextual information. By using self-attention mechanism, Non-local Networks [14] can use the information of the whole image to enhance the feature of points at any position, yet greatly increasing the computational complexity. To reduce complexity for both time and space, CCNet [8] propose a criss-cross attention module which can capture contextual information from full-image in a more efficient and effective way. In short, the semantic segmentation method mentioned above can be used to extract the waterline. But the widely used cross-entropy loss for semantic segmentation task does not make the network pay attention to the classification of boundary pixels, which is unfriendly for waterline extraction task. Meanwhile, as a dual task of semantic segmentation, edge detection is obviously helpful for waterline extraction, because waterline is made up of many semantic boundaries.

In this paper, we propose a joint multi-task framework which uses semantic information to enhance edge detail features to extract waterline inspired by BiseNetV2 [16]. As shown in Fig. 2 The proposed network contains two main branches: a semantic branch and a detail branch. The semantic branch has a deeper network to extract high-level semantic information. The detail branch has a shallower network and a larger resolution to retain more detail feature. In particular, we design an information aggregation module to effectively integrate the features from two branches. Besides, a new benchmark dataset for waterline extraction has been collected to train the proposed network. The main contributions of this paper are summarized as follow:

- We introduced a dataset with carefully annotated for waterline extraction task. This is the first dataset for waterline extraction tasks.

- A robust CNN architecture for waterline extraction is proposed. The model has been trained from the scratch, without pretrained weights. On the dataset we introduced, our method outperforms other comparison methods.

The rest of the paper is organized as follow. Section 2 summarizes recent work on semantic segmentation and edge detection. The proposed network is described in Sect. 3. The experiment settings and experiment result are presented in Sect. 4. Finally, conclusions and future work are given in Sect. 5.

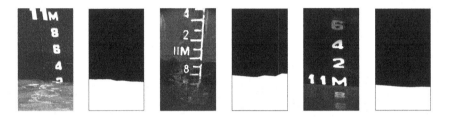

Fig. 1. Examples of the dataset proposed in this paper. The label is marked in the form of a semantic mask. The groundtruth of boundary can be easily obtained by a sobel filter

2   Related Work

Semantic segmentation and edge detection are two interrelated tasks. Semantic edges often surround the segmentation mask. Therefore, the accuracy of the prediction of edge pixels will affect the final segmentation result. Besides, the high-level semantic information obviously can also improve the accuracy of edge detection.

Semantic Segmentation. Fully convolutional network [10] based methods first make a breakthrough in semantic segmentation task. In deeplabv2 [2], atrous convolution is proposed to capture long-distance semantic information. It is a method improving the network's receptive field without sacrificing resolution. In order to fuse low-level and high-level information, Unet [11], Refinenet [9], Deeplabv3+ [3] adopt an encoder-decoder structure. Besides, some work devoted to fuse multi-scale contextual information to improve the representation ability of the features. In Deeplabv3 [4], ASPP module uses different dilation convolution to obtain multi-scale contextual information. PSPNet [19] aggregates features based on different sub-regions to mine global contextual information. Recently, there are many effective methods based on self-attention mechanism. PSANet [18] learns an attention mask adaptively and connects each pixels on the feature map with other pixels to alleviate local neighborhood constraint. DANet [5] puts forward a position attention module and a channel attention module, which respectively model the semantic interdependence in spatial and channel.

Edge Detection. HED [15] proposes an end-to-end structure to obtain more accurate edge prediction maps through a multi-scale integrated learning method. CASENet [17] extends the network proposed in HED [15]. The category edge features on the top layer are fused with the bottom features supervised by a multi-label loss function. DFF [7] proposes a dynamic feature fusion method. This method assigns adaptive weights to each position separately, aiming to generate a fused edge map which is adaptive to the specific content of each image. RPCNet [20] uses the relevance of semantic segmentation and edge detection to improve network performance. The PCM module in RPCNet [20] captures multi-scale global context information for one task to boost another task in a recurrent way.

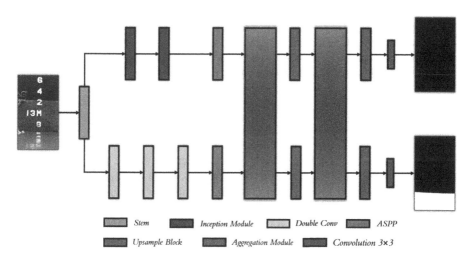

Fig. 2. Overall structure of the proposed network. The network has two main branches. Shallower branch has higher resolution and retain rich details. Deeper branches are used to extract high-level semantic information. The information of the two branches is fully integrated through the aggregation module. As a dual task, both edge label and semantic mask are used to co-supervise the generation of edge map.

3   Network Architecture

This section introduces the proposed network for waterline extraction in detail. Our architecture consists of two main branches: an detail branch and a semantic branch, which are fused by an information aggregation layer. The detail branch is supervised by edge label and the semantic branch is supervised by semantic mask. In this way, two tasks are coupled together and boost each other.

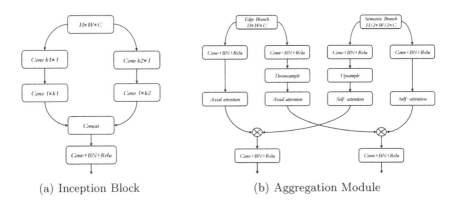

(a) Inception Block   (b) Aggregation Module

Fig. 3. Key module of the proposed network.(a)Inception Block. Features are respectively passed through two groups of asymmetric convolution with different kernel size. (b) Aggregation Module. Notation: Conv is convolution operation with 3×3 kernel size; BN denotes the batch normalization; Downsample use maxpooling; Upsample use transposed convolution; ⊗ means element-wise multiplication

3.1 Detail Branch

This branch is used to extract edge features, thus shallower network depth and higher resolution are required. Due to the interference of the full load line and water stains near the real waterline, the network needs a larger receptive field to capture contextual information. Larger convolution kernels and dilate convolution are two commonly used way. For large convolution kernel, inspired by Inception-v4 [13] network, we split two parallel N×N convolution kernels into 1×N and N×1 parts respectively. This strategy reduces the network parameters greatly. Besides, the asymmetric convolution kernel is more suitable for thin and long targets such as waterlines. We call it Inception Block , as shown in Fig. 3(a). Finally, an ASPP module follows to align the channel dimension.

3.2 Semantic Branch

This branch is parallel to the detail branch. The main function of this branch is to obtain high-level semantic information. Thus, commonly used semantic segmentation network can be placed here. Considering the computation cost, we choose a tiny structure like DeepLabV3 [4]. It only contains four residual blocks followed by an ASPP module.

3.3 Aggregation Module

Taking advantage of the attention mechanism, we propose an information aggregation module, as illustrated in Fig. 3(b). The input of this module is the feature map of two branches passing through ASPP module. The feature map from detail branch and sematic branch have $\frac{1}{8}$ and $\frac{1}{16}$ size of the original respectively.

These two features are each convolved twice with resolution unchanged. Then, two of these four intermediate feature are down-sampled and up-sampled once respectively to align the resolution of the other two. Afterwards, these four intermediate features all go through an attention module to enhance the features. In particular, the two intermediate features of the semantic branch use nonlocal self-attention mechanism [14] to obtain global context information, while the two intermediate features of the detail branch use the column-direction axial attention [8] to enhance the distinction of features on both sides of the waterline. Finally, intermediate features with the same resolution apply element-wise multiplication to fuse information from the two branches.

3.4   Loss Function

As shown in Fig. 2, The proposed network has two coupled tasks. After an epoch of training, the network can output a heatmap $H \in \mathbb{R}^{H \times W}$ and a segmentation mask $M \in \mathbb{R}^{H \times W}$.

Boundary Loss. Since the edge pixels of the waterline only occupy a very small part of the image, there is a serious imbalance of positive and negative points during training. Therefore, we relax the edge extraction task into learning a heatmap near the waterline. Similar to CenterNet [21], we spread the points on the waterline by a Gaussian kernel to the area near the waterline to form a heatmap label denoted as G. Therefore, we follow CenterNet [21] to define a boundary loss:

$$L_H = \frac{-1}{N} \sum_{x,y} \begin{cases} (1 - H_{x,y})^\alpha log(H_{x,y}), & if \quad Y_{x,y} = 1 \\ (1 - G_{x,y})^\beta (H_{x,y})^\alpha log(1 - H_{x,y}), & otherwise \end{cases} \quad (1)$$

where α and β is hyperparameters used to balance the difficult and easy samples as well as the positive and negative samples. In our experiments, we set $\alpha = 2$ and $\beta = 4$.

Dual Task Loss. For heatmap H, we can use soft-argmax instead of argmax to extract a predicted waterline map H' so as to maintain the differentiability of the loss function. For segmentation mask M, We can make difference with its Gaussian blur result to easily get an predicted waterline map $\triangledown M$. Thus, we can compute smoothl1 loss between these two map, which is:

$$L_D = \sum_{x,y} \left| \triangledown M_{x,y} - H'_{x,y} \right|_1 \quad (2)$$

Continuity Loss. Due to the continuity constraint of the waterline, two adjacent columns of the output map should have similar responses. As illustrated in Boundary Loss, the continuity of the waterline can be implicitly constrained by the continuity of the heatmap in column dimension. Thus, we compute smoothL1 loss between the two adjacent columns of the predicted heatmap as follows:

$$L_{str} = \sum_{i=1}^{W-1} |H_{:,i} - H_{:,i+1}|_1 \qquad (3)$$

where W represents the width of the image.

Total Loss Function. Besides, We use the classic cross entropy loss (L_{BCE}) to measure the error of the output of semantic branch. Finally, the integrated loss function can be formulated as below:

$$L = L_H + L_{BCE} + \lambda_1 L_D + \lambda_2 L_{str} \qquad (4)$$

In our experiments, we empirically set $\lambda_1 = 1$ and $\lambda_2 = 100$.

4   Experiments

4.1   Dataset

An important contribution of this paper is proposed a carefully annotated dataset for waterline extraction task. This dataset is obtained by extracting key frames from 69 videos collected at some actual port, such as Port of Dalian, etc. It contains 360 waterline pictures of 1280×720 pixels each. Label of these images is accurately annotated in the form of semantic mask. Figure 1 shows examples of this dataset. Through the label image, we can use the sobel operator to extract boundary which can be seen as groundtruth of waterline. From the introduced dataset, 60 images have been randomly selected for testing and the 300 remainders for training and validation.

4.2   Train Setting

The proposed network is trained from scratch using kaiming initialization [6] manner. We adopt 8 batchsize and use Adam optimizer with 0.0003 weight decay to train our model. The initial learning rate is set to 0.001 with a cosine annealing strategy. Besides, we train the model for 40K iterations on the proposed dataset. The training process takes around 1 days on a TITAN X GPU with cuda 10.0. The input images are resized to 512×288. We conduct experiments based on PyTorch 1.4.

4.3   Evaluation Metric

For the waterline extraction task, the evaluation is defined as the mean value of the ordinate difference under each abscissa between the predicted waterline and groundtruth, denoted as MOD (mean ordinate difference). Meanwhile, in order to compare with the semantic segmentation method, we also adopt mIOU to evaluate the effectiveness of the network.

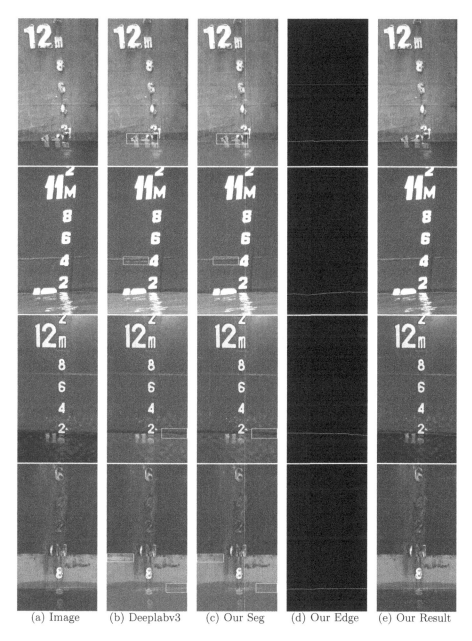

(a) Image   (b) Deeplabv3   (c) Our Seg   (d) Our Edge   (e) Our Result

Fig. 4. Visualization results on the proposed dataset among DeepLabv3 [4] and our network. (a) Original image; (b) segmentation result of DeeplabV3 [4]; (c) segmentation result of our network; (d) edge prediction of our network; (e) waterline extraction result

4.4   Results

We compared our method with the existing semantic segmentation based methods, and the experimental results are shown in Table 1. It can be seen that our network achieves the state-of-the-art on the MOD indicator.

Table 1. Comparison with state-of-the-art on the proposed dataset.

Methods	Backbone	MOD	mIOU
U-Net [11]	–	0.81	99.3
U-Net++ [22]	–	0.95	99.4
DeeplabV3 [4]	ResNet18	0.87	99.4
DeeplabV3 [4]	ResNet50	0.84	99.6
Ours	–	**0.72**	**99.6**

As mentioned in the introduction, waterline extraction determines the accuracy of water gauge reading, which may cause economic problems. Figure 4 shows the experiment result of our network and DeeplabV3 [4]. These results show the advantage of our method compared to the semantic segmentation method. The first row of Fig. 4 shows that semantic segmentation model can not accurately extract the waterline especially near the water scale which is fatal to the water gauge reading. The second row of Fig. 4 shows that the semantic segmentation method will be affected by the full load line of the ship, thus requires post-processing to eliminate this effect. However the edge branch of our method can directly extract the waterline to avoid this problem. The third row of Fig. 4 shows that in the position where the water is clear, method based on semantic segmentation cannot accurately classify pixels near the waterline.

5   Conclusions

A joint multi-task model for waterline extraction is proposed. Up to our knowledge, it is the first DL based approach for waterline extraction task. A large number of experiment results and comparisons with state-of-the-art semantic segmentation based approaches show the effectiveness of the proposed network. Without any pretrained model, it outperforms the state-of-the-art approaches. Besides, we introduced a carefully annotated dataset for waterline extraction. Future work will be focused on adding the connectivity constraints of water and ship areas in the network to improve the accuracy of waterline extraction.

Acknowledgements. This work was supported in part by the National Natural Science Foundation of China (Grant No. 61976208) and Coal Science and Technology Research Institute Co., Ltd Technological Innovation Project(2019CX-I-03).

References

1. Canny, J.: A computational approach to edge detection. IEEE Trans. Pattern Anal. Mach. Intell. **6**, 679–698 (1986)
2. Chen, L.-C., et al.: DeepLab: semantic image segmentation with deep convolutional nets, atrous convolution, and fully connected CRFs. IEEE Trans. Pattern Anal. Mach. Intell. **40**(4), 834–848 (2017)
3. Chen, L.-C., et al.: Encoder-decoder with atrous separable convolution for semantic image segmentation. In: Proceedings of the European Conference on Computer Vision (ECCV), pp. 801–818 (2018)
4. Chen, L.-C., et al.: Rethinking atrous convolution for semantic image segmentation. arXiv preprint arXiv:1706.05587 (2017)
5. Fu, J., et al.: Dual attention network for scene segmentation. In: Proceedings of the IEEE/CVF Conference on Computer Vision and Pattern Recognition, pp. 3146–3154 (2019)
6. He, K., et al.: Delving deep into rectifiers: surpassing human-level performance on imagenet classification. In: Proceedings of the IEEE International Conference on Computer Vision, pp. 1026–1034 (2015)
7. Hu, Y., et al.: Dynamic feature fusion for semantic edge detection. arXiv preprint arXiv:1902.09104 (2019)
8. Huang, Z., et al.: CCNet: criss-cross attention for semantic segmentation. In: Proceedings of the IEEE/CVF International Conference on Computer Vision, pp. 603–612 (2019)
9. Lin, G., et al.: RefineNet: multi-path refinement networks for highresolution semantic segmentation. In: Proceedings of the IEEE Conference on Computer Vision and Pattern Recognition, pp. 1925–1934 (2017)
10. Long, J., Shelhamer, E., Darrell, T.: Fully convolutional networks for semantic segmentation. In: Proceedings of the IEEE Conference on Computer Vision and Pattern Recognition, pp. 3431–3440 (2015)
11. Ronneberger, O., Fischer, P., Brox, T.: U-net: convolutional networks for biomedical image segmentation. In: Navab, N., Hornegger, J., Wells, W.M., Frangi, A.F. (eds.) MICCAI 2015. LNCS, vol. 9351, pp. 234–241. Springer, Cham (2015). https://doi.org/10.1007/978-3-319-24574-4_28
12. Sobel, I.E.: Camera Models and Machine Perception. Stanford University, Stanford (1970)
13. Szegedy, C., et al.: Inception-v4, inception-resnet and the impact of residual connections on learning. In: Thirty-First AAAI Conference on Artificial Intelligence (2017)
14. Wang, X., et al.: Non-local neural networks. In: Proceedings of the IEEE Conference on Computer Vision and Pattern Recognition, pp. 7794–7803 (2018)
15. Xie, S., Tu, Z.: Holistically-nested edge detection. In: Proceedings of the IEEE International Conference on Computer Vision, pp. 1395–1403 (2015)
16. Yu, C., et al.: BiseNet v2: bilateral network with guided aggregation for real-time semantic segmentation. arXiv preprint arXiv:2004.02147 (2020)
17. Yu, Z., et al.: CaseNet: deep category-aware semantic edge detection. In: Proceedings of the IEEE Conference on Computer Vision and Pattern Recognition, pp. 5964–5973 (2017)
18. Zhao, H., et al.: PSANet: point-wise spatial attention network for scene parsing. In: Proceedings of the European Conference on Computer Vision (ECCV), pp. 267–283 (2018)

19. Zhao, H., et al.: Pyramid scene parsing network. In: Proceedings of the IEEE Conference on Computer Vision and Pattern Recognition, pp. 2881–2890 (2017)
20. Zhen, M., et al.: Joint semantic segmentation and boundary detection using iterative pyramid contexts. In: Proceedings of the IEEE/CVF Conference on Computer Vision and Pattern Recognition, pp. 13666–13675 (2020)
21. Zhou, X., Wang, D., Krähenbühl, P.: Objects as points. arXiv preprint arXiv:1904.07850 (2019)
22. Zhou, Z., Rahman Siddiquee, M.M., Tajbakhsh, N., Liang, J.: UNet++: a nested U-net architecture for medical image segmentation. In: Stoyanov, D., et al. (eds.) DLMIA/ML-CDS -2018. LNCS, vol. 11045, pp. 3–11. Springer, Cham (2018). https://doi.org/10.1007/978-3-030-00889-5_1

Face and Body and Biometrics

Comparing Facial Expression Recognition in Humans and Machines: Using CAM, GradCAM, and Extremal Perturbation

Serin Park[1] and Christian Wallraven[2(✉)]

[1] Department of Artificial Intelligence, Korea University, Seoul, Korea
`bvcxz565@korea.ac.kr`
[2] Department of Artificial Intelligence & Department of Brain and Cognitive Engineering, Korea University, Seoul, Korea
`wallraven@korea.ac.kr`

Abstract. Facial expression recognition (FER) is a topic attracting significant research in both psychology and machine learning with a wide range of applications. Despite a wealth of research on human FER and considerable progress in computational FER made possible by deep neural networks (DNNs), comparatively less work has been done on comparing the degree to which DNNs may be comparable to human performance. In this work, we compared the recognition performance and attention patterns of humans and machines during a two-alternative forced-choice FER task. Human attention was here gathered through click data that progressively uncovered a face, whereas model attention was obtained using three different popular techniques from explainable AI: CAM, GradCAM and Extremal Perturbation. In both cases, performance was gathered as percent correct. For this task, we found that humans outperformed machines quite significantly. In terms of attention patterns, we found that Extremal Perturbation had the best overall fit with the human attention map during the task.

Keywords: Facial expression recognition · AffectNet · Humans versus machines · Human-in-the-loop

1 Introduction

Facial expression is a natural and powerful tool of communication among humans. Facial expressions are instantly processed by humans conveying a wealth of messages: a smiling face spreads happiness, and a sad face makes our heart ache. There is evidence that some emotional facial expressions are largely universal [6], that is, they are recognized well in different cultures and associated with similar semantic content. Recent work, however, has cast some doubt to the degree of this universality [10,13] and the degree to which facial expressions are actually a reliable signal of an internal mental state [1], but that does not lessen the importance of facial expressions in human-to-human communication [22].

© Springer Nature Switzerland AG 2022
C. Wallraven et al. (Eds.): ACPR 2021, LNCS 13188, pp. 403–416, 2022.
https://doi.org/10.1007/978-3-031-02375-0_30

Because of its importance to humans, facial expression recognition is also a major topic in the field of machine learning. If machines would be able to interpret human facial expression correctly - and possibly make appropriate facial expressions in return - human-to-machine interaction would become more natural and efficient. Recognition of facial expression by machines is called automatic facial expression recognition, or automatic FER. Automatic FER has come a long way, from hand-crafted approaches to the current end-to-end deep learning models that locate and recognize facial expressions [16]. Nonetheless, there still is a long way to go: current algorithms are good enough at recognizing laboratory-controlled facial expression images, but they struggle to recognize expressions from naturalistic images [18,25].

This leads us to the natural question: do humans and machines process facial expression images differently? And if they do, can we teach machines to act more like humans? In this paper, we adopted a human-in-the-loop (HIL) paradigm to address this question: we first collected click data from human participants to gather those spatial locations that may be important for disambiguating an expression in a two-alternative forced-choice task. Click data are reported to be a cost-efficient substitute for eye-tracking, and reflect the regional attention well [5,14]. For automatic FER, we trained an ensemble of deep neural networks on AffectNet [19], a large, in-the-wild facial expression dataset, and compared its activation map with human click data using three different explainability or visualization methods. We also tried to further fine-tune the models with the human attention map to see whether this would improve the FER performance.

2   Related Work

2.1   Automatic FER

After the advent of deep learning, FER has typically been implemented with deep neural networks due to their superior performance and robustness over the past years [16]. In this section, we will go through some of the most popular datasets of FER and their benchmarks.

FER datasets can be broadly categorized as either controlled or in-the-wild. Controlled datasets are posed by trained actors and photographed in the lab with regular illumination. The extended Cohn-Kanade dataset (CK+; [17]) is a classic example of a controlled dataset. It contains 593 video sequences from 123 individuals that start from neutral expression and culminate in the intended expression (one of seven categories: anger, contempt, disgust, fear, happiness, sadness, and surprise). In contrast, in-the-wild datasets are crawled from the web by searching for emotion-related keywords. This type of dataset is typically larger than controlled datasets, and noisier in terms of identity, illumination, etc. FER+ [2], a re-labeled version of FER2013 [11], has been a popular early dataset in the field, with 28,709 training images, 3,589 validation images and 3,589 test images, consisting of the same seven expressions as the CK+ dataset.

Currently, AffectNet [19] is the largest publicly-available labelled dataset on facial expressions (see Dataset section below for detailed information).

FER models have reached excellent performance on controlled datasets: on CK+, Frame Attention networks proposed by [18] have attained 99.7% accuracy. However, FER models perform less well with in-the-wild datasets: the state-of-the-art (SOTA) accuracy on the FER+ dataset with cleaned and updated labels is 89.75% reached by a PSR model on seven expressions [29]. SOTA on the AffectNet dataset, in contrast, is only 65.74% for seven of the eight included emotion categories [25]. Given that FER systems in practical use, such as humanoid robots and surveillance systems, will not be fed with regular illuminations, frontal head position and exemplary expressions, it is important to improve FER accuracy on such in-the-wild datasets.

2.2 Human FER

As automatic FER is an effort to mimic the natural capacity of humans to recognize facial expressions, one must look back on humans to get insight for the models. One thing to note is that humans are not necessarily better than deep neural networks in the task of classifying images. Human performance on the (non-updated) FER2013 dataset was $65\pm5\%$ [11], while the then-SOTA model, ResMaskingNet [23] reached 76.82%. However, this does not mean machines have outperformed humans in facial expression recognition in general. As stated above, recognizing someone's facial expression in the real world represents quite different challenges.

One of the key differences between humans and computers in FER is that humans pay attention to a limited region in the face, while computers treat all pixels equally in the initial phase. Humans distribute most of their attention to the eyes and mouth [20,22], which partly explains the efficiency with which humans recognize facial expression. Interestingly, the region of interest can differ depending on culture [12]. East Asians focus on the eyes, while Western Caucasian also pay attention to the mouth region. This difference leads East Asians to perform less well when discriminating 'fear' from 'disgust', in which pair the mouth region holds the key information.

2.3 Transfer Learning

Transfer learning has two major approaches: the first approach is to pretrain and then fine-tune. Fine-tuning is a common practice in training neural networks. As it is difficult to collect large datasets for specific problems, researchers often train their networks first on ImageNet, a large-scale object classification dataset that contains 1.2 million images with 1000 classes [4]. ImageNet-pretrained models are also available in deep learning libraries. Fine-tuning may be done several times: [21] introduced cascaded fine-tuning, where the researchers first trained a deep CNN model on ImageNet dataset, an auxiliary dataset related to emotion recognition, and finally on the target dataset.

Another approach is Knowledge Distillation, also known as Teacher-Student model. It was originally developed as a model compression method [3]. The Teacher network first learns the representations and outputs prediction labels. Then the Student network is trained on the prediction labels of Teacher. One key aspect of Knowledge Distillation is that it can transfer knowledge across models with different structure. It even enables human-machine transfer learning: [26] implemented this type of learning, albeit indirectly. The researchers first trained a Teacher model on an FER dataset and obtained a saliency map for each image by visualizing the activations of the Teacher model. Then the researchers masked the images by leaving only the most important parts of the image based on the saliency maps - usually around the eyes and mouth - and used the masked images to train the Student model. The masked images initially helped accelerate the training, but the acceleration was retained only if the training data was switched to unmasked images after a certain point - there was no effect on accuracy, however. The critical aspect was that the researchers validated the masked images by comparing them to eye-tracking results by human observers. As the saliency maps of Teacher model were shown to be similar to human attention maps, this work is an indirect example of human-machine transfer learning.

3   Dataset

We chose the AffectNet dataset [19] to train our models for two reasons. First, it is the largest labelled dataset for facial expressions, containing a total of 440,601 labelled images in eight categories: neutral, happy, sad, surprise, fear, disgust, anger, and contempt. Second, it seems to be a difficult dataset to improve on: it was collected by web-based crawling methods, and each image was labeled by one, though expert, human annotator. Therefore, the AffectNet dataset contains in-the-wild images that may be mislabelled or vague. Specifically, out of 36,000 images that were annotated by two human annotators to calculate agreement, their agreement was only 60.7 percent. Moreover, the dataset is highly imbalanced: the largest class, happy, contains 143,991 images while the smallest class, contempt, contains only 5,119 images. This imbalance reflects the real-world proportion of expression occurrences; one does observe happy expressions more often than one observes contempt.

The baseline for AffectNet was measured with AlexNet [15]. As the test set is not publicly available, the validation set, which contains 500 images for each expression, is used as the benchmark dataset. Baseline accuracy with weighted loss was 58% on the validation set. The state-of-the-art is an SL + SSL in-panting-pl model [24], with an average accuracy of 61.72% for eight emotion categories. Table 1 summarizes major results on AffectNet benchmarks and the baseline. In cases where one paper listed several methods with slight differences on the ranking, we only chose one method with the best result. Moreover, we only list methods that were tested on all eight emotion categories, as we will focus also on eight categories in this paper.

Table 1. SOTA and baseline results on AffectNet dataset

Method	Accuracy	Reference
SL + SSL in-panting-pl (B0)	61.72	[24]
Distilled student	61.60	[27]
Multi-task EfficientNet-B0	61.32	[25]
RW loss	61.03	[7]
PSR	60.68	[29]
Baseline (weighted loss)	58.0	[19]

For the human experiment, hand-picked images from the AffectNet validation set were used (see Fig. 1 for example images). For each of the eight facial expression categories, 35 images were chosen that were deemed to be good representatives of the intended expressions. The total number of images was therefore 280. All computational experiments used the full training set of AffectNet and the validation set minus our 280 images.

Fig. 1. Sample images used for human experiment

4   Human Experiment

4.1   Participants

24 Korea University undergraduates were recruited by an online advertisement (12 female, mean age 23.75 ± 3.33 years (SD) - all had normal or corrected-to-normal vision). Of the 24 participants, two had to be excluded from statistical analyses; one being an outlier (overall accuracy more than $3\,\sigma$ lower compared to the sample mean), and the other having skipped an entire block due to mistake.

4.2   Methods and Task

The 280 experimental images were blurred by an opencv function (cv2.blur) with $k = 70$, and converted to grayscale, so that the expression could not be recognized by just looking at the blurred image. Human participants were asked to click on these blurred images to reveal circular parts. The revealed parts were not blurred and in original colors. From the revealed parts, participants had to determine which expression the picture portrayed. There was no limit to the number of clicks, but the participants were asked to make as few clicks as possible. Participants were seated in a quiet room in front of a monitor at a distance of roughly 57 cm. The faces subtended roughly 4.5° of visual angle.

The response options were given in a two-alternative forced-choice (2AFC) paradigm, one being the correct label and the other the false label. For one picture, the false label was fixed across all participants, so there was a fixed picture set for a pair of labels; such as 'happy' versus 'sad'. Moreover, participants were instructed to pay attention to the option pair before clicking on the image and use that information to guide clicks. This instruction was given in order to find key regions for discriminating between a pair of expressions. For example, the mouth region is crucial for discriminating 'fear' from 'surprise' [12]. There was a total of 280 trials, as 35 images were selected from each of the 8 categories. Order of trial was randomized for each participant. The trials were split into 4 sessions of 70 trials each with breaks in-between.

4.3   Results

The average accuracy across all participants in this 2AFC task was 83.9%. The confusion matrix (Fig. 2) illustrates the response pattern of participants. The numbers in the cells are actual normalized values, but the colormap was based upon square roots of the values in order to highlight the differences among non-diagonal values. The confusion pattern shows that some pairs of emotions are confused more often than others: 'contempt' is mistaken for 'neutral', 'fear' for 'surprise', 'anger' for 'disgust', and 'disgust' for 'contempt'.

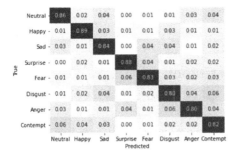

Fig. 2. Human experiment confusion matrix

Next, we plotted the accuracy for each pair of expressions as a heatmap (Fig. 3a). 'True' labels (on the y axis) mean the true label for a given image, and 'false' labels (on the x axis) are the false options in the 2AFC experiment. This matrix is not symmetric since an image with 'happy' as true label and 'sad' as false label is qualitatively different from an image with 'sad' as true label and 'happy' as false label. Same-label pairs do not exist in the experiment, but were included as empty cells for a more legible visualization of pair structures. We also explored two other variables as a function of expression pairs: the number of clicks before label decision for one image, and the time taken between the first click and the label decision of one image (Figs. 3b,c). As in the accuracy heatmap, same-label pairs were included as empty cells. A clear positive correlation was observed between number of clicks and time, $r = .93$, $p < .001$. Significant negative correlations were observed between number of clicks and accuracy, $r = -.56$, $p < .001$, and between time and accuracy, $r = -.65$, $p < .001$.

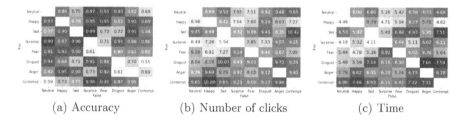

(a) Accuracy   (b) Number of clicks   (c) Time

Fig. 3. Accuracy, number of clicks and time as a function of pairs

Next, we analyzed the pattern of clicks to investigate the strategies participants used. For visualization, clicks were color-coded according to their sequence: the first click was coded in red, the last click in yellow, and the clicks in between were given interpolated colors. We first obtained the colored click map for one picture, clicked by one participant, and averaged the click maps from all participants on the same picture, given that the label choice was correct. We found that participants mostly click the left eye first, then the right eye, and finally the mouth. In the case of images with low accuracy, the last few clicks were often around the left eye; which means people go back to the left eye when the stimulus is difficult to classify. Figure 4a is an example of an image with high accuracy, where the trend to start from the left eye and to end at the mouth is clear. Figure 4b is an example of an image with low accuracy, where the last click is often on the left eye.

5   Algorithms

5.1   Model Training

To compare the human FER results with those of our DNN, the multiclass problem of classifying eight expression categories of the AffectNet dataset was split

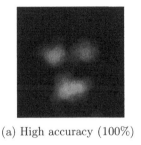
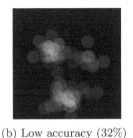

(a) High accuracy (100%)   (b) Low accuracy (32%)

Fig. 4. Visualization of click sequence in images with high and low accuracy (Color figure online)

into a set of binary classification problems. Specifically, there were 28 classifiers (all possible pairs in eight emotions; $\binom{8}{2}$) such as 'happy' versus 'sad', etc. For all classifiers, a ResNet-50 model was used with cross-entropy-loss and Adam optimizer with a base learning rate of 0.0001. Images were augmented by horizontal flip, small degrees of shifting, scaling, rotating, and changes in brightness and contrast. The batch size was 64. The classifiers were trained with original AffectNet training dataset restricted to the two categories in question, and the larger class was undersampled to match the smaller class. Therefore, the size of the dataset was different for each model. Because of this difference, all models were trained until they reached training accuracy of 90 (with maximum epoch of 150), rather than for a fixed number of epochs, to enable fair comparison.

The trained binary classifiers were fine-tuned with the click-revealed images used in the human experiment. There were only 10 source images for each classifier, but as there were 22 participants, the size of fine-tuning dataset could be as large as 220, if the accuracy was 100 percent. The images were also augmented by shifting the click mask by one pixel in eight directions relative to the image. Lastly, we also gave unmasked versions of hand-picked images to the models to prevent catastrophic forgetting. These unmasked, or original, images were augmented in the same manner that was used in pretraining.

5.2   Model Results

We ensembled the prediction results from 28 binary classifiers by simple vote and weighted vote methods (Fig. 5a, b). In the simple vote method, each classifier votes for a class for each test sample. The class with the most votes becomes the predicted label. In the weighted vote method, the largest output value from the fully connected layer of each classifier becomes the weighted vote [9]. This value reflects the confidence of the model. With the train-up-to-90 classifiers, accuracy was 49% for simple vote and a similar level of 50% for weighted vote.

Additionally, we tested a set of classifiers trained for 30 epochs to compare the pattern of prediction (Fig. 6a, b). The performance was similar, with 48% for simple vote and 49% for weighted vote. However, classifiers trained for a set number of epochs showed a greater bias towards 'happy' in the confusion matrix. This tendency was more pronounced in the weighted vote method than in simple vote. This is because 'happy', the representation of which is learned in a relatively short time, gave high confidence while the confidence was low for other expressions.

We also trained a multiclass model for comparison (Fig. 7). In this model, we implemented weighted cross entropy loss instead of undersampling. The number of epochs was 40, with other hyperparameters staying the same. The total accuracy of multiclass model was 54%, which is higher than the ensemble model. However, the two minor classes, 'disgust' and 'contempt', showed higher recall rates for the ensemble model (Fig. 5b). The pattern of confusion of the multiclass model was similar to Fig. 6a, where each pair is trained for the same number of epochs and the simple vote method is used. Overall, the ensemble method showed relatively similar performance across different classes, although the average accuracy dropped by 4%.

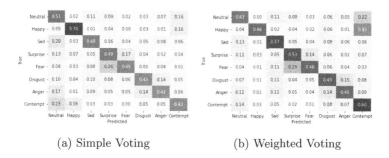

(a) Simple Voting   (b) Weighted Voting

Fig. 5. Ensembled results of pretrained models trained up to 90% train accuracy

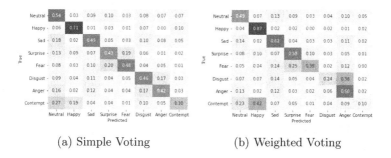

(a) Simple Voting   (b) Weighted Voting

Fig. 6. Ensembled results of pretrained models trained for 30 epochs

Lastly, we fine-tuned the models with masked images. Contrary to initial expectations, the overall accuracy *decreased*, to 43% for simple vote and 44%

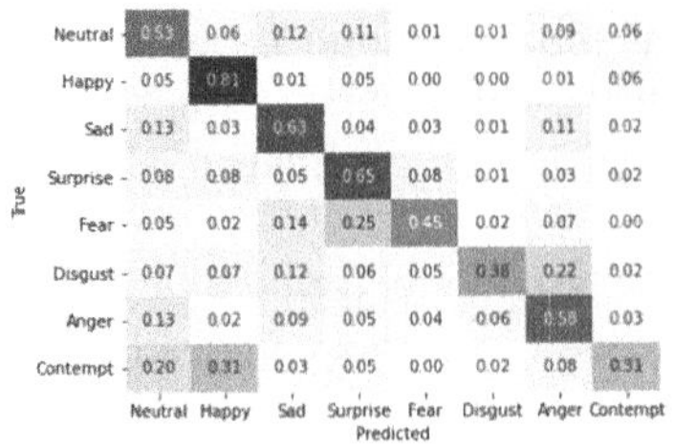

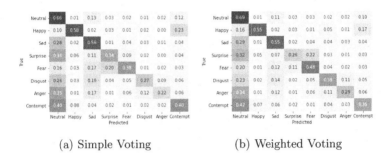

Fig. 7. Multiclass model for comparison

for weighted vote. Varying the ratio of masked and unmasked images did not improve performance. In the confusion matrix (Fig. 8a, b), we observed a strong bias towards the 'neutral' expression.

(a) Simple Voting   (b) Weighted Voting

Fig. 8. Ensembled results of finetuned models

5.3   Comparing Humans and Models

We first looked at correlations of the confusion matrices for the different computational models and the human confusion matrix shown in Fig. 2. There was a positive correlation between human and trained-up-to-accuracy-90 simple-vote model (Fig. 5a), $r = .93$, $p < .001$, and weighted-vote model (Fig. 5b), $r = .92$, $p < .001$. We also found a positive correlation between human and trained-for-30-epochs simple-vote model (Fig. 6a), $r = .91$, $p < .001$, and weighted-vote model (Fig. 5b), $r = .80$, $p < .001$. Lastly, we found a positive correlation between human and multiclass model (Fig. 7), $r = .91$, $p < .001$. This result supports our claim that although the ensemble model has lower average accuracy than multiclass model, its pattern of confusion is slightly more similar to that of humans than multiclass model.

We visualized the activations of pretrained models with three visualization techniques: CAM [30], GradCAM [28] and Extremal Perturbation [8]. Figure 9 demonstrates visualizations of each method over the same image.

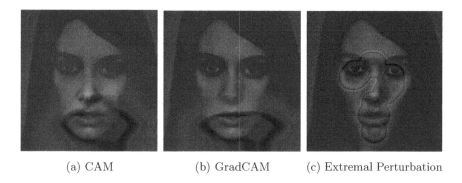

(a) CAM   (b) GradCAM   (c) Extremal Perturbation

Fig. 9. Saliency maps for each method

To see how similar each method is to the human attention map, we computed dice coefficients between human attention maps and model saliency maps. The dice coefficient is given by two times the area of overlap between two binary masks, divided by the total number of 1's in both masks. The attention, or saliency, maps were averaged within expression pairs, normalized and scaled to integer values between 0 and 255. The averaged masks were thresholded at value of 50; that is, values below 50 were set to 0 and values over 50 were set to 1.

Figure 10 illustrates dice coefficients of three different visualization methods in a box plot. If the dice coefficient is close to 1, it means the method is similar to human attention maps. The plot reveals that Extremal Perturbation has the highest mean dice coefficient value. One-way analysis of variance (ANOVA) verifies this observation, as there is a highly significant difference among variables, $F = 85.45$, $p < .001$. Pairwise Tukey analysis reveals that Extremal Perturbation had significantly higher dice coefficients than CAM, $t = 10.31$, $p < .001$, and GradCAM, $t = 12.12$, $p < .001$. There was no significant difference between CAM and GradCAM, $t = 1.81$, $p > .05$. Additional analysis shows that the effect of facial expression was not significant, $F = 1.34$, $p > .05$ and hence that all eight expressions were more similar at equivalent levels for Extremal Perturbation compared to the other two methods.

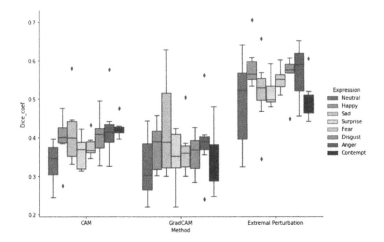

Fig. 10. Dice coefficients between human attention map and model saliency maps

6 Conclusion and Future Work

Our work compared human attention maps represented by click data, and model saliency maps using three different visualization methods: CAM, GradCAM, and Extremal Perturbation. We found that Extremal Perturbation had the best fit with the human attention. It will be interesting to extend this comparison also to other, more standard N-AFC FER tasks, in which humans need to disambiguate between more than two expressions.

Our computational experiments showed that the ensemble models of binary classifiers for FER did not perform as well as the standard multiclass model. However, by training the binary classifiers until they reach training accuracy of 90% and combining the classification results by weighted vote method, we obtained a model that is less biased towards major expressions. Interestingly, we failed to improve the model using attentional information from humans as using the masked images as fine-tuning dataset proved an inadequate method for guiding the attention of a CNN-based model - this is in some way similar to the work by [26] who also found little to no improvement when using masked images. In the future, we will work on incorporating the attention mechanism to our model to channel the model's attention to meaningful regions more effectively.

Lastly, our participants pool was limited in that the participants were all East Asians. According to previous research [12], East Asians tend to focus only on the eyes compared to Western Caucasians, and are thus less accurate at discriminating between 'surprise' and 'fear', 'anger' and 'disgust', respectively. In Fig. 4, we can actually see some evidence for this, with the mouth region often being the last to be revealed, which may be in line with this aforementioned research. Future experiments with Western Caucasian participants may show a different pattern of results.

Acknowledgments. This work was supported by Institute of Information Communications Technology Planning Evaluation (IITP; No. 2019-0-00079, Department of Artificial Intelligence, Korea University) and National Research Foundation of Korea (NRF; NRF-2017M3C7A1041824) grant funded by the Korean government (MSIT).

References

1. Barrett, L.F., Adolphs, R., Marsella, S., Martinez, A.M., Pollak, S.D.: Emotional expressions reconsidered: challenges to inferring emotion from human facial movements. Psychol. Sci. Publ. Interest **20**(1), 1–68 (2019)
2. Barsoum, E., Zhang, C., Ferrer, C.C., Zhang, Z.: Training deep networks for facial expression recognition with crowd-sourced label distribution. In: Proceedings of the 18th ACM International Conference on Multimodal Interaction, pp. 279–283 (2016)
3. Buciluă, C., Caruana, R., Niculescu-Mizil, A.: Model compression. In: Proceedings of the 12th ACM SIGKDD International Conference on Knowledge Discovery and Data Mining, pp. 535–541 (2006)
4. Deng, J., Dong, W., Socher, R., Li, L.J., Li, K., Fei-Fei, L.: ImageNet: a large-scale hierarchical image database. In: 2009 IEEE Conference on Computer Vision and Pattern Recognition, pp. 248–255. Ieee (2009)
5. Egner, S., Reimann, S., Hoeger, R., Zangemeister, W.H.: Attention and information acquisition: comparison of mouse-click with eye-movement attention tracking. J. Eye Move. Res. **11**(6), 1–27 (2018)
6. Ekman, P., Keltner, D.: Universal facial expressions of emotion. In: Segerstrale U.P., Molnar P. (eds.) Nonverbal Communication: Where Nature Meets Culture, pp. 27–46 (1997)
7. Fan, X., Deng, Z., Wang, K., Peng, X., Qiao, Y.: Learning discriminative representation for facial expression recognition from uncertainties. In: 2020 IEEE International Conference on Image Processing (ICIP), pp. 903–907. IEEE (2020)
8. Fong, R., Patrick, M., Vedaldi, A.: Understanding deep networks via extremal perturbations and smooth masks. In: Proceedings of the IEEE/CVF International Conference on Computer Vision, pp. 2950–2958 (2019)
9. Galar, M., Fernández, A., Barrenechea, E., Bustince, H., Herrera, F.: An overview of ensemble methods for binary classifiers in multi-class problems: experimental study on one-vs-one and one-vs-all schemes. Pattern Recogn. **44**(8), 1761–1776 (2011)
10. Gendron, M., Roberson, D., van der Vyver, J.M., Barrett, L.F.: Perceptions of emotion from facial expressions are not culturally universal: evidence from a remote culture. Emotion **14**(2), 251 (2014)
11. Goodfellow, I.J., et al.: Challenges in representation learning: a report on three machine learning contests. In: Lee, M., Hirose, A., Hou, Z.-G., Kil, R.M. (eds.) ICONIP 2013. LNCS, vol. 8228, pp. 117–124. Springer, Heidelberg (2013). https://doi.org/10.1007/978-3-642-42051-1_16
12. Jack, R.E., Blais, C., Scheepers, C., Schyns, P.G., Caldara, R.: Cultural confusions show that facial expressions are not universal. Curr. Biol. **19**(18), 1543–1548 (2009)
13. Jack, R.E., Garrod, O.G., Yu, H., Caldara, R., Schyns, P.G.: Facial expressions of emotion are not culturally universal. Proc. Natl. Acad. Sci. **109**(19), 7241–7244 (2012)

14. Kim, N.W., et al.: Bubbleview: an interface for crowdsourcing image importance maps and tracking visual attention. ACM Trans. Comput.-Hum. Interact. (TOCHI) **24**(5), 1–40 (2017)

15. Krizhevsky, A., Sutskever, I., Hinton, G.E.: ImageNet classification with deep convolutional neural networks. Adv. Neural. Inf. Process. Syst. **25**, 1097–1105 (2012)

16. Li, S., Deng, W.: Deep facial expression recognition: a survey. IEEE Trans. Affect. Comput. (2020)

17. Lucey, P., Cohn, J.F., Kanade, T., Saragih, J., Ambadar, Z., Matthews, I.: The extended Cohn-Kanade dataset (ck+): a complete dataset for action unit and emotion-specified expression. In: 2010 IEEE Computer Society Conference on Computer Vision and Pattern Recognition-Workshops, pp. 94–101. IEEE (2010)

18. Meng, D., Peng, X., Wang, K., Qiao, Y.: Frame attention networks for facial expression recognition in videos. In: 2019 IEEE International Conference on Image Processing (ICIP), pp. 3866–3870. IEEE (2019)

19. Mollahosseini, A., Hasani, B., Mahoor, M.H.: AffectNet: a database for facial expression, valence, and arousal computing in the wild. IEEE Trans. Affect. Comput. **10**(1), 18–31 (2017)

20. Moon, H.J.: Facial expression processing with deep neural networks: from implementation to comparison with humans. Master's thesis, Korea University, Seoul, Korea (2019)

21. Ng, H.W., Nguyen, V.D., Vonikakis, V., Winkler, S.: Deep learning for emotion recognition on small datasets using transfer learning. In: Proceedings of the 2015 ACM on International Conference on Multimodal Interaction, pp. 443–449 (2015)

22. Nusseck, M., Cunningham, D.W., Wallraven, C., Bülthoff, H.H.: The contribution of different facial regions to the recognition of conversational expressions. J. Vis. **8**(8), 1–1 (2008)

23. Pham, L., Vu, T.H., Tran, T.A.: Facial expression recognition using residual masking network. In: 2020 25th International Conference on Pattern Recognition (ICPR), pp. 4513–4519. IEEE (2021)

24. Pourmirzaei, M., Esmaili, F., Montazer, G.A.: Using self-supervised co-training to improve facial representation. arXiv preprint arXiv:2105.06421 (2021)

25. Savchenko, A.V.: Facial expression and attributes recognition based on multi-task learning of lightweight neural networks. arXiv preprint arXiv:2103.17107 (2021)

26. Schiller, D., Huber, T., Dietz, M., André, E.: Relevance-based data masking: a model-agnostic transfer learning approach for facial expression recognition. Front. Comput. Sci. **2**(6) (2020)

27. Schoneveld, L., Othmani, A., Abdelkawy, H.: Leveraging recent advances in deep learning for audio-visual emotion recognition. Pattern Recogn. Lett. (2021)

28. Selvaraju, R.R., Cogswell, M., Das, A., Vedantam, R., Parikh, D., Batra, D.: Gradcam: visual explanations from deep networks via gradient-based localization. In: Proceedings of the IEEE International Conference on Computer Vision, pp. 618–626 (2017)

29. Vo, T.H., Lee, G.S., Yang, H.J., Kim, S.H.: Pyramid with super resolution for in-the-wild facial expression recognition. IEEE Access **8**, 131988–132001 (2020)

30. Zhou, B., Khosla, A., Lapedriza, A., Oliva, A., Torralba, A.: Learning deep features for discriminative localization. In: Proceedings of the IEEE Conference on Computer Vision and Pattern Recognition, pp. 2921–2929 (2016)

Pose Sequence Generation with a GCN and an Initial Pose Generator

Kento Terauchi and Keiji Yanai[✉]

Department of Informatics, The University of Electro-Communications, Tokyo, Japan
`terauchi-k@mm.inf.uec.ac.jp`, `yanai@cs.uec.ac.jp`

Abstract. The existing methods on video synthesis have succeeded in generating higher quality videos by using guide information such as human pose skeletons, segmentation masks and optical flows as auxiliary information. Some existing video generation methods on human motion adopts a two-step video generation consisting of generation of pose sequences and video generation from pose sequences. In this paper, we focus on the first stage, the generation of pose sequences, in the whole processing of video generation of human motion. We incorporate a Graph Convolutional Network (GCN) and an initial pose generator into the model to model poses more explicitly and to generate pose sequences naturally. The experimental results show that the proposed method can generate better quality pose sequences than the conventional methods by improving the initial pose generation and introducing GCN.

Keywords: Video generation · Human pose sequence generation · GCN · VAE

1 Introduction

In recent years, image generation has achieved great success with the development of Generative Adversarial Networks (GAN) and Variational Auto Encoder (VAE). GANs and VAEs have been applied to various image translation tasks by conditioning on labels, images, sounds and texts. However, video generation is more difficult task than still image synthesis because it requires temporal modeling in addition to spatial modeling. Unconditional video generation is a difficult task in general. Then, many existing video generation methods employ guide information such as motion flows to synthesize a video. Some guide-based video synthesis methods have succeeded in generating higher quality videos by using guide information. There are various types of videos to be generated, such as videos of people, videos of natural scenery such as cloud flow, and videos of driving scenery in a city. In the case of human motion video generation, most of the existing video generation methods such as Cai et al. [2] adopt a two-step video generation consisting of two stages: the generation of pose sequences and the generation of videos from pose sequences. In this paper, we focus on the first stage, the generation of pose sequences, in the whole processing of video generation of human motion.

© Springer Nature Switzerland AG 2022
C. Wallraven et al. (Eds.): ACPR 2021, LNCS 13188, pp. 417–430, 2022.
https://doi.org/10.1007/978-3-031-02375-0_31

The main objective of ours is to generate pose sequences with actions corresponding to input labels. To do that, we propose to use a Graph Convolutional Network (GCN) [10] to model human poses more explicitly and enable natural pose sequence generation. GCN is often used as a method for action recognition. However, there are still few methods that use GCN for generating pose sequences. In this paper, we propose a model that incorporates GCN and takes the structure of poses into account. In addition, we add an initial pose generator to the network of Action2Motion [5] which we use as a base method in this work. The experimental results show that the proposed method can generate better quality pose sequences than the conventional methods.

2   Related Work

2.1   Image Generation

Image generation methods have achieved great success in recent years with the development of VAE [7] and GAN [4]. GANs can generate high-quality images by alternately training generators and descriptors in an adversarial manner. Generator tries to generate a plausible image. Discriminator tries to distinguish whether the input image is real or generated fake. The VAE reconstructs the image by maximizing the variational lower bound, while the autoencoder forces the latent variables to be normally distributed. In recent years, various improvements of GANs, such as StyleGAN [6] and BigGAN [1], have achieved remarkable success in generating high-resolution images. Some VAE models have also been proposed, such as VQ-VAE2 [11], which can generate images with high accuracy comparable to GAN. In video generation, the quality of individual frames contributes greatly to the overall quality of the video. Therefore, image generation methods are often applied to video generation.

2.2   Video Generation

Video generation methods include unconditional video generation from noise and generation using flow and segmentation as guides. In unconditional video generation, VGAN [15] divides the generation into foreground and background. TGAN [13] considers the movement of the latent space with time. MoCoGAN [14] separates the latent space into motion and content, and DVDGAN [3] enables high-quality video generation by training on a large amount of data. However, these methods often have difficulties in generation quality and computational complexity. On the other hand, the guide-based generation methods can simplify the generation and improve the quality of the generation. There are several methods such as a human pose based method [2], a flow based method [12], a segmentation based method [16] and a method that adds 3D information to the guide [9]. In the guide-based method, the generation can be manipulated by editing the guide. In this study, we consider video generation in two stages: pose sequence generation and video generation from pose sequences, In particular, we aim to make the generation of pose sequences more natural.

2.3   Pose Sequence Generation

The generation of pose sequences has several promising applications, such as the use of pose guides as a preliminary step in the generation of videos, and the behavior of 3D models. There are existing studies of pose sequence generation. For example, overall generation using CNNs, sequential generation using RNNs, and reference-based [17] which enables various motion generation by cutting out several references and interpolating between them. Cai et al. [2] deals with two stages of video generation: pose sequence generation and video generation from pose sequences, as shown in Fig. 1. For the generation of pose sequences, a model that learns the movement of latent variables and a model that sequentially generates pose sequences from latent variables are trained using adversarial loss with a discriminator. The model can also be used for interpolation and prediction of pose sequences by searching for latent variables corresponding to a certain pose through optimization. For generating pose sequences, a generator only considers time variation by moving latent variables. On the other hand, in our study, we use GRU and Graph Convolutional Network (GCN) to consider both temporal and structural information simultaneously.

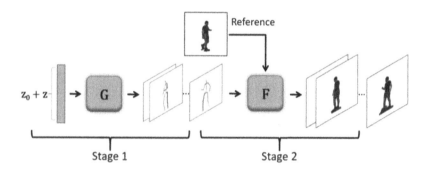

Fig. 1. Cai et al. (cite from [2])

Action2Motion [5] focuses only on the generation of pose sequences, which are generated from conditioning on action labels only. While the prior distribution of VAEs usually follows a normal distribution, Action2Motion assumes that the prior distribution changes as time changes, the architecture infer the prior distribution from the information of the previous time step. In practice, as shown in the Fig. 2, the architecture consist of the encoder of the previous frame, the encoder of the next frame and the decoder (in the Fig. 2, described as Prior, Posterior and Generator). The architecture introduces Prior Loss which brings the distributions of the outputs of the encoder of the previous frame and the encoder of the next frame closer together. pose sequence is reconstructed by the decoder. In the decoder, the GRU is used to capture the temporal information. Overall architecture is trained with Prior Loss and MSE Loss. During testing, the encoder of the previous frame produces an output similar to the encoder of the next frame. From the pose of the previous frame, the pose of the next frame can be generated sequentially. The architecture uses the representation of the body's center coordinate and the angle of each joint. This paper also introduces HumanAct12, a dataset that focuses only on the generation of pose sequences. HumanAct12 is temporally smoother and less noisy than the pose sequence annotations obtained from motion capture in the previous datasets. In our sequential generation model, we modify the generation of the initial frame based on Action2Motion and introduce GCN into the decoder to generate a more natural pose sequence.

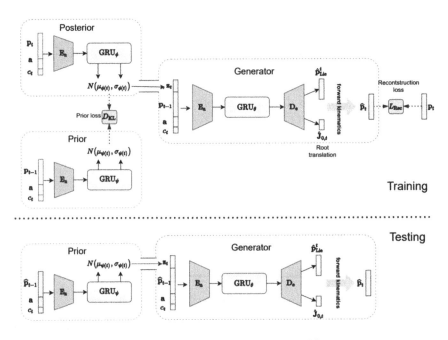

Fig. 2. Action2Motion. (cite from [5])

2.4   Graph Convolution Network

Graph Convolutional Network (GCN) [10] enables convolution on graphs with complex shapes, unlike CNNs which have grid-like relationships. Attempts to convolve human poses with GCNs have been made in action recognition [8], and 3D pose estimation from 2D in [18]. However, there are still few studies using GCN for pose generation. In this study, we apply GCN to the generation of pose sequences. By capturing both time and structure, we hope to make the generation of pose sequences more realistic.

3 Method

We propose a method for generating pose sequences corresponding to a given motion category. The proposed model is generating frames one by one sequentially based on Action2Motion [5]. We use GRU and GCN to consider both time and structure at the same time. The training loss functions and pose representation are also based on Action2Motion.

3.1 Proposed Model

In the proposed model, two changes are made on the model of Action2Motion: we add (1) an initial pose generator, and (2) GCN to the decoder. We aim to improve the quality of generation by these changes. The basic architecture is the same as that of Action2Motion, which consists of a previous frame encoder $E_p r$, a next frame encoder $E_p o$, and a decoder D. We add an initial frame encoder and an initial condition decoder that consider the first frame. By incorporating GCN into the decoder, we aim to learn a model with more expressive power.

Initial Pose Generator. In Action2Motion, when the initial frame is generated, the information of the previous frame is treated as zero, which reduces the diversity of the initial frame of the generated pose sequence. We believe that special treatment of the initial frame is necessary. So we propose to add an initial pose generator to the model of Action2Motion. We encode the first pose with the initial frame encoder so that it is normally distributed like VAE. This makes it possible to generate a variety of frames from noise. In addition, when generating the first frame, we give the information decoded by the initial frame condition decoder from the latent space as a condition for the decoder. The whole architecture is shown in Fig. 3.

Let the length of the pose sequence be T, the number of joints be J, and the number of categories be C. The pose sequence of the data set is $P = \{p_1, p_2, ..., p_T\}$, the i-th pose representation is $p_i \in \mathbb{R}^{J \times 3}$, and the generated pose sequence is $\hat{P} = \{\hat{p}_1, \hat{p}_2, ..., \hat{p}_T\}$. The conditional vector for the i-th pose, $c_i \in \mathbb{R}^C$, consists of (α, t_i) where α_i is an one-hot vector on action categories, and $t_i \in \mathbb{R}$ is a scalar value on relative duration time.

We obtain the initial latent variable, z_f, by reparameterization from the VAE output of the initial frame encoder, $(\mu_f, \sigma_f^2) = E_f(P, c_1)$ Next, we generate the output of the initial frame condition decoder, $\hat{p}_0$, by $\hat{p}_0 = D_f(z_f)$, Using them, the initial frame, $\hat{p}_1$, is generated by the formula, $\hat{p}_1 = D(z_f, \hat{p}_0, c_1)$. After the second frame, in the same way as Action2Motion, we obtain the VAE latent values, (μ, σ^2), using the formula, $(\mu, \sigma^2) = E(p_{i-1}, c_i)$. Then we reparameterize it as z, and use the formula, $\hat{p}_i = D(z, p_{i-1}, c_i)$, to generate the pose $\hat{p}_i$.

Decoder. The layer structure of the decoder is shown in Fig. 3. The decoder takes latent representations and conditions as its inputs and provide them into the two layers of GRU and the two fully connected layers, in the same way as

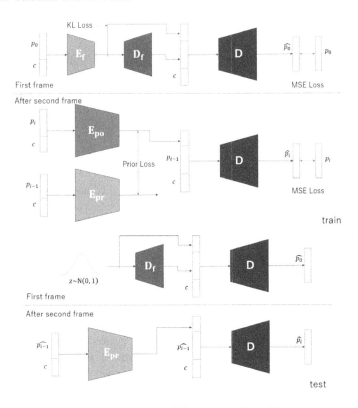

Fig. 3. Overview of the proposed model.

Action2Motion. Then, the decoder embeds it in the pose representation. It learn the structural representation by using three layers of GCN to get a complex representation. We uses a multi-scale GCN that convolves information for each edge in the graph connection. Finally, the output is obtained by passing through a fully connected layer with different weights for each joint. We can maintain the semantic consistency of each joint by passing a fully connected layer to each joint.

3.2   Loss Functions

The objective function uses MSE Loss and Prior Loss as in Action2Motion. KL Loss is used to make the output of the initial frame encoder closer to a normal distribution.

$$L_f = -\frac{1}{2} \sum_{j=1}^{dim(z_f)} (1 + \log \sigma_j^2 - \mu_j^2 - \sigma_j^2) \qquad (1)$$

The KL loss allows models to generate the initial frame from noise (Fig. 4).

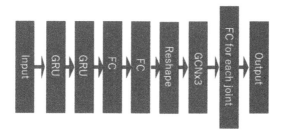

Fig. 4. The layer structure of the decoder.

3.3   Pose Representation

The representation of the pose sequence to be learned is similar to the representation in Action2Motion. It consists of the 3D Cartesian coordinates of the center joint of the body and the angular representation of each bone. The angular representation is a Lie algebraic representation, and the rotation is represented by three parameters. When converting to 3D coordinates, the bones connected from the central joint of the body are tilted to the angle of the representation in turn, and the position of the joint moved by the length of the bone is obtained, and the coordinates of the neighboring joint are obtained. In this case, the length of the bones is adjusted manually. By not including the length of the bones in the pose representation, the model can generate stable motions independent of the body size.

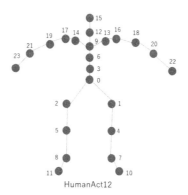

Fig. 5. Location of the joint in HumanAct12.

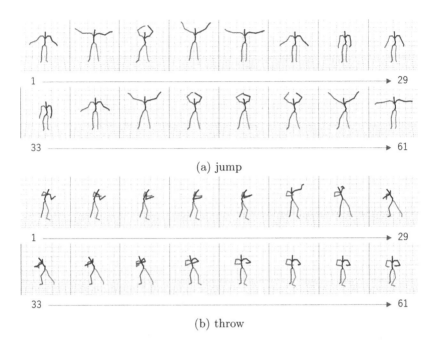

(a) jump

(b) throw

Fig. 6. The example of pose sequence in HumanAct12.

4   Experiments

We report the results of actual training using the model described in this paper. We evaluate the results qualitatively and quantitatively in order to confirm that the model is able to generate pose sequences corresponding to the categories. The baseline to be compared is Action2Motion [5]. We use HumanAct12 [5] as the training dataset. We use the Adam optimizer to repeat the 6000 epoch training. We also evaluate "Ours (IPG only)" by adding only the initial pose generator (IPG), and "Ours (GCN only)" by incorporating only GCN in the decoder as ablation studies.

4.1   Dataset

HumanAct12. HumanAct12 is the dataset presented in Action2Motion. HumanAct12 is a dataset for action recognition and motion generation that contains 1191 pose sequences ranging from 9 to 403 frames in length with 12 coarse categories and 34 detailed categories. Each pose sequence consists of 24 joints. Each joint is shown in Fig. 5. The data used for generation are randomly selected sequences and fixed-length frames are randomly cut out from the sequences. If the pose sequence is less than a fixed length frame, the last frame is padded. Some examples of pose sequences are shown in Fig. 6. For the categorical conditioning, we use 12 coarse categories.

4.2 Qualitative Evaluation

Examples of the generated results are shown in Fig. 7 and Fig. 8 which corresponds to "eating" and "running', respectively. The positions of the 3D joints are drawn in 3D space, and the poses are represented by straight lines connecting the key points. The figures shows the results of (a) the ground-truth and generated videos by (b) Action2Motion and (c) our proposed method. Each human motion sequence is represented with every 4 frames among the total 64 frames. Each of them is generated from different noise vectors using the trained model. The proposed model is able to generate motions similar to the dataset, and even complex motions such as eating and running are well generated. There are reasonable movements such as the correspondence of the relationship between hands and feet. Compared to Action2Motion, the proposed model is temporally smoother and more natural in its generation.

4.3 Interpolation of Latent Space

To show that the model is not simply storing a data set, we interpolate the latent space. We show that a latent variable in the middle of two latent variables generates a pose sequence in the middle of two pose sequences. If interpolation can be achieved, we can say that the learned model has acquired a continuous representation in the latent space. We generate pose sequences using the learned model from two latent variables generated from random numbers and their intermediate latent variables, respectively. We interpolate in two settings, within the same action and between different actions, and in the interpolation between different actions, we interpolate the action labels at the same time.

The results of interpolation within the same action are shown in Fig. 9, and the results between different actions are shown in Fig. 10. The figures show the results with every 8 frames with the leftmost image as the first frame. The pose sequence in the middle row is generated by interpolating the latent variables that generate both the pose sequences in the top row and the bottom row. The interpolation in Fig. 9 is generated from two kinds of "warming-up" action sequences, and the interpolation in Fig. 10 is generated from the "jumping" and "sitting" action sequences. For each interpolation of both the same action and the difference actions, the pose sequence generated from the average of the two latent variables inherits the features of both pose sequences generated from the two latent variables. From this, we can say that interpolation has been achieved.

4.4 Quantitative Evaluation

Similar to Action2Motion, we use the following four metrics for evaluation, FID, Accuracy, Diversity, and Multimodality. All the measures are measured by sampling 3000 pose sequences from the dataset and the generated data. The results are shown in Table 1. The proposed method, the results of which are represented as "Ours (FULL)" in the table, outperforms the existing methods in FID while

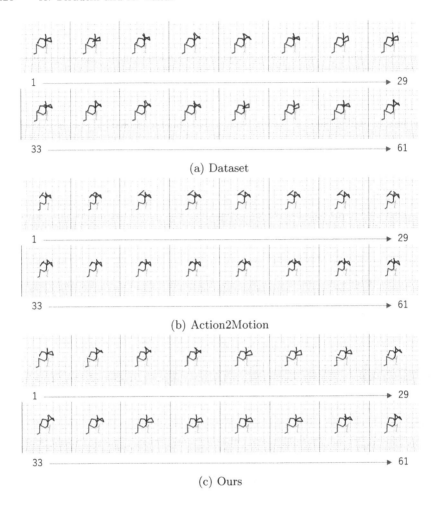

(a) Dataset

(b) Action2Motion

(c) Ours

Fig. 7. The results of generating pose sequence conditioned on "eat" action.

maintaining the same accuracy. This means that the proposed method is able to generate clear pose sequences more naturally than the existing methods. Note that Diversity and Multimodality should be close to the value of groundtruth (GT), since both too large value of them and too small value of them are not good. Each evaluation metric is explained below.

FID measures the distance between the distributions of the real data and the generated data. We use the feature vectors extracted from the trained model of action recognition. For feature extraction, we use the trained models available on the Action2Motion GitHub. The lower the FID, the closer to the data set and the higher the quality of the generation.

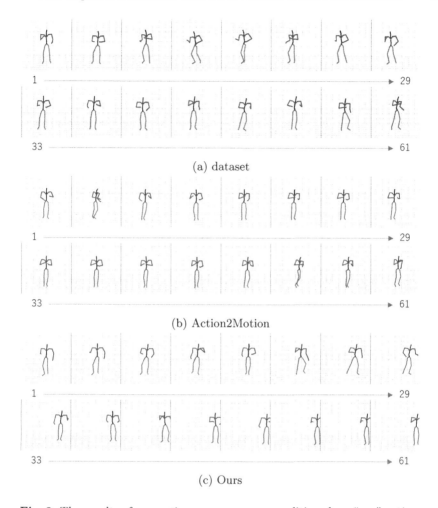

Fig. 8. The results of generating pose sequence conditioned on "run" action.

Accuracy is calculated as classification accuracy by classify the generated pose sequences with the trained action classification model. We use the same model as the model used for FID computation. The higher accuracy, the more clearly the pose sequences with distinct actions are generated.

Diversity is measured as the variance of the pose sequences generated by all the action conditions. With this measure, we judge if the generated sequences are diverse or not. However, even if unnatural sequences are generated, the diversity might be large. Therefore, the diversity value can be an indicator of diverse generation only when the indices of FID and accuracy are good.

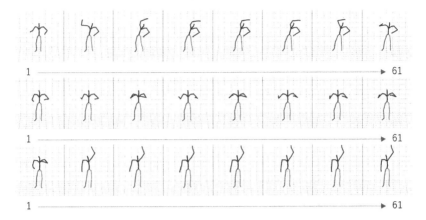

Fig. 9. Interpolation within the "warm-up" action.

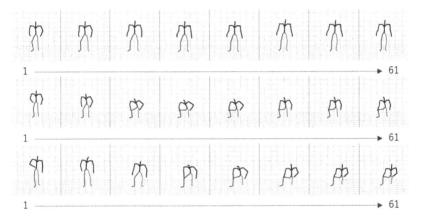

Fig. 10. Interpolation between "jump" action and "sit" action.

Multimoldality measures the diversity of pose sequences generated by each action category condition. Unlike the evaluation of diversity over all the action conditions, we measure the diversity within the same action category. In this measure, we can see whether diversity is maintained within a category or not.

4.5   Ablation Study

In this research, two changes are made to Action2Motion: (1) adding IPG (Initial Pose Generator) to the encoder and (2) adding GCN (Graph Convolutional Network) to the decoder. With these two changes, we tried to improve the quality of generation. We examine the impact of these two changes on the quality of generation. We also conducted two evaluations: Ours (IPG only) with only (1) changed, and Ours (GCN only) with only (2) changed.

Table 1. The results of quantitative evaluation.

Method	Accuracy↑	FID↓	Diversity→	Multimodality→
Groundtruth (GT)	0.997	0.092	6.857	2.449
Action2Motion	0.923	2.458	7.032	2.870
Ours (FULL)	**0.924**	2.252	**6.962**	**2.861**
Ours (IPG only)	0.864	**1.979**	6.924	3.388
Ours (GCN only)	0.542	13.599	5.933	3.309

The results are shown in Table 1. Ours (IPG only) outperformed the baseline regarding FID. Its accuracy was inferior to Ours (FULL), and it could not generate a clear pose sequence. Ours (GCN only) failed to generate a clear pose sequence because both Accuracy and FID are by far less than others.

5   Conclusion

In this study, we proposed a model that explicitly captures the structural information by considering the initial frame with the initial pose generator and incorporating GCN. The qualitative results showed that the proposed method was capable of generating complex and diverse motions. Quantitatively, the proposed method outperformed the existing methods and showed more natural generation.

As future works, we plan to make additional evaluations on other datasets, since we have evaluated our method on only one kinds of the dataset. In addition, we like to study a model for generating videos from pose sequences, and actually generate videos from generated poses.

Acknowledgement. This work was supported by JSPS KAKENHI Grant Number 17H06100 and 21H05812.

References

1. Brock, A., Donahue, J., Simonyan, K.: Large scale GAN training for high fidelity natural image synthesis. In: Proceedings of International Conference on Learning Representations (2019). https://openreview.net/forum?id=B1xsqj09Fm
2. Cai, H., Bai, C., Tai, Y., Tang, C.: Deep video generation, prediction and completion of human action sequences. In: Proceedings of of European Conference on Computer Vision, pp. 366–382 (2018)
3. Clark, A., Donahue, J., Simonyan, K.: Adversarial video generation on complex datasets. arXiv preprint arXiv:1907.06571 (2019)
4. Goodfellow, I., et al.: Generative adversarial nets. In: Advances in Neural Information Processing Systems, pp. 2672–2680 (2014)
5. Guo, C., et al.: Action2motion: conditioned generation of 3D human motions. In: Proceedings of ACM International Conference Multimedia (2020)

6. Karras, T., Laine, S., Aila, T.: A style-based generator architecture for generative adversarial networks. In: Proc. of IEEE Computer Vision and Pattern Recognition, pp. 4401–4410 (2019)
7. Kingma, D., Welling, M.: Auto-encoding variational Bayes. In: Proceedings of International Conference on Learning Representations (2014)
8. Liu, Z., Zhang, H., Chen, Z., Wang, Z., Ouyang, W.: Disentangling and unifying graph convolutions for skeleton-based action recognition. In: Proceedings of IEEE Computer Vision and Pattern Recognition, pp. 143–152 (2020)
9. Mallya, A., Wang, T.C., Sapra, K., Liu, M.Y.: World-consistent video-to-video synthesis. In: Proceedings of European Conference on Computer Vision (2020)
10. Niepert, M., Ahmed, M., Kutzkov, K.: Learning convolutional neural networks for graphs. In: Proceedings of International Conference on Machine Learning, pp. 2014–2023 (2016)
11. Razavi, A., van den Oord, A., Vinyals, O.: Generating diverse high-fidelity images with VQ-VAE-2. In: Advances in Neural Information Processing Systems, pp. 14866–14876 (2019)
12. Ren, Y., Li, G., Liu, S., Li, T.H.: Deep spatial transformation for pose-guided person image generation and animation. IEEE Trans. Image Process. (2020)
13. Saito, M., Matsumoto, E., Saito, S.: Temporal generative adversarial nets with singular value clipping. In: Proceedings of IEEE International Conference on Computer Vision, pp. 2830–2839 (2017)
14. Tulyakov, S., Liu, M., Yang, X., Kautz, J.: MoCoGAN: decomposing motion and content for video generation. In: Proceedings of IEEE Computer Vision and Pattern Recognition (2018)
15. Vondrick, C., Pirsiavash, H., Torralba, A.: Generating videos with scene dynamics. In: Advances in Neural Information Processing Systems, vol. 29, pp. 613–621 (2016)
16. Wang, T., et al.: Video-to-video synthesis. In: Advances in Neural Information Processing Systems (2018)
17. Xu, J., Xu, H., Ni, B., Yang, X., Wang, X., Darrell, T.: Hierarchical style-based networks for motion synthesis. In: Proceedings of European Conference on Computer Vision (2020)
18. Zhao, L., Peng, X., Tian, Y., Kapadia, M., Metaxas, D.N.: Semantic graph convolutional networks for 3D human pose regression. In: Proceedings of IEEE Computer Vision and Pattern Recognition, pp. 3420–3430 (2019)

Domain Generalization with Pseudo-Domain Label for Face Anti-spoofing

Young Eun Kim and Seong-Whan Lee[✉]

Department of Artificial Intelligence, Korea University, Seoul, Republic of Korea
{ye_kim,sw.lee}@korea.ac.kr

Abstract. Face anti-spoofing (FAS) plays an important role in protecting face recognition systems from face representation attacks. Many recent studies in FAS have approached this problem with domain generalization technique. Domain generalization aims to increase generalization performance to better detect various types of attacks and unseen attacks. However, previous studies in this area have defined each domain simply as an anti-spoofing datasets and focused on developing learning techniques. In this paper, we proposed a method that enables network to judge its domain by itself with the clustered convolutional feature statistics from intermediate layers of the network, without labeling domains as datasets. We obtained pseudo-domain labels by not only using the network extracting features, but also using depth estimators, which were previously used only as an auxiliary task in FAS. In our experiments, we trained with three datasets and evaluated the performance with the remaining one dataset to demonstrate the effectiveness of the proposed method by conducting a total of four sets of experiments.

Keywords: Face anti spoofing · Domain generalization · Meta learning

1 Introduction

As face recognition (FR) has been widely studied over the past few decades [1–5], face recognition techniques have been applied to many real-word applications, such as surveillance and biometric systems. Unlike other biometric authentication systems, face-to-face authentication does not require expensive equipment and is also possible with regular RGB cameras. However, FR systems are vulnerable to presentation attacks [6–9]. Presentation attack is an attack in which someone attempts to authenticate using paper photos or videos of a face of other person. Typical presentation attacks include printed photo attacks, replay

This work was supported by Institute of Information & communications Technology Planning & Evaluation (IITP) grant funded by the Korea government (MSIT) (No. 2019-0-00079, Artificial Intelligence Graduate School Program (Korea University)).

attacks that play videos in front of authentication cameras using tablets or laptops, and 3d mask attacks, but various kinds of unseen attacks have recently been made to breach the security. Thus, needs for technique to detect face presentation attacks has recently emerged and actively studied in the name of face anti-spoofing (FAS) for the security of authentication systems.

Prior work on FAS can be largely divided into two methods: temporal-based methods and texture-based methods. In temporal based method, early works used particular liveness facial motions, such as mouth motion [10] and eye-blinking [11,12] as spoofing cues. However, temporal-based methods is vulnerable to the attack of which an attacker punctures only the eyes or mouth of a photograph and allows the actual eye and mouth to replace it. The Texture based method extracts handcrafted features such as Local Binary Pattern (LBP) or Histogram of oriented Gradients (HoG) and uses traditional classifiers such as support vector machine (SVM) or linear discriminant analysis (LDA) to classify them to genuine face and spoof face [13,14]. Texture based methods aim to learn the fine textures shown when a picture is printed and to learn the textures of the devices used for attack. Furthermore, beyond the methods using handcrafted features and traditional classifiers, deep learning-based methods were first proposed with convolutional neural networks [15]. In [18], pixel-wise labeling was proposed demonstrating even better performance. However, while these existing studies have shown good performance on intra-dataset testing, they have shown significant degradation of performance on the cross-dataset testing. This means that existing methods is not robust on unseen attacks.

Research to improve the generalization performance of data of unseen domains has also evolved, called domain generalization (DG) [28–31]. In FAS, studies have also shown to learn domain-invariant features by adapting several domain generalization techniques. Techniques such as adversarial learning, feature disentangling, and meta-learning were widely used to improve generalization performance. Adversarial learning [41] uses minmax games to make domain indistinguishable features using domain discriminator. For example, [19], one discriminator and triplet loss were used together. Feature division performs tasks by focusing on the spoof-relevant part, assuming that features extracted from the network can be distinguished between those containing a lot of domain-relevant information and those containing spoof-relevant information. For the first time in the [21], the technique of metal learning for domain generalization was applied to anti-spoofing by using depth regression as an auxiliary task.

However, previous DG-focused studies have all defined each domain as dataset and focused on learning techniques. This is because each dataset has a different device or filming environment used in the attack. However, each dataset also contains different types of attacks, such as high quality attacks and low quality attacks or printed attacks and video replay attacks. The more datasets are used, the more likely they are to be included in other datasets, but the more similar types of attacks are to be classified as the same domain.

In this paper, we do not simply define dataset as domain, but we propose to define domain by checking the style features of each dataset through output in the middle layer of the network, based on which we cluster. The [27] states that

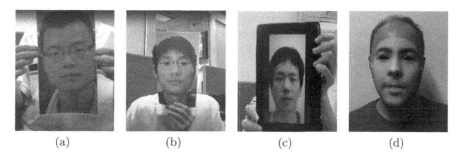

Fig. 1. Various types of face presentation attacks (a) printed photo attack, (b) cut photo attack, (c) video replay attack and (d) 3D mask attack

the late feature of the middle layer of the network reflects the style information of the image, and the [26] applies the late feature and adversarial learning of the middle layer to the domain generalization task. However, adversarial learning has the disadvantage of being unstable in learning, and setting different number of clustering groups can change the structure of the discriminator network, which can lead to performance degradation. Using this motif, we apply meta-learning techniques to extract domain-invited and spoof-relevent features from the network with a defined pseudo domain label. This provides stable learning, as well as the need to label domain if dataset is obtained by web-crawling (Fig. 1).

2 Related Work

2.1 DG Based Face Anti-spoofing Methods

Domain generalization technique was widely used to improve the generalization performance of anti-spoofing algorithms against unseen attacks. Studies using Adversarial learning to extract domain-invariant features include [19] and [20]. [20] used as discriminators of which the number was same with the number of domains to allow the network to create domain-invariant features with a minimax approach. In [19], the framework named SSDG is designed to generate domain invariant features by one discriminator. By passing adversarial learning only on the real image, the real image allows feature distribution to be distributed similarly regardless of its domains. [23] synthesized images by mixing the content features and livness features. By exchanging the liveness features of the real person and the attack, [23] got different reconstructed images with the same content but their liveness attributes are changed.

Previous studies using meta learning include [21] and [52]. Most similar to our study is the framework of [21], which has a distribution that first proposed domain generalization metal learning to anti-spoofing. [52] proposed an unsupplied domain adaptation method. Autoencoder is used to obtain domain information of data at the time of inference, and binary classification is used by classifiers based on domain information. Among those works, the ones most related is

[21]. The similarity is that we also used meta learning for domain generalization. However, we have significant difference in the aspect of defining domains. With our proposed method, the number of domain groups can be defined as much as we want.

2.2 Meta Learning for Domain Generalization (MLDG)

Meta learning presents a technique that makes it applicable to any model rather than creating a new deep learning model for domain generalization performance. Learning to generalize describes the analysis of MLDG. The objective of MLDG is:

$$\underset{\Theta}{\operatorname{argmin}} \mathcal{F}(\Theta) + \beta \mathcal{G}\left(\Theta - \alpha \mathcal{F}'(\Theta)\right), \tag{1}$$

where $\mathcal{F}(\cdot)$ is the loss from the meta-train domains, $\mathcal{G}(\cdot)$ is the loss from the meta-test domains and $\mathcal{F}'(\Theta)$ is the gradient of the training loss $\mathcal{F}(\Theta)$. It means meta learning will tune such that after updating the meta-train domains, performance is also good on the meta-test domains.

For another perspective view that [38] is describing is that it we can get another analysis by doing the first order Taylor expansion for the second term in Eq. 1 as follows:

$$\mathcal{G}(x) = \mathcal{G}(\dot{x}) + \mathcal{G}'(\dot{x}) \times (x - \dot{x}), \tag{2}$$

where $\dot{x}$ is an arbitrary point that is close to x. The multi-variable form x is a vector and $\mathcal{G}(x)$ is a scalar.

Using Taylor expansion in Eq. 2, Eq. 1 can be modified as follows:

$$\underset{\Theta}{\operatorname{argmin}} \mathcal{F}(\Theta) + \beta \mathcal{G}(\Theta) - \beta \alpha \left(\mathcal{G}'(\Theta) \cdot \mathcal{F}'(\Theta)\right) \tag{3}$$

This reveals that we want to minimize the loss on both meta-train and meta-test domains, and maximize the dot product of $\mathcal{F}'(\Theta)$ and $\mathcal{G}'(\Theta)$. Recall the dot operation computes the similarity of two vectors. Since $\mathcal{F}'(\Theta)$ and $\mathcal{G}'(\Theta)$ are gradient of losses in two sets of domains, the similar direction means the direction of improvement in each set of domains is similar.

The DGML strategy in [38] is used during training stage using pseudo-domain labels which were assigned to training data.

3 Method

3.1 Overview

In order to split domains of data without domain labels, we clustered the style features of each data iteratively. Our method can be divided into two main processes. First, for every epoch, data are divided into N domains using the mean and variance of the mid-level features of the feature extractor and mid-level features of the depth estimator. Second, model-agnostic meta-learning (MAML) is exploited to generalize on domains. The framework of our method is illustrated in Fig. 2.

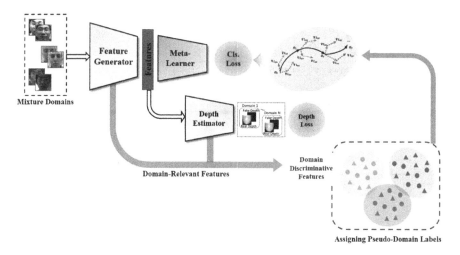

Fig. 2. Overview of the proposed framework. The stacked convolutional feature statistics from feature generator and depth estimator is clustered into N groups and assigned pseudo-domain labels

3.2   Splitting Domains

Existing DG-based anti-spoofing studies define domains as datasets. However, if dataset are obtained through web Crawling, it is difficult to know the domain label and time is spent labeling it. We received a motivation from the previous study, [26], and use middle-level feature of the model to divide in respect to the domain of data. To define a domain, the middle-level feature is clustered with clustering model and labeled with N domains. The reason for using middle-level features is that in previous studies, middle-layer features are known to reflect the style of data [27]. We stacked the convolutional feature statistics of 5th layer, 9th layer of the feature extractor and the last layer of depth estimator, respectively. Then we adopted principal component analysis (PCA) to reduce the dimension of the stacked convolutional features into 256 dimensions. With the reduced style feature, clustering method like K-nearest neighbor (KNN) or gaussisan mixture model (GMM) was used to cluster source domain into N pseudo domains.

3.3   Meta Learning for Domain Generalization

In domain generalization, meta-learning performs three main steps repeatedly: meta-train, meta-test, and meta-optimization. Before performing meta-learning step, $(N-1)$ domains are randomly selected, and the remaining 1 domain is defined as a meta-test set. In the meta-train phase, $(N-1)$ sets of meta-parameters obtained by performing 1 step gradient description based on each loss for $(N-1)$ datasets are obtained. Then, we use the meta-parameter of each domain to obtain the loss of data from the meta-test domain and perform the full optimization (Fig. 3).

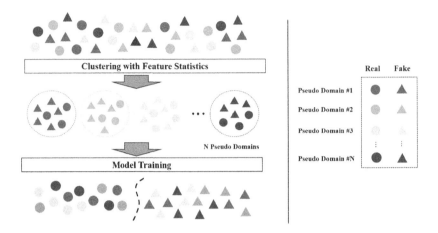

Fig. 3. Domain generalization with clustered convolutional feature statistics containing style information. Training data are clustered into N pseudo-domain groups and trained in a way that classifies liveness well.

Meta-train. We sampled batches in every meta-train domain D_{trn}, denoted as $\widehat{S}_i(i = 1, \ldots, N-1)$, and we conducted the cross-entropy classification and depth regression in every meta-train domain. Cross entropy loss is calculated as follows:

$$\mathcal{L}_{Cls(\widehat{S}_i)}(\theta_F, \theta_M) = \sum_{(x,y)\sim\widehat{S}_i} y \log M(F(x)) + (1-y)\log(1-M(F(x))), \quad (4)$$

where F and M denote feature extractor and meta learner, respectively. θ_F is the parameters of the feature extractor, and θ_M is the parameters of the meta learner. In each meta-train domain, we can obtain the updated meta learner's parameter, meta-parameters as $\theta_{M_i}' = \theta_M - \alpha\nabla_{\theta_M}\mathcal{L}_{Cls(\widehat{S}_i)}(\theta_F, \theta_M)$.

Meanwhile, loss for depth estimator is calculated as follows:

$$\mathcal{L}_{\text{Dep}(\widehat{S}_i)}(\theta_F, \theta_D) = \sum_{(x,I)\sim\widehat{S}_i} \|D(F(x)) - I\|^2, \quad (5)$$

where D denotes depth estimator, θ_D is the parameter of the depth estimator and I are the pre-calculated face depth maps for input face images. We used the dense face alignment network named PRNet [42] to obtain depth maps of real faces, and depth maps of all zeros are set as the supervision for fake faces. Depth loss in meta train step is not used to update meta parameters, but used in meta optimization step.

Meta-test. In Meta-test phase, we sampled batch in the one remaining meta-test domain D_{val}, denoted as $\tilde{S}$. To generalize well to unseen attacks of various senarios, we use meta-parameters which was obtained from meta-train phase to calculate the classification losses:

$$\sum_{i=1}^{N-1} \mathcal{L}_{Cls(\widetilde{S})} \left(\theta_F, \theta'_{M_i} \right) = \sum_{i=1}^{N-1} \sum_{(x,y) \sim \widetilde{S}} y \log M'_i(F(x)) + (1-y) \log \left(1 - M'_i(F(x)) \right) \quad (6)$$

The depth loss is also calculated like meta-train:

$$\mathcal{L}_{\mathrm{Dep}(\widetilde{S})} \left(\theta_F, \theta_D \right) = \sum_{(x,I) \sim \widetilde{S}} \| D(F(x)) - I \|^2 \quad (7)$$

By using meta parameters in calculating classification loss on meta-test domain, we can obtain the generalized direction of gradients of meta-test loss.

Meta-optimization. To update the parameter of feature extractor, meta learner and depth estimator, we summarize all the learning information in the meta-train and meta-test as follows:

$$\theta_M \leftarrow \theta_M - \beta \nabla_{\theta_M} \left(\sum_{i=1}^{N-1} \left(\mathcal{L}_{Cls(\widehat{S}_i)} \left(\theta_F, \theta_M \right) + \mathcal{L}_{Cls(\widetilde{S})} \left(\theta_F, \theta'_{M_i} \right) \right) \right) \quad (8)$$

$$\theta_F \leftarrow \theta_F - \beta \nabla_{\theta_F} \left(\mathcal{L}_{\mathrm{Dep}(\widetilde{S})} \left(\theta_F, \theta_D \right) + \sum_{i=1}^{N-1} \left(\mathcal{L}_{Cls(\widehat{S}_i)} \left(\theta_F, \theta_M \right) \right. \right.$$
$$\left. \left. + \mathcal{L}_{Dep(\widehat{S}_i)} \left(\theta_F, \theta_D \right) + \mathcal{L}_{Cls(\widetilde{S})} \left(\theta_F, \theta'_{M_i} \right) \right) \right) \quad (9)$$

By doing meta-train, meta-test and meta-optimization stage iteratively, we can extract generalized feature which are related to spoof discriminative information and discard spoof-irrelevant information.

4   Experimental Evaluation

4.1   Experimental Settings

Datasets. Four public face anti-spoofing datasets are utilized to evaluate the effectiveness of our method: OULU-NPU [6], CASIA-MFSD [7], Idiap Replay-Attack [8], and MSU-MFSD [9]. Following the setting in [21], one dataset is treated as one domain in our experiment. we randomly selected three datasets as source domains for training and the remaining one as the target domain for testing. Thus, we have four testing tasks in total: O&C&I to M, O&M&I to C, O&C&M to I, and I&C&M to O. Area under curve (AUC) is used as the evaluation metric. Also, t-SNE visualization is also reported to further evaluate performance.

Table 1. Comparison with state-of-the-art face anti-spoofing methods on four testing sets.

Methods	O&C&I to M		O&M&I to C		O&C&M to I		I&C&M to O	
	HTER (%)	AUC (%)	HTER (%)	AUC (%)	HTER (%)	AUC (%)	HTER (%)	AUC (%)
LBPTOP	36.9	70.8	42.6	61.5	49.5	49.5	53.1	44.0
MS_LBP	29.7	78.5	54.2	44.9	50.3	51.6	50.2	49.3
Binary CNN	29.2	82.8	34.8	71.9	34.4	65.8	29.6	77.5
Auxiliary (ALL)	–	–	28.4	–	27.6	–	–	–
Auxiliary (Depth)	22.7	85.8	33.5	73.1	29.1	71.6	30.1	77.6
MMD-AAE	27.0	83.1	44.5	58.2	31.5	75.1	40.9	63.0
MADDG	17.6	88.0	24.5	84.5	22.1	84.9	27.9	80.0
SSDG	16.7	90.5	23.1	85.5	18.2	90.6	25.2	81.8
RFM	13.8	93.9	20.2	88.1	17.3	90.4	16.4	91.1
Self-DA	15.4	91.8	24.5	84.4	15.6	90.1	23.1	84.3
Ours	13.8	93.1	20.3	87.6	18.4	88.4	16.6	90.7

Implementation Details. The size of face image is $256 \times 256 \times 6$, where we extracted RGB and HSV channels of each face image. The Adam optimizer is used for the optimization. The learning rate α, β are set to 0.001. The batch size is 7 per domain, and thus 21 for 3 training domains totally. For a new testing sample, its classification score l is calculated for testing as follow: $l = M(F(x))$, where F and M are the trained feature extractor and meta learner. The number of clustering group was set to three.

4.2 Experimental Comparison

Compared Methods. We compare several state-of-the-art face anti-spoofing methods as follows: LBPTOP [48]; Multi-Scale LBP [49]; Binary CNN [15]; Auxiliary [50]: This method learns a CNN-RNN model to estimate the face depth from one frame and rPPG signals through multiple frames. To fairly compare our method only using one frame information, we also compare the results of its face depth estimation component (denoted as Auxiliary(Depth)); MMD-AAE [51]; SSDG [19]; MADDG [20]: This method uses adversarial learning for domain generalization; RFM [21]: This method uses meta learning which is similar to our works; SelfDA [52]: This method is for domain adaptation, but similar with domain generalization in that it doesn't have target domain information.

Comparison Results with SOTA Face Anti-spoofing Methods. From comparison results in Table 1, it can be seen that the proposed method outperforms most of the state-of-the-art face anti-spoofing methods. Moreover, as shown in Fig. 4, we randomly select 1000 samples of target dataset and plot the t-SNE visualizations to analyze the feature space learned by our proposed method. Even though it didn't reach at the best result, this method has advantages that it doesn't require domain labels and can adjust the number of domain we are going to use in meta-learning.

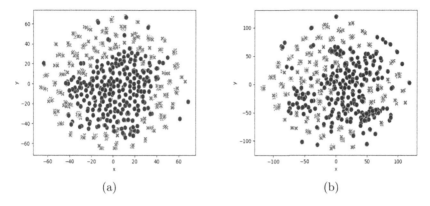

(a)   (b)

Fig. 4. The t-SNE visualization of our model with assigning pseudo-domain labels. Blue colors are fake test images and orange colors are real images. (a) t-SNE plot which is tested with CASIA-FASD and trained on Oulu-NPU, Idiap Replay attack, MSU-MFSD. (b) t-SNE plot which is tested with Idiap Replay attack and trained on Oulu-NPU, CASIA-FASD, MSU-MFSD. (Color figure online)

5   Conclusion

In this paper, we cluster using the average and variance of the late features extracted from the feature extractor and the depth estimator, and define N pseudo-domains. It also applied meta learning with a dataset of psuedo domain defined for Domain generalization. In the meta train phase, each loss was obtained for a different domain and N meta-parameters for one step optimization, and eventually the meta test found a direction in which the loss was minimized for the new dataset. Although this study did not show high performance compared to the method of SOTA, it has the advantage of not requiring domain labeling unlike conventional methods. Also, domain can be defined separately by the number of domains desired.

References

1. Deng, J., Guo, J., Xue, N., Zafeiriou, S.: ArcFace: additive angular margin loss for deep face recognition. In: CVPR (2019)
2. Wen, Y., Zhang, K., Li, Z., Qiao, Yu.: A discriminative feature learning approach for deep face recognition. In: Leibe, B., Matas, J., Sebe, N., Welling, M. (eds.) ECCV 2016. LNCS, vol. 9911, pp. 499–515. Springer, Cham (2016). https://doi.org/10.1007/978-3-319-46478-7_31
3. Zhang, X., Zhao, R., Qiao, Y., Wang, X., Li, H.: AdaCos: adaptively scaling cosine logits for effectively learning deep face representations. In: CVPR (2019)
4. Wang, H., et al.: CosFace: large margin cosine loss for deep face recognition. In: CVPR (2018)
5. Liu, W., Wen, Y., Yu, Z., Li, M., Raj, B., Song, L.: SphereFace: deep hypersphere embedding for face recognition. In: CVPR (2017)

6. Boulkenafet, Z., Komulainen, J., Li, L., Feng, X., Hadid, A.: OULU-NPU: a mobile face presentation attack database with real-world variations. In: International Conference on Automatic Face and Gesture Recognition (FG), pp. 612–618. IEEE (2017)

7. Zhang, Z., Yan, J., Liu, S., Lei, Z., Yi, D., Li, S.Z.: A face antispoofing database with diverse attacks. In: International Conference on Biometrics (ICB), pp. 26–31 (2012)

8. Chingovska, I., Anjos, A., Marcel, S.: On the effectiveness of local binary patterns in face antispoofing. In: International Conference of Biometrics Special Interest Group (BIOSIG), pp. 1–7 (2012)

9. Wen, D., Han, H., Jain, A.K.: Face spoof detection with image distortion analysis. Trans. Inf. Forensics Secur. (TIFS), pp. 746–761 (2015)

10. Kollreider, K., Fronthaler, H., Faraj, M.I., Bigun, J.: Real-time face detection and motion analysis with application in "liveness" assessment. IEEE Trans. Inf. Forensics Secur. $2(3)$, 548–558 (2007)

11. Pan, G., Sun, L., Zhaohui, W., Wang, Y.: Monocular camera-based face liveness detection by combining eyeblink and scene context. Telecommun. Syst. 47, 215–225 (2011)

12. Lin, S.G., Pan, Z., Wu, S.L.: Blinking-based live face detection using conditional random fields. In: International Conference on Biometrics (ICB) (2007)

13. Määttä, J., Hadid, A., Pietikäine, M.: Face spoofing detection from single images using micro-texture analysis. In: Biometrics International Joint Conference on IEEE, pp. 1–7 (2011)

14. Komulainen, J., Hadid, A., Pietikainen, M.: Context based face anti-spoofing. In: IEEE Sixth International Conference on Biometrics: Theory, Applications and Systems (BTAS), pp. 1–8 (2013)

15. Yang, J., Lei, Z., Li, S.Z.: Learn convolutional neural network for face anti-spoofing. arXiv preprint arXiv:1408.5601 (2014)

16. Patel, K., Han, H., Jain, A.K.: Cross-database face antispoofing with robust feature representation. In: You, Z., et al. (eds.) CCBR 2016. LNCS, vol. 9967, pp. 611–619. Springer, Cham (2016). https://doi.org/10.1007/978-3-319-46654-5_67

17. Li, L., Feng, X., Boulkenafet, Z., Xia, Z., Li, M., Hadid, A.: An original face anti-spoofing approach using partial convolutional neural network. In: 2016 Sixth International Conference on Image Processing Theory, Tools and Applications (IPTA), pp. 1–6. IEEE (2016)

18. George, A., Marcel, S.: Deep pixel-wise binary supervision for face presentation attack detection. In: 2019 International Conference on Biometrics (ICB), pp. 1–8. IEEE (2019)

19. Jia, Y., Zhang, J., Shan, S., Chen, X.: ArcFace: additive angular margin loss for deep face recognition. In: CVPR (2019)

20. Shao, R., Lan, X., Li, J., Yuen, P.C.: Multi-adversarial discriminative deep domain generalization for face presentation attack detection. In: CVPR (2019)

21. Shao, R., Lan, X., Yuen, P.C.: Regularized fine-grained meta face anti-spoofing. In: AAAI (2020)

22. Wang, J., Zhang, J., Bian, Y., Cai, Y., Wang, C., Pu, S.: Self-domain adaptation for face anti-spoofing. In: AAAI (2021)

23. Zhang, K.-Y., et al.: Face anti-spoofing via disentangled representation learning. In: Vedaldi, A., Bischof, H., Brox, T., Frahm, J.-M. (eds.) ECCV 2020. LNCS, vol. 12364, pp. 641–657. Springer, Cham (2020). https://doi.org/10.1007/978-3-030-58529-7_38

24. Yu, Z., Li, X., Niu, X., Shi, J., Zhao, G.: Face anti-spoofing with human material perception. In: Vedaldi, A., Bischof, H., Brox, T., Frahm, J.-M. (eds.) ECCV 2020. LNCS, vol. 12352, pp. 557–575. Springer, Cham (2020). https://doi.org/10.1007/978-3-030-58571-6_33

25. Jourabloo, A., Liu, Y., Liu, X.: Face de-spoofing: anti-spoofing via noise modeling. In: ECCV (2018)

26. Matsuura, T., Harada, T.: Domain generalization using a mixture of multiple latent domains. In: AAAI (2019)

27. Li, Y., Wang, N., Liu, J., Hou, X.: Demystifying neural style transfer. In: IJCAI (2017)

28. Li, H., Pan, S.J., Wang, S. and Kot, A.C.: Domain generalization with adversarial feature learning. In: CVPR (2018)

29. Li, Y., et al.: Deep domain generalization via conditional invariant adversarial networks. In: ECCV (2018)

30. Ding, Z., Yun, F.: Deep domain generalization with structured low-rank constraint. IEEE Trans. Image Process. (TIP) **27**(1), 304–313 (2017)

31. Motiian, S., Piccirilli, M., Adjeroh, D.A., Doretto, G.: Unified deep supervised domain adaptation and generalization. In: ICCV (2017)

32. Tang, H., Chen, K., Jia, K.: Unsupervised domain adaptation via structurally regularized deep clustering. In: CVPR (2020)

33. Cui, S., Wang, S., Zhuo, J., Li, L., Huang, Q., Tian, Q.: Towards discriminability and diversity: batch nuclear-norm maximization under label insufficient situations. In: CVPR (2020)

34. Xu, R., Li, G., Yang, J., Lin, L.: Larger norm more transferable: an adaptive feature norm approach for unsupervised domain adaptation. In: ICCV (2019)

35. Finn, C., Abbeel, P., Levine, S.: Model-agnostic meta-learning for fast adaptation of deep networks. In: ICML (2017)

36. Li, Z., Zhou, F., Chen, F., Li, H.: Meta-SGD: learning to learn quickly for few shot learning. arXiv (2017)

37. Hsu, K., Levine, S., Finn, C.: Unsupervised learning via meta-learning. In: ICLR (2019)

38. Li, D., Yang, Y., Song, Y.-Z., Hospedales, T.M.: Learning to generalize: meta-learning for domain generalization. In: AAAI (2018)

39. Liu, X., Thermos, S., O'Neil, A., Tsaftaris, S.A.: Semi-supervised meta-learning with disentanglement for domain-generalised medical image segmentation. In: de Bruijne, M., et al. (eds.) MICCAI 2021. LNCS, vol. 12902, pp. 307–317. Springer, Cham (2021). https://doi.org/10.1007/978-3-030-87196-3_29

40. Yin, M., Tucker, G., Zhou, M., Levine, S., Finn, C.: Meta-learning without memorization. In: ICLR (2020)

41. Bai, T., Luo, J., Zhao, J., Wen, B., Wang, Q.: Recent advances in adversarial training for adversarial robustness. In: IJCAI (2021)

42. Feng, Y., Wu, F., Shao, X., Wang, Y., Zhou, X.: Joint 3D face reconstruction and dense alignment with position map regression network. In: ECCV (2018)

43. Yu, Z., et al.: Searching central difference convolutional networks for face anti-spoofing. In: CVPR (2020)

44. Zhang, Y., Qiu, Z., Liu, J., Yao, T., Liu, D., Mei, T.: Customizable architecture search for semantic segmentation. In: CVPR (2019)

45. Yang, X., et al.: Face antispoofing: model matters, so does data. In: CVPR (2019)

46. Xiong, F., AbdAlmageed, W.: Unknown presentation attack detection with face RGB images. In: 2018 IEEE 9th International Conference on Biometrics Theory, Applications and Systems (BTAS), pp. 1–9. IEEE (2018)

47. Atoum, Y., Liu, Y., Jourabloo, A., Liu, X.: Face anti-spoofing using patch and depth-based CNNs. In: 2017 IEEE International Joint Conference on Biometrics (IJCB), pp. 319–328 (2017)
48. Tiago, P., et al.: Face liveness detection using dynamic texture. EURASIP J. Image Video Process. (2014)
49. Määttä, J., Hadid, A., Pietikäinen, M.: Face spoofing detection from single images using micro-texture analysis. In: Proceedings of the IEEE International Joint Conference on Biometrics (IJCB) (2011)
50. Liu, Y., Jourabloo, A., Liu, X.: Learning deep models for face anti-spoofing: binary or auxiliary supervision. In: CVPR (2018)
51. Li, H., Pan, S.J., Wang, S., Kot, A.C.: Domain generalization with adversarial feature learning. In: CVPR (2018)
52. Wang, J., Bian, Y., Cai, Y., Wang, Pu, S.: Self-domain adaptation for face anti-spoofing. In: AAAI (2021)
53. Yang, H.-D., Lee, S.-W.: Reconstruction of 3D human body pose from stereo image sequences based on top-down learning. Pattern Recogn. **40**(11), 3120–3131 (2007)
54. Roh, M.-C., Kim, Park, J., Lee, S.-W.: Accurate object contour tracking based on boundary edge selection. Pattern Recogn. **40**(3), 931–943 (2007)
55. Lee, S.W., Bülthoff, H.H., Poggio, T.: Biologically Motivated Computer Vision. Springer, Heidelberg (2003). https://doi.org/10.1007/3-540-36181-2
56. Ahmad, M., Lee, S.-W.: Human action recognition using multi-view image sequences features. In: Proceedings of 7th IEEE International Conference on Automatic Face and Gesture Recognition, pp. 523–528 (2006)
57. Lee, S.-W., Song, H.-H.: A new recurrent neural-network architecture for visual pattern recognition. In IEEE Trans. Neural Netw. **8**(2), 331–340 (1997)

Face Anti-spoofing via Robust Auxiliary Estimation and Discriminative Feature Learning

Pei-Kai Huang, Ming-Chieh Chin, and Chiou-Ting Hsu[✉]

Department of Computer Science, National Tsing Hua University, Hsinchu, Taiwan
alwayswithme@gapp.nthu.edu.tw, cthsu@cs.nthu.edu.tw

Abstract. Face anti-spoofing is critical to applications which heavily rely on the authenticity of detected faces. Recently, auxiliary information, such as facial depth maps and rPPG signals, have been successfully included to boost the performance of face anti-spoofing. Consequently, the quality of auxiliary estimation is key to the effectiveness of live/spoof classification. In this paper, we focus on the robustness of auxiliary estimation and the discriminability of latent features. We propose to estimate the auxiliary information along with the training of live/spoof classifier in an adversarial learning framework. We include additional constraints in the contrastive loss and propose a discriminative batch-contrastive loss to learn the latent features. Both the auxiliary information and the discriminative latent features are included into the live/spoof classification. In addition, because not all the auxiliary supervisions are equally reliable, we propose an adaptive fusing strategy to fuse the estimation results from different auxiliary-supervised branches. Experimental results on several benchmark datasets show that the proposed method significantly outperforms previous methods.

Keywords: Face anti-spoofing · rPPG signal · Facial depth map · Adversarial learning · Contrastive loss

1 Introduction

Presentation attack (PA), such as Print Attack (i.e., printing a face on a paper) and Replay Attack (i.e., replaying a face video on digital devices), poses a serious threat to the security of facial recognition systems. Many face anti-spoofing methods, including the earlier methods [5,6,10] and the recent deep-learning based methods [9,12,16,18,25,27], have been developed to counter the attacks.

Recently, the auxiliary information, such as facial depth maps and Remote Photoplethysmography (rPPG) signals, has been successfully included to supervise the live/spoof classification and achieves substantial improvement. The advantages of using auxiliary supervision is evident. Intuitively, we should be able to perceive the uneven depth from live faces but can merely distinguish a planar depth from spoof faces. The rPPG signals, which measures the human blood volume changes in optical information, characterize human cardiovascular

© Springer Nature Switzerland AG 2022
C. Wallraven et al. (Eds.): ACPR 2021, LNCS 13188, pp. 443–458, 2022.
https://doi.org/10.1007/978-3-031-02375-0_33

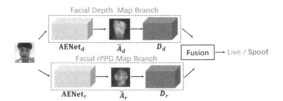

Fig. 1. The proposed framework consists of two auxiliary supervised branches: facial depth map branch and facial rPPG map branch, where $\mathbf{AENet_d}$ and $\mathbf{AENet_r}$ are the auxiliary estimation networks, $\mathbf{D_d}$ and $\mathbf{D_r}$ are the corresponding discriminators, and $\bar{\mathbf{A}}_d$ and $\bar{\mathbf{A}}_r$ are the estimated facial depth map and rPPG map, respectively. The final detection result is derived by adaptive fusion of the two branches.

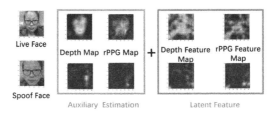

Fig. 2. Two branches of auxiliary estimation as well as the latent features are all included into the live/spoof classification.

signals and serve as a distinguishing feature to classify live and spoof videos. For example, in [18], the facial depth map is estimated first and then used to guide the spatial alignment of feature maps for the subsequent rPPG estimation. In [1,15,18], different auxiliary estimations are combined to detect spoof faces.

In this paper, we focus on the robustness of auxiliary estimation. The two auxiliary supervisions, i.e., facial depth map and facial rPPG map, are included in the proposed framework. Unlike previous methods, we propose using two parallel branches of adversarial learning networks to learn auxiliary information independently, as shown in Fig. 1. We also propose a discriminative batch-contrastive loss to increase the discriminability of latent features. As shown in Fig. 2, we include both the auxiliary estimation and the latent features to promote the live/spoof classification. Finally, we develop an adaptive fusion strategy to accommodate different reliabilities of the two branches. Our experimental results on **OULU-NPU**, **SiW**, **CASIA-MFSD** and **Replay-Attack** show that we achieve a state-of-the-art performance on **OULU-NPU** and a competitive result on **SiW**.

2   Related Work

Previous anti-spoofing methods generally fall into three categories:

Texture-Based Methods. Traditional texture-based methods have been developed using various hand-crafted feature, such as LBP [2,5,6,10], SIFT [21], and SURF [6]. Some other methods [13,20,26] utilize deep-learning based features to improve the anti-spoofing performance. However, because these methods rely on the learned textural features, they tend to capture arbitrary texture patterns (e.g., screen bezel) instead of discriminative live/spoof features.

Depth-Based Methods. Depth-based methods [1,12,18,25] have been shown to be very effective for face anti-spoofing. Atoum *et al.* [1] first demonstrated the benefits of using depth estimation for face anti-spoofing. Liu *et al.* [18] utilized the depth estimation to supervise the live/spoof classification, and Jourabloo *et al.* [12] proposed the face de-spoofing via the depth estimation.

Temporal-Based Methods. Most of the temporal-based methods [9,14,16,17] measure the rPPG signals from different face regions to detect live faces. However, because the estimation of rPPG signals is very sensitive to environmental illumination and human motion, many efforts need to be taken to ensure the reliability of rPPG signals. For example, in [18], the authors proposed using the depth information to guide the rPGG estimation.

3   Proposed Method

The goal of this paper is to discriminate live and spoof faces via robust auxiliary supervisions. We include two auxiliary information, including facial depth and facial rPPG signals, to supervise the live/spoof classification. As shown in Fig. 1, the proposed framework consists of two branches: a facial depth map branch and an rPPG map branch. We develop the two branches by using the same adversarial learning network, where each includes an auxiliary estimation network **AENet** and a discriminator **D**.

Note that, the proposed framework is very different from that in [18], where the depth map is estimated first via a CNN and is then used to guide the spatial alignment of feature maps for the subsequent rPPG estimation. In contrast to this sequential pipeline, our framework is developed using two parallelly processing branches. Our motivation comes from that, although the facial depth is one of the main distinguishing features between live and spoof faces under presentation attacks (PA), the depth maps estimated from spoof faces are not always planar with zero values. In addition, because the "ground-truth depths" for live faces are estimated from the off-the-shelf methods, the resultant depths tend to be noisy for non-frontal faces and may not always serve as a good supervision. Therefore, instead of concatenating the two auxiliary estimations consecutively, we propose to process the two branches independently.

As to aggregating the two auxiliary estimations, unlike previous methods [1,15,18], which linearly combine them using empirically determined parameters, we argue that different auxiliary supervisions are not equally reliable under different scenarios. Moreover, we also observe that the latent features learned in the estimation networks **AENet** characterize discriminative information as well as the estimated auxiliary information. Therefore, we include the latent features into the live/spoof classification and propose an adaptive fusion strategy to accommodate different reliabilities of the two branches.

3.1   Auxiliary Information

We adopt two auxiliary information, including facial depth map and facial rPPG map, to supervise the proposed anti-spoofing model. As described in [18,25], facial depth has been shown to be one of the most discriminative spatial features for face anti-spoofing. On the other hand, rPPG signals, which analyze the blood volume changes in optical information, characterize the temporal discrepancy between live and spoof facial videos [15,16]. Below, we describe how we construct the "ground truth" of the two auxiliary information to supervise the training of $\mathbf{AENet_d}$ and $\mathbf{AENet_r}$.

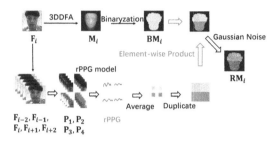

Fig. 3. Estimation of rPPG supervision.

Facial Depth Map. The proposed facial depth branch aims to detect spoof faces in terms of pixel-wise depth. To train the depth map estimation network $\mathbf{AENet_d}$, we first use the-state-of-the-art 3D dense face alignment methods (3DDFA) [11,30] to estimate the ground truth of the facial depth. Next, we adopt the same setting as in the previous methods [18,25] by using the the estimated depth and the zero values as the ground truth of the live faces and the spoof faces, respectively, to train the depth estimation network $\mathbf{AENet_d}$.

Facial rPPG Map. In the facial rPPG branch, our goal is to detect spoof faces in terms of rPPG signals. As shown in Fig. 3, to estimate the facial rPPG map of the i-th frame $\mathbf{F}_i$, we include a number of consecutive frames $\mathbf{F} = [\mathbf{F}_{i-2}, \mathbf{F}_{i-1}, \mathbf{F}_i, \mathbf{F}_{i+1}, \mathbf{F}_{i+2}]$ as the input (5 frames are involved in our experiments) and decompose each frame into several subregions. Four subregions $\mathbf{P}_1, \mathbf{P}_2, \mathbf{P}_3$, and $\mathbf{P}_4$ are shown in Fig. 3. Next, we use the rPPG model [24] to estimate the signal of each subregion and then average the results obtained from the consecutive frames in $\mathbf{F}$. Furthermore, to locate the facial region, we threshold the facial depth map $\mathbf{M_i}$ obtained by 3DDFA [11,30] into a binary mask $\mathbf{BM_i}$ and conduct element-wise product of $\mathbf{BM_i}$ with the averaged rPPG values. Finally, to better approximate the rPPG map of live faces, we add the Gaussian noises $N(0, 0.01)$ to construct the facial rPPG map $\mathbf{RM}_i$ for live faces. As to the spoof faces, we simply set the whole facial rPPG map $\mathbf{RM}_i$ with values of zeros.

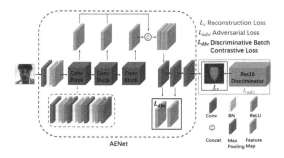

Fig. 4. Architecture of the adversarial learning network in one single branch. Three loss terms are defined to train the network: $\mathcal{L}_r$ is used to estimate the auxiliary information under the auxiliary supervision, $\mathcal{L}_{adv}$ is introduced to improve the estimation robustness of **AENet**, and $\mathcal{L}_{dbc}$ is used to increase the discriminability of the latent features.

3.2 Network Architecture

Figure 1 shows the proposed framework, which consists of one facial depth map branch and one rPPG map branch. We develop each of the two branches using the same network architecture, as shown in Fig. 4. To improve the robustness of the auxiliary estimation, we propose to take advantage of adversarial learning by including a discriminator **D** to guide **AENet** (the Auxiliary Estimation Network) to learn the auxiliary information to be as discriminative as possible.

In Fig. 4, the network **AENet** includes multiple convolutional blocks to extract a pyramid of multi-scale feature representation. Each convolutional block consists of convolutional layers, batch normalization layers, ReLU activation functions and a pooling layer. The feature maps of all the convolutional blocks are resized to 64×64 and are then concatenated together. Similar to the ResNet structure, we use the bypass connections in **AENet** to extract features from layers of different depths. As to the discriminator **D**, we use Res18 as the backbone and add a fully connected (FCN) layer to its original last FCN layer to classify the auxiliary information into 1 for live faces and 0 for spoof faces, respectively.

3.3 Auxiliary Estimation and Discriminative Feature Learning

Adversarial learning generally consists of a feature encoder and a domain-specific discriminator. In this work, we train **AENet** to estimate the auxiliary information and to extract the discriminative latent features. The live/spoof faces discriminator **D** is trained to predict how likely a sample comes from live/spoof videos. By playing the min-max game, the discriminator **D** gradually guides **AENet** to learn robust auxiliary estimation, under the supervision of auxiliary information. Furthermore, we propose a new loss term: the discriminative batch-contrastive loss, to increase the discriminability of the latent features.

Auxiliary Estimation. We first define the reconstruction loss $\mathcal{L}_r$ to train **AENet** to approximate the "ground truth" by,

$$\mathcal{L}_r = ||\mathbf{A} - \bar{\mathbf{A}}||_1^2, \tag{1}$$

where $\mathbf{A}$ is the "ground truth" auxiliary information, $\bar{\mathbf{A}} = \mathbf{AENet}(\mathbf{F}_i; \Theta)$ is the estimated auxiliary information, Θ is the network parameter, and $\mathbf{F}_i$ is the i-th frame.

Adversarial Training. Although we use the reconstruction loss $\mathcal{L}_r$ to constrain **AENet** under the auxiliary supervision, the discriminability of the auxiliary information is still far from satisfactory. We believe the main reason comes from the limited number of training data in one mini-batch. Therefore, to enforce **AENet** to focus on discriminability between live and spoof faces, we include the discriminator $\mathbf{D}$ to guide **AENet** under the adversarial loss $\mathcal{L}_{adv}$:

$$\mathcal{L}_{adv} = (y - 1)log(1 - \mathbf{D}(\bar{\mathbf{A}})) - ylog(\mathbf{D}(\bar{\mathbf{A}})), \tag{2}$$

where y is the class label of face, i.e., $y = 1$ for live face and $y = 0$ for spoof face.

Discriminative Batch-Contrastive Loss. In addition, inspired by the idea of batch-contrastive loss [28], we expect to further increase the discriminability of the latent features in **AENet** via another loss term. The original contrastive loss [8] is designed to learn a latent space so that the intra-class distance is smaller and that the inter-class distance is larger than a margin. In [28], a batch-based contrastive loss is proposed and additionally includes the center loss to reduce the intra-class distance. However, because the "class centers" are updated according to the samples within each mini-batch, if the calculated "class centers" locate closely to each other, the additional center loss can hardly improve the discriminability. To tackle this issue, we explicitly define the center of spoof faces to be $\mathbf{0}$ in the latent space. In our two auxiliary-supervised branches, because both the depth map and the rPPG map for spoof faces are assumed to be zero, we can readily push the spoof features in both latent spaces towards zero values. The proposed discriminative batch-contrastive loss $\mathcal{L}_{dbc}$ is defined by,

$$\mathcal{L}_{dbc} = \begin{cases} \sum_i ||f(\mathbf{F}_i) - \mathbf{0}||_2^2, \forall i \in \{1, ..., p\}, y_i = 0 \\ \sum_i max(||\mathbf{m} - f(\mathbf{F}_i)||_2^2, 0), \forall i \in \{1, ..., p\}, y_i = 1 \\ \sum_{\{i|y_i=1\}} max(||\mathbf{c} + \mathbf{m} - f(\mathbf{F}_i)||_2^2, 0) + \sum_{\{i|y_i=0\}} ||f(\mathbf{F}_i) - \mathbf{0}||_2^2, otherwise \end{cases} \tag{3}$$

where y_i is the class label of the i-th frame $\mathbf{F}_i$ in the mini-batch of size p, $f(\cdot)$ is the feature extractor, $\mathbf{m} = \tau * \mathbf{1}$, τ is the margin, and $\mathbf{c} = \frac{\sum_{\{i|y_i=0\}} f(\mathbf{F}_i)}{\sum_{\{i|y_i=0\}} 1}$ is the center of the spoof faces in the mini-batch.

In Equation (3), there exist three cases within a randomly sampled mini-batch. First, if all the samples in the mini-batch are spoof faces, i.e., all with the class label $y = 0$, then we push their latent features to be close to $\mathbf{0}$. In contrast, if all the samples in the mini-batch are live faces with $y = 1$, then we push their latent features to be away from that of spoof faces by at least a margin τ. Otherwise, if the mini-batch includes samples from both classes, then our goal is two-fold: to push the latent features to approach their corresponding class centers, and to keep them away from that of the other class by at least a margin τ.

In comparison with the contrastive loss $\mathcal{L}_c$ [8], the proposed $\mathcal{L}_{dbc}$ not only constrains the inter-class distance to be larger than a margin, but also constrains the latent features to be close to their class centers. In addition, in comparison with the batch-contrastive loss $\mathcal{L}_{bc}$ [28], we explicitly enforce the features of spoof class to be near zero values to further enlarge inter-class distance. In Sect. 4.2, we will show experimental comparisons of $\mathcal{L}_{dbc}$ with the contrastive loss $\mathcal{L}_c$ and the batch-contrastive loss $\mathcal{L}_{bc}$.

Total Loss. Finally, we include the reconstruction loss L_r, the adversarial loss L_{adv}, and the discriminative batch-contrastive loss $\mathcal{L}_{dbc}$ to define the total loss of each branch by:

$$\mathcal{L}_T = \mathcal{L}_r + \mathcal{L}_{adv} + \mathcal{L}_{dbc}. \tag{4}$$

3.4   Live/Spoof Classification

During the inference stage, most methods [12,18,25,27] measured the detection score in terms of either the estimated auxiliary information or the classification output. The latent features, however, are hardly included in the final live/spoof classification. Observing that the latent features implicitly capture discriminative information, we believe they should contribute as much as the auxiliary information in the classification. Especially, as described in Sect. 3.3, we strive to increase the discriminability of latent features; the overall detection performance is expected to significantly benefit from both the latent features as well as the auxiliary estimation.

Single Branch Detection. We first formulate the face anti-spoofing detection score of one single branch by,

$$s_{all} = s_{ae} + \alpha s_{ef}, \tag{5}$$

which incorporates both the auxiliary estimation score s_{ae} and the latent features score s_{ef} defined by

$$s_{ae} = \frac{\sum_{h=1}^{H} \sum_{w=1}^{W} |\bar{\mathbf{A}}_{hw}|}{HW}, \tag{6}$$

and

$$s_{ef} = \sum_{l=1}^{L} \frac{\sum_{c=1}^{C_l} \sum_{h=1}^{H_l} \sum_{w=1}^{W_l} \mid f(\mathbf{F}_i)_{lchw} \mid}{C_l H_l W_l}, \tag{7}$$

where $\bar{\mathbf{A}} \in \mathbb{R}^{1 \times H \times W}$ is the estimated auxiliary information with one channel, $\mid \cdot \mid$ is the absolute value function, $f(\mathbf{F}_i)_l$ is the l-th latent feature map, L is the number of latent feature map and is set as 2 in our experiments (as shown in Fig. 4), and C, H, and W refer to the channel number, height, and width, respectively.

Detection by Adaptive Fusion. With the two single-branch scores s_{all_d} and s_{all_r}, like most of the previous methods [1,15,18], we can simply fuse them by a weighted summation to derive the final detection score. However, because the two auxiliary information is not equally reliable under different scenarios, the adequacy of this fusing method is doubtful. For example, in the scenarios with partially occluded faces, the facial rPPG branch may fail to estimate robust rPPG signals; on the other hand, in the cases with non-frontal faces, the estimated depths tend to be inaccurate. Therefore, we propose a simple and adaptive fusing method by:

$$s_{final} = \begin{cases} \beta s_{all,d} + (1-\beta)s_{all,r}, if \ ave_{D_d,D_r} \geq T \quad and \quad \mathbf{D}_d(\bar{\mathbf{A}}_\mathbf{d}) \geq \mathbf{D}_r(\bar{\mathbf{A}}_\mathbf{r}), or, \\ \qquad\qquad\quad if \ ave_{D_d,D_r} < T \quad and \quad \mathbf{D}_d(\bar{\mathbf{A}}_\mathbf{d}) \leq \mathbf{D}_r(\bar{\mathbf{A}}_\mathbf{r}); \\ \beta s_{all,r} + (1-\beta)s_{all,d}, if \ ave_{D_d,D_r} \geq T \quad and \quad \mathbf{D}_d(\bar{\mathbf{A}}_\mathbf{d}) < \mathbf{D}_r(\bar{\mathbf{A}}_\mathbf{r}), or, \\ \qquad\qquad\quad if \ ave_{D_d,D_r} < T \quad and \quad \mathbf{D}_d(\bar{\mathbf{A}}_\mathbf{d}) > \mathbf{D}_r(\bar{\mathbf{A}}_\mathbf{r}), \end{cases} \tag{8}$$

where

$$ave_{D_d,D_r} = \frac{\mathbf{D}_d(\bar{\mathbf{A}}_\mathbf{d}) + \mathbf{D}_r(\bar{\mathbf{A}}_\mathbf{r})}{2}, \tag{9}$$

is the average of the outputs of the two discriminators $\mathbf{D}_d$ and $\mathbf{D}_r$, T is a threshold, and β ($\beta > 0.5$) is the fusing parameter to give one of the single-branch scores a larger weight.

The rationale behind Equation (8) is to assign a larger weight β to the branch with a better auxiliary estimation. Specifically, if ave_{D_d,D_r} is larger than T, then the input sample is more likely to be a live face; therefore, we assign the branch with a larger score a larger weight. On the other hand, if ave_{D_d,D_r} is smaller than T, then the input is more likely to be a spoof face; similarly, we assign a larger weight to the branch with better estimation (note that, in this case, the smaller branch score indicates better estimation). The threshold T is set as 0.5 and β is empirically set as 0.715 in all our experiments.

Table 1. Ablation study of the depth branch **AENet$_d$** on **OULU-NPU** Protocol 1, by using different contrastive loss terms with the latent feature score $s_{ef,d}$.

Abbreviation	Contrastive loss term			APCER (%)	BPCER (%)	ACER (%)
	$\mathcal{L}_c$	$\mathcal{L}_{bc}$	$\mathcal{L}_{dbc}$			
AENet$_d$, $\mathcal{L}_c$	✓			4.17	0.83	2.50
AENet$_d$, $\mathcal{L}_{bc}$		✓		2.92	1.67	2.29
AENet$_d$, $\mathcal{L}_{dbc}$			✓	**2.50**	**0.83**	**1.67**

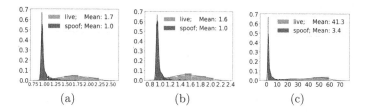

(a)   (b)   (c)

Fig. 5. Distribution of the latent feature score $s_{ef,d}$ from the depth branch **AENet$_d$** on the **OULU-NPU** Protocol 1, using different contrastive loss terms: (a) $\mathcal{L}_c$, (b)$\mathcal{L}_{bc}$, and (c) $\mathcal{L}_{dbc}$. X-axis is $s_{ef,d}$, and Y-axis is the normalized number of samples.

4 Experiments

4.1 Experimental Setting

Dataset. We evaluate our method on the face anti-spoofing databases: **OULU-NPU** [3], **SiW** [18], **CASIA-MFSD** [29], and **Replay-Attack** [7]. To have a fair comparison with previous methods, we follow the same settings and conduct intra-testing on **OULU-NPU** and **SiW** and cross-testing [20] on **CASIA-MFSD** and **Replay-Attack**, respectively.

Table 2. Ablation study of the depth branch **AENet$_d$** on **OULU-NPU** Protocol 1, under different combinations of the total loss $\mathcal{L}_T$ and the detection score $s_{all,d}$.

Total loss $\mathcal{L}_T$			Branch score $s_{all,d}$		APCER (%)	BPCER (%)	ACER (%)
$\mathcal{L}_r$	$\mathcal{L}_{adv}$	$\mathcal{L}_{dbc}$	$s_{ae,d}$	$s_{ef,d}$			
✓			✓		2.08	3.33	2.71
			✓	✓	2.29	3.33	2.81
✓	✓		✓		2.92	0.83	1.88
			✓	✓	2.92	0.83	1.88
✓		✓	✓		2.50	1.67	2.08
			✓	✓	2.50	0.83	1.67
✓	✓	✓	✓		2.29	0.83	1.56
			✓	✓	2.50	0.00	**1.25**

Table 3. Comparison of single branch detection vs. adaptive fusion detection on **OULU-NPU** Protocol 3.

Branch	APCER (%)	BPCER (%)	ACER (%)
AENet$_d$	2.01 ± 0.92	0.83 ± 0.91	1.42 ± 0.77
AENet$_r$	2.29 ± 1.95	0.83 ± 2.04	1.55 ± 1.99
AENet$_d$ + AENet$_r$	$\mathbf{1.38 \pm 1.78}$	$\mathbf{0.28 \pm 0.68}$	$\mathbf{0.83 \pm 0.86}$

Evaluation Metrics. We follow the protocols and evaluation metrics defined in the face anti-spoofing databases. The Attack Presentation Classification Error Rate $APCER$ [23] measures the errors among all the attack videos. The Bona Fide Presentation Classification Error Rate $BPCER$ [23] evaluates the errors among all the live videos. $ACER = \frac{APCER+BPCER}{2}$ [23] is the average of $APCER$ and $BPCER$.

Implementation Details. We implement the proposed framework with PyTorch. To train the discriminator **D**, we set a constant learning rate of $1\mathrm{e}{-}3$ for 30 epochs. During the training phase of **AENet**, we fix the discriminator **D** and set a constant learning rate of $1\mathrm{e}{-}4$ for 100 epochs. The mini-batch size for training **D** and **AENet** are 10 and 5, respectively. Five consecutive frames $\{\mathbf{F}_i\}_{i=1}^{5}$ are sampled from each video in our experiments. The margin τ in Eq. (3) is set as 50.

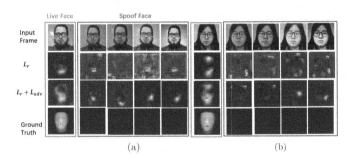

(a)   (b)

Fig. 6. Examples of auxiliary estimation on **OULU-NPU** Protocol 1. (a) and (b) are different subjects. $\mathcal{L}_r$ and $\mathcal{L}_r + \mathcal{L}_{adv}$ indicate that the model is trained without and with the adversarial loss $\mathcal{L}_{adv}$, respectively.

Table 4. Detection results of intra testing on **OULU-NPU** Protocols 1–4. For a fair comparison, the results of STASN [27] reported here are trained without using any external dataset.

Protocol	method	APCER (%)	BPCER (%)	ACER (%)
1	CPqD [4]	2.9	10.8	6.9
	GRADIANT [4]	1.3	12.5	6.9
	Auxiliary [18]	1.6	1.6	1.6
	FDS [12]	**1.2**	1.7	1.5
	STASN [27]	**1.2**	2.5	1.9
	DSGTDL [25]	2.0	**0.0**	1.0
	Ours	1.67	**0.00**	**0.83**
2	MixedFASNet [4]	9.7	2.5	6.1
	GRADIANT [4]	3.1	1.9	2.5
	Auxiliary [18]	2.7	2.7	2.7
	FDS [12]	4.2	4.4	4.3
	STASN [27]	4.2	**0.3**	2.2
	DSGTDL [25]	2.5	1.3	1.9
	Ours	**0.69**	1.67	**1.18**
3	MixedFASNet [4]	5.3 ± 6.7	7.8 ± 5.5	6.5 ± 4.6
	GRADIANT [4]	2.6 ± 3.9	5.0 ± 5.3	3.8 ± 2.4
	Auxiliary [18]	2.7 ± 1.3	3.1 ± 1.7	2.9 ± 1.5
	FDS [12]	4.0 ± 1.8	3.8 ± 1.2	3.6 ± 1.6
	STASN [27]	4.7 ± 3.9	0.9 ± 1.2	2.8 ± 1.6
	DSGTDL [25]	3.2 ± 2.0	2.2 ± 1.4	2.7 ± 0.6
	Ours	$\mathbf{1.38 \pm 1.78}$	$\mathbf{0.28 \pm 0.68}$	$\mathbf{0.83 \pm 0.86}$
4	Massy HNU [4]	35.8 ± 35.3	8.3 ± 4.1	22.1 ± 17.6
	GRADIANT [4]	5.0 ± 4.5	15.0 ± 7.1	10.0 ± 5.0
	Auxiliary [18]	9.3 ± 5.6	10.4 ± 6.0	9.5 ± 6.0
	FDS [12]	$\mathbf{1.2 \pm 6.3}$	6.1 ± 5.1	5.6 ± 5.7
	STASN [27]	6.7 ± 10.6	8.3 ± 8.4	7.5 ± 4.7
	DSGTDL [25]	6.7 ± 7.5	3.3 ± 4.1	5.0 ± 2.2
	Ours	5.41 ± 6.40	$\mathbf{2.50 \pm 2.74}$	$\mathbf{3.96 \pm 3.90}$

Table 5. Detection results of intra testing on **SiW** [18] Protocols 1-3.

Protocol	Method	APCER (%)	BPCER (%)	ACER (%)
1	Auxiliary [18]	3.58	3.58	3.58
	STASN [27]	–	–	1.00
	DSGTDL [25]	0.64	0.17	0.40
	Ours	**0.14**	**0.00**	**0.07**
2	Auxiliary [18]	0.57 ± 0.69	0.57 ± 0.69	0.57 ± 0.69
	STASN [27]	–	–	0.28 ± 0.05
	DSGTDL [25]	**0.00 ± 0.00**	**0.04 ± 0.08**	**0.02 ± 0.04**
	Ours	**0.00 ± 0.00**	0.08 ± 0.10	0.04 ± 0.05
3	Auxiliary [18]	8.31 ± 3.81	8.31 ± 3.80	8.31 ± 3.81
	STASN [27]	–	–	12.10 ± 1.50
	DSGTDL [25]	**2.63 ± 3.72**	**2.92 ± 3.42**	**2.78 ± 3.57**
	Ours	6.82 ± 2.95	4.19 ± 1.33	5.51 ± 0.80

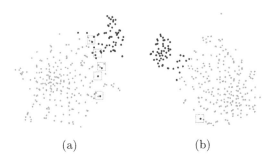

(a)   (b)

Fig. 7. t-SNE [19] visualization of latent depth features on the testing videos of **OULU-NPU** Protocol 1, using the total loss (a) w/o $\mathcal{L}_{dbc}$, and (b) $w/$ $\mathcal{L}_{dbc}$. The live and spoof faces are represented by green and red colors, respectively. The misclassified samples are highlighted by the blue dotted squares. (Color figure online)

4.2 Ablation Study

Comparison Between Different Contrastive Loss Terms. In Table 1, we compare using different contrastive losses to train the depth branch **AENet$_d$** on the **OULU-NPU** Protocol 1. That is, in Eq. (4), we replace the proposed discriminative batch-contrastive loss $\mathcal{L}_{dbc}$ with the contrastive loss $\mathcal{L}_c$ [8] or the batch-contrastive loss $\mathcal{L}_{bc}$ [28]. The margin τ is set as 50 for all three cases. The improved performance in all the metrics $APCER$, $BPCER$ and $ACER$ verifies the superiority of $\mathcal{L}_{dbc}$ over $\mathcal{L}_c$ and $\mathcal{L}_{bc}$. In Fig. 5, we show the distributions of latent feature score $s_{ef,d}$ of the three contrastive losses. The proposed $\mathcal{L}_{dbc}$, by explicitly pushing the spoof features toward zero values, better enlarges the inter-class distance between live and spoof faces than $\mathcal{L}_c$ and $\mathcal{L}_{bc}$.

Comparison Between Different Losses and Detection Scores. In Table 2, we compare using different combinations of the total loss $\mathcal{L}_T$ to train the depth branch $\mathbf{AENet_d}$ and using different detection scores in the inference stage on **OULU-NPU** protocol 1.

First, by comparing the cases of $\mathcal{L}_r$ vs. $\mathcal{L}_r + \mathcal{L}_{adv}$, we show that the adversarial learning framework indeed encourages $\mathbf{AENet}$ to focus on discriminative auxiliary information and improves the performance over the case $\mathcal{L}_r$. In Fig. 6, we use two more examples to demonstrate the efficacy of $\mathcal{L}_{adv}$. As shown in Fig. 6, the auxiliary estimation scores $s_{ae,d}$ in the case of $\mathcal{L}_r + \mathcal{L}_{adv}$ substantially increase the discrepancy between live and spoof faces than using $\mathcal{L}_r$ alone.

Next, we compare $\mathcal{L}_r$ with $\mathcal{L}_r + \mathcal{L}_{dbc}$. The performance improvement of $\mathcal{L}_r + \mathcal{L}_{dbc}$ verifies the superiority of the proposed discriminative batch-contrastive loss $\mathcal{L}_{dbc}$. Moreover, because $\mathcal{L}_{dbc}$ increases the discriminability of latent features, we see that inclusion of the latent feature score $s_{ef,d}$ in the inference stage significantly improves the performance. In Fig. 7, we use t-SNE to visualize the latent depth features obtained without and with the proposed $\mathcal{L}_{dbc}$. The visualization result of Fig. 7 (b) shows that $\mathcal{L}_{dbc}$ greatly enlarges the inter-class distance than in Fig. 7 (a).

Finally, when $\mathcal{L}_r$, $\mathcal{L}_{adv}$, and $\mathcal{L}_{dbc}$ are all included in the total loss, the overall improvement demonstrates the effectiveness of the proposed auxiliary estimation and discriminative latent feature learning.

Effectiveness of Adaptive Fusion. Table 3 compares the detection results of one single branch with the adaptive fusion. The significant improvement of the adaptive fusion shows that the proposed scheme is widely applicable to different scenarios.

4.3   Intra Testing and Cross Testing

Tables 4 and 5 show the comparison with previous methods [4,12,18,25,27] on **OULU-NPU** and **SiW**, respectively. With the robust auxiliary estimation and discriminative feature learning, the proposed method outperforms previous methods on **OULU-NPU** and achieves promising performance on **SiW**.

Table 6 gives the cross testing results on **CASIA-MFSD** and **Replay-Attack**. The results show that, the proposed method enables a good generalization from **CASIA-MFSD** to **Replay Attack** and is comparable with other methods from **Replay Attack** to **CASIA-MFSD**. As mentioned in [12], the latter case, where the models are trained on low-resolutional data but tested on higher resolutional data, remains a big challenge for cross testing.

Table 6. The detection results of cross testing between **CASIA-MFSD** and **Replay-Attack**. The evaluation metric is ACER (%).

Method	Train	Test	Train	Test
	CASIA-MFSD	Replay-attack	Replay-attack	CASIA-MFSD
LBP-1 [10]	55.9		57.6	
LBP-TOP [10]	49.7		60.6	
Motion [10]	50.2		47.9	
Motion-Mag [2]	50.1		47.0	
CNN [26]	48.5		45.5	
Spectral cubes [22]	34.4		50.0	
LBP-2 [5]	47.0		39.6	
FDS [12]	28.5		41.1	
Colour texture [6]	30.3		37.7	
STASN [27]	31.5		30.9	
Auxiliary [18]	27.6		**28.4**	
DSGTDL [25]	**17.0**		**22.8**	
Ours	**24.71**		30.90	

5   Conclusion

This paper proposes an effective anti-spoofing method via robust auxiliary estimation and discriminative feature learning. Under the auxiliary supervisions of facial depth and rPPG signals, we develop a framework with two parallel branches of adversarial learning networks followed by an adaptive fusion. By including the discriminative batch-contrastive loss into the adversarial learning, we successfully improve the robustness of auxiliary estimation and the discriminability of latent features. Moreover, we include both the estimated auxiliary information and the latent features in the live/spoof detection and design an adaptive fusion strategy to fuse different auxiliary-supervised branches. Experimental results on several benchmark datasets show the superiority of the proposed method over previous methods.

References

1. Atoum, Y., Liu, Y., Jourabloo, A., Liu, X.: Face anti-spoofing using patch and depth-based CNNs. In: 2017 IEEE International Joint Conference on Biometrics (IJCB), pp. 319–328 (2017). https://doi.org/10.1109/BTAS.2017.8272713
2. Bharadwaj, D., Vatsa, S.: Computationally efficient face spoofing detection with motion magnification. In: Proceedings of the IEEE Conference on Computer Vision and Pattern Recognition Workshops, pp. 105–110 (2013)
3. Boulkenafet, Z., Komulainen, J., Li, L., Feng, X., Hadid, A.: OULU-NPU: a mobile face presentation attack database with real-world variations, May 2017

4. Boulkenafet, Z., et al.: A competition on generalized software-based face presentation attack detection in mobile scenarios. In: 2017 IEEE International Joint Conference on Biometrics (IJCB), pp. 688–696. IEEE (2017)
5. Boulkenafet, Z., Komulainen, J., Hadid, A.: Face anti-spoofing based on color texture analysis. In: 2015 IEEE International Conference on Image Processing (ICIP), pp. 2636–2640. IEEE (2015)
6. Boulkenafet, Z., Komulainen, J., Hadid, A.: Face spoofing detection using colour texture analysis. IEEE Trans. Inf. Forensics Secur. **11**(8), 1818–1830 (2016)
7. Chingovska, I., Anjos, A., Marcel, S.: On the effectiveness of local binary patterns in face anti-spoofing. In: 2012 BIOSIG-Proceedings of the International Conference of Biometrics Special Interest Group (BIOSIG), pp. 1–7. IEEE (2012)
8. Chopra, S., Hadsell, R., LeCun, Y.: Learning a similarity metric discriminatively, with application to face verification. In: 2005 IEEE Computer Society Conference on Computer Vision and Pattern Recognition (CVPR 2005), vol. 1, pp. 539–546. IEEE (2005)
9. Ciftci, U.A., Demir, I., Yin, L.: FakeCatcher: detection of synthetic portrait videos using biological signals. IEEE Trans. Pattern Anal. Mach. Intell. 1 (2020). http://dx.doi.org/10.1109/TPAMI.2020.3009287
10. de Freitas Pereira, T., Anjos, A., De Martino, J.M., Marcel, S.: Can face anti-spoofing countermeasures work in a real world scenario? In: 2013 International Conference on Biometrics (ICB), pp. 1–8. IEEE (2013)
11. Guo, J., Zhu, X., Yang, Y., Yang, F., Lei, Z., Li, S.Z.: Towards fast, accurate and stable 3D dense face alignment. In: Proceedings of the European Conference on Computer Vision (ECCV) (2020)
12. Jourabloo, A., Liu, Y., Liu, X.: Face de-spoofing: anti-spoofing via noise modeling. In: Proceedings of the European Conference on Computer Vision (ECCV), pp. 290–306 (2018)
13. Li, L., Feng, X., Boulkenafet, Z., Xia, Z., Li, M., Hadid, A.: An original face anti-spoofing approach using partial convolutional neural network. In: 2016 Sixth International Conference on Image Processing Theory, Tools and Applications (IPTA), pp. 1–6 (2016). https://doi.org/10.1109/IPTA.2016.7821013
14. Li, X., Komulainen, J., Zhao, G., Yuen, P.C., Pietikäinen, M.: Generalized face anti-spoofing by detecting pulse from face videos. In: 2016 23rd International Conference on Pattern Recognition (ICPR), pp. 4244–4249 (2016)
15. Lin, B., Li, X., Yu, Z., Zhao, G.: Face liveness detection by RPPG features and contextual patch-based CNN. In: Proceedings of the 2019 3rd International Conference on Biometric Engineering and Applications, pp. 61–68 (2019)
16. Liu, S.Q., Lan, X., Yuen, P.C.: Remote photoplethysmography correspondence feature for 3D mask face presentation attack detection. In: Proceedings of the European Conference on Computer Vision (ECCV), September 2018
17. Liu, S., Yuen, P.C., Zhang, S., Zhao, G.: 3D mask face anti-spoofing with remote photoplethysmography. In: Leibe, B., Matas, J., Sebe, N., Welling, M. (eds.) ECCV 2016. LNCS, vol. 9911, pp. 85–100. Springer, Cham (2016). https://doi.org/10.1007/978-3-319-46478-7_6
18. Liu, Y., Jourabloo, A., Liu, X.: Learning deep models for face anti-spoofing: binary or auxiliary supervision. In: Proceedings of the IEEE Conference on Computer Vision and Pattern Recognition, pp. 389–398 (2018)
19. Van der Maaten, L., Hinton, G.: Visualizing data using t-sne. Journal of machine learning research 9(11) (2008)

20. Patel, K., Han, H., Jain, A.K.: Cross-database face antispoofing with robust feature representation. In: You, Z., et al. (eds.) CCBR 2016. LNCS, vol. 9967, pp. 611–619. Springer, Cham (2016). https://doi.org/10.1007/978-3-319-46654-5_67

21. Patel, K., Han, H., Jain, A.K.: Secure face unlock: spoof detection on smartphones. IEEE Trans. Inf. Forensics Secur. **11**(10), 2268–2283 (2016). https://doi.org/10.1109/TIFS.2016.2578288

22. Pinto, A., Pedrini, H., Schwartz, W.R., Rocha, A.: Face spoofing detection through visual codebooks of spectral temporal cubes. IEEE Trans. Image Process. **24**(12), 4726–4740 (2015)

23. International Standard Organisation: Information Technology-biometric Presentation Attack Detection-part 1: Framework. ISO, Geneva, Switzerland (2016)

24. Tsou, Y.Y., Lee, Y.A., Hsu, C.T.: Multi-task learning for simultaneous video generation and remote photoplethysmography estimation. In: Proceedings of the Asian Conference on Computer Vision (2020)

25. Wang, Z., et al.: Deep spatial gradient and temporal depth learning for face anti-spoofing. In: Proceedings of the IEEE/CVF Conference on Computer Vision and Pattern Recognition, pp. 5042–5051 (2020)

26. Yang, J., Lei, Z., Li, S.Z.: Learn convolutional neural network for face anti-spoofing. arXiv preprint arXiv:1408.5601 (2014)

27. Yang, X., et al.: Face anti-spoofing: model matters, so does data. In: Proceedings of the IEEE/CVF Conference on Computer Vision and Pattern Recognition, pp. 3507–3516 (2019)

28. Zhang, G., Xu, J.: Discriminative feature representation for person re-identification by batch-contrastive loss. In: Asian Conference on Machine Learning, pp. 208–219. PMLR (2018)

29. Zhang, Z., Yan, J., Liu, S., Lei, Z., Yi, D., Li, S.Z.: A face antispoofing database with diverse attacks. In: 2012 5th IAPR International Conference on Biometrics (ICB), pp. 26–31. IEEE (2012)

30. Zhu, X., Liu, X., Lei, Z., Li, S.Z.: Face alignment in full pose range: a 3D total solution. IEEE Trans. Pattern Anal. Mach. Intell. (2017)

PalmNet: A Robust Palmprint Minutiae Extraction Network

Bing Liu[1,2], Zheng Wang[1,2], and Jufu Feng[1,2(✉)]

[1] Key Laboratory of Machine Perception (Ministry of Education),
Department of Machine Intelligence, Peking University,
Beijing, People's Republic of China
`fjf@cis.pku.edu.cn`
[2] School of Electronics Engineering and Computer Science, Peking University,
Beijing 100871, People's Republic of China

Abstract. Minutiae is the crucial foundation of palmprint recognition due to their discriminant and persistence. However, disturbed by complex latent noise, wide creases, and various frequency changes, it still challenging to extract palmprint minutiae. To address these issues, a robust palmprint minutiae extraction framework, PalmNet, is proposed. Specifically, considering the complex noise on the latent palmprint that is difficult to model, we avoid directly extracting the minutiae on the original image, but based on the Gabor enhanced map. Further, to make up for amplitude information missing in the Gabor enhanced phase field, we fuse phase and amplitude features to boost model performance. The orientation field is an inherent property of palmprints. Accurate orientation field estimation can benefit minutiae extraction and Gabor enhancement. Therefore, to recover the orientation field disturbed by wide crease, we make use of deep feature expression power and orientation consistency strategy to estimate orientation field. This two-stage method combines palmprint prior knowledge and has better interpretability, which can help us understand and analyze the total framework. Experiments on public LPIDB v1.0 and THUPALMLAB palmprint database demonstrate that our proposed algorithm outperforms the state-of-the-art. Notably, our algorithm improves the rank-1 recognition rate from 91.7% to 99.6% on the THUPALMLAB database.

Keywords: Palmprint recognition · Minutiae extraction · Deep learning

1 Introduction

Latent palmprint identification is especially paramount for law enforcement since approximately 30% of the latent found in a crime scene origin from palms [5,14]. Due to stable discriminant and persistence over time, compared with other features, minutiae play an essential role in this process. Although latent palmprints share some common problems with latent fingerprints [9], such as complex latent

© Springer Nature Switzerland AG 2022
C. Wallraven et al. (Eds.): ACPR 2021, LNCS 13188, pp. 459–473, 2022.
https://doi.org/10.1007/978-3-031-02375-0_34

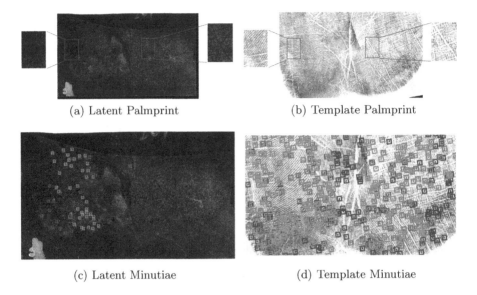

(a) Latent Palmprint   (b) Template Palmprint

(c) Latent Minutiae   (d) Template Minutiae

Fig. 1. Minutiae extraction performance. Red squares denote predicted minutiae by PalmNet and blue squares denote ground truth. (Color figure online)

appearance and poor ridge structures, latent palmprints have unique characteristics of numerous wide creases and frequency changes.

To extract palmprint minutiae, many studies [18, 21, 22, 26] design algorithms directly based on the original input images. Although end-to-end models are friendly to training, their accuracy degrades significantly in latent palmprints because of complex background noises and poor image quality. Figure 1 shows a pair of minutiae extraction results (c) and (d) on a latent palmprint (a) and responding template palmprint (b). The texture on the left box in (b) is very clear, the image quality is very good, and it is easy to extract minutiae from this area. For the right box in (b), affected by a large number of creases, if we directly extract minutiae on the original image, it will generate numerous pseudo minutiae in this area. Both two boxes in (a) are blurry and ridge lines are not clear, which leads the number and confidence of minutiae in (c) are much smaller than (d). In summary, the end-to-end minutiae extraction on the original image depends heavily on image quality and is not robust.

Alternatively, two-stage strategy based on Gabor enhancement [8] is proved to be effective for removing latent noises and improving image quality [1, 6, 9, 15]. Compared with end-to-end learning strategy, two-stage strategy incorporates more expert prior knowledge and has better interpretability. However, these hand-crafted algorithms fail in practical applications due to a lack of robust features. As shown in Fig. 2(a)–(b), AFIS [24] and VeriFinger [25] are well-known commercial software based on hand-crafted features. Both of them produce numerous false and missing minutiae.

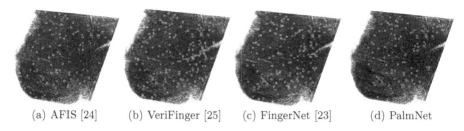

(a) AFIS [24]   (b) VeriFinger [25]   (c) FingerNet [23]   (d) PalmNet

Fig. 2. Minutiae extraction performance on LPIDB v1.0 latent palmprint images. (a) AFIS [24] and (b) VeriFinger [25] produce numerous false and missing minutiae. (c) FingerNet [23] predicts more fakes in the thenar area. (d) Our PalmNet has a reliable extraction. Red squares denote predicted minutiae and blue squares denote ground truth. (Color figure online)

Inspired by deep learning feature representation ability, some researchers introduce deep features to replace traditional hand-crafted features [17, 22, 23, 27]. However, for more difficult palmprints, there is little deep minutiae extraction work specialized on it. Because local similarity exists between palmprint and fingerprint, it is a topic worthy of discussion on deep fingerprint minutiae extraction. FingerNet [23] and MinutiaeNet [17] are typical representatives. Both of them learn minutiae deep representation based on Gabor enhancement. Two important parameters of Gabor filters are ridge orientation and frequency. However, these deep learning methods based on Gabor enhancement are not optimized for processing wide creases and frequency changes; thus, they cannot estimate accurate orientation and frequency. In other words, Gabor won't work if they are directly applied to palmprints and easily bring many fakes and leaks to minutiae extraction like Fig. 2(c).

In this paper, aiming at solving the above issues, we propose a two-stage robust palmprint minutiae extraction framework named PalmNet. To recover actual ridge disturbed by creases and frequency changes, we focus on improving the orientation field and frequency field. Meanwhile, proper orientation and frequency field can also benefit for Gabor enhancement to remove latent noise. In detail, we predict orientation field probability distribution at each pixel and assign the corresponding orientation according to the probability and orientation consistency. For frequency estimation, Discrete Fourier Transform (DFT) is computed on each 16×16 image patch to decompose multiple sets of orientation and frequency parameters. Then, we can complete frequency selection based on the orientation most consistent with the acquired orientation field. Naturally, we can generate Gabor enhanced phase field based on orientation field and frequency field to extract minutiae. Phase field mainly describes the ridge texture structure and the amplitude field reflects the confidence between the local image and filter, which includes quality information [6]. To make up for the missing amplitude information in phase field, we fuse the amplitude field for minutiae extraction. This fusion strategy uses the complementarity of phase and amplitude model, and extensive experiments show the effectiveness of PalmNet.

The main contributions of this paper are summarized:

- To the best of our knowledge, we first introduce deep learning to palmprint minutiae extraction and propose PalmNet, which learns robust orientation and frequency representation to alleviate wide creases disturb, frequency changes, and remove noises.
- We propose to fuse the amplitude model to make up for the missing amplitude information in the phase model, which boosts minutiae extraction results.
- Extensive experiments demonstrate that PalmNet achieves superior minutiae extraction performance on both live-scan and latent palmprints benchmarks.

2   Related Work

Palmprint minutiae extraction is of critical foundation in palmprint recognition and matching. Traditional palmprint minutiae extraction algorithms can be divided into two categories: (i) **End-to-end**: Some researchers [18,21,26] extract minutiae on raw image and then design hand-crafted detectors. However, due to the latent noises and wide creases, these methods are easy to attack. (ii) **Two stage**: To remove latent noise and ensure that the minutiae extraction algorithm is robust w.r.t. the input palmprint images' quality, many researchers [1,4,9] detect minutiae based on the Gabor enhanced ridge-line skeleton, then apply some simple structural rules to remove spurious minutiae. Furtherly, Feng *et al.* [6] decompose Gabor convolution responses to obtain phase field and amplitude field, where the phase field is used to detect minutiae and the amplitude field is used to measure minutiae's reliability. However, these traditional methods using hand-crafted features cannot accurately estimate orientation and frequency parameters, leading to a false Gabor enhancement result.

To learn more robust features for above minutiae extraction problem, some deep learning based methods have gotten researchers' attention [17,19,22,23,27]. We also borrow ideas from these methods. Tang *et al.* [22] utilize a fully convolutional network to detect minutiae. However, this end-to-end network is similar to a black box, and suffers from poor interpretability and limited generalization. FingerNet [23] and MinutiaeNet [17] combine fingerprint domain knowledge with a deep learnable network. However, limited by changeable frequency, creases disturb, and missing amplitude information, they still fail on latent palmprint minutiae extraction. Zhou *et al.* [27] extract minutiae directly from raw fingerprint images to speed up. However, this shallow and light network could not resist latent fingerprint complex noise, so it's hard to generalize to real law enforcement. Our paper pays attention to orientation and frequency feature representation and model fusion to solve these issues.

3   PalmNet

Since accurate Gabor enhancement relies on accurate orientation and frequency estimation modules. Before these modules are trained, the result of Gabor

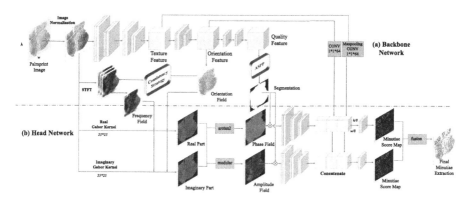

Fig. 3. The architecture of PalmNet. (a) Backbone Network contains orientation field, frequency field, and segmentation modules. (b) Head Network has Gabor enhanced phase and amplitude field and minutiae fusion result.

enhancement is not credible, and the training of minutiae extraction on the enhancement is also not meaningful. Thus, we design PalmNet mainly contains two parts. In the first part, we call the backbone network, aim to estimate accurate orientation field, frequency field, and segmentation. After the backbone network converges, its parameters are frozen. For the second part, we extract minutiae on Gabor enhanced phase and amplitude field and fuse their minutiae score maps to boost performance. Figure 3 shows the complete network pipeline.

3.1   Gabor Amplitude-Phase Model

In the classical Gabor Amplitude-Phase model, the 2D complex Gabor filter is introduced. Its form is

$$g_{\omega,\theta}(x,y) = \frac{1}{\sqrt{\sigma_{\theta_\perp}}} e^{-\frac{v^2}{2\sigma_{\theta_\perp}^2}} \cdot \frac{1}{\sqrt{\sigma_\theta}} e^{-\frac{u^2}{2\sigma_\theta^2}} e^{iwu}, \tag{1}$$

where, $u = x\cos\theta + y\sin\theta, v = -x\sin\theta + y\cos\theta$, and ω, θ denote the frequency and orientation of the filter, respectively, which could be pre-calculated in Sect. 3.2. $\sigma_\theta, \sigma_{\theta_\perp}$ are parameters along the orientation of θ and its perpendicular orientation. Convolute the palmprint with complex Gabor filter, we could obtain that

$$I_g(x_0, y_0) = \sum_{(x,y)\in D} f'(x,y) * g_{\omega,\theta}(x,y) = A(x_0, y_0) e^{i\varphi(x_0, y_0)}, \tag{2}$$

where, $A(x_0, y_0)$ denotes the amplitude, $\varphi(x_0, y_0)$ is the phase, $f'(x,y)$ is the local image after mean-variance normalization, and D denotes the local area. Worth mentioning, the amplitude $A(x_0, y_0)$ is the convolution result of the image and the Gabor filter $g_{\omega,\theta}$, its response is higher when the ridge is clear, which can fit the Gabor filter well. Hence, the amplitude $A(x_0, y_0)$ contains image quality

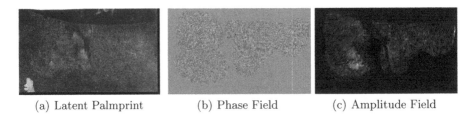

(a) Latent Palmprint   (b) Phase Field   (c) Amplitude Field

Fig. 4. Latent palmprint and its phase and amplitude fields from the Gabor Amplitude-Phase model.

information. Figure 4 shows a latent palmprint and corresponding phase field and amplitude field. From this figure, we can conclude that the phase field improves latent palmprint quality and describes more clearly ridges. In the amplitude field, the response in the good quality area is significantly larger than that in the poor quality area. They can reflect the ridge structure information and quality information respectively. Hence, we fuse phase and amplitude fields to detect minutiae in the following paper.

3.2   Backbone Network

As the network deepens, we define texture feature (TF), orientation feature (OF), and quality feature (QF) according to the semantics. The primary layer of the backbone network is stacked by residual blocks [7], and we implement convolution with a stride to replace pooling operation.

Orientation Field Module. Standard ridge orientation range is $[0°, 180°)$. Because the palmprint area is much larger than a fingerprint, for example, the size of a full template palmprint is about $2,048 \times 2,048$ pixels. To save GPU memory, we discrete $[0°, 180°)$ to a N-class classification task ($N \leq 180$). For each pixel (x, y), its orientation probability $P_{x,y} = [p_0, p_1, \cdots, p_{N-1}]$, where the p_i indicates the probability that orientation value is $\lfloor \frac{180}{N} \cdot i \rfloor$. In practice, we set N = 90. Although the dispersion inevitably causes a $2°$ error, it is still acceptable, which is a trade-off between GPU memory and accuracy.

Orientation Field Loss. There is rare available labeled data of palmprint orientation field. To solve these issues, we adopt a combination of weak labels and strong labels to generate training pseudo labels. For weak labels, we firstly use FingerNet [23] to generate initial orientation field $P_{x,y}^{*}{}'$. Given un-oriented minutiae directions are the same as the corresponding orientation field, we replace minutiae neighborhood in $P_{x,y}^{*}{}'$ with expert marked minutiae directions as our strong labels. Multi-class cross-entropy loss models the probability distribution similarity between predicted orientation field $P_{x,y}$ and pseudo label $P_{x,y}^{*}$:

$$L_{ori} = -\frac{1}{|M|} \sum_{M} \sum_{i=0}^{N-1} p_i^* \log p_i, \qquad (3)$$

where M denotes foreground regions, $|\cdot|$ denotes the number of foreground pixels, p_i and p_i^* indicates the predicted and label probability.

Following [23], considering orientation coherence is a strong palmprint domain prior knowledge and plays a role in the orientation field smooth, so we define a coherence loss function by Eq. (4).

$$L_{coh} = \frac{|M|}{\sum_M \frac{\sqrt{((\sin 2\theta)*1_3)^2+((\cos 2\theta)*1_3)^2}}{\sqrt{(\sin 2\theta)^2+(\cos 2\theta)^2}*1_3}} - 1, \tag{4}$$

where $*$ denotes convolution operation; $\sin 2\theta$ and $\cos 2\theta$ are double angle representation of orientation field; 1_3 is an all-ones matrix with size of 3×3.

Frequency Field Module. To estimate the frequency field more intuitively, we transform normalized palmprint image $I(x, y)$ into the frequency domain space. Specifically, $I(x, y)$ is divided into non-overlapping 16×16 patches. Then, the DFT, $F(\mu, \sigma)$, of the resulting image is computed on each patch. Since a 2D sine wave can model the ridge structure:

$$I(x, y) = a * \sin(2\pi f(\cos(\theta)x + \sin(\theta)y + \phi), \tag{5}$$

where f, θ, a, ϕ represent the frequency, orientation, amplitude, phase, and (μ, σ) is the sine wave position. Thus, the task of estimating local ridge frequency is equivalent to calculate the parameters of sine wave [9]. These decomposed waves are sorted in the decreasing order of amplitude, and top-3 waves are recorded: the first wave, the second wave, and the third wave.

Consistency Strategy. Motivated by frequency and orientation are closely related parameters, accurate orientation estimation will also improve frequency estimation. We represent top-3 frequency and orientation parameters sets as $\{[f_0, \theta_0], [f_1, \theta_1], [f_2, \theta_2]\}$ and select frequency f_i corresponding to the orientation θ_i which is closest to the orientation field obtained in the *Orientation Field Module* as the final frequency.

$$f = f_i, \quad \min_i |\theta_i - O(x, y)|, \tag{6}$$

where, $i = 0, 1, 2$, represents top-3 parameter subscript. $O(x, y)$ denotes orientation field obtained in the *Orientation Field Module* .

Segmentation Module. The purpose of segmentation is to distinguish the foreground and background of a palmprint. The foreground is usually a regular orientational texture, which has a remarkable coincidence with the orientation field. Therefore, we let the segmentation module and orientation field module share common features.

Segmentation Loss. Similarly, there is no manually-annotated segmentation labels. We consider generating pseudo-labels from the minutiae marked by experts. Considering that the minutiae marked by the experts must be in the foreground area of the palmprint, we use the convex hull composed of minutiae as the weak segmentation labels. We adopt dice loss [20] to learn the module.

$$L_{seg} = \frac{2\sum(S * \hat{S})}{\sum(S + \hat{S})},$$ (7)

where S is the predicted segmentation and $\hat{S}$ is the responding pseudo label.

Full Loss. Finally, all previous loss terms are combined linearly: .

$$L = \lambda_1 L_{ori} + \lambda_2 L_{coh} + \lambda_3 L_{seg}.$$ (8)

3.3 Head Network

After the backbone network converges, we freeze backbone weights and start training the head network. As we state in Sect. 3.1, amplitude image contains image quality information and the phase image reflects image texture information. In our next experiment, we use the complementary characteristics and extract minutiae based on these two images, and further merge minutiae predicted score maps. Figure 3(b) describes the architecture of the head network.

Phase and Amplitude Field Module. The core of this module lies in the orientation and frequency estimation and the design of Gabor filter. In practice, we first use orientation and frequency estimation results calculated in Sects. 3.2, and then convolute on palmprint using generated a group of Gabor filter based on these two parameters. Next, we assign a unique Gabor enhanced result for each position. Finally, we obtain phase and amplitude field by:

$$\begin{aligned} I_p &= arctan2(\frac{I_{real}}{I_{imag}}) \\ I_a &= \sqrt{I_{real}^2 + I_{imag}^2}, \end{aligned}$$ (9)

where, $I_p, I_a, I_{real}, I_{imag}$ denotes phase, amplitude, enhanced real and imaginary image respectively.

Minutiae Module. For minutiae detection, we take the phase field and amplitude field as input and design two same networks as shown in Fig 3(b). We fuse many middle-layer features, and the output is four feature maps: minutiae direction, minutiae X offset, minutiae Y offset, and minutiae score map.

Minutiae Direction. Similar to the orientation field, since the minutiae period is $[0, 360°)$, we discrete original direction every $2°$ and predict a 180-d direction probability distribution for representation.

Minutiae X, Y Offset. The minutiae feature map is $1/8$ scale of the original image. When it is restored to the original image coordinate system, to avoid the position error by downsampling, it is necessary to regress the offsets in X and Y axes.

Minutiae Score Map. It's a matrix of size $\frac{H}{8} \times \frac{W}{8}$. Each pixel of the matrix is a value between 0–1, indicating the probability that the corresponding 8×8 area contains minutiae.

Score Map Fusion. We directly add these two score maps predicted by phase and amplitude field mainly contain two reasons: (i) Some minutiae may have a high prediction probability in one network, while a low probability in another network. In addition, complementarity can be used to improve recall; (ii) For the minutiae with high predicted probabilities in both networks, they are still very high after addition, indicating current minutiae is confirmed by both networks.

Minutiae Representation. We give the details of minutiae representation from the score map, direction map and X, Y offset. Specifically, we represent n minutiae in a palmprint by an $n \times 3$ array. For i-th minutia, we use $[x_i, y_i, o_i]$ to denote its position coordinates (x_i, y_i) and direction (o_i). Firstly, the coordinates on the score map can be easily removed by a proper threshold value. Then, use the position with the highest probability of X and Y in the corresponding position on the offset map as the offset of the precise coordinates, and add this offset to the score map coordinates. In this way, we can get accurate pixel-level minutiae coordinates. The minutiae direction of the corresponding position can be obtained by Eq. (10).

$$o_i = \lfloor \frac{360}{N} \rfloor \cdot argmax(P_d), \tag{10}$$

where, $P_d = [p_0, p_1, \cdots, p_{N-1}]$ denotes minutiae direction vector. In our experiment, we set $N = 180$.

Loss Function. The minutiae label was marked by experts. We use multi-class cross-entropy to classify minutiae direction, L_2 loss to regress minutiae position (X, Y offsets). Considering minutiae distribution is sparse in a palmprint, especially in a latent palmprint. To balance positive and negative samples ratio, we use focal loss [13] to constraint minutiae score map.

$$L_d = -\frac{1}{|\boldsymbol{D}|} \sum_{\boldsymbol{D}} \sum_{i=0}^{N-1} \boldsymbol{Q}_i \log \boldsymbol{P}_i$$

$$L_2 = \frac{1}{|\boldsymbol{D}|} \sum_{\boldsymbol{D}} \|(\boldsymbol{P} - \boldsymbol{Q}) * \boldsymbol{D}\|_2^2 \tag{11}$$

$$L_s = \begin{cases} -\alpha(1 - \boldsymbol{P})^\gamma \log \boldsymbol{P}, & \boldsymbol{Q} = 1 \\ -(1 - \alpha)\boldsymbol{P}^\gamma \log(1 - \boldsymbol{P}), & otherwise, \end{cases}$$

where, L_d, L_2 and L_s loss are applied to minutiae direction, position, score map, respectively. $\boldsymbol{P}$ is predicted feature map, and $\boldsymbol{Q}$ is ground truth. $\boldsymbol{D}$ is minutiae 8×8 neighborhood. $\gamma \geq 0$ is a focusing parameter, and α is a weight parameter.

In the end, we take the total loss for joint training.

$$L_{final} = \lambda_4 L_d + \lambda_5 L_2 + \lambda_6 L_s. \tag{12}$$

4   Experiment

4.1   Database

Training data is collected from real crime scenes, including about 200 pairs of latent palmprints and their matched live-scan palmprints. We also collect 543 live-scan palmprint images using a commercial palmprint scanner of JY503. To avoid overfitting, we crop them into 512×512 patches and implement data augmentation in Sect. 4.2. All images are 500 ppi with expert marked minutiae.

Test set is conducted on LPIDB v1.0 [16] and THUPALMLAB [3], which are the most popular benchmarks for 500ppi latent and live-scan palmprint studies. LPIDB v1.0 contains 380 latent palmprints from 100 different palms of 51 donors but with different sizes. THUPALMLAB contains 1,280 palmprint images from 80 individuals (two palms per person and eight impressions per palm). Each palmprint is $2,040 \times 2,040$ pixels in size. It should be noted that only LPIDB v1.0 has ground truth minutiae marked by experts, and THUPALMLAB does not have any annotations, so it can only be used for identification experiments.

4.2   Implementation Details and Hyper-parameters

In order to stabilize the optimization, PalmNet is trained on a two-stage procedure. Firstly, we let PalmNet learn ridge properties with orientation field and segmentation constraints. After a few epochs, we add minutiae losses. This is because the Gabor enhancement module needs an accurate orientation field and frequency field to work properly. Before the orientation field module is well trained, the result of Gabor enhancement is not credible, and the training of the minutiae module does not make much sense.

In the first stage of training, according to the confidence of the label and the value range and importance of the loss function, we set the weighted hyper-parameters λ of the loss function as: $\lambda_1 = 1$, $\lambda_2 = 1$, $\lambda_3 = 5$.

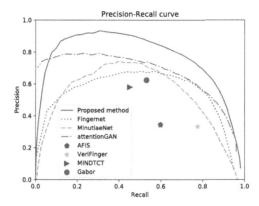

Fig. 5. Precision-Recall curves of different minutiae extraction algorithms on LPIDB v1.0. Dataset.

In the training of the second stage, we keep the weighted value of the orientation field and the segmentation loss unchanged, and increase the weighted value of the minutiae loss function: $\lambda_4 = 0.5$, $\lambda_5 = 0.5$, $\lambda_6 = 10$.

We use data augmentation protocol by randomly translation and rotation and randomly applied horizontal and vertical flipping. By following [2], we also randomly (10% probability) apply color distortion on an image. Our network is trained with an Adam optimizer [10]. Compared with the traditional stochastic gradient descent (SGD), Adam adaptively adjusts the learning rate according to the gradient, which can save the time of hyper-parameter tuning. Adam's hyper-parameters are set as follows: $lr = 0.001$, $\beta_1 = 0.9$, $\beta_2 = 0.999$, $\epsilon = 1e - 8$.

All the networks are implemented in TensorFlow and trained on the server with an Nvidia GeForce GTX 1080Ti GPU.

4.3 Evaluation

Minutiae Extraction Performance. We compare minutiae extraction performance with published approaches on LPIDB v1.0 datasets. Following [17,23], a predicted minutia is called true if its distance to ground truth is less than 15 pixels, and its angle is less than 30°. Figure 5 presents the precision-recall curves.

MINDTCT [11], VeriFinger [25] and AFIS [24] are well-known commercial software which anyone can download and use on custom applications. Gabor algorithm [6] extracts minutiae on the Gabor phase image. Due to the wider crease and more frequent changes in palmprints, even current mainstream fingerprint deep learning methods [17,23] still cannot extract palmprint minutiae accurately. AttentionGAN [14] aims to recover the orientation field to improve minutiae; however, it is designed for live-scan palmprints and cannot be applied for latent palmprints. Our method improves orientation and frequency and fuses palmprint multi-models to resist latent noise, achieving state-of-the-art performance. Figure 6 shows more visual results.

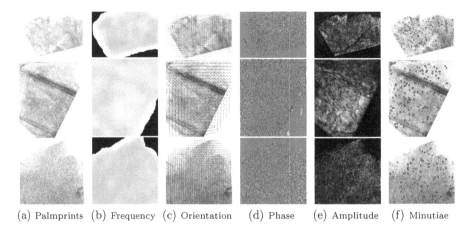

(a) Palmprints (b) Frequency (c) Orientation   (d) Phase   (e) Amplitude   (f) Minutiae

Fig. 6. Visual results of PalmNet. From left to right: (a) Latent Palmprints (b) Frequency (c) Segmented Orientation Field (d) Phase (e) Amplitude (f) Minutiae. From top to bottom, they represent the three areas of palm prints: interdigital, hypothenar, and thenar region. Among them, the thenar region has wide creases, which is the hardest region in a palm to identify.

Identification Performance. Figure 7 shows Cumulative Match Characteristic (CMC) curves on the public THUPALMLAB dataset to test whether Palm-Net could increase the palmprint identification performance. The matching strategy is based on MetricNet [12]. The gallery contains about 10,160 palmprints (160 palms in THUPALMLAB and our 10,000 in-house databases). The query is the left 1,120 prints. Our algorithm achieves a rank-1 identification rate of 99.6%, which is higher than others.

Ablation Performance Model Fusion. We compare the minutiae extraction performance of single phase model, single amplitude model, and two fused model on LPIDB v1.0 and plot precision-recall curve in Fig. 8. From Fig. 8, we can confirm that a single phase or amplitude model reflects the part of the palmprint character. When this complementary information is fused, it can boost final extraction performance.

Consistency Strategy. To explore the impact of consistency strategy for orientation and frequency field, we provide ablation studies with/without consistency in Table 1. The results are reported on LPIDB v1.0 and indicate the effectiveness of the consistency strategy.

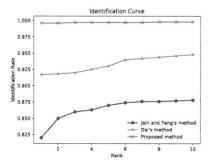
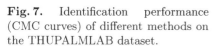

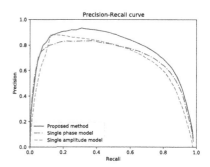

Fig. 7. Identification performance (CMC curves) of different methods on the THUPALMLAB dataset.

Fig. 8. Precision-Recall curves of single phase model, single amplitude model, and fused model on LPIDB v1.0. Dataset.

Table 1. Comparison w/o consistency strategy on orientation (ori) and frequency (fre) field for minutiae extraction on LPIDB v1.0 datasets.

Strategy	Precision	Recall	F1 Score
w/o ori+w/o fre	0.663	0.672	0.667
w/o ori+ w fre	0.702	0.697	0.699
w ori+w/o fre	0.736	0.691	0.713
Ours	**0.737**	**0.731**	**0.734**

4.4   Conclusion and Future Work

In this paper, we propose a deep network, PalmNet, for palmprint minutiae extraction. We creatively fuse phase and amplitude models to boost extraction performance. To remove latent noise, overcome wide creases interference orientation field and frequency changes, we combine palmprint consistency prior knowledge with learnable orientation and frequency distribution to select appropriate parameters. Extensive experiments show PalmNet achieves state-of-the-art performance.

Future work can be further improved by (i) designing a learnable frequency module, (ii) using larger palmprint datasets for network training, and (iii) compressing model and improving efficiency.

References

1. Cappelli, R., Ferrara, M., Maio, D.: A fast and accurate palmprint recognition system based on minutiae. IEEE Trans. Syst. Man Cybern. Part B (Cybern.) **42**(3), 956–962 (2012)

2. Chen, T., Kornblith, S., Norouzi, M., Hinton, G.: A simple framework for contrastive learning of visual representations. In: International Conference on Machine Learning, pp. 1597–1607. PMLR (2020)

3. Dai, J., Feng, J., Zhou, J.: Robust and efficient ridge-based palmprint matching. IEEE Trans. Pattern Anal. Mach. Intell. **34**(8), 1618–1632 (2011)

4. Dai, J., Zhou, J.: Multifeature-based high-resolution palmprint recognition. IEEE Trans. Pattern Anal. Mach. Intell. **33**(5), 945–957 (2010)

5. Dewan, S.K.: Elementary, Watson: Scan a palm, find a clue. The New York Times, p. 1 (2003)

6. Feng, J., Liu, C., Wang, H., Sun, B.: High-resolution palmprint minutiae extraction based on Gabor feature. Sci. China Inf. Sci. **57**(11), 1–15 (2014)

7. He, K., Zhang, X., Ren, S., Sun, J.: Deep residual learning for image recognition. In: Proceedings of the IEEE Conference on Computer Vision and Pattern Recognition, pp. 770–778 (2016)

8. Hong, L., Wan, Y., Jain, A.: Fingerprint image enhancement: algorithm and performance evaluation. IEEE Trans. Pattern Anal. Mach. Intell. **20**(8), 777–789 (1998)

9. Jain, A.K., Feng, J.: Latent palmprint matching. IEEE Trans. Pattern Anal. Mach. Intell. **31**(6), 1032–1047 (2008)

10. Kingma, D.P., Ba, J.: Adam: a method for stochastic optimization. arXiv preprint arXiv:1412.6980 (2014)

11. Ko, K.: User's guide to NIST biometric image software (NBIS) (2007)

12. Li, R., Song, D., Liu, Y., Feng, J.: Learning global fingerprint features by training a fully convolutional network with local patches. In: 2019 International Conference on Biometrics (ICB), pp. 1–8. IEEE (2019)

13. Lin, T.-Y., Goyal, P., Girshick, R., He, K., Dollár, P.: Focal loss for dense object detection. In: Proceedings of the IEEE International Conference on Computer Vision (2017)

14. Liu, B., Feng, J.: Palmprint orientation field recovery via attention-based generative adversarial network. Neurocomputing **438**, 1–13 (2021)

15. Maltoni, D., Maio, D., Jain, A.K., Prabhakar, S.: Handbook of Fingerprint Recognition. Springer, London (2009). https://doi.org/10.1007/978-1-84882-254-2

16. Morales, A., Medina-Pérez, M.A., Ferrer, M.A., García-Borroto, M., Robles, L.A.: LPIDB v1. 0-latent palmprint identification database. In: IEEE International Joint Conference on Biometrics, pp. 1–6. IEEE (2014)

17. Nguyen, D.-L., Cao, K., Jain, A.K.: Robust minutiae extractor: integrating deep networks and fingerprint domain knowledge. In: 2018 International Conference on Biometrics (ICB), pp. 9–16. IEEE (2018)

18. Rao, A.T., Ramaiah, N.P., Mohan, C.K.: Palmprint recognition based on minutiae quadruplets. In: Raman, B., Kumar, S., Roy, P.P., Sen, D. (eds.) Proceedings of International Conference on Computer Vision and Image Processing. AISC, vol. 460, pp. 117–126. Springer, Singapore (2017). https://doi.org/10.1007/978-981-10-2107-7_11

19. Sankaran, A., Pandey, P., Vatsa, M., Singh, R.: On latent fingerprint minutiae extraction using stacked denoising sparse autoencoders. In: IEEE International Joint Conference on Biometrics, pp. 1–7. IEEE (2014)

20. Sudre, C.H., Li, W., Vercauteren, T., Ourselin, S., Jorge Cardoso, M.: Generalised dice overlap as a deep learning loss function for highly unbalanced segmentations. In: Cardoso, M.J., et al. (eds.) DLMIA/ML-CDS -2017. LNCS, vol. 10553, pp. 240–248. Springer, Cham (2017). https://doi.org/10.1007/978-3-319-67558-9_28

21. Tan, Z., Yang, J., Shang, Z., Shi, G., Chang, S.: Minutiae-based offline palmprint identification system. In: 2009 WRI Global Congress on Intelligent Systems, vol. 4, pp. 466–471. IEEE (2009)
22. Tang, Y., Gao, F., Feng, J.: Latent fingerprint minutia extraction using fully convolutional network. In: 2017 IEEE International Joint Conference on Biometrics (IJCB), pp. 117–123. IEEE (2017)
23. Tang, Y., Gao, F., Feng, J., Liu, Y.: FingerNet: an unified deep network for fingerprint minutiae extraction. In: 2017 IEEE International Joint Conference on Biometrics (IJCB), pp. 108–116. IEEE (2017)
24. Važan, R.: Source AFIS SDK (2014)
25. Verifinger. Neuro-technology (2010)
26. Wang, R., Ramos, D., Fierrez, J.: Latent-to-full palmprint comparison based on radial triangulation under forensic conditions. In: 2011 International Joint Conference on Biometrics (IJCB), pp. 1–6. IEEE (2011)
27. Zhou, B., Han, C., Liu, Y., Guo, T., Qin, J.: Fast minutiae extractor using neural network. Pattern Recogn. **103**, 107273 (2020)

Multi-stage Domain Adaptation for Subretinal Fluid Classification in Cross-device OCT Images

Tian Li[1], Kun Huang[1], Yuhan Zhang[1], Mingchao Li[1], Weiwei Zhang[2], and Qiang Chen[1(✉)]

[1] School of Computer Science and Engineering, Nanjing University of Science and Technology, Nanjing, China
chen2qiang@njust.edu.cn
[2] Department of Ophthalmology, The First Affiliated Hospital with Nanjing Medical University, Nanjing, China

Abstract. Optical coherence tomography (OCT) is a practical basis that is widely used for computer-aided retinal diagnosis, and OCT images from different devices show obvious intensity distribution differences. Recently, deep learning based models have achieved promising results for the classification tasks on single-device OCT images. However, when the models trained on source domain images are transferred for the classification of the target domain images from another OCT device, we can observe significant performance degradation. Re-annotating target domain images and fine-tuning models are inefficient. In this paper, we propose a multi-stage domain adaptation method (MSDA), which can learn generalized and effective domain invariant information for cross-device OCT classification from labeled source domain images and unlabeled target domain images. Specifically, task-independent feature alignment (TiFA) module firstly maps OCT images with different distributions to the same latent space, where the original image information is effectively preserved. Then, the downstream task-specific feature alignment (TsFA) module further distills out category-associated features from the output of TiFA. The experimental results demonstrate that the proposed MSDA improves the subretinal fluid classification performance of cross-device OCT images.

Keywords: Subretinal fluid classification · Multi-stage domain adaptation · Feature alignment · Cross-device images

1 Introduction

The leakage from the retinal capillaries accumulates in the retinal intercellular space can result in a swelling of the central retina, which is macular edema [8]. It

This study was supported in part by National Natural Science Foundation of China (62172223, 61671242), in part by Key R & D Program of Jiangsu Science and Technology Department (BE2018131) and the Fundamental Research Funds for the Central Universities (30921013105).

© Springer Nature Switzerland AG 2022
C. Wallraven et al. (Eds.): ACPR 2021, LNCS 13188, pp. 474–487, 2022.
https://doi.org/10.1007/978-3-031-02375-0_35

causes sudden and severe visual impairment, even loss of vision. The treatment regimen needs to be effective in distinguishing the types of fluid that cause macular edema [7,17], such as intraretinal fluid (IRF), subretinal fluid (SRF), and pigment epithelial detachment (PED). Optical Coherence Tomography (OCT) is a non-invasive medical imaging tool [3] that can provide high-resolution images of fluids that cause macular edema and has been widely applied in computer-aided diagnosis (CAD). However, the OCT imaging devices used in the clinic may come from different manufacturers. The data distribution of images captured from different devices are variations that presents challenges to CAD.

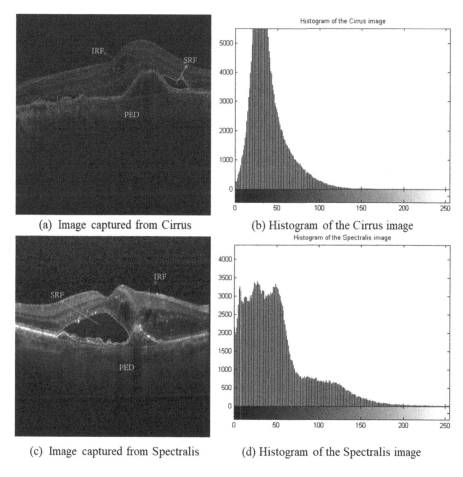

(a) Image captured from Cirrus   (b) Histogram of the Cirrus image

(c) Image captured from Spectralis   (d) Histogram of the Spectralis image

Fig. 1. Examples of images from different devices and their histograms

Figure 1 shows two OCT images captured from different devices and their grayscale histograms, where the one is from Cirrus (Carl Zeiss Meditec, Dublin, CA, USA) and another is from Spectralis (Heidelberg Engineering, Heidelberg,

Germany). Although fluid classification in OCT images captured by various devices is easy for experienced clinicians, CAD often performs poorly. It is an option that manually annotates the target domain image and fine-tunes the original model, but it is time-consuming and expensive, particularly for medical images. Therefore, it is of great significance to research a method that learns models from OCT images captured by one device and adapts them to another device without adding additional manual annotations.

Domain adaptation (DA) is proposed to solve the problem of domain shift caused by data distribution discrepancy of images from different domains. A typical domain adaptation setting consists of a well-labeled source domain and an unlabeled target domain. In general, the two domains are interconnected, i.e., sharing the same semantic space, but drawn from distinctive data distributions [9]. Recently, the domain adaptive methods have developed rapidly. One of them uses a style-transfer of the source images [10,11,23] for classification. These methods often have fake generation used in medical images, which leads to inaccurate classification. Another tends to match the distribution of the source domain and the target domain in the feature space [16,19,19]. These methods obtain domain-invariant features for classification by adversarially fooling the domain discriminator. However, the domain-invariant features obtained by such methods are noisy, which contains task-independent information. It is negatively impacting our ultimate task.

To compensate for these shortcomings, we proposed a multi-stage domain adaptation method (MSDA) suitable for subretinal fluid classification in cross-device OCT images. Our method contains a task-independent feature alignment (TiFA) module and a task-specific feature alignment (TsFA) module. Specifically, the TiFA module includes dual encoders, decoders, and discriminators. The TsFA module includes two feature extractors, a discriminator and a classifier. Firstly, we use the TiFA module for mapping features to the same latent space, where the original image information is effectively preserved. Then, the downstream TsFA module further distills out category-associated features from the output of TiFA and use them for classification. There are benefits to our approach. On the one hand, we input the obtained domain-invariant features into the classifier instead of the translated images, which get rid of the error in classification caused by fake generation to our tasks. On the other hand, we perform two-stage feature alignment to reduce the noise in the domain-invariant features. The contributions of our paper are summarized as follows:

- We proposed a novel multi-stage domain adaptation method (MSDA), which is the first solution of the subretinal fluid classification in cross-device OCT images.
- Our method combines feature-based domain adaptation and image-based domain adaptation efficaciously and obtains noise-free domain-invariant features.
- We evaluated our method for fluid classification tasks in cross-device OCT images. In many settings, our method outperforms other methods.

2   Related Work

Domain Adaptation (DA). Domain adaptation is the ability to apply an algorithm trained in one source domain to a different target domain. Recently, there has been much research on visual unsupervised domain adaptation after Ben-David [1] studied how the common representation between the two domains makes the two domains appear to have similar distributions to achieve effective domain adaptation. These methods have been developed mainly in several directions: statistical differences-based approaches and adversarial training-based approaches, etc. These methods are focused on finding a mapping from the representation of the source domain to those of the target or getting domain-invariant representation shared between the domains. Maximum mean discrepancy(MMD) [2] is a widely used method of measuring domain distribution difference. MMD-based approaches map features from the target domain and the source domain to the same meaningful space and then closing the distance between the representation distributions of the two domains in this space. Ghifary et al. [4] combined MMD and neural network for domain adaptation for the first time, minimizing the representation discrepancy of the source and target domains in the hidden layer based on MMD minimization. Subsequently, JAN et al. [13] proposed the method that measure the discrepancy of the joint distribution of the last few layers of the network, and RTN [12] introduce pseudo-labels based on the above methods, which use MMD to align the edge distribution and conditional distribution of the target domain and the source domain. In addition to MMD, some other metrics are also used, Sun et al. [18] proposed the CORAL metric, which not only aligns the mean of the source and target domains but also aligns the variance compared to MMD.

After the Generative Adversarial Network (GAN) was proposed [5], adversarial training is widely used in domain adaptation and has achieved excellent success. The generator aligns the distribution of the source domain and the target domain in the data space or feature space through the adversarial training of the domain discriminator. DANN [19] is a domain adversarial training method that aims to generate domain-invariant features using a gradient reversal layer by deceiving a domain discriminator. ADDA [19] uses the same ideology, first which uses the data of the source domain to pre-train a classifier, then uses the structure of GAN to map the data of the target domain to the source domain, and finally uses the pre-trained classifier for the classification of the target domain. Saito et al. proposed method MCD [16] focus on task-specific decision boundaries. The above methods all use the discriminator in the feature space, and the discriminator can also be used in the data space. The development of GAN is very rapid, which has made a breakthrough in unsupervised domain adaptation (UDA), CoGAN [11] used a weight-sharing strategy to learn a common representation across domains. Inspired by this, UNIT [10] assumed that there exists a shared-latent space in which a pair of corresponding images from different domains could be mapped to the same latent representation. Cycle-GAN introduced cycle-consistency loss [23], which is a breakthrough, and then there are many methods based on this, like MADAN [22], which aligns the

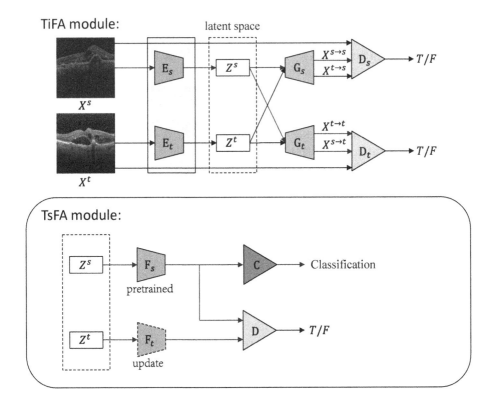

Fig. 2. The architecture of our proposed multi-stage domain adaptation method (MSDA). Our method has two modules: task-independent feature alignment (TiFA) and task-specific feature alignment (TsFA).

distribution at the feature level and pixel-level at the same time. In addition, [14,15] applied cycleGAN to the medical image field. OP-GAN [20] and DAST [21] used self-supervision on this basis. Hou et al. [6] combined knowledge distillation with UDA and visualized adapted knowledge.

3   Method

In this section, the detail of our proposed method is shown in Fig 2. Our model consists of a task-independent feature alignment (TiFA) module and a task-specific feature alignment (TsFA) module, described in detail in the following subsections, respectively. The TiFA module is used to align features preliminarily, where the original image information is effectively preserved. We use the TsFA module to distills out category-associated features from the output of TiFA and use them for classification.

3.1 Task-Independent Feature Alignment Module

Initially, we define OCT images captured from one device as X^s and captured from another device as X^t. Following Ben-David et al.'s theory [1], we define the distribution of inputs X^s and X^t as source domain and target domain, respectively.

As illustrated in Fig 2, inspired by UNIT [10], we use a task-independent feature alignment module to align features. The TiFA module contains two encoders E_s and E_t, two decoders G_s and G_t and two discriminators D_s and D_t. Firstly, we input X^s and X^t into the E_s and E_t and get features Z^s and Z^t, as $Z^s = E_s(X^s)$ and $Z^t = E_t(X^t)$. Then we input Z^s and Z^t into G_s to get reconstructed images $X^{s \to s}$ and transformed images $X^{t \to s}$, as $X^{s \to s} = G_s(Z^s)$ and $X^{t \to s} = G_s(Z^t)$. We do the same with G_t, and we get reconstructed images $X^{t \to t} = G_t(Z^t)$ and transformed images $X^{s \to t} = G_t(Z^s)$. The TiFA employs two discriminators D_s and D_t for adversarial training. For the input images X^s and X^t, D_s and D_t should output true. For the images generated by G_s and G_t, the discriminators should output false.

We use the Kullback-Leibler (KL) divergence loss $\mathcal{L}_{KL}$ to align the features of the two domains. The $\mathcal{L}_{KL}$ constraints that the distribution of the features to the prior distribution, which can be expressed as:

$$\mathcal{L}_{KL} = \mathrm{KL}(Z^s \,\|\, P) + \mathrm{KL}(Z^t \,\|\, P) \tag{1}$$

where $\mathrm{KL}(\cdot)$ is KL Divergence and P is the zero mean Gaussian distribution.

We use the reconstruction loss $\mathcal{L}_{rec}$ to constraints the information of the features could be used to reconstruct original images. The reconstruction loss $\mathcal{L}_{rec}$ is expressed as:

$$\mathcal{L}_{rec} = \left\| X^s - X^{s \to s} \right\|_2 + \left\| X^t - X^{t \to t} \right\|_2 \tag{2}$$

The GAN loss is used for making sure that the transformed images $X^{t \to s}$ and $X^{s \to t}$ can fit into the distribution of source domain and target domain, respectively. The GAN loss is expressed as:

$$\begin{aligned}
\mathcal{L}_{GAN} &= \mathcal{L}_{GAN_s} + \mathcal{L}_{GAN_t} \\
&= \log\left(D_s\left(X^s\right)\right) + \log\left(1 - D_s\left(X^{t \to s}\right)\right) \\
&\quad + \log\left(D_t\left(X^t\right)\right) + \log\left(1 - D_t\left(X^{s \to t}\right)\right)
\end{aligned} \tag{3}$$

Furthermore, we carried out cycle generation for the transformed images $X^{s \to t}$ and $X^{t \to s}$, and define the cycle features as $Z^{t \to s} = E_s(X^{t \to s})$ and $Z^{s \to t} = E_t(X^{s \to t})$. We use $\mathcal{L}_{cyc\_KL}$ to constraint $Z^{t \to s}$ and $Z^{s \to t}$, the cycle KL loss $\mathcal{L}_{cyc\_KL}$ can be expressed as:

$$\mathcal{L}_{cyc\_KL} = \mathrm{KL}(Z^{t \to s} \,\|\, P) + \mathrm{KL}(Z^{s \to t} \,\|\, P) \tag{4}$$

We define the cycle transformed images as $X^{s \to t \to s}$ and $X^{t \to s \to t}$, and we use a cycle consistency loss $\mathcal{L}_{cyc}$ to constraints that the content of transformed images should be same as original images. The $\mathcal{L}_{cyc}$ is expressed as:

$$\mathcal{L}_{cyc} = \left\| X^s - X^{s\to t\to s} \right\|_2 + \left\| X^t - X^{t\to s\to t} \right\|_2 \qquad (5)$$

The overall objective function of our TiFA module can be written as:

$$\min_{E_s, E_t, G_s, G_t} \max_{D_s, D_t} (\lambda_1 \mathcal{L}_{KL} + \lambda_2 \mathcal{L}_{cyc\_KL} + \lambda_3 \mathcal{L}_{cyc} + \lambda_4 \mathcal{L}_{GAN} + \lambda_5 \mathcal{L}_{rec}) \qquad (6)$$

where the hyper-parameters λ_1, λ_2, λ_3, λ_4 and λ_5 control the weights of the objective functions.

After training, The encoders E_s and E_t in our TiFA module can map OCT images from different domains into a latent space while keeping their original information.

3.2   Task-Specific Feature Alignment Module

Since the features Z^s and Z^t obtained by E_s and E_t in TiFA module are only task-independent initial alignment, we use a TsFA module to future distills out category-associated features. Note we define the category label corresponding to X^s as Y^s. The training procedure includes two different steps.

Pre-training. We pre-train a feature extractor F_s and classifier C for the features Z^s.

The C and F_s are jointly trained for the accurate classification of feature representations Z_s extracted from input OCT images. The optimization problem is the minimization of the following cross-entropy loss $\mathcal{L}_0$:

$$\mathcal{L}_0 = -Y^s \log C(F_s(Z^s)) \qquad (7)$$

Adversarial Training. We distill out category-associated features by adversarial training a feature extractor F_t and a discriminator D. This F_t can then be cascaded of the classifier C previously trained to perform inference on the features Z^t.

As shown in Fig. 2, firstly, we use the pre-trained F_s as an initialization for F_t and fix F_s, then F_t and D are trained in an adversarial manner. Once the D cannot distinguish whether the features belong to source domain and target domain, it is considered that the obtained features are domain-invariant. Our F_t and D are optimized according to an adversarial loss $\mathcal{L}_{adv}$, which can be expressed as:

$$\begin{aligned} \mathcal{L}_{adv} &= \mathcal{L}_{adv\_D} + \mathcal{L}_{adv\_F_t} \\ &= -\log\left(D\left(F_s\left(Z^s\right)\right)\right) + \log\left(D\left(F_t\left(Z^t\right)\right)\right) \end{aligned} \qquad (8)$$

4   Experiments

In this section, we evaluate our approach on OCT image datasets. The evaluation results demonstrate that the proposed method shows better performance than some of the state-of-the-art methods, like DANN [19], ADDA [19], MCD [16] and the method proposed by Hou et al. [6].

4.1   Materials

The OCT image datasets used in our experiments comes from MICCAI RETOUCH CHALLENGE 2017. These OCT images are captured either by Cirrus (Carl Zeiss Meditec, Dublin, CA, USA) or Spectralis (Heidelberg Engineering, Heidelberg, Germany) devices, both widely applied in clinics. The B-scans produced by each device differ substantially from each other in many aspects, in addition to the difference in scanning light source (Cirrus is 840 nm and Spectralis is 880 nm), the difference in resolution (1024 × 512 pixels for Cirrus B-scans, 496 × 512 pixels for Spectralis B-scans) and signal distribution caused by the difference in axial (Cirrus is 5 μm and Spectralis is 7 μm) and lateral (Cirrus is 10 μm and Spectralis is 14 μm) resolution, the difference in noise style caused by the optimization of the signal-to-noise ratio (SNR) of Spectralis and so on. In this dataset, Cirrus and Spectralis both collected OCT images of 24 patients, but Cirrus obtained 128 B-scans for each patient, and Spectralis obtained 49 B-scans for each patient. Table 1 shows the details about the datasets. Since each image may contain more than one type of fluid, we set a three-digit label for each image, the first digit indicates whether there is an IRF, the second digit indicates whether there is an SRF, and the third digit indicates whether there is a PED.

Table 1. The different types of fluid distribution in the dataset (In label, the first digit indicates whether there is an IRF, the second digit indicates whether there is an SRF, and the third digit indicates whether there is a PED).

Label	Number of images from Cirrus	Number of images from Spectralis
000	1504	465
001	119	30
010	180	55
011	334	123
100	679	267
101	70	75
110	87	87
111	99	74
Total	3072	1176

To be more in line with actual medical application scenarios, we conduct the patient-independent experiment. For the patient-independent evaluation, the datasets are divided into a random choice of patients rather than B-scans. Thus, the training and testing sets are independent. In the classification network part, we randomly use the OCT images from 19 (for Cirrus including $19 \times 128 = 2432$ B-scans) or 20 patients (for Spectralis including $20 \times 49 = 931$) as the training set, and the OCT images from the remaining 5 (for Cirrus including $5 \times 128 = 640$ B-scans) or 4 patients (for Spectralis including $4 \times 49 = 196$) as the test set. This evaluates the model capability on the patient level instead of B-scans. We use the nearest neighbor interpolation method to resize the images to 512×512 to ensure that the input of the networks is consistent.

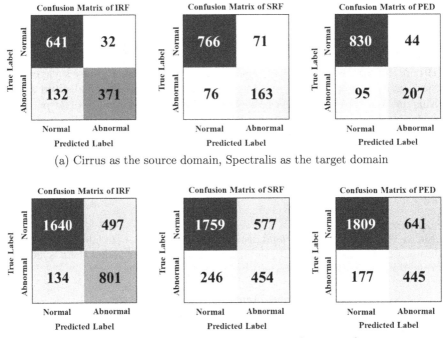

(a) Cirrus as the source domain, Spectralis as the target domain

(b) Spectralis as the source domain, Cirrus as the target domain

Fig. 3. Confusion matrix of IRF, SRF and PED

4.2 Experiment Protocols

As shown in Fig. 2, our method mainly consists of two modules, i.e., the TiFA module and the TsFA module. In this subsection, we describe the details of our implementation.

TiFA Module. The TiFA module contains dual encoders E_s and E_t, decoders G_s and G_t and discriminators D_s and D_t. Specifically, the E_s and E_t are implemented by five convolutional layers, the size of the convolution kernel size is 5, the stride size is 3, and the Leaky rectified linear unit (Leaky LeRU) is used as the activation function. The G_s and G_t are implemented by five deconvolutional layers with a convolution kernel size of 6 and stride size of 6 for image generation. The D_s and D_t are implemented by four convolutional layers with the

Table 2. Evaluation results of several domain adaptation models

Method		Cirrus→Spectralis			Spectralis→Cirrus		
		Accuracy	Sensitivity	Subset_acc	Accuracy	Sensitivity	Subset_acc
Source only	IRF	0.7185	0.5626	0.4685	0.6563	0.6781	0.4349
	SRF	0.7219	0.2979		0.82	0.4557	
	PED	0.7704	0.1192		0.7347	0.3424	
	Avg	0.7369	0.3266		0.737	0.4921	
DANN [19]	IRF	0.7092	0.5388	0.4804	0.6813	0.6652	0.4268
	SRF	0.75	0.5841		0.7591	0.1486	
	PED	0.8095	0.3079		0.6436	0.1125	
	Avg	0.7562	0.4769		0.6947	0.3088	
ADDA [19]	IRF	0.7229	0.3837	0.5893	0.7119	0.4963	**0.5205**
	SRF	0.9014	0.823		0.8177	0.6943	
	PED	0.8529	0.606		0.8076	0.3328	
	Avg	0.8257	0.6042		**0.7791**	0.5078	
MCD [16]	IRF	0.6718	0.3598	0.4838	0.7021	0.6759	0.5023
	SRF	0.7738	0.6608		0.7692	0.004	
	PED	0.8197	0.5629		0.7995	0.492	
	Avg	0.7551	0.5278		0.7569	0.3906	
Hou et al.'s method [6]	IRF	0.7628	0.6382	0.4957	0.7021	0.0214	0.5008
	SRF	0.7347	0.115		0.7709	0.0314	
	PED	0.7721	0.1225		0.7969	0.0338	
	Avg	0.7565	0.2919		0.7566	0.0289	
MSDA (Ours)	IRF	0.8605	0.7376	**0.6896**	0.7946	0.8567	0.5117
	SRF	0.875	0.7758		0.7321	0.6486	
	PED	0.8818	0.6854		0.7337	0.7154	
	Avg	**0.8724**	**0.7329**		0.7535	**0.7402**	

convolutional kernel size of 5 and the stride size of 2, and a fully connected (FC) layer, and the final outputs are activated by the sigmoid function. We optimize TiFA module by stochastic gradient descent (SGD), and we set the batch size as 8 and the learning rate as 10^{-4}. The hyperparameters in the objective functions are set to $\lambda_1 = 0.01$, $\lambda_2 = 0.01$, $\lambda_3 = 10$ and $\lambda_4 = 1$.

TsFA Module. The TsFA module contains two feature extractors F_s and F_t, a discriminator D and a classifier C. Specifically, we deploy VGG-11 as the backbone network of F_s and F_t. The classifier C is implemented by a standard softmax classifier. The discriminator D is implemented by FC-Sigmoid. We optimize TiFA module by SGD, and we set the batch size to 8 and the learning rate as 10^{-4}.

4.3 Performance Evaluation

The evaluation of the proposed method is carried out on OCT images with subretinal fluid by accuracy, sensitivity, and subset accuracy. Consequently, the accuracy and sensitivity are computed as follows:

$$\text{Accuracy} = \frac{TP + TN}{TP + FP + TN + FN} \tag{9}$$

$$\text{Sensitivity} = \frac{TP}{TP + FN} \tag{10}$$

Moreover, subset accuracy is the most strict metric for evaluating each image, indicating the percentage of samples that have all their labels classified correctly, which is computed as follows:

$$\text{Subset\_accuracy} = \sum_{i=1}^{N} \frac{Y_i \cap P_i}{N} \tag{11}$$

where Y_i is the ground truth of the image, P_i is the predicted output, and N is the number of images.

Since the task of our model is to classify the subretinal fluid, FN (diagnosing the patient as healthy and will miss the best treatment time) is more severe than FP, and the model should be more inclined to find all positive samples. That is, on the premise of ensuring accuracy, we hope that the model has high sensitivity.

4.4   Results and Discussion

We evaluated the performance of our proposed method to classify subretinal fluid on the OCT image datasets mentioned in Sect. 4.1. As shown in Table 2, all classes demonstrated practical accuracy and sensitivity, and all samples also have persuasive subset accuracy. When the source domain is a dataset from Cirrus, the confusion matrix to test the target domain is shown in Fig. 3.

We also compared our method with some related work, such as DANN [19], ADDA [19], MCD [16] and Hou et al.'s method [6], as shown in Table 2. The former three methods all directly get a generator that aligns the distribution of the source domain and the target domain in the data space or feature space through the confrontation of the domain discriminator. DANN [19] achieves the feature alignment between the source and target domains through a gradient reversal layer. ADDA [19] is aimed at the entire feature extractor. MCD [16] pays attention to the category boundary. Hou et al.'s method [6] is to turn the original target image into the source-style image. Our method first maps the images of the two domains to the same latent space and then obtains domain invariant features without task-independent information through adversarial training again.

Although the accuracy of each type of edema and the subset accuracy of all samples in ADDA is slightly better than our method, its sensitivity is far lower than our method, which indicates that it tends to predict abnormal samples as normal, which is of significant risk in the disease diagnosis scenario. Therefore, considering the accuracy and sensitivity of each type of fluid and the subset accuracy of all samples, our method outperforms all methods compared.

4.5   Ablation Study

In this section, We carried out ablation studies by adding one component to evaluate the benefits of each module. We further design the following three approaches for comparison:

1) Without adaptation. We perform fully supervised training E_s, F_s and C on the source domain images and then directly use them to test the target domain images.
2) TiFA. We add TiFA module based on 1) to observe its effect.
3) TsFA. We further add the TsFA module.

Table 3. Results of ablation studies

Method	W/O adaptation	TiFA	TsFA	Avg_acc	Avg_sen	Subset_acc
Cirrus to Spectralis	✓			0.7369	0.3266	0.4685
		✓		0.7526	0.5339	0.4838
		✓	✓	0.8724	0.7329	0.6896
Spectralis to Cirrus	✓			0.737	0.4921	0.4349
		✓		0.7511	0.4907	0.4528
		✓	✓	0.7535	0.7402	0.5117

Our method contains TiFA module and TsFA module, and we report the MSDA ablation study in Table 3 to show the contribution of each term. As we can see, each module is essential to our MSDA. After our first feature alignment with the TiFA module, the classification performance improved, but not significantly.This is because the features after initial alignment are disturbed by other information besides the category information needed for classification. The performance of our method has been significantly improved after the addition of TSFA module to align the features and distill the category information in the features.

5   Conclusion

Solving the problem of data analysis acquired across devices is of great significance in medical applications. In this article, we propose a multi-stage domain adaptation to classify retinal fluids for cross-device OCT images, which maps the images acquired by the two devices to the same latent space and then distills out category-associated features. We evaluated our method on the cross-device fluid classification tasks and compared the performance with those of some related works, demonstrating the effectiveness of the proposed network architecture. In our future work, we will investigate the more challenging domain adaptation on OCT images classification.

References

1. Ben-David, S., Blitzer, J., Crammer, K., Kulesza, A., Pereira, F., Vaughan, J.W.: A theory of learning from different domains. Mach. Learn. **79**(1), 151–175 (2010)
2. Borgwardt, K.M., Gretton, A., Rasch, M.J., Kriegel, H.P., Schölkopf, B., Smola, A.J.: Integrating structured biological data by kernel maximum mean discrepancy. Bioinformatics **22**(14), e49–e57 (2006)
3. Duker, J.S., Waheed, N.K., Goldman, D.: Handbook of Retinal OCT: Optical Coherence Tomography E-Book. Elsevier, Amsterdam (2013)
4. Ghifary, M., Kleijn, W.B., Zhang, M.: Domain adaptive neural networks for object recognition. In: Pham, D.-N., Park, S.-B. (eds.) PRICAI 2014. LNCS (LNAI), vol. 8862, pp. 898–904. Springer, Cham (2014). https://doi.org/10.1007/978-3-319-13560-1_76
5. Goodfellow, I.J., et al.: Generative adversarial networks. arXiv preprint arXiv:1406.2661 (2014)
6. Hou, Y., Zheng, L.: Visualizing adapted knowledge in domain transfer. arXiv preprint arXiv:2104.10602 (2021)
7. Jaffe, G.J., et al.: Macular morphology and visual acuity in the comparison of age-related macular degeneration treatments trials. Ophthalmology **120**(9), 1860–1870 (2013)
8. Johnson, M.W.: Etiology and treatment of macular edema. Am. J. Ophthalmol. **147**(1), 11–21 (2009)
9. Li, J., Chen, E., Ding, Z., Zhu, L., Lu, K., Shen, H.T.: Maximum density divergence for domain adaptation. IEEE Trans. Pattern Anal. Mach. Intell. **43**, 3918–3930 (2020)
10. Liu, M.Y., Breuel, T., Kautz, J.: Unsupervised image-to-image translation networks. arXiv preprint arXiv:1703.00848 (2017)
11. Liu, M.Y., Tuzel, O.: Coupled generative adversarial networks. arXiv preprint arXiv:1606.07536 (2016)
12. Long, M., Zhu, H., Wang, J., Jordan, M.I.: Unsupervised domain adaptation with residual transfer networks. arXiv preprint arXiv:1602.04433 (2016)
13. Long, M., Zhu, H., Wang, J., Jordan, M.I.: Deep transfer learning with joint adaptation networks. In: International Conference on Machine Learning, pp. 2208–2217. PMLR (2017)
14. Oulbacha, R., Kadoury, S.: MRI to CT synthesis of the lumbar spine from a pseudo-3D cycle GAN. In: 2020 IEEE 17th International Symposium on Biomedical Imaging (ISBI), pp. 1784–1787. IEEE (2020)
15. Romo-Bucheli, D., et al.: Reducing image variability across oct devices with unsupervised unpaired learning for improved segmentation of retina. Biomed. Opt. Express **11**(1), 346–363 (2020)
16. Saito, K., Watanabe, K., Ushiku, Y., Harada, T.: Maximum classifier discrepancy for unsupervised domain adaptation. In: Proceedings of the IEEE Conference on Computer Vision and Pattern Recognition, pp. 3723–3732 (2018)
17. Schmidt-Erfurth, U., Klimscha, S., Waldstein, S., Bogunović, H.: A view of the current and future role of optical coherence tomography in the management of age-related macular degeneration. Eye **31**(1), 26–44 (2017)
18. Sun, B., Feng, J., Saenko, K.: Return of frustratingly easy domain adaptation. In: Proceedings of the AAAI Conference on Artificial Intelligence, vol. 30 (2016)
19. Tzeng, E., Hoffman, J., Saenko, K., Darrell, T.: Adversarial discriminative domain adaptation. In: Proceedings of the IEEE Conference on Computer Vision and Pattern Recognition, pp. 7167–7176 (2017)

20. Xie, X., Chen, J., Li, Y., Shen, L., Ma, K., Zheng, Y.: Self-supervised CycleGAN for object-preserving image-to-image domain adaptation. In: Vedaldi, A., Bischof, H., Brox, T., Frahm, J.-M. (eds.) ECCV 2020. LNCS, vol. 12365, pp. 498–513. Springer, Cham (2020). https://doi.org/10.1007/978-3-030-58565-5_30
21. Yu, F., Zhang, M., Dong, H., Hu, S., Dong, B., Zhang, L.: DAST: unsupervised domain adaptation in semantic segmentation based on discriminator attention and self-training. In: Proceedings of the AAAI Conference on Artificial Intelligence, vol. 35, pp. 10754–10762 (2021)
22. Zhao, S., Li, B., Yue, X., Gu, Y., Xu, P., Hu, R., Chai, H., Keutzer, K.: Multi-source domain adaptation for semantic segmentation. arXiv preprint arXiv:1910.12181 (2019)
23. Zhu, J.Y., Park, T., Isola, P., Efros, A.A.: Unpaired image-to-image translation using cycle-consistent adversarial networks. In: Proceedings of the IEEE International Conference on Computer Vision, pp. 2223–2232 (2017)

SaME: Sharpness-aware Matching Ensemble for Robust Palmprint Recognition

Xu Liang[1], Zhaoqun Li[3], Dandan Fan[2,3], Jinyang Yang[1], Guangming Lu[1(✉)], and David Zhang[1,2,3(✉)]

[1] Harbin Institute of Technology, Shenzhen 518055, China
luguangm@hit.edu.cn
[2] Shenzhen Institute of Artificial Intelligence and Robotics for Society, Shenzhen 518129, China
[3] The Chinese University of Hong Kong, Shenzhen 518172, China
davidzhang@cuhk.edu.cn

Abstract. Pose and illumination variations in unconstrained palmprint recognition cause critical problems in terms of region of interest (ROI) misalignment, defocus blur, and underexposured or overexposured imaging. However, most existing methods do not consider these quality factors when performing ROI matching; thus, palmprint recognition performance is sensitive to variations of palm poses and ambient light conditions. To address these problems, we propose the SaME strategy for robust contactless palmprint recognition. We have designed the sharpness-aware matching ensemble framework to exploit the advantages of different types of features while avoiding their limitations. First, we designed a quality scoring method based on an effective palmprint sharpness indicator. Second, a multi-feature extraction scheme was designed to take advantage of coarse-grained and fine-grained features. Finally, a quality-aware matching ensemble model is proposed to realize robust palmprint recognition. We conducted experiments on five contactless databases, and the results demonstrate that the proposed SaME framework can reduce the equal error rate (EER) significantly without complex ROI alignment. In addition, the EER value was less than 0.5% on the COEP×5 dataset that was generated with considerable quality variations.

Keywords: Contactless palmprint recognition · Image quality assessment · Matching ensemble · Matching boosting · Quality-aware matching

This work was supported in part by the NSFC under Grants 62176077 and 62172347; in part by the Guangdong Basic and Applied Basic Research Foundation under Grant 2019Bl515120055, in part by the Shenzhen Key Technical Project under Grant 2020N046, in part by the Shenzhen Fundamental Research Fund under Grant JCYJ20210324132210025, in part by the Open Project Fund (AC01202005018) from Shenzhen Institute of Artificial Intelligence and Robotics for Society, and in part by the Medical Biometrics Perception and Analysis Engineering Laboratory, Shenzhen, China.

C. Wallraven et al. (Eds.): ACPR 2021, LNCS 13188, pp. 488–500, 2022.
https://doi.org/10.1007/978-3-031-02375-0_36

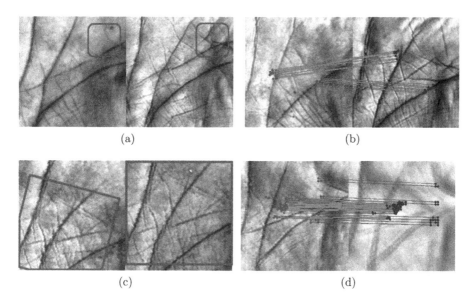

(a)   (b)

(c)   (d)

Fig. 1. Typical problems in contactless palmprint recognition: (a) interclass similarity caused by similar principal lines; (b) interclass similarity caused by similar regions; (c) intraclass variation caused by ROI misalignment; and (d) intraclass dissimilarity caused by motion blur.

1   Introduction

Due to the natural interaction mode, touchless palmprint recognition has become one of the most popular biometrics. Various devices and applications have been proposed based on palmprint recognition techniques. For example, related turnstiles and attendance devices are widely used in daily lives. In addition, given a palm image, people cannot tell to whom it belongs; thus, palmprint is not that much privacy sensitive compared to face recognition in which expressions, hairstyles, and makeups are captured. However, for touchless palmprint recognition systems, the palmprint images are captured in an open space; thus, localization variations, illumination changes, and image blur occur frequently. These factors have result in two major problems, *i.e.*, interclass similarity and intraclass variation.

As shown in Fig. 1, the interclass matches are affected by the similarities caused by principal lines or local regions, and intraclass matches are affected by large ROI misalignment or low-quality imaging. Fine-grained local features with nearest neighbor (NN) matching can solve the misalignment problem; however, they are sensitive to image quality variations. Coarse-grained features are robust to quality variations; however, they cannot handle ROI misalignment. Thus, we seek to a method that can exploit the advantages of these two types of features to achieve improved robustness and discrimination simultaneously. In traditional methods [1–4], the final decision (*i.e.*, genuine or impostor) is obtained by simply

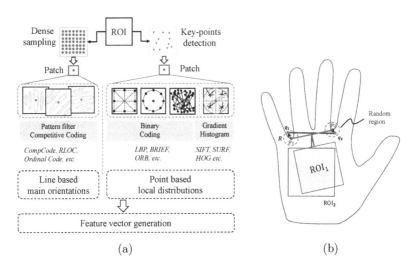

Fig. 2. Frameworks of the (a) feature extraction and (b) ROI localization schemes.

comparing the matching score to a *threshold*, which means that the 1D score space is only divided into two intervals, *i.e.*, a genuine interval and an impostor interval. However, this scheme is insufficient to achieve high accuracy in real-world scenarios. In addition, the matching scores obtained from high-quality ROI image pairs and blurred image pairs have different meanings. Thus, in this study, the boosting tree model is utilized to divide high-dimensional matching score space into different confidence intervals by considering quality indicators of the matching scores. Our primary contributions are summarized as follows:

(1) A sharpness-based matching score (SMS) is proposed based on a sharpness indicator and the Gaussian scale space (GSS).
(2) A multi-feature extraction framework is proposed to exploit the advantages of both coarse-grained and fine-grained features.
(3) A quality-aware matching ensemble framework is developed to achieve high robustness in unconstrained environments.

2   Related Work

Figure 2a shows the framework of current texture-based feature extraction schemes. As can be seen, the key feature extraction procedures can be divided into two steps, *i.e.*, (1) how to generate the keypoints and (2) how to encode the image patch centered at the keypoint. For the first step, two schemes can be used to generate keypoints. The first scheme is dense sampling with a fixed stride [1–6], and the second scheme involves searching for distinctive points using special strategies, *e.g.*, corner detection [7,8] or scale extrema-points detection [9]. After obtaining the key points, three schemes can be used to generate corresponding feature vectors, *i.e.*, (1) using directional filters to extract the corresponding convolution responses [1–5], (2) selecting predefined pixels in the image patch and encoding their relative magnitudes into a list of binary codes [8,11,12], and (3) utilizing all pixels in the image patch to generate a gradient histogram according to their grayscale values [6,9,13]. Based on these texture-based features, many palmprint recognition methods have been proposed to effectively encode and robustly match palmprint patterns. Among them, direction representation (DR)-based methods have achieved better performance [1–5,14,15]. This strategy attempts to extract the main directions of the local regions via convolution operations using directional filter banks, and many commonly used palmprint recognition methods that are based on this strategy, *e.g.*, CompCode [2], RLOC [4], and BOCV [14] have been proposed. Then, improved approaches [5,16–20] were also proposed based on the DR strategy. However, DR-based methods have two shortcomings, *i.e.*, they only have high responses to principal lines and only support point-to-point matching because the single main direction is not a distinctive feature. Thus, such methods cannot be used to perform NN matching between two region of interest (ROI) images. As a result, when the ROI is localized with translations and rotations (see Fig. 2b), verification accuracy is reduced immediately. Unfortunately, ROI misalignment is more serious in touchless palmprint recognition compared to illumination change and image blur. ROI misalignment leads to high false reject rate (FRR) and will greatly reduce the user's experience in real-world applications. Recently, many studies have developed methods [21–24] to handle the misalignment problem. Among these methods, a method that employs scale invariant local features combined with NN matching has achieved good performance [22,23]. Fine-grained local feature descriptors, *e.g.*, LBP [11], HOG [6], SIFT [9], DSIFT [10], SURF [13], FAST [7], BRIEF [12], and ORB [8], have good characteristics in terms of describing the detailed information of the image patch. These descriptors are sufficiently distinctive; thus, they can be utilized for NN matching. This strategy can find the pose relation between two ROI images automatically and align them via perspective transformation. However, they are not always sufficiently robust in real-world applications, because the keypoints detection and matching algorithms used in such frameworks are sensitive to image quality degradation and loss of detail textures [23,25]. For example, illumination change, motion blur, and defocus blur can significantly reduce the number of intraclass matches. However, these situations occur commonly in touchless environment; thus, fine-grained features are also insufficient to achieve robust palmprint recognition.

As analyzed above, a matching ensemble framework is required to achieve high robustness because a feature is only good at dealing with one specific matching task. The decision tree model can separate the high-dimensional space flexibly by splitting each attribute hierarchically, and each branch represents a specific interval; thus, the tree-based framework is suitable for our task to effectively fuse decisions from different features. Here, attributes are matching scores. Once a matching score, *i.e.*, a single attribute, falls into the confidence interval of the current tree node; the node can make its decision directly; otherwise, the node

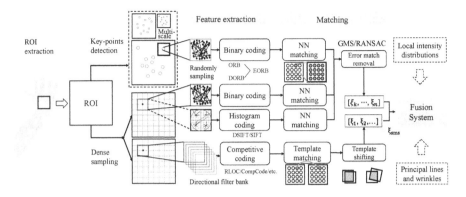

Fig. 3. Framework of multifeature extraction and matching.

will seek help from its child nodes (other features). The proposed method is detailly introduced in the following.

3   Method

3.1   Framework of SaME

The proposed SaME scheme contains five main steps, *i.e.*, ROI extraction, keypoints generation, feature extraction, matching and matching ensemble (ME). As shown in Fig. 5, a gallery database stores the feature templates of each registered ROI image. When a new probe/query ROI image is input, first, the templates of different types of features are extracted, and then they are utilized to match against with each sample in the gallery. After feature matching, the obtained matching scores are concatenated to form a score vector $x = [\xi_1,\ldots,\xi_i,\ldots,\xi_n], i \in \{1,n\}$, where n is the number of features and ξ_i is the matching score of feature-i between two ROIs. Then, vector x is input to the proposed ME model to obtain the final fused prediction.

3.2   Multifeature Extraction

The multi-feature extraction framework is shown in Fig. 3. Based on the above analysis, CompCode, OrdinalCode, RLOC, SIFT, DSIFT, and ORB were selected to extract and match the coarse-grained and fine-grained features. This feature set has covered the types of the commonly used feature extraction and matching schemes (as shown Fig. 2a). In addition, an enhanced-ORB (EORB) algorithm was designed to further increase the robustness of the feature. Here, EORB combines ORB and dense ORB (DORB); and the EORB matching score is defined as $\xi_{eorb} = \mathcal{P}(\xi_{orb} + \xi_{dorb})$, where $\mathcal{P}$ represents post-processing operations. Compared with ORB, the keypoint detection process in DORB is replaced by dense sampling.

3.3   Sharpness-Based Matching Score

The captured touchless palmprint image can be considered a single image in the GSS which is defined as follows:

$$L(\sigma) = G(\sigma) * I, \tag{1}$$

where I is an ideal image, L is the corresponding blurred image at σ in the GSS, and $*$ is the convolution operation. According to the Gaussian scale pyramid (GSP) [9], σ is generated as follows:

$$\sigma = \lambda\sigma_0 = 2^k\sigma_0, \quad k = o + s/S, \tag{2}$$

where σ_0 is the base scale, λ is a variable to change the scale, S is the number of layers in each octave, and o and s are the octave and layer indices of the GSP, respectively. Thus, k increases linearly, and λ increases exponentially. According to our experiments, the optimal settings of SIFT for palmprint recognition are $o = [-1, 0]$, $s = [0, 1, 2, 3]$, and $S = 4$; thus, $k \in [-1, 0.75]$. Based on a previous sharpness evaluation study [26], we selected EAV (denoted ε) as the sharpness indicator for palmprint images. The EAV of an ROI image is defined as: $\varepsilon = \mathrm{eav}(I) = 1/(m \times n) \cdot \sum_{i=1}^{m \times n} \sum_{j=1}^{8} |df_{ij}/dx_{ij}|$, where $m \times n$ is the size of image I, df is the difference in gray values between two pixels i and j, and dx represents the distance of the two pixels. Note that pixel j is one of the eight neighbors of pixel i. Accordingly, the mean EAV value of one dataset is defined as follows:

$$\bar{\varepsilon} = 1/N \cdot \sum_{i=0}^{N} \varepsilon_i, \tag{3}$$

where N is the number of ROI images in the dataset. Using Eq. (1) and Eq. (2), the GSPs of all images in a given dataset can be generated. Then, for each GSP location k (as defined in Eq. (2)), the corresponding $\bar{\varepsilon}$ value can be calculated from the corresponding blurred dataset. Figure 4a shows the $\bar{\varepsilon}$ curves obtained from different contactless palmprint databases. According to the Taylor formula, the relationship between $\bar{\varepsilon}$ and k can be defined as follows:

$$\bar{\varepsilon} = f(k) = f(k_0) + f'(k_0)(k - k_0) + \cdots + \frac{f^n(k_0)}{n!}(k - k_0)^n + R_n(k), \tag{4}$$

where $R_n(k)$ is the Lagrange residual term of order n. According to this definition, $\bar{\varepsilon}$ represents the sharpness of the captured image, and k is the ROI image's location in the GSP. To avoid overfitting, we set the model as simple as possible, $i.e.$, the first-order approximation is utilized to fit the data. Without loss of generality, let $k_0 = 0$ (which means $s = o = 0$) and $n = 1$. Then, we obtain the following:

$$\bar{\varepsilon} \approx f'(0) \cdot k + f(0) = a \cdot k + b, \tag{5}$$

where, a and b can be obtained via linear regression (Fig. 4a). The initial blur level of the captured palmprint image is affected by dot per inch and depth

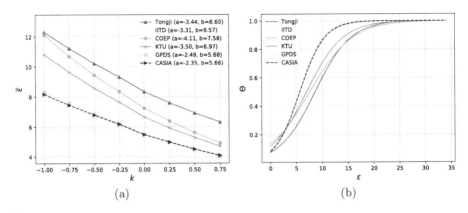

Fig. 4. The relation between the sharpness indicator and the image quality. (a) Mean EAV curves obtained from different databases in the GSP. (b) SQI curves obtained by the parameters learned from corresponding databases.

of focus; thus, slop a and intersect b of different databases are determined by their imaging systems. However, once the palmprint image acquisition device is established, the system model is fixed. Then, a and b can be obtained via regression learning.

In the GSP, a larger scale σ results in lower sharpness; thus, the quality score should be inversely proportional to σ. Accordingly, the sharpness-based quality indicator (SQI) of a palmprint ROI image is defined as follows:

$$\Theta = \frac{1}{1 + e^k} \approx \frac{1}{1 + e^{(\beta \cdot \varepsilon + \gamma)}}, \tag{6}$$

where $\beta = 1/a$ and $\gamma = -b/a$. SQI is denoted by Θ in the remainder of this paper. The corresponding quality curves are shown in Fig. 4b. As can be seen, $\Theta \in (0, 1)$. Given two ROI images, the EAV values ε_1, ε_2 of them can be calculated, and the corresponding quality indicators Θ_1, Θ_2 can also be calculated using Eq. (6). Then, the SMS between them is defined as follows:

$$\xi_{(\text{ROI}_1, \text{ROI}_2)} = \min(\Theta_1, \Theta_2). \tag{7}$$

3.4   Matching Ensemble

Given two ROI images, according to Eq. (7) and Eqs. (S1)–(S3)[1], the matching scores ξ_{comp}, ξ_{rloc}, ξ_{sift}, ξ_{dsift}, ξ_{orb}, ξ_{dorb}, ξ_{eorb}, and ξ_{sms} can be obtained. Then, the ME model is defined as follows:

$$\hat{y} = \phi(x) = \sum_{k=1}^{K} f_k(x), \tag{8}$$

---

[1] The *Supplementary Material* is available at https://github.com/xuliangcs/same.

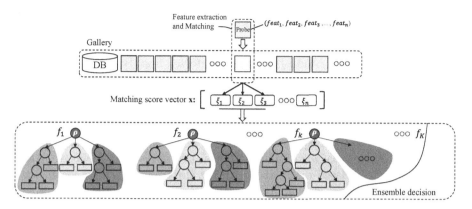

Fig. 5. Framework of SaME.

where $x = [\xi_1, \xi_2, \ldots, \xi_n]$ is the matching score vector generated by various features, *i.e.*, $[\xi_{\text{comp}}, \xi_{\text{rloc}}, \xi_{\text{sift}}, \xi_{\text{dsift}}, \xi_{\text{orb}}, \xi_{\text{dorb}}, \xi_{\text{eorb}}, \xi_{\text{sms}}]$, f_k is the k-th decision tree, K is the number of trees, and $\hat{y}$ is the prediction score. The labels (denoted y) of the genuine and impostor ROI matching are given as 1 and -1, respectively. The k-th regression tree is defined as follows:

$$f_k(x) = \Gamma_\varrho^k(x) = \begin{cases} \tau_1^k(x), & \xi_{\text{sms}} \leq t_1, \\ \tau_2^k(x), & t_1 < \xi_{\text{sms}} < t_2, \\ \tau_3^k(x), & \xi_{\text{sms}} \geq t_2, \end{cases} \tag{9}$$

where $\Gamma^k = \{\tau_i^k\}, i \in \{1, 2, 3\}, k \in \{1, \cdots, K\}$, and $\varrho(\cdot)$ is the sharpness-aware node that selects a subtree from set Γ^k according to ξ_{sms}. Without loss of generality, subtree $\tau_i^k(x) = \omega_{q(x)}$, where q is a mapping function from R^n to ς (from input x to a leaf index). $\omega \in R^T$ controls the outputs of τ_i^k; here, T is the number of leaves of the tree τ_i^k. For each tree, the output of x is selected from ω via ς, and leaf index $\varsigma \in \{1, \cdots, T\}$. Note that node ϱ is fixed as the root node during tree establishment. The split points of ϱ are fixed according to the SMS distribution of the training set (see Fig. 6b). After the training samples are separated by ϱ according to ξ_{sms}, the regression trees $\tau_i^k, k \in \{1, 2, \cdots, K\}$ can be learned using XGBoost [27] which is one of the most widely used boosting trees implementation. Finally, three sets of boosting trees are obtained; as shown in Fig. 5, trees of the same set are in the same color.

The proposed SaME framework can achieve higher robustness than the existing methods because SaME utilized much more low-quality images for training. However, most existing palmprint databases were collected under relatively ideal conditions; thus, we should design an ROI augmentation method to obtain sufficient data variations to fully train the ensemble tree subsets.

3.5   ROI Augmentation Strategy

As shown in Fig. 2b, while localizing the ROI, the coordinates of the two finger valley points (denoted p_1 and p_2) should be detected first. Based on the tangent line $\overline{p_1 p_2}$, the standard ROI region could be localized using a previously proposed method [1, 24]. Considering the true nature of ROI variations in touchless palmprint recognition, we generated more ROI images from the original palm image rather than simply rotating the existing ROI images [4]. Specifically, after obtaining points p_1 and p_2, we add randomly translations to the two points within the circle regions with radius R. Then, two new points (denoted q_1 and q_2) were obtained. Based on q_1 and q_2, using the traditional ROI localization method, a new ROI region, e.g., ROI_2 in Fig. 2b, was generated. As a result, the new ROI images were localized with sufficient translations, rotations, and scale variations. In this study, R was set to $0.1 \times \overline{p_1 p_2}$ and two randomly localized ROI images were generated. In addition, two blurred ROI images were generated from the standard ROI image via Gaussian convolution. In summary, five ROI images were extracted from each palm image in the original database.

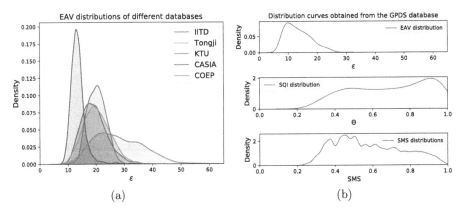

Fig. 6. Quality-related distributions: (a) EAV distributions obtained from different databases, and (b) distributions of EAV (ε), SQI (Θ), and SMS on the GPDS database.

4   Experimental Results

4.1   Sharpness-Based Quality Indicator

Here, assume that σ_c is the initial image smoothing level generated by the camera, and the corresponding GSP location is denoted k_c. As shown in Fig. 4a, the mean EAV curves on different databases do not overlapped perfectly because the initial shifts, i.e. k_c, are inevitably introduced to the imaging sensor even the camera lens focus well. Figure 6a also shows this phenomenon. For simplicity, the parameters β, γ obtained from the IITD database were selected to calculate the palmprint SQI; thus, $a = -3.31$, $b = 9.57$, and $SQI = 1/(1 + e^{-0.3\varepsilon + 2.89})$.

Accordingly, the SQI and SMS distributions on the GPDS database are shown in Fig. 6b, it can be found that SQI stretches the mid-low sharpness range compared to EAV.

Table 1. EERs (%) on different databases obtained by different methods.

Refs	Methods	IITD	KTU	GPDS	COEP	COEP×5
[2]	CompCode	1.122	0.290	6.133	1.740	21.804
[3]	OLOF	1.447	0.559	5.333	2.275	20.748
[4]	RLOC	0.954	0.290	5.156	1.293	19.702
[5]	LLDP	1.184	1.511	7.566	2.632	21.439
[23]	SIFT+RANSAC	0.164	0.640	1.330	0.312	0.502
[32]	PalmNet	0.395	0.775	10.00	1.606	16.388
[33]	ORB+GMS	0.356	1.192	1.366	0.354	0.783
–	EORB	0.060	0.331	0.290	**0.305**	0.994
–	ME	0.009	0.083	0.041	0.309	**0.333**
–	SaME	**0.003**	**0.050**	**0.029**	**0.305**	0.339

4.2   Recognition Performance of the Proposed SaME

The IITD [28], KTU [29], GPDS [30], and COEP [31] touchless palmprint databases were used to evaluate the EERs. Here, for the IITD and COEP databases, the ROI images were extracted using a previously reported method [24]. For the KTU and GPDS databases, the official ROI images were used. In this experiment, each database was divided into training and test sets. Here, each hand was treated as a separate category. For each database, palm images of the first half individuals were set as the training set, and palm images of the remaining individuals were set as the test set. Note that each ROI image in the test set matched all other images in the test set to generate test matching scores. In addition, the training matching scores were generated using the training dataset in the same manner. The EERs listed in Table 1 were obtained from the test matching scores (without class-based aggregation). The values of (t_1, t_2) were set to (0.6, 0.95) for the IITD and COEP×5 databases, (0.9, 0.95) for the KTU database, (0.6, 0.65) for the GPDS database, and (0.98, 0.99) for the COEP database. For the boosting trees in the ME model, K was set to 10 and the maximum height of the trees was set to six. As shown in Table 1, the proposed SaME achieved lower EERs on most datasets than the compared methods, including ME. Note that the ME-based method learns the boosting trees directly without using the sharpness information (ξ_{sms}). Thus, the results demonstrate that SMS is useful in terms of improving recognition performance.

In addition to the above mentioned original databases, the COEP×5 database was generated to obtain large variations using the ROI augmentation method introduced in Sect. 3.5. Figure 7 shows the detection error tradeoff curves obtained by different methods. As can be seen, the proposed SaME and ME methods were more robust than the compared methods when the dataset contains large variations in sharpness, rotation, translation, and scale (Fig. 7b).

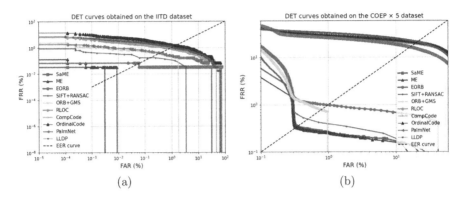

(a)   (b)

Fig. 7. DET curves obtained by different methods on the (a) IITD and (b) COEP×5 datasets.

5   Conclusion

In this paper, we have proposed the SaME approach, which is a unified framework that exploits the advantages of different features for touchless palmprint recognition. In addition, a sharpness indicator, *i.e.*, SQI, was proposed for the boosting trees to get better understanding of the meaning of the matching scores obtained from ROI images with different qualities. Further more, a new ROI augmentation strategy was designed for model training. The experimental results obtained on various databases, *e.g.*, the IITD, KTU, GPDS, COEP, and COEP×5 databases, demonstrate that the proposed SaME framework is effective in terms of improving the accuracy and robustness of existing palmprint recognition systems.

References

1. Zhang, D., Kong, W.-K., You, J., Wong, M.: Online palmprint identification. IEEE Transactions on Pattern Analysis and Machine Intelligence. **25**(9), 1041–1050 (2003)
2. Kong W.-K., Zhang D.: Competitive coding scheme for palmprint verification. In: Proceedings of the 17th International Conference on Pattern Recognition, pp. 520–523. IEEE, Cambridge (2004)
3. Sun Z., Tan T., Wang Y., Li S.: Ordinal palmprint representation for personal identification. In: Proceedings of IEEE Conference on Computer Visual Pattern Recognition-CVPR 2005, pp. 279–284. IEEE Computer Society, Los Alamitos (2005)

4. Jia, W., Huang, D.-S., Zhang, D.: Palmprint verification based on robust line orientation code. Pattern Recognit. **41**(5), 1504–1513 (2008)
5. Luo, Y.-T., et al.: Local line directional pattern for palmprint recognition. Pattern Recognit. **50**, 26–44 (2016)
6. Dalal, N., Triggs, B.: Histograms of oriented gradients for human detection. In: IEEE Computer Society Conference on Computer Vision and Pattern Recognition-CVPR 2005, vol. 1, pp. 886–893. IEEE, Los Alamitos (2005)
7. Rosten, E., Porter, R., Drummond, T.: Faster and better: a machine learning approach to corner detection. IEEE Trans. Pattern Anal. Mach. Intell. **32**(1), 105–119 (2008)
8. Rublee, E., Rabaud, V., Konolige, K., Bradski, G.: ORB: an efficient alternative to SIFT or SURF. In: International Conference on Computer Vision-ICCV 2011, pp. 2564–2571. IEEE, Los Alamitos (2011)
9. Lowe, D.G.: Distinctive image features from scale-invariant keypoints. Int. J. Comput. Vis. **60**(2), 91–110 (2004). https://doi.org/10.1023/B:VISI.0000029664.99615.94
10. Vedaldi, A., Fulkerson, B.: VLFeat: An open and portable library of computer vision algorithms. The VLFeat Software Package. https://www.vlfeat.org/api/dsift.html. Accessed 1 Oct 2021
11. Ojala, T., Pietikainen, M., Maenpaa, T.: Multiresolution gray-scale and rotation invariant texture classification with local binary patterns. IEEE Trans. Pattern Anal. Mach. Intell. **24**(7), 971–987 (2002)
12. Calonder, M., Lepetit, V., Strecha, C., Fua, P.: BRIEF: binary robust independent elementary features. In: Daniilidis, K., Maragos, P., Paragios, N. (eds.) ECCV 2010, Part IV. LNCS, vol. 6314, pp. 778–792. Springer, Heidelberg (2010). https://doi.org/10.1007/978-3-642-15561-1_56
13. Bay, H., Tuytelaars, T., Van Gool, L.: SURF: speeded up robust features. In: Leonardis, A., Bischof, H., Pinz, A. (eds.) ECCV 2006, Part I. LNCS, vol. 3951, pp. 404–417. Springer, Heidelberg (2006). https://doi.org/10.1007/11744023_32
14. Guo, Z., Zhang, D., Zhang, L., Zuo, W.: Palmprint verification using binary orientation co-occurrence vector. Pattern Recognit. **30**(13), 1219–1227 (2009)
15. Jia, W., et al.: Palmprint recognition based on complete direction representation. IEEE Trans. Image Process. **26**(9), 4483–4498 (2017)
16. Fei, L., Xu, Y., Tang, W., Zhang, D.: Double-orientation code and nonlinear matching scheme for palmprint recognition. Pattern Recognit. **49**, 89–101 (2016)
17. Zhang, L., Li, L., Yang, A., Shen, Y., Yang, M.: Towards contactless palmprint recognition: a novel device, a new benchmark, and a collaborative representation based identification approach. Pattern Recognit. **69**, 199–212 (2017)
18. Fei, L., Zhang, B., Zhang, W., Teng, S.: Local apparent and latent direction extraction for palmprint recognition. Inf. Sci. **473**, 59–72 (2019)
19. Fei, L., Zhang, B., Xu, Y.: Learning discriminant direction binary palmprint descriptor. IEEE Trans. Image Process. **28**(8), 3808–3820 (2019)
20. Zhao, S., Zhang, B.: Learning salient and discriminative descriptor for palmprint feature extraction and identification. IEEE Trans. Neural Netw. Learn. Syst. **31**(12), 5219–5230 (2020)
21. Li, W., Zhang, B., Zhang, L., Yan, J.: Principal line-based alignment refinement for palmprint recognition. IEEE Trans. Syst. Man Cybern. **42**(6), 1491–1499 (2012)
22. Morales, A., Ferrer, M.A., Kumar, A.: Towards contactless palmprint authentication. IET Comput. Vis. **5**(6), 407–416 (2011)

23. Wu, X., Zhao, Q., Bu, W.: A SIFT-based contactless palmprint verification app-roach using iterative RANSAC and local palmprint descriptors. Pattern Recognit. **47**, 3314–3326 (2014)
24. Liang, X., Zhang, D., Lu, G., Guo, Z., Luo, N.: A novel multicamera system for high-speed touchless palm recognition. IEEE Trans. Syst. Man Cybern. Syst. **51**(3), 1534–1548 (2021)
25. Tian C., Xu Y., Zuo W., Lin C.-W., Zhang D.: Asymmetric CNN for Image Super-resolution. IEEE Trans. Syst. Man Cybern. Syst. early access (2021). https://doi.org/10.1109/TSMC.2021.3069265
26. Zhang, K., Huang, D., Zhang, B., Zhang, D.: Improving texture analysis perfor-mance in biometrics by adjusting image sharpness. Pattern Recognit. **66**, 16–25 (2019)
27. Chen, T., Guestrin, C.: XGBoost: a scalable tree boosting system. In: Proceedings of the 22nd ACM SIGKDD International Conference on Knowledge Discovery and Data Mining-KDD 2016, pp. 785–794 (2016)
28. Kumar A.: Incorporating cohort information for reliable palmprint authentication. In: The Sixth Indian Conference on Computer Vision, Graphics and Image Pro-cessing, pp. 583–590. IEEE Computer Society, Los Alamitos (2008)
29. The KTU Contactless Palmprint Database. https://ceng2.ktu.edu.tr/~cvpr/contactlessPalmDB.htm. Accessed 1 Oct. 2021
30. GPDS100 Contactless Hands Database. https://gpds.ulpgc.es/. Accessed 1 Oct 2021
31. COEP Contactless Palmprint Database. https://www.coep.org.in/resources/coeppalmprintdatabase. Accessed 1 Oct 2021
32. Genovese, A., Piuri, V., Plataniotis, K.N., Scotti, F.: PalmNet: Gabor-PCA convo-lutional networks for touchless palmprint recognition. IEEE Trans. Inf. Forensics Secur. **14**(12), 3160–3174 (2019)
33. Bian, J., Lin, W.Y., Matsushita, Y., Yeung, S.K., Nguyen, T.D., Cheng, M.M.: GMS: grid-based motion statistics for fast, ultra-robust feature correspondence. In: 2017 IEEE Conference on Computer Vision and Pattern Recognition-CVPR 2017, pp. 2828–2837. IEEE, New York (2017). https://doi.org/10.1109/CVPR.2017.302

Weakly Supervised Interaction Discovery Network for Image Sentiment Analysis

Lifang Wu, Heng Zhang, Ge Shi$^{(\boxtimes)}$, and Sinuo Deng

Faculty of Information Technology, Beijing University of Technology, Beijing, China
tinkersxy@gmail.com

Abstract. Visual sentiment is subjective and abstract, and it is very challenging to locate the sentiment features from images accurately. Some researchers devote themselves to extracting visual features but ignore the relation features. However, sentiment reaction is a comprehensive action of visual content, and regions may express different emotions and contribute to the image sentiment. This paper takes the abstract sentiment relation as the starting point and proposes the Weakly Supervised Interaction Discovery Network that couples detection and classification branch. Specifically, the first branch detects sentiment maps with the cross-spatial pooling strategy, which generates the representations of emotions. Then, we employ a stacked Graph Convolution Network to extract the interaction feature from the above features. The second branch utilizes both interaction and visual features for robust sentiment classification. Extensive experiments on six benchmark datasets demonstrate that the proposed method exceeds the state-of-the-art methods for image sentiment analysis.

Keywords: Visual sentiment analysis · Sentiment classification · Convolutional neural networks · Graph convolution network

1 Introduction

The development of social networks has attracted many researchers to dig and explore the emotional information in social media. There have been some applications, such as advertising, education, and other fields. Among them, because images can express human emotions and ideas more intuitively, image sentiment analysis has gradually become an essential part of the field of emotion computing.

The sentiment is a vague and subjective abstract concept, and analyzing image sentiment is a challenging task. In the existing research of image sentiment analysis, researchers devote themselves to accurately extracting the sentimental information contained in the image. In 2016, some researchers applied deep learning to sentiment feature extraction and achieved a good performance. Later, Yang et al. [14] put forward the concept of "Affective Region." They extract features from regions with strong sentiment in the image and supplement

© Springer Nature Switzerland AG 2022
C. Wallraven et al. (Eds.): ACPR 2021, LNCS 13188, pp. 501–512, 2022.
https://doi.org/10.1007/978-3-031-02375-0_37

fine-grained features utilizing feature fusion strategy such as concatenation or pooling. Later, with the help of a saliency detection tool, Wu et al. [12] propose to extract the local sentiment feature from the salient region and achieve remarkable performance improvement. The above two methods assume that the image sentiment comes from the corresponding local region, ignoring the emotional connection between different regions. Further, Yang et al. [13] propose the Weakly Supervised Coupled Networks (WSCNet) to obtain the emotional regions of the image and get the "Sentiment Map" to describe the emotion interaction. However, they adopt the weighted sum strategy to represent the relationship among emotions, which simplifies the emotion interaction. As shown in Fig. 1, in the emotional response of human beings, areas with corresponding emotion makes a non-negligible contribution to sentiment, and there is still hard-to-describe sentiment interaction information among the regions.

Fig. 1. Examples of image sentiment. We label sentiment regions with heat maps, and extract the sentiment interaction features according to the emotional relations of Mikel's emotion model.

To solve this problem, we propose an end-to-end model to extract and utilize emotional interaction characteristics. Inspired by the work of Yang et al. [13], instead of dragging the boxes of objects in the image, we use an emotion map to describe the weight of the region in the image that stimulates the corresponding emotion. Specifically, for the feature maps obtained in the convolutional neural network, a cross-spatial pooling strategy is adopted to obtain the spatial information and the regions in the highlight image to stimulate corresponding emotions. Then, we use a topological diagram to define and describe the emotional relationship, take the regional features corresponding to multiple emotions as nodes, and take the weight between categories in the emotion model as the corresponding "sentiment map". Then, GCN is used to update and aggregate the node features and obtain the emotional interaction features. Finally, we integrate the visual features representing the scene information with the interactive features representing the sentiment interaction information to realize the prediction of emotion categories. Our method only needs the image-level labels of the sentiment in the training process, making full use of the existing image emotion image datasets.

Our contributions are as follows:

Firstly, we propose to describe the sentiment interaction at the cognitive level with a graph and define the emotional relationship with the results of psychological research. For an input image, we transform it into a graph and demonstrate the effectiveness of sentiment relation knowledge.

Secondly, we propose a model that makes full use of sentiment interaction features rather than visual features. We use the weakly supervised sentiment region detection method to identify the interaction semantics extracted from the visual semantics at the cognitive level, which effectively utilizes sentiment interaction features and reduces data preprocessing steps.

Finally, our method achieves state-of-the-art. It is proved that the extensive use of cognitive features and visual features can promote image sentiment analysis.

2   Related Work

2.1   Visual Sentiment Prediction

The sentiment is an abstract and subjective concept. Accurate extraction of emotional features in images is one of the difficulties in image sentiment analysis. Some researchers are working to bridge the "affective gap" between visual content and sentiment. Inspired by psychological research, Machajdik and Hanbury [6] realized the task of image emotion classification by utilizing the hand-craft features, such as color, texture, composition, and so on. Based on [11], Sun et al. proposed the sentiment region based on the object proposal method and realized sentiment classification using corresponding depth features.

Further, Yang et al. [14] proposed to utilize the Affective Region (AR) with the help of instance segmentation tools. By fusing the features of AR and original images, they get a better classification performance. Wu et al. [12] utilize a saliency detection algorithm to enhance local features and improve classification performance in a large margin.

These methods focus on extracting features at the visual level and ignoring affective relationships at the cognitive level. Later, with the help of instance segmentation, Wu et al. proposed to leverage the sentimental interaction information among objects. However, the gap between object and sentiment limits the improvement of this method.

Different from previous works, we propose an end-to-end approach. This model aims to extract the sentimental relation features from sentiment semantics, which avoids the loss of information between object semantics and sentiment semantics and omits data preprocessing steps.

2.2   Weakly Supervised Detection

Compared with the objective existence of objects, sentiment is subjective and fuzzy. Therefore, the semantic level information extraction of objects cannot fully express the emotional information in the image. Besides, few works concentrating on end-to-end CNN frameworks for weakly supervised object detection without additional localization information.

There is a work concentrating on weakly supervised sentiment detection [13], they proposed joint sentiment detection and classification and achieved an improvement with the "Sentiment Map". Specifically, they proposed the cross-spatial pooling strategy to summarize the feature maps of the network into "sentiment map", which is a weighted sum of the features of different emotions. This method effectively overcomes the problem of weak feature differentiation caused by the fuzziness of human emotion, but there are still some limitations in the exploration of emotional relationships. In the absence of sentimental domain knowledge, the response values of feature maps may not fully represent the interaction among sentiments. We utilize the convolutional network and cross-spatial pooling strategy to detect the sentiment regions and design an interaction feature extraction method based on GCN to make use of the relational information in the sentiment regions.

2.3   Graph Convolutional Network

Graph neural networks were proposed by Gori et al. [5] and further developed by Scarselli et al. [8]. However, due to the limitations of methods and computer technology, this method needs many computing resources on massive data, which is challenging to realize. Further, Bruna et al. [2] proposed the graph convolution networks, which attracts the attention of researchers in various fields.

Different from the CNN model, the graph describes the relations among nodes by building a relational model. Chen et al. [4] proposed to utilize the inter-dependent object information from labels in multi-label image classification. However, this method needs the annotation of image objects, which requires a lot of human resources.

In this paper, we employ the graph structure to capture and explore the sentimental interaction information. Specifically, we couple the sentiment detection and classification tasks. With the help of weakly supervised sentiment region detection, we employ a stacked GCN model to capture the sentiment interaction feature in images.

3   Method

This section aims to develop an algorithm to extract the sentimental relation information with only image-level labels. An overview of our proposed Weakly Supervised Interaction Discovery Network is illustrated in Fig. 2. The proposed WSINDNet learns both detection and classification tasks with two branches. We employ the detection branch to generate the sentiment regions and utilize GCN to leverage the sentiment interaction information, which is then fed into the classification branch to fuse the holistic as the relational representations.

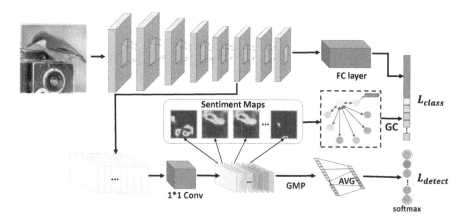

Fig. 2. Overview of the Weakly Supervised Interaction Discovery Network. During training, the model needs only image-level sentimental labels and we adopt a joint training strategy to couple the detection and classification branches.

3.1   Sentiment Map Detection

Unlike the target of the location task, the response map of emotions is independent due to the fuzziness of human emotions. The same area in the image may express multiple emotions, and one emotion can also correspond to different regions. Inspired by the work of Yang et al. [13], we also adopt the cross-spatial pooling strategy to realize the weakly supervised sentiment region detection.

Specifically, we employ VGGNet as the backbone, and utilize the feature maps to generate the sentiment regions. Let $\{(x_i, y_i)\}_{i=1}^{N}$ be a collection of training examples, where x_i is an image, and y_i is the corresponding sentiment label. For each instance, let $F \in \mathbb{R}^{w \times h \times n}$ be the feature maps of the last convolution layer, where w and h are the spatial size (width and height) of the feature maps, and n is the number of feature channels. As shown in Fig. 2, the 1×1 convolution layer is used as k detectors to capture the high response regions for each emotion category which results in $F' \in \mathbb{R}^{w \times h \times kC}$. By summarizing all the information to a image-level score, the cross-spatial pooling strategy achieves the weakly supervised region detection regardless of the input size:

$$v_c = \frac{1}{k} \sum_{i=1}^{k} \boldsymbol{G}_{\max}\left(f_{c,i}\right), c \in \{1, \cdots, C\} \tag{1}$$

where $f_{c,i}$ is the i-th feature map of c-th emotion. $G_{\max}$ represents the Global Max Pooling (GMP), which is utilized to identify the discriminative parts of the feature maps and generate a $1 \times 1 \times kC$ vector. k represents an average pooling operation to maximize the discriminative feature and results in the vector

$\mathbf{v} \in \mathbb{R}^C$, which is fed into a C-class soft-max layer to supervise the detection performance.

$$L_{detect} = -\frac{1}{N} \sum_{i=1}^{N} \sum_{c=1}^{C} \mathbf{1}\,(y_i = c) \log v_c \qquad (2)$$

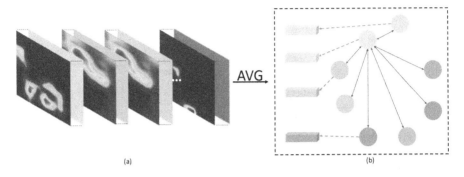

(a)   (b)

Fig. 3. An example of sentiment graph: (a) An object segmentation result, where the object are distinguished by different color overlay. (b) A sentiment graph structure, where the nodes represent objects of corresponding color and edges reflect the similarity of nodes in the sentiment space.

Unlike Yang et al., we aim to leverage the sentiment interaction and did not sum the feature map of multiple emotions into a sentiment map. We retain the F' by average pooling and get corresponding heatmaps of emotions, which is repeat to $w \times h \times n$ and make Hadamard product with F to highlight the features of connected regions. Then, As shown in Fig. 3, we employ an average pooling operation to generate the feature vectors corresponding to each emotion category.

3.2   Sentiment Interaction Extraction

Sentiment Graph. In the introduction, we introduced the contribution of sentiment interaction to human emotion. As an abstract and subjective logical response, sentiment is difficult to capture and extract. In addition to the visual features, we propose the Sentiment Graph to define and extract the relation features in the image. Specifically, we construct a unique undirected graph with emotion categories as nodes, describe the relationship between emotions with an adjacency matrix, and extract the sentiment interaction features with stacked GCNs.

To accurately describe the emotional relationship between nodes, we take the distance between emotions in Mikels' emotional model to measure emotional similarity and reciprocal emotional distance as the adjacency matrix in the Sentiment Graph. At the same time, although the sentiment distance can effectively represent emotional similarity, it cannot reflect the difference between the positive and negative, so we put forward the method in Formula 3 to calculate the sentiment relationship:

$$A_{ij} = \begin{cases} \frac{1}{dis_{ij}} + 1, & \text{if } S_i * S_j < 0 \\ \frac{1}{dis_{ij}}, & \text{otherwise} \end{cases} \mathbf{1}\,(y_i = c)\log v_c \qquad (3)$$

where A_{ij} is a element of adjacency matrix A, S_i, S_j represent the polarities of i-th, j-th emotion and dis_{ij} is the sentiment distance between them.

Interaction Extraction. To simulate the sentimental interaction, we select GCN to propagate and aggregate the representation of objects under the supervision of sentiment relations. Specifically, we employ the stacked GCNs, in which the input of each layer is the output H^l from the previous layer, and output the new node feature H^{l+1}. The feature of the first GCN layer H^0 is generated from the detection branch introduced above.

Formula (4) shows the feature update process of layer l, where $\tilde{A}$ describes the relationship among nodes. H^l is the output of the previous layer $l-1$, and H^{l+1} is the output of the current layer, W^l is the weight matrix of the current layer, and σ is the nonlinear activation function.

$$H^{l+1} = \sigma(\tilde{D}^{-\frac{1}{2}}\tilde{A}\tilde{D}^{-\frac{1}{2}}H^l W^l) \qquad (4)$$

In addition, $\tilde{D}$ is the degree matrix of $\tilde{A}$, and obtained by Eq. (5).

$$\tilde{D}_{ii} = \sum_j \tilde{A}_{ij} \qquad (5)$$

3.3   Joint Training Strategy

Sentiment Classification Branch. Like previous works [11,12,14,15,17], we select VGGNet as the backbone to capture the deep feature of images. To highlight the effect of sentiment interaction and make a fair comparison with previous works, we keep this branch as simple as possible. Previous studies have demonstrated the sentimental feature extraction capability of VGGNet with 16 layers [10]. We select it as the backbone to supplement the global context information missing in the interactive features. Besides, we changed the last fully connected layer from 4096 to 2048 and get the image feature F_h.

From the perspective of image representation, the original convolutional feature F_h represents the holistic feature of the image. The sentiment interaction feature provides fine-grained features that contain sentiment interaction information. We use the concatenate operation to fuse the two features, which results in $F = [F_h; F_s]$. F_s represents the sentiment interaction feature generated from the GCN model. The classification is carried out by minimizing the following loss function:

$$L_{class} = -\frac{1}{N} \sum_{i=1}^{N} (y_i * log\hat{y}_i + (1 - y_i) * log(1 - \hat{y}_i)) \tag{6}$$

Joint Training. We adjust the joint training strategy to couple the sentiment detection and classification task. By minimizing the collective loss function, we can detect the sentiment regions with the image-level label and leverage the sentiment regions to extract the sentiment interaction information to facilitate classification. The joint loss function is described in Formula 7.

$$L = L_{class} + \lambda L_{detect} \tag{7}$$

4   Experiment

4.1   Datasets

We evaluate our method on five public datasets: **FI** [17], **Flickr** [1], **Emotion-ROI** [7], **Twitter I** [16] and **Twitter II** [1]. FI is collected from Flickr and Instagram. The researchers select eight emotion categories (i.e., amusement, anger, awe, contentment, disgust, excitement, fear, sadness) as keywords to query images, and they get about 90,000 raw images with noise. Then, they employ 225 Amazon Mechanical Turk (AMT) workers to annotate the emotion and result in 23,308 images. Flickr contains 484,258 images from Flickr, which are labeled by a corresponding adjective and noun pairs (ANP) automatically. Though Flickr has an enormous data scale, automatic labeling makes it less reliable. Emotion-ROI contains 1,980 images with six emotion labels (i.e., anger, disgust, fear, joy, sadness, surprise), which are annotated manually with 15 regions that can evoke human emotions. Twitter I and Twitter II are annotated with sentiment labels (positive and negative) by AMT workers, consisting of 1296 and 603 images. Specifically, following [13], we conduct training and testing on the three subsets of Twitter I: 'Five agree', 'At least four agree', and 'At least three agree', which are filtered based on the annotation results. For example, 'Five agree' means that the five AMT workers label the same sentiment to a given image.

4.2   Baselines

To demonstrate the performance of our proposed method, we compare our approach against several previous works, including methods using traditional features, CNN-based methods, and CNN-based methods with a local feature branch.

- The global color histograms (**GCH**) extract 64-bin RGB histogram as image representation, and the local color histogram features (**LCH**) [9] divide image into 16 blocks and calculate 64-bin RGB histogram for each block.
- Borth et al. [1] introduced semantic information by **SentiBank**, and they filtered 1,200 ANPs as the presentation of sentiment semantic.

- **DeepSentibank** [3] employs CNN to realize both ANPs prediction and sentiment classification. We utilize a pre-trained DeepSentiBank to extract 2089-dimension deep features from the last fully-connected layer and realize sentiment prediction by LIBSVM.
- You et al. [16] build a potentially cleaner dataset and proposed **PCNN** trained with weakly supervised data and achieve a generalization improvement.
- Yang et al. [14] proposed the 'Affective Regions' with the help of instance segmentation, which contain reach sentiment and object information, and the design three fusion strategy to fuse the 'Affective Regions' and image feature.
- Wu et al. [12] proposed to utilize the salient regions in sentiment analysis by salient detection algorithm and achieved a significant performance improvement.

4.3   Implementation Details

Following previous works [14], we select VGG-16 [7] as backbone and initialize it with pre-trained model on ImageNet. We randomly crop and resize the input images into 224×224 with random horizontal flipped for data enhancement. SGD is selected as the optimizer, and Momentum is 0.9. The initial learning rate is 0.01, which drops by a factor of 10 per 20 epoch. We set the hyper-parameters λ to be 0.1, which is tuned on the FI validation set.

To make a fair comparison, we adopted the same split for five datasets with Yang et al. [14]. At the same time, we also convert the dataset labels with emotion categories to the sentiment labels. For example, EmotionROI has six emotion categories: anger, disgust, fear, joy, sadness, and surprise. Images with labels of anger, disgust, fear, sadness are relabeled as negative, and those with joy and surprise are labeled as positive. Also, different datasets have different emotion categories. We select the detection branch training parameters of FI, the larger manually annotated dataset, as the initialization weight of other datasets.

Table 1. Sentiment classification performance on FI, Flickr, Twitter I, Twitter II, EmotionROI. Results with bold indicate the best accuracy compared with other algorithms.

Method	FI	Flickr	Twitter I			Twitter II	EmotionROI
			Twitter I-5	Twitter I-4	Twitter I-3		
GCH	–	–	67.91	97.20	65.41	77.68	66.53
LCH	–	–	70.18	68.54	65.93	75.98	64.29
SentiBank	–	–	71.32	68.28	66.63	65.93	66.18
DeepSentiBank	61.54	57.83	76.35	70.15	71.25	70.23	70.11
VGGNet [10]	70.64	61.28	83.44	78.67	75.49	71.79	72.25
PCNN	75.34	70.48	82.54	76.50	76.36	77.68	73.58
Yang [14]	86.35	71.13	88.65	85.10	81.06	80.48	81.26
Wu [12]	88.84	72.39	89.50	86.97	81.65	80.97	83.04
Ours	**89.18**	**74.53**	**91.25**	**87.96**	**84.34**	**81.32**	**83.33**

4.4   Classification Results

As shown in Table 1, we evaluate the performance of our proposed WSIDNet against different methods on five datasets. Compared with the hand-crafted features, CNN-based models can extract the sentimental feature from images. Our proposed method performs favorably against the state-of-the-art methods for sentiment classification, e.g., about 2.14% improvement on Flickr and 1.75% on TwitterI-5 datasets, which illustrates that WSIDNet can learn more discriminative representation for sentiment classification.

4.5   Ablation Study

The ablation study results on five datasets are shown in Table 2. Compared with backbone, our WSIDNet further improves the classification performance by 6.13% and 7.59% on FI and TwitterI-3 datasets. These results suggest that the sentiment interaction feature can effectively provide the information at the cognitive level.

Table 2. The model performance comparison across image datasets.

Method	FI	Flickr	Twitter I			Twitter II	EmotionROI
			Twitter I-5	Twitter I-4	Twitter I-3		
Backbone	83.05	70.12	84.35	82.26	76.75	76.99	77.02
WSIDNet	**89.18**	**74.53**	**91.25**	**87.96**	**84.34**	**81.32**	**83.33**

4.6   Detection Results

Figure 4(a) shows the detected sentiment maps for a joy image from the Emotion-ROI generated by the sentiment detection branch. Compared with the Emotion Stimuli Map that human annotates, the heat maps of amusement, excitement, and contentment have a high consistency with ground truth. In particular, awe tends to come from the natural landscape, so it is different from other emotions that express positive categories. In the classes of negative emotion, anger and fear focus on the boy's clenched fist, while disgust comes from the soil. Besides, the scene of the boy leaving expresses more sadness.

We also display some poor results of the detection branch. As shown in Fig. 4(b), the detection results of the negative sentiment are concentrated in the debris accumulation in the image, which is significantly different from the marked area in the ground truth. This indicates that the image does not necessarily contain all the emotion categories, and the performance of weakly supervised sentiment detection is still limited.

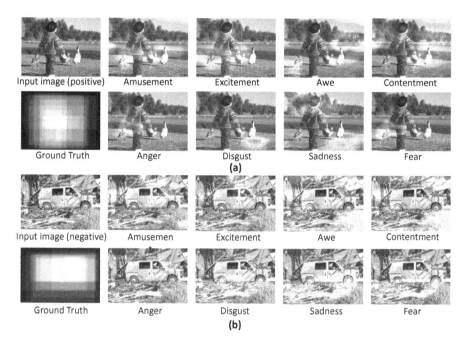

Fig. 4. Detected sentiment maps of the proposed WSIDNet on the EmotionROI. (a) detection results the detection branch (b) Poor results of the sentiment region detection branch with wrong and incomplete detection locations

5   Conclusion

This paper addresses fuzzy and subjective emotion in visual emotion analysis by utilizing sentiment interaction information. In particular, we propose a Weakly Supervised Interaction Discovery Network, an end-to-end model to couple the detection and classification task. Firstly, we adjust the cross-spatial pooling operation to realize automatic detection of sentiment and design a "sentiment graph" to model the sentiment relation, which takes the emotion as nodes and defines the adjacency matrix with the sentiment distance. Then, we employ a stacked GCN model to aggregate and update node features to obtain the expression of sentiment interaction. We evaluated the model's performance on five public datasets, and our approach exceeded the best available. Also, how to make more effective use of cognitive object interaction information is still a challenging problem.

Acknowledgement. This work was supported in part by Beijing Municipal Education Committee Science Foundation (KM201910005024), Beijing Postdoctoral Research Fundation (Q6042001202101).

References

1. Borth, D., Ji, R., Chen, T., Breuel, T., Chang, S-F.: Large-scale visual sentiment ontology and detectors using adjective noun pairs. In: ACM MM (2013)
2. Bruna, J., Zaremba, W., Szlam, A., LeCun, Y.: Spectral networks and deep locally connected networks on graphs. In: 2nd International Conference on Learning Representations, ICLR 2014, pp. 61–80 (2014)
3. Chen, T., Borth, D., Darrell, T., Chang, S.-F.: Deepsentibank: Visual sentiment concept classification with deep convolutional neural networks. arXiv preprint arXiv:1410.8586 (2014)
4. Chen, Z.M., Wei, X.S., Wang, P., Guo, Y.: Multi-label image recognition with graph convolutional networks. In: Proceedings of the IEEE/CVF Conference on Computer Vision and Pattern Recognition, pp. 5177–5186 (2019)
5. Gori, M., Monfardini, G., Scarselli, F.: A new model for learning in graph domains. In: Proceedings. 2005 IEEE International Joint Conference on Neural Networks, vol. 2, pp. 729–734. IEEE (2005)
6. Machajdik, J., Hanbury, A.: Affective image classification using features inspired by psychology and art theory. In: ACM MM (2010)
7. Peng, K.-C., Sadovnik, A., Gallagher, A., Chen, T.: Where do emotions come from? predicting the emotion stimuli map. In: ICIP (2016)
8. Scarselli, F., Gori, M., Tsoi, A.C., Hagenbuchner, M., Monfardini, G.: The graph neural network model. IEEE Trans. Neural Netw. **20**(1), 61–80 (2008)
9. Siersdorfer, S., Minack, E., Deng, F., Hare, J.: Analyzing and predicting sentiment of images on the social web. In: Proceedings of the 18th ACM international conference on Multimedia, pp. 715–718 (2010)
10. Simonyan, K., Zisserman, A.: Very deep convolutional networks for large-scale image recognition (2015)
11. Sun, M., Yang, J., Wang, K., Shen, H.: Discovering affective regions in deep convolutional neural networks for visual sentiment prediction. In: ICME (2016)
12. Wu, L., Qi, M., Jian, M., Zhang, H.: Visual sentiment analysis by combining global and local information. Neural Process. Lett. **51**(3), 2063–2075 (2019). https://doi.org/10.1007/s11063-019-10027-7
13. Yang, J., She, D., Lai, Y.-K., Rosin, P.L., Yang, M.-H.: Weakly supervised coupled networks for visual sentiment analysis. In: CVPR (2018)
14. Yang, J., She, D., Sun, M., Cheng, M.-M., Rosin, P.L., Wang, L.: Visual sentiment prediction based on automatic discovery of affective regions. IEEE Trans. Multimedia **20**(9), 2513–2525 (2018)
15. You, Q., Jin, H., Luo, J.: Visual sentiment analysis by attending on local image regions. In: AAAI (2017)
16. You, Q., Luo, J., Jin, H., Yang, J.: Robust image sentiment analysis using progressively trained and domain transferred deep networks. In: AAAI (2015)
17. You, Q., Luo, J., Jin, H., Yang, J.: Building a large scale dataset for image emotion recognition: the fine print and the benchmark. In: AAAI (2016)

Joint Multi-feature Learning for Facial Age Estimation

Yulan Deng[1], Lunke Fei[1(✉)], Jie Wen[2], Wei Jia[3], Genping Zhao[1],
Chunwei Tian[4], and Ting Ke[1]

[1] School of Computer Science and Technology, Guangdong University of Technology,
Guangzhou, China
flksxm@126.com
[2] School of Computer Science and Technology, Harbin Institute of Technology
(Shenzhen), Shenzhen, China
[3] School of Computer and Information, Hefei University of Technology, Hefei, China
[4] School of Software, Northwestern Polytechnical University, Xi'an, China

Abstract. Age estimation from face images has attracted much attention due to its favorable of many real-world applications such as video surveillance and social networking. However, most existing studies usually directly extract aging-feature, which ignore the high age-related factors such as race and gender information. In this paper, we propose a joint multi-feature learning method for robust facial age estimation by extensively exploring age-related features. Specifically, we first specially learn the race and gender features from face images, which are two highly related information for age estimation of an individual. Then, we jointly learn the aging-feature by concatenating these race-specific and gender-specific information maps with the original face images. To fully utilize the continuity and the order of age labels, we form a regression-ranking age estimator to predict the final age. Experimental results on three benchmark databases demonstrate the superior performance of our proposed method on facial age estimation in comparison with other state-of-the-art methods.

Keywords: Age estimation · Multi-feature learning ·
Regression-ranking fusion · Convolutional neural networks

1 Introduction

Age estimation is to identify a human age from face images, which is an important problem for numerous practical applications, such as video surveillance, social networking, and human-computer interaction. So far, there have been a variety of age estimation methods [1, 2]. In general, there are two stages for age estimation: aging-feature extraction and aging-feature estimator. For aging-feature extraction, the objective is to extract more aging-features from face images to make age information separable. In recent years, a number of aging-feature extraction methods

© Springer Nature Switzerland AG 2022
C. Wallraven et al. (Eds.): ACPR 2021, LNCS 13188, pp. 513–524, 2022.
https://doi.org/10.1007/978-3-031-02375-0_38

were proposed, and they can be classified into two categories: hand-crafted feature and learning-based feature. Representative hand-crafted feature representations include Local Binary Pattern (LBP) [3], Histogram of Oriented Gradients (HOG) [4] and Biologically Inspired Features (BIF) [5]. Generally, hand-crafted feature descriptors usually require strong prior knowledge. Due to this, the recent studies mainly focus on learning-based feature such as CNN-based deep-learning feature because of its great success on various computer vision tasks [6,7]. For example, Tan et al. [8] proposed a deep hybrid-aligned network to extract aging-feature. Liu et al. [9] employed a very deep architecture VGG-16 network to learn deep aging-feature.

For aging-feature estimator, it mainly converts the aging-feature into exact age numbers. In general, aging-features estimator can be grouped into three categories: classification-based methods, regression-based methods, and ranking-based methods. Representative classification-based methods include Support Vector Machines (SVM) [10], Random Forests (RF) [11] and k Nearest Neighbors (KNN) [12]. Classification-based methods equally treat each age number as a class so that they ignore inherent relationship of age labels. Therefore, the costs of classifying a young subject as middle-aged subject and old subject are the same. Due to this, many methods [1,13] formulated the aging-feature estimator as a regression problem because of continuous property of human age. For example, Agustsson et al. [14] proposed a nonlinear regression network for age estimation. Geng et al. [15] proposed a CPNN algorithms to learn age regression distributions. In recent years, ranking-based methods have been introduced to age estimation [16,17], which mainly use the ordinal relationship among age labels. For example, Chen et al. [17] proposed a ranking-CNN model with a series of basic networks and their binary outputs are aggregated for the final age prediction.

Compare with aging-feature estimator, aging-feature extraction significantly affects the performance of final age estimation accuracy because the aging information of face images are usually affected by many factors such as race and gender [18]. Figure 1 shows some face images with different genders and races, where peoples with similar ages look very different ages because of gender and race differences. How to extract discriminative and robust features for reliable age estimation remains a challenging problem [19,20].

In this paper, we propose a new aging-feature descriptor by exploring multiple aging-related features for robust age estimation. We first form two high aging-related feature maps by specially learning the gender and race information of an individual. Then, we concatenate these feature maps with the original face image to jointly learn the aging-feature descriptor. Finally, we use a regression-ranking age estimator to predict the final age. We conduct comparative experiments on three widely used databases to demonstrate the effectiveness of the proposed method.

The main contributions can be summarized as follows:

– We propose a joint multi-feature learning method for age estimation by exploring multiple aging-related features such as gender and race information, such that more discriminative aging-feature can be obtained in the final feature descriptor.

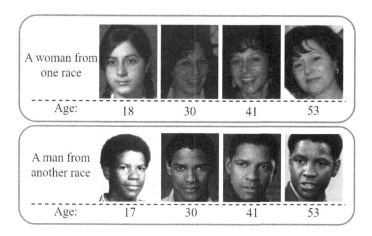

Fig. 1. Face images of people from different genders and races.

- We design a regression-ranking age estimator to predict the final age, so that the continuity and order properties of the age label can be simultaneously utilized.
- We conduct extensive experiments on three widely used databases. The experimental results show that our proposed method outperforms the other state-of-the-art age estimation methods.

The remainder of this paper is organized as follows. Section 2 reviews the related work. Section 3 elaborates our proposed method. Section 4 presents the experimental results. Section 5 offers the conclusion of this paper.

2   Related Work

In this section, we briefly review two related topics including multi-feature age estimation and age estimator.

2.1   Multi-feature Age Estimation

In the past, most age estimation methods [3,4] only considered a single age feature. However, the aging process is a complex process that is affected by many factors such as gender and race factors. To learn the more discriminative and robust features for age estimation, a few multi-feature-based methods were proposed recently [21–23], which aimed to learn and fuse multiple features. For example, Antipov et al. [22] presented a deep learning model for age estimation by fusing the general and children-specialized features. Yaman et al. [21] proposed a multimodal age estimation method by combining ear and profile face. Yang et al. [24] utilized a two-stream model to learn and integrate different age features for age estimation. The extensive experimental result show that the multi-feature method obtained the more discriminative and robust age features and achieved a better performance compared with other single-feature based methods. Unlike most existing multi-feature descriptors combining multimodal features, in this paper, we simultaneously extract and fuse multi-type features from single-model face images for age estimation.

2.2 Age Estimator

After obtaining aging features, age estimator mainly converts the aging features into exact age numbers. In the past, age estimator was modeled as a classifier. For example, Zheng et al. [25] proposed a PCANet to estimate human age based on the softmax loss. Soumaya et al. [26] presented an autoencoder network to classify age label based on unsupervised learning. Note a fact that age label is a continuous value rather than a set of discrete classes [27]. Thus, to make use of the continuity of age labels, regression-based methods were proposed for age estimation in recent years. For example, Rothe et al. [1] first used expected value on the softmax probabilities and then calculate the regression age. Zhang et al. [13] presented an age representation as a distribution over two discrete adjacent bins. To better exploit the ordinal relationship among age labels, a few ranking based methods were proposed recently. For example, Xie et al. [16] proposed an ordinal ensemble learning network for age estimation. Chen et al. [17] proposed a ranking-CNN model that contains a series of basic CNNs, which converted age estimation problem into multiple binary classification tasks. In this work, we simultaneously use regression and ranking age prediction schemes to engineer the age-feature estimator.

3   Proposed Method

In this section, we first present the overall framework of the proposed method. Then, we illustrate the multiple type aging-related features learning and the regression-ranking estimator of the proposed method.

3.1   The Framework of the Proposed Method

In general, peoples of different genders or from different races, as shown in Fig. 1, usually have different appearance and age characteristics. In other word, gender and race are two most important factors for age estimation of an individual. Due to this, we aim to learn more robust aging-feature by exploring the potential gender and race information from the original images. Figure 2 shows the basic idea of the proposed method, which mainly consists of two parts: multiple type aging-related features learning and regression-ranking age estimator. In the first part, we first specially learn the gender-specific and race-specific information from face images, which are the two high aging-feature related factors for age estimation. Then, we integrate the gender and race features into the original face images to jointly learn the aging-feature, so that more discriminative aging-feature can be obtained in the final feature descriptor. In the second part, to simultaneously utilize the continuity and the order of age labels, we engineer the regression and ranking age prediction schemes to form the age estimator. In the following, we present the detailed procedures of the two parts of the proposed method.

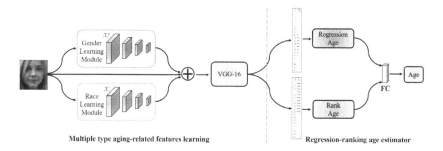

Fig. 2. The pipeline of our proposed method. First, we learn multiple aging-related information including gender-specific and race-specific features, and then combine them with the original images to jointly learning the aging-related feature descriptor. Lastly, we form a regression-rank estimator to predict the final age.

3.2   Multiple Type Aging-Related Features Learning

To extensively exploit the aging-related features, we first specially learn race and gender features and then fuse them with the original map to jointly learn the robust aging-feature. Figure 2 (left part) illustrates the multi-type feature learning network, where both gender and race learning modules are composed of 4 convolution blocks and each convolution block includes a convolutional layer, a non-linear activation, a batch normalization and a pooling layer. For the convolutional layer, we respectively use 32 and 64 kernels with the size of 5×5, stride of 1 pixel and 0 padding for the first and second layers to learn the coarse features. Then, we use the following two layers to learn the subtle features, which respectively use 64 and 128 kernels with the size of 3×3, stride of 1 and 1padding. And the outputs of the convolutions add an element-wise nonlinear activation function to normalize the front results. Without a loss of generality, we use the ELU function as the nonlinear activation function to deactivate the output of the convolutional layer. For the batch normalization, we use the subtractive and divisive normalization operations [27] to normalize each feature map. For the pooling layer, we use the maximum pooling operation to generate the feature representative map.

The gender and race features learning modules respectively exploit gender-specific and race-specific information from the original images. Inspired by the spatial attention mechanism [28] that the feature map of the first convolution layer contains more discriminative features, we select the feature maps from the first convolution layers of gender and race modules, and embed them into the original image for further aging-feature learning. Specifically, let $X_i, X_i^g, X_i^r \in R^{1 \times w \times h}$ be the original image, gender and race feature map respectively, and $\oplus$ denotes channel-connection operation, $newmap = [[X_i], [X_i^g], [X_i^r]] \in R^{3 \times w \times h}$ is formed and input into the next VGG-16-based network to further learn the final aging-feature.

3.3   Regression-Ranking Age Estimator

Due to the fact that the practical age label is continuous and ordinal rather than a set of discrete and independent classes, we engineer our proposed age estimator as an end-to-end regression and ranking task. Specifically, we modify the VGG-16 network to make it have two outputs: the age probability $\{p_i \in [0,1] \,|\, i = 1, 2, ..., n\}$ and the age ranking $\{p_j = 0/1 \,|\, j = 1, 2, ..., n\}$. For regression, the age number can be computed as

$$reg\_age = \sum_{i=1}^{n} J_i * P_i = [1, ..., a_n] * [p_1, ..., p_n]^T, \tag{1}$$

where J_i is the age label and P_i denotes the probability of input image belonging to the age of J_i. For ranking, the age number is predicted as follows:

$$ranking\_age = \sum_{j=1}^{n} [p_j > 0], \tag{2}$$

where $[\cdot]$ denotes the truth-test operator, which is 1 if the inner condition is true, and 0 otherwise. Age regression and age ranking respectively estimate the age from age continuity and age order properties, such that they are complementary for the final age number estimation. After age regression and age ranking, we further forward them to a fully connected layer to estimate the final age as follows:

$$age = \alpha_1 \sum_{i=1}^{n} J_i * P_i + \alpha_2 \sum_{i=1}^{n} [p_j > 0], \tag{3}$$

where α_1 and α_2 are two parameters of fully connected layer to balance the effects of continuity and order of age label and make a good trade-off between them.

4   Experiments

In this section, we evaluate the proposed method on three widely used databases in comparison with several state-of-the-art methods. All our modules were implemented within the pytorch framework and the Adam was used as the optimizer. The learning rate and batch size were empirically set to 0.001 and 16, respectively, and the Reduce LR on Plateau algorithm was used to automatically adjust the learning rate. The parameters of the proposed architecture were all initialized with the Xavier initialization. All experiments were performed under the same platform with GTX2060 s graphics card (including 2,176 CUDA cores), i5-9600KF CPU, 32 GB RAM and 1 TB hard disk drive.

4.1   Datasets and Preprocessing

We use three databases, including MORPH2, FG-NET, and LAP, to conduct our comparative experiments. Of them, MORPH2 is one of the most widely used datasets for evaluating age estimation, which contains 55,134 face images of 13,617 subjects with the age ranging from 16 to 77. FG-NET is another benchmark dataset that contains 1,002 face images of 82 individuals with the age ranging from 0 to 69. LAP was released in 2015 at the ChaLearn Looking at people challenge, which contains 4,691 face images with detailed age information. Table 1 tabulates the information of three databases as well as their experimental settings.

Table 1. The basic information and experimental settings of the three databases.

Datasets	Instances	Training (80%)	Testing (20%)	Age range
MORPH2	55,000	44,000	11,000	16–77
FG-NET	1,002	800	200	0–69
LAP	4,691	3,612	1,079	3–85

As shown in Table 1, the training images of FG-NET, MORPH2 and LAP databases are extremely insufficient. For example, FG-NET contains no more than eight hundred training images, which is far from enough to train a deep learning network. To enlarge the sample sets, we first flip each image to obtain two mirror-symmetric samples and then rotate them by $\pm 5°$ and $\pm 10°$. Moreover, we add Gaussian white noise with variance of 0.001, 0.005, 0.01, 0.015 and 0.02 on the original and the synthetic samples, so that each image is finally extended to 40 samples. To reduce the error caused by illumination variation and different posture, we use illumination equalization [31] to normalize illumination in the experiments. After that, all face images were first processed by a face detector [29] and a few non-face images would be removed. Then, we use AAM [30] to align all faces, according to the eyes center and the upper lip. Finally, all face images are cropped into the size of 224 × 224 and then fed into the network. Some aligned images are shown in Fig. 3.

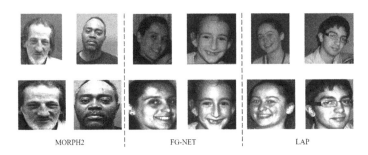

MORPH2   FG-NET   LAP

Fig. 3. Some of the original and aligned images from MORPH2, FG-NET and LAP databases.The first row is the original image, and the second row is the aligned image.

4.2 Comparisons with the State-of-the-art

To evaluate the performance of our proposed method on age estimation, we compare the proposed method with four representative age estimation methods including DHAA [8], C3AE [13], AGEn [31], and GA-DFL [9]. Following the standard age estimation proposal [1], we first train our method based on training samples. Then, we predict the age number of the testing samples to calculate the Mean Absolute Error (MAE) [31], Table 2 tabulates the age estimation results of different methods on the three databases.

Table 2. The MAEs of different age estimation methods on the MORPH2, FG-NET and LAP databases.

Methods	Estimator	MORPH2	FG-NET	LAP
DHAA [8]	Regression	2.48	2.59	3.05
C3AE [13]	Regression	2.75	2.95	–
AGEn [31]	Rank	2.52	2.96	2.94
GA-DFL [9]	Rank	3.25	3.93	3.37
Ours	Regression-Rank	**2.42**	**2.56**	**2.86**

It can be seen from Table 2 that our proposed method consistently outperforms the four comparison methods by achieving obviously lower MAEs. This is because our proposed method first specially extracts the gender-specific and race-specific information from the original face images, which can provide more instructive aging-related information than the original images for the final aging-feature learning. By integrating these multi-type features with complementary information, more discriminative and robust aging-feature can be obtained in final feature descriptor. Another possible reason is that the proposed method adaptively fuses the regression and ranking age estimator, which can fully utilize the continuity and the ordinal relationship of age labels.

4.3 Ablation Analysis

To better evaluate the effectiveness of the gender and race feature learning sub-modules, we conduct the following comparative experiments by removing one or both of them from our proposed method. Specifically, we take the proposed method with only original aging-specific feature learning model as the baseline, and referred the gender and race learning sub-modules to as baseline+Gender, baseline+Race and baseline+Gender+Race (i.e., the proposed method), respectively.

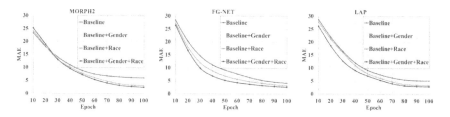

Fig. 4. The MAEs of the proposed method with embedding different gender and race features learning modules.

Figure 4 shows the MAEs of the proposed methods with different combinations of gender and race feature learning modules. It clearly shows that Baseline+Gender and Baseline+Race consistently outperform the baseline method, demonstrating the effectiveness of both the gender and race feature learning procedures. Moreover, our proposed method with both gender and race feature learning modules yields the best result. Therefore, the multi-feature jointly learning module of the proposed method can exploit more discriminative and robust aging-feature than a single learning module for age estimation.

To validate the effectiveness of our regression-ranking age estimator, we compare regression, ranking and regression-ranking estimator on age estimation task, respectively. Figure 5 depicts the MAEs of the three different estimators on the three databases. We can see that our fusion estimator outperforms both regression only or ranking only estimators. This is because regression-ranking fusion aging-feature prediction technique can make a good tradeoff between the continuity and ordinal relationship of age for the aging-features prediction.

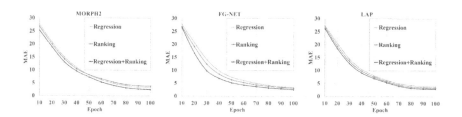

Fig. 5. The MAEs of the proposed method based on different estimators.

5 Conclusion

In this paper, we have proposed a joint multi-feature learning method for reliable facial age estimation. To extract more robust aging-feature, we first specially exploit high aging-related gender and race features and then fuse these multi-type features with the original face images to jointly learn the final aging-feature. To fully utilize the continuous and orderly property of age, we combine the regression and ranking loss to form a fusion-based age estimator for the final aging-feature prediction. Experimental results on several benchmark datasets demonstrated that the proposed method achieves a very competitive age estimation performance compared with state-of-the-art methods.

Acknowledgement. This work was supported in part by the National Natural Science Foundation of China under Grants 62176066, 62076086 and 62006059, in part by the Guangzhou Science and technology plan project under Grant 202002030110, in part by the Natural Science Foundation of Guangdong Province under Grant 2019A1515011811.

References

1. Rothe, R., Timofte, R., Van Gool, L.: Deep expectation of real and apparent age from a single image without facial landmarks. Int. J. Comput. Vis. **126**(2), 144–157 (2016). https://doi.org/10.1007/s11263-016-0940-3
2. Niu, Z., Zhou, M,. Wang, L., Gao, X., Hua, G.: Ordinal regression with multiple output CNN for age estimation. In: IEEE Conference on Computer Vision and Pattern Recognition, pp. 4920–4928 (2016)
3. Ojala, T., Pietikainen, M., Maenpaa, T.: Multiresolution gray-scale and rotation invariant texture classification with local binary patterns. IEEE Trans. Pattern Anal. Mach. Intell. **24**(7), 971–987 (2002)
4. Dalal, N., Triggs, B.: Histograms of oriented gradients for human detection. In: IEEE Conference on Computer Vision and Pattern Recognition, pp. 4920–4928 (2016)
5. Guo, G., Mu, G., Fu, Y.: Human age estimation using bio-inspired features. In: IEEE Conference on Computer Vision and Pattern Recognition, pp. 112–119 (2009)
6. Antipov, G., Baccouche, M.: Effective training of convolutional neural networks for face-based gender and age prediction. Pattern Recognit. **72**(1), 15–26 (2017)
7. Pei, W., Dibeklioğlu, H., Baltrušaitis, T., Tax, D.M.: Attended end-to-end architecture for age estimation from facial expression videos. IEEE Trans. Image Process. **29**, 1972–1984 (2019)
8. Tan, Z., Yang, Y., Wan, J., Guo, G.: Deeply-learned hybrid representations for facial age estimation. In: International Joint Conferences on Artificial Intelligence, pp. 3548–3554 (2009)
9. Liu, H., Lu, J., Feng, J., Zhou, J.: Group-aware deep feature learning for facial age estimation. Pattern Recognit. **66**, 82–94 (2017)
10. Chen, P.H., Lin, C.J., Schölkopf, B.: A tutorial on v-support vector machines. Appl. Stoch. Models Bus. Ind. **21**(2), 111–136 (2005)
11. Shen, W., Guo, Y., Wang, Y., Zhao, K., Wang, B.: Deep differentiable random forests for age estimation. IEEE Trans. Pattern Anal. Mach. Intell. **43**(2), 404–419 (2021)

12. Gunay, A., Nabiyev, V.V.: Automatic age classification with LBP. In: International Symposium on Computer and Information Sciences, vol. 1, pp. 1–4 (2008)
13. Zhang, C., Liu, S., Xu, X., Zhu, C.: C3AE: exploring the limits of compact model for age estimation. In: IEEE Conference on Computer Vision and Pattern Recognition, pp. 12587–12596 (2019)
14. Agustsson, E., Timofte, R., Van Gool, L.: Anchored regression networks applied to age estimation and super resolution. In: IEEE International Conference on Computer Vision, pp. 1643–1652 (2017)
15. Geng, X., Yin, C., Zhou, Z.H.: Facial age estimation by learning from label distributions. IEEE Trans. Pattern Anal. Mach. Intell. **35**(10), 2401–2412 (2013)
16. Xie, J.C., Pun, C.M.: Deep and ordinal ensemble learning for human age estimation from facial images. IEEE Trans. Inf. Forensics Secur. **15**, 2361–2374 (2020)
17. Chen, S., Zhang, C., Dong, M., Le, J., Rao, M.: Using ranking-CNN for age estimation. In: IEEE Conference on Computer Vision and Pattern Recognition, pp. 5183–5192 (2017)
18. Duan, M., Li, K., Li, K.: An ensemble CNN2ELM for age estimation. IEEE Trans. Inf. Forensics Secur. **13**(3), 758–772 (2017)
19. Fei, L., Zhang, B., Xu, Y., Tian, C., Rida, I., Zhang, D.: Jointly heterogeneous palmprint discriminant feature learning. IEEE Trans. Neural Netw. Learn. Syst. 1–12 (2021). https://doi.org/10.1109/TNNLS.2021.3066381 (2021)
20. Fei, L., Zhang, B., Zhang, L., Jia, W., Wen, J., Wu, J.: Learning compact multifeature codes for palmprint recognition from a single training image per palm. IEEE Trans. Multimedia **23**, 2930–2942 (2021)
21. Yaman, D., Irem Eyiokur, F., Kemal Ekenel, H.: Multimodal age and gender classification using ear and profile face images. In: IEEE Conference on Computer Vision and Pattern Recognition Workshops, pp. 2414–2421 (2019)
22. Antipov, G., Baccouche, M., Berrani, S.A., Dugelay, J.L.: Apparent age estimation from face images combining general and children-specialized deep learning models. In: IEEE Conference on Computer Vision and Pattern Recognition Workshops, pp. 96–104 (2016)
23. Wang, L., Huang, J., Yin, M., Cai, R., Hao, Z.: Block diagonal representation learning for robust subspace clustering. Inf. Sci. **526**, 54–67 (2020)
24. Yang, T.Y., Huang, Y.H., Lin, Y.Y., Hsiu, P.C., Chuang, Y.Y.: SSR-Net: a compact soft stagewise regression network for age estimation. In: International Joint Conference on Artificial Intelligence, pp. 1078–1084 (2018)
25. Zheng, D.P., Du, J.X., Fan, W.T., Wang, J., Zhai, C.M.: Deep learning with PCANet for human age estimation. In: Huang, D.-S., Jo, K.-H. (eds.) ICIC 2016, Part II. LNCS, vol. 9772, pp. 300–310. Springer, Cham (2016). https://doi.org/10.1007/978-3-319-42294-7_26
26. Zaghbani, S., Boujneh, N., Bouhlel, M.S.: Age estimation using deep learning. Comput. Electr. Eng. **68**, 337–347 (2018)
27. Li, K., Xing, J., Su, C., Hu, W., Zhang, Y., Maybank, S.: Deep cost-sensitive and order-preserving feature learning for cross-population age estimation. In: IEEE Conference on Computer Vision and Pattern Recognition, pp. 399–408 (2018)
28. Woo, S., Park, J., Lee, J.-Y., Kweon, I.S.: CBAM: convolutional block attention module. In: Ferrari, V., Hebert, M., Sminchisescu, C., Weiss, Y. (eds.) ECCV 2018, Part VII. LNCS, vol. 11211, pp. 3–19. Springer, Cham (2018). https://doi.org/10.1007/978-3-030-01234-2_1
29. Simonyan, K., Zisserman, A.: Very deep convolutional networks for large-scale image recognition. arXiv preprint arXiv:1409 (2018)

30. Cootes, T.F., Edwards, G.J.: Active appearance models. IEEE Trans. Pattern Anal. Mach. Intell. **23**(6), 681–685 (2001)
31. Tan, Z., Wan, J., Lei, Z., Zhi, R., Guo, G., Li, S.Z.: Efficient group-n encoding and decoding for facial age estimation. IEEE Trans. Pattern Anal. Mach. Intell. **40**(11), 2610–2623 (2017)

Is CNN Really Looking at Your Face?

Hiroya Kawai[1]($\boxtimes$), Takashi Kozu[1], Koichi Ito[1], Hwann-Tzong Chen[2], and Takafumi Aoki[1]

[1] Graduate School of Information Sciences, Tohoku University, 6-6-05, Aramaki Aza Aoba, Sendai 9808579, Japan
hiroya@aoki.ecei.tohoku.ac.jp
[2] Department of Computer Science, National Tsing Hua University, 101, Section 2, Kuang-Fu Road, Hsinchu 300044, Taiwan

Abstract. Face recognition has dramatically improved its performance with the advent of deep learning, especially Convolutional Neural Networks (CNNs), while they have raised a new issue: the difficulty in interpreting the results. The question is what CNN looks at in a face image to identify a person. To answer this question, this paper presents a simple and novel analysis of deep face recognition based on facial parts. We evaluate the recognition accuracy of face images with specific regions masked using face segmentation labels. Our analysis clarifies what CNNs really need in face images for face recognition. The paper concludes with an application of face recognition models to general visualization methods and the problems contained in some classical face image datasets.

Keywords: Face recognition · Face parsing · CNN · Biometrics

1 Introduction

Face recognition has received much attention in recent years as one of the most promising solutions for recognizing individuals [12]. Face recognition is more convenient and cost effective than other biometric recognition such as fingerprint recognition and iris recognition, since face images can be captured at a distance using a standard camera. Therefore, face recognition is in great demand as person authentication in video surveillance, smart shopping, interactive robots, and any portable devices like smartphones. The main research topic in face recognition is to improve the recognition accuracy, since variations in pose, facial expression, illumination, etc., degrade the performance of face recognition [6,9]. The performance of face recognition has improved dramatically with the advent of deep learning, especially convolutional neural networks (CNNs), and the availability of large-scale face image datasets [22]. On the other hand, the interpretability of the results obtained by CNNs is extremely poor compared to typical methods using handcrafted feature descriptors, since a CNN model with a large number of parameters is optimized as a black box through training. The question naturally arises, then, "what is CNN looking at to understand faces?"

© Springer Nature Switzerland AG 2022
C. Wallraven et al. (Eds.): ACPR 2021, LNCS 13188, pp. 525–539, 2022.
https://doi.org/10.1007/978-3-031-02375-0_39

In this paper, we explore this fundamental, yet still unresolved problem of deep face recognition using a simple and novel analysis. We propose an analysis method based on face parsing to interpret the results of deep face recognition. Face parsing computes pixel-wise label maps for different semantic components such as eyes, nose, mouth, hair, etc. In addition to these components, our analysis method also covers the background. Binary masks are generated based on the semantic labels obtained by face parsing, and CNN models for face recognition are trained and evaluated by applying these masks to face images. Through the evaluation of the recognition accuracy and visualization of CNN models based on various combinations of mask patterns, in face recognition, we demonstrate that the contours of the face and facial parts are important, and that the mouth, eyes, and eyebrows are sensitive to pose changes and aging. Our analysis also clarifies that images of only hair and background without a face can be used for verifying individuals in several famous face image datasets. In addition, we also provide an application of our analysis method which is a new visualization method dedicated to face recognition model, and we show that the visualization results are more reliable than those obtained by general visualization methods for CNN models.

2   Related Work

We briefly summarize the relevant literature on face recognition, visualization of CNNs, and face parsing in the following.

2.1   Face Recognition

The most traditional approach of face recognition is extracting geometric features from a face image and matching them. A lot of keypoints are detected from a face image, and the distances and angles among the keypoints are used as features [9]. Face recognition methods using handcrafted feature descriptors extracted from around keypoints such as Local Binary Patterns (LBPs) have been proposed since the advent of machine learning methods such as Support Vector Machines (SVMs) [1,2]. Recently, deep learning-based face recognition has become the mainstream. The methods for training CNNs using loss functions focusing on the distance between features in the feature space have been mainly proposed, such as FaceNet [18] and ArcFace [5]. The biggest difference between these deep learning-based methods and the traditional methods is the input to the discriminator. While traditional methods require the input of feature descriptors extracted based on keypoints, recent CNN-based methods require the direct input of face images. CNNs can achieve high recognition accuracy by automatically extracting features suitable for face recognition, however, it is not clear what kind of facial features CNNs use for face recognition.

2.2   Visualization of CNNs

The difficulty in interpreting CNNs is one of the common challenges in computer vision. The visualization of the feature map using the class activation

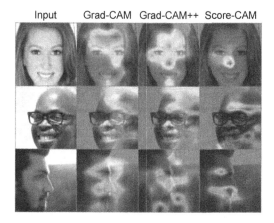

Fig. 1. Example of visualization of deep face recognition using ResNet-50 by Grad-CAM [19], Grad-CAM++ [4], and Score-CAM [21].

map [4,19,21] allows us to analyze which regions CNNs pay attention to in object recognition. On the other hand, such visualization methods have little effect when the target object covers most of the image, as in face recognition. Figure 1 shows examples of visualization of a face recognition model using three major methods: Grad-CAM [19], Grad-CAM++ [4], and Score-CAM [21], where ResNet-50 [7] is used as a face recognition model. Some results focus on particular facial parts, such as forehead, nose, mouth, and chin; however, the interpretation of the whole results is difficult since the focusing areas are not clear.

2.3 Face Parsing

Face parsing is one of the semantic segmentation methods, which computes pixel-wise label maps for different semantic components such as eyes, nose, mouth, hair, etc. Many highly accurate segmentation methods using deep learning have been proposed, and the accuracy of face parsing has been improved as well [14,15]. Face parsing has been applied to face attribute estimation [3,10] and face image generation and transformation [11,13]. To the best of our knowledge, there is no work that uses face parsing to analyze and improve the performance of face recognition.

3   Datasets

The datasets used in this paper for face parsing and face recognition are described below.

3.1 Datasets for Face Parsing

In this paper, we use two typical face parsing datasets: CelebAMask-HQ [11] and Landmark guided face Parsing (LaPa) [15]. CelebAMask-HQ dataset consists of

Fig. 2. Examples of face images in two face parsing datasets [11,15] and four face recognition datasets [8,16,20,23].

30,000 face images with 19 classes manually annotated semantic labels. The size of face images are 1,024 × 1,024 pixels, and most of them are high-quality and front facing. The semantic labels with 512 × 512 pixels include the basic face parts (hair, skin, eyes, eyebrows, nose, mouth, ears, etc.) and accessories (eyeglasses, earrings, necklace, etc.). LaPa dataset consists of 22,168 face images with 11 classes manually annotated semantic labels. The size of the face image is 450 × 450 pixels, and the dataset includes some images of low-quality and different face orientations. The semantic labels with the same size as face images do not include ears (which are labeled as part of the skin instead) and any accessories. We used six classes of semantic labels by combining several classes: *background, skin, eyebrows, mouth, nose,* and *eyes.* In CelebAMask-HQ, ears are combined with *skin.* In both datasets, the left and right sides are combined into one class, e.g., right eye and left eye are combined into *eyes,* upper lip and lower lip are combined into *mouth,* and other classes such as *hair, neck,* etc. are combined into *background.* The upper part of Fig. 2 shows some examples of face images in CelebAMask-HQ and LaPa.

3.2   Datasets for Face Recognition

In this paper, we use six face image datasets: CASIA-Webface [23] is used for training, and LFW [8], AgeDB [16], CFP [20], CALFW [25], and CPLFW [24] are used for test. CASIA-WebFace [23] is a famous medium-scale face dataset, which consists of 494,414 images from 10,575 persons. Labeled Faces in the Wild (LFW) [8] is a standard dataset, which consists of 13,233 images from 5,749 persons. In-the-wild Age Database (AgeDB) [16] is a dataset, which considers aging and consists of 16,488 images from 568 persons. In AgeDB, we use AgeDB-30, which is a pair of faces with an age difference of 30 years. Celebrities in Frontal-Profile in the Wild (CFP) [20] is a dataset, which considers face orientation and consists of 7,000 images from 500 persons. In CFP, we use CFP-FP, which is a pair of frontal and profile faces. Cross-Age LFW (CALFW) [25] and Cross-Pose LFW (CPLFW) [24] are datasets created based on LFW, which consists of 11,652 and 12,174 images from 5,749 persons. For each dataset, the face image pairs in the LFW are updated so that the differences in face orientation and age become larger. The lower part of Fig. 2 shows some examples of face images in CASIA-Webface [23], LFW [8], AgeDB [16], and CFP [20].

4   Face Parsing for Face Recognition

The face image used in face recognition is different from the image used in face parsing. Face parsing focuses on high-resolution and high-quality face images to assign a facial part label to each pixel. Face recognition, on the other hand, focuses on face images with low resolution, unnatural colors such as grayscale, and different face poses to evaluate the robustness of the face recognition methods. Therefore, in order to perform face parsing for face recognition, it is necessary to consider a method that performs accurate part segmentation on the face images used to evaluate the performance of face recognition. A simple CNN model can be used for face recognition instead of the complex CNN models that are generally used for face parsing since features are generally extracted after the faces are aligned. Therefore, in this paper, we propose a face parsing method using U-Net [17]. U-Net consists of encoder and decoder networks with shortcut connections between them at multiple levels. The U-Net used in the proposed method is a smaller version with 75% fewer output channels in each layer. Pixel-wise cross-entropy loss is used as the loss function.

To perform face parsing on face images used in face recognition, it is necessary to consider the variations in intensity values. Therefore, we apply three preprocessings to the input images: RandomGrayscale, ColorJitter, and GaussianBlur. In RandomGrayscale, a color image is randomly converted to a grayscale image. In ColorJitter, the intensity, hue, and saturation of the image are changed randomly. The rate of change is randomly selected from a predefined range. In this paper, we set this range as $[0.5, 1.5]$. In GaussianBlur, a Gaussian filter with a predefined kernel size is applied to the image. The standard deviation of the filter is randomly selected from a predefined range. In this paper, we set this range as $[0.1, 2.0]$. The execution probabilities for RandomGrayscale, ColorJitter, and GaussianBlur are set to 0.1, 0.8, and 0.8, which are determined empirically. We also apply pixel value normalization to $[-1.0, 1.0]$ and RandomHorizontalFlip to the input image in training.

CelebAMask-HQ dataset is randomly separated into 80% (24,000 images) for training and 20% (6,000 images) for validation. LaPa dataset is also separated into 18,168 images for training, 2,000 images for validation, and 2,000 images for test according to the recommended experimental protocol. All input images are aligned by the similarity transform and resized to 112×112 pixels. We use a

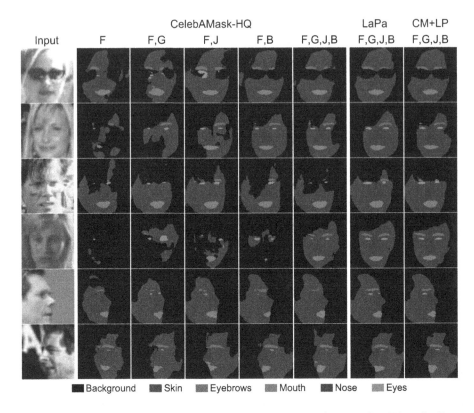

Fig. 3. Qualitative comparison of segmentation results (F: RandomFilp, G: Ran-domGrayscale, J: ColorJitter, and B: GaussianBlur), where "CM+LP" indicates that the mixed dataset of CelebAMask-HQ and LaPa is used for training.

standard mini-batch SGD for training with a batch size of 64. The initial value of the learning rate is 0.1 and is multiplied by 0.1 if the validation loss does not improve in five consecutive epochs. The training is completed if the validation loss does not improve in 10 consecutive epochs.

Figure 3 shows the results for different combinations of preprocessing and different datasets. All the three preprocessings are effective in improving the seg-mentation accuracy of face images. GrayScale and ColorJitter are effective for images with unnatural colors, while GaussianBlur is effective for low-resolution and blurred images. In addition, the segmentation accuracy of all face images, especially profile faces, is significantly improved when trained on the LaPa dataset. On the other hand, mixing the two datasets for training is not effective. In the CelebAMask-HQ dataset, all eyeglasses are annotated as a separate class from the skin, while in the LaPa dataset, only sunglasses are annotated as back-ground. This difference in annotation criteria results in a slight decrease in the segmentation accuracy for background and skin. From the above, U-Net trained

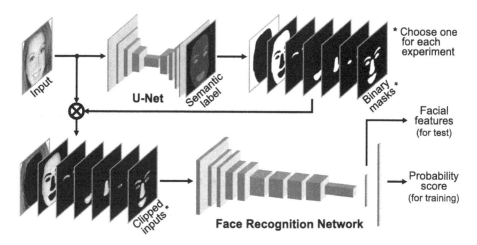

Fig. 4. An overview of the proposed analysis method, where the case of the editing strategy (a) Clipping Part is presented.

on the LaPa dataset with all the preprocessings applied is used for analyzing face recognition.

5   Face Recognition with Face Parsing

In this section, we describe an analysis method for deep face recognition using face parsing. The purpose of the analysis is to identify where the deep face recognition models look or should look in a face image. We propose a method to analyze the face recognition model based on the facial part masks by combining the trained face parsing model with the face recognition model. Figure 4 shows an overview of the proposed analysis method. The face parsing model described in the previous section is used to estimate semantic labels from a face image, where seven binary masks, *background*, *skin*, *eyebrows*, *mouth*, *nose*, *eyes*, and *parts* (without *background* and *skin*), are obtained based on the semantic labels. The input face image is then edited based on the resulting binary mask and input to the face recognition network. In this paper, we consider the following four types of editing strategies to analyze face recognition models from various perspectives.

(a) Clipping Part: This strategy evaluates which part is used for face recognition by clipping the target part from the face image. We multiply the face image by a binary mask in which pixels in the target part are set to 1 and the others to 0 as shown in Fig. 5(a).

(b) Masking Part: This strategy is the inverse of (a) and evaluates whether the target part is required for face recognition or not. We multiply the face image by a binary mask in which pixels in the target part are set to 0 and the others to 1, resulting in an image missing only the target part as shown in Fig. 5(b).

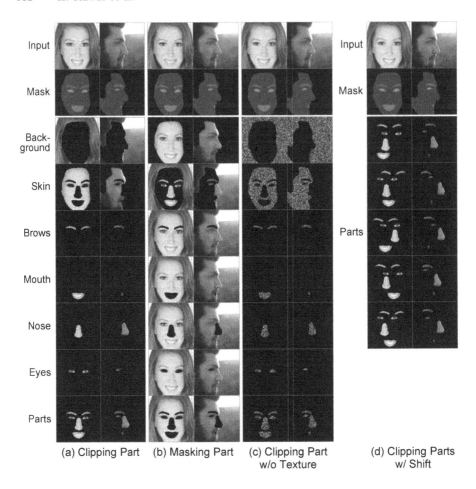

Input

Mask

Back-
ground

Skin

Brows

Mouth

Nose

Eyes

Parts

Input

Mask

Parts

(a) Clipping Part   (b) Masking Part   (c) Clipping Part   (d) Clipping Parts
w/o Texture   w/ Shift

Fig. 5. Examples of face images obtained with each editing strategy.

(c) **Clipping Part without Texture**: This strategy evaluates whether the texture is necessary for face recognition by clipping the part as in (a) and replacing the texture with random noise. The generated image does not contain any texture information, but only the shape information of the target part as shown in Fig. 5(c).

(d) **Clipping Parts with Shift**: This strategy evaluates whether the positional information of parts is necessary for face recognition by randomly shifting the target parts as shown in Fig. 5(d). Note that we add different fixed values to the vertical shift value of each part so that the parts do not overlap after shifting.

6   Experiments and Discussion

In this section, we describe the experiments to analyze deep face recognition using face parsing. We discuss two types of analysis: the importance of each part of the face, and the importance of each feature (shape, texture, and position of parts), and then we introduce an application of the analysis method.

6.1   Experimental Settings

The architecture of the face recognition network is based on ResNet-50 [7], which is a widely used CNN architecture. Note that, in this paper, we employ an improved version of ResNet-50 proposed in the first version of the ArcFace paper [5], which uses a special convolution block (BatchNormalization-Conv-BN-PReLU-Conv-BN) and a special classifier (BN-Dropout-FullyConnected-FC-Softmax) to obtain a 512-dimensional facial feature vector. Cross entropy is used as the loss function, Stochastic Gradient Descent (SGD) is used to optimize the weights, and a batch size and the number of epochs are set to 64 and 34. The learning rate is initialized at 0.0125 and multiplied by 0.1 at the beginning of epochs 20, 28, and 32. The input image is aligned to 112×112 pixels by similarity transform estimated from five keypoints: both eyes, nose, and both ends of mouth, normalized to $[-1, 1]$ pixel values, and then flipped randomly in the horizontal direction.

The evaluation metrics in this experiment are summarized below. In strategies (a) and (b), we evaluate the models using face images edited in the same way as during training. In strategies (c) and (d), we evaluate the model using textured instead of untextured face images, or face images with each part shifted by a fixed value instead of a random value, to eliminate the effect of randomness. In this experiment, we evaluate the accuracy of face recognition according to 10-fold cross validation. 6,000 pairs of face images (3,000 genuine pairs and 3,000 impostor pairs) are created according to the official experimental protocol for each dataset and divided equally into 10 sets. Note that CFP-FP has 7,000 pairs. The cosine similarity score between 512-dimensional feature vectors extracted from two face images is computed. For each of the 10 sets, the threshold of the score that maximizes the verification accuracy is calculated, and the average of the accuracy of the 10 sets is reported.

6.2   Experimental Results

Table 1 summarizes the verification accuracy of the model trained using images with different editing strategies, where "baseline" indicates that the model is trained using the original images, and "bg." indicates that the target part is *background*. A part of the results is also summarized graphically in Fig. 6.

Table 1. Verification accuracy of models trained using edited face images.

Method	Target	Accuracy [%]				
		LFW	AgeDB-30	CALFW	CFP-FP	CPLFW
Baseline	–	99.10	92.53	91.90	94.74	86.83
(a) Clipping part	Bg	94.48	74.50	81.63	79.31	77.68
	Skin	**98.82**	**90.93**	**90.73**	**92.07**	**83.97**
	Brows	90.60	72.35	78.57	75.69	69.47
	Mouth	81.02	67.88	73.28	69.60	62.28
	Nose	92.63	83.18	84.50	82.47	75.15
	Eyes	82.62	70.18	76.18	65.40	59.88
	Parts	97.75	90.13	89.73	88.21	79.95
(b) Masking part	Bg	99.12	92.48	91.65	93.59	85.25
	Skin	98.77	90.27	90.63	90.54	83.80
	Brows	99.12	**92.93**	**91.70**	94.36	86.38
	Mouth	**99.18**	92.10	91.63	93.86	86.42
	Nose	99.03	91.48	91.05	93.30	85.78
	Eyes	99.12	92.13	91.52	**94.37**	**86.45**
	Parts	98.80	90.83	91.00	92.86	85.40
(c) Clipping part w/o texture	Bg	85.93	65.98	71.85	67.26	65.42
	Skin	**93.42**	**75.42**	**80.62**	**76.83**	**72.08**
	Brows	77.35	65.87	68.37	62.70	59.03
	Mouth	65.38	56.90	60.12	56.79	54.05
	Nose	69.00	57.55	61.10	58.21	54.93
	Eyes	68.37	60.18	62.00	55.46	53.92
	Parts	87.57	72.88	76.48	71.06	65.78
(d) w/Shift	Parts	98.08	90.48	89.98	89.27	81.35

6.3 Discussion on Facial Parts

The importance of facial parts in face recognition is discussed based on the experimental results. The model trained on *skin* exhibits the highest accuracy, except for the baseline trained on the original face images. Therefore, *skin* has the highest potential for face recognition in facial parts. The next best model is the one trained on *nose*. *nose* has a texture similar to *skin*, and its shape is useful for verifying profile faces, while it is highly sensitive to illumination changes. Surprisingly, the model trained on *background* has the highest accuracy among the facial parts except for *skin* in LFW and CPLFW, especially for LFW, its accuracy is greater than 94%. In LFW, the number of images per person is small, and most genuine pairs consist of face images taken at the same time and place, which can be verified using only the background and hair. On the other hand, in datasets with aging, such as AgeDB, it is difficult to verify only the background and hair since the background and hair are different even if they are genuine pairs. This fact suggests that the background and hair have sufficient potential for face recognition, and CNNs take the initiative to use them in training. The models trained on other facial parts,

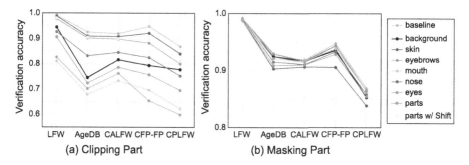

Fig. 6. Comparison of verification accuracy of models trained using clipped or masked face images.

i.e., *eyebrows*, *mouth*, and *eyes*, have worse accuracy than *skin* and *nose*, especially for AgeDB-30, since these parts change significantly with aging and facial expression changes. The models trained on *eyes* are also sensitive to changes in face orientation since it is difficult to recognize eyes in profile faces. The accuracy of the model trained on *parts*, which is combined with the four facial parts of *eyebrows*, *mouth*, *nose*, and *eyes*, is slightly lower than that of *skin*. In particular, the accuracy of face recognition is degraded for datasets that contain large changes in face orientation due to the difficulty of accurate face parsing for profile faces. We expect that the accuracy improvement in face parsing allows us to achieve high accuracy in face recognition even if only some small facial parts are used. We also notice that *eyebrows*, *mouth*, and *eyes* are not always important in face recognition and can be substituted by other regions. CNNs have the potential to recognize individuals using only their faces since the degradation in accuracy of face recognition due to background masking is limited. The models trained by masking *skin* or *nose* exhibit a significant degradation in face recognition accuracy, and therefore these parts are important in face recognition.

6.4   Discussion on Facial Features

The importance of facial features, i.e., shape, texture, and position of parts, in face recognition is discussed based on the experimental results. The degree of decreased accuracy due to texture removal varies depending on the facial parts, however, texture is crucial in face recognition since all the models exhibit a significant degradation in accuracy due to texture removal. In particular, the degradation in accuracy when the *nose* texture is removed is extremely large compared to other facial parts. This is due to the instability of the boundary between *nose* and *skin* compared to other parts, which results in inconsistent annotations in the face parsing datasets. The model trained on *skin* without texture exhibits over 93% accuracy in LFW. This indicates that the shape of the face and facial parts is important for face recognition using CNN as well as the background and hair texture. Note that *skin* without texture includes not only the contours of the face, but also the contours of the facial parts as shown in Fig. 5(c). The positional relationship among the facial parts is not essential for face recognition since the accuracy of face recognition is not degraded even if each part moves randomly.

7   Application to Visualization

In this section, we present an example of the application of our analysis method to CNN visualization. In the previous section, we have evaluated the potential of facial parts and features in face recognition using face images applying the same mask pattern during training and test. Our analysis method becomes a facial part-based visualization method that can be used for any pretrained face recognition model by applying a mask to the face images only during test. This visualization method is inspired by Score-CAM [21]. In Score-CAM, a lot of masks are generated by normalizing each channel of the feature vectors output from the middle layer of CNN. These masks are applied to the original image and input to CNN to generate an activation map by calculating a weighted sum of feature vectors with the probability scores of the target class as weights after applying softmax. This is based on the assumption that high probability scores for the target class can be obtained by inputting a masked image with the important regions being kept into CNN. We replace the mask generated from the feature vectors in Score-CAM with the mask of facial parts based on the semantic labels obtained from face parsing.

Figure 7 shows the visualization results from the proposed visualization method compared with the general visualization methods for CNN [4,19,21]. The five on the left in this figure show the visualization results for the models in "baseline" of Table 1, i.e., the models trained on the original face images. The results of the proposed method for the three face images on the left suggest that this model may identify individuals based on the accessories such as hats and sunglasses. The two remaining results of the proposed method suggest that CNN uses the characteristic shapes of the mouth and nose for identification. The general visualization methods provide less meaningful results, while the proposed method provides results that can be interpreted intuitively. The rest of the figure shows the result of visualizing the trained model on facial parts. It is expected that regions of the same part used for training are activated on the map; however, the general visualization methods provide different results. On the other hand, the proposed method provides almost the expected results. The proposed method visualizes CNNs based on the six facial parts, making it difficult to visualize details compared to the general visualization methods that visualize CNNs pixel by pixel. We expect this problem to be improved by using all the class labels in the face parsing dataset or by splitting the large area into multiple classes.

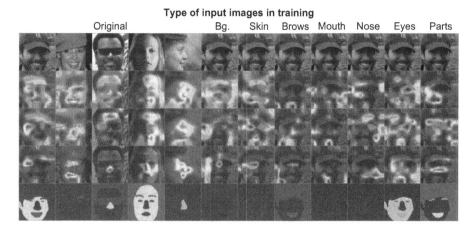

Fig. 7. Comparison of the visualization result. From top to bottom, input images, activation maps by Grad-CAM [19], Grad-CAM++ [4], Score-CAM [21], and the proposed method are shown. The activation maps show that the closer to red they are, the more important they are for identification.

8 Conclusion

This paper proposes an analysis method using face parsing to interpret the results of deep face recognition. The U-Net based face parsing model is designed specifically for low-quality images in the dataset for face recognition, and the semantic labels estimated by this model can be used to crop or mask some facial parts of the face image. Through the training and test of CNN models using facial parts, we have clarified what information CNN needs for face recognition and the surprising problem that high recognition accuracy can be achieved with only background and hair on several famous face image datasets. In addition, we have applied our face parsing method to a visualization method and demonstrated that it is more reliable than general visualization methods. In future work, we plan to develop a novel face recognition method combined with a face recognition model that requires only small facial parts and a face image generator that replaces the face with a non-existent face except for the facial parts.

References

1. Ahonen, T., Hadid, A., Pietikäinen, M.: Face recognition with local binary patterns. In: Pajdla, T., Matas, J. (eds.) ECCV 2004. LNCS, vol. 3021, pp. 469–481. Springer, Heidelberg (2004). https://doi.org/10.1007/978-3-540-24670-1_36
2. Ahonen, T., Hadid, A., Pietikäinen, M.: Face description with local binary patterns: application to face recognition. IEEE Trans. Pattern Anal. Mach. Intell. **28**(12), 2037–2041 (2006)
3. Benini, S., Khan, K., Leonardi, R., Mauro, M., Migliorati, P.: Face analysis through semantic face segmentation. Signal Process. Image Commun. **74**, 21–31 (2019)

4. Chattopadhay, A., Sarkar, A., Howlader, P., Balasubramanian, V.N.: Grad-CAM++: generalized gradient-based visual explanations for deep convolutional networks. In: Proceedings of the IEEE Winter Conference on Applications Computer Vision, pp. 839–847, June 2018

5. Deng, J., Guo, J., Xue, N., Zafeiriou, S.: ArcFace: additive angular margin loss for deep face recognition. In: Proceedings of the IEEE Conference on Computer Vision and Pattern Recognition, pp. 4685–4694, June 2019

6. Ding, C., Tao, D.: A comprehensive survey on pose-invariant face recognition. ACM Trans. Intell. Syst. Technol. **7**(3), 37:1-37:42 (2016)

7. He, K., Zhang, X., Ren, S., Sun, J.: Deep residual learning for image recognition. In: Proceedings of the IEEE Conference on Computer Vision and Pattern Recognition, pp. 770–778 (2016)

8. Huang, G.B., Ramesh, M., Berg, T., Learned-Miller, E.: Labeled faces in the wild: a database for studying face recognition in unconstrained environments. Technical report 7–49, University of Massachusetts, Amherst, October 2007

9. Jafri, R., Arabnia, H.R.: A survey of face recognition techniques. J. Inf. Process. Syst. **5**(2), 41–68 (2009)

10. Khan, K., Attique, M., Khan, R.U., Syed, I., Chung, T.S.: A multi-task framework for facial attributes classification through end-to-end face parsing and deep convolutional neural networks. Sensors **20**(2), 21–31 (2020)

11. Lee, C.H., Liu, Z., Wu, L., Luo, P.: MaskGAN: towards diverse and interactive facial image manipulation. In: Proceedings of the IEEE Conference on Computer Vision and Pattern Recognition, pp. 5548–5557, June 2020

12. Li, S., Jain, A.: Handbook of Face Recognition. Springer, London (2011). https://doi.org/10.1007/978-0-85729-932-1

13. Li, Y., Liu, S., Yang, J., Yang, M.H.: Generative face completion. In: Proceedings of the IEEE Conference on Computer Vision and Pattern Recognition, pp. 3911–3919, June 2017

14. Lin, J., Yang, D.C., Zeng, M., Wen, F., Yuan, L.: Face parsing with RoI tanh-warping. In: Proceedings of the IEEE Conference on Computer Vision and Pattern Recognition, pp. 5654–5663, June 2019

15. Liu, Y., Shi, H., Shen, H., Si, Y., Wang, X., Mei, T.: A new dataset and boundary-attention semantic segmentation for face parsing. In: Proceedings of the AAAI Conference on Artificial Intelligence, vol. 34, no. 7, pp. 11637–11644 (2020)

16. Moschoglou, S., Papaioannou, A., Sagonas, C., Deng, J., Kotsia, I., Zafeiriou, S.: AgeDB: the first manually collected, in-the-wild age database. In: Proceedings of the IEEE Conference on Computer Vision and Pattern Recognition Workshops, pp. 1997–2005, June 2017

17. Ronneberger, Olaf, Fischer, Philipp, Brox, Thomas: U-Net: convolutional networks for biomedical image segmentation. In: Navab, Nassir, Hornegger, Joachim, Wells, William M.., Frangi, Alejandro F.. (eds.) MICCAI 2015. LNCS, vol. 9351, pp. 234–241. Springer, Cham (2015). https://doi.org/10.1007/978-3-319-24574-4_28

18. Schroff, F., Kalenichenko, D., Philbin, J.: FaceNet: a unified embedding for face recognition and clustering. In: Proceedings of the IEEE Conference on Computer Vision and Pattern Recognition, pp. 815–823, June 2015

19. Selvaraju, R.R., Cogswell, M., Das, A., Vedantam, R., Parikh, D., Batra, D.: Grad-CAM: visual explanations from deep networks via gradient-based localization. In: Proceedings of the IEEE International Conference on Computer Vision, pp. 618–626, October 2017

20. Sengupta, S., Cheng, J., Castillo, C., Patel, V., Chellappa, R., Jacobs, D.: Frontal to profile face verification in the wild. In: Proceedings of the IEEE Winter Conference on Applications Computer Vision, pp. 1–9, February 2016

21. Wang, H., et al.: Score-CAM: score-weighted visual explanations for convolutional neural networks. In: Proceedings of the IEEE Conference on Computer Vision and Pattern Recognition Workshops, pp. 111–119, June 2020

22. Wang, M., Deng, W.: Deep face recognition: a survey. Neurocomputing **429**, 215–244 (2021)

23. Yi, D., Lei, Z., Liao, S., Li, S.Z.: Learning face representation from scratch. CoRR abs/1411.7923, November 2014

24. Zheng, T., Deng, W.: Cross-pose LFW: a database for studying cross-pose face recognition in unconstrained environments. Technical report, Beijing University of Posts and Telecommunications, February 2018

25. Zheng, T., Deng, W., Hu, J.: Cross-age LFW: a database for studying cross-age face recognition in unconstrained environments. CoRR abs/1708.08197, August 2017

NFW: Towards National and Individual Fairness in Face Recognition

Yufei Sun, Yong Li$^{(\boxtimes)}$, and Zhen Cui

Nanjing University of Science and Technology, Nanjing, China
{yufeisun,yong.li,zhen.cui}@njust.edu.cn

Abstract. Face recognition has been a long-standing research field and especially boosted by the development of convolutional neural network (CNN). However, existing CNN based FR methods are known to exhibit bias - subjects in a certain demographic group can be better recognized than other groups. While previous works mostly focus on the fairness among different races, we argue that it is essential and favorable to measure the national as well as individual fairness of existing FR methods. As to achieve this, we contribute a dataset called National Faces in the World (NFW) to measure the fairness of representative state-of-the-art FR methods across different countries and individuals. We make comprehensive comparisons on our proposed NFW dataset and illustrate different degrees of bias of existing FR methods. We hope to facilitate more fair FR research with the proposed NFW. The dataset will be public for the whole research community at https://github.com/God-BlessYou/NFW.

Keywords: Deep learning · Face recognition · Machine learning fairness

1 Introduction

With rapid progress of deep learning technology, face recognition (FR) has achieved great success [5,12,17,25]. Until now, the technology of face recognition can be found in our daily life almost everywhere. For example, paying by face is being popular and bringing many conveniences for people don't have to take cash and the only thing one need to do when shopping is showing his or her face in front of the webcam captured by the vending machine. Face recognition is also helpful in arresting crimes and public area supervision. Nevertheless, despite the high FR accuracy it brings, many research works have revealed that current FR methods are biased [1,2,15,19,23,30]. In other words, FR systems are known to exhibit discriminatory behaviors against certain demographic groups. As a whole, this can be classified into two cases including group fairness and individual fairness. When a group can be split into many subgroups, subgroup fairness can be defined similarly. In this work, we do not distinguish groups and subgroups for convenience.

© Springer Nature Switzerland AG 2022
C. Wallraven et al. (Eds.): ACPR 2021, LNCS 13188, pp. 540–553, 2022.
https://doi.org/10.1007/978-3-031-02375-0_40

Group fairness means that models should have stable performance with no respect to a specific group of samples, which is a challenge for many face recognition models. For instance, black people turn out to show lower performance than whites, and females often have lower accuracy than males while adults could be recognized more easily than the younger and the older. Besides, unfairness in the face recognition systems may lead to an enormous impact on daily life. For example, ethnic discrimination will arise when people from a specific demographic group are easy to be recognized as crimes than ones in other groups. From the legal perspective, there are several regulations to prevent such discrimination, such as Article 7 of the Universal Declaration on Human Rights, Article 14 of the European Convention of Human Rights, or the General Data Protection Regulation (GDPR) [24].

Individual fairness means that models are supposed to treat every individual equally. For face recognition, people with similar image distribution should get similar performance. The problem of individual fairness in face recognition has been proposed earlier [30], but few research efforts have been made in the face recognition field due that the distributions of images from different identities vary dramatically both in quantity and quality. Thus, the evaluation dataset on individual fairness in face recognition is still a vacancy in the research community.

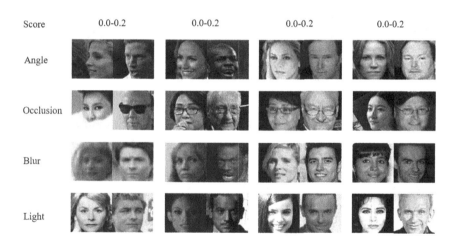

Fig. 1. Images with different quality scores in NFW. The quality scores are normalized between [0,1]. The higher the value, the better the image quality. We consider four aspects of angle, occlusion, blur, and light.

The causes of bias in face recognition are various. From the perspective of datasets, models could encode task-independent information of samples in training sets. Generally speaking, different groups of people in a dataset often tend to have different distributions of samples, which makes deep learning models perform differently on these groups. For example, models inherently encode gender information during training which has nothing to do with the face recognition task. On the other hand, deep learning algorithms themselves are usually hard to learn an unbiased feature space due to the non-linearity activation function applied in the convolutional neural network. The other reason that leads to a biased model is the nature of people. According to the 2019 National Institute of Standards and Technology (NIST) reports on face recognition [8], people of some special demographics (such as African) are inherently difficult to recognize for the color of facial skin covers some distinguishable face feature.

While previous works of fairness literature mainly focus on races [6,7,26,27], genders [1,15] and ages [13], we argue that people from different countries also give different performances and that people even from the same nationality with similar image quality also don't lead to similar accuracy in the evaluation of face recognition models. For example, the TPR of identities from Spain is usually the highest and that of people from China is the lowest over 20 countries in our experiments. To boost the fairness research both in quality and granularity, we build a benchmark for fair face recognition which contains 1K identities from 20 countries based on which we validate the existence of bias of existing state-of-the-art recognition models in both national and individual levels.

The motivations of evaluating national and individual fairness are as follows: (1) We aim to encourage more fairness research in more various levels, beside the ethnicities/races and genders. (2) In most cases, similar individuals should be treated equally. For example, in the case of paying by face, faces with similar poses are supposed to give similar recognition accuracy. Otherwise, it may bring some people inconvenience. (3) From the other perspective, by realizing individual fairness, group fairness can be further improved when individuals from different groups have similar poses, emotions, and so on. (4) To the best of our knowledge, there are few datasets that can be used to evaluate individual fairness in the face recognition research community.

Our main contributions are two folds: (1) We propose an evaluation dataset called NFW for face recognition to measure the national and individual-level bias of recognition models. And to the best of our knowledge, we are the first to explore and uncover the bias of face recognition models in the granularity of nationality and individuals. (2) We do extensive experiments to make comprehensive comparisons of several state-of-the-art face recognition algorithms on the proposed NFW dataset and show their different degrees of bias.

2   Related Work

Biases in Face Recognition. Several recent studies have uncovered common biases of deep models for face recognition. The NIST2019 Face Recognition Vendor Test (FRVT) [8] reported that black men invariably gave lower false-negative identification rates than white women and women invariably gave higher false-negative rates than men. Moreover, people with colored skin were inherently difficult to recognize for existing algorithms, and better image quality reduced the false-negative rates and performance discrepancy. Besides, adults were invariably simpler to recognize than the younger and the older. Wang et al. [27] found people with colored skin tended to be easily impacted by noise, especially for African and Asian. Xu et al. [29] treated the normalized classifier matrix as class centers and mitigated racial biases by keeping a consistent FPR on the classifier for every training sample. Li et al. [16] utilized racial information and mitigated racial biases by incorporating face recognition and race classification tasks with several asymmetrical transformer modules. [1] found a significant difference in the recognition accuracy of DCNNs on male and female faces. They analyzed the gender inequality in face recognition accuracy and found that the phenomenon of the impostor and genuine distributions for women shifting closer towards each other was general across datasets of African-American, Caucasian, and Asian faces. In other words, deep models even trained on a balanced dataset still suffered from bias. GenderShades [4] explored gender classification on African faces to further scholarship on the impact of phenotype on gender classification and found that male subjects were more accurately classified than female subjects and lighter subjects were more accurately classified than darker individuals.

Datasets for Face Recognition. Face recognition models benefit from large-scale training databases. Some large-scale face datasets have been proposed for training efficient face recognition models. Commonly used MS1M [9] contains 10 million images of 100K subjects, and all the images were downloaded from websites with unbalanced gender and age distribution so models trained on the dataset inevitably learn biased features. GlobalFace and BalancedFace [26] are the other two popular training sets. GlobalFace has more than 2.6 million images of people around the world and the population is similar to the real-world distribution, while BalancedFace contains 1.3 million face images of four races including African, Indian, Caucasian, and Asian. Each race of the dataset has an equal number of identities and images. Frequently used evaluations of face recognition includes LFW [11], MegaFace [14] and IJB [18,28]. The main metric of these face benchmarks is the accuracy of face verification. AgeDB [20] has 16488 images with age and gender labels and is often used for age-invariant face recognition. CALFW [32] has 3K front faces with large inner-class discrepancy along ages. CPLFW [31] is composed of 3K front faces with large inner-class variance along with poses. RFW [27] is the most relevant dataset with our NFW. It is a popular dataset to perform fairness measurement among four different races (African, Indian, Caucasian, and Asian) with about 3K identities and 10K images each race which leads to 3K hard positive pairs as well as negative pairs. BFW [22] contains eight different demographics of ethnic attributes and is also frequently used to evaluate race bias in face recognition. However, none of the above face benchmarks is able to measure the bias on the national or individual level in face recognition, and the lack of such benchmark limits the research community to develop recognition models with high accuracy as well as low discrepancy over different groups and individuals of people. To this end, we contribute a dataset called National faces in the World (NFW) on which we validate the existence of bias of existing face recognition models. It is worth noted that the proposed dataset can be used to perform the evaluation of individual fairness as well as national fairness because of our special building strategies.

The rest parts of the paper are as follows. In Sect. 3, we go into details of the proposed dataset and make a comprehensive analysis of its statistical attributes. In Sect. 4, we evaluate several state-of-the-art face recognition models and show their different degrees of bias both on the nationality and individual levels. In Sect. 5, we draw the overall conclusions and show some promising research directions on NFW in the future.

3   NFW: National Face In-the-World

3.1   Image Collection

Intuitively, there are many ways to build a face verification benchmark with country labels. For example, one may match parts of the popular BalancedFace and GlobalFace [26] datasets with country labels as an augmentation. However, it's non-trivial for two main reasons: 1) there are few (about 4K) identities in BalancedFace that have country information according to our scrapping result from IMDB[1] website. 2) most people come from power countries like American which means that the number of countries will be extremely small and we are not able to make overall evaluation on as many countries as we expect. To overcome these challenges, we collected totally about 17 million faces on the internet. These images belong to 360K identities around the world. The IMDB website provides helpful information about the nationality of some celebrities. After filtering identities with unknown nationality and manually replacing city labels with responding countries, we got 5.8 million images of 40K identities from more than 200 countries.

3.2   Image Filtering

Then we remove the same identities with BalancedFace [26] using a ResNet101 backbone model to calculate the cosine similarity between two identities based on the extracted mean 512-dimension embeddings of images from the two identities. Two identities are judged as the same person as long as the cosine similarity of the embeddings of them is larger than a predefined threshold. Empirically, we found that when the threshold is set to 0.3, there are already many wrong matched identities. So we chose 0.3 as the cosine similarity threshold to clean our collected images. After the collision, we got 30139 identities that have no overlapping with BalancedFace, and we will give the collided identities list in NFW so that models trained on other datasets can also perform the fairness evaluation.

---

[1] http://imdb.com/.

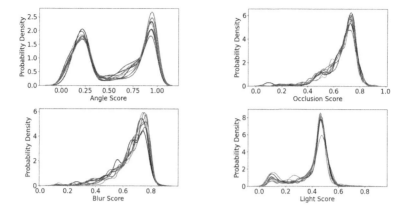

Fig. 2. The similar distribution of quality scores for 10 randomly selected countries in NFW. To make the quality distribution more similar across different countries, we filter images with all 4 quality scores in predefined intervals. For the score of angle, we choose a mixed gaussian with two means 0.2 and 0.9.

Our goal is to build a benchmark that can be used to perform national and individual fairness evaluations simultaneously. So we must choose identities with similar image quality and at the same time, we are supposed to reduce or eliminate the effect of different gender and age distribution. Besides, we must keep the balance of identity and image numbers in selected countries. Firstly, to keep the similar distribution of image qualities for each individual, we measure image qualities with models from [21]. The image qualities take 4 factors into consideration, i.e. angle, occlusion, blur, and light. The quality score ranges from 0.0 to 1.0 for all 4 dimensions. Figure 1 shows some images under different qualities and Fig. 2 shows the quality distribution of 10 randomly selected countries. By statistical comparison and analysis, we found that there is a large discrepancy for the whole collected database in different countries but for the first 30 countries, the deviation of image qualities can be ignored. So we chose identities from the first 30 countries as candidates.

We intuitively found that the light score is between 0.4 and 0.6 for almost all the images and the discrepancy of images with occlusion, blur or light score in [0.4, 1.0] can be ignored. The main factor of image quality is the angle, or in other words, the pose.

3.3   Identity Selection

To avoid saturated performance and reduce interaction of quality metrics mentioned above, we first select 15 images with angle quality in (0, 0.3] and 15 images with angle quality in (0.3, 1.0] for each identity while keeping the other three quality scores in [0.4, 1.0]. An identity is abandoned if there are not so many images satisfied. After filtering images with quality score, there are a total of 353425 images of 10329 identities left. It is not enough to just filter identities with image quality. To reduce the effect of other factors, we keep the gender distribution balanced during the building of NFW, and we estimate face attributes with tools from [10]. Besides, every country has a similar age distribution and most of the selected images are between 25 and 55 years old, which means that images in each country are subject to independent identical distribution along with age. Last but not least, we manually remove noisy samples of each identity, and those with too many noisy images are simply dropped. After removing countries whose identity numbers are less than 50, we finally get 20 countries in total. Figure 3 shows the age distribution in the final countries.

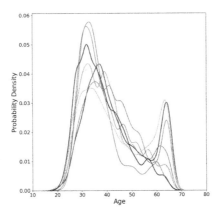

Fig. 3. Age distribution of 10 randomly selected countries in NFW. To reduce the interaction of age and country, we further consider the similarity of age distribution in different countries. Notably, the age estimation can be of great uncertainty and intuitively faces in an age interval with length 10 could be extremely similar.

Considering the balance of gender, identity, and image number during the evaluation of national fairness, although there are so many countries to which the collected identities and images belong, more than 60% of them are American and English and there won't be enough countries to perform the fairness evaluation if the threshold of the number of identities in each country is too high (e.g. 100). To keep a balanced identity and image number across countries, Our final NFW dataset contains 25049 face images of 1K identities with 15 to 30 images for each identity and 50 identities for each country with close numbers of women and men. Table 1 shows the number of male and female identities in each country.

Table 1. The number of males and females in every country.

Country	Male	Female	Images	Country	Male	Female	Images
USA	25	25	1272	China	27	23	1165
UK	25	25	1241	Mexico	25	25	1267
Canada	25	25	1235	Korea	25	25	1179
France	25	25	1255	Japan	26	24	1250
Germany	25	25	1264	Philippines	25	25	1303
India	25	25	1299	Brazil	25	25	1245
Italy	25	25	1232	Sweden	26	24	1272
Australia	25	25	1295	Russian	25	25	1229
Spain	25	25	1293	Argentina	25	25	1240
Poland	25	25	1253	Czech	25	25	1260

3.4 Pair Selection

For individual fairness evaluation, all the images under an identity contribute to his/her own positive pairs, and we simply regard images from two different identities as negative pairs. In this way, we finally got 308987 positive pairs and about 0.31 billion negative pairs for face verification. As for national fairness, to avoid saturated performance caused by the limited number of identities and image pairs, we chose some hard pairs with a ResNet101 model pretrained on large-scale face dataset, calculating the cosine similarities of all the candidate pairs based on their 512-dimension embeddings. Specifically, we follow RFW [27] to chose 3000 positive pairs and 3000 negative pairs. For each identity, we chose 60 hard positive pairs according to their cosine similarity. And we chose 1500 easy negative pairs and 1500 hard ones for each country in the same way. Figure 4 shows the distribution of cosine similarity of negative pairs in the countries and Fig. 5 shows some hard pairs in NFW.

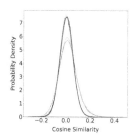

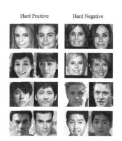

Fig. 4. The similar distribution of cosine similarity of negative pairs in 10 random selected countries.

Fig. 5. Sample of hard pairs in NFW.

4   Experiments on NFW

Experimental Settings. For national fairness, We chose several state-of-the-art face recognition models as baselines including ArcFace [5], CosFace [25], Xu et al. [29], RL-RBN-arc and RL-RBN-cos [26]. For Individual fairness, we make detailed comparisons on ArcFace, CosFace, and Xu et al. [29]. For the model of RL-RBN, we use their pre-trained models and for others, we employed the ResNet34 network. All models are trained on BUPT-BalancedFace. The learning rate starts from 0.1 and is multiplied by 0.1 at epoch 16, 24, 28, and the training process is stopped at epoch 32. We use SGD [3] optimizer with a batch size of 512, and the weight decay is set to 0.0005.

Evaluation for National Bias. The accuracy and ROC are two common metrics for face verification. The TPR (True Positive Rate) is defined as the ratio of positive pairs truly predicted to the total number of positive pairs. And the FPR (False Positive Rate) is defined as the ratio of negative pairs predicted as positives to the total number of negative pairs. For national bias, we follow RFW [27] using the Standard deviation (Std) to measure the discrepancy of recognition accuracy in different countries.

Evaluation for Individual Bias. Calculating the Std of accuracies for all the identities is improper to measure the individual bias because the number of identities inherently decreases the Std value. So, the individual bias is alternatively measured as the Std of the individual TPRs and FPRs. Given a specified FPR (global FPR), we can calculate the threshold of cosine similarity from all the negative pairs. Then we can get the individual TPRs and FPRs by comparing the similarities of individual pairs with the threshold. Finally, we are able to calculate the Std of individual TPRs and FPRs. Note that before calculating the Std of individual FPRs, we must divide the individual FPRs by the specified global FPR because the individual FPRs are usually much less than 1 and have the same magnitude as the global FPR.

4.1   Results on National Bias

Table 2 shows the mean and std of accuracy for the evaluated models. The mean accuracies are similar to those on RFW but the Std is much larger, and maybe this is because race or ethnicity is a coarse-grained definition for demographics and fails to fully reflect the real-world population distribution at a national level. What's more, the discrepancy of specific demographics is actually decreased because of the large number of samples in each race. Figure 6 shows the mean ROC of each model. The overall results are consistent with previous works of literature for racial bias.

Table 2. The **Mean** and **Std** of verification accuracies (%).

Country	ArcFace [5]	CosFace [25]	CIFP [29]	RL-RBN-arc [26]	RL-RBN-cos [26]
USA	97.12	**97.40**	97.27	94.93	95.62
UK	98.40	**98.53**	98.32	95.08	96.37
Canada	97.15	**97.85**	97.73	93.15	95.82
France	97.58	97.10	**98.70**	95.70	95.67
Germany	97.53	97.72	**98.73**	94.48	95.38
India	96.73	96.58	**97.52**	95.62	95.25
Italy	97.18	**98.23**	98.10	94.13	93.85
Australia	98.12	97.70	**98.30**	93.88	95.32
Spain	97.13	**98.00**	97.97	94.57	94.63
Poland	94.67	96.20	**96.38**	89.02	91.68
China	93.55	94.47	**95.83**	89.03	89.37
Mexico	96.52	96.02	**97.75**	92.52	93.05
Korea	90.50	90.23	**93.73**	86.65	86.87
Japan	96.42	**97.32**	96.05	94.70	93.02
Philippines	94.17	**94.93**	93.82	91.17	91.57
Brazil	93.02	93.95	**94.13**	90.68	90.82
Sweden	96.23	97.72	**97.73**	94.03	94.07
Russian	97.77	97.90	**98.37**	93.78	95.33
Argentina	94.78	94.65	**97.58**	93.57	94.65
Czech	96.20	**96.57**	96.45	93.22	94.30
Mean↑	96.04	96.40	**97.08**	93.01	93.63
Std↓	1.95	2.00	**1.48**	2.40	2.40

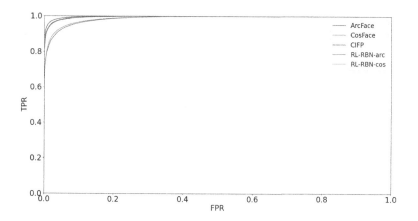

Fig. 6. The national mean ROC of each method.

4.2   Results on Individual Bias

Because there are few research works on the individual bias in face recognition, we go into more details on TPR and FPR as well as the Std of them, which helps to validate the existence of individual bias and make comprehensive comparisons on the selected models.

Table 3. The **thresholds** of cosine similarity for each method at different global FPRs.

Global FPR	ArcFace [5]	CosFace [25]	Xu et al. [29]
1e$-$3	0.32	0.26	**0.19**
1e$-$4	0.40	0.33	**0.24**
1e$-$5	0.46	0.39	**0.30**
1e$-$6	0.51	0.44	**0.34**
1e$-$7	0.55	0.47	**0.38**

Table 3 shows the thresholds of cosine similarity of negative pairs calculated by each model at different global FPRs. The lower the thresholds are, the stronger power the models have to distinguish similar negative pairs. We chose a minimum FPR as 1e–7 for that we have a total of 0.31 billion negative pairs. We make a comparison of thresholds under different FPRs and find that the thresholds vary dramatically across different models, which means our NFW dataset can better distinguish the performance of similar face recognition models.

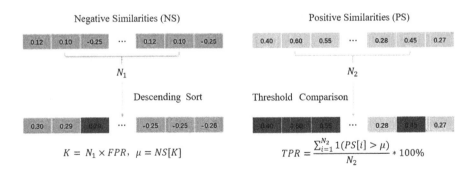

Fig. 7. An illustration for calculating individual TPR at a given FPR. Given FPR = 0.0001, then K = $N_1 \times 0.0001$, and $\mu = NS[K]$ is the threshold for the expected FPR, so TPR@FPR can be calculated by the threshold.

Table 4 shows the Mean and Std of individual TPRs of each model at different global FPRs. Steps to calculate individual TPR at a specific FPR are illustrated in Fig. 7. Generally speaking. The mean TPR on NFW is close to RFW, while

Table 4. The **Mean/Std of individual TPRs** for each method at different global FPRs.

Global FPR	RL-RBN-arc [26]	RL-RBN-cos [26]	CIFP [29]
1e−3	99.67/0.7	99.77/0.4	**99.88/0.27**
1e−4	97.61/2.73	98.33/1.81	**99.03/1.08**
1e−5	91.64/6.24	93.46/4.86	**95.71/3.00**
1e−6	80.96/10.24	83.72/8.95	**88.64/5.85**
1e−7	68.52/13.25	73.59/11.71	**76.71/9.6**

the standard deviation is much higher. Besides, it becomes higher when the global FPR is getting lower for all the evaluated models, which validates the challenging fact of our NFW benchmark.

Table 5. The **Mean/Std of individual FPRs** for each method at different global FPRs.

Global FPR	RL-RBN-arc [26]	RLRBN-cos [26]	CIFP [29]
1e−3	1.0054/0.62	1.0049/0.63	**1.0046/0.52**
1e−4	1.0079/0.98	1.0084/1.00	**1.0043/0.89**
1e−5	1.0142/1.55	1.0139/1.57	**1.0071/1.44**
1e−6	1.0274/2.67	1.0300/**2.44**	**1.0156**/2.59
1e−7	1.0632/5.14	1.0358/4.88	**1.0286/4.80**

Table 5 shows the Mean and Std of individual FPRs (divided by global FPR) of each model at different global FPRs. We can see clearly that the FPRs of all the models are almost the same given the global FPR. This is because the threshold of cosine similarity is chosen by the k-th larger negative similarity (Fig. 7), and the relative similarities of most pairs will be kept regardless of specific models. On the other hand, the standard deviation is close to that of their TPRs when the global FPR is the same, which validates the advantage of the balance between positive pairs and negative pairs in our NFW dataset.

5   Conclusions and Future Work

In this paper, we propose to expand the fairness research area with national fairness in face recognition. And we release a face dataset NFW to measure the bias of face recognition models at both national and individual levels. Our comprehensive experiments show the different degrees of bias in several state-of-the-art recognition algorithms. Besides, because most of the training data have no label of countries, unsupervised methods are showing excellent performance recently in various vision tasks, which will be our future exploration. We hope NFW can draw more research attention to national and individual fairness and we believe it will boost more efficient and fair algorithms in the research community.

References

1. Albiero, V., Zhang, K., Bowyer, K.W.: How does gender balance in training data affect face recognition accuracy? In: 2020 IEEE International Joint Conference on Biometrics (IJCB), pp. 1–10. IEEE (2020)
2. Barocas, S., Hardt, M., Narayanan, A.: Fairness in machine learning. Nips Tutor. **1**, 2 (2017)
3. Bottou, L.: Large-scale machine learning with stochastic gradient descent. In: Lechevallier, Y., Saporta, G. (eds.) Proceedings of COMPSTAT 2010, pp. 177–186. Springer, Heidelberg (2010). https://doi.org/10.1007/978-3-7908-2604-3_16
4. Buolamwini, J., Gebru, T.: Gender shades: intersectional accuracy disparities in commercial gender classification. In: Conference on Fairness, Accountability and Transparency, pp. 77–91. PMLR (2018)
5. Deng, J., Guo, J., Xue, N., Zafeiriou, S.: ArcFace: additive angular margin loss for deep face recognition. In: Proceedings of the IEEE/CVF Conference on Computer Vision and Pattern Recognition, pp. 4690–4699 (2019)
6. Gong, S., Liu, X., Jain, A.K.: Jointly de-biasing face recognition and demographic attribute estimation. In: Vedaldi, A., Bischof, H., Brox, T., Frahm, J.-M. (eds.) ECCV 2020. LNCS, vol. 12374, pp. 330–347. Springer, Cham (2020). https://doi.org/10.1007/978-3-030-58526-6_20
7. Gong, S., Liu, X., Jain, A.K.: Mitigating face recognition bias via group adaptive classifier. arXiv preprint arXiv:2006.07576 (2020)
8. Grother, P., Ngan, M., Hanaoka, K.: Face Recognition Vendor Test (FVRT): Part 3, Demographic Effects. National Institute of Standards and Technology (2019)
9. Guo, Y., Zhang, L., Hu, Y., He, X., Gao, J.: MS-Celeb-1M: a dataset and benchmark for large-scale face recognition. In: Leibe, B., Matas, J., Sebe, N., Welling, M. (eds.) ECCV 2016. LNCS, vol. 9907, pp. 87–102. Springer, Cham (2016). https://doi.org/10.1007/978-3-319-46487-9_6
10. Han, H., Jain, A.K., Wang, F., Shan, S., Chen, X.: Heterogeneous face attribute estimation: a deep multi-task learning approach. IEEE Trans. Pattern Anal. Mach. Intell. **40**(11), 2597–2609 (2017)
11. Huang, G.B., Mattar, M., Berg, T., Learned-Miller, E.: Labeled faces in the wild: a database for studying face recognition in unconstrained environments. In: Workshop on Faces in 'Real-Life' Images: Detection, Alignment, and Recognition (2008)
12. Huang, Y., et al.: Curricularface: adaptive curriculum learning loss for deep face recognition. In: Proceedings of the IEEE/CVF Conference on Computer Vision and Pattern Recognition, pp. 5901–5910 (2020)
13. Huang, Z., Zhang, J., Shan, H.: When age-invariant face recognition meets face age synthesis: a multi-task learning framework. arXiv preprint arXiv:2103.01520 (2021)
14. Kemelmacher-Shlizerman, I., Seitz, S.M., Miller, D., Brossard, E.: The megaface benchmark: 1 million faces for recognition at scale. In: Proceedings of the IEEE Conference on Computer Vision and Pattern Recognition, pp. 4873–4882 (2016)
15. Krishnan, A., Almadan, A., Rattani, A.: Understanding fairness of gender classification algorithms across gender-race groups. arXiv preprint arXiv:2009.11491 (2020)

16. Li, Y., Sun, Y., Cui, Z., Shan, S., Yang, J.: Learning fair face representation with progressive cross transformer. arXiv preprint arXiv:2108.04983 (2021)
17. Liu, W., Wen, Y., Yu, Z., Li, M., Raj, B., Song, L.: SphereFace: deep hypersphere embedding for face recognition. In: Proceedings of the IEEE Conference on Computer Vision and Pattern Recognition, pp. 212–220 (2017)
18. Maze, B., et al.: IARPA Janus benchmark-C: face dataset and protocol. In: 2018 International Conference on Biometrics (ICB), pp. 158–165. IEEE (2018)
19. Mehrabi, N., Morstatter, F., Saxena, N., Lerman, K., Galstyan, A.: A survey on bias and fairness in machine learning. arXiv preprint arXiv:1908.09635 (2019)
20. Moschoglou, S., Papaioannou, A., Sagonas, C., Deng, J., Kotsia, I., Zafeiriou, S.: AgeDB: the first manually collected, in-the-wild age database. In: Proceedings of the IEEE Conference on Computer Vision and Pattern Recognition Workshops, pp. 51–59 (2017)
21. Ou, F.Z., et al.: SDD-FIQA: unsupervised face image quality assessment with similarity distribution distance. arXiv preprint arXiv:2103.05977 (2021)
22. Robinson, J.P., Livitz, G., Henon, Y., Qin, C., Fu, Y., Timoner, S.: Face recognition: too bias, or not too bias? In: Proceedings of the IEEE/CVF Conference on Computer Vision and Pattern Recognition Workshops, pp. 0–1 (2020)
23. Terhörst, P., et al.: A comprehensive study on face recognition biases beyond demographics. arXiv preprint arXiv:2103.01592 (2021)
24. Voigt, P., von dem Bussche, A.: The EU General Data Protection Regulation (GDPR). Springer, Cham (2017). https://doi.org/10.1007/978-3-319-57959-7
25. Wang, H., et al.: CosFace: large margin cosine loss for deep face recognition. In: Proceedings of the IEEE Conference on Computer Vision and Pattern Recognition, pp. 5265–5274 (2018)
26. Wang, M., Deng, W.: Mitigating bias in face recognition using skewness-aware reinforcement learning. In: Proceedings of the IEEE/CVF Conference on Computer Vision and Pattern Recognition, pp. 9322–9331 (2020)
27. Wang, M., Deng, W., Hu, J., Tao, X., Huang, Y.: Racial faces in the wild: reducing racial bias by information maximization adaptation network. In: Proceedings of the IEEE/CVF International Conference on Computer Vision, pp. 692–702 (2019)
28. Whitelam, C., et al.: IARPA Janus benchmark-B face dataset. In: Proceedings of the IEEE Conference on Computer Vision and Pattern Recognition Workshops, pp. 90–98 (2017)
29. Xu, X., et al.: Consistent instance false positive improves fairness in face recognition. In: Proceedings of the IEEE/CVF Conference on Computer Vision and Pattern Recognition, pp. 578–586 (2021)
30. Zemel, R., Wu, Y., Swersky, K., Pitassi, T., Dwork, C.: Learning fair representations. In: International Conference on Machine Learning, pp. 325–333. PMLR (2013)
31. Zheng, T., Deng, W.: Cross-pose LFW: a database for studying cross-pose face recognition in unconstrained environments. Technical report, Beijing University of Posts and Telecommunications, 5 (2018)
32. Zheng, T., Deng, W., Hu, J.: Cross-age LFW: a database for studying cross-age face recognition in unconstrained environments. arXiv preprint arXiv:1708.08197 (2017)

Adversarial Learning and Networks

Unsupervised Fabric Defect Detection Based on DCGAN with Component-Encoder

Zhoufeng Liu[✉], Chengli Gao[✉], Chunlei Li, Ning Huang, and Zijing Guo

Zhongyuan University of Technology, Zhengzhou 45007, China
{lzf,gaochengli}@zut.edu.cn

Abstract. Deep learning technology has been proven applicable in fabric defect detection, but the detection performance relies on the large-scale labeled training sets. However, it is a tedious task to construct these annotated datasets in the industrial production line. To alleviate this issue, an unsupervised fabric defect detection model based on generative adversarial network (GAN) with component-encoder is proposed. Firstly, a component encoder is integrated into the deep convolutional generative adversarial network (DCGAN) for easily training the acquired positive sample image instead of random noise, and it is easier for the model to fit the data distribution of the samples. And to ensure the authenticity of the reconstructed image, two loss functions are adopted for the original DCGAN. In the testing stage, the test image patches are input into the trained model to generate the normal image patches. Finally, the residual image obtained by subtracting the original image from the reconstructed image is segmented to localize the defect region. Experimental results on the fabric dataset demonstrate the proposed model can locate the defect region well.

Keywords: Fabric defect detection · DCGAN · Unsupervised learning · Encoder · Image processing

1 Introduction

Fabric defects have a negative impact on the fabric quality, which may result in the economic losses. Therefore, fabric defect detection plays an essential role in the control of production quality [1–3]. However, the traditional way of manual detection suffers from the low detection accuracy and speed. In addition, the detection performance is greatly influenced by subjective factors, such as personal experience, fatigue. The detection method based on machine vision provides a promising solution.

Traditional automatic detection methods usually apply image texture analysis techniques to detect the abnormal regions, such as structural-based method [4], statistical-based method [5], and filter-based method [6]. Structural methods commonly regard the texture model as a composition of texture primitives which are

© Springer Nature Switzerland AG 2022
C. Wallraven et al. (Eds.): ACPR 2021, LNCS 13188, pp. 557–568, 2022.
https://doi.org/10.1007/978-3-031-02375-0_41

arranged by certain spatial placement rules, thus the defect detection can be verified by inferencing the arrangement rules of texture primitives. Statistical methods utilized the spatial distribution feature of gray values to localize the defects, such as histogram statistics [7,8], autocorrelation functions [9,10], co-occurrence matrices [11] and local binary patterns (LBP) [12], etc. Filter-based approaches transform the fabric image into the frequency domain, and use the energy of the filter responses to detect defects. However, the fabric images often suffer from the severe noise, deformation and scale-variety [13]. Thus, these factors may lead the above detection methods to have low detection accuracy, and lack of self-adaptivity.

Deep learning-based technology had a strong feature learning ability, which has attracted more and more researcher's attention. In recent years, methods based on deep learning have been performed remarkably in image classification and object detection [14–18], which have provided a new solution for defect detection. Many scholars have exploited some methods of deep learning for defect location. Compared with the traditional method, the method deep learning-based uses multilayer neural networks to automatically learn high-level features from a large amount of training data.

Generally speaking, defect detection methods based on deep learning technology can be categorized into three classes, according to their learning strategies: (i) supervised learning-based methods, (ii) transfer learning-based methods, and (iii) unsupervised learning-based methods. For supervised learning, Wang et al. [19] applied the sliding window detection method to identify the defect by position. Although the accuracy rate is high, the detection speed is slow due to the use of sliding window traversal. In [20], Chen et al. used deep convolutional neural networks (CNNs) combined with SSD, YOLO and other network methods to build a cascaded detection network. Although the above methods have achieved good defect detection performance, supervised learning training requires a large number of non-defect and defect samples, so this method is more suitable for surface defect detection task with a large number of samples. Transfer learning pretrains a model through a common large dataset, then fine-tunes it using specific defective samples. Gopalakrishnan et al. [21] employed a Deep Convolutional Neural Network (DCNN) trained on the 'big data' ImageNet database, and transfer that learning to automatically detect cracks in surface pavement images. Zhu et al. [22] presented a vision-based method for bridge defects detection using transfer learning and convolutional neural networks (CNNs), which could automatically analyze and identify a large volume of collected images.

The above work did achieve good performance, but it depended on a large number of labeled datasets. Due to all kinds of fabric style and the variety of defect pattern, it is difficult to collect and label large-scale image sets. Compared with supervised learning, unsupervised learning does not need a large number of labeled samples for training. Unsupervised learning, which can realize detection under the premise of only normal training dataset, has strong adaptability.

GAN [23] is an unsupervised learning method proposed by Goodfellow et al. It has been proved that it can be used in the task of surface defect detection [24–26]. In [24], the author used positive samples to realize the defect detection process by artificially generating defects. Although this method achieves good detection performance, since real defects are different in class and scale, artificially generated defects may not be able to simulate real defects. In some defect detection scenarios, it may lead to a decrease in defect detection performance. Liu et al. [27] proposed a based on multistage GAN fabric defect detection model. Because the defect detection part of the model is still in a supervised learning mode, the problem of data annotation still needs to be considered. Thus, it is difficult to consider the actual application scenarios.

Considering the above situations, we propose an unsupervised fabric surface defect detection method based on DCGAN with component-encoder. The model does not need to labeled dataset and only uses positive samples for training. The purpose of introducing the encoder component is to use fabric samples as input instead of random noise, which makes model training easier and fits sample data distribution faster. At the same time, in order to generate more realistic image, feature loss and reconstruction loss are added into the model on the basis of the original loss function. Firstly, the proposed fabric defect detection model is trained on non-defective samples in the training phase. The trained model can reconstruct the input samples without defects. Then, in the test phase, the model only learns the data distribution of the non-defective fabric image, so it is impossible to reconstruct the defective position for the input defective image. Finally, the difference image between the reconstructed image and the original image is obtained, and the defective area is segmented by threshold segmentation.

The contributions of this paper are as follows:

1. The unsupervised defect detection model is adopted in this paper. This makes a sense for industrial sites, where defect detection and labeling are difficult.
2. A component-encoder is added to the deep convolution generative adversarial network, which takes the positive sample image as input to enable the model to capture the data distribution and reconstruct the image at a faster speed.
3. In the original training model, feature loss and reconstruction loss are added to make the reconstructed image of the model more realistic.

2   Proposed Methods

In this section, we first introduce fabric defect detection pipeline before discussing the details of the two main modules: 1) deep convolutional generative adversarial network with encoder component, 2) image defect segmentation. And next, the training objectives of the network model are also detailed.

2.1   Framework Description

As noted above, in real-world applications, insufficient labeled datasets are significant challenges for fabric detection methods. Given such circumstances, we propose a based on DCGAN with a component-encoder method for fabric defect detection, which is capable of training a detection model on existing defect-free fabric samples and segments defect in the test phase.

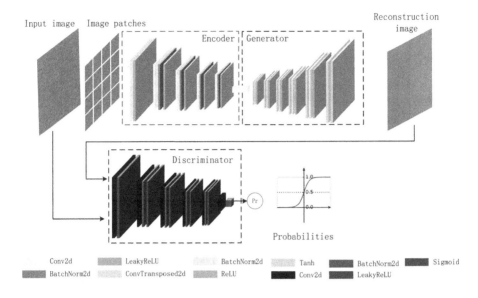

Fig. 1. The training framework of the proposed model.

Figure 1 depicts the proposed fabric defect detection training model. The input of the model is one defect-free fabric dataset. Specifically, we design a DCGAN with an encoder component for unsupervised defect detection. The purpose of adding an encoder component to the DCGAN model is to train the network with an image as input, not noise. The encoder can compress the input image into latent space representation. DCGAN takes these potential spatial representations with image information as input, which makes the whole network model easier to train. At the same time, to make the model reconstruct a more realistic image, in addition to the original adversarial loss, feature loss and reconstruction loss are added.

The reconstructed image is shown in Fig. 2. The clear texture can be seen from the reconstructed image in Fig. 2. So the reconstruction ability of the model is confirmed.

Figure 3 describes the testing phase of the model. As we can see, in addition to the discriminator, only the generator and encoder participate in the test phase. Firstly, the input image is reconstructed by the trained-well model. Secondly, the reconstructed image is compared with the original input image to obtain a residual image. Finally, through threshold segmentation, the final defect detection result is obtained. Threshold segmentation will be introduced in details in the experiment part. The reconstructed defective image is shown in Fig. 4.

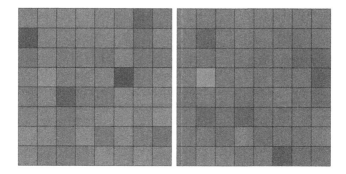

Fig. 2. Reconstruction of non-defective image.

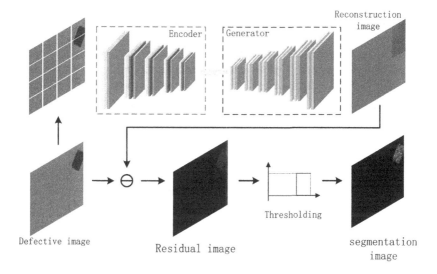

Fig. 3. The test framework of the proposed model.

Fig. 4. The reconstructed defective image.

Generally speaking, the whole experiment process can be described as follows. Firstly, the positive sample image is input into the network model, and the model is trained to reconstruct the image. Then, in the test phase, the image with the defect is input into the trained model. Since the model only learned the positive sample, it can not reconstruct the defective position. Finally, the residual image is obtained by subtracting the original image and the reconstructed image, and the defect is segmented by threshold segmentation method.

2.2 Training Objective

To work out the goal of training, in addition to the original adversarial loss, there are also feature loss and reconstruction loss. The loss functions are presented as follows:

Adversarial Loss. As shown in Eq. (1), this loss function reduces the difference between the input image x and generated fake image $G(x')$ as much as possible when training generator G, whereas discriminator D distinguishes the original input image x, and fake image $G(x')$, generated by generator G as much as possible. The goal is to minimize the adverse loss of generator G and maximize the adverse loss of discriminator D. The adversarial loss can be expressed as:

$$L_{adv}(G, D) = E_{x \sim P_x(x)}\left[\log D(x)\right] + E_{x' \sim P_{x'}(x')}\left[\log\left(1 - D\left(G\left(x'\right)\right)\right)\right] \quad (1)$$

where E represents the expected distribution, P_x represents the distribution of training samples of real image, x' represents the output of the real image x after being encoded by the encoder, $P_{x'}$ represents the distribution of x', $D(x)$ denotes the probability from the real image distribution $P_x(x)$.

Feature Loss. In [28], the authors have proposed a new objective function. The motivation is to make the images generated realistic by the generator. The features of the middle layer after the discriminator and the real images after the discriminant network are the same as far as possible. Based on this idea, it is assumed that f is the feature map to judge the output of the network middle layer. And then the feature loss function is:

$$L_{fea} = \|f_x - f_{x'}\|_2^2 \quad (2)$$

where f_x denotes the feature of real image x from the middle layer after the discriminator; $f_{x'}$ represents the feature of x' from the middle layer after the discriminator.

Reconstruction Loss. To provide generator G with better image reconstruction ability, the proposed method uses a reconstruction loss function to represent the difference between x and $G(x')$ pixels. It is defined as the L_1 distance between the input x, and generated fake image $G(x')$. This ensures that the generated image is consistent with the input image as much as possible. The equation of reconstruction loss of generator is defined as:

$$L_{rec} = \frac{1}{N} \|x - G(x')\| \tag{3}$$

where N represents the number of input defective images x and the number of reconstructed images $G(x')$ respectively.

In the training process, the model can be trained by the weighted summation of the above three loss functions. The definition of the weighted summation loss function is as follows:

$$L_{total} = \lambda_{adv}L_{adv} + \lambda_{fea}L_{fea} + \lambda_{rec}L_{rec} \tag{4}$$

where λ_{adv}, λ_{fea}, and λ_{rec} are the weights of three loss functions. And their values are set to 1, 1, 40.

3   Experiments

In this section, we describe the experiment in details, including qualitative and quantitative evaluation of the performance of the proposed method, and the parameter setting of experiment.

3.1   Datasets

The whole fabric dataset contains 352 images of non-defective fabrics and 200 images of defective fabrics. Unlike the original DCGAN input-Gaussian noise, the DCGAN with an encoder component can take an image as input. The defect-free image is easier to obtain than the defect image, which is also in line with the practical application. In fabric dataset, only non-defective fabric samples are used for model training, and defective samples are used for the model test. There are 5632 patches extracted from 352 defect-free fabric images whose size is 512×512. And there are 200 defective fabric images. The size of the image patch is set to 128×128 in order to be consistent with the network model input. The final output is spliced into 512×512 size.

3.2   Defect Detection

Once the model is trained, it can be used to detect defects. The encoder and generator participate in the test phase, while the discriminator is not involved.

In the test, a fabric image with the size of 512×512 is cropped into 16 image patches with size of 128×128 before the image is sent to the test model (Fig. 5). The trained model can reconstruct each image patch except the defective image patch. And then the reconstructed image patches are reorganized into 512×512 size images in sequence. The reconstructed image is subtracted from the original image to obtain a residual image. It can be expressed as:

$$I_{residual} = abs(I_{org} - I_{rec}) \tag{5}$$

where $I_{residual}$ represents the residual image.

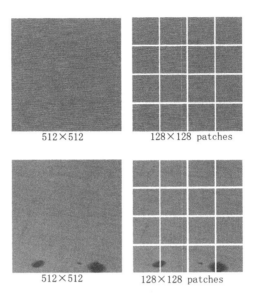

512×512   128×128 patches

512×512   128×128 patches

Fig. 5. The cropping images.

Threshold segmentation is performed on the residual image to segment the defect location. The selection of the threshold is very important, which is related to the detection performance of the model. Inspired by [29], the threshold value of threshold segmentation is selected as: $T_{(i)} = \mu_{(i)} + \gamma \times \sigma_{(i)}$. where μ is the residual image mean value, σ is the image standard deviation, and γ is a constant. According to the experiment, when γ is selected as 4.5, the defect segmentation effect is the best. In this paper, μ, σ and T can be described as:

$$\mu_{(i)} = \frac{\sum I_{residual(i)}}{n} \tag{6}$$

$$\sigma_{(i)} = \sqrt{\frac{\sum I_{residual(i)} - \mu_{(i)}}{n}} \tag{7}$$

$$T_{(i)} = \frac{\sum I_{residual(i)}}{n} + \gamma \times \sqrt{\frac{\sum I_{residual(i)} - \mu_{(i)}}{n}} \tag{8}$$

where n represents the number of $I_{residual(i)}$ pixels of all residual images participating in the calculation.

3.3 Evaluation Metrics

In this work, we evaluate the performance of the proposed network and existing two unsupervised defect detection models by using four evaluation metrics, including the Precision and Recall, mean F-measure (meanF), and Mean Absolute Error (MAE).

$$Precision = \frac{TP}{TP + FN} \tag{9}$$

$$Recall = \frac{TP}{TP + FP} \tag{10}$$

$$F_\beta = \frac{(1 + \beta^2) \times Precision \cdot Recall}{\beta^2 \times Precision + Recall} \tag{11}$$

$$MAE = \frac{1}{HW} \sum_{i=1}^{H} \sum_{j=1}^{W} |P_{ij} - G_{ij}| \tag{12}$$

where TP represents the number of correctly detected defect pixels, FP denotes the number of falsely detected defect pixels and FN is the number of falsely detected background pixels. F-measure reflects the overall performance of pixel classification. MAE indicates the average pixel-wise absolute difference between the prediction P and the ground truth G. where W and H represent the width and height of the image respectively.

3.4   Implementation Details

During the training stage, we processed the original image dataset, and a 512×512 image was divided into 16 image patches with size of 128×128. Our network is trained for 100 epochs with an NVIDIA GTX 1080 Ti GPU. The code was implemented using Python 3.6 with packages Pytorch 1.4.0, Numpy, and OpenCV.

3.5   Comparison with Other Methods

We compare the proposed algorithm with two state-of-the-art defect detection methods, including the AnoGAN, GANomaly. All methods are trained and tested with the same dataset. During training, AnoGAN and GANomaly also model non-defective samples. During testing, these methods generate the corresponding reconstructed image. Then we get the image after segmentation defect by pixel comparison.

Table 1. Quantitative evaluation. mean F-measure (meanF, larger is better), Mean Absolute Error (MAE, smaller is better), Precision (Precision, larger is better), and Recall (Recall, larger is better). The best results on our dataset are highlighted in boldface.

Method	meanF	MAE	Precision	Recall
AnoGAN	0.0571	0.0059	0.0985	0.1005
GANomaly	0.4967	0.0034	**0.7895**	0.3150
Ours	**0.5232**	**0.0033**	0.7418	**0.3652**

Quantitative Evaluation. Table 1 shows the quantitative comparison results in terms of Mean F-measure, MAE, Precision, Recall. As can be seen from the results, the performance of the proposed model is more significant. In particular, in terms of the Mean F-measure, MAE and Recall, the performance is improved by 2.65%, 0.01% and 5.02% over the second-best method GANomaly, respectively.

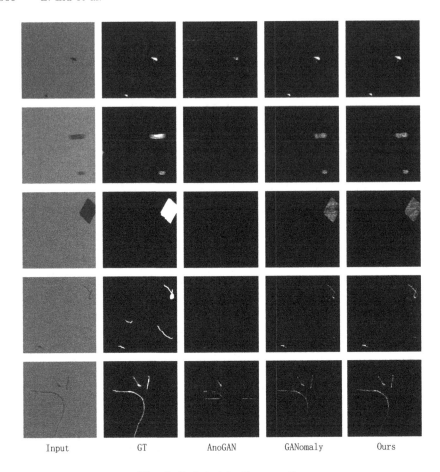

| Input | GT | AnoGAN | GANomaly | Ours |

Fig. 6. Defect detection results.

Qualitative Evaluation. To further illustrate the superior performance of the method, Fig. 6 shows the visual comparison of the proposed method and other defect detection methods. It can be seen that the proposed method can accurately segment the defects of fabric defects.

4   Conclusion

In this paper, a fabric defect detection framework based on a deep convolution generative adversarial network with an encoder component is proposed. Firstly, the defect-free image patch is input into DCGAN with an encoder component to make the model easier to train. Secondly, the image is input into the trained encoder and generator to reconstruct the image. Finally, the residual image is obtained by comparing the reconstructed image with the original image, and then the defect image is segmented by threshold segmentation. Extensive evaluations demonstrate the effectiveness of the network. Although the unsupervised defect detection model can effectively detect defects, it is still difficult to detect some easily confused defects which are highly similar to the texture background in appearance. In the future, we will explore some deep learning-based strategies to improve the difference between foreground and background regions.

Acknowledgement. This work was supported by NSFC (No. 61772576, No. 62072489, U1804157), Henan science and technology innovation team (CXTD2017091), IRTSTHN (21IRTSTHN013), Program for Interdisciplinary Direction Team in Zhongyuan University of Technology, ZhongYuan Science and Technology Innovation Leading Talent Program (214200510013).

References

1. Ngan, H.Y.: Automated fabric defect detection-a review. Image Vis. Comput. **29**(7), 442–458 (2011)
2. Hanbay, K.: Fabric defect detection systems and methods-a systematic literature review. Optik **127**(24), 11960–11973 (2016)
3. Cohen, F.S.: Automated inspection of textile fabrics using textural models. IEEE Trans. Pattern Anal. Mach. Intell. **13**(08), 803–808 (1991)
4. Wen, W.: Verifying edges for visual inspection purposes. Pattern Recogn. Lett. **20**(3), 315–328 (1999)
5. Kim, C.W.: Hierarchical classification of surface defects on dusty wood boards. Pattern Recogn. Lett. **15**(7), 713–721 (1994)
6. Campbell, J.G.: Automatic visual inspection of woven textiles using a two-stage defect detector. Opt. Eng. **37**(9), 2536–2542 (1998)
7. Yuan, X.C.: An improved Otsu method using the weighted object variance for defect detection. Appl. Surf. Sci. **349**, 472–484 (2015)
8. Aminzadeh, M.: Automatic thresholding for defect detection by background histogram mode extents. J. Manuf. Syst. **37**, 83–92 (2015)
9. Wood, E.J.: Applying Fourier and associated transforms to pattern characterization in textiles. Text. Res. J. **60**(4), 212–220 (1990)
10. Haralick, R.M.: Statistical and structural approaches to texture. Proc. IEEE **67**(5), 786–804 (1979)
11. Haralick, R.M.: Textural features for image classification. IEEE Trans. Syst. Man Cybern. **6**, 610–621 (1973)
12. Ojala, T.: A comparative study of texture measures with classification based on featured distributions. Pattern Recogn. **29**(1), 51–59 (1996)
13. Zhai, W., Zhu, J., Cao, Y.: A generative adversarial network based framework for unsupervised visual surface inspection. In: 2018 IEEE International Conference on Acoustics, Speech and Signal Processing (ICASSP), CONFERENCE 2018, pp. 1283–1287. IEEE (2018). https://doi.org/10.1109/ICASSP.2018.8462364
14. He, K., Zhang, X., Ren, S.: Deep residual learning for image recognition. In: Proceedings of the IEEE Conference on Computer Vision and Pattern Recognition, CONFERENCE 2016, pp. 770–778. CVPR (2016)
15. Huang, G., Liu, Z.: Densely connected convolutional networks. In: Proceedings of the IEEE Conference on Computer Vision and Pattern Recognition CVPR, CONFERENCE 2017, pp. 4700–4708. CVPR (2017)

16. Krizhevsky, A.: ImageNet classification with deep convolutional neural networks. In: Advances in Neural Information Processing Systems 25, pp. 1097–1105 (2012)
17. Simonyan, K.: Very deep convolutional networks for large-scale image recognition. arXiv preprint arXiv:1409.1556 (2014)
18. Szegedy, C., Liu, W.: Going deeper with convolutions. In: Proceedings of the IEEE Conference on Computer Vision and Pattern Recognition, CONFERENCE 2015, pp. 1–9. CVPR (2015)
19. Wang, T.: A fast and robust convolutional neural network-based defect detection model in product quality control. Int. J. Adv. Manuf. Technol. **94**(9), 3465–3471 (2018)
20. Chen, J.: Automatic defect detection of fasteners on the catenary support device using deep convolutional neural network. IEEE Trans. Instrum. Meas. **67**(2), 257–269 (2017)
21. Gopalakrishnan, K.: Deep convolutional neural networks with transfer learning for computer vision-based data-driven pavement distress detection. Constr. Build. Mater. **157**, 322–330 (2017)
22. Zhu, J.: Vision-based defects detection for bridges using transfer learning and convolutional neural networks. Struct. Infrastruct. Eng. **16**(7), 1037–1049 (2020)
23. Goodfellow, I.: Generative adversarial networks. Commun. ACM **63**(11), 139–144 (2020)
24. Zhao, Z., Li, B., Dong, R., Zhao, P.: A surface defect detection method based on positive samples. In: Geng, X., Kang, B.-H. (eds.) PRICAI 2018. LNCS (LNAI), vol. 11013, pp. 473–481. Springer, Cham (2018). https://doi.org/10.1007/978-3-319-97310-4_54
25. Hu, G.: Unsupervised fabric defect detection based on a deep convolutional generative adversarial network. Text. Res. J. **90**(3–4), 247–270 (2020)
26. Niu, S., Lin, H.: DefectGAN: weakly-supervised defect detection using generative adversarial network. In: 2019 IEEE 15th International Conference on Automation Science and Engineering (CASE), CONFERENCE 2019, pp. 127–132. IEEE (2019). https://doi.org/10.1109/COASE.2019.8843204
27. Liu, J.: Multistage GAN for fabric defect detection. IEEE Trans. Image Process. **29**, 3388–3400 (2019)
28. Salimans, T.: Improved techniques for training GANs. Adv. Neural. Inf. Process. Syst. **29**, 2234–2242 (2016)
29. Xie, X.: TEXEMS: texture exemplars for defect detection on random textured surfaces. IEEE Trans. Pattern Anal. Mach. Intell. **29**(8), 1454–1464 (2007)

Proactive Student Persistence Prediction in MOOCs via Multi-domain Adversarial Learning

Sreyasee Das Bhattacharjee$^{(\boxtimes)}$ and Junsong Yuan$^{(\boxtimes)}$

State University of New York at Buffalo, Buffalo, USA
{sreyasee,jsyuan}@buffalo.edu

Abstract. Automatic evaluation of a student's STEM learning profile to understand her persistence is of national interest. In this paper, we propose an early "dropout" and behavior prediction model that can identify the potentially 'marginalized' student learning patterns to facilitate early instructional intervention in Massive Open Online Courses (MOOC) learning platform. Note that in the MOOC setting, building a comprehensive learning profile of the students is particularly more challenging due to the lack of available information and constrained communication modes. Unlike most existing works, which ignore these environmental constraints of missing information to formulate an over-simplified problem of 'one-time' prediction task in a supervised setting, the proposed model introduces a continual automated monitoring and proactive estimation process, which transforms its decision making capacity over time with evolving data patterns. In a semi-supervised scenario, the Multi-Domain Adversarial Feature Representation (mDAFR) strategy promotes the emergence of features, which are discriminative for the main learning task, while remaining largely invariant to the data sources (course from which the data was captured) in consideration. This ensures an enhanced distributed learning capacity over different course environments. Compared to transfer learning, mDAFR reports 11–15% improved classification accuracy in KDDCup dataset, and demonstrates a competitive performance against several state-of-the-art methods in both KDDCup and MOOCDropout datasets.

Keywords: Multi-feature learning · Adversarial learning · Domain adaptation · Classification · MOOC

1 Introduction

As we march into this new era of Fourth Industrial Revolutions as World Economic Forum calls it [29], it reflects on how education is evolving at a faster pace than ever before, to suit the increasing demand for the right skills. Massive Open Online Courses (MOOCs), such as Coursera, Edx are turning increasingly popular for their online course offerings. However, despite ensuring more

© Springer Nature Switzerland AG 2022
C. Wallraven et al. (Eds.): ACPR 2021, LNCS 13188, pp. 569–583, 2022.
https://doi.org/10.1007/978-3-031-02375-0_42

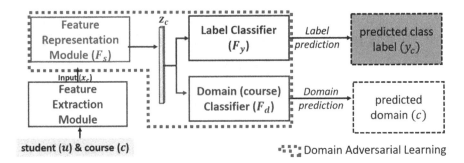

Fig. 1. Workflow Diagram for the proposed method that takes into consideration of both students' course related activity details & learning behavior patterns to design a multi-domain adversarial learning, which is discriminative of the underlying category information y_c for an input sample $\mathbf{x}_c$, however invariant to the underlying course (or domain) specification (c), from which the sample was originated. During test time, F_y is used to make the persistence behavior prediction for the student u.

flexible, personalized, and collaborative learning environment compared to traditional classroom-based course offerings, attrition remains to be a challenge for the MOOC courses [13]. Recent surge of success in artificial intelligence (AI) that aims to automate several complex tasks in manufacturing, transportation, e-commerce, health care, and financial markets, triggers a fundamental research question on its applicability to support an evolving education system. Although efficient data processing tools and sophisticated multimodal data analytic algorithms have been instrumental to demonstrate impressive performances in the domains of anomaly detection, signal processing, and multimodal data analytic research [1], it is still not evident, how to utilize the power of AI most effectively to assist each actor in the STEM life cycle (student, instructors, councilors, college professionals) to augment their respective capacities toward mitigating the attrition in the educational environment.

In fact, depending on the course requirement details and the student's individual learning style, learning patterns may slightly vary across courses (like comparing activities in two courses 'Introduction to Physics' Vs 'Introduction to CS1') [10]. However, the course completion objectives may remain same for all the courses the student is presently enrolled in. Therefore, to ensure generalized performance across multiple course environments, we introduce a multi-domain adversarial feature representation learning module that cannot discriminate across the single training (*Source*) and multiple testing (*Target*) domains, and yet makes an accurate early prediction on students' persistence behavior. While most existing methods addressing this problem formulate it as a one-time prediction task and perform some post-hoc analysis [15], in a practical scenario it is important to note that the behavioral processes like self-determination and self-efficacy may evolve over a relatively short time-period. Often the change is triggered by certain surrounding environmental conditions (like the subtle presence of microaggression in a TA's response), which may frequently create some differentiated impacts on a young mind. The identification of a potentially 'marginalized' student profile is useful only if such a prediction is accurate and early enough. This would help to design appropriate intervention by the course instructors or other concerned authorities to reduce the overall attrition rate. While prediction at a fixed time-stamp may not be of much help, the proposed method employs a continual automated monitoring process, which learns the sequential activity patterns over time to ensure an early and timely risk identification more accurately. Figure 1 gives a workflow overview of the proposed Multi-Domain Adversarial Feature Representation (mDAFR) learning method. The primary contributions of the work may be summarized as:

1. *Sequential Learning Activity Analysis for Early Detection* that may proactively identify the 'marginalized' profiles at every pre-defined interval to facilitate a timely instructional intervention for personalized assistance.
2. *Understanding Learning Behavior within Student Contexts* is facilitated by clustering them into groups using the explainable k-means algorithm ExKMC [9], which not only reflects different types of learning patterns observed in the student population, but also helps understand the student-specific unique activity details, which may have impacted the clustering configurations. ExKMC enhances interpretability of the model's prediction by visualizing each cluster configuration using a small decision tree, wherein the cluster assignment of each sample is interpreted by a short sequence of single-feature thresholds.
3. *Multi-Domain Adversarial Feature Representation Learning* that in a semi-supervised setting, utilizes annotated samples from a *Source* course and promotes the emergence of features, which are discriminative for the main learning task and invariant to the *domain shifts* over multiple smaller *Target* courses.
4. *Evaluating Generalization Performance across Diverse Course Environments* using two large scale MOOC datasets in Instructor-led course settings.

The rest of the paper is organized as follows: Sect. 2 briefly describes some related works; The proposed method is described in Sect. 3; Sect. 4 and Sect. 5 respectively presents the experimental results and the follow-up discussions; and the conclusion is in Sect. 5.

2 Related Works

Although MOOC has shown tremendous potential for ensuring an enhanced accessibility to distance and lifelong learners, from the research perspective, digital activity details of participants offer a tremendous amount of data to describe students' individual learning patterns including watching video lectures, participation in discussion forums, timely submission of assignments, etc. Evidences show that these may be investigated to predict student completion [13] or engagement [4]. In this section, we briefly describe the related methods to predict dropout using students' learning activities and patterns. Since the proposed method develops a multi-domain adversarial feature representation learning model, we will also discuss related works based on adversarial learning.

Modelling MOOC Dropouts based on Learning Activity Details: A significant amount of research have explored the problem in K-12 settings [6, 28]. With the recent development in educational technologies and resources, MOOC is rapidly becoming more popular to the global learner community as a steady alternative that offers a more flexible as well as a personalized learning environment. However, the success rate of MOOC learners is often lower than that achieved by students in a physical classroom setting [16]. In fact, high dropout rate in MOOC appears to be a prominent issue, requiring immediate attention [27]. A set of recent works use deep neural network models to address the dropout prediction task in MOOC environment for predicting whether a user is likely to dropout in the next weeks [18,26]. To enable a more accurate time-stamped analysis, some works [7,24] model the sequential feature information to build variants of Recurrent Neural Network (RNN) models. Jeon et al. [15] present a multi-layer representation module based on Branch and Bound (BB) algorithm from the raw clickstream data. However, to ensure interpretability, useful sequence information is lost. A comprehensive literature review covering the recent progress in addressing the task of MOOC-based dropout prediction problem can be found in [2].

Adversarial Domain Invariant Learning: The proposed work is also related to Generative Adversarial Network (GAN) [12]. Existing methods develop generative models for domain adaptation or domain generalization. Both these models propose to learn an effective classifier useful for the target domain by leveraging a large collection of source domain labeled data. However, several domain adaptation techniques [3,25] utilize its limited access to the labeled data and unlabeled data generated from the target domain to learn the target data pattern. While the evolving data characteristic and the availability of large annotated sample collection in *Target* domain pose additional challenges for our problem setting, the category sets in both *Source* and *Target* domains are identical in our scenario. Given this, we develop a novel variant of multi-domain adversarial feature representation learning model that promotes emergence of a learned descriptor, while demonstrating significant invariance to the underlying course context. This is critical as often a student's individual learning behaviour and sense of persistence have a uniformly dominant influence in all the courses, the student has recently been enrolled, wherein other course-specific details may not be equally discriminative.

3   Proposed Method

In particular we have $\mathbf{x}_c \overset{def}{=} \{\mathbf{x}_c^{(t)}\}_{t=1}^T \in \mathbb{R}^{m \times T}$, where the learning activity at a given time-stamp $t \in \{1, ..., T\}$ and $c \in \mathcal{C}$, is represented in terms of a compact m dimensional descriptor $\mathbf{x}_c^{(t)}$ that may capture student data from two different

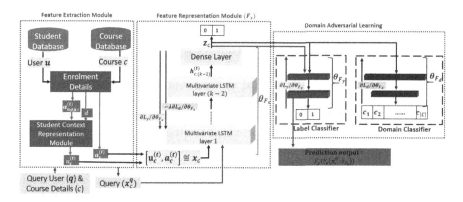

Fig. 2. For each $c \in \mathcal{C}$ and student $u \in \mathcal{U}$, a sample $\mathbf{x}_c \in \mathcal{D}_c \subset \mathbb{R}^{m \times T}$ represents the learning activity in terms of a T-length sequence. At a given time-stamp $t \in \{1, ..., T\}$ for course $c \in \mathcal{C}$, it captures both *Course Activity* ($\mathbf{a}_c^{(t)}$), and *Student Context* ($\mathbf{u}_c^{(t)}$) as its components. In our experiments, we have a new time-stamp on every *third* day in the entire span of the course duration, wherein the last day of the course is denoted by T. The figure illustrates an overview of the proposed Multi-Domain Adversarial Feature Representation (mDAFR) learning method to ensure a domain invariant descriptor $\mathbf{z}_c$ with minimized *domain shift* across several course settings in $\mathcal{C}$. During testing phase, $F_y(F_s(\mathbf{x}_c^q; \theta_{F_s}); \theta_{F_y})$ is used to predict the labels for the query $\mathbf{x}_c^q$, for any $c \in \mathcal{C}$.

perspectives: (1) An overall *Student Context* that reports a holistic understanding of student's overall working style in the course and its comparative pattern against the overall course population at the time-stamp t. This component is denoted by $\mathbf{u}_c^{(t)}$ and the details of its derivation are described in Sect. 3.1; and (2) *Course Activity Descriptor* that reports the student's course-specific learning activity details (like 'access', 'navigate', 'video views' etc.) for $c \in \mathcal{C}$ at the time instant t and denoted by $\mathbf{a}_c^{(t)}$. The details of the specific types of features that we use to build $\mathbf{a}_c^{(t)}$ is discussed in Sect. 4.2. We concatenate these two components to describe a student's comprehensive learning pattern $\mathbf{x}_c^{(t)}$ at a given time instant t. The label $y_c = 0$ (or $y_c = 1$) represents the fact that the student described by the multivariate sequence vector $\mathbf{x}_c$ successfully completed all course requirements (or dropped out) of the course $c \in \mathcal{C}$ within the course lifespan $[1, T]$. In addition to making a summative evaluation of an input query $\mathbf{x}_c$, by designing an effective multi-domain adversarial sequence modelling scheme, the proposed method also enables proactive evaluation, wherein for a predefined $\eta > 0$ and a subsequence $\mathbf{x}_c^{t_0} \stackrel{def}{=} [\mathbf{x}_c^{(t_0 - \eta)}, ..., \mathbf{x}_c^{(t_0)}]$ of $\mathbf{x}_c$ describing the student's course-specific learning history at time t_0 ($t_0 > \eta$), the system can also make an early prediction on their 'marginalization' score highlighting their dropout risk. The entire dataset $\mathcal{D} = \cup_{c \in \mathcal{C}} \mathcal{D}_c$ is comprised of multiple course-specific collections of students' activity details.

Note that for each course-specific collection $\mathcal{D}_c$, the sample population representing each of the two classes, may be highly unbalanced, like in a practical scenario, students dropping out of a course in the middle, would be comparably a rare phenomenon. Therefore, a dataset with nearly uniform distribution for samples representing both the categories ('successful completion' and 'dropping out') may not be always possible. To address such data scarcity, Transfer Learning (TL) (or more specifically termed as semi-supervised Domain Adaptation) is often found as a solution, where a ML model learned using the data collection from a *Source* domain (e.g. a course with plenty of labeled data), is transferred to a *Target* domain (e.g. a course for which the dataset is more unbalanced, or the dataset size is not reasonably large enough to build a sophisticated ML/DL model from scratch) to be finetuned in the context of the *Target* domain [20]. However, this risks the transferred neural network model prone to catastrophic forgetting [17,30].

While some existing works propose to directly combine the data gathered from multiple courses to compensate for such data imbalance, subtle yet critical course-specific fine-grained context details preserved within a learned feature descriptor may not be reasonable generalizable and thus may negatively impact on the prediction performance. Therefore, our model relies on the theory of domain adaptation [10], which suggests that the predictions must be made on the feature descriptors that cannot discriminate among multiple domains. To this effect, given a collection of annotated samples $\mathcal{D}$, we design an effective and efficient domain adversarial feature representation learning model that promotes emergence of a learned descriptor, which is discriminative to the main task (i.e. identifying profiles potentially at the risk for dropping out) and also optimized to demonstrate invariance to the underlying data distribution variance observed across *Source* and multiple potential *Target* domains. An overview of the proposed algorithm is illustrated in Fig. 2.

3.1 Feature Extraction

The entire set of students in our data collection is represented as $\mathcal{U}$. In order to gain a better understanding of a student's overall learning behavior at a given time-stamp t compared to the whole class population, the *Course Activity Descriptor* reports the student's course-specific learning activity details (like 'access', 'navigate', 'video views' etc.) for $c \in \mathcal{C}$ at the time instant t. For each $u \in \mathcal{U}$, the *Course Activity Descriptor* is denoted by $\mathbf{a}_c^{(t)}$, the details of which is discussed in Sect. 4.2. Given $\mathbf{a}_c^{(t)}$, the overall *Student Context* descriptor $\mathbf{u}_c^{(t)}$, is designed to capture a holistic understanding of student's overall working style in the course c and its comparative pattern against the overall course population at the time-stamp t.

Toward facilitating the derivation of a comprehensive student-specific learning pattern, a clustering analysis is performed to capture an aggregated understanding of the student's learning pattern from all the courses the student is currently enrolled in. For a given $u \in \mathcal{U}$, an aggregated learning activity in course c is represented as: $\mathbf{a}_{agg,c}^{(t)} = \sum_{n=1}^{t} \mathbf{a}_c^{(n)}$. We use the explainable k-means algorithm ExKMC [9] that takes inputs k as an estimated cluster number and the entire data collection $\mathcal{U}$ represented using the set $\{\mathbf{a}_{agg,c}^{(t)}\}$, to partition into

k clusters $\{\mathcal{U}_k\}_{k=1}^5$. Following Silhouette Analysis [23], the number of clusters is set to be $k = 5$. The primary objective of ExKMC is to generate an explainable k-means clustering using a threshold tree with a specified number of leaves. In fact, the clustering algorithm is initiated by building a threshold tree with k leaves using the Iterative Mistake Minimization (IMM) algorithm [5]. IMM first runs a standard k-means algorithm, producing a set of k centers that are given as an additional input. Then, given a budget of k' leaves, it greedily expands the tree to reduce the clustering cost. At each step, the clusters form a refinement of the previous clustering by adding more thresholds to allow for more flexibility in the data partition and employ a surrogate cost to enable multiple leaves to correspond to the same cluster. The main idea is that by fixing the centers between steps, we can more efficiently determine the next feature-threshold pair to add. The surrogate cost is non-increasing throughout the execution as the number of leaves k' grows. When $k' = n$, then the k-means cost matches that of the reference clustering. In our experiments, we have used $k' = 2k$. In fact, extending the tree to use k' leaves with ExKMC leads to a lower-cost result that better approximates the reference clustering and helps find an explainable clustering with high accuracy, while using only $O(k)$ leaves for k-means clustering. Note that in this specific application scenario, just tagging a student as 'marginalized' based on their cluster assignment may be risky and may also prove biased. Thus, an additional interpretation supporting the system prediction on a student's cluster assignment may be significant.

Student Context Descriptor: The overall *Student Context* vector is defined as $\mathbf{u}_c^{(t)} \stackrel{def}{=} \left[u_{c,1}^{(t)}, ..., u_{c,5}^{(t)}, d \right] \in \mathbb{R}^6$, where $u_{c,k}^{(t)}$ represents the probability that the student u belongs to cluster $\mathcal{U}_k$. The term $d \stackrel{def}{=} 1 - \frac{E_u}{E_f + E_u}$ computes the student's overall *Persistence Score*, by computing the ratio between the number of dropped out courses E_u and the total number of courses that the student has enrolled, including the ones that the student has completed. The term E_f represents the number of courses the student has completed by now. Note that the *Persistence Score* is 1 until a student drops out of a course. When demographic data (e.g. age group, gender, education level) $\mathbf{g}_u$ is available for each student $u \in \mathcal{U}$, we further cluster samples (represented using an augmented vector $[\mathbf{a}_{agg,c}^{(t)}, \mathbf{g}_u]$) within each $\mathcal{U}_k$ into 5 different groups $\{\mathcal{U}_{k,l}^d\}_{l=1}^5$. The resulting *Demography Context* vector for u is defined as $\mathbf{d}_c^{(t)} \stackrel{def}{=} \left[d_{c,1}^{(t)}, ..., d_{c,5}^{(t)} \right]$, where $d_{c,k}^{(t)}$ represents the Gower distance between u and the cluster center of $\mathcal{U}_{k,l}^d$. Then, the overall *Demography Aware Student Context* uses a combined representation as $\mathbf{u}_c^{(t)} \stackrel{def}{=} \left[u_{c,1}^{(t)}, ..., u_{c,5}^{(t)}, d_{c,1}^{(t)}, ..., d_{c,5}^{(t)}, d \right] \in \mathbb{R}^{11}$.

3.2 Feature Representation

The feature representation module in Fig. 2 uses a specific *Source* $\in \mathcal{C}$, for which the course-specific subcollection $\mathcal{D}_{sr} \subset \mathcal{D}$ is used to learn the feature representation module F_s that can effectively identify the potentially 'marginalized' students in the course c. Typically a larger subcollection of course-specific samples with a balanced distribution across various classes is considered as a *Source* subcollection D_{sr}. In Sect. 4.3, we report results using different choices of *Source* domains from C. Long Short-Term Memory (LSTM) network model, a variant of Recurrent Network Model (RNN), is used as the feature extractor module [14]. Given a sample $\mathbf{x}_c = \{\mathbf{x}_c^{(t)}\}_t \in \mathcal{D}_{sr}$, passed as an input to F_s, each of its recurrent layers is designed to propagate historical information via a chain-like neural network architecture that integrates the current input and the hidden state $\mathbf{h}^{(t-1)}$ at $(t-1)^{th}$ time stamp [19] along with the gating functions into its state dynamics [14].

As shown in Fig. 2, F_s has a stack of $(k-2)$ LSTM layers, followed by the $(k-1)^{th}$ layer as a fully connected dense layer and k^{th} layer as a softmax layer. For each sample $\mathbf{x}_c$, the intermediate $(k-2)^{th}$ layer output $\{\mathbf{h}_{c,(k-2)}^{(t)}\}_{t=1}^{N_c}$ is fed as an input to the $(k-1)^{th}$ dense layer of F_s and produces $\mathbf{z}_c \in \mathbb{R}^n$ as a compact derived sample descriptor (the dimension n of $\mathbf{z}_c$ depends on the $(k-1)^{th}$ layer size of F_s), which is learned to be discriminative of its underlying category information y_c^i. However, having been an effective representative of several course-specific learning activity patterns, which may not generalize well across multiple courses. Each LSTM layer coupled with dropout layer has 64 hidden units. With Rectified Linear unit (ReLU), the FC layer has 16 units.

3.3 Multi-domain Adversarial Feature Representation (mDAFR) Learning

Note that the entire dataset $\mathcal{D}$ is essentially a collection of samples collected from different courses, where the samples representing a student's learning pattern in course $c \in \mathcal{C}$ belongs to its sub-collection $\mathcal{D}_c$. In a practice setting, not all these course-specific subcollections may have sufficiently large annotated collection to build a indigenous course-specific model from scratch. Therefore, in practical settings, the samples of $\mathcal{D}$ are typically originated from two types of courses (or domains): the data collection from *Source* domain denoted by $\mathcal{D}_{sr}$, which has comparably larger collection of samples representing each label; and $(|\mathcal{C}| - 1)$ smaller subcollections representing samples from *Target* domains $\{\mathcal{D}_{tar,j}\}_{j=1}^{(|\mathcal{C}|-1)}$. Therefore, $\mathcal{D}$ can be decomposed as $\mathcal{D} = \{\mathcal{D}_{sr}\} \cup \{\mathcal{D}_{tar,j}\}_{j=1}^{(|\mathcal{C}|-1)}$. The proposed mDAFR model aims to leverage the larger collection of *Source* data (student activity details from the source sr) and smaller unlabelled sample collections of multiple *Target* domains (student activity details from multiple target *tar* courses) to build a robust classifier. Note that while there may exist multiple distributions representing the data patterns of the *Source* and various *Target* domains, which are all unknown, they all represent the identical set of semantic categories. Hence, given a test sample $\mathbf{x}_c$ our ultimate goal is to design a model that can accurately predict its label y_c irrespective of its originating domain in $\mathcal{C}$.

The mDAFR module employs a deep feed-forward architecture that for each input $\mathbf{x}_c$, predicts its label $y_c \in \{0, 1\}$ and its underling domain $c \in \mathcal{C}$ [10]. As shown in Fig. 2, the input vector $\mathbf{x}_c$ is passed through the initial feature representation module F_s to generate a n-dimensional derived descriptor $\mathbf{z}_c \in \mathbb{R}^n$, which is then transformed by a mapping F_y to the label y_c. The proposed domain invariant feature representation module uses F_s (trained using $\mathcal{D}_{sr} \subset \mathcal{D}$) as the initial feature representation module. In order to achieve domain invariance, we also introduce a multiclass domain classifier module F_d that can predict the originating domain of the input sample. The weight parameters of all the $(k-1)$ layers (except the last Softmax layer) of F_s represented by θ_{F_s} along with the network parameters θ_{F_y} (and θ_{F_d}) of F_y (and F_d) are further updated jointly using a combined loss term defined as below [10]:

$$
E(\theta_{F_s}, \theta_{F_y}, \theta_{F_d}) = \frac{1}{|\mathcal{D}_{sr}|} \sum_{i=1}^{|\mathcal{D}_{sr}|} \mathcal{L}_y^i(\theta_{F_s}, \theta_{F_y}) - \lambda \Bigg(\frac{1}{|\mathcal{D}_{sr}|} \sum_{i=1}^{|\mathcal{D}_{sr}|} \mathcal{L}_d^i(\theta_{F_s}, \theta_{F_d}) +
$$

$$
\frac{1}{(|\mathcal{C}|-1)|\mathcal{D} \setminus \mathcal{D}_{sr}|} \sum_{j}^{(|\mathcal{C}|-1)} \sum_{i=1}^{|\mathcal{D}-tar,j|} \mathcal{L}_d^i(\theta_{F_s}, \theta_{F_d}) \Bigg) \quad (1)
$$

where, the empirical classification loss on a labeled example x_c^i from course c is denoted as $\mathcal{L}_y^i$ and the domain discrimination loss is denoted as $\mathcal{L}_d^i$. They are defined as $\mathcal{L}_y^i(\theta_{F_s}, \theta_{F_y}) = \mathcal{L}_y(F_y(F_s(x_c^i; \theta_{F_s}); \theta_{F_y}), y_i)$ and $\mathcal{L}_d^i(\theta_{F_s}, \theta_{F_d}) = \mathcal{L}_d(F_d(\mathcal{R}(F_s(x_c^i; \theta_{F_s})); \theta_{F_d}), c)$, where c (and y_i) represents the course (and ground truth persistence category details) information for x_c^i. The term $\mathcal{L}_y$ (e.g. multinomial) and $\mathcal{L}_d$ (e.g. multi-class cross-entropy loss) are the corresponding loss functions. In all experiments, we use $\lambda = 1$. A 'pseudo function' $\mathcal{R}(\mathbf{x})$ is introduced by defining two (incompatible) equations describing its forward and backpropagation behavior [10] as $\mathcal{R}(\mathbf{x}) = \mathbf{x}$ and $\frac{dR}{d\mathbf{x}} = -\mathbf{I}$. The joint learning using the combined loss term defined in Eq. (1) can be implemented using Stochastic Gradient Descent by optimizing the saddle points $\theta_{F_s}^0, \theta_{F_y}^0, \theta_{F_d}^0$ as, $(\theta_{F_s}^0, \theta_{F_y}^0) = \underset{\theta_{F_s}, \theta_{F_y}}{\arg\min}\, E(\theta_{F_s}, \theta_{F_y}, \theta_{F_d}^0)$ and $\theta_{F_d}^0 = \underset{\theta_{F_d}}{\arg\max}\, E(\theta_{F_s}^0, \theta_{F_y}^0, \theta_{F_d})$. This enables the system attain an equilibrium between the classification performance, the mitigating system's ability for domain discrimination. This results in obtaining a domain invariant feature representation that may influence a more accurate label prediction task.

Early Prediction: For any $c \in \mathcal{C}$ and a given query $\mathbf{x}_c^q$ of length t_0 such that $\eta < t_0 < T$, during the testing phase, we decompose it into $(t_0 - \eta + 1)$ equal sized subsequences $\{\mathbf{x}_{c,i}^q\}_{i=1}^{(T-\eta+1)}$. Each $\mathbf{x}_{c,i}^q$ as a query, depicts the learning activity pattern for η consecutive time stamps, extracted from the original sequence $\mathbf{x}_c^q$. Then an average 'marginalization' score of $\{F_y(F_s(\mathbf{x}_{c,i}^q; \theta_{F_s}); \theta_{F_y})\}_{i=1}^{(t_0-\eta+1)}$ is used to classify $\mathbf{x}_c^q$. In our experiments, we use $\eta = 5$ to obtain 4 different partial subsequences from each $\mathbf{x}_c$ (or $\mathbf{x}_c^q$), each of which is treated as a separate training sample, labeled same as $\mathbf{x}_c$.

4   Experiments

4.1   Dataset

We use KDDCup[1] and the recent MoocDropout[2] dataset for our experiments. The information contained in both the datasets is of three types: 1) Object/module data; 2) log data; and 3) label data to specify course completion or dropout. Object/module data comprises of course/module-specific details (e.g. chapter, course info, peer-grading, course, video, dictation, problem, start and end of each module etc.).

KDDCup dataset is a collection of event and relation-based activity details of 39 Instructor-paced mode courses, which include the information of a total of $200,904$ enrollments and $112,448$ unique students. The MoocDropout dataset contains 698 Instructor-paced courses. This data collection has the log details for $1,319,032$ video activities, $10,763,225$ forum participation activities, $2,089,933$ assignment activities, $738,0344$ web page access related activities. Among the total $200,904$ student population, $159,223$ students dropped out before completing the course and $41,681$ completed all the requirements of their enrolled course within a given timeframe.

MoocDropout also provides students' demographic information (age, gender, education level), which, as described in Sect. 3.1, is used to describe the *Demographic Context* of students. In the instructor paced environment (IPE) of 698 courses, it has the log details for $50,678,849$ video activities, $443,554$ forum participation activities, $7,773,245$ assignment activities, $9,231,061$ web page access related activities. Among the total $467,113$ student population, $372,088$ students dropped out before completing the course and $95,025$ completed all the

Table 1. Performance comparison of the proposed mDAFR model against the Transfer Learning [31] in KDDCup dataset: In each experimental iteration a specific *Source* collection (indexed as sr) and each of the other 38 courses is treated as a *Target* domain. Columns 2–7 report the performance of the proposed method for each iteration that uses a specific sr as a source collection. Column 8 reports the average performance, that computes the mean of Columns 2–7. Similarly, Columns 2–7 in Row 2 report the performance of another set of experimental iterations, where transfer learning method is adopted for each iteration using a specific sr as a source collection to learn the base model which is then transferred to each of the other 38 *Target* locations and the base model learned at sr is finetuned by the entire non-source subcollection $\mathcal{D}\backslash\mathcal{D}_{sr}$ and finetuned model is used to classify the samples from the entire test collection across all the courses in $\mathcal{C}$.

	$sr = 6$	$sr = 11$	$sr = 13$	$sr = 16$	$sr = 18$	$sr = 22$	Average
Proposed method	0.864	0.895	0.853	0.884	0.875	0.872	**0.874**
Transfer learning [31]	0.689	0.782	0.793	0.748	0.766	0.801	0.763

---

[1] https://www.biendata.xyz/competition/kddcup2015/.
[2] http://moocdata.cn/data/user-activity.

requirements of their enrolled course within a given timeframe. The other subset of the dataset reports the details of 515 courses in the self-paced environment (SPE). This has the log details for $38,225,417$ video activities, $90,815$ forum participation activities, $3,139,558$ assignment activities, $5,496,287$ web page access related activities. Among the total $218,274$ student population, $205,988$ students dropped out before completing the course and $12,286$ completed all the requirements of their enrolled course within a given timeframe. IPE courses follow a similar offering pattern as the conventional classrooms, however in SPE individual students follow their individual learning schedules, which can be more than 16 weeks, typically fixed for any IPE course. The learning activities in SPE courses also include video watching (watch, stop, and jump), forum discussion (ask questions and replies), assignment completion (with correct/incorrect answers, and reset), and web page clicking (click and close a course page). The label data contains information on whether the student has completed the course or not, where label 1 indicates that the student dropped out, and 0 indicates that the student completed the course.

4.2   Implementation Details

Given the activity information of all unique enrolments in the entire course collection in the dataset, 14 features are derived to represent the action of a student at any time instance t: access; discussion; navigate; page close; problem, video; wiki; server; browser; chapter; sequential; total time; and session. The time span of each course was divided in 7 nearly equal-sized segment, in which each segment was of 4 consecutive days except the last one, which was either 2 or 3 days depending on the month length. The *Course-Specific Feature Representation Module* described in Sect. 3.2 consists of $(k-2) = 3$ LSTM layers, each of which was paired with a dropout layer with a dropout ratio as 0.1. For compactness, each LSTM layer coupled with its corresponding dropout layer is treated as 1 layer. The number of hidden units in each layer was set to be 64. The $(k-1)^{th}$ Fully Connected (FC) layer is designed with 16 units and defined with Rectified Linear unit (ReLU) activation. The learning of this course-specific feature representation module occurs with 60 epochs with 20% of the training samples are used for validation at every learning epoch. To deal with data imbalance, the samples from the two classes were assigned weights derived using Sklearn [21] util function class_weight() so that the training data collection appears as a balanced representation of both the classes.

4.3   Results and Comparative Study

We use accuracy as an evaluation metric that computes the ratio of the correct predictions over all the predictions made by a classifier, for reporting the performance [11]. To compare the performance against that of several methods reported by [8], we use F1 score that is the harmonic mean of the precision and recall with its best value reached at 1 for perfect precision and recall [11].

Table 2. Average Performance of the proposed method (mDAFR) with F1 score (in %) as the evaluation metric, in KDDCup and MoocDropout dataset. To perform an equivalent comparison with other methods, mDAFR model is finetuned in an active learning setting with a small fraction of the annotated *Target* samples and Column mDAFR(A) reports the result. The result is compared against the average performance obtained by using several off-the-shelf classifiers that includes Support Vector Machine (SVM), Random Forest (RF), Gradient Boosting Decision Tree (GBDT), Context-aware Feature Interaction Network (CFIN) [8], Deep sequential (a combination of Convolution Neural Network and LSTM, denoted as ConRec), Deep Feed Forward Neural Network (DNN-3), and Simple-LSTM [22].

Dataset	mDAFR(A)	mDAFR	CFIN	SVM	RF	GBDT	ConRec	DNN-3	Simple-LSTM
KDDCup	93.45	88.68	92.27	91/65	91.73	91.88	0.86	0.85	0.84
MoocDropout	92.27	87.53	90.48	82.86%	83.11	85.18	0.76	0.75	0.73

Table 1 reports the accuracy scores [11] to compare the performance of the proposed method against transfer learning [31] using 6 different courses as the *Source* domain, for which there are at least 800 samples representing the minority category (i.e. usually the *dropped out* category in this scenario). This specific problem scenario being prone to a severe data imbalance issue, not all $\mathcal{D}_c$ for $c \in \mathcal{C}$ may be an appropriate representative of the problem spectrum with a reasonable number of samples from each category in consideration. In a typical transfer learning setting, the base model is learned using the *Source* course data and transferred to each of the *Target* course environment for later finetuning and the resulting finetuned model is used classify the samples from the entire test collection across all the courses in $\mathcal{C}$. As observed, the proposed method demonstrates a significantly robust performance compared to transfer learning using a variety of choices for the source collections $sr = 6, 11$, etc. In fact, a comparison of the average performances reported in Column 8, clearly demonstrates the effectiveness of the proposed method over the traditional transfer learning method that frequently suffers from catastrophic forgetting and thereby fails to remain equally effective for the *Source* domain sr, on which the model was originally learned. However, the proposed mDAFR model remains to be invariant of the underlying domain information, from which the query sample was originated. The proposed method attains around 11% improved accuracy score over the transfer learning method.

Table 2 uses F1 score to report the performance of the proposed method against the state-of-the-art results described by [8], which in a supervised setting, use the combined training collection of $\mathcal{D}$ (comprising of 10–30 times more 'annotated' training samples representing students' learning activity across all the courses in two datasets) to train a Context-aware Feature Interaction Network (CFIN) in a strictly supervised setting. Note that in KDDCup dataset, CFIN obtains F1 Score of 92.27%. However, the proposed mDAFR model uses significantly smaller course-specific annotated collection $\mathcal{D}_{sr}(\subset \mathcal{D})$ to present a competitive average F1 score 88.68% over all choices of $sr \in \{6, 11, 13, 16, 18, 22\}$.

To compare the performances improvement of the proposed method in an equivalent experiment setting as in CFIN, the mDAFR model is then finetuned in an active learning environment[1] with the *Target* course data, wherein mDAFR required only 1–3% of the total *Target* annotated samples, we achieve a significant performance gain. In KDDCup dataset, the finetuned model obtains 93.45% F1 score. A similar average performance is also observed for the MoocDropout, where Instructor-paced courses with more than 1000 samples were chosen as the *Source* classes to report 92.27% average F1 Score.

5   Conclusion

The proposed method designs a continual monitoring system that employs a multi-domain adversarial feature representation (mDAFR) strategy to early identify the potentially 'marginalized' students, who may need personalized instructional support. While domain-adaptation offers a promise to assist educators in their effort for personalize pedagogical approach by highlighting some determining feature attributes, the proposed student-centric model benefits all participants involved in the course life-cycle. In addition to encouraging the emergence of features that are more exclusive and discriminative to the main learning task and invariant to the *domain shifts*, across a variety of courses, the proposed mDAFR model is also suitable for interactive learning in a distributed data environment, wherein the model can be learned in a large *Source* course and can be easily customized with a smaller data collection of *Target* courses. This shows a greater promise to be adopted in a real-life setting, where an extensive data sharing (specifically the annotated data) across departments/schools/universities may be an issue due to its confidentiality concerns. By facilitating a more personalized interaction with a small set of identified 'marginalized' student profiles, the proposed model offers practical assistance to help improve student retention.

References

1. Bhattacharjee, S.D., Tolone, W.J., Paranjape, V.S.: Identifying malicious social media contents using multi-view context-aware active learning. Future Gener. Comput. Syst. **100**, 365–379 (2019)
2. Borrella, I., Caballero, S., Ponce-Cueto, E.: Predict and intervene: addressing the dropout problem in a MOOC-based program, pp. 1–9 (June 2019). https://doi.org/10.1145/3330430.3333634
3. Chen, S., Zhou, F., Liao, Q.: Visual domain adaptation using weighted subspace alignment. In: 2016 Visual Communications and Image Processing (VCIP), pp. 1–4. IEEE (2016)
4. Dascalu, M.D., et al.: Before and during COVID-19: a cohesion network analysis of students' online participation in moodle courses. Comput. Hum. Behav. **121**, 106780 (2021)
5. De Raedt, L., Blockeel, H.: Using logical decision trees for clustering. In: Lavrač, N., Džeroski, S. (eds.) ILP 1997. LNCS, vol. 1297, pp. 133–140. Springer, Heidelberg (1997). https://doi.org/10.1007/3540635149_41

6. Dupéré, V., Dion, E., Leventhal, T., Archambault, I., Crosnoe, R., Janosz, M.: High school dropout in proximal context: the triggering role of stressful life events. Child Dev. **89**(2), e107–e122 (2018)

7. Fei, M., Yeung, D.: Temporal models for predicting student dropout in massive open online courses. In: 2015 IEEE International Conference on Data Mining Workshop (ICDMW), pp. 256–263 (2015)

8. Feng, W., Tang, J., Liu, T.X.: Understanding dropouts in MOOCs. In: Proceedings of the AAAI Conference on Artificial Intelligence, vol. 33, pp. 517–524 (2019)

9. Frost, N., Moshkovitz, M., Rashtchian, C.: ExKMC: expanding explainable *k*-means clustering. arXiv preprint arXiv:2006.02399 (2020)

10. Ganin, Y., Lempitsky, V.: Unsupervised domain adaptation by backpropagation. In: Proceedings of the 32nd International Conference on International Conference on Machine Learning, ICML 2015, vol. 37, pp. 1180–1189. JMLR.org (2015)

11. Godbole, S., Sarawagi, S.: Discriminative methods for multi-labeled classification. In: Dai, H., Srikant, R., Zhang, C. (eds.) PAKDD 2004. LNCS (LNAI), vol. 3056, pp. 22–30. Springer, Heidelberg (2004). https://doi.org/10.1007/978-3-540-24775-3_5

12. Goodfellow, I.J., et al.: Generative adversarial networks. arXiv preprint arXiv:1406.2661 (2014)

13. Halawa, S., Greene, D., Mitchell, J.: Dropout prediction in MOOCs using learner activity features. Proc. Second Eur. MOOC Stakehold. Summit **37**(1), 58–65 (2014)

14. Hochreiter, S., Schmidhuber, J.: Long short-term memory. Neural Comput. **9**(8), 1735–1780 (1997)

15. Jeon, B., Park, N., Bang, S.: Dropout prediction over weeks in MOOCs via interpretable multi-layer representation learning. arXiv preprint arXiv:2002.01598 (2020)

16. Jordan, K.: Massive open online course completion rates revisited: assessment, length and attrition (June 2015). https://doi.org/10.13140/RG.2.1.2119.6963

17. Li, Z., Hoiem, D.: Learning without forgetting. CoRR abs/1606.09282 (2016). http://arxiv.org/abs/1606.09282

18. Nagrecha, S., Dillon, J.Z., Chawla, N.V.: MOOC dropout prediction: lessons learned from making pipelines interpretable. In: Proceedings of the 26th International Conference on World Wide Web Companion, pp. 351–359 (2017)

19. Pascanu, R., Gülçehre, Ç., Cho, K., Bengio, Y.: How to construct deep recurrent neural networks. CoRR abs/1312.6026 (2013)

20. Patricia, N., Caputo, B.: Learning to learn, from transfer learning to domain adaptation: a unifying perspective. In: Proceedings of the IEEE Conference on Computer Vision and Pattern Recognition, pp. 1442–1449 (2014)

21. Pedregosa, F., et al.: Scikit-learn: machine learning in Python. J. Mach. Learn. Res. **12**, 2825–2830 (2011)

22. Prenkaj, B., Velardi, P., Distante, D., Faralli, S.: A reproducibility study of deep and surface machine learning methods for human-related trajectory prediction. In: Proceedings of the 29th ACM International Conference on Information & Knowledge Management, pp. 2169–2172 (2020)

23. Rousseeuw, P.J.: Silhouettes: a graphical aid to the interpretation and validation of cluster analysis. J. Comput. Appl. Math. **20**, 53–65 (1987)

24. Tang, C., Ouyang, Y., Rong, W., Zhang, J., Xiong, Z.: Time series model for predicting dropout in massive open online courses. In: Penstein Rosé, C., et al. (eds.) AIED 2018, Part II. LNCS (LNAI), vol. 10948, pp. 353–357. Springer, Cham (2018). https://doi.org/10.1007/978-3-319-93846-2_66

25. Tzeng, E., Hoffman, J., Saenko, K., Darrell, T.: Adversarial discriminative domain adaptation. In: Proceedings of the IEEE Conference on Computer Vision and Pattern Recognition, pp. 7167–7176 (2017)
26. Wang, W., Yu, H., Miao, C.: Deep model for dropout prediction in MOOCs. In: Proceedings of the 2nd International Conference on Crowd Science and Engineering, pp. 26–32 (2017)
27. Whitehill, J., Mohan, K., Seaton, D., Rosen, Y., Tingley, D.: MOOC dropout prediction: how to measure accuracy? In: Proceedings of the Fourth 2017 ACM Conference on Learning@ Scale, pp. 161–164 (2017)
28. Wood, L., Kiperman, S., Esch, R., Leroux, A., Truscott, S.: Predicting dropout using student- and school-level factors: an ecological perspective. Sch. Psychol. Q. **32**, 35–49 (2017). https://doi.org/10.1037/spq0000152
29. World Economic Forum, W.: Fourth industrial revolution (2020). https://www.weforum.org/agenda/archive/fourth-industrial-revolution
30. Xiao, Z., Wang, L., Du, J.Y.: Improving the performance of sentiment classification on imbalanced datasets with transfer learning. IEEE Access **7**, 28281–28290 (2019). https://doi.org/10.1109/ACCESS.2019.2892094
31. Zhuang, F., et al.: A comprehensive survey on transfer learning. Proc. IEEE **109**(1), 43–76 (2020)

Author Index

Author Index

Printed in the United States
by Baker & Taylor Publisher Services